DIETRICH BONHOEFFER WORKS, VOLUME 9

The Young Bonhoeffer: 1918–1927

This series is a translation of
DIETRICH BONHOEFFER WERKE
Edited by
Eberhard Bethge†, Ernst Feil,
Christian Gremmels, Wolfgang Huber,
Hans Pfeifer, Albrecht Schönherr,
Heinz Eduard Tödt†, Ilse Tödt

This volume has been made possible through the generous support of the National Endowment for the Humanities, the Aid Association for Lutherans, Lilly Endowment, Inc., the Stiftung Bonhoeffer Lehrstuhl, the Bowen H. and Janice Arthur McCoy Charitable Foundation, the Lusk-Damen Charitable Gift Fund, Dr. John and Cleo Young, The Lutheran Theological Seminary at Philadelphia and numerous members and friends of the International Bonhoeffer Society.

DIETRICH BONHOEFFER WORKS

General Editor
Wayne Whitson Floyd Jr.

DIETRICH BONHOEFFER

The Young Bonhoeffer

1918–1927

Translated from the German Edition
Edited by
HANS PFEIFER
In Cooperation with
CLIFFORD J. GREEN AND CARL-JÜRGEN KALTENBORN

English Edition
Edited by
PAUL DUANE MATHENY, CLIFFORD J. GREEN,
AND MARSHALL D. JOHNSON

Translated by
MARY C. NEBELSICK
WITH THE ASSISTANCE OF
DOUGLAS W. STOTT

FORTRESS PRESS   MINNEAPOLIS

DIETRICH BONHOEFFER WORKS, Volume 9

Originally published in German as *Dietrich Bonhoeffer Werke*, edited by Eberhard Bethge et al., by Chr. Kaiser Verlag in 1986; Band 9, *Jugend und Studium: 1918–1927*, edited by Hans Pfeifer in cooperation with Clifford J. Green and Carl-Jürgen Kaltenborn. First English-language edition of *Dietrich Bonhoeffer Works*, Volume 9, published by Fortress Press in 2003.

Jacket design: Cheryl Watson
Cover photo: Dietrich Bonhoeffer. © Chr. Kaiser/Gütersloher Verlagshaus, Gütersloh.
Internal design: The HK Scriptorium, Inc.

Library of Congress Cataloging-in-Publication Data

Bonhoeffer, Dietrich, 1906–1945.
    [Jugend und Studium: 1918–1927. English]
    The young Bonhoeffer : 1918–1927 / Dietrich Bonhoeffer ; translated from the German edition edited by Hans Pfeifer in cooperation with Clifford J. Green and Carl-Jürgen Kaltenborn ; English edition edited by Paul Duane Matheny, Clifford J. Green, and Marshall D. Johnson ; translated by Mary C. Nebelsick with the assistance of Douglas W. Stott.
    p. cm. — (Dietrich Bonhoeffer works ; v. 9)
    Includes bibliographical references (p.) and indexes.
    ISBN 0-8006-8309-9 (alk. paper)
    1. Bonhoeffer, Dietrich, 1906–1945—Childhood and youth. 2. Theologians—Germany—Biography. I. Matheny, Paul D. (Paul Duane) II. Green, Clifford J. III. Johnson, Marshall D. IV. Title. V. Series: Bonhoeffer, Dietrich, 1906–1945. Works. English. 1986 ; v. 9.

BR45.B6513 1986 vol. 9
[BX4827.B57]
230'.044 s—dc21
[230'.044'092 B]   2002032510

The paper used in this publication meets the minimum requirements of American National Standard for Information Sciences—Permanence of Paper for Printed Library Materials, ANSI Z329.48-1984.

Manufactured in Canada
07   06   05   04   03   1   2   3   4   5   6   7   8   9   10

CONTENTS

GENERAL EDITOR'S FOREWORD
TO DIETRICH BONHOEFFER WORKS

SINCE THE TIME that the writings of Dietrich Bonhoeffer (1906–45) first began to be available in English after World War II, they have been eagerly read both by scholars and by a wide general audience. The story of his life is compelling, set in the midst of historic events that shaped a century.

Bonhoeffer's leadership in the anti-Nazi Confessing Church and his participation in the *Abwehr* resistance circle make his works a unique source for understanding the interaction of religion, politics, and culture among those few Christians who actively opposed National Socialism. His writings provide not only an example of intellectual preparation for the reconstruction of German culture after the war but also a rare insight into the vanishing world of the old social and academic elites. Because of his participation in the resistance against the Nazi regime, Dietrich Bonhoeffer was hanged in the concentration camp at Flossenbürg on April 9, 1945.

Yet Bonhoeffer's enduring contribution is not just his moral example but his theology as well. As a student in Tübingen, Berlin, and at Union Theological Seminary in New York—where he also was associated for a time with the Abyssinian Baptist Church in Harlem—and as a participant in the European ecumenical movement, Bonhoeffer became known as one of the few figures of the 1930s with a comprehensive and nuanced grasp of both German- and English-language theology. His thought resonates with a prescience, subtlety, and maturity that continually belies the youth of the thinker.

In 1986 the Chr. Kaiser Verlag, now part of Gütersloher Verlagshaus, marked the eightieth anniversary of Bonhoeffer's birth by issuing the first of the sixteen volumes of the definitive German edition of his writings, the *Dietrich Bonhoeffer Werke* (*DBW*). The final volume of this monumental critical edition appeared in Berlin in the spring of 1998.

Preliminary discussions about an English-language edition (*DBWE*) began even as the German series was beginning to emerge. As a consequence, the International Bonhoeffer Society, English Language Section, formed an editorial board, initially chaired by Robin Lovin, assisted by Mark Brocker, to

xiii

undertake this project. Since 1993 the *Dietrich Bonhoeffer Works* translation project has had its institutional home at the Lutheran Theological Seminary at Philadelphia, under the leadership of its general editor and project director—Wayne Whitson Floyd Jr.—and its executive director—Clifford J. Green. The editorial office is located in Norfolk, Virginia, at Talbot Hall, the offices of the Episcopal Diocese of Southern Virginia, where Dr. Floyd serves as the Director of the Anglican Center for Theology and Spirituality.

The *Dietrich Bonhoeffer Works* provides the English-speaking world with an entirely new, complete, and unabridged translation of the written legacy of one of the twentieth century's most notable theologians. The success of this edition is based foremost upon the gifts and dedication of the translators producing these new volumes, upon which all the other contributions of this series depend.

The *DBWE* includes a large amount of material appearing in English for the first time. Key terms are now translated consistently throughout the corpus, with special attention being paid to accepted English equivalents of technical theological and philosophical concepts.

This authoritative English edition strives, above all, to be true to the language, the style, and—most importantly—the theology of Bonhoeffer's writings. Translators have sought, nonetheless, to present Bonhoeffer's words in a manner that is sensitive to issues of gender in the language it employs. Consequently, accurate translation has removed sexist formulations that had been introduced inadvertently or unnecessarily into earlier English versions of his works. In addition, translators and editors generally have employed gender-inclusive language, insofar as this was possible without distorting Bonhoeffer's meaning or dissociating him unduly from his own time. To avoid introducing into Bonhoeffer's text gender-exclusive grammatical constructions that were absent in the original German (such as the generic use of the masculine pronoun 'he'), the *DBWE* translations have followed the tradition of using 'they' and other plurals following a singular antecedent. This usage is commended by both *The Chicago Manual of Style* and *The American Heritage Dictionary,* and counts as precedents the works of Oliver Goldsmith, George Eliot, and Shakespeare, who himself wrote such lines as "God send everyone their heart's desire."

At times Bonhoeffer's theology sounds fresh and modern, not because the translators have made it so, but because his language still speaks with a hardy contemporaneity even after more than half a century. In other instances, Bonhoeffer sounds more remote, a product of another era, not due to any lack of facility by the translators and editors, but because his concerns and rhetoric are in certain ways bound inextricably to a time that is past.

Volumes include introductions written by the editor(s) of each volume of the English edition, footnotes provided by Bonhoeffer, editorial notes added by the German and English editors, and afterwords composed by the editor(s) of the German edition. In addition, volumes provide tables of abbreviations used in the editorial apparatus, as well as bibliographies that list sources used by Bonhoeffer, literature consulted by the editors, and other works related to each particular volume. Finally, volumes contain pertinent chronologies, charts, and indexes of scriptural references, names, and subjects.

The layout of the English edition has retained Bonhoeffer's manner of dividing works into chapters and sections, as well as his original paragraphing (exceptions are noted by a ¶-symbol to indicate any paragraph break added by the editors of the English edition or by conventions explained in the introductions written by the editor[s] of specific volumes). The pagination of the *DBW* German critical edition is indicated in the outer margins of the pages of the translated text. Where material has been inserted from DBW 17, which provided supplemental material not available at the time of the original publication of a given German volume, the page numbers in the margin are preceded by the numeral 17. Such material appears in chronological order by its date of composition and is indicated by placing a lower case letter after its identifying item number. At times, for the sake of precision and clarity of translation, a word or phrase that has been translated is provided in its original language, set within square brackets at the appropriate point in the text. Biblical citations come from the New Revised Standard Version (NRSV), unless otherwise noted. Where versification of the Bible used by Bonhoeffer differs from the NRSV, the verse number in the latter is noted in the text in square brackets.

Each volume in Series-B of the *DBWE*, numbered 9-16, contains collected writings from a particular period of Bonhoeffer's life. These volumes, themselves appearing in chronological order, are then each divided into three main parts, each of which also is arranged chronologically: (1) Letters, Journals, Documents; (2) Essays, Seminar Papers, Papers, Lectures, Compositions; (3) Sermons, Meditations, Catechetical Writings, Exegetical Writings. Each item within each part—each separate letter, note, essay, sermon, etc.— is numbered consecutively from the start of each of the three major parts. In editorial notes these items are labeled by the DBWE volume number, then the major part number in that volume, then the individual item number, and finally the page number in that volume. Thus, *DBWE* 9 (1/109): 179, editorial note 1, would refer to the English Edition, volume 9, part 1, item number 109, page 179, editorial note 1.

Bonhoeffer's own footnotes—which are indicated in the body of the text by plain, superscripted numbers—are reproduced in precisely the same numerical sequence as they appear in the German critical edition, complete with his idiosyncrasies of documentation. In these, as in the accompanying editorial notes, existing English translations of books and articles have been substituted for their counterparts in other languages whenever available. The edition of a work that was consulted by Bonhoeffer himself can be ascertained by consulting the bibliography at the end of each volume. When a non-English title is not listed individually in the bibliography (along with an English translation of the title), a translation of each title has been provided for the English reader within the footnote or editorial note in which it is cited.

The editorial notes, which are indicated in the body of the text by superscripted numbers in square brackets—except *DBWE* volume five where they are indicated by plain, superscripted numbers—provide information on the intellectual, ecclesiastical, social, and political context of Bonhoeffer's pursuits during the first half of the twentieth century. These are based on the scholarship of the German critical edition; they have been supplemented by the contributions of the editors and translators of the English edition. Where the editors or translators of the English edition have substantially augmented or revised a German editor's note, the initials of the person making the change(s) appear at the note's conclusion, and editorial material that has been added in the English edition is surrounded by square brackets. When any previously translated material is quoted within an editorial note in altered form—indicated by the notation [trans. altered]—such changes should be assumed to be the responsibility of the translator(s).

Bibliographies at the end of each volume provide the complete information for each written source that Bonhoeffer or the various editors have mentioned in the current volume. References to the archives, collections, and personal library of materials that had belonged to Bonhoeffer and that survived the war—as cataloged in the *Nachlaß Dietrich Bonhoeffer* and collected in the Staatsbibliothek in Berlin—are indicated within the *Dietrich Bonhoeffer Works* by the abbreviation *NL* followed by the corresponding reference code within that published index.

The production of any individual volume of the *Dietrich Bonhoeffer Works* requires the financial assistance of numerous individuals and organizations, whose support is duly noted on the verso of the half-title page. In addition, the editor's introduction of each volume acknowledges those persons who have assisted in a particular way with the production of the English edition of that text. A special note of gratitude, however, is owed to all those prior translators, editors, and publishers of various portions of Bonhoeffer's literary legacy who heretofore have made available to the English-speaking world the writings of this remarkable theologian.

This definitive English edition depends especially upon the careful scholarship of all those who labored to produce the critical German edition, completed in April 1998, from which these translations have been made. Their work has been overseen by a board of general editors—responsible for both the concept and the content of the German edition—composed of Eberhard Bethge†, Ernst Feil, Christian Gremmels, Wolfgang Huber (spokesperson for the German editorial board), Hans Pfeifer (who still serves as the ongoing liaison between the German and English editorial boards), Albrecht Schönherr, Heinz Eduard Tödt†, and Ilse Tödt.

The present English edition would be impossible without the creativity and unflagging dedication of the members of the Editorial Board of the *Dietrich Bonhoeffer Works* (Victoria Barnett, Mark Brocker, Keith W. Clements, Wayne Whitson Floyd, Clifford J. Green, John W. de Gruchy, Barry A. Harvey, Geffrey B. Kelly, Reinhard Krauss, Michael Lukens, and H. Martin Rumscheidt), as well as the members of its Advisory Committee (James H. Burtness, Barbara Green, James Patrick Kelley, Robin W. Lovin, Nancy Lukens, Paul Matheny, and Mary Nebelsick).

The deepest thanks for their support of this undertaking is owed, as well, to all the various members, friends, and benefactors of the International Bonhoeffer Society; to the National Endowment for the Humanities, which supported this project during its inception; to the Lutheran Theological Seminary at Philadelphia and its former Auxiliary who established the Dietrich Bonhoeffer Center on its campus, specifically for the purpose of facilitating these publications in the early years of this project; to the Episcopal Diocese of Southern Virginia, which generously provides office space to the General Editor, and especially to the Advisory Board of the Anglican Center for Theology and Spirituality, which graciously allows the General Editor time for his role in the DBWE; and to our publisher, Fortress Press, as represented with uncommon patience and *Gemütlichkeit* by Michael West, Rachel Riensche, Jessica Thoreson, and Ann Delgehausen. The privilege of collaboration with professionals such as these is fitting testimony to the spirit of Dietrich Bonhoeffer, who was himself always so attentive to the creative mystery of community—and that ever deepening collegiality that is engendered by our social nature as human beings.

Special mention must be made of the priceless contribution made to all Bonhoeffer scholarship, especially the *Dietrich Bonhoeffer Werke*, by Eberhard Bethge, who died on March 18, 2000. Eberhard was Dietrich's student, then friend and collaborator, and later his editor and biographer. His impact on this English Edition of the *Dietrich Bonhoeffer Works*—and all those persons whose labor has brought it about—is immeasurable. All who meet Dietrich Bonhoeffer in the form of his printed words owe a never-ending debt of gratitude to this remarkable human being, Eberhard Bethge, who almost single-handedly was responsible for assuring that Bonhoeffer's legacy would endure for us and generations to come.

Wayne Whitson Floyd Jr., General Editor and Project Director
January 27, 1995
The Fiftieth Anniversary of the Liberation of Auschwitz
Sixth revision on September 11, 2002

Abbreviations

AB (DBWE 2)	*Act and Being* (*DBWE,* English edition)
D (DBWE 4)	*Discipleship* (*DBWE,* English edition)
DB	*Dietrich Bonhoeffer: Eine Biographie,* German edition
DB-ER	*Dietrich Bonhoeffer: A Biography* (Fortress Press, 2000 revised edition)
DBW	*Dietrich Bonhoeffer Werke,* German edition
DBWE	*Dietrich Bonhoeffer Works,* English edition
E (DBW 6)	*Ethics* (*DBW,* German edition)
FP	*Fiction from Prison*
FP (DBWE 7)	*Fiction from Tegel Prison* (*DBWE,* English edition)
GS	*Gesammelte Schriften* (Collected writings)
LPP	*Letters and Papers from Prison,* 4th edition
LW	[Martin] *Luther's Works,* American edition
NL	*Nachlaß Dietrich Bonhoeffer*
NRS	*No Rusty Swords*
NRSV	The *New Revised Standard Version* of the Bible
SC (DBWE 1)	*Sanctorum Communio* (*DBWE,* English edition)
TF	*A Testament to Freedom*
WA	*Weimar Ausgabe* (Weimar edition), Martin Luther
WA Br	*Weimar Ausgabe Briefwechsel* (Weimar edition, letters), Martin Luther

PAUL DUANE MATHENY

EDITOR'S INTRODUCTION
TO THE ENGLISH EDITION

DIETRICH BONHOEFFER BELONGED to an extraordinary family who rose above the deception pervading their culture and society during his life. His times also were extraordinary in the degree to which historical events and cultural and political realities rose to an incredible pitch of madness and violence. Distant as those years often seem from the preoccupations particular to our generation, there is something remarkably human and familiar about the struggles Bonhoeffer faced during his lifetime.

In the midst of such tumultuous times the best and the worst human qualities are forced to the fore. Such periods call for voices that rise out of the context of suffering and confusion and remind us of who we are and who God has called us to be. The din of seemingly demonic voices was deafening for most; yet for some, the voices of justice, truth, and compassion were still heard during events that evoked the most dramatic human passions possible.

Dietrich Bonhoeffer was to put his life on the line for justice. This volume gives witness to the journey that would lead to his theological and political engagement, and eventually his death. This witness recounts a way of life that forged a man of spiritual and theological integrity and Christian compassion.

The most immediate context of Bonhoeffer's formative years was the life of his home and family, yet it extends also to friends, church, and community. We must consider the intellectual influences on him, the social and cultural challenges of the world he lived in, and his budding pastoral convictions and career expectations.

Dietrich Bonhoeffer's Home Life

Bonhoeffer's early life was bound to his family and the society in which it was enmeshed. He had seven brothers and sisters: Karl-Friedrich, Walter, Klaus, Ursula, Christel, Sabine (his twin), and the eighth child, Susanne. He was the most athletic of his siblings; as a result he protected the young ones, and they sought his careful but strong hand when they needed it. His entire family

1

encouraged him to be diligent. As a result he became the most talented musician of the siblings and grew accustomed early in life to writing down his thoughts and ideas. Social life was important. A large, financially and socially privileged Berlin family such as his was expected to host many parties. These events were festive, with no expense spared in creating the best atmosphere for the family's circle. Attention to detail marked every event.[1] In such an atmosphere many friends and visitors felt at ease. For many the Bonhoeffer home was a welcoming and joyous place, especially for children. Bonhoeffer's parents loved surprises and events for their children, and there were many of both. It was an atmosphere where everyone mattered.

Summer was regularly spent on vacation. First they traveled to Wölfelgrund, during the time they lived in Breslau, and later they summered in a house in Friedrichsbrunn in the eastern Harz Mountains.[2] There they spent many bright and cheerful holidays with friends and family. In the large garden in Friedrichsbrunn they could do anything they liked. Dietrich studied mushrooms and plants, and in the evenings the village children would join them for games. This son had turned into a gifted athlete. Here in sports he found exuberance in tests of his own strength. In the evenings they watched the mists and the stars. Under the rowan (mountain ash) trees, he used to sit and read stories, especially those that were lighthearted and humorous.[3] He was a young man with simplicity of feeling and an unusual sense of selflessness.

His family members and their friends liked Dietrich Bonhoeffer. They appreciated his caring and careful manners and his energetic attitude. His family was healthy, as was Dietrich, both spiritually and physically. He did not have a particular best friend, although he was surrounded by people who were close and who enriched his life through their concern for him and their involvements in his life. The intellectual and emotional energy of their life together carried over into everyday family activities. This was to continue throughout his entire lifetime and was in evidence even during the years of the war.[4]

Bonhoeffer was eager to learn and to be useful to his parents, his family, and his friends. His parents were devoted to their children and eager to encourage whatever talents they had. Nonetheless, he was not particularly precocious in skills necessary for school, often struggling with his writing and other academic skills. Even so he soon demonstrated athletic, musical, and linguistic skills that would distinguish him. Bonhoeffer had a talent for learning foreign languages. In his family, being distinguished was not viewed as

---

[1.] See Leibholz-Bonhoeffer, *The Bonhoeffers: Portrait of a Family*, 8–9; see also Emmi Bonhoeffer, "The House on Wangenheimstrasse," in Dietrich Bonhoeffer, *FP* 134–37.

[2.] See *DB-ER* 16.

[3.] See *DB-ER* 16–18; see also Leibholz-Bonhoeffer, *The Bonhoeffers*, 7–9.

[4.] See *DB-ER* 852. Bonhoeffer enjoyed playing the host, even when he was in prison.

extraordinary; it was expected. The pressure to perform and grow in intellectual life was great. Yet there was little noticeable competition among the children. They supported each other, and their parents did not permit complaining of any kind, a characteristic that Dietrich displayed throughout his life. In such an environment the family thrived. Bonhoeffer's childhood was full of joy and vitality. Some might even call it sheltered from the pain that surrounded them, but this did not mean that he did not learn the power of compassion and understanding. This was evidenced repeatedly in the interplay between the members of his family, the household, and their friends.

Later in life he was to note that his childhood years had sheltered him from the dark side of life, the shadow lands.[5] Although his early years probably had not been overly protective, they had buffered him from the suffering of the world. Yet it was his ability to grow in compassion that was to mark his life and theology, as his life's journey led him from a privileged and joyous home into a world that knew suffering as deeply as any has known it.

The Family of Dietrich Bonhoeffer

Dietrich Bonhoeffer had a distinguished, privileged, and scholarly family heritage.[6] Although he did not stem from the nobility, his was not a typical middle-class existence, but rather was related to circles of lower nobility and to the intellectual elite of his time.[7] His father, Karl Ludwig Bonhoeffer, was a professor of psychiatry. His grandfather, Karl Alfred von Hase, had been a professor of practical theology, and his great-grandfather, Karl August von Hase, one of the most accomplished professors of church history of the nineteenth century. Many of his relatives also had achieved prominence in the intellectual and cultural circles of Berlin society. Dietrich's uncle Hans von Hase, for example, was a highly respected pastor. Another relative, Richard Schöne, was the general director of the Royal Prussian Museums in Berlin. Yet another, Richard von Volkmann, was a novelist and surgeon general of the Prussian Army. And still another, Rüdiger Count von der Golz, was a lieutenant general. The ideals and expectations for any member of such a family were high indeed.

The first home he knew was at Scheitniger Park in Breslau, near the hospital clinic where his father was professor of psychiatry and neurology and

---

[5.] See *GS* 3:490–95 and the letter of Susanne Dreß, *DB-ER* 19–20.

[6.] See Bosanquet, *The Life and Death of Dietrich Bonhoeffer*, 17–23. Bonhoeffer's family has its roots in Schwäbisch Hall, a free city before the establishment of the German nation. The family had been prominent leaders there for more than three hundred years. By the eighteenth century, they had become academics, lawyers, theologians, and medical doctors.

[7.] See *DB-ER* 3–13.

director of the hospital for nervous diseases. Work was important to his father and therefore to the rest of the family. His father's role in the family demanded respect; nonetheless, Karl Bonhoeffer did not let convention hinder him from developing loving and fatherly relations with his children. Manners were strictly enforced; the father was never to be contradicted. Yet in spite of his apparent strictness Professor Bonhoeffer was not perceived by family members as overly stern but as mild-tempered, sympathetic, and indeed sensitive to the feelings of others. Karl Bonhoeffer had a keen eye for what was genuine. He showed his respect, a value honored by all the family, especially for what was warmhearted and unselfish.

The Bonhoeffer family believed in standing by the weak.[8] In spite of their privileged existence, humility was an important value. Karl Bonhoeffer rejected hollow phrases, clichés, and platitudes. Dietrich embraced this value early in his life, and he was later to be very grateful for his father's restraining hand.[9] This can be seen even at school. In a paper written in 1923, near the end of his secondary school education, Bonhoeffer compared two of the greatest Roman lyrical poets, Catullus and Horace.[10] His preference of Catullus over Horace is evidence of how deeply the value of humility was ingrained. Catullus's humility and romance are praised with an effusion of adjectives over the discerning and ambitious nationalism of Horace. Bonhoeffer could identify with a man who had written for a small circle of friends. The nationalist Horace, to the contrary, was derided for his self-centeredness.[11] The sort of pride that could be justified in a person was to depend, according to Bonhoeffer, on what was right and respectful, not on selfish ambition.

Even though they had a number of maids, a chauffeur, and tutors, little extravagance was allowed in the Bonhoeffer home and there were no aristocratic pretensions to social distance and class. The children were devoted to the household employees and showed them consideration.[12] Everything was well arranged for the children's advancement and enrichment, intellectual and spiritual, and to this end they were educated at home. The circle of home life was given meticulous stewardship,[13] and the value of each person in the household in preserving these goals was appreciated and recognized.

[8.] See Leibholz-Bonhoeffer, *The Bonhoeffers*, 10–11.

[9.] See *DB-ER* 15–16. Concerning the influence of his father on his theological path, see *LPP* 275, *DB* 246, and Green, *Bonhoeffer: A Theology of Sociality*, 105ff.

[10.] See below, "Gymnasium Paper on Catullus and Horace Written to Fulfill Requirements for Graduation," 2/2:198–214.

[11.] See below, 2/1:201.

[12.] Note how frequently they are mentioned in Dietrich Bonhoeffer's letters. Dietrich even went to visit a relative of his childhood governess when he was in Cuba (*DB-ER* 151); see also Bosanquet, *The Life and Death of Dietrich Bonhoeffer*, 28–29. Bonhoeffer loved Käthe Horn, who had taken care of him as a child. Maria Horn was Paula Bonhoeffer's right hand (Zimmermann and Smith, eds., *I Knew Dietrich Bonhoeffer*, 17–18).

[13.] See *DB-ER* 17 and Leibholz-Bonhoeffer, *The Bonhoeffers*, 6.

All family members, too, had their roles in this stewardship. Women at that time were not expected to be scholars, but Dietrich's mother understood the life of the mind and chose to become trained as a teacher. With responsibility for arranging the education of the children, she decided that Dietrich and Sabine were to be taught at home by Miss Käthe Horn. Nevertheless, she watched over their development with love, showing a particular talent for making stories interesting and captivating, something that Bonhoeffer inherited, as shown by his ability later to engage children and youth.[14]

His mother had a strong personality and effectively carried out her responsibilities. A gregarious, warmhearted, and unaffected person, she loved the society of friends and her family. Unlike her husband, she did not love nature the way a scientist would. She loved instead to celebrate the community of her family, enjoying especially music and literature, surprises, and parties. Bonhoeffer may have inherited his appreciation of a spirited sentimentality from his mother. For example, when comparing Horace with Catullus, he praised Catullus for putting his all into his experience and chided Horace for his absurd desire to cultivate culture for the future.[15] Like his mother, Dietrich grew to desire the richness of life. As a young student he was to argue that the fullness of life, its emotions and passions, rather than mere ideas, is what conquers the world. Culture for culture's sake robbed life. Like his father, Bonhoeffer appears to have learned to be careful and balanced and, like his mother, to be in love with life and people. It was a powerful combination in later life.

The cultural traditions and roots of his family went back several generations. His grandmother, Klara von Hase, who by marriage became Countess Kalckreuth, had been a pupil of Clara Schumann and Franz Liszt; and although at a relatively early age he chose to study theology instead, Dietrich was at one point himself attracted to a musical career.[16] The family's circle of acquaintances in earlier generations had even included Goethe. Moreover, the life of the young Bonhoeffer was populated by the constant presence of authors, professors, pastors, noblemen, and soldiers—past and present – whose presence served to reinforce particular humanistic values, as well as a national ethos.[17] Later in life he was to carry the family chronicle

---

[14.] An assessment of his children's sermons and catechesis indicates this; see below, 1/114:187.

[15.] See below, "Catullus and Horace," 2/2:214.

[16.] See below, 1/25:46, and Leibholz-Bonhoeffer, *The Bonhoeffers*, 34. It almost happened that he studied with the famous musician Leonid Kreutzer (*DB-ER* 25).

[17.] See Leibholz-Bonhoeffer, *The Bonhoeffers*, 5 and *DB-ER* 3–6, 9, 11.

with him into prison and relive it in the sketch of his Tegel novel. He knew that he had inherited much, and he felt deeply an obligation to maintain the tradition.

Life Expectations

His options in life were those that his family and culture offered. It was expected that he would contribute to his society and culture either as a musician, soldier, or academic. We do not know the extent to which he examined each of these alternatives. There is, however, no doubt that the political and military conflicts of his age had an influence on him.[18] A child during the war years of 1916–17, Dietrich played soldiers in the garden. During his university years, he joined up for military training, like so many of his family circle before.[19] And in the spring of 1918, when his brother Walter, only eighteen years old, left home voluntarily to serve as an ensign on the western front, Dietrich, then only twelve, sang a song for his brother wishing him Godspeed.[20] Years later when he announced to his students in Finkenwalde his opposition to war, they were noticeably surprised. They asked how a German Lutheran could even think of avoiding military service to his nation.[21] In his earlier years, he certainly had felt the same as his students. But soon there were signs that his mind was changing about this traditional and honored activity. In his essays on honor and his children's sermon on Psalm 24:7, we find this young man, destined one day to play the role of the conspirator, reflecting on what it meant to be a person of integrity and honor. This did not mean cowardice, nor could it mean brutality, in a person. On the one hand, the sensitivities of a spirited young man were being honed by increasing familiarity with the wisdom of the gospel.[22] On the other hand, the profound impact of the death of his brother Walter certainly had freed him to be able to think more deeply about the nature of war than his tradition would have otherwise easily allowed.

Bonhoeffer wanted to lead a life both honoring the tradition he loved so much and keeping the religious faith he was coming to embrace so passionately. At fourteen, when he took confirmation classes, the question arose in his mind as to whether he should become a minister. He often read the Bible, and the Christian culture that his home life imparted seemed to come more naturally to him than to others. His interest in theology became appar-

---

[18.] See Leibholz-Bonhoeffer, *The Bonhoeffers*, 3–5, 32–33. The image of his family members whose lives had been affected by World War I was certainly an important memory of his youth.

[19.] See below, 1/45–50:69–74.

[20.] See Bosanquet, *The Life and Death of Dietrich Bonhoeffer*, 35–37.

[21.] See *DB-ER* 431–33.

[22.] See below, 3/10:509–14, on Psalm 24:7; 3/6:476–88, a catechesis on Luke 9:57-62; and 3/15:529–40, his meditation and catechesis on honor.

ent at an early age.[23] He found himself discovering through faith a whole new perspective on life.

Dietrich clearly anticipated a rich life comparable to the one he had enjoyed at home. Still, while very young, he realized that he had to decide upon his career path and already began making his plans for the future while still in his early teens. He asked himself what would make him strong in mind, experience, and faith. While his early years of education had been at home, in 1913 he began to attend the Friedrich-Werder Gymnasium, where he studied the classics of German education. This curriculum was designed to prepare him for an academic career, a choice that fitted him well, since serious academic study seemed as inevitable to him as his life of faith.

When he entered the university at Tübingen, he spent his time gathering a broad picture of theological and philosophical study. His social circle was for a time centered mostly on the Hedgehog fraternity (the *Igel*), a student society with semi-political late-nineteenth-century origins. His father had belonged to the Hedgehog, and it was only natural that Dietrich would join as well.

It was within this circle that Bonhoeffer experienced "military service" in a postwar territorial training organization called "The Black Reichswehr." Technically, it was illegal, but had been deemed necessary due to Germany's military helplessness after the First World War. It was here that the nationalist and antidemocratic stream of German society was experienced by the young man.

These rumblings still seemed uneventful for him as he made plans to travel to Italy, the mecca of cultured Germans.[24] Family history connected Bonhoeffer to Rome. His great-grandfather Karl August von Hase had made many trips to Rome in an effort at conciliation with the Roman Catholic Church and had received his hereditary peerage as a result.[25] But there may have been an even more compelling reason to take this journey. Italy was believed by many to have an almost mystical power to awaken the mind for spiritual and emotional enrichment. This trip was intended by his family to be for the young Bonhoeffer a moment of spiritual and intellectual awakening, both opening him to the majesty of the Renaissance and, like Goethe, stripping him of the bourgeois simplicity of his upbringing. And it did both. As he gazed on the architectural and artistic beauty of this amazing culture, the young man gained his first vision of the church's glory. In Rome he discovered the church at the heart of the world—an impression that was to transform his life and send him searching for a concept of the church consistent with this experience. Here lie the roots of Bonhoeffer's later preoc-

---

[23.] See Zimmermann and Smith, eds., *I Knew Dietrich Bonhoeffer*, 30–32.
[24.] See Bosanquet, *The Life and Death of Dietrich Bonhoeffer*, 51.
[25.] See *DB-ER* 6–7, 56–58.

cupation with the idea of the church. Indeed, it can be argued that much more than his time at university, his journey to Italy was to have a profound effect on his commitment to the church, its integrity and life. It lent color and passion to his understanding of the Christian life.[26]

Keeping the World at Bay

Bonhoeffer was born into a world in disarray, veering toward destruction. His secure family life stood in strong contrast to the political and social chaos that churned around it. Rejecting the demonic voices of nationalist irrationalism, Bonhoeffer turned to the sources of his intellectual heritage, a heritage that he believed encouraged openness to new ideas and experiences, including a love of art and culture, as well as love of travel, which was never to abandon him.

Dietrich's journey to Italy and especially Rome reflects the cultural leanings of Weimar Germany, which was fascinated more by ancient than contemporary Rome. Like Goethe a century before, he traveled to Italy to breathe in the art and life of a world that was profoundly human. Although he ostensibly traveled abroad to study, he actually spent little if any time in an academic setting.[27] He did, however, go prepared to experience the full breadth of ancient Rome and its Renaissance glory in the arts and culture. Here he discovered the ingenuity of the humanistic mind.

Like a dream suddenly broken off, his journey was abruptly ended due to the political realities of his time, when he traveled to war-torn Tripoli. There he confronted the brutal logic and incomprehensibility of war.[28] His first visit out of Europe was both transformative and unpleasantly shattering. The world could not be kept at bay.

A Young Man Chooses to Become a Theologian and a Pastor

Bonhoeffer's experience in Libya was not the first event in his life to penetrate the boundary between his world and its political turmoil that churned

---

[26.] See *DB-ER* 57–65, especially 58–62; see below, 1/57:84, a diary entry in which Bonhoeffer wrote, "The great Pan is not dead." On this trip he discovered that the horizons of ancient Roman culture were still very much in play. These were intellectually and emotionally stirring times for Bonhoeffer, the memory of which was still important to him in prison (see *LPP* 238).

[27.] We have little knowledge of the institution where Bonhoeffer was supposed to have matriculated. See below, 1/71, editorial note 2. We do not even know whether he matriculated.

[28.] See below, 1/57:82–109, "Italian Diary"; also see below, the letters to Walter Dreß: (1/89a:144f; 1/89b:145f; 1/93a:150; 1/93b:150; 1/94a:152; 1/96a:157; 1/96b:157f; 1/97a:161; 1/97b:161; 1/97e:163; 1/97f:164; 1/99a:166; 1/99b:167f; 1/99c:168f; 1/102a:173; 1/102b:173; and 1/105a:177.

around his family. Although his home had kept the world at bay for much of his childhood, the world had abruptly invaded his life a second time. The first time had been the death of his brother Walter near Marcel Cave during World War I.[29] His family was devastated, especially his mother, who apparently experienced a mental breakdown due to the loss.[30] Walter had been considered highly talented and was deeply loved by his brothers and sisters. The grief of the entire family was profound. By the time of the young Bonhoeffer's later journey to Rome and Tripoli, he was older and more mature, seeking to put the pieces together from a deeper perspective. Bonhoeffer began to sense how vulnerable all were to the violent political realities of a social world that had lost its way.

The challenge of coming to terms with his world led to Bonhoeffer's serious engagement with the intellectual and spiritual issues of his day. He was later to seek out Wilhelm Dreier, Richard Widmann, and Walter Dreß, pastors and theologians within the circle of his family, as a way to frame a new understanding about his world that could make sense to him. The diary of his Italian trip is replete with reflections on the future of Christianity, especially the possible demise of Protestantism. His essay on Horace and Catullus, written while still at the Gymnasium, had struggled with the problem of death while affirming the richness of life and the virtue of service to culture and nation.

The decision to pursue a theological career was not an easy one. He had been the athlete and musician of the family, reflecting a deeply ingrained love for life and art. Dietrich never spoke directly about this decision, so we have little to report with historical confidence about the factors that went into his decision. Even though he was descended from theologians and was related to a pastor, Hans von Hase, he had little firsthand experience with the institutional church up to this point in his development,[31] except for the confirmation classes that he and a few friends had attended. His family was Christian by tradition but not active in the church.

What compelled him to make his career decision is unclear. There is little doubt, however, that his reflections on the meaning of death played a role.[32] The theme of death is raised often in the material contained in this volume—in his children's sermons, in his papers on Luther, as well as in his essay on honor. Catullus's decision to die for love impressed him greatly as a sentimental young man, and he reacted strongly on the basis of emotion. Later he was to observe a deeper wisdom in the thoughts of a dying Luther.

[29.] See Bosanquet, *The Life and Death of Dietrich Bonhoeffer*, 36–37.
[30.] See below, 1/3:22, editorial note 4.
[31.] See *DB-ER* 34–36.
[32.] See *DB-ER* 28, 38–41; cf. Leibholz-Bonhoeffer, *The Bonhoeffers*, 32–33.

In any case, the value of a life of purpose and faith is a theme that runs throughout Bonhoeffer's work and life story. His letters, essays, meditations, and sermons in this volume betray his yearning for integrity. Honor for him came to mean obedience to God, a topic that appears throughout his theology, even during these early years.[33] It was here also that he found joy and satisfaction.

The Church and the World

The love of the world that was such an important part of Bonhoeffer's childhood was expressed by his father in the love of nature through science and by his mother in the love of culture through society. This son inherited both parental proclivities. Yet although he never lost this love of the world, it was a newly found love—the love of God—that was to determine his future. And the community where he was to express this love was not that of science or society but that of the church.

In his "Italian Diary" from 1924 he reflects seriously about the crisis of the liberal Protestant church and the ability of the Catholic church to address the concrete needs of its adherents.[34] A year later, in his "Seminar Paper on Luther's Feelings about His Work," Bonhoeffer reflects on the integrity of the Protestant cause. Its strength, he writes, is built upon the recognition of the need for submission to God, a recognition he found expressed most profoundly in the life and thought of Martin Luther.[35] Yet for Bonhoeffer being a Christian never meant a denial of the world and its joys. His 1926 "Commemorative Paper for Adolf von Harnack," entitled "'Joy' in Early Christianity," is witness to Bonhoeffer's commitment to the life-enriching strength of faith in God.[36] Joy and submission are both elements of the love for God that Bonhoeffer was discovering.

Dietrich's reflections, especially those in his diary and in his sermons, give evidence of a profound awareness of the complex landscape of the religious life of the church. They are precursors to his later thoughts on the struggle between the ecumenical movement and the Confessing Church. The Catholic church and the national church of Germany both had become

---

[33.] His two essays on Martin Luther in this volume (see below, "Seminar Paper on Luther's Feelings about His Work," 2/5:257–84, and "Seminar Paper on the Holy Spirit according to Luther," 2/10:325–70) are replete with indications that Bonhoeffer viewed Luther as a model of Christian integrity. We find the theme of Christian integrity in his "Seminar Paper on 1 Clement" (see below, 2/4:216–56) as well as in his "Paper on John and Paul" (see below, 2/13:395–404). Christ for Bonhoeffer is not a religious hero but the Lord who redeems. True honor comes from obedience to God.

[34.] See below, "Italian Diary," 1/57:88–91, 106f, and Bosanquet, *The Life and Death of Dietrich Bonhoeffer*, 52–54, 63–65.

[35.] See below, 2/5:257–84.

[36.] See below, 2/11:370–85.

churches domesticated by their culture, in Bonhoeffer's view. They no longer proclaimed the life-giving truth about the gospel that expected true honor, true joy, and true submission, all of which are found in God.

Understanding Bonhoeffer's Legacy

Carl Friedrich von Weizsäcker has called Bonhoeffer's path in life a "journey to reality."[37] The materials in this volume illuminate the formative steps in the journey from Bonhoeffer's stimulating and loving childhood home to the cold and heartless walls of a prison. They reveal the beginning of a life journey that opened the reality of God to Bonhoeffer—and through his life and work to us. Always surrounded by friends, Bonhoeffer was to face the challenges of his time with profound human integrity and a deep sense of the presence of God. The first stages, articulated in this volume, reveal those elements that formed the person we have come to know mainly through his later writings and life.

Bonhoeffer's sermons and essays below make it abundantly clear that he was ahead of his generation in the Weimar Republic, most of whom felt that all was well with the tradition that had wed church and state, culture and war. Bonhoeffer was ready for the theological and political struggle that was to come. He stood prepared with an unclouded vision, while the German intelligentsia were shaken by their general capitulation to the Nazi tide. His unshaken faith and persistent integrity stood in the face of the cruel will of nationalist fanaticism. Bonhoeffer could live in such a world with good humor and grace and yet without compromise. He chose to suffer affliction for the people of God instead of the easy road of racial privilege. He became a mentor for the faithful of the future, because he was groomed to be such a human being; we are privileged to watch the first moments of that development in these pages.

The Foundations of a Life of Faith

The reader of this volume will discover strands of thought and influence that continue into Dietrich Bonhoeffer's subsequent life as a pastor and theologian. There are too many to recount here. Discovered in these pages is the early life of an original thinker who rose quickly to the level of a systematic and rigorous proponent of theological and spiritual insights. Some of his early academic essays demonstrate significant scholarly skill. Others, such as his catechetical essays and his works on biblical interpretation and the Holy Spirit and eschatology, demonstrate his willingness to go beyond the perspectives of his teachers and develop insights of his own. His sermons and his addresses to children reveal much about his spiritual and intellectual strug-

---

[37.] Carl Friedrich von Weizsäcker (quoted in *DBW* 9:1).

gles and open for the reader the wisdom Bonhoeffer was learning to share with those he loved and cared for most.

Description and Organization of Material[38]

This volume consists primarily of letters written by and to Bonhoeffer, plus diplomas, official papers, a diary, essays, academic papers, notes, and outlines for reports, children's talks, catechetical works, and early sermons. Bonhoeffer never expected to see any of this written material in print. As is often the case with student work, the actual manuscripts and papers were not all in good condition. Some were prepared as academic papers, but most were not. Some seem to be—and are—unfinished. They are nonetheless important documents. The selection of letters for inclusion was the prerogative of the editors of the original German edition of *DBW* 9; they chose writings from Bonhoeffer's youth and education that were especially characteristic biographically, historically, and theologically.

Approximately two-thirds of the letters Bonhoeffer wrote during this period are included here, but only a few of the letters he received. Many of his more personal writings are not included. All of the texts, except for a very long letter from Wilhelm Dreier, have been included without abridgement. Newly discovered letters (not originally included in *DBW* 9 [1986], but published in the supplemental volume to the German edition, *DBW* 17, *Register und Ergänzungen* [1999]), have been added here due to their importance for his theological development. So that the numbering of the letters in *DBWE* 9 will continue to correspond to that of the original *DBW* 9 German edition, and so that these additional letters can nevertheless appear here in chronological order, they are numbered with supplementary lower case Arabic letters following each numbered correspondence immediately preceding them chronologically.

The material in this volume is organized into three parts. Part 1 contains the letters, a diary, his official papers, and documents; Part 2 includes his school essays, university papers, reports, notes, and graduation theses (statements that he argued as part of his public oral defense for his degree); and Part 3 contains his sermons, children's addresses, meditations, and catechetical works. This division reveals the varied types of literary work and the different literary styles he was learning to master as a young man. The material in each of the three parts is in chronological order. Any questions about the dating of a text are reported in the editorial notes. As with Part 1, material from the supplemental volume of the German edition, *DBW* 17, has been included here also in Parts 2 and 3. The page numbers in the margins that are preceded by the number 17 refer to this volume.

[38.] This section is based upon the Foreword of the German edition of this volume, *DBW* 9:2-6.

The Bonhoeffer papers are now in the manuscript department of the Staatsbibliothek, or State Library, in Berlin. In the 1980s a microfiche set of the Bonhoeffer papers was made by the Bundesarchiv in Koblenz. The microfiche set includes material from this period not published in this volume; these are listed in an appendix below. For a catalog of the Bonhoeffer literary estate and an index to the microfiche, see Dietrich Meyer and Eberhard Bethge, *Nachlaß Dietrich Bonhoeffer: Ein Verzeichnis—Archiv, Sammlung, Bibliothek.*

When possible the texts are presented in their final form. Except in a few cases, the abbreviations used by Bonhoeffer are clarified either by spelling them out or by using abbreviations recognizable to English-speaking readers. When Bonhoeffer corrected a text, the emendation is noted when it demonstrates the development of his thought; it is then included in either the body of his text or in the editorial notes.

Editorial notes contain explanations, notes from Bonhoeffer's teachers and professors, and discursive comments.[39] In Parts 2 and 3 an effort was made by the editors of the German edition to include the sources used by Bonhoeffer, as well as translations of material quoted by Bonhoeffer in French, Latin, and Greek. A bibliography of material used by Bonhoeffer is included in this volume along with a bibliography of material used by his correspondents and the editors.

Part 1 presents special difficulties in identifying the names of persons, geographical data, historical events, and references to plays on words and colloquialisms. These were not always clear. Biographical information on persons mentioned in Bonhoeffer's material or the editorial notes has been included in the Index of Names. Eberhard Bethge's notes from Bonhoeffer's *Gesammelte Schriften,* the first edition of Bonhoeffer's collected writings published in German, were used with his permission by the editors of the German critical edition.

Translation Issues

A number of translation problems and issues need to be mentioned. Most of the material in this volume has never been translated before. This volume contains a variety of literary genres, from the formal academic to the colloquial to a diary written at times in a completely disjointed fashion. Each style created its own set of problems. The decision was made to try to match as closely as possible the style that Bonhoeffer chose, without adding to or improving the original text. Although at times this can lead to lack of clarity and roughness in the translation, in a scholarly edition such as this it is more

---

[39.] Notes added by editors of the English edition are indicated by placing them in square brackets, followed by the initials of the editor who added material at that point.

important to keep the style of the original than to improve on Bonhoeffer's own efforts. When phrasing, style, and sentence structure allowed, the original has been followed rather closely.

Almost all titles, forms of address, official designations, place-names, and occupations have been rendered in English equivalents for the convenience of the reader, who may be struck by both the similarity and the difference between the cultural and linguistic contexts of Bonhoeffer's time and ours. In his diary, sermons, and children's addresses, Bonhoeffer often left certain things unspoken, making it necessary for his reader to fill in the gaps. Bonhoeffer often phrased his sermons for maximum effect upon his German congregations. Translating his phrasing "as is" would not have the same effect on an English-speaking audience. In such cases, the translation has sought to find phrasing in English that would approximate as closely as possible the German phrasing and meaning.

The academic essays presented a different set of problems. Some, such as his "Paper on the Historical and Pneumatological Interpretation of Scripture," or his "Paper on Reason and Revelation," were not formal essays but rather texts that he prepared for oral presentation to his seminar or simply as notes to himself. They have been left in their unfinished state, so that the tone and flavor of their translation would not be lost by polishing his grammar or syntax. The same editorial policy has governed the treatment of Bonhoeffer's colloquial style of address to children.

Apparatus and Helps

Appendices 1 and 2 provide a description for the process of "Dating the Manuscripts" and a "Chronology of *The Young Bonhoeffer: 1918–1927*." Appendix 3 provides an overview of the "Lectures and Seminars in Which Bonhoeffer Participated" as a university student. Appendix 4, a list of "Unpublished Material from This Period," catalogs all other known letters, diary material, essays, reports, notes, sermons, catechetical writings, and addresses from this time period that are not included in this volume, but that are cataloged in the *Nachlaß Dietrich Bonhoeffer* (see Bibliography). Appendix 5 provides a table providing a "List of Texts Published in Both *Gesammelte Schriften* and *DBWE* 9." Finally, the Bibliography of *The Young Bonhoeffer: 1918–1927* differs somewhat from the bibliographies in the volumes of the English edition published thus far. It is organized in three sections, which include "Literature Used by Bonhoeffer," "Literature Mentioned by Bonhoeffer's Correspondents," and "Literature Consulted by the Editors" of both the German and English editions. Three indices complete the volume: "Index of Scriptural References," "Index of Names" (including short biographical identifications of almost all persons listed), and "Index of Subjects."

Acknowledgments

The *DBW* volume editors and several colleagues all contributed to the original editing of the various papers, sermons, and other texts in the critical edition that is the basis for this translation. The editorial apparatus of this present volume is based upon their work, including the constant support and advice of Renate and Eberhard Bethge, without which *DBW* 9, originally published in 1986, would not have been possible.

Their work is acknowledged here, rather than in editorial notes as in the German volume. The numbers after their names indicate the pieces on which they worked.

Herbert Anzinger: 2/4; 2/14; 3/9

Clifford Green: 2/5; 2/10; 3/1; 3/5; 3/6; 3/7; 3/15; 3/16

Carl-Jürgen Kaltenborn: 2/4; 2/11; 2/13; 2/14; 2/16; 2/17; 2/17a; 2/17b; 3/13; 3/14; 3/15; 3/16

Theodor Mahlmann: 2/8; 2/12

Hans Pfeifer: 2/1; 2/2; 2/6; 2/7; 2/8; 2/9; 2/11; 2/12; 2/13a; 2/15; 2/16; 3/1; 3/2; 3/3; 3/4; 3/5; 3/6; 3/7; 3/8; 3/9; 3/10; 3/11; 3/12; 3/16a

Joachim von Soosten: 2/5; 2/9; 2/10

Paul D. Matheny and Mary C. Nebelsick would like to express special thanks for the hard work and advice of Robert Osborn of Duke University, whose attention accompanied the text, its translation, and its initial editorial preparation with patience and scholarly insight. Their thanks also go to the library staff of Ernst Miller White Library at Louisville Presbyterian Theological Seminary for the graciousness and support shown during the first stages of the translation and editing. Library staffs at Vanderbilt Divinity School and Roanoke College also provided valuable assistance. The patience and understanding of Westhampton Christian Church in Roanoke, Virginia, while Dr. Matheny, their pastor, devoted so much time to this undertaking, are also deeply appreciated.

Prior to the completion of much of the editorial work on *DBWE* 9, and even before the translation itself could be refined for publication, Paul Matheny and Mary Nebelsick each assumed new teaching positions at Union Theological Seminary in the Philippines, and subsequent to their move were not available to conclude their tasks. Translation of the front and back matter of this volume, including the Editor's Afterword to the German edition and all the indexes, were provided by Douglas W. Stott. Dr. Marshall Johnson, former Editorial Director of Fortress Press, agreed to assume the editorial role for this volume in medias res, including resolving issues of translation as well as correcting and completing the editorial apparatus. His long-practiced editorial gifts and meticulous attention to detail contributed significantly to this publication. Special thanks are owed to Dr. Evan Burge, Warden Emeritus of

Trinity College, Melbourne, who, during the final stages of manuscript preparation, completed a speedy review and correction of translations of Latin quotations in the two Luther papers and the Graduation Theses, and answered numerous queries about Latin terms. Dr. Clarke Chapman of Moravian College assisted with numerous details in the editorial notes, working especially on the letters in Part One. Hans Pfeifer and Clifford Green, two of the editors of the original German edition, along with Victoria Barnett, from the *DBWE* Editorial Board, and Wayne Whitson Floyd, the General Editor of the English-language edition, devoted considerable time and skill to completing the necessary editorial revisions of the manuscript and making it ready for publication in its final form.

The Young Bonhoeffer:
1918–1927

PART 1
Letters, Diary, Documents

A. The First World War and the Beginning of the Republic. Final School Years. January 1918–March 1923

---

1. To Julie Bonhoeffer[1]

January 23, 1918

Dear Grandmama,

Please come on February 1 so you'll already be here on our birthday.[2] It would really be a lot nicer if you were here. Please decide at once and come on the 1st.

Karl-Friedrich[3] is writing to us more often. Recently he wrote that he won the first prize in a race in which all of the junior officers of his company competed. The prize was 5 marks.

Recently we all spent the evening at the Schöne's.[4] First, we had a wonderful sausage soup—as you know, they had just slaughtered a pig. Next, we had the roast of veal that Aunt Johanna[5] brought with her from Timmendorf. With it there were vegetables, asparagus and carrots; then there were wonderful preserves and coffee.[6] Later we made music, conversed, and

---

[1.] *NL* A 3/2 (1); handwritten letter dated "23.1.1918" mailed from Berlin-Grunewald, Wangenheimstrasse 14, which since March 1916 had been the home of the Bonhoeffer family (see *DB-ER* 28). Bonhoeffer's paternal grandmother, Mrs. Julie Bonhoeffer, neé Tafel, lived in Tübingen, Neckarhalde 38.

[2.] February 4, 1906, is the day the twins Dietrich and Sabine Bonhoeffer were born.

[3.] Karl-Friedrich, Dietrich's brother, was in the military.

[4.] The Richard Schöne family lived at Wangenheimstrasse 13–15.

[5.] Johanna Schöne, daughter of Richard and Helene Schöne.

[6.] This description of a festive meal is set against the background of the catastrophic food shortage in the war year 1917–18, during which the twelve-year-old Dietrich often experienced "incredible hunger." See Sabine Leibholz, *The Bonhoeffers: Portrait of a Family*, 53; also Karl Bonhoeffer, "Lebenserinnerungen," 90.

finally tea and cheesecake were brought in. Around 10 o'clock the three of us[7] went home with Miss Käthe.[8] The others followed at around 10:45. Besides all this, there was a very good wine, of which everyone was served quite a lot.——

Today Miss Käthe and Ursel[9] went to see *Don Carlos*.[10] It was a splendid production. Walter[11] will return on Sunday. Today we were given 17 fine flounder from Boltenhagen[12] on the Baltic Sea, which we will eat this evening. We have already invited Aunt Tony Volkmann[13] and Aunt Johanna Schöne to dinner. Please come soon.

Best wishes,
Your grandson,
Dietrich

2. To Ursula Bonhoeffer[1]

Dear Ursel,

We have already been here a whole day, and it has gone by terribly quickly. Mr. Qualmann was not waiting for us when we arrived in Klütz[2] on Sunday a quarter of an hour late. Only a bus and a number of private cars were there, so we waited until 3:45. When Miss Horn[3] telephoned Boltenhagen and asked why Mr. Qualmann had not come he said that seats had been reserved for us on the incredibly full bus. He told us that another vehicle filled with people would be returning (to the station) at any minute and we

---

[7.] The three youngest children: Dietrich Bonhoeffer, Sabine Bonhoeffer (married name Leibholz), and Susanne Bonhoeffer (married name Dreß).

[8.] Katharina Horn, sister of Maria Horn (see below, letter 2), taught the twins many years (see *DBW* 10:192).

[9.] Ursula Bonhoeffer; married name Schleicher.

[10.] [A play by the German poet and playwright Friedrich Schiller.] [PDM]

[11.] Walter Bonhoeffer, Dietrich's brother, was in the military.

[12.] A Baltic Sea spa between Lübeck and Wismar. For many years the Bonhoeffer family vacationed there. See below, 1 / 2:21.

[13.] Tony, or Toni, Volkmann was the adopted daughter of Dr. Richard Volkmann, who was related to the Hase family.

[1.] *NL* A 3/3(1); undated handwritten letter mailed from Boltenhagen, the Qualmann's guesthouse; the estimated date is June 17, 1918. Among the travelers were Maria Horn (see below, editorial note 3); Hans-Christoph von Hase; and Dietrich, Sabine, and Susanne Bonhoeffer.

[2.] The last train station before Boltenhagen.

[3.] From 1908 until her marriage to Dr. Richard Czeppan in 1923 (see below, 1/11:000, editorial note 4) Maria Horn, called Hörnchen , was a teacher in Bonhoeffer's home. Her piety, shaped by the community of the Herrnhutter Brethren, influenced the development of Bonhoeffer as a young child. She remained a lifelong friend of the family.

could take it. Well, about 4:15 a vehicle finally arrived and we reached Boltenhagen around 5 o'clock. The sea was pretty stormy, and the waves crashed against the beach with a vengeance. So we drank our afternoon tea and then returned to the beach. Then, however, we wanted to buy our shovels, so we went to a kiosk and got everything. We also bought a flag. From the kiosk we went immediately to Breaker's Bridge and then walked homeward along the beach. I can't even tell you how many jellyfish had washed ashore. At any rate, we were constantly bending down to throw them back into the water. They come in all different sizes—fat, thin, round, and in every shape imaginable. Then we had to eat supper. Afterwards we went out once more to the sea and then to bed. On Sunday, we got up at 7:30. First we ate breakfast. Everyone had an egg, ham, butter, milk, and sausage. After this we ran to the beach and built our own wonderful sand castle. Next, we made a rampart around the wicker beach chair. Then we worked on the fortress. While we left it alone for 4–5 hours for dinner and tea, it was completely washed away by the sea. But we had taken our flag with us. After tea we went back down and dug canals. I don't know what they look like today. Then it began to rain, and we watched Mr. Qualmann's cows being milked.

I hope you are feeling better. Thank Mama very much for the things for me.

Best wishes,
Your Dietrich

3. To Julie Bonhoeffer[1]   12

Dear Grandmama,

Yesterday evening while we were sitting on the beach we saw two airplanes fly overhead. Both were seaplanes. Both flew very low. Then suddenly one flew very high and the next moment it dived down headfirst. I thought it had made a nosedive, which they often practice in Grunewald. Soon we saw a thick black pillar of smoke rising above the ground, and we knew this meant that the plane had crashed! We went toward the other airplane, which in the meantime had landed on the water and had moved toward land. Others came by and reported that only one person had been in the airplane; but the pilot from the other airplane said that two people had to have been in it. Then everyone searched again and somebody said that the pilot had completely burned up but the other had jumped out and had sustained only a hand injury. Afterwards he came over and we saw that his entire eyebrows were singed. Then we went away again.[2]

[1.] *NL* A 3/2(3); undated handwritten letter mailed from Boltenhagen. Postmarked July 3, 1918.

[2.] On the same day, Bonhoeffer wrote his parents (*NL* A 3/1(4)) that their acquaintance, Otto von Weddingen, a famous U-boat commander, lived in Boltenhagen.

As we lay in bed that evening, we fell asleep quickly. Then we all woke up one after the other, because the sea suddenly raged very violently. It washed away our entire fortress and penetrated 20 meters inland. The wicker beach chairs were covered over with sand up to the seats. It is too bad that the weather is unpleasant today as well, so we are sitting inside. We have had several days of nice weather and have gone swimming. We also built two rafts for ourselves.

In the afternoon a few days ago (Sunday), we slept in our sand castle and all got very sunburned. In the afternoon we walked to Ternewitz.[3] First we had a little piece of cake and then asked for bread. We told her we had bread coupons, but she said she could not give us any bread. Afterwards, I went in again and wanted to get everyone another piece of cake, but she said she had only one piece left. When I begged her for bread, she said she would give it to us this one time, but she did not do so willingly.

On Friday we will return to Berlin. We can get for you only dried soup and coffee additive at 4 marks a pound. Absolutely nothing else can be had here except when one can barter something, such as petroleum, fabric, or other items.

Karl-Friedrich's military training course is finished on July 3, but he came home early on the 2nd.

We have to take a nap every afternoon. Two other boys are also here. One is 10 years old and the other 14. A little Jewish boy is also here. We play more often with the other two. Yesterday evening we had a quartet and we played writing games.

Everything was lit up with spotlights again yesterday evening, certainly because of the pilots. I had left my boat in the wicker beach chair, but when we came out today, the sea had washed it far away down the beach.

The food lately has been splendid. We always save a bit of cheese and honey for Karl-Friedrich. Tomorrow, the last day, we also plan to make a garland out of oak leaves for Walter's grave.[4]

Best wishes to you.
Your grandson,
Dietrich

[3.] Approximately 4 km east of Boltenhagen.

[4.] Walter Bonhoeffer died on March 28, 1918, as a result of a wound received during World War I at Marcel Cave in France.

4. To Hans Christoph von Hase[1]

July 15, 1918

Dear Hans-Christoph,

I waited all day long for a letter from you and none came. Why don't you write? Perhaps you've written and the letter has not arrived. If you don't, I can't come. I'm not even mentioned anymore when a visit to you is discussed. Only the girls are spoken of. So write as often as you can.   14

It would be a great shame if I could not come, because then our wonderful plans would be ruined. And that would be a shame.

Did your sisters like the things? We are now making an underground cave and underground passages that go from one side of the arbor to the cave. We've done this so that when we roughhouse with Klaus[2] again we can either bring rescuers to the cave or we can attack the enemy from the rear. We will make a wall, a ditch, and a very deep hole in front of the cave so that when anyone falls in we can pull them directly into the hole.

Please give my greetings to Uncle Hans, Aunt Elizabeth, and the cousins.[3] Don't forget to write.

Best wishes,
Yours,
Dietrich.

5. To His Sisters and Brothers and Maria Horn[1]

Friday, [September] 12, 1918

Dear brothers and sisters and Dear Miss Horn,

I just found out that the letter that I wrote to you hasn't even been sent yet and that the first part is missing. Dear Bina,[2] I thank you very much for your card. I don't know if I already wrote you that we found partridge eggs, and that four have already hatched. We had to help two because they couldn't get   15

[1.] *NL* A 3/3(2): handwritten letter dated "den 15.7.1918" mailed from Berlin-Grunewald. Also previously published in *DB-ER* 28. Hans-Christoph von Hase often spent his vacation with Bonhoeffer until his student years; see, e.g., *DB-ER* 28.

[2.] Klaus Bonhoeffer.

[3.] Hans von Hase, brother of Paula Bonhoeffer and Bonhoeffer's godfather, was superintendent of the church district of Liegnitz (Legnica); he married Ada (née) Schwarz. Elisabeth von Hase was the sister of Hans von Hase and Paula Bonhoeffer. Hans von Hase's home was in Waldau, 2 km west of Liegnitz. The cousins were Klara, Dorothea, Renate, Rosemarie, and Traute von Hase.

[1.] *NL* A 3/3(3); handwritten letter dated "Freitag, den 12.[9.] 1918" mailed from Waldau; the month is inferred [although September 12, 1918, was on Thursday, not Friday].

[2.] Sabine Bonhoeffer.

out. The hen under which we placed them is not showing them how they should eat, and we don't know how to teach them. I now help Hänschen[3] more often when he brings in the animals. I always go first. That means I steer the animals to the hay bales that need to be loaded, and recently I even drove the wagon a good piece around quite a few turns.

Yesterday Klärchen[4] and I rode horses. It was very nice. We glean[5] here often and successfully, and so gather quite a lot. Today I want to thresh again and let it go through the separator. The reason one gets so much is that we always get permission to glean on fields that haven't been counted. And naturally everything goes much faster there.

Didn't you get the card asking for the Latin book? Now I always have to take lessons with Hänschen. Regrettably, the fruit harvest is not particularly good. However, to make up for it, the beet and wheat crops are wonderful. The potatoes are also doing very well. There is quite a lot of fruit in the garden, especially apricots and grapes. The plums are all right, but there is only one-tenth the amount of pears of what there was last year. Although they are much larger than last year, they are not big enough to compensate for their small number.

This afternoon we want to go boating on the lake at Pansdorf.[6] By the way, I am arriving in Berlin, Charlottenburg train station, at 12:40, but without Christel.[7] She will arrive in the afternoon by way of Breslau. I won't travel by way of Breslau because I would have only a half-hour stopover, and that would mean three hours of unnecessary travel. So until Sunday.

My best wishes to you and the maids.
Yours,
Dietrich

16   **6. To His Parents**[1]

Dear Parents,

Yesterday we took my gleanings to be ground up. There will even be 10–15 pounds more than I had thought, depending on how fine it will be ground. Actually there should be 18 pounds more, but who knows how they will grind it.

[3.] Hans Christoph von Hase.

[4.] Klara von Hase.

[5.] This refers to gleanings from the grainfields after the harvest, a welcome addition to meager foodstuffs in the winter of 1918–19.

[6.] Two km west of Waldau.

[7.] Christine Bonhoeffer, later married to von Dohnanyi.

[1.] *NL* A 3/1(6); undated handwritten postcard mailed from Waldau. Postmarked September 30, 1918.

This morning we cooked. The weather here is magnificent, with sunshine almost the whole time. In the next few days we will harvest the potatoes. By the way, the potatoes are really not as bad and are not at all as rotten as has been reported at home. I work every day here with Hänschen and Uncle Hans translating Latin. Will you come to Breslau this time, dear Mama, since Karl-Friedrich is not on active duty?[2] If you do, please pick me up in Waldau.

My best regards to you and to everyone else.
Yours,
Dietrich

7. To Julie Bonhoeffer[1]

Sunday, December 8, 1918

Dear Grandmama,

Mama is doing much better now.[2] In the morning she still feels very weak, but in the afternoon she feels quite steady again. Sadly, she still eats hardly anything. Mr. Senz[3] believes that she must lie in bed for eight more days and then get up for an hour at a time. So she will probably be able to spend Christmas with us, even if she can't be with us the whole day. Recently we got the news that we would billet soldiers: two regular soldiers. Well, we got everything ready in one of the girls' rooms but no one came the entire day. The girls lay down in their old beds, but suddenly, around 1:30 at night, the doorbells rang shrilly. We didn't know what the reason could be. As we came out of our rooms, we saw that it was our billeted soldiers, and they were not two regular soldiers but an officer and his servant. So they had to sleep together. But the next day I had to give up my room to the lieutenant. He will probably stay there four to eight days, but we don't know yet exactly.

Mr. Gauwald,[4] a comrade of Karl-Friedrich's, is also here. He was captured and escaped. Once, when no watchman was posted, he left the camp and walked without a map in the direction of our positions. For five days, he had nothing to eat other than a few wild plums.

Ursel told me that I should tell you what I would like for Christmas. I am out of stationery and postcards, so I would naturally love to have some. At the

17

[2.] This was due to a temporary delay in placing troops on the front.

[1.] *NL* A 3/2(5); handwritten letter dated "Sonntag, den 8.12.18" mailed from Berlin-Grunewald.
[2.] After Walter's death (see above, 1/3:22, editorial note 4) his mother became very ill.
[3.] Bonhoeffer's family doctor.
[4.] Difficult to decipher in the original manuscript; perhaps "Hauwald". The identity of this person is unknown.

moment the weather here is pitiful. There is heavy fog all around and the air is extremely wet and cold.

Today Klaus and I are going to see Theodor Dietrich,[5] who lies wounded here in the Charitée.[6] Eight days ago all the children were at the Krückmann's.[7] On Monday Aunt Elisabeth and Uncle Benedict[8] will be traveling to Waldau.

Best wishes to you.
Gratefully,
Your grandson Dietrich

18   **8. To Julie Bonhoeffer**[1]

Dear Grandmama,

Many thanks for the fine stationery and postcards. They really are wonderful. The postcards in the little book are especially nice. I was so happy to receive them. Once again all of us received a tremendous number of things. I received an additional piece for my "Jung-Deutschland" game,[2] which has battle plans from this war. Then I was also given several books. "Im Wasgenwald,"[3] which you gave Walter for Christmas in 1917, came from Walter's bookshelf. All of us received a plate of goodies as well. In addition, I received various other things.

The day before yesterday it snowed, but sadly everything had melted by the 24th and today the weather is pretty nasty. But it is really very good that snow is not lying on the ground, because otherwise the transportation problems[4] would be much more difficult. Sadly, Theodor Dietrich[5] did not come to our house, because he had to have a sliver of bone removed on the 23rd; but we went to see him and brought him his Christmas presents. He is doing very well again, and so we think he might be able to come to our house on New Year's Eve.

[5.] A second cousin on the Bonhoeffer side of the family.

[6.] The correct spelling is "Charité," the hospital and clinic of the University of Berlin.

[7.] Emil Krückmann, Professor of Ophthalmology and since 1912 director of the eye clinic at the University of Berlin.

[8.] Elisabeth and Benedict von Hase (known as Uncle Bubi).

[1.] *NL* A 3/2(6); undated handwritten letter mailed from Berlin-Grunewald. Postmarked December 25, 1918.

[2.] Cf. below, pages 1/12:30 and 3/4:465.

[3.] A novel by Baron Ferdinand von Raesfeld subtitled *Jäger - und Kriegsroman aus dem Grenzland* ("Hunting and War Novel from the Frontier").

[4.] This refers to the German Armistice Commission's forced agreement on December 1–2, 1918, to surrender Germany's best and heaviest locomotives by the order to submit to the French ultimatum and to attain an extension of the armistice.

[5.] The identity of this person is not known (cf. above, 1/7:25).

On the 27th Oluf and Püppi Krückmann[6] are coming over to spend the whole day with us. I thank you again very much for your presents.

My best regards to you.
Your grateful grandson,
Dietrich

9. To Julie Bonhoeffer[1]

19

January 11, 1919

Dear Grandmamama,

So far Mama is feeling pretty good again in spite of these disturbances. For a while she lived with the Schönes across the street. Since then, she has been doing significantly better. You will certainly have read in the newspaper about the attack on the Halensee train station.[2] It wasn't too dangerous, but we could hear it quite clearly because it happened at night. The whole thing lasted about an hour. Then these fellows were pushed back. When they tried it again around 6 o'clock in the morning, they only got bloody heads. This morning we heard artillery fire. We don't know yet where it came from. At the moment it is thumping again, but it seems to be only in the distance.

Karl-Friedrich will finally be released from the Charitée. He might yet take some kind of part in this, but Mama and Papa are not yet in complete agreement with him. At the moment, thank God, the government's troops are doing better. Our vacations are being extended until the 17th of the month, either because of the disturbances or because of the shortage of coal. Our school has so little that it lasts only a short time. Hopefully all of these things will come to an end soon.

Many kind regards to you.
Your grateful grandson,
Dietrich

[6.] Children of Emil Krückmann (see above, 1/7:26, editorial note 7).

[1.] *NL* A 3/2(7); handwritten letter dated "den 11.1.1919" mailed from Berlin-Grunewald. Also previously published in part in *DB-ER* 30.

[2.] The Halensee train station was about 800 meters as the crow flies from Bonhoeffer's room. The attack on the station was made by the "Revolutionary Communist Party/Spartacus Federation," founded on December 30–31, 1918, which wanted to hinder the election of the National Assembly and to establish a soviet republic in Germany. For this reason an armed revolt as well as a general strike took place in Berlin; the unrest lasted until January 12, 1919.

20   **10. To Julie Bonhoeffer**[1]

Grunewald, February 10, 1919

Dear Grandmama,

Thank you many times for the fine Ulmer bread[2] and the book. The animal tales are terribly funny. We read them together after dinner once. I like them quite a lot. The Ulmer bread also tasted wonderful. I also received a lot of other things: my broken watch was returned, a fountain pen, stilts, many books on composers, and an awful lot to eat.

We go ice-skating quite a lot here, but that will probably have to end because now it is beginning to thaw. Sometimes we go sledding. Mama is getting quite well again. She shall probably go to Kissingen for a month in May.

Once again Aunt Hannah[3] had Georg Konrad brought home from his training in Berau,[4] because she didn't like his being there. We aren't suppose to talk about the fact that she sent for him, because he is being told that he can't complete his training there.

By the way, I didn't have any afternoon classes on my birthday. I actually didn't go because I had a horrible boil. Right after that I got lumbago, so that Friday was the first day I could go back.

It surely is absurd[5] that Scheidemann is Minister-President and Ebert should be the Provisional President.[6]

My best wishes.
Gratefully, your grandson
Dietrich

[1.] *NL* A 3/2(8); handwritten dated "den 10.II.1919."

[2.] See below, 1/14a:32, editorial note 3.

[3.] Hannah Countess of Goltz (born von Hase), sister of Paula Bonhoeffer.

[4.] Her son had gone to Berau in the southern part of the Black Forest near Walshut for paramilitary training.

[5.] This word, *toll* in German, is mostly used by Bonhoeffer in a negative sense; cf. 1/24, 1/44, and 1/48. The initial shock over this political development yielded soon to a generally more positive assessment of the new republic, as Bonhoeffer's indignation over the murder of Rathenau demonstrates. See *DB-ER* 33; cf. below, page 49.

[6.] He is referring here to Philipp Scheidemann and Friedrich Ebert.

11. To His Parents[1]   21

May 20, 1919

Dear Parents,

Recently, the principal suddenly came into Latin class.[2] He asked some
questions in between. My turn came and I knew the answer. We have already
taken tests in Latin, mathematics, and French. In Latin, I got a 3, the third
best grade in the class. In mathematics, I got a 2-. It was the best grade and
Maria[3] got it as well. In French, I got a 3, which was also among the best
grades. All in all, I am probably the best student in the class, along with
Maria. The class is just simply terrible; they simply don't know anything
except a little history.

Klaus is over at Czepan's[4] home today and was invited to stay for supper.
Czepan asked Klaus to stay and play some music with him after supper.

What do you think of the terms of peace?[5] I hardly believe that one can   22
accept them in their present form. Considering the demonstrations we had,
it might lead to a nationwide protest movement. To be sure, one has to keep
in mind that our enemies might eventually halt food shipments until we
accept. If the Saar and Upper Silesia are relinquished, complete economic
collapse would follow. But naturally, the same would happen if we didn't get
any food. I hope that Ebert will call a general vote so that he doesn't have to
bear the responsibility alone.

It has just chimed 9 o'clock. I have to go to bed.

Many best wishes.
Yours,
Dietrich

[1.] *NL* A 3/1(7); handwritten letter dated "den 20.V.19" mailed from Berlin. Also previously published in part in *DB-ER* 31.

[2.] The principal, Dr. Wilhelm Vilmar, was a frequent guest of the historian Hans Delbrück, whose family were friends of the Bonhoeffer family and lived in the neighborhood
(see *Fiction from Tegel Prison*, 165ff.). Bonhoeffer had just transferred that Easter from
Friedrich-Werder Gymnasium to Grunewald Gynmasium [both are secondary schools in
the humanities that prepare students in the classical disciplines for entrance to a univer-
sity].[PDM] Cf. below 1/31:52f. and 1/36:60, and the Festschrift, *75 Jahre Walther Rathenau-
Oberschule (previously Grunewald-Gymnasium) 1903–1978*.

[3.] Maria Weigert lived at Wangenheimstraße 12, next door to the Bonhoeffer family.

[4.] Richard Czeppan was a teacher of Klaus Bonhoeffer and until 1919 of Dietrich Bonhoeffer. He was a friend to both and often Bonhoeffer's piano partner.

[5.] On May 7, 1919, the German representatives received the terms of peace following
World War I.

12. To Julie Bonhoeffer[1]

August 15, 1919

Dear Grandmama,

Congratulations on your birthday.[2] I wish you a very good upcoming year.

Ursel and Karl-Friedrich are coming home Sunday. We are really looking forward to seeing them. It is a shame that they will have to leave again so soon.

It was very nice in Friedrichsbrunn,[3] but it was too bad that I got sick just when Mama and Klaus arrived.

Yesterday we were in the Natural History Museum with our class. Our student council has decided that one day each month should be free for educational trips, and so we went to the Natural History Museum. Other classes also took regular field trips.

Today is certainly the hottest day in the year, at least in Berlin. It is 26° [79° F] in the shade; that is more than 30° [86° F] in the sun. I can't go swimming today, however, because I have a piano lesson. We play tennis pretty often, either by ourselves or with some others from our school.

Sadly, I won't be at home for Susi's birthday party. I have a rowing class and I certainly can't miss it. Klaus might be able to skip class, but he doesn't yet know if he can because he didn't go the last time. I also joined the Boy Scouts here. Every Sunday morning we do exercises, play war games,[4] and such. It is always very nice. I won't be able to go next time, however, because my brother and sister are coming and of course we are going to pick them up.

Christel has been attending our Grunewald school since the long vacation. At this point, there are already quite a few girls there. One is in the Unterprima R5, one in the Obersekunda R and Christel is in (Obersekunda) H. In our class there are two girls, and in the Untersekunda R there are also two.[5] So altogether there are eleven. Perhaps another girl may come into our class. There are eleven boys and two girls in our class.

A friend visited me on Saturday. We played a few writing games and then talked. It was very nice. Once again I wish you a very good year. Please say hello to my parents and my brothers and sisters.

Best regards.
Your grateful grandson,
Dietrich

[1.] *NL* A 3/2(10); handwritten letter dated "den 15.8.1919" mailed from Berlin.

[2.] Her birthday was August 21.

[3.] A community in the Harz Mountains, where the Bonhoeffer family owned a home, a former forest ranger's house, which since 1913 they had used as a summer dwelling.

[4.] See above, page 26, and below, page 465.

[5.] The nine high school grades of a gymnasium in Bonhoeffer's time were named Sexta, Quinta, Quarta, Untertertia, Tertia (or Obertertia), Untersekunda, Obersekunda, Unterprima, and Oberprima. Thus, the girls in question are all in the last four years of Gymnasium.[WF]

13. To Julie Bonhoeffer[1]

December 22, 1919

Dear Grandmama,

I wish you an absolutely joyous holiday and am sending you a folder for
the letters of 1920. Recently Uncle Otto[2] visited us; and soon after that
Lothar[3] came over. He wanted to see Krückmann because of his eyes. Dr.   24
Krückmann was very impressed by Lothar, and said it was wonderful how
much he was able to accomplish with what little he had. Lothar went home
again on Wednesday evening.

We received our report cards this Christmas. I had the best report card of
the boys. One girl in our class got an even better report card. At present, the
weather is terrible here. It rains one moment and snows the next so that a
miserable slush follows.

The Boy Scouts will give a performance on Sunday afternoon and I will
play the piano. I will play an Impromptu by Schubert, a Trio by Haydn and a
piece with someone who plays cello. Today I am going to a concert given by
a piano player. I am already looking forward to it very much. The boy playing the piano is only 15 years old. I am also taking dancing lessons this year.
We are learning modern dances.

Once again, joyous holidays and a happy New Year to you, dear Grandmamama.

Your grateful grandson,
Dietrich

14. To Julie Bonhoeffer[1]

Dear Grandmama,
Thank you very much for the nice book you sent me. I have already begun to
read it and I like it very much. I received many other things as well: *Der Wer-
wolf* by Alexis, *Die Schwarze Galeere* by Raabe, *Knulp* by Hesse,[2] a sled, and
many more things.

[1.] *NL* A 3/2(11); handwritten letter mailed from Berlin dated "den 22.XII.19."

[2.] Otto Bonhoeffer, director of a unit of I. G. Farben, brother of Karl Bonhoeffer.

[3.] Lothar Bonhoeffer, son of Otto Bonhoeffer, had been wounded and almost blinded in 1914 during the war.

[1.] *NL* A 3/2(12); undated handwritten letter mailed from Berlin, Christmas 1919.

[2.] These are three popular German novels by Willibald Alexis, Wilhelm Raabe, and
Hermann Hesse.

Sadly, Ursel has been sick; nevertheless she was able to come downstairs. Today she has a temperature of only 36°.[3] Saturday, many people will come to our house, and we will probably dance and play games as well. Today the Goltzes[4] are coming over for dinner. On Saturday afternoon, I will play in a performance given by the Boy Scouts. Mr. Schäffer, Karl-Friedrich's piano teacher, composed a piece for Christmas that we played for Mama and Papa.

We would all be very happy if you came to visit us soon. Then you would still be here for our birthday. Your saltwater pretzels taste terrific. Papa gave us each some. Because of the coal, our vacation will probably be extended approximately 14 days.

All my best to you.
Your grateful grandson,
Dietrich

17:17   14a. To Julie Bonhoeffer[1]

February 9, 1920

Dear Grandmama,

Thank you very much for the lovely Ulmer bread and the marmite.[2] Both tasted wonderful. I also received many other things, a lot of musical pieces, a biography of Beethoven, and many other books. I was given a sausage and some bread ration coupons[3] from Waldau.[4] On the afternoon of our birthday we invited our friends over. First we played in the garden, because the weather was so nice. Then we went in and played inside, and then even danced a little.—Yesterday morning we took a lovely walk in the Grunewald. The sun shone beautifully, and everything[5] was covered with frost. Our parents return home from Breslau tomorrow evening. Klaus

---

[3.] Difficult to decipher in the original manuscript; perhaps "369." The first would be 96.8° F, the other 98.4° F.

[4.] Refers to the family of Rüdiger Count von der Goltz; see above, 1/10:28, editorial note 3.

[1.] *NL Dreß*. Cf. Reinhart Staats and Matthias Wünsche, "Dietrich Bonhoeffer's Abschied von der Berliner 'Wintertheologie'," 265ff. First previously published in *Zeitschrift für Neuere Theologiegeschichte/Journal for the History of Modern Theology* 4 (1997): 265ff. Transcribed by Eberhard Bethge. This is a thank-you letter dated "d[en] 9.11.[19]20" following the birthday of Dietrich and his twin sister, Sabine, on February 4.

[2.] Ulmer bread is a Swabian specialty. Marmite (a popular spread made of malt extract that is best on bread) contained nutrients growing children needed during the food shortage that accompanied the war.

[3.] Coupons were used for bread during and after the war.

[4.] Home of Bonhoeffer's uncle, Superintendent Hans von Hase. Cf. above, 1/4:23, editorial note 3.

[5.] Difficult to decipher; perhaps reads "all things."

will complete his final examinations for his school graduation certificate on the 17th. We are all so sorry that Aunt Emilie[6] is so sick and had to go stay in the hospital. Please greet her when you can and many kind regards to you from

Gratefully.
Your grandson,
Dietrich

14b. To Julie Bonhoeffer[1]   17:18

April 2, 1920

Dear Grandmama,

Christel, Klaus, and I arrived here in Friedrichsbrunn[2] yesterday. We all traveled fourth class,[3] and therefore it was terribly full. Christel was the only one who had a seat until we reached Magdeburg. The rest of us sat on suitcases. We had a three-hour stopover in Magdeburg, and we visited the cathedral[4] there. Liddy[5] and I were able to get a seat in Magdeburg, while the others had to stand in the next coach. We did, however, arrive pretty much on time. The others walked a bit of the way to meet us. We'll probably go to Treseburg today. The weather is very nice. Mrs. Klaaßen, a seamstress, is taking care of the house. All of our girls[6] have left and the new ones won't come until the 15th. We got our report cards on Wednesday. I had the best one[7] of all the boys. Only Maria Weigert[8] did better.—I have to close now, because we want to take a walk.

Best wishes and have a happy holiday.[9]
Your grandson,
Dietrich

[6.] The identity of this person is not known.

[1.] *NL* Dreß; handwritten with pencil dated "d[en] 2.IV.[19]20." Writing paper embossed with the letters "D.B." First previously published in *Zeitschrift für Neuere Theologiegeschichte/Journal for the History of Modern Theology* 4 (1997): 269. Transcribed by Eberhard Bethge.

[2.] Vacation home of the Bonhoeffer family in the Harz Mountains.

[3.] Fourth class was at that time the least expensive way to travel the National Railway.

[4.] Magdeburg Cathedral was constructed 1209–1363.

[5.] The identity of this person is not known.

[6.] Maids working for the household.

[7.] Refers to grade-point average.

[8.] Classmate who lived next door to the Bonhoeffer family on the Wangenheimstraße; see above, 1/11:29.

[9.] Easter 1920.

15. To Klaus Bonhoeffer[1]

July 20, 1920

Dear Klaus,

At long last I must also write to you. Until now I have written only once. Before we traveled here, I took a two-day canoe trip with several students from my class. (By the way, did you understand the card we wrote with Justus[2] and Bornitz[3] during the canoe trip?) We were in a thoroughly crazy mood. We traveled to the neighborhood of Ketzin[4] and spent the night outside. Although it was terribly hot during the day, it became so cold around 3:00 that I had to wrap myself in a cover with someone else. Early in the morning, around 4:30, having already bathed, we went home.

We have had great luck with the weather since we have been here. The sun has shone almost the whole time. We even want to go to the Auerberg[5] tomorrow. I hope that I can find the route we traveled the last time on the map, because the others don't know how to get there.

This year there are unbelievably many mushrooms. We are already drying them. Ask Grandmama if she would like us to dry some for her for her birthday. Recently we went to Hänichen[6] to get raspberries and we found 15 pounds of mushrooms on the side of the road.

Stalls are already being erected for the shooting match. Hänschen[7] is helping Mr. Sanderhoff with them. Leni Küstermann's father[8] is also here, and we often go walking with him. Maybe I'll take a trip with him to Brocken.[9] We'll start at the Bodetal train station,[10] because he doesn't want to be gone overnight.

We have an awful lot to read here, which is nice because we otherwise don't. I have already read *Ein Kampf um Rom*, Augustine, and Tolstoy's *Gespräche* with Teneromo, and now I want to read *Stechlin*. Are you familiar with Tolstoy's *Gespräche?* In it there is a story entitled "Die Zwei Greise."[11]

[1.] *NL* A 4/3(2), handwritten letter dated "den 20.VII.1920" mailed from Friedrichsbrunn.

[2.] Justus Delbrück, son of Hans Delbrück.

[3.] Most likely Gerhard Bornitz, a schoolmate of Hans von Dohnanyi.

[4.] About 13 km northwest of Potsdam on the Havel River.

[5.] At Stolberg in the southern part of the Harz Mountains.

[6.] Refers to the Hänichen health resort at Alexisbad in the Harz Mountains.

[7.] Hans-Christoph von Hase.

[8.] Karl Brückner from Meiningen, father of Helene Küstermann, called Leni, who often visited the Bonhoeffer home with her daughters.

[9.] See 1/16:35f.

[10.] Second train station in Thale, 5 km southwest of Quedlinburg.

[11.] These were two popular German novels, *Ein Kampf um Rom* by Felix Dahn and *Der Stechlin* by Theodor Fontane. *Gespräche mit Tolstoi*, by J. Teneromo, mentions the legend of the "Die Zwei Greise" ("two old men"), who speak about the corruption of truth through participation in social injustice. The young Bonhoeffer may not be aware that Tolstoy refers to himself here.

Tolstoy's version, however, is not at all like the real story and it is very odd. I don't understand at all what it is supposed to mean.

What happened to my bike was despicable. Someone stole it from me in the space of 2 minutes. When are you actually going to take the trip with Karl-Friedrich? When are you coming back? We are not coming back until August 8. But I think we'll be caught up then in the crazy vacation turmoil.

Please give everyone the best from all. And my best wishes also to you.

Yours,
Dietrich

16. To His Parents[1]   27

July 29, 1920

Dear Parents,

Yesterday I returned from my trip. It was truly wonderful. Early Monday morning around 3, we got up and hiked toward Thale. First, we traveled to Blankenburg. From there, we went further toward Elbingerode. This stretch was simply glorious; it ran constantly through valleys, woods, and ravines. We traveled with the rack railway, because we were climbing sharply. With it we went from Elbingrode over Rübeland toward Dreiannen-Hohne;[2] and then came the prettiest stretch: from Dreiannen-Hohne toward the Brocken. We climbed higher and higher and saw many different villages lying beneath us in the valley. Schierke[3] certainly lies in a wondrously beautiful spot. The higher we went, the clearer it became. When we finally reached the summit it was like winter; one's fingers froze completely and the wind blew so strong up in the observation tower that one could hardly stand. Mr. Brückner told us the whole time, "Just don't catch a cold." The next day he had such a bad head cold that he could hardly talk. After an hour we traveled toward Dreiannen-Hohne and from there we traveled toward Nordhausen. This ride was also wonderfully beautiful. It reminded me immediately of the Thuringian forest that we passed when we went to Tübingen. Again and again there were woods filled with birches[4] and spruce. Afterwards it went through the "golden meadow"[5] until it reached Nordhausen. This is an extremely beautiful old town with a magnificent Romanesque cathedral. We were in it. It is obvi-

---

[1.] *NL* 4/1 (2); handwritten letter dated "den 29.VII.1920" mailed from Friedrichsbrunn.

[2.] Thale, Blankenburg, Dreiannen-Hohne are places on the train route from Quedlinburg to Brocken. Bonhoeffer was confused about the order of Rübeland and Elbingerode.

[3.] A village 5 km southeast of Brocken.

[4.] Difficult to decipher in the original manuscript.

[5.] The fruitful Helme valley lies between Nordhausen and Sangerhausen on the southern border of the eastern part of the Harz Mountains.

28

ously still used as a Catholic church. It truly was the first time that I had been in a Catholic church, and I was completely surprised by the splendor. The entire altar was covered with gold, and there were paintings of the saints and the Virgin Mary everywhere. They had probably been painted a long time ago. Having seen this, one can understand how something like it can attract simple people.

Afterwards we also went to the City Hall, which is also a very old structure. Then we walked on the city wall that separates the old city from the new city. When we returned we went past the house in which the inventor of the pianoforte was born and died. His name was Schröter.[6] Then we went to the hotel and to bed.

The next morning we traveled to Kelbran and hiked up the Kyffhäuser Mountains.[7] Something very interesting is there. The warriors of 1870 erected a 40–50 meter high monument to the old Kaiser on the mountain. From there we have a beautiful view of the entire "Golden Meadow" in the Thuringian forest. Friedrichsbrunn cut off the view of the Auerberg. From Kyffhäuser we hiked toward Rothenburg, a fortress built around 1100. It had been destroyed during the Peasants' War, so we couldn't see much of it. We also had a nice view of Roßla,[8] Kelbra, and the surrounding villages and cities from there. Finally we went from Rothenburg back to Kelbra. We traveled together to Sangerhausen and there we went our separate ways. Mr. Brückner traveled to Erfurt and I traveled to Suderode.[9] The others had come a little ways to meet me, so it was about 8 when I arrived at home.

By the way, how are Grandmama and Christel? Is Grandmama coming or not? This year the vacation went by so terribly fast. I had planned to read so much more. I recently read *Stechlin.* I thought it was very good; the individuals are portrayed brilliantly. I want to read *Der weimarische Musenhof.*[10]

Best wishes from everyone and especially from your grateful
Dietrich

[6.] Christoph Gotthard Schröter.

[7.] The Kyffhäuser Mountains are south of the "Golden Meadow." Kelbran is 5 km northwest of the Kyffhäuser Mountains.

[8.] Four km mortheast of Kelbra.

[9.] Bad Suderode today is an eastern part of Gernrode, on the northern border of the eastern Harz Mountains.

[10.] A work by Wilhelm Bode.

17. To His Parents[1]   29

August 23, 1920

Dear Parents,

Today, after confirmation class, Priebe[2] came to me and said that he wanted me to tell you that the congregation of Grunewald wants to publish a commemorative book for all of those who fell in the war. Every person who fell will have a page of honor in which his life, his parentage, etc., will be mentioned. Would you please briefly write all of that down?

It is very nice to be here alone for a little while. In the evenings we play music most of the time or at least spend time together. As a precaution, we let all the blinds down in the evening. Isn't that unbelievable? Even women have now become robbers, as was recently reported in the Grunewald paper.

Today Ursel received an informal invitation from several girls from the Pestalozzi-Froebel-House.[3] We have played music there also. One of them sang very prettily. Yesterday morning I went to see the Klinger exhibit[4] in the old museum. No one else could spare the time to go. It was simply wonderful. It was comprised solely of drawings. But I believe they are the most beautiful I have ever seen—at least in some respects, especially the one "Vom Tode."[5] There is also another art exhibit at the Lehrter Train Station, but it is not supposed to be very good. I must close now because I have to go to bed and go to school around 4 o'clock tomorrow.

Best wishes to you and to everyone else.
Yours,
Dietrich

18. To His Parents[1]   30

November 1, 1920

Dear Parents,

The people from Friedrichsbrunn arrived the day before yesterday. I picked them up at the Potsdam train station. Miss Horn had to leave again at

---

[1.] *NL* A 4/1(3); handwritten letter dated "den 23.VIII.20" mailed from Berlin-Grunewald.

[2.] Hermann Priebe was the pastor of the Berlin-Grunewald parish.

[3.] A school of home economics founded in 1873 for kindergarten teachers and social workers.

[4.] Max Klinger.

[5.] Both etchings, "On Death I and II," stem from the years 1889, 1898, and 1910. On this cf. *GS* 6:232ff. and *DB-ER* 37–41. The other etching he mentions below is in a Berlin train station.

[1.] *NL* A 4/1(4); handwritten letter dated "den 1.XI.20" mailed from Berlin-Grunewald. The date is probably incorrect; it is more likely September 1, 1920. This letter is also previously published in part in *DB-ER* 42.

5 o'clock the next day. Miss Polte[2] arrived yesterday evening. Aunt Elisabeth will not continue on her journey until the day after tomorrow. Yesterday Uncle Otto arrived for an hour at vespers. He sends you his love.

We've done something terribly funny in school. Our Greek teacher told us that he would give us a test in the near future. He gave us some vocabulary words to study for the test and said that it would be impossible for us to find the passage. We said we would find the text. He thought we would never be able to find it but that we should go ahead and try. Well, I used the dictionary, found it, and told every one else in the class. Our Greek teacher was away for a few days and asked the Latin teacher to dictate the test to us. Somehow he had heard from Justus that we had already found the passage, and he reported this to the whole staff except the Greek teacher. So we all have decent grades, and he knows *nothing*.

By the way, have you written to Priebe about the commemorative book? Please do it fairly soon.[3]

Our principal assigned us totally idiotic essays again. All are to be based on phrases. One is, "What the trees tell me." He naturally expects terribly long-winded phrases.[4] I'll let Christel write the treatise for me, that is, very scientifically about the anatomy and physiology of the trees; and this will then be what the trees tell me.

I thank you very much, dear Mama, for the letter.

All my best.
Yours,
Dietrich

[2.] A seamstress who sewed for the Bonhoeffer family in Breslau, now Wroclaw, and occasionally came to Berlin to sew.

[3.] See 1/17:37.

[4.] Cf. *LPP* 275. [Bonhoeffer talks about 'phraseology' in his prison writings; his father had taught him to avoid imprecise and pretentious language.] [PDM]

19. Certificate of Confirmation[1]   31

Certificate of Confirmation
Romans 1:16
Οὐ γὰρ ἐπαισχύνομαι τὸ εὐαγγέλιον τοῦ Χριστοῦ· δύναμις γὰρ
θεοῦ ἐστιν εἰς σωτηρίαν παντὶ τῷ πιστεύοντι.[2]

Dietrich Bonhoeffer
born on *February 4, 1906*, baptized on *March 18, 1906*,
was confirmed in this local Protestant church
on *March 15, 1921*
Berlin-Grunewald, *March 15, 1921*.
Protestant Parish
H. Priebe
Pastor

(Official seal)[3]

20. From Richard Czeppan[1]

Ratibor, March 15, 1921

Dear Dietrich,

I send you many greetings as you celebrate your confirmation today. This day is especially important for you, a future theologian. It is the day you enter the Protestant church as a fully entitled member.

As a small surprise, Klaus will hand you a very interesting little book of writings on   32
historical theology. It comes from my war library, and it was with me on the western front.

Yesterday afternoon I departed on one of the many trains for voters leaving from the colorfully decorated train station in Silesia. Bands played patriotic songs as we departed.[2] They were also present at the smaller train stations en route to the larg-

---

[1.] *NL* D 11(7); a printed form with handwritten cursive entries. Between the heading and the declaration of confirmation is a picture of the church at Grunewald. March 15, 1921, was Palm Sunday. See *DB-ER*, 36–37.

[2.] "For I am not ashamed of the gospel (of Christ); it is the power of God for salvation to everyone who has faith, to the Jew first and also to the Greek" (Rom. 1:16). Until the 6th ed. of Nestle, *Novum Testamentum Graece* (1906) the τοῦ Χριστοῦ after εὐαγγέλιον was a component of the text. Later it appeared only in the apparatus. Ἰουδαίῳ τε πρῶτον καὶ Ἕλληνι ("to the Jew first and also to the Greek") was missing at the end of the citation.

[3.] Text of the seal: "Seal of the Protestant Parish of Berlin-Grunewald."

[1.] *NL* C 9(2); handwritten letter dated "15.III.21" mailed from Ratibor, today Ratibórz, a district capital in Upper Silesia, on both sides of the Oder River.

[2.] The Treaty of Versaille required, among other things, that in Upper Silesia a vote be taken concerning future inclusion in the German Empire. Because all citizens born there had a right to vote in their homeland, the national railroad sent special trains to the voting

er cities. Real enthusiasm prevailed. This gave one hope that the voter turn out would be good. I believe that we can get 80% of the population to vote. This percentage will probably be even higher in my hometown of Ratibor.

The passport and luggage control at the border was nothing but a show. Two Italian soldiers with metal helmets and rifles conducted the control in public. It was not very rigorous.

Today I arrived in Ratibor shortly after 6. The sun emerged gloriously from behind a wall of haze. Hopefully, this is a lucky symbol for voting results.

I am making this journey with a friend who earned his doctorate in oriental studies before the war. During the war he was in Constantinople.

My relatives will arrive in the next few days.

A 95-year-old citizen of Ratibor is expected. In my voting-train there were old people who had to be propped up and driven to the polls.

Spring 1921 will be known for a great political victory. Something joyful is finally taking place in the current gloomy times.

With wishes for a healthy and happy celebration for you and your esteemed relatives, I send my regards.

Yours,
R. Czeppan

33   **21. To Julie Bonhoeffer**[1]

April 7, 1921

Dear Grandmama,

Originally I wanted to write you a letter without the usual beginning, but this would have meant that it never would have gotten written. So take this one instead.

On Thursday morning, around 4 o'clock, we set out from Friedrichsbrunn and traveled in the direction of Thale, and so we were already in Berlin at 2, even with a 2-hour wait in Magdeburg.

It was very pretty in Friedrichsbrunn. We had nice weather almost the whole time. This allowed us to go walking a lot. I ate whipped cream there for the first time since the end of the war. We helped put out forest fires on three consecutive days while we were there. The first fire was in Friedrichsbrunn. We saw the second fire when we were hiking toward Siptenfelde.[2] It was a small fire, and the person who set it was caught. He had set many fires

---

stations. The vote on March 20, 1921, was in favor of Germany; in Ratibor it passed with a three-quarters majority.

[1.] *NL* A 4/2(3); handwritten letter dated "den 7.IV.21" mailed from Berlin-Grunewald.
[2.] Six km west of Alexisbad in the Harz Mountains.

and is obviously mentally incompetent. The third fire was the most terrible. Papa and we three boys were taking a day trip to Ballenstadt. When we were about half an hour outside of the city, we came to a big oak tree. It was on fire and the forest fire had spread out over approximately 800 meters.[3] In the beginning, we and two others were the only ones there. We didn't know what to do. Then the forest ranger came. We helped him lay a back fire. The greatest danger was past after an hour and a half. When several people with pickaxes arrived we were able to continue our walk.

Today was the first day I went to school again properly. Up until now, it has been very nice because we had classes with other teachers. Soon it will be boring again.

This evening the Anschütz's are coming with Lilo.[4] I have to let her have my room.

I also received a book from Aunt Lina[5] for my confirmation. It had belonged to great-grandfather Hase. I received Bismark's *Gedanken und Erinnerungen* from my godfather Heine.[6] On April 18 we are having a party commemorating Luther's public appearance at Worms.[7]

34

All the best.
Your grandson,
Dietrich

22. From Klaus Bonhoeffer[1]

Dear Dietrich,

Thank you very much for your letter. I just learned indirectly from Christel, through Justus, that you have had the flu for a very long time. I hope that you are better and that you get through the convalescent stage. It really isn't any big loss that you have missed school for so long. Are you actually having warm summer weather? The climate is very strange here. If the sun runs the risk of shining for half a day, it instantly becomes idiotically hot and humid. Then it threatens to storm, although it rarely does.

[3.] Difficult to decipher in the original manuscript; it could also read "400" or "500."

[4.] Lilo was Gerhard Anschütz's daughter.

[5.] The identity of this person is not known. Perhaps he refers to his great-aunt Pauline Countess von Kalckreuth. Karl August von Hase's *Gnosis oder protestantisch-evangelische Glaubenslehre für die Gebildeten in der Gemeinde* was in Bonhoeffer's library, with Hase's name inscribed therein.

[6.] Prof. Dr. Med. Leopold Heine, Breslau, from whom Dietrich received the German original of Otto von Bismark's autobiographical work, *The Memoirs, Being the Reflections and Reminiscences of Otto, Prince von Bismarck.*

[7.] "Appearance at Worms" replaced "posting of the theses."

[1.] *NL* D, 1/11(22); Bonhoeffer's handwriting transcribed by Emmi Bonhoeffer. During the summer semester of 1921 Klaus Bonhoeffer studied law at Heidelberg University.

The day before yesterday I took a very nice trip with Justus through the Odenwald region. We took quite a few roundabout paths on our way toward Hirschhorn, an extremely beautiful old town in the Neckar Valley. The ruins of a fortress and a monastery are perched on the steep Neckar bank. One only has to walk in any direction at all and one soon comes to an extremely beautiful area. I especially love the paths high up along the Bergstraße.[2] From there one has a view of the Rhine plateau. It is always very pretty from far away, due to the extremely wonderful misty atmosphere present there. Only in this way can I explain the region's remarkable light.

I have now reached the point again where I can take regular trips. We all became sedentary directly after the Pentecost holidays. Georg Konrad is constantly together with his fraternity brothers. He didn't spend much time with them the whole time Wanda was here.[3] Soon I will go with him to a student's duel and see for myself how they fence and cut their faces. Several of his fraternity brothers are said to fence very well. G. K. does not have to join until next summer. At the present time he takes fencing lessons almost every day. In most fraternities, it is business as usual, just as it was before the war. In the evenings, around 11:30, the place is crawling with drunken students. Sometimes they are very amusing. Recently I made an appointment with one early in the morning, i.e., at 8 o'clock at the university. He didn't come, because he had partied so much that he couldn't find his way home and had to spend the night on the bank of the Neckar. The next day, around 11 o'clock, he was dragged out of bed by the others. He still had his boots on. This kind of thing is all right once or twice. It is amazing that so many have not thought of a more reasonable sport by now!

Yesterday, I attended a Russian balalaika concert. Twenty balalaika players played folk songs. Accompanying them were dancers wearing Russian costumes. One man danced so wildly that at the end it was almost as if he were crazy. During several occasions he jumped up in the air at least 1 1/2 meters, and yelled and cried. The woman danced more quietly and was very graceful in spite of her knee boots.

I have to race over to one of my classes. Uncle Gerhard[4] is coming over to visit you on Friday night. He will probably write to you about it.

My best.
Your Klaus

[2.] [The Bergstraße is a small stretch of land leading from Darmstadt to Heidelberg, famous for its warm climate, wines, and fruit.][PDM]

[3.] Georg Conrad Count von der Goltz and Wanda Hjort, whom he later married.

[4.] Cf. above, 1/21:41, editorial note 4.

23. To Julie Bonhoeffer[1]

May 3, 1921

Dear Grandmama,

We just received your lovely letter and were very happy to hear from you. Thank you very much.

We have already received a letter from Ursel from Arendsee.[2] The door to her room is 1.2 meters high but there is only enough space in it for a bed and a bedside table (no chair!) and it has windows on three walls and a view of the sea. She has to get up at 5 o'clock in the morning to make 270 sandwiches for the children. All in all she likes it a lot. Klaus has not really written a detailed letter yet. I wonder if he will come visit you at Pentecost?

I might take a several-day bicycle trip to Mecklenburg with Dr. Czeppan. He is a former teacher of mine. It will, however, be very expensive, because one can't carry anything on a bicycle.—Regarding the trip to visit you, we have thought something like this: I will travel 4th [class] and will make several stopovers. The first day I will go as far as Meinigen, where we have many relatives.[3] I will stay there for one day and if the trains run at convenient times will go from there to Stuttgart. I might be able to spend the night in Stuttgart as well. This way the trip will be far less expensive. Otherwise it would cost 160 marks.

I hope that there are good connections from Meinigen to Stuttgart, so I won't have to make another stop. I would prefer this, even though you do get to know a region if you are forced to spend some time there.

H. Ludloff[4] is now attending our university. He visits us every Sunday but was not able to live with us because he had already rented a room. Susi is a shining star at the school she is now attending. Recently she was able to explain something to the girls that the teachers had not been able to convey to them.

On one recent evening, I went with Sabine to the Peoples Theater. We saw a truly distinguished production of Sophocles' *Antigone*. The chorus was especially good. They really have to do a terrific amount of work to learn their parts. On Sunday I will hear the "Eroica." Czeppan has invited me to go with him. Bärbel Hildebrandt[5] has not had a fever for a week now, but her

36

[1.] *NL* A 4/2(1); handwritten letter dated "3.V.21." mailed from Berlin-Grunewald. [It appears to have been written before Pentecost, whereas the letter preceding it from Klaus (1/22:42) mentions that the Pentecost holidays are over.] [WF]

[2.] Baltic Sea resort; today it is known as Kühlungsborn in the Doberau district.

[3.] Among others, the Brückner family, the Leubuscher family, and the Küstermann family.

[4.] Hanfried Ludloff, a friend of Karl-Friedrich Bonhoeffer's, studied physics.

[5.] Bärbel Hildebrandt, best friend of Christine Bonhoeffer.

body is so swollen that her regular clothes can't be buttoned. On Sunday, she will have been in bed for three months!

37   I have now composed a choral piece for four voices with a trio based on the text of Psalm 42:6.[6] We might perform it as a surprise for our parents on Pentecost. It is too bad that Klaus and Ursel are away at this time. Recently we have had good weather most of the time. It is not at all like the weather at your place.

What will the entente say to our offer?[7] Surely nothing very favorable. Yet I also believe that they fear communism too much to invade as a result of our refusal.[8]

My very best, dear Grandma.
Yours,
Dietrich

I am looking forward to Tübingen very much.

24. To His Parents[1]

Dear Parents,

I was really very upset that I had to stay in bed again, but now the worst appears to be over. Today, however, Sabine kept me company by staying in bed with some kind of stomachache. Yesterday she vomited every time she ate anything and again after her outing. She really must have done something to upset her stomach while she was out. At noon today she had a temperature of 38° [100.4° F]. She sleeps rather much but is quite lively the rest of the time and tells jokes. Perhaps as early as tomorrow I'll get up a little or, if that's not possible, I'll get up the day after tomorrow. This is very frustrating because of school. Once again I'll have to do make up work.

38   Have you had a chance to write to Waldau about the bicycle? It must be very urgent because they telephoned here. The people at the store thought I wouldn't be able to sell it here, because no one wants to buy English prod-

---

[6.] "Why are you cast down, O my soul, and why are you disquieted within me? Hope in God; for I shall again praise him, my help and my God. My soul is cast down within me; therefore I remember you from the land of Jordan and of Hermon, from Mount Mizar" (Ps. 42:5-6).

[7.] On April 27, 1921 the Indemnity Commission [the entente of which Bonhoeffer wrote] determined that the amount of German reparations was 132 million gold marks. On the following day they gave an ultimatum to the German ambassador in London. The German leaders protested without success.

[8.] The ultimatum threatened an occupation of the Ruhr.

[1.] *NL* A 4/1(11); handwritten undated letter mailed from Berlin at the end of August 1921.

ucts at the moment.[2] It was completely remodeled according to German standards at the time I got it, so there shouldn't be any problems with the tires or anything else that would prevent us from giving it to the people in Waldau.

We received a card from Klaus on the same day his long letter from you arrived. He writes as if he is really very happy, and he will see quite a lot if he is always able to stay with different people for very short periods of time.

What is the real response to Erzberger's[3] assassination in southern Germany? There will be a lot going on here when he is buried on Wednesday. Mr. Weigert, who had previously convicted Hirschfeld for attempting to shoot Erzberger,[4] does not think it is possible that he did it again. Hirschfeld would only have been given a leave of absence if he were sick. By the way, it is crazy that we don't subscribe to the newspaper. Without one we don't learn anything at all about all these things. As it is now each one of us buys a paper every day. It is much more expensive this way.

My very best.
Yours gratefully,
Dietrich

25. To Sabine Bonhoeffer[1]   39

May 23, 1922

Dear Sabine,

Thank you very much for your letter. I actually wanted to wait a while before writing to you so that you would get my letter at a time when you would not be getting a letter from any of the rest of us. This, however, will never happen because you will be getting Ursel's letter soon and I have to answer your letter sometime. So, first to your questions:

Mama will treat me to riding lessons if you can be patient. I will bring a whip along as well.

[2.] In response to the London ultimatum (cf. above, 1/23:44, editorial note 7) there was a total boycott of English goods.

[3.] Matthias Erzberger had resigned as finance minister in March 1920 after the Helfferich trial (see below, editorial note 4); he was murdered by two former marine officers on August 26, 1921.

[4.] Ottwig von Hirschfeld attempted to murder Erzberger in January 1920 as he left the Moabit county court following a lawsuit summons against Dr. Karl Helfferich, who had been charged because of his writing "Away with Erzberger." See Krummacher and Wucher, *Die Weimarer Republik*, 99f. and Eschenburg, *Matthias Erzberger*, 118.

[1.] *NL* Appendix A 5(1); Bonhoeffer's handwriting transcribed by Sabine Leibholz. The letter dated "23.5.1922" was mailed from Berlin.

I took French lessons with a Miss Lindauer. Grandmama will know about it, of course.[2] We had already made elaborate plans for my summer vacation because we could not arrange to have Susi stay with anyone at all. We were trying to decide if I should go with Hans-Christoph to Siebenbürgen[3] or with the Gilberts[4] to Salzburg. But the problem was solved in another way. Susi might go with the Ficks[5] to Innsbruck; Ursel to Elmau and the rest stays the same. Karl-Friedrich has plans to see Kärnten, Steiermark, and perhaps (!!!) a bit of Italy. Klaus probably wants to go to the Alps.

It is not certain yet if Papa will travel to Geneva; but it is probable. Munich is probably out of the question at this point. We are all pretty angry.[6] Uncle Hans will visit us for approximately four weeks after Pentecost. I am really looking forward to it.

Yesterday morning the unveiling of the monument for those killed in action took place in Spandau. It is a very beautiful monument depicting a fallen man with a steel helmet, similar to the "Dying Gaul."[7] Next to him is the imperial eagle.[8] The orations that followed were not particularly pleasant. Still the evening turned out to be very nice. The Brandts, Miss Rubba, Lene Delbrück, the Schleichers and Lotte Leu[9] were there. We played a little music and sang.

It is very nice that you are now playing in a string orchestra there. How is your Okkarina playing? Eight days ago, I auditioned for Kreutzer.[10] He cannot take me on as a student, however, because he teaches only those who want to be trained as professional musicians. He seemed to like it very much, however, because he praised Miss Grußendorff's[11] school. He said that I should go ahead and stay with her for the rest of the year, and after finishing high school I should enter the school of music and study with him.

[2.] Sabine Bonhoeffer spent several months with her grandmother during the summer of 1922.

[3.] So-called "trips to the frontier" were "a matter of honor" in the Youth Movement after 1918.

[4.] Felix and Mary Gilbert. Mary Gilbert was a friend of Ursula Bonhoeffer's.

[5.] Rudolf Fick. The Ficks owned a vacation home in Innsbruck.

[6.] The father had not accepted a call to Munich. See Karl Bonhoeffer, *Lebenserinnerungen*, 96.

[7.] [The "Dying Gaul" is a sculpture, c. 230 B.C.E., in the Capitoline Museum, Rome.] [PDM]

[8.] On May 21, 1922, the monument "Die Wacht" (The Watch), sculpted by Prof. August Schreitmüller, was unveiled in Spandau. The monument was moved to Stabburggarten, where it can be seen today.

[9.] Irene Brandt, Klaus Brandt, Klaus Bonhoeffer, Miss Rubba (the identity of this person is not known), Lene Delbrück, Rüdiger Schleicher, and his brother Jörg (cf. below, letter 32, editorial note 3), and Charlotte Leubuscher, called Lotte Leu.

[10.] Leonid Kreutzer.

[11.] The Bonhoeffer children's piano teacher.

We, Klaus, Ursel, Scheicher, [. . .] and I, attended *St. Matthew's Passion* on Saturday. It was not as good as last time, but, since it cost only 12 marks, one could become reacquainted with it again cheaply. Emmi[12] left the day before yesterday. She was very content.

Since she left, much too much food is being prepared at home. Anna[13] still has to readjust.

By the way, when you go to Stuttgart you have to go visit Eugen Bonhoeffer. It certainly is especially nice there. Just be sure to write him first. Susi is in great distress in school. She has an enormous amount of work to catch up on. At present, she has gone swimming. We are now getting ready to perform *Egmont* in school. Ulla Andreae[14] has been selected to play Klärchen, and I have been asked to play Egmont.

I still do not know if I am going to do it, since it is very difficult to perform   41 well.

How is Grandmama? I am really looking forward to spending the summer vacation with you. Please give her my love. I still haven't made any plans for Pentecost. Maybe Max[15] will decide to go hiking. If he doesn't, I might go with them.

Please give my best regards to the Gaupps,[16] to [. . .][17] and all the others.

My best wishes to Grandmama and to you.
Yours,
Dietrich

26. To His Parents[1]

June 7, 1922

Dear Parents,

The day before yesterday I got back from the heath. It truly was astoundingly beautiful. We[2] certainly had magnificent weather. It rained only on the first day of the Pentecost holiday. But during that day it was particularly

---

[12.] Emmi Delbrück, daughter of Hans Delbrück, later married to Klaus Bonhoeffer.

[13.] Cook in the Bonhoeffer house.

[14.] Ursula-Ruth Andreä was the niece of Walther Rathenau and Bonhoeffer's classmate. See Marion Yorck von Wartenburg, *Die Stärke der Stille*, 13ff. [*Egmont* is the famous play by Johann Wolfgang von Goethe. [PDM]

[15.] Max Delbrück.

[16.] Robert Gaupp, was a student friend of Karl Bonhoeffer; their families remained close.

[17.] Illegible.

[1.] *NL* A 4/1(12); handwritten letter dated "den 7.VI.22" mailed from Berlin-Grunewald.

[2.] At Pentecost Bonhoeffer went on a trip with Max Delbrück.

impressive on the heath. The dark color of the vegetation, the birch trees rising above, and the junipers, which almost look like cypresses, were all particularly beautiful in the pouring rain. At that point we were near Wilsede.[3] Afterwards we went to Soltau where we stayed for two days. From there we took the trip to the prehistoric mounds that I wrote you about.

42

It is too bad that much of the heath is being farmed even though the yield is very poor. We also went to one of the many moors, but it was disappointing that we did not get to go to a high moor. The many herds of small sheep with their shepherds are astonishingly pretty. The people were always very nice and friendly, but very frugal. We were not able to get a single glass of milk on the whole heath, because they could sell it in town for more money. The old farmhouses with the old engravings and furniture were also very interesting. In every house I entered there were incredible amounts of ham to be smoked that still hung from the ceiling. In spite of the unfruitful land, I believe that the people are becoming very prosperous on their cattle alone. On the last day we also visited a 900-meters-deep potash mining pit near Hannover. It was very interesting. We whizzed down with unbelievable speed almost in a free fall. In a strange way, one did not notice it at all in the dark. One rode so quietly that one thought one could just as easily stand up. Below ground we walked around through huge salt vaults wearing workmen's clothing and carrying carbide lamps. They now work underground almost exclusively with locomotives and hardly use horses at all. They have only three left.

Yesterday Uncle Hans came to visit. Today he left again for Rügen. He actually looked very good. The two people are still here, a public school teacher and a civil servant for the railroad.[4] They hardly know any German, so we have hardly gotten to know each other. Otherwise nothing has happened as far as I know.

All the best from everyone to Grandmama and Sabine.
But especially from your grateful,
Dietrich

By the way, Diels died.[5]

[3.] This is a nature preserve in the moors of Lüneburg, 20 km north of Soltau.

[4.] The identity of this person is not known.

[5.] Hermann Diels had been a professor of Classical Philosophy in Berlin since 1882; Bonhoeffer's teacher Walther Kranz indexed Diels's book on the pre-Socratics.

27. To Sabine Bonhoeffer[1]   43

Dear Sabine,

Many thanks for your letter. In two weeks I will be with you. I am really looking forward to emerging from the "hole" for an extended period of time. In all probability I will arrive on the 7th. Perhaps I'll get there in the morning, if I travel at night, or I might get there in the afternoon. But do not change your plans to go dancing,[2] as my plans are not yet definite. Christel also wrote today saying I should travel through Heidelberg.[3] If I do, it will be even later.

We had a very exciting day yesterday. Around 9 o'clock in the morning while I was still at home, the director of the girls' school[4] telephoned. He urgently wanted to speak to Mama. He said that Susi had fallen from a ladder during gymnastics, was unconscious, and was bleeding from her backbone. Naturally, we were dreadfully frightened and Mama, Uncle Hans, and Klaus ran to the school. I stayed here and summoned an ambulance from Mrs. Meyer. The ambulance brought Susi here after a good half hour. Papa could not be reached. But a nurse from the Grunewald Sanitarium was here. Naturally it was not half as bad as the silly director had said. There was nothing wrong with her backbone. She slipped from a loose step on a ladder and probably fainted during the fall due to shock. Papa examined her again. She seems to have pulled some muscles. It was lucky that it happened the way it did. This morning the gymnastics teacher came to visit and brought a chocolate bar to console her.

After we had gotten over the shock I went to school and arrived after the third period. I just arrived when one heard a peculiar crack in the courtyard. Rathenau had been assassinated[5]—barely 300 meters away from us! What a   44 pack of right-wing Bolshevik scoundrels! He was murdered merely because he did not appeal to some conceited, idiotic ass. People are responding with crazed excitement and rage here in Berlin. They are having fistfights in the Reichstag.

[1.] *NL* Appendix A 5(2); Bonhoeffer's handwriting transcribed by Sabine Leibholz. The probable date is June 25, 1922; it was sent from Berlin to Tübingen.

[2.] At the Stuttgartia, the fraternity of Gerhard von Rad. See below, 1/29:51, editorial note 3.

[3.] Christine and Klaus Bonhoeffer were studying at the University of Heidelberg.

[4.] The Bismarck Lyceum in Grunewald.

[5.] Walther Rathenau was the foreign minister who concluded the Treaty of Rapallo. On June 24, 1922, in the Königsallee while driving to the Ministry, he was shot to death by two former army officers, members of the "Organization Consul"; cf. *DB-ER* 33–34. [The "Organization Consul" was a secret organization of antidemocratic rightists, headed by Captain Arthur Ehrhardt, whose brigade helped to form the SA.] [PDM]

Uncle Hans wants to leave on Tuesday, but a general strike[6] has just been called. Recently I went with Czeppan to the "Versunkenen Glocke."[7] It was a very nice production, except for some of the scenery. I'll probably see you on the 7th, dear Sabine (but I won't arrive on the holiday train).
My best wishes to Mama[8] and to you.

Yours,
Dietrich

28. To His Parents[1]

July 7, 1922

Dear Parents,

I arrived here exactly on time and found everyone in very good shape. I was able to sleep very well, especially with the pillow. One man actually began to talk about politics as soon as he had entered the railway compartment. He was really very narrowmindedly right-wing. I almost believe he could belong to the C association.[2] The only thing he had forgotten was his swastika. I was on the verge of joining in, but I preferred to let it be.

Grandmama thanks you very much for the things, as does Sabine, who is terribly excited about our travel plans. She apparently does not place too much importance on the party at the Hedgehog house. Tonight she is going to the Stuttgarter's.[3] She could not cancel her plans at this late date. We will also visit Mrs. Wild.[4] A "Queen of the Night" is blooming in her garden. All the best to all.

Gratefully,
Dietrich

I forgot my toiletries.

45

[6.] Cf. Schwarz, *Die Weimarer Republik*, 83ff.
[7.] Gerhart Hauptmann's *Der versunkene Glocke* (The Sunken Bell) was first performed in 1896 in Berlin.
[8.] Must mean "Grandmama."

[1.] *NL* A 4/1 (13); handwritten postcard dated "7.VII.1922" from Tübingen.
[2.] The identity of this person is not known, perhaps the "Organization Consul" mentioned above, 1/27:49, editorial note 5.
[3.] Cf. above, 1/27:49, editorial note 2.
[4.] The identity of this person is not known.

29. To Hans von Dohnanyi[1]

July 19, 1922

Dear Hans,[2]

Christel wrote that we really should make our plans definite, so we have decided to meet in Freiburg. It seemed to be the only possible place to meet if one didn't want to lose a whole day. The train connections are terrible. We have to change trains as many as five times to get there. I hope that you agree. In addition, we wanted to meet each other there on July 31, because otherwise Rad[3] can't come. We will have to forgo the Blauen, but it is not supposed to be particularly pretty. On July 1 we will go up to the Belchen[4] and then hike in the direction of the Bodensee. This stretch will take until the 3rd. We want to be sure to be there at noon on the 4th and stay until the 6th. In the afternoon on the 6th: Bregenz-Bludenz or even further. We really have to show the others the Scesaplana. I would like to climb it again. How about you? The 7th, 8th, 9th only in the Alps, and on the 10th home to Tübingen. Maybe it will be all right at Grandmama's. I'm practically certain it will be, but don't write to anyone about it. I'll send you more precise information. Then we could go home together on the 12th. By the way, on July 31 you will reach Freiburg at 1:02, and we will arrive at the main train station at 3:52. Your train will leave Heidelberg at exactly 8:00.

Write to me if you really want to make any changes. Make sure to include the train schedules and write everything down exactly, since coordinating everything is the hardest part. However, I hope the plans suit you. That's everything. I hope you can read it all. Is Leibholz coming?[5] Czeppan is also staying nearby. It is still a mystery to me how we're going to stay in huts while we're in the Alps. Write to me and Christel again in any case, so that we can be sure to be in agreement. See you again in 1½ weeks!

Yours,
Dietrich

[1.] *NL* A 4/3(3); handwritten postcard dated "den 19.VII.22" mailed from Tübingen.

[2.] Hans von Dohnanyi, later married to Christine Bonhoeffer.

[3.] Gerhard von Rad. With help from his grandmother, who was a friend and neighbor of Julie Bonhoeffer's in Tübingen, he became acquainted early on with the Bonhoeffer children. He studied in Tübingen from the summer semester of 1922 until the winter semester of 1923–24.

[4.] Blauen and Belchen, the highest points of the southern part of the Black Forest.

[5.] Gerhard Leibholz, called Gert.

30. To Julie Bonhoeffer[1]

August 18, 1922

Dear Grandmama,

I wish you many happy returns of the day on your 80th birthday and hope that during the entire coming year you will be as lively and healthy as I hope you are on your birthday. I'm really disappointed that I can't be there with you now. Instead, I have to sit here in school again. We could have played something musical together. I hope that you will have better weather for your birthday celebration than we have at present. It has rained the whole day. We will also be celebrating your birthday here. Mama told us that we will order ice cream.

Toni Volkmann was here yesterday evening. At the moment she is traveling to Friedrichsbrunn to spend some time in a cottage with a few friends. I was asked to send you her love.

My paper on Euripides[2] is going well. I think I'll be able to submit it in 4–6 weeks. If I've done a good job I won't have to do another thing for the *Abitur*,[3] because the paper will count even more than the examination.

47   On Sunday Susi has invited a lot of people over to celebrate your birthday early.

Once again, I wish you all the best for the coming year.

Gratefully,
Dietrich

[1.] *NL* A 4/2(4); handwritten letter dated "den 18.VIII.22" mailed from Berlin-Grunewald.

[2.] Cf. "Euripides' Philosophie" ("Euripides' Philosophy") (*NL* A 5/2).

[3.] This is the graduation examination for the German public school system. It is similar to high school graduation in the United States.

31. *Abitur* Report Card[1]

Drafted by
Reform-Realgymnasium and Reform-Gymnasium in Berlin-Grunewald

Certificate of Completion
awarded by the Gymnasium

Dietrich Bonhoeffer, born on the 4th of February, 1906, in Breslau, son of University Profes-
sor Privy Counsellor of Medicine Dr. Karl Bonhoeffer who lives in Berlin-Grunewald, attended
our school for four years and two of those years were spent in the first form of the Gym-
nasium.

I. Behavior and Diligence

Behavior:	*Very Good*
Diligence:	*Good*

He was exempted from the oral examination.

II. Knowledge and Skills

Religion:	*Good*	
German:	*Performance in class: Good*	*Good*
	Written Examination: Very Good	
Latin:	*Good*	
Greek:	*Good (with more difficult requirements)*	

English:	*Sufficient*	
Hebrew:	*Good*	
History: }		
Geography: }	*Sufficient*	
Philosophy:	*Good*	
Mathematics:	*Class Performance: Sufficient*	*Sufficient*
	Written Examination: Good	

48

Singing:	*Good*	
Gymnastics:	*Performance in class: Very Good*	*Very Good*
	Examination: Good	

Handwriting:	*Insufficient*

[1.] *NL* D 14. A copy of a log entry at the school; printed form with handwritten cursive entries. Headings for subjects present on this form, in which Bonhoeffer received no grades, are not listed here. The school was "a so-called intermediate school; after complet-ing the lower second form, one could choose to add subjects to the regular curriculum or one could choose to study the regular subjects more intensively" (Yorck von Wartenburg, *Die Stärke der Stille*, 13; cf. 14f.). See also Sombart, *Jugend in Berlin*, 15f.

On the basis of the above results and because he is now leaving this institution, the examination committee, who have signed their names below, have awarded him
the Certificate of Completion
of a Gymnasium.
Dietrich Bonhoeffer intends to *study Theology.*
The school dismisses him *with the best wishes.*
Berlin-Grunewald, *March 1, 1923*

The examination committee
  Sattert   National Commisioner
  Dr. Dottermann[2]   Representative of the Board of Trustees
  Dr. Vilmar[3]   Director
Grunow, Honorable Assistant Headmaster   *Havenstein, Assistant Headmaster*[4]
Simons, Assistant Headmaster   *Dr. Fritz Resa, Honorable Assistant Headmaster*
Prof. Dr. Kappus, Assistant Headmaster[5]   *Dr. Kranz, Assistant Headmaster*[6]
Heiniger, Assistant Headmaster   *Noetzky, Assessor of the Educational Council*

[2.] Difficult to decipher in the original manuscript; perhaps: "Dr. Boltermann," headmaster of the Bismarck Gymnasium.

[3.] Cf. above, 1/11:29, editorial note 2.

[4.] Martin Havenstein, German scholar and philosopher, Bonhoeffer's philosophy teacher.

[5.] Carl Kappus, Bonhoeffer's Hebrew teacher. Cf. Yorck von Wartenburg, *Die Stärke*, 15.

[6.] Walther Kranz.

B. Student Life in Tübingen.
April 1923–February 1924

---

32. To His Parents[1]

Dear Parents,

Our trip[2] was so nice that one couldn't have wished for it to be any better. We traveled alone for the most part, except when another man got in with us for a couple of hours. At any rate, we were always able to stretch out on the benches. Shortly before we came to Suhl we had to stop for 50 minutes because a defect in the machinery had been discovered. Although we arrived in Stuttgart 50 minutes late we still met up with Jörg Schleicher.[3] We went home with him because our train didn't continue through to Tübingen, even though we were assured twice during the trip that it did. Moreover, our connection pulled away in front of our noses. So, we didn't arrive here till 2:30. Jörg came with us. We found everyone here well and healthy. The first thing I did was to go shopping. Then we noticed to our great dismay that we had probably left the coffee at home. I've just finished washing and drying the dishes alone, while Christel was doing some more shopping. Hag[4] also just came in and Jörg will probably come over this evening as well.

Shortly after we pulled out of Berlin a train conductor stopped by. When he saw that we were unpacking our lunches, he said that we should go right ahead and unpack completely, as he wouldn't mind sharing a roll with us. He was delighted when we gave him some chocolate and two rolls.

[1.] *NL* A 7/1(1); undated handwritten letter mailed from Tübingen at the end of April 1923; previously published in *GS* 6:26.

[2.] Bonhoeffer traveled to Tübingen with Christine, who studied biology there; at first they lived with their grandmother.

[3.] Jörg Schleicher was the brother of Rüdiger Schleicher, who married Ursula Bonhoeffer the next month.

[4.] Erich Haag was a member of the "Hedgehog" fraternity (see *DB-ER* 48–51).

By the way, the train traveled along a very peculiar route. Instead of going through Meiningen we went through Grimmenthal[5] and then Heilbronn, but I believe the train has to go through Tübingen when it travels from Stuttgart to Immendingen.

Please give my love to Grandmama and tell her we took care of the letters. The fruit trees here have almost lost their blooms already. The lilies of the valley are emerging and cowslips can be seen everywhere. By the way, the weather here isn't very nice; it is cool and a bit rainy. Please send our love to the engaged couple,[6] especially from the Schleichers.[7]

My best wishes to everyone.
Gratefully yours,
Dietrich

33. To His Parents[1]

Dear Parents,

Yesterday evening I was up at the Hedgehog fraternity house[2] and took a look at it, and this afternoon I went rowing with a few of the Hedgehogs. I talked to Hag[3] about the whole matter, and he said that students from Würtemberg had to stay at least three semesters but that northern Germans had to stay only two. I liked the people fairly well and would like very much to join them for the one semester that I am here. Now, I don't know what you would think about my staying here for a second semester.[4] I told Hag that I couldn't give him a definite answer but would write to you immediately. When I told him that I was afraid that I might not be able to practice the piano this winter, he replied that the house had just gotten a new piano and that I could play it anytime I wanted to. Pressel[5] told me the same thing.

51

[5.] Five km east of Meiningen.

[6.] Ursula Bonhoeffer and Rüdiger Schleicher.

[7.] Jörg and Otto Schleicher, M.D., Stuttgart; Otto was the father of Jörg and Rüdiger Schleicher.

[1.] *NL* 7/1(2); undated handwritten letter mailed from Tübingen at the beginning of May 1923; previously published in *GS* 6:27f.

[2.] See 1/36:60, editorial note 2.

[3.] Cf. above, 1/32:55, editorial note 4.

[4.] Inflation made a second semester away from home difficult to finance (see below, 1/34:58, editorial note 6). The Swabians were expected to stay in the fraternity house for three semesters. The first semester was called the "fox" semester; the second was the first active semester; and during the third semester, one was to be prepared, as a rule, to be an officer of the fraternity. Those who were not from Swabia were not often considered for such positions in the fraternity.

[5.] Wilhelm Pressel was a member of the Hedgehog fraternity and a friend of Rüdiger Schleicher's.

Furthermore, they play quite a bit of music there. Tomorrow, I'll play a trio with two others. Please write as soon as you can and tell me what you think about my staying here for a second semester. I want to be able to give my final decision as soon as possible. I don't want to continue accepting their invitations if I won't be staying after all. Furthermore, I would naturally like to stay a second semester on account of the faculty alone because I've not yet been able to hear some of the docents lecture whom I am very anxious to hear.

Your card came today, dear Mama. Thank you very much. Please greet everyone from me and please write to me very soon even if it is a very short letter, because I want to tell them soon about the decision.

My lectures began on Wednesday, at least some of them. Up until now I have found Schlatter[6] the most interesting. Hauer's[7] "History of Religion" begins tomorrow. I am really looking forward to it.

Very best wishes.
Gratefully yours,
Dietrich

34. To His Parents[1]   52

Dear Parents,

It is 7:30. I was just awakened from my afternoon nap by a monstrous cloudburst. Since I am leaving tomorrow, as you know, I want to write to you to tell you how things are. The trip went very well.[2] I stayed with Grandmama until she went to bed. When I returned in the morning she was unexpectedly lively. She was also very happy.

Well, I was already at Miss Jäger's today.[3] She would like me to move in as early as Wednesday, but I might have to wait 8 days, because she is still expecting lodgers. At any rate it is settled. The room is really very inexpensive, 6000 marks for everything. I told Mrs. Koken no.[4]

[6.] Adolf Schlatter, Professor of New Testament.

[7.] Jakob Wilhelm Hauer was a scholar and missionary, who in 1924 founded the "German Faith Movement," *Deutsche Glaubensbewegung*, a collection of different groups committed to the Nordic-Volkish worldview.

[1.] *NL* A 7/1(3); undated handwritten letter mailed from Tübingen during the latter half of May 1923; previously published in *GS* 6:28.

[2.] He is speaking of his return trip after the marriage of Ursula and Rüdiger Schleicher, on May 15, 1923, in Berlin.

[3.] Bonhoeffer's landlady; see below, 1/35:58.

[4.] Difficult to decipher in the original manuscript; the identity of this person is not known.

I purchased Müller's book[5] at once, because the price had already increased since the last time I looked at it. I didn't want to wait until it cost even more.[6] With a 25% reduction in price it cost a little over 70 thousand. I am very happy to have it. Thank you again very much for it. Nothing else has happened in the 10 hours I have been here. Hopefully, my alarm clock will wake me up at 5:30 tomorrow morning. We are traveling to Ellwangen. It will not be very pleasant if the weather remains as it is since it has been raining without interruption.

I still have to go quickly to the student dormitory for a preliminary discussion of tomorrow's activities.

Best wishes to everyone. All my best to you.
Gratefully yours,
Dietrich

53   **35. To His Parents**[1]

Dear Parents,

I already wrote you about all this, but yesterday evening I found the still unmailed letter in the dining room. On the day after I arrived back I had to go on a recruitment trip for the students' self-help organization to an area near Hall. It was a very beautiful and, judging from our success, a very rich Catholic area. The people were actually all very friendly and accommodating. However, I spoke to many students who had collected money in the Protestant parishes, and they told me that they were treated completely differently. Hardly anyone gave them anything. Tuesday Grandmama and Christel came by to visit me, as you know. I have been living at Miss Jäger's, Uhlandstraße 10, since yesterday evening. The room is little, quiet, and very bare with only four naked walls, a table, a bed, two chairs, and two windows; but, for the start these are the most important items, though I'd like to put flowers or something else in here. However, one can work much better here because everything is so quiet and no one interrupts you.

I immediately bought Müller's *Kirchengeschichte* on the first day. It already costs 70 thousand instead of 55,000 marks. But I thought it would cost even more as time went by, so I bought it right away. I am extremely happy to have

---

[5.] D. Karl Müller, *Kirchengeschichte*.

[6.] The value of German currency had slowly declined since the end of the war. Early in the year 1923 galloping inflation had set in. In July of that year the dollar was worth 353,581 paper marks; by October a dollar was worth 25,271,400,000 paper marks.

[1.] *NL* A 7/1(4); undated handwritten letter mailed from Tübingen at the end of May 1923; previously published in *GS* 6:29f.

it. One works much better from a printed book than one does from course lectures, and after all Müller lectures from large extracts taken from his book.

I chose my fraternity body guard on Thursday.[2] I chose Schmid,[3] the son of the resident philosopher, who is in his third semester and is studying zoology. He also plays violin a lot, so we play music together quite a bit.

Pressel constantly raves about the lovely days in Berlin, and everywhere I go people ask me about the wedding.—Rüdiger's friend Scharpf is getting married today.[4] I wonder if Rüdiger knows about it.

Unfortunately, food is getting to be more and more expensive here. Bread already costs 1100 marks, and I was sorry to learn that the others by mistake ate all of my sausage except for a little piece.

It is relatively inexpensive to play tennis here, just 5000 marks for the whole semester. It is too bad that I don't have my racket; renting costs a good deal. Christel is playing tennis today with another student.

On Thursday in Rottenburg I attended the Corpus Christi procession, which made a great impression on me. It was the first time I saw such a large procession. (Rottenburg is, of course, the bishop's seat.) It really makes a very distinct impression when you hear the approaching people in the procession praying from a long way off. Accompanying them are young girls wearing white dresses and wreaths. The streets are full of flowers and birch branches. Pictures of the saints, the Virgin Mary, and Jesus hang from the windows. Everyone seems to be earnestly participating. The whole thing is a large religious folk festival. To a great extent, however, the theatrical aspect was very negligible. Now I have to go to dinner. Give my love to everyone, especially the married couple.

My best.
Gratefully yours,
Dietrich

[2.] Whoever enters the fraternity as a new member is called a *Fux*, or "Fox" and must choose an older fraternity brother to become his special caretaker, called a *Leibbursche* or "personal body guard."

[3.] Fritz Schmid studied natural science at Tübingen when Bonhoeffer was a student there. His father, Wilhelm Schmid, Professor of Classical Philosophy in Tübingen, had been a member of the Hedgehog fraternity starting the winter semester 1877–78.

[4.] Walter Scharpff, M.D.

55

36. Curriculum Vitae[1]

In Breslau on February 4, 1906, I, with my twin sister, saw the light of day as the son of the university professor the Venerable[2] Mr. Karl Bonhoeffer and my mother, née von Hase. I left Silesia when I was six years old, and we moved to Berlin where I entered the Friedrich-Werder Gymnasium. Due to our move to Grunewald, I entered the school there, where I passed my Abitur at Easter 1923.

From the time I was thirteen years old it was clear to me that I would study theology. Only music caused me to waver during the past two years. I am now studying here in Tübingen for my first semester, where I took the customary step for every dutiful son and became a Hedgehog. I have chosen Fritz Schmid to be my personal bodyguard. I have nothing else to share about myself.

Dietrich Bonhoeffer

37. To His Parents[1]

Thursday, June 7

Dear Parents,

I am now most comfortably settled into my room and am very happy that I live here instead of at Mrs. Koken's. I go over to see Grandmama every day, or every other day, when I go up to the house.[2] I am just beginning to notice how terribly expensive everything is. Everything is constantly getting more expensive, and I fear that I won't be able to manage with the amount of money I have. Recently I had to pay 14,000 marks for 1 pound of sausage.

56

It costs more than 10,000 marks to have your clothes washed once, and the meals at the house are also getting expensive. I myself have to buy the tea and coffee that my landlord and landlady make for me. I would appreciate it if you would send me a little bit of money or sausage or something like that because, as you know, I still have to pay for my room and for fencing.[3]

[1.] *NL* Appendix A 17; handwritten entry in the Foxes' book of the Hedgehog fraternity in the summer semester of 1923.

[2.] *Alter Herr*, literally "old man" or "elder," was the designation of former members of a fraternity, who after their studies, formed a special club. They were called the Elder Union by the Hedgehog fraternity and through this club remained connected to the "active" students.

[1.] *NL* A 7/1(5); handwritten letter dated "Donnerstag den 7.Juni" mailed from Tübingen, 1923; previously published in *GS* 6:30f.

[2.] He refers here to the house of the Hedgehog fraternity on the hill behind the squared-stone walls of the castle Twingia (see *DB-ER* 48).

[3.] See below, the German editor's "Afterword."

I now have to visit many of our older members. It is very boring and robs me of my Sunday or Thursday mornings.

By the way, Professor Schmid[4] sends you his best regards. He met you at a festival on Founders' Day. I now spend a lot of time with Fritz Schmid. There at the house we play a lot of good music. There are not many concerts here, as you know, so it makes it very nice.

Do we have a book on logic at home? I would very much like to have one to work with. And I believe that you, Papa, told me that you have the Sigwart,[5] didn't you? If it is there, could Sabine bring it with her when she comes at the beginning of July? Please give her and the married couple[6] and everyone else my love.

Best wishes to you all.
Gratefully yours,
Dietrich

38. To Paula Bonhoeffer[1]

July 19, 1923

Dear Mama,

Thank you very much for your letter. My suits are in the following condition: The sedge linen one is really too small and the seams are ripped open everywhere. The khaki fits. The blue one and the new light one fit as well, but the old light one is very dirty and probably needs to be dry-cleaned. The pants are also wearing very thin and now and again little holes can be seen in them. We don't have any material to patch them with. The pants of the light suit that you sent me are too small. At the moment I am wearing the khaki suit, but when it gets dirty I will have to wear the good light one, since the other one is really too drab. So I would appreciate it if I were to get another summer suit for Friedrichsbrunn; the one being cleaned won't be ready by then and I have to have it for Berlin. So maybe another larger linen one would be good, or something else with short pants.

As far as boots go, I wear the Haferlschuhe[2] regularly. So everything is fine there. We bought a hat for 60,000. All my underwear is in good condition. I received the 70 thousand. I thank you very much.

57

[4.] Cf. above, 1/35:59, editorial note 3.

[5.] Christoph Sigwart, author of *Logik*.

[6.] Ursula and Rüdiger Schleicher.

[1.] *NL* A 7/1(6); handwritten postcard dated "den 19.VII.23" mailed from Tübingen; previously published in *GS* 6:31f.

[2.] [*Haferlschuhe* are a type of sturdy walking shoe that originated in the early nineteenth century.] [PDM]

By the way, the cost of transportation will increase by 250%. Lectures end on the 31st. Please give my best to Papa and all the others.

And my very best wishes to you.
Gratefully,
Dietrich

Mrs. Schorpff sends her best wishes to you and Rüdiger.

39. To His Parents[1]

Friedrichsbrunn, August 16, 1923

Dear Parents,

Yesterday I put Susi on the express train in Halberstadt, and she even got a good seat. It was too bad that the train was late, because it made it impossible for me to see the cathedral. I then walked home, passing through the Witches' Dancing Place[2] just as the sun went down behind the farthest mountains. As it did so, it delineated the cliffs wonderfully. The others have gone in every direction. This afternoon I might go swimming in the Erichsberg pool because it is incredibly hot today, although it is threatening to storm. At the moment the girls have gone out, and Klaus and Justus will leave shortly. Maybe I'll take a short walk. Otherwise I read quite a bit; but sadly I have noticed that I brought far too little with me so I'll probably go to the pastor and borrow something. I'm currently reading Schleiermacher's *Reden über Religion*,[3] which I find much more interesting the second time around. I am working through it systematically because I want to take a lecture course on it next semester. Hans is coming tomorrow, and Christel and Grete[4] want to meet him in Treseburg. They then want to hike back with him by way of Thale, where Hans wants to put his nephew on the train to Berlin. Justus will be hiking in the Harz for three more days. He wants to meet up with Klaus in Halberstadt on the way back. They want to see Halberstadt together and then travel to Berlin. Should we stay fourteen more days? I'm really looking forward to the piano and my books again. Is Aunt

---

[1.] *NL* A 7/1(7); handwritten letter dated "den 16. August 23"; previously published in *GS* 6:32f. A letter from Christine Bonhoeffer to her parents is found on the same sheet of paper.

[2.] [The cathedral in Halberstadt is St. Stephen's Cathedral (1239).] [WF] The Hexentanzplatz, or Witches' Dancing Place, is a plateau above the Bode River chasm. [This area of the Harz Mountains is associated with the fables of the witches' dance in Jakob Grimm's fairy tales and in the Walpurgis Night scene in Goethe's *Faust*.] [WF]

[3.] Bonhoeffer owned a critical edition of Schleiermacher's *On Religion: Speeches to Its Cultured Despisers*.

[4.] Hans and Margarete von Dohnanyi. In 1930 Margarete married Karl-Friedrich Bonhoeffer.

Elisabeth actually coming, and if so when? Toni and Miss Böse[5] want to know, of course. Furthermore, Christel tells me that Toni is going to tell you horror stories about the difficulty of buying groceries. It isn't nearly that bad, however; one can get everything one wants more easily than in Berlin, and there are no difficulties with money. You don't need to worry about it. Otherwise, Miss Böse and Aunt Toni are very content and cozy; they have settled in very well. Anna[6] was so enchanted by the Witches' Dancing Place that she assures me over and over again that she will never forget it and that she will always want to go back. The people from the Ruhr[7] are very quiet and orderly, and one hardly notices them.

At present we are learning about the political situation from the "Vorwärts,"[8] which we subscribe to with a park ranger. The rise of the value of the dollar to seven million marks has caused great unease among the workers in Thale. I heard about it recently when I rode on the train with some of them.

All the best from everyone, especially your grateful
Dietrich

40. To His Parents[1]

Friedrichsbrunn, August 23, 1923

Dear Parents,

I was asked to write you and tell you when we'll arrive home. The Dohnanyis have to go back on the 28th; we thought we would go with them. We'll leave from Thale around 12:35, travel first to Halberstadt, tour the town for a few hours, leave there at 7:20, and get to Berlin at 11:10. The packages are being sent today.

Yesterday, Mrs. Hansen[2] from Quedlinburg, was here at Aunt Elisabeth's. We took her over a little bit of the wooded glade and then had a wonderful moonlight walk on the Georg's summit. It rains most of the day, and this makes it even more magnificent at night. We were at the Witches' Dancing Place again, this time under a full moon. One evening recently Anna[3] was with us on a walk. She was thrilled by the "Romanesque" landscape, which was "just exactly like a beautiful postcard." In general she seems to have

59

[5.] Toni Volkmann and her friend Miss Böse.

[6.] This is a cook for the Bonhoeffer family.

[7.] Refugees from the Ruhr, which was occupied on January 11, 1923.

[8.] A Social Democratic Party newspaper. [The word "Vorwärts" means "forward!" The newspaper was the central voice of the SDP at that time.] [PDM]

[1.] *NL* A 7/1(8); handwritten letter dated "den 23. August 23"; first previously published in *GS* 6:33f.

[2.] Elisabeth Hansen, née Brückner, was Bonhoeffer's second cousin.

[3.] See above this page, editorial note 6.

recovered well and doesn't complain at all about headaches. Aunt Toni will probably wait with Aunt Elisabeth for the Rüdigers.[4] Aunt Toni has been stung so badly in her ear by a horsefly that the whole ear is quite swollen.

Unfortunately, Sabine has already told you all the details about our wonderful trip. (It wasn't any more expensive than 2 days here at the house, because the train is still so inexpensive.) It was wonderful to be able to visit both old cities. Thank you very much for making it possible.

Aunt Toni just told me very unhappily that I should write that her estimate of 10 million wasn't high enough. We need ½ million every day for bread. Because your letter, with the information about what we should send you, hasn't arrived yet, it will cost more to send the packages. We have mailed most of our things on ahead so that we can ourselves carry as many of the others as possible. The trip also costs ½ million. And so she would like to ask for an additional 10 million. But then, maybe it would be better if we left earlier, because two separate households are certainly more expensive than one, and it really has been very nice.

My and everybody else's very best wishes to you as well as to the Rüdigers and everyone else.
Gratefully yours,
Dietrich

41. To His Parents[1]

October 27, 1923

Dear Parents,

I have now learned what the exact price of our meals will be. Each meal costs 1 billion. One can order meals for 2–3 weeks in advance. That is very advantageous because, after all, the prices will increase in relationship to the dollar. Of course, I don't have that much money on hand. I had to spend 6 billion for bread. Margarine costs 20 M.[2] Furthermore I have to pay 35 M for university fees by November 6, 1/2 M for the semester courses, and 15 M for student fees. Then the library fees, health insurance, etc. I have to pay the Hedgehog fraternity 40 pfennigs every month. I've already paid 20.

[4.] Bonhoeffer is referring to the Rüdiger Schleicher family.

[1.] *NLA* 7/1(9); handwritten postcard dated "den 27. Oktober 23" mailed from Tübingen, previously published in *GS* 6:34.

[2.] "M" is normally an abbreviation for the *mark,* the basic German currency. Here it is apparently an abbreviation for a billion marks. Concerning further quotations of prices in this letter, on October 16, 1923, the German Annuity Office was created. It restored the currency with the help of the stabilized mark [*Rentenmark*]. Indeed, the stabilized mark was circulated after November 15, 1923. It was in use into 1924 in conjunction with the paper mark.

The Old Testament commentary cannot be obtained anywhere here. It   61
would be out of the question anyway, due to the current book prices.

Heim's lectures on dogmatics[3] that I am attending are based on an outline he has prepared. It costs 1 mark 50 pfennigs. I had borrowed the outline
from a fellow student, but he needs it back. These are my current needs. The
numbers are horrendous, but when these are taken care of I really won't
need much more. Should I exchange the Swiss francs? Hopefully they will at
least hold on to their value. By the way, the 5-franc bills are going to be
recalled, in case you have any more. Grandmama is not doing very well at
present; she is sleeping poorly and has many headaches and dizzy spells.
Today she lay in the sun on the balcony for a long time and it helped her a
great deal. She sends you her best wishes, as do I.

Gratefully yours,
Dietrich

42. To His Parents[1]

Tübingen, November 3, 1923

Dear Parents,

I want to write to you once more before the next increase in postal rates.
Grandmama had another argument with Ba.,[2] who behaved very vulgarly.
Grandmama had inquired at the government agency in charge of rental
agreements about how high the basic rent could be. Thereupon Ba. demanded a one-fifth increase in rent without giving a reason. He kept referring to
negotiations that had taken place in the spring. I told him that he had to
have a written record of these negotiations. He said he neither had nor need-   62
ed to have a written record of them. "Besides," he said, "he had often said
that Grandmama should look for another apartment." We told him that this
was out of the question. He would get the money only if he could substanti-
ate his claim in writing. At that he stood up, "bid us farewell," said that
Grandmama should seek accommodations elsewhere, and raced out the
door. We were at the lawyer's this afternoon. The lawyer knew nothing about
the agreement that Ba. claimed to have made with him. He said that we
should just ignore Ba. and not pay more rent. Ba. is becoming increasingly
drunken and miserly and takes advantage of Grandmama whenever he can.

[3.] Karl Heim's lectures on dogmatic theology were published as *Leitfaden der Dogmatik zum Gebrauch von akademischen Vorlesungen* (cf. *GS* 1:63–64 and *GS* 3:138ff.; partial English translation in *NRS* 347ff.). Bonhoeffer later was critical of Heim (see *GS* 1:63f. and *GS* 3:138ff.).

[1.] *NL* A 7/1(10), handwritten letter dated "den 3. November 1923"; first previously published in *GS* 6:34f.

[2.] The identity of this person is not known.

Grandmama always takes these things very seriously. She constantly talks about not wanting to stay here. She wants to move to Stuttgart or to a rest home here. In addition, when I told her about our plan, she said that she would like to come for a visit, but she couldn't expect you to have her stay forever. And I don't believe that the reason is that she can't decide to give up her apartment, because she has thought of other possibilities. Instead she really thinks that another person cannot be added to the household. I believe it would be reassuring if you would write to her. Her pension is also low. She received 85 billion in October and the rent alone cost 65. She can afford it only because she has dollars. Every month she gets 10. Nights are evidently not very easy for her, at least she says she is sleeping very poorly. She is very noticeably upset by the winter and Ba.

I am pretty well provided with supplies. I bought 1 pound of margarine, 1 pound of cheese and marmalade, as well as 50 dinners in advance. They now cost 2½ billion, and I paid 1 billion for them 3 days ago. The only thing that is now terribly expensive is laundry. One starched shirt cost 15 billion several days ago. At the moment a complaint against the university bursar's office is in progress. It is charged with being negligent when it gave students the details about the university fees. There is also a complaint against it because some students have to pay these fees on the 1st of November while others have to wait until the 12th of November to pay them. It is fairly certain that little will come of this.—By the way, Jutta Köhler is engaged to a lecturer named Jessen.[3]

63

A seminar class given by Groos[4] on the *Kritik der reinen Vernunft* began today. I liked it a lot. I haven't yet purchased Heim's book for 1.5 M. I am hoping that the money will keep its value. I hope there won't be any riots in Berlin.[5] As you know, reports of the riots are all exaggerated here but, although it seems funny, you are more apt to believe them when the news affects you directly. The news that we get here is always one day old, and this is also upsetting.

Today Otto Koffka[6] suddenly showed up at my place. He is also studying here and has turned out to be very nice. I wasn't able to find out anything

---

[3.] Jutta Köhler and Dr. Otto Jessen.

[4.] Karl Groos's seminar on Kant's *Critique of Pure Reason* (see below, 1/2/6:307, editorial note 7).

[5.] This was no idle concern. In Bavaria on September 26, 1923, the monarchist Gustav Ritter von Kahr was named General Staff Commissioner. He challenged the German government under Chancellor Gustav Stresemann and proceeded aggressively against the left wing in Bavaria. He kept in contact with General Ludendorff and Hitler, who were preparing the Putsch of November 8 and 9, 1923. In western, central, and northern Germany, communist riots were anticipated. In Hamburg a similar insurrection was put down on October 22–24. In the Rhineland there were separatist riots on October 21 and 22 under the protection of the French occupation.

[6.] A fellow student who was interested in the Hedgehog fraternity.

from Karl-Friedrich's friend Walker because the lists have already been buried.[7] Every day I wait for my package to arrive. I hope nothing has happened to it. I urgently need my shoes.—The Heidenhains send you their best, as does Hilde.[8] She was unable to keep her position, is now here, and is looking for another one. Can Ursel help? Klaus will probably take his examinations in the next few days. How is Rüdiger doing? Please give everyone my and Grandmama's best regards, the Czeppan's too. All the best to you.

Gratefully yours,
Dietrich

43. To Helene Yorck von Wartenburg[1]   64

Tübingen, November 3, 1923

Dear Aunt Helene,

Mama wrote to me from Berlin and told me that you had sent me some wonderful books. I am extremely delighted to hear this. I had longed for Köstlin's[2] book for a long time so that I could complete my library on Luther. I believe I now have all the major works that were written about him. The absence of Köstlin's book was the only regrettable gap. I am therefore particularly pleased that you have given it to me. I thank you as well for the two Gospels. Unfortunately, Mama did not give me any particulars on them.

At present I am delighted to be here in Tübingen. I am very grateful to my parents, who have made it possible for me to study here in spite of the difficult times. Almost all the lectures in my area this semester are particularly enticing. I am at the university almost all day. Grandmama,[3] with whom I live, sends you fond greetings. She is fairly healthy and, to our delight, very vigorous.

[7.] In those months, rebellious acts were expected; indeed November 9, 1923, was the day of Hitler's attempt to seize power in Germany by an act of rebellion. Bonhoeffer's cryptic phrase, the "burying of lists" probably refers to the hiding of the names of persons who would be prepared to fight against such a rebellion (possibly by literally burying them in watertight containers), for they would themselves be in danger of being put into prison by the allied forces, since military training of students was strictly against the Versailles Treaty.

[8.] Hilde Heidenhain was the daughter of Martin Heidenhain. The two families had been friends ever since the Bonhoeffers had lived in Breslau.

[1.] *NL* A 7/2(1); handwritten letter dated "den 3. November 1923"; previously published in *GS* 6:35ff. Helene Countess Yorck von Wartenburg was the sister of Bonhoeffer's grandmother Klara von Hase (see *DB-ER* 4–5 and 14).

[2.] Julius Köstlin, *Life of Luther.*

[3.] Having his own room had become too expensive; cf. above, 1/34:58, editorial note 6.

We hope that she will decide to move in with us for good, because it is very difficult and painful for her to be alone. She also has a very melancholy maid who doesn't make her situation any easier.

In the last few days we've stocked up on winter provisions. We got potatoes and wood. Up until now we have been lucky that the weather has been warm here, almost like summer. It is too bad that the weather changed yesterday and we had to begin heating. We are sitting in the thick fog that rises from the Neckar valley and can hardly see our hands in front of our faces when we are on our lovely balcony, from which we usually have a magnificent view of the whole valley.

65

I have to go to the philosophy seminar. Good-bye for now, dear Aunt Helene. As far as it is possible, take good care of yourself. All the best to you for every good thing.

Gratefully yours,
Dietrich

44. To His Parents[1]

November 8, 1923

Dear Parents,

I just received Karl-Friedrich's money and bought cheese and a few shoelaces. Thank you very much, dear Mama, for your letter. It is soothing to know that it is not as bad at home as is reported.[2] However, the most recent news reports don't give one any idea what will happen now. It's a nuisance that I have to go on a rural solicitation trip for the students' kitchen tomorrow, of all days. Now I won't be able to hear anything more about the situation and, what is especially hard, I won't be able to hear anything from you. I hope Sabine is feeling well again. On this solicitation trip, I will be traveling to Küntzelsau,[3] where the church is being dedicated. The weather is beautiful, but I hope the trip doesn't last too long since I don't like being without a newspaper for several days, even though its sensationalism isn't exactly comforting.

As far as I can remember, I never did receive the blue bank book that you've written about, dear Mama. I received only the money. Sabine was with me, as you know.

[1.] *NL* A 7/1(11); handwritten postcard dated "den. 8.11.23" mailed from Tübingen; previously published in *GS* 6:36f.

[2.] See above, 1/42:66, editorial note 5.

[3.] Location of church of Pastor Konstantin Boeckheler, and later his son Nathaniel.

Grandmama is not feeling well. The political situation also distresses her quite a bit and she still worries far too much about supplies. She'll write to you again before the prices rise.

All my best regards to everyone and especially to you.   66
Gratefully yours,
Dietrich

Are my portfolio and fur hat still coming?

45. To Karl Bonhoeffer[1]

Wednesday, November 14, 1923

Dear Papa,

Your card came today. Many thanks. I got back yesterday evening. When I arrived at the university today I learned that the military exercises in the afternoon have been canceled, because they would have had to take place in Tübingen. Here they run the risk of being spied upon. Instead, all of the fraternities in Tübingen, almost without exception, are leaving tomorrow morning for Ulm. There they will take part in 14 days of training.[2] Many of the other students are going as well. At first I said that I could not possibly take part and would complete the training sometime during vacation. But when I learned that the Control Commissions of the Entente would be watching over the training exercises beginning on December 1, I thought again. I then spoke to a couple of people who are also going. The Hedgehog fraternity and really all of the other fraternities are going in full strength. I also spoke with Rad.[3] He, however, has received a deferral due to weakness. They all strongly advised me to participate in it as soon as possible. The situation is this: the imperial army, with the personal permission of Reinhardt,[4]   67
is training students and other people in Ulm and Constance. The training lasts for 14 days. It is ridiculous that these cannot be scheduled to coincide

---

[1.] *NL* A 7/1(12), handwritten letter dated "Mittwoch, den 14. November 1923" mailed from Tübingen; previously published in *GS* 6:37f.

[2.] Beginning in March 1919 "Student Reserve Security Companies" were trained according to the wishes of the government of Württemberg. They were put into action on April 1, 1919, in Stuttgart during a general strike. The fraternities formed the individual platoons of these companies. At that time Wilhelm Pressel led a platoon with students of the Hedgehog fraternity (cf. *DB-ER* 50). Because of these activities Karl-Friedrich Bonhoeffer did not join the Hedgehog fraternity (see *DB-ER* 49). Following this pattern, the students of Tübingen were called up again in the face of the uprisings feared by the government.

[3.] Gerhard von Rad was in the hospital this year because of a stubborn bronchitis.

[4.] General Walther Reinhardt.

with vacation. You have to tell them one day in advance if you are not going. Naturally, no coercion will be brought to bear if one's situation is critical. The sole purpose is to train as many people as possible before the Control Commission[5] is put in place—At present I have told them I would go for the following reasons. There is a one-day notice period and every member of the Hedgehog fraternity who has studied at the university for 7 semesters or less is going. If fewer persons came than had been registered, problems would arise. I said I would go until approximately Tuesday when I expected to hear what you had to say about this situation. If you had any specific objections I would then return to Tübingen.

At first, I thought that I could do this at another time and that it would be better not to interrupt the semester. I now think, however, that the sooner one gets this over with the better; then one can have the secure feeling that one can help in crises.

Grandmama is sad that she will be alone for 14 days, but says I should go ahead and go. Jörg Schleicher is also taking part. Please write me your opinion immediately.

Thank Mama very much for her dear letter and card. My best to everyone. All my best regards to you.

Gratefully yours,
Dietrich

68   **46. To His Parents**[1]

Ulm, November 16, 1923

Dear Parents,

You will have received my last letter in the meantime. Today I am a soldier. Yesterday, as soon as we arrived, we were invested with a uniform and were given our equipment. Today we were given grenades and weapons. Until now, to be sure, we have done nothing but assemble and disassemble our beds. Tomorrow our tour of duty begins. We get up at 5:30 and begin duty at 6:30. It lasts until 11:00. We're free until 2:00. We have duty until 5:00 or 5:30. Then we're finished.

[5.] In 1922–23, the student "Reserve Security Companies" were transformed into paramilitary groups whose mission was to defend property and inhabitants in the case of unrest. The allies announced that they would establish a commission that would keep this movement under control.

[1.] *NL* A 7/1(13); handwritten letter dated "den 16. November 23" mailed from the barracks in Wilhelmsburg, Ulm; previously published in *GS* 6:38f.

We can go out at night or do anything else we want to do. The food is excellent. There is no pay, but I really don't need anything. I brought along a lot to read. One really does have enough time to get much work done.

It is too bad that it is so difficult to get a newspaper. But for the moment it seems the situation will remain calm. If anything happens, I can get away at any time.

Sabine is certainly doing well. Hörnchen is really tormented by her sciatic nerve.—Every day I hope to find Jörg, who is also in the military somewhere. My address is: Jaeger (not stud. theol.) D.B. Ulm 13, Inf. Reg. 10 Company, 1 Corps.

My best to everyone. And best regards to you.
Gratefully yours,
Dietrich

47. To His Parents[1]   69

November 20, 1923

Dear Parents,

I was delighted to receive the letters. One of them is from you, dear Mama, with the news that you approve of this situation. The training certainly does not commit me to anything else at all. Only the citizens of Württemberg will be summoned to this regiment if the need arises. It is inconceivable that northern Germans would be asked to participate. Until now the exercises have not been very taxing at all. There are approximately 5 hours of marching, shooting, and gymnastics daily, and 3 instruction periods, as well as other things. The rest of the time is free.

We live 14 to a room. It is too bad that the nicest member of the Hedgehog fraternity[2] received a deferral today. The only thing that the examination found amiss were my eyes. I'll probably have to wear glasses when I fire a weapon. The Lance Corporal who trains us is very good-natured and nice. The attitude of these people is much different from what I imagined, and they are not only this way to us. The troops of the imperial army are certainly treated much differently from what they were before.

The food is quite decent. Although it is not exactly plentiful, one gets full because there is a lot of meat. I received Sabine's letter today. I thank her warmly and will write her again soon. It's really grand that Klaus is satisfied with the results of his examinations. Christel is certainly having a ridiculous

---

[1.] *NL* A 7,1(14); handwritten letter dated "den 20. November 23" mailed from Ulm; previously published in *GS* 6:39f.
[2.] Probably Udo Weynand.

time with her ears. Luckily Hörnchen has been delivered from her situation. Please thank Karl-Friedrich for me. This way I received 4½ billion today and exchanged them at once for loans.

I have to go to an instruction course now.

All my regards to everyone and to you my best wishes.
Gratefully yours,
Dietrich

70

48. To Sabine Bonhoeffer[1]

Ulm, November 24, 1923

Dear Sabine,

Thank you very much for your letter. I received it when it was forwarded to me here. It gave me even more pleasure because one often gets bored here. It is hard to pull oneself together to do something important. I think it is crazy and silly of you not to play the violin at all anymore. How were your lessons with Eberhardt?[2] I had heard a lot about him being an especially good teacher. You could surely find half an hour a day to practice. At the very least, practice a trio for Christmas so that we can play one together.

How I will be able to play, though, is a mystery to me. At the moment I have a bandage on every finger. Also they are not getting any more limber here. We have a wide variety of duties. Yesterday was the first time I found it very exhausting. We practiced ground maneuvers with assaults and such. It is especially horrible to throw oneself down on the frozen field with a rifle and a knapsack. Tomorrow we have a big marching exercise with all our equipment, and on Wednesday we have a battalion maneuver. After that the fortnight will soon be over. The oily spots on this paper do not, it happens, come from the pancakes we had at noon but from cleaning a rifle. We get up at 5:30, have duty until 11:30, and then again from 2–6 o'clock. Then one can go to bed if one doesn't have anything to sew, clean, or write. The way they divide our rations is also strange. In the morning, we get only coffee and dry bread. In contrast, at noon the food is very nutritious and most of the time it is plentiful. In the evenings we get coffee again and either cheese, honey, or sausage. At any rate, the rations don't cause one to decline. From what I have seen of it until now, Ulm is a charming old town. We are on a hillock that overlooks the whole town. The dawn is especially pretty from here. Recently I had an astonishingly beautiful view of the Alps from the Münster

71

tower. We saw clearly the Säntis and the Bavarian Alps. I have to go on duty

---

[1.] *NL* Appendix A 5(3); dated "den 24. November 1923." Bonhoeffer's handwriting transcribed by Sabine Leibholz.

[2.] The identity of this person is not known.

now. Give my love to everyone. Thank Hörnchen and Czeppan for the card
they sent me.

My best to you.
Yours,
Dietrich

49. To His Parents[1]

Sunday, November 25, 1923

Dear Parents,

Today, Sunday, nothing is going on. I will probably spend the whole day
here because it is foggy and the barracks look woeful. Until recently the
weather was splendid, but now there finally seems to be an end to it. Yesterday, it began to rain a little. We had a very interesting field drill and marching exercise yesterday. The only unpleasant thing about it was the blisters
that I and most of the others got from running in knee-high boots. But, all
in all, for the 2–3 weeks that we are here, these training sessions are naturally more meaningful for us than the rifle drills and similar things. I received
your letter with the money yesterday, dear Mama. Thank you very much. The
money came at the right time, and I had waited fervently for news. I really
find it so extreme that Becker[2] has become a French citizen that I can hardly believe it. It is not yet clear how long our training will last. We actually registered for only 14 days, but it will probably last 3 weeks at most. I think it is
possible that those who want to leave can conclude their training exercises
after 14 days. After that, according to what I heard, there will be private
training exercises, i.e., something that would really not even be necessary for
us. I will be back in Tübingen on Thursday the 6th at the latest. The fur hat
will hardly be necessary anymore. The semester will end on the 15th of
December. Then I would travel on the 16th and be there for Klaus's lecture.
Should I get anything for Christmas for Grandmama in Tübingen? It is, after
all, nearer and less expensive.

Yesterday I met a member of the Hedgehog fraternity, Rector Schott,[3]
who knows you well, dear Papa. He sends you his best regards.

I just heard that one of our people has been severely injured by a machine
gun. He is being taken to the hospital. He is the son of Kraus[4] in Kennen-

72

[1.] *NL* A 7/1(15); handwritten letter dated "den 25. November 23" mailed from Ulm;
previously published in *GS* 6:40f.
[2.] The identity of this person is not known. With reference to the sharp comment in
reference to the separatist movement, see above, 1/42:66, editorial note 5.
[3.] Emil Schott.
[4.] Paul Kraus.

burg, who is also a member of the Hedgehog fraternity. His knee seems to be completely shattered. I'll go see him this afternoon. It is horrible for him because he is in his 7th semester, and he was able to sacrifice the 3 weeks only with great difficulty.

It has been rumored here that Stresemann has resigned.[5] One doesn't hear anything that is at all accurate here.

Please give my best wishes to everyone.

Next Sunday is the first Sunday of Advent!

Warmest wishes.
Gratefully yours,
Dietrich

50. To His Parents[1]

Tübingen, December 1, 1923

Dear Parents,

Well, today I am a civilian. I am very happy to be here again. I told the lieutenant on Wednesday that I wanted to leave after two weeks. The students are now beginning to stand watch and to have barracks duty. I didn't exactly find it necessary to play truant from the semester any longer. It was, after all, very reasonable to perform one's duty for two weeks. We began with group training, and then progressed fairly quickly to proper field duty and to shooting exercises. To train to do these things was, after all, the main point. When your letter came on Friday, dear Papa, my case was already under review, but I handed them your letter as well. As far as fatigue is concerned, the exercises were far easier for me than they were for all the other students in our quarters. I was, therefore, surprised by your news. Yesterday morning I received my discharge papers. I traveled to Tübingen in the afternoon and arrived around 7:30. It is wonderful to eat once again with a knife and a fork at a table with place settings, to sleep alone in one's own bed, and especially to take a warm bath. But, in spite of it all, I believe the two weeks made quite an impact on me. I did only physical work, and have muscles and disfigured hands to show for it. All in all, the weather was nice up there. The scenery was often very beautiful when snow was on the ground. I remember a particularly beautiful morning when we and several other companies, M.G.s[2] etc.,

---

[5.] He indeed resigned after being rejected in a vote of confidence on November 23, 1923.

[1.] *NL* A 7/1(16); handwritten letter dated "den 1. Dezember 23"; previously published in *GS* 6:41ff. and partially in *DB-ER* 53.

[2.] ["Machine guns"][WF]

began a maneuver while it was still extremely dark. The rising sun caused the dark contours to stand out beautifully against the snow. Half an hour later one could see the Alps magnificently clearly and close at hand.[3]

On the whole, the Imperial Army makes a very good impression. Although almost everyone is intensely reactionary, they are very companionable and decent to us students. Everyone is just waiting for the moment when Ludendorff will pull off the matter with more effective[4] support, i.e., the support of the Imperial Army. This is the complete opposite opinion of all the people up at the house, who want to murder Ludendorff. Today it seems that everyone is stirred up in one direction or other.

When I returned I found Grandmama in good health. The maid's situation, however, is getting worse, and she cries without cause or interruption. From now on Grandmama has to pay her rent in gold (12 marks). I received your last shipment of money addressed to Christel. By the way, Christel said she wanted to write to me about something, and I'm awaiting her letter so she should go ahead and write. I was at the Heidenhains' this afternoon. They send you their regards, as does Miss Rothmann.[5]—At the moment   74
Grandmama is busy knitting children's trousers. I don't know if they are intended as a Christmas present or as something else.

You'll probably spend the evening together on this first Sunday of Advent. I'll continue to read *Wilhelm Meister*[6] aloud to Grandmama, so we'll finish it by the end of the semester. Tomorrow I'll finally return to the college. My fond greetings to all of you from Grandmama and me.

Gratefully yours,
Dietrich

51. To Paula Bonhoeffer[1]

Dear Mama,

Please accept my heartfelt thanks for your Advent greeting. I was delighted by it. It made me as happy as your letter did that arrived today. I found out what Grandmama would like us to give her. She really needs a walking stick and a pair of gloves. As far as groceries are concerned, she needs powdered milk. I've pretty much gotten over the flu. Grandmama is spending the after-

---

[3.] See below, 1/57:86 and 95.

[4.] "More effective" than was the case with the Hitler putsch of November 9, 1923.

[5.] The identity of this person is not known.

[6.] Johann Wolfgang von Goethe, *Wilhelm Meisters Lehrjahre* (1791).

[1.] *NL* A 7,1(17); undated handwritten postcard mailed from Tübingen, postmarked December 5, 1923; previously published in *GS* 6:43.

noon at the Heidenhain's. I have to hurry to the University. By the way, classes end on the 15th, so I can be home on the 17th. Please convey my best regards to everyone. All my regards.

Gratefully yours,
Dietrich
The maid wears the same size as Grandmama.

75 **52. To Sabine Bonhoeffer**[1]

To Sabine: Please forward this quickly

Dear Sabine,

Can it be true that you haven't planned to do anything at all for Klaus's [. . .][2] teacher trainee? Tell me! I would really like to know! What kind of a trio piece should we play? We will surely do something! I won't be able to play anything alone, because I am terribly out of practice. If possible, ask Mama to give us tickets to the Christmas oratorio and then go pick them up. I really would like to listen to a beautiful concert again; there is nothing at all like that here. What do you want for Christmas? Perhaps a "Liedermann-Knackfuß"?[3] There is an antiquarian one here that I could afford. Or Little Knights? Cinnamon Stars?[4] I will bring Papa some of those anyway. I don't know what I should give Mama at all, or Papa. Write me if you can think of anything.

I'm arriving home early on December 7,[5] probably laden down with Grandmama's Christmas presents. When is Rüdiger going to finish his doctorate? Could he possibly have finished it already? Please answer these many questions for me soon. I have to go now.

Best wishes.
Yours,
Dietrich

[1.] *NL* Appendix (A 592); undated. Bonhoeffer's handwriting transcribed by Sabine Leibholz. Date ca. December 10, 1923.

[2.] Illegible.

[3.] This probably refers to Knackfuß and Zimmermann's *Allgemeine Kunstgeschichte.*

[4.] [Little Knights, *Springerle,* and Cinnamon Stars, *Zimtsterne,* are traditional German Christmas cookies.] [WF]

[5.] Bonhoeffer must mean December 17, 1923.

53. To His Parents[1]

December 12, 1923

Dear Parents,

As soon as your card came I immediately went to Ba.[2] The situation has been taken care of quite well. He admitted that it was a mistake and nervously apologized. He seems to have had a terribly bad conscience. Miss Ba. couldn't refrain from offering friendly overtures and apologies. I believe, however, that he'll try the same thing again the next time. Because of him Grandmama really does not have an easy time of it.

I've thought it over and I can travel just as easily on Saturday as on Sunday, since I don't have any college classes on Saturday afternoon. Then I won't miss the warm bath that I've been looking forward to. I also received a written invitation to Czeppan's big party, so I'll be able to go to it as well.

Grandmama has had lumbago for the past few days, but she is feeling better today. She is wearing herself out with all the Christmas preparations and won't be dissuaded from them. She always says that you are best able to develop a resistance to an illness if you participate in everything, and so she does a lot of shopping and visiting.

By the way, our maid wears shoe size 40–41. She has a generous figure and an equally large shoe size.

Please give the Rüdigers my fond greetings. We would like to know when he'll finish his doctorate. I'm really looking forward to being with you again. Grandmama also sends her love. My best regards to all of you and very much to Aunt Elizabeth.

Gratefully yours,
Dietrich
I have a key and an alarm clock.[3]

[1.] *NL* A 7/1(18); handwritten postcard dated "den 12.12.23" mailed from Tübingen; previously published in *GS* 6:43.

[2.] See above, 1/42:65f.

[3.] Difficult to decipher in the original manuscript.

77   **54. To Sabine Bonhoeffer**[1]

February 5, 1924

Dear Sabine,

This time I'm writing you a longer letter than I did on your birthday. Mother and Father say[2] that you've written to me as well, so I'm disappointed that nothing has arrived yet. I received all sorts of fabulous and magnificent things for my birthday. Surely you know about the books. I received something else that you won't even be able to guess at, a splendid guitar. I'm sure you'll be jealous because it has a wonderful tone. Papa had given me 50 marks for anything else that I wanted, so I bought a guitar and am very happy about it. And just so you won't get over your astonishment, I'll tell you about the next completely unbelievable occurrence. Just think, it is possible that next semester—I will be studying in Rome!! Of course, nothing is at all certain yet, but it would be absolutely the most fabulous thing that could happen to me. I can't even begin to imagine how great that would be! Our parents want to ask Axel Harnack[3] about this possibility. At any rate they are seriously considering it. All of you can certainly shower me with advice; but don't be too envious while you are doing it. I'm already making inquiries everywhere around here. Everyone is telling me that it is very inexpensive. Papa has still thinks that I really should postpone it. Nevertheless, after thinking about it, I want to do it so much that I can't imagine ever wanting to do it more than I do now. But go ahead and do your best to dissuade me so that it will make an impression on me. If I do go to Rome I wouldn't even return home at Easter but would travel directly from here so that the trip won't be so long. Talk about it a lot at home; it can only help things. Keep your ears open as well.

78   We celebrated my birthday very quietly yesterday, i.e., we didn't do anything grand. We just sat comfortably together and thought about Rome now and then. You will certainly have celebrated your birthday on a much larger scale. I very nearly forgot to thank you for your fabulous efforts at composing my birthday poem. It is remarkable that you used so many different allusions and it turned out exactly right. Our parents will certainly tell you everything else. I am feeling better again. After classes are over, I'll meet our parents at Walz.[4]

Please give everyone my love, because I can't possibly write anyone else today. Thank everyone in the meantime for me. We're looking forward to

---

[1.] *NL* A 7/2(4); handwritten letter dated "5. Februar 24" mailed from Tübingen; previously published in *GS* 6:43f.

[2.] His parents visited Bonhoeffer on his birthday in Tübingen, because he had fallen while ice-skating and had suffered a concussion (see *DB-ER* 56).

[3.] Axel von Harnack, son of Adolf von Harnack.

[4.] Confectioner's shop and café in Tübingen, Kronenstraße 19.

seeing Rüdiger. "Who knows when we'll see each other again?!" Best wishes, and don't be too envious.

Yours,
Dietrich
Please give Grete[5] my best regards.

55. To His Parents[1]

February 12, 1924

Dear Parents,

I finally met the student at the ASTA,[2] whose job it is to help anyone who wants to study abroad. By chance, it was someone who had been near Rome, so he could give me some very useful information. First the unpleasant things. In Rome there is no semester system. Instead the year runs from November 1 of one year to November 1 of the following year, so it would be difficult to get credit for one semester. Now the pleasant things. First, studying there really is much less expensive. It is strange that the fees are less expensive for foreigners. Food and lodging are both very inexpensive and easy to find. Furthermore, many Germans live there. There is an Italian, i.e., papal university there and a Germanicum,[3] and one can be admitted to both. This student will write to them immediately and ask for specific information about everything. Travel within Italy is less expensive than it is here. The only thing that is expensive is the visa: 15–20 marks. He advised me not to live in a hostel but in a room. It is less expensive and more secure, because one's things would be stolen in a hostel. All in all, he said, studying there would not be more expensive than studying here, and he claimed he knew this for certain.

I am very anxious to hear what you think about the matter now. I know a member of the Hedgehog fraternity[4] here who might also go to Rome, but that is also very tentative.

79

[5.] Grete von Dohnanyi.

[1.] *NL* A 7/1(19); handwritten letter dated "12. Februar 1924" mailed from Tübingen; previously published in *GS* 6:44f.

[2.] [*Allgemeiner Studentenausschuß*. This is a general administrative organization addressing various student needs at the university, composed of the elected representatives of the general student body of a university.] [WF]

[3.] The Pontificia Universitas Gregoriana is the papal university. It was founded in 1551 as the "Collegium Romanum" by Julius III at the urging of Ignatius Loyola. The "Collegium Germanicum," the German Theological Seminary, was founded in 1552 by Julius III and placed under the leadership of the Jesuits.

[4.] Udo Weynand.

Grandmama is doing fine. The days have worn her out remarkably little. Rüdiger will leave in an hour, and I am sitting in the library during an hour break between classes. Please be sure to write back soon.

Best regards to you and everyone else.
Gratefully yours,
Dietrich

56. To His Parents[1]

Tübingen, February 18, 1924

Dear Parents,

80
Yesterday and the day before yesterday Held[2] and I were in the Black Forest. We walked from Kniebis to Hornisgrinde.[3] It was magnificent as well as inexpensive. It was the last free Saturday–Sunday that we will have here. On the next one, we will probably take the wagon ride and pay for it out of the 50 marks. In two Saturdays I will, as you know, already be on my way home. We wanted to make good use of this past Saturday. The weather was beautiful. Above us lay an enormous amount of snow so that the only thing one saw was glittering ice and blue sky. The trees were completely covered in ice, so you could see truly fantastic figures brought into relief against the sky.

It is wonderful that Klaus is already traveling to Italy and especially that he is going directly south through Naples. I am still waiting, ever more anxiously, for news from Rome, from you, and from the man at the University's ASTA office who, as you know, was going to make inquiries for me. I would naturally like to have some concrete information by the end of the semester so that I could tell the people here something definite. Your card just came, dear Mama, saying that Axel Harnack will write to the German pastor.[4] That will certainly be very good. Pressel[5] is also going there during the Easter vacation with a small group of travelers from Tübingen.

By the way, I made inquiries about Karl-Friedrich's Baltic friend for him. His address is: Dr. N.[6] Walker, Derendingen, bei Eckhof. Thank Sabine very

---

[1.] *NL* A 7/1 (20); handwritten dated "den 18. Februar 1924"; previously published in *GS* 6:45f.

[2.] Robert Held.

[3.] Kniebis, a high plain in the northern part of the Black Forest, east of Offenburg; Hornisgrinde, fifteen km northwest of Kniebis near Achern.

[4.] Pastor Dr. Ernst Schubert was the pastor of the German parish in Rome. See below, 1/71.

[5.] See above, 1/33:56, editorial note 5.

[6.] Difficult to decipher in the original manuscript; perhaps "W."

much for me for her birthday letter and poem. I may write to her again, but I might postpone it for 14 days.

I am in a great quandary about how to transport my lute. After all, I already have two suitcases and a backpack. Perhaps I'll have to check one suitcase through to Rome so I won't have to mail any packages.

Grandmama is well and sends her love. I hope that you, dear Mama, will soon be well again. I haven't had the flu a second time.

The very best wishes to you and the whole household.
Gratefully yours,
Dietrich

C. Trip to Italy.
April–June 1924

57. Italian Diary[1]

Diary

Departed form Berlin on April 3 in the evening. Ursel's illness[2] cast a shadow over the preparations. I took Italian lessons from R. Czeppan,[3] and occasionally conversed with Aunt Elisabeth. I knew the Baedecker[4] by heart by the beginning of the trip. I first thought about this trip when I was sick in bed in Tübingen, when I heard the news that my parents would travel to Rome. They had just arrived in Tübingen when I presented my plan to them. They were not completely opposed to it, so I dreamed about my travel plans and sought traveling companions. At first, Weynand was to be my one faithful companion, but even he left me in the lurch. So it finally began on the third of April. I had begun a paper in Berlin that I will continue to work on in Rome.[5]

[1.] *NL* A 8; handwritten diary of April 3—June 4, 1924; previously published in *GS* 6:58-90. The fact that both letters and a diary concerning the trip to Italy have survived invites one to read the contemporaneous texts in parallel. While Bonhoeffer's diary was used to express his immediate impressions and notions, the letters and cards present the result of an initial sorting out of his thoughts. It might be helpful to compare the diary entries during Holy Week and the contemporaneous letter to his parents (see below, page 91f. and 1/61:110) and particularly the letters from North Africa (see below, 1/65:115f. and 1/66:116f.) with the diary, page 5:98f. Note that the letters to his parents say nothing about the "shock" repeatedly noted in the diary or of the situation "without measure" (page 98) during his stay in Libya. In order to facilitate the comparison, references to corresponding contemporaneous texts are noted at appropriate places.

[2.] She suffered from a high fever after giving birth.

[3.] See below, 1/75:125.

[4.] Bonhoeffer used the tour guide by Karl Baedeker, *Mittelitalien und Rom.*

[5.] Title and content unknown.

The trip went through Munich, Kufstein, Brenner, Bozen, Verona, Bologna, and Florence to Rome. It feels strange when one first crosses the Italian border. Fantasy begins to transform itself into reality. Will it really be nice to have all one's wishes fulfilled? Or might I return home completely   82 disillusioned after all? But reality is, quite certainly, more beautiful than fantasy. That was demonstrated for the first time in the Bozen rose garden. Suddenly, one steps out of the scenic wintry Alps into an extremely wide, luxuriously flowering valley. In the distance, in the red glow of the sunset, one sees the magnificently beautiful Dolomites. Changed trains in Bozen. For the first time, the train was full of Italians. Night had fallen again. Extremely cheerful activity prevailed in the train car. The Italians are very charming to strangers and like to chat with them. We arrived in Bologna around 2 o'clock at night and proceeded to trek into town with a group of 4 men (among them a Catholic theology student and a banker),[6] where the liveliness continued. We soon met a man from whom we asked directions, and he guided us through the whole city himself. On the main street, long colonnades, then, at the cathedral and marketplace, beautiful clear moonlight. It was extremely and astoundingly beautiful. I had my first Italian conversation with this man. To my surprise it went very well. 7 o'clock in the morning, Florence, then finally 2:20 in Rome. Before entering the city one sees St. Peter's standing there, a singularly solemn moment. However, the knavery already began at the train station. We arrived at the Pincio[7] in the Via Lazio in our cab accompanied by an Italian lad. We had to pay the fare for him when we reached our destination, and then he also demanded, but did not receive, a big tip. The first thing we were told there was that our rooms had been ready for two days and "fara prezzo."[8] After this beginning, visits to Signora Jocca[9] and Axel von Harnack, neither of whom was at home.

Then, for the first time to St. Peter's. The first impression was in this case not the greatest—as usual when you paint something in your mind for years with the brightest colors of the imagination. Afterwards it looks much more   83 natural in reality. Nevertheless, at first sight you are immediately overwhelmed. The absence of pews allows the architecture to stand out much more forcefully. The dome with the "Tu es Petrus . . ." is the first thing that

---

[6.] The Catholic theological seminarian Platte-Platenius (no further identification is available) was with the group, as were the banker and Klaus and Dietrich Bonhoeffer, who were traveling together.

[7.] A park established in the years following 1890, on the northernmost hill of Rome above the Piazzo del Popolo.

[8.] "They had to be paid for."

[9.] She was the German wife of an Italian; her address was given to the brothers so they would know someone in Rome.

clearly impresses itself on one's consciousness out of the vastness of space, but otherwise I haven't gotten a unified view of the whole so far.[10]

Around 7 o'clock, home through enormous bustle on the streets, cars at furious speeds, announcers whose shouts cause one to think of terrible cries for help, children with their "Santo." A child throws his copper coin into the air, calls out "Santo," lifts his cap and hopes for a good outcome. Depending on the side facing upward the coin belongs to him or to his partner. The shops are built directly on the street. Women with baskets of flowers and the colorful oil carts juggled through the masses with much screaming and skill. It is confusing, and even if one does come from Berlin it isn't any easier to find one's way around. Finally, even after making it home on time, we dared to venture into the city again after we ate. The later it gets, the greater the turmoil in the streets. The worst things are the cars on the narrow, crooked streets.

Sunday the 6th was our first trip to the Colosseum. This building has such power and beauty that, from the moment one sees it, one knows one has never seen nor been able to imagine anything like it. Antiquity is not completely dead. It becomes very clear after only a few moments how false is the statement Πᾶν ὁ μέγας τέθνηκεν.[11] The Colosseum is overgrown, entwined with the most luxurious vegetation, palm trees, cypress, pine, herbs, and all sorts of grasses. I sat there for almost an hour. Then we went on to the Forum. It was closed because of the elections, but it made a powerful impression on me from the outside. The view from the Arch of Severus[12] on the Palatine captivated me the whole time. I went home with the thought running through my head, "the great Pan is not dead."

An afternoon invitation to Signora Jocca's. To my great dismay I had mislaid all of my travel money for an hour and so was late to the event. Mother and child were still there. Conversation half-German, half-Italian. A short walk. Cars with fascists throwing pamphlets onto the streets are everywhere.

Monday afternoon, St. Peter's, with our traveling companion the Catholic seminarian. *Monday* morning, Forum and Palatine. Next to the Pincio. The Palatine is probably the most beautiful place in Rome: the magnificent grounds, the spacious view, the ancient remains of the buildings that are often still well preserved make the place fabulous. Afterwards, the Capitoline, which disappointed me with its Renaissance style. Why didn't one leave the few old ruins there with the grand freestanding staircase, as such it would still have been more beautiful than this reconstruction. There really is a massive difference between classical antiquity and its rebirth.

[10.] "You are Peter . . ." (Matt. 16:18); cf. the postcard to his parents dated April 6, 1924 (below, number 58).

[11.] "The great Pan is dead." Plutarch, *Moralia.* See also Dietrich Bonhoeffer, *Predigten—Auslegungen—Meditationen,* 1:148.

[12.] Triumphal arch of Emperor Septimus Severus, built 203 C.E. on the eastern side of the Forum.

Tuesday afternoon, the Pantheon. The outside of this building is a wonderful uniform architectural structure, but the inside has been atrociously decorated by one of the popes. This pope, along with many other popes, lacked any sense of style and good taste. (I am happy that there is an admission charge.) So, unfortunately, the effect of the whole is considerably diminished. Afterwards we went to Signora Jocca. *Tuesday* morning, Terme Museum with Babs.[13] A fragment of a sleeping Fury impressed me the most. Only the head, carved in relief, is preserved. Likewise, the original bust of Aristotle. In the afternoon, St. Pietro in Vincola[14] with Michelangelo's Moses. It didn't particularly appeal to me. The chain with which St. Peter is supposed to have been bound is exhibited here. Thereupon to the much more beautiful St. Maria Maggiore.[15] Large Basilica. Vespers were just being held by the Canons. I stole into the corner of the small side chapel and was able to follow everything. Afterwards Klaus went home. In addition, I spent a short time at St. Peter's. In front of the entrance you are brought back to earth by some impudent trader who wants to palm his wares off on you. Here I struck a bargain for 20 postcards for 2 lira = 40 pfennigs. Unfortunately, the weather is erratic.

Wednesday (Vatican collection, no longer a chance to see it) Sistine Chapel, terribly full. Only foreigners. Nonetheless the impression is indescribable.—Afternoon, Pincio, a most magnificent view. Ponte Molle,[16] of the beautiful view one can't see anything any longer. Evening, honored Axel at the Trevi Fountain[17] in a trattoria, guitar player, etc.

Thursday, April 10, Santa Maria sopra Minerva.[18] Michelangelo and Bernini's statues of Christ with the cross are situated at the altar.[19] In addition Lippi, among others. The church is Gothic, which is very remarkable here. Afternoon, the Lateran Church. I think that only the part behind the

[13.] The identity of this person is not known.

[14.] Basilica with three naves, built 442 C.E.

[15.] One of the five patriarchal churches from the 5th century, rebuilt in the 16th–17th centuries. The mosaics were from the 5th century.

[16.] Ponte Milvio, called Ponte Molle, built for the Via Flaminia, 220 B.C.E. Renovated in stone in 109 C.E. and 312 C.E. Constantine fought the decisive battle against his opponent Maxentius on this bridge and was victorious.

[17.] The Trevi Fountain is a monumental baroque fountain. It is believed that whoever throws a coin in this fountain will return to Rome.

[18.] It was built on the ruins of Domitian's temple to Minerva in 800 and renovated in 1280. It is Rome's only medieval Gothic church.

[19.] Michaelangelo completed only one sculpture of Christ. [Santa Maria's statue of Christ the Redeemer was started by Michaelangelo in 1519 and completed by one of his students.] [WF] The sculpture of John the Baptist is by an unknown artist. [It is interesting that Bonhoeffer did not mention the most striking object at the altar of Santa Maria sopra Minerva, the body of St. Catherine of Siena (1347–80), which lies in clear view beneath the main altar!] [WF]

confessional is beautiful. The prophets,[20] from the Bernini school, take the feeling of mystery out of the well-lit space; afterwards, the Callistus catacombs,[21] with a bad tour given by a Dominican, then also the Via Appia.— Evening with our comrades from the pensione: a Russian, Levintoff, who played the piano very well; his fiancé, who is from Italy; his sister-in-law, from Greece; their friend, from France; two friends, and our German-Russian table-mate.

Friday, early: Villa Borghese. The lower halls are poorly organized. Above are the fabulous originals: Titian, *Sacred and Profane Love*; Raphael, *Deposition*, etc.; Leonardo; Andrea del Sarto; and artists from the Netherlands.

Today was the first day I resolved to write. Until now I've been too exhausted from looking at so many things. This afternoon at Trajan's Forum. The column is magnificent, but the rest looks like a harvested vegetable garden. I had had great expectations from Baedeker's description but was very disappointed. Therefore we had nothing more pressing to do than to get on a train and ride to San Paolo fuori le mura.[22] A magnificent old basilica that regrettably has often been restored, in construction exactly like the Lateran: 5 nave aisles and 1 transept, the apse here is somewhat smaller. This church on the whole is purer in style and more uniform than the Lateran[23] and is kept darker. When we entered, we heard organ music and singing from one of the side chapels. It was almost evening, full of atmosphere. Magnificent cloisters. The columns, which are all different from one another, are painstakingly decorated with mosaics. The impression is a bit oriental. After this we walked along the Via Antica Ostiensis and watched a splendid sunset. The sun gradually turned from the shrillest yellow into red and blue. Large tattered shreds of clouds, developing peculiar red tints, emerged and glittered across the sky. The sky then turned deep blue and clouds became black. In the foreground the deep green cypresses and pines could be still seen while the houses of the city, as always, appeared yellowish in the evening light.

Until now I have not written anything about our living arrangements. We live in a clean house in the immediate vicinity of the Pincio. The room is fairly

---

[20.] Actually the sculpture Bonhoeffer saw in St. John Lateran, the oldest Christian basilica and the cathedral of Rome, is of an apostle.

[21.] These are on the Via Appia, with several papal graves from the 3rd and 4th centuries.

[22.] St. Paul's Without the Walls, one of the five patriarchal churches, was built in 324 C.E. under Constantine. After a fire in 1828 it was rebuilt according to the original plans. [The five patriarchal basilicas: St. Peter's (Patriarch of Constantinople), St. Paul's Without the Walls (Patriarch of Alexandria), St. John Lateran (Cathedral of the Pope, Patriarch of the West), St. Mary Major (Patriarch of Antioch), and St. Lawrence Without the Walls (Patriarch of Jerusalem), each of which dates to the 4th century C.E.] [WF]

[23.] St. John Lateran, one of the five patriarchal basilicas, was founded by Constantine; today's baroque form dates from the middle of the 6th century.

clean as well. In Italy it seems that one has to freeze in bed. I don't, of course, but everyone else does. Regrettably, we are compelled to be here at meal-times; otherwise for the sake of price and variety we would go to a trattoria more often. Our landlord and landlady speak only Italian. I find this very useful, particularly since Klaus doesn't begrudge me the opportunity to speak. He keeps himself in noble ignorance of the language. At table, the tower of Babel comes to life: Italians, Russians, French, English, and we Germans. The Russians are able to speak the most languages, the English the least. Then come the Germans.

Saturday, the 12th. When we got up it was raining. Read a little in Heiler.[24] Then it cleared up and we went to Maria dei Capuccini.[25] It is a long passage with several individual sections that are decorated with the bones of 4000 dead monks. Some completely desiccated corpses are seated upright and are framed by the bones, probably the abbots.[26] This was begun in 1627, and in 1870 it was forbidden by the state. The Catholic belief in the resurrection seems thwarted by this (note the burning of heretics). I must explore the prehistory of this religious phenomenon—Then Palazzo Barberini,[27] with few but much more beautiful galleries: Andrea del Sarto, Reni, Titian. One just can't grasp the artistic qualities of the Dutch painters in these surroundings. I am just now noticing that while I was unable to grasp the true meaning of Italian painting in Berlin, here I am unable to grasp the true significance of the Dutch artists, whom I admire most when I am in Berlin. It is odd how quickly the different atmosphere, flora, and other surroundings seem self-evident and make one feel at home.

Returning home, I found our bill. It completely delighted me. It was 1/3 less than I had expected, so I could proceed into the next week without hesitation. We were so happy we went to a trattoria at the Trevi Fountain, drank some excellent white wine [Vino Bianco], and ate domestic cheese with Maria Weigert. Then, once again, on to the Forum, where I spent an hour sitting on an overturned pillar, dreaming magnificent dreams. The sky had become clear blue. The three columns of the Temple of Castor and Pollux were the only things silhouetted against it. I also had a good robust local wine in my stomach. Everything contributed to a magnificent hour that transplanted me into the classical world. Then the Palatine with the most beautiful view. However, the sunset seen from the Pincio is even more beautiful. A

87

[24.] Most likely this refers to Friedrich Heiler, *Der Katholizismus.*

[25.] Our Lady of the Conception of the Capuchins was built in the 1620s; it was a church of the Capuchin monastic order, one of the three Franciscan groups comprising the Order of Friars Minor.

[26.] The Capuchin monks do not call their head an abbot, [but rather custode, or guardian]. [WF]

[27.] Begun in 1626 by Carlo Maderna, completed in 1633 by Borromini and Bernini, it contains the Galleria Nazionale d'Arte Antica, the National Gallery of Ancient Art.

carriage ride to the Pincio, where at 7:45 dusk was already falling heavily. During the day, the sky here is not very different in color from the sky at home. At night, or rather at dusk, the sky is nothing like the sky at home. Then the deep blue sky becomes a background for the glowing orange trees. The blue is a violet blue. It is unlike anything we have experienced. It is already 10:30. To finish the day I just drank a quarter of a liter of wine with Klaus.—Tomorrow morning, Mass at St. Peter's. I am looking forward to it very much.

Palm Sunday: I am sitting in the Colosseum in magnificent weather. It is 4 o'clock. This morning: Mass from 10 to 12:30 in Saint Peter's performed by a cardinal. The most astonishing thing was the boys' choir. In some respects, they had trained voices, like women, as if they were eunuchs.[28] To a marked degree, however, they still had splendidly expressive children's voices. It would be absurd to compare them with the Berlin Cathedral Choir. In the Catholic church Palm Sunday is infused completely with the expectation of the Passion. The complete Passion story is read as a dialogue between the evangelists, Jesus, Pilate, etc., and the choir. In contrast, at home Palm Sunday is a day of greatest joy. The thought of the events that follow Palm Sunday naturally has an effect on the celebration, but in reality we only think of them involuntarily. In addition to the cardinal many other important religious, seminarians, and monks stood at the altar. The universality of the church was illustrated in a marvelously effective manner. White, black, yellow members of religious orders—everyone was in clerical robes united under the church. It truly seems ideal. During the grand processions the palms, large yellow, braided branches, were blessed. I was fortunate to stand next to a Catholic woman who had a Missal, so that I could follow everything. The Credo of the choir was magnificent. Therein is truly the most beautiful part of every Mass, the conceptus de spiritu sancto natus ex Maria virgine.[29] At this point the voices were very tender and melodious. I have probably never heard the likes of it before. Well, now I have to go to the Trinità dei Monti[30] to the Vespers, sung by the nuns.

Once again I have put off writing for two days. So on Sunday afternoon in the Trinità dei Monti it was almost indescribable. Around 6 o'clock approximately 40 young girls who wanted to become nuns entered in a solemn procession wearing nun's habits with blue or green sashes. The organ began to

[28.] Actually, the admittance of eunuchs into the Sistine Chapel Choir was forbidden during Leo XIII's papacy (1878–1903).

[29.] Bonhoeffer cites the Latin of the Apostles' Creed, "conceived by the power of the Holy Spirit, born of the Virgin Mary," but here the text of the Nicene Creed was probably sung, "Incarnatus est de Spiritu sanct ex Maria virgine" ("by the power of the Holy Spirit he became incarnate from the virgin Mary").

[30.] The church called Trinità dei Monti was founded in 1495 by Franciscans upon the Pincio.

play. With unbelievable simplicity, grace, and great seriousness they sang Evensong while a priest officiated at the altar. The impression left by these novices[31] was even greater than would have been left by real nuns, because every trace of routine was missing. The ritual was truly no longer merely ritual. Instead, it was worship in the true sense. The whole thing gave one an unparalleled impression of profound, guileless piety. When the door opened after the short half hour one had the most magnificent view overlooking the domes of Rome while the sun was setting. Then I also went for a bit of a walk on the Pincio. The day had been magnificent. It was the first day on which something of the reality of Catholicism began to dawn on me—nothing romantic, etc.—but I think I'm beginning to understand the concept of 'church.'[32]

Monday, the 14th. Morning in the Vatican, only the antiquities. As at the first, I couldn't detain myself in the entrance halls but eagerly went at once into the Belvedere. When I saw the Laocoon[33] there for the first time, a chill actually went through me. It is unbelievable. I spent a lot of time there and in front of the Apollo.[34] Then I had to tear myself away and go to other things. I don't want to list them here. The head of Pericles was marvelous, as were many others.

In the afternoon: Maria Maggiore. Important day of confession. All the confessionals are occupied and densely surrounded by people praying. It is gratifying to see so many serious faces; nothing that you can say against Catholicism applies to them. The children also confess with true fervor. It is   90 very touching to see that for many of these people confession has not become an obligation, but a necessity. Confession does not necessarily lead to scrupulous narrowness, although this can and may often happen especially with very serious people. It is also not merely pedagogy, but is the only way for primitive people to be able to speak to God. For those people who are religiously astute, it is the concretization of the idea of the church that is fulfilled in confession and absolution.

Tuesday, the 15th, morning, Capitoline Museum. The "Lupa Capitolina" and the "Boy Extracting a Thorn"[35] inspired me the most. In addition, a

---

[31.] Probably not novices but rather students of the Franciscan boarding school, Sacré Coeur, in the nunnery (see Baedeker, cited above; also see *LPP*, 218); the singing at this place had earlier been praised by Felix Mendelssohn-Bartholdy.

[32.] See below, 1/93:148f., and Bonhoeffer, *Predigten, Auslegungen, Meditationen*, 1:165f.

[33.] [Laocoön and His Sons is a 1st century C.E. marble (attributed by Pliny to the sculptors Agesander, Athenodorus, and Polydorus) that depicts the Trojan priest Laocoön in an event from Vergil's Aeneid (Book 2).][WF] See *LPP*, 194 and 212.

[34.] Apollo of Belvedere, of Leochares, approximately 350 B.C.E.

[35.] The Capitoline Wolf, an Etruscan bronze from the 5th century B.C.E. [depicts the she-wolf that legend says nursed Romulus and Remus; the figures of the two boys were a Renaissance addition][WF]; "Boy Extracting a Thorn," bronze statue from the 1st century B.C.E.

splendid head of a "Vecchia"[36] is there. Otherwise it was not too impressive for my taste; i.e., "the Dying Gaul" should not be forgotten.—Afternoon, to Maria Maggiore again. Here for the second time I met a small boy who came with his father to confession. Apparently, he had forgotten something in his previous confession. He came out of the confessional rather distraught. Or it could be that his father was raising the child to be an excessively scrupulous person, which is the worst crime one can commit against a child in relation to the church. I will probably come to this church more often to observe the life of the church rather than to look at it from an artistic standpoint, even though it is among the most beautiful of churches.

Wednesday the 16th, morning. We were together in the Villa Farnesina[37] to look at the Raphaels. They are badly renovated with a background of Prussian blue, so that it is hard for one to be enraptured by them. In the adjoining gallery is the *Galatea*, which is especially beautiful.

Afternoon, at home. Then, a short walk to Gesù,[38] where the reading of the Lamentations[39] had just begun. This magnificent church was illuminated by slowly darkening altar candles and a small number of gaslights. People had partially decorated its secondary altar situated on the right. It looked like a sea of flowers. At the front stood white-robed Jesuits who performed elaborate ceremonies.[40]

Maundy Thursday, early, St. Peter's around 10 o'clock. Led to one's place by the verger Eusebius. The celebrations had already begun. At the altar the cardinal, at both sides of the altar the students of the seminaries, priests, bishops, etc., were seated according to rank. It seems that the pope won't come this year. First the Mass, then a magnificent communion service for all the clergy. The choral song accompanying it was unbelievably impressive.

Afternoon, St. Peter's again. Once again it began with Lamentations, of course different ones for each day; then the Miserere. Because my Missal didn't correspond very well to the reading, it was difficult to follow. Then a great procession to the papal altar. Each of the religious and seminarians received a stick with a tuft on the end of it, to hold in their hands. Then the procession began. First the cardinal, then one after the other all the other participants climbed up the altar steps and—after the altar had been cleared of everything around it (covering, crucifix) as a symbol for the theft of Jesus' garments – they swept the altar clean, as a sign of cleansing/purifi-

91

[36.] "An old woman."

[37.] This villa, built by Peruzzi from 1505 to 1511, is in the part of the city called Trastevere, with frescoes by Raphael and his students, e.g., *Triumph of Galatea*, etc.

[38.] La Chièsa del Gesù was built from 1568 until 1575 to be the primary church of the Jesuits. It houses the grave of Ignatius Loyola.

[39.] Selected sections of Lamentations of Jeremiah are sung during the mourning Mass on the afternoons of Maundy Thursday, Good Friday, and Holy Saturday.

[40.] Cf. the postcards to his parents and to Sabine on April 16, 1924 (below, 1/59:109f. and 1/60:110).

cation.[41] Thereupon they processed to the Chapel of the Holy of Holies, accompanied by beautiful singing.

Good Friday, early, St. Peter's, around 9 o'clock. Again good seats. Reading of the Gospel. Then the extraordinarily festive adoration of the cross [adoratio cruces]. The celebrant himself takes the cross down from the altar. Thereupon, adoration by all clergy who knelt and kissed the cross. Accompanying it, magnificent singing and choral response, then a procession to the Most Holy, where the cross will be buried in an urn. Until the Saturday of Holy Week there will no longer be a Holy of Holies.[42]

Afternoon: in St. Peter's again, around 4:30, with our Catholic seminarian Platte-Platenius. I understood the order of the Mass for the first time, because he had the Roman Missal with him. The liturgy was extremely well organized. It is interesting how the Catholic church interprets certain psalms according to its own ends, even when they have a completely different historical significance.[43] The "Christus factus," "Benedictus" (Luke 1-2) and Miserere (Psalm 50) by the choir were simply indescribable. Three solos for the alto were performed by a eunuch; two of them usually sing in the choir. The eunuchs all belong to one order, which sends especially outstanding individual singers to all the choirs. There is something about the way they sing that is thoroughly inhuman, English, dispassionate, and united with a peculiar rapturous ecstasy. On the way back, a long discussion with Platte-Platenius about the meaning of sacrifice in the Catholic church. Modern Catholicism symbolizes what is not comprehensible. It is understandable that he can't comprehend this. Protestantism allows the symbols to fall away at this point. It has fewer traditions and is more honest. Platte-Platenius had the presumption to maintain the view that modern Catholicism is fundamentally the same as early Christianity. The traditions of 19 centuries had clarified it. It seems to me more probable that the traditions of 1900 years have spiritualized it and, to that extent, have clarified it; yet, in this clarification they have falsified the original, which was much more meaningful. Thus the justification for the Reformation, which opposes the Catholic church from another standpoint.[44]

92

[41.] This is a description of the custom of stripping the altar on Maundy Thursday and leaving it bare until the start of the Easter Vigil. The liturgical symbolism is Jesus being stripped of his garments and the penitential stripping away of human sins. It also speaks to the bleakness of the events that follow: the agony in the garden, the betrayal, the flight of the disciples, all a prelude to the passion to be commemorated on Good Friday.

[42.] Until the beginning of the Easter Vigil late on Holy Saturday, there would be no visible decorated altar, and no more bread and wine would be consecrated for Holy Communion.[WF]

[43.] Concerning the discussion on Catholicism, cf. below 1/57:93, 3/14:525ff., and Bonhoeffer, *Predigten, Auslegungen, Meditationen*, 1:165f.

[44.] Crossed out, "In Catholicism the objective fact certainly never plays the most important part."

Easter Saturday: the morning in the Lateran. It was a pity that the consecration of the fire was already over by 8 o'clock. Then the consecration of the
baptismal water followed in the baptistery. The baptismal font, beautifully
decorated, surrounded by clergy, among them the celebrant Cardinal Pamphili, the representative of the pope.[45] A delightfully lively joyous mood was
present among the clerics; a joyous expectation of the grand "Gloria" in the
Mass, i.e., of the announcement of the resurrection. This anticipatory mood
seems strange to us who celebrate Holy Saturday under the impression of
Good Friday. In this way, two different types of people clearly differentiate
themselves from one another. One type always stands under the impression
of that which is coming and thus loses the objectivity needed for the present
moment. The second type has this objectivity to an exceptional degree.
Prophets, visionaries, and expectant individuals belong to the first type. The
objective, often more profound individuals, who enjoy life to the fullest
degree, belong to the other. One type is more speculative, the other more
pensive, brooding. After the consecration of the water, a procession once
again took place in the church: consecration of the 7 theological orders.[46]
First the cutting of the tonsure of the youngest; then the first ordination to
doorkeeper (touching the key, ringing the bells); then the ordination to
reader or lector (touching the book), to exorcist (touching the book of
incantations); and the ordination to acolyte (touching the candle and the
chalice). After the 4 minor orders, the 3 major orders: the subdeacons, who
must vow to follow the path of celibacy and to follow the breviary; deacons,
who may preach; and finally, the priesthood. All these three at the last come
together in the preface.[47] Ordination to the priesthood falls into several
parts: (1) as with all the others, donning the vestments and the blessing, (2)
the anointing and binding of hands, (3) touching the chalice and plate[48]
with bound hands, and (4) communion and conveying of the power to forgive sins.

Afternoon, went to an Armenian celebration of the resurrection.[49] The
impression was that of an eastern fairy-tale play. The whole ceremony was

---

[45.] Apparently he means Basilio Pompilij. See also below, 1/61:110f.

[46.] Following the Council of Trent, the traditional seven orders of ministry in the
Roman Catholic Church were priests, deacons, subdeacons, acolytes, exorcists, readers,
and doorkeepers.

[47.] It appears that Bonhoeffer is describing a point in the ordination ceremony when
all those being admitted into the major holy orders join together at the saying of the Proper Preface, the prayer that comes at the start of the Canon of the Mass.[WF]

[48.] He means here the paten; the eighteen-year-old Protestant's limited understanding of what is occurring is betrayed by the fact that not once does Bonhoeffer mention the
actual ordination by the laying on of hands by the bishops and the other priests who participate in ordaining the new clergy.

[49.] He is speaking of a rite of the Armenian church that is united with the Roman
Catholic Church; the service probably was in St. Niccolò da Tolentino.

carried out with enormous pomp and skillful display. The choir was good, the melodies old and interesting. The only soprano, a boy who was about 12 years old, sang the melody with a powerful and beautiful voice. He held out against the entire men's choir. The young people were dressed in brown skirts with a red upper vestment, or a red skirt with a colorfully stitched top. Both bishops wore white robes (stitched with gold), wearing imposing miters. Their long white beards and their sharply defined serious faces made a very dignified impression. The repeated opening and closing of the curtain hanging in front of the altar, which was illuminated with candles in a very poetic manner, produced a peculiar theatrical impression. The faces of the young people, who were between 17 and 20, were refined and serious.

94

After church met Marion Winter.[50] Went home with Platte-Platenius. Long, mutually animated discussion. He tried to attack Kant; but in doing so fell, against his will, into the usual Catholic vicious circles [circuli vitiosi]. In addition, he believes in the proof of God based on the teleology of the world as knowledge, thereby, of course, always confusing logical and faith-based "knowledge." Thus, reasoning in circles. He would really like to convert me and is quite honestly convinced of his method. In this way, through dialectical artifice, which he, however, doesn't use as such, he accomplishes the least! Following these discussions, I find I am once again much less sympathetic to Catholicism. Catholic dogma veils every ideal thing in Catholicism, without knowing that this is what it is doing. There is a huge difference between confession and dogmatic teachings about confession—unfortunately also between 'church' and the 'church' in dogmatics.

Easter morning at 10 o'clock, High Mass in St. Peter's. The priest was with me again and I could therefore follow everything. The Sistine Chapel choir sang; one can hardly conceive of anything so magnificent. It was even more beautiful than the choir had been up until now. Yet I can't say that this particular worship service made a strong impression on me.

The afternoon at the Joccas', the *Spring Sonata* was performed.[51] A curious sensation to hear such a characteristically un-Italian piece played on Italian soil with Italian ardor and lightheartedness.

In the evening, preparation for the trip to Sicily. I part from Rome with a heavy heart, even if it is only for 14 days, even if it will take me to Naples and Sicily. It had already become dearer and more familiar to me in 2½ weeks than any other city. It had enabled me to learn more in 2 weeks than any other city. It is an unimaginable thought that I might have to leave it for a long time, as will happen in 6 weeks.

[50.] Former classmate, later Countess Yorck von Wartenburg; see *DB-ER* 34 and Yorck von Wartenburg, *Die Stärke*, 14.

[51.] This may refer to Beethoven's Violin Sonata, no. 9, which is nicknamed the "Spring Sonata."[WF]

95   Sicily [52]

Palermo: on the 21st, in the morning. We boarded the train to Naples. The weather was still moderate when we arrived at 1:30. After a long search for a trattoria I was directed to a "buona trattoria" that was, to be sure, as unbelievably filthy as the nastiest farmhouse in Germany. Hens, cats, dirty children, and unpleasant aromas surrounded us. Dried clothes fluttered all around us. But hunger, fatigue, and ignorance of the countryside induced us to sit down. Of course, we ate dry pasta [pasta asciutta] and drank ½ liter of some disgustingly sweet sticky wine. After a bit of bargaining we paid our bill. We got up relieved and went to redeem our tickets for the sea passage. After that we went shopping for the sea voyage. According to Klaus, these are the necessities of life: Schnaps, lemons, chocolate bars, sardines, oranges, among other things. We then went to a restaurant to have the last rites administered, where we once again ate pasta asciutta, and boarded the ship. Nothing was of any help for Klaus. After only 4 hours he lay there and had had more than enough; the sea made great demands on him, and he was able to hold out against it only for a short time. It invited me to perform my duty only at the first sight of the magnificent sunny mountainous cliffs. All in all, it was very gracious. We arrived at 8:30. Remarkably, the moon had risen while we were at sea. Like a golden fish, it rose gradually out of the sea. It was a fantastic vision. Regrettably the sunrise was obscured. The approach toward and arrival at Sicily were wondrously beautiful. The harbor there lay under a magnificent sun. A room at the Hotel Veronica was offered to us while we were still at the harbor. We drove to it in a carriage. After having tea for breakfast, we went immediately to bed. Although we intended to sleep for half an hour, we slept until 1 o'clock. We went to a restaurant, ate dinner, and then went to the cathedral. From the outside it was extremely beautiful, but I was truly shocked at the interior. This was supposed to be the world-famous

96   cathedral in which Friedrich II and Henry VI lay buried! [53] But, this really was it, one couldn't change the fact, so I endeavored somehow to appreciate it. The absence of style won out, however, and it just couldn't be done. Here one couldn't even appreciate it from a loftier perspective, as one could so often do in Rome. Even the historical perspective, which can so often do wonders, failed. I went out and redoubled my enthusiasm for the exterior. To be sure, the architecture was difficult to take in at a glance, but the whole thing at least gave the impression of uniformity.—After having our travel

---

[52.] Cf. below, 1/62:112, a letter to his parents on April 22, 1924.

[53.] Palermo Cathedral, built by the Normans in 1170, was altered in the interior in late baroque style; a cupola was added to the building's exterior. [In it are buried Emperor Frederick II (1194–1250) and Henry VI Hohenstaufen (1265–97), Holy Roman Emperor and King of Sicily.] [WF]

tickets stamped, we proceeded to the English Gardens. (By the way, it cost only 27 marks Brenner–Brenner, 3rd class.) Here we actually strolled under palm trees for the first time. In Rome the palm tree is much more of an ornamental tree. Here it is truly a street tree.

In the evening we lay in bed and decided to take a look at our finances. To our not inconsiderable astonishment I was 400 lira short and Klaus was missing 150 lira. After we counted and recounted, we went to sleep very depressed. When we awoke on *Wednesday the 23rd* I discovered, after recounting my money, that the evening before I had miscounted it to my disadvantage. Although Klaus was not able to account for his money, we were both very happy. We hoped to stay the course with Klaus's 170 lira and my 800 lira. With a few curses and aphorisms about the reprehensibility and other unpleasant aspects of money, we applied ourselves to our day's work. First we went to our trattoria on the Via Roma and then to San Giovanni dei Eremiti.[54]

Again, I haven't written in 5 days—very eventful ones.[55] So in the morning we went on to San Giovanni. It appealed to me tremendously, because its appearance is thoroughly oriental. Unbelievably alluring sweet scents rose out of the garden from all sorts of wonderful flowers. A person anticipates   97 the Orient without realizing that soon one would take oriental surroundings for granted. I had fantasized about the Orient just as I had fantasized about Italy while still in Germany. I always discover that these fantasies are so completely different from the reality. They are so much more grandiloquent and colorful. Only reality can first make the picture concrete; one's horizon is never expanded through fantasy, for the sole reason that concrete perspectives are missing. One can read anything one wants about a country, and yet every image remains a picture painted on one's own native canvas in the most magnificent colors. Now, when this native background is no longer present even the most magnificent colors are washed away. One can stand firmly in the Orient only when one's native prejudices as well as the magnificent fantasies of something completely new and immeasurable by our standards have all fallen away. Only then does the earlier, vague picture slowly begin to solidify and become concrete. In this way a new world is born in oneself. It grows on every street corner. Old veils fall away and much more beautiful things become real. A person's first trip to the Orient can be compared to a magnificent sunrise.[56] Magnificent fog heralds the coming of the sun in fantastic colors, but it only heralds it. Quietly, but only in the remote distance, one anticipates what will be. The veils become increasingly magnificent, but the first ray of the sun barely arrives when the clouds and the fog

---

[54.] The church San Giovanni degli Eremiti, St. John of the Hermits, was built in 1132 by the Normans in the style of a mosque [over the ruins of a preexistent Gregorian monastery and of an ancient building, presumably iself a mosque.] [WF]

[55.] The date of writing is therefore April 26 or 27, 1924.

[56.] Cf. above, 1/50:75 and 1/57:86.

already begin to flee. The bigger the ball of sun becomes, the more the fog melts into oblivion. Finally the sun is there in all its magnificence. All fantasies were in vain because the sun is present as an existing entity. We stand there mute and must accept it as it is. But I am really still in Palermo, and I still have to go to Girgenti[57] and Syracuse. I want to do this quickly because I am being urged on toward Africa.

98

In Palermo we also went to Monreale.[58] It didn't make any particular impression on me. The Capella Palatina[59] affected me completely differently. It is the castle's chapel and is built in the Norman style. Here one can make interesting observations about the meaning and boundaries of mosaic decorations. Without a doubt mosaics are primarily decorative in character. Because of this, it appears to me that the enormous mosaics in St. Peter's do not fulfill their original purpose. Naturally, their churchly import is completely different. An enormous amount of mysticism is contained in ornamentation. This is another aspect of mosaics. There is in the ornamentation of sacred stories, no doubt, an unconscious impulse to establish these historical things metaphysically. Naturally, the mosaics are also of particular interest in *art history*.—Monte Pellegrino[60] at dusk. The following evening Santa Maria di Gesù. Scenically, it is probably the most beautiful spot in Italy that I have seen up to now.

Friday the 25th, *departure to Girgenti*. The first really serious discussion about Africa with my traveling companions. In Girgenti, after arranging for a place to stay, off to the temples.[61] I found it regrettable that during the whole period I couldn't get into the mood to appreciate classical culture on its own terms. I appreciated the scenic qualities much more. The fact that the architectural monuments were overrated could not be blamed on the famous reputation of the temples. It is certainly my fault that I could not appreciate them. I am still supersaturated from Rome. Scenery has now become more important than classical antiquity. We got to know 3 German "Wandervögel"[62] in Girgenti: a student, an art dealer who is a very sympathetic and intelligent man, and an artisan. We took them all to Africa with us. We did several things together.[63]

[57.] Under Mussolini, this city was renamed Agrigento.

[58.] Monreal Cathedral, built in 1174, displays Roman and Arabic influences; the interior is fully bedecked with mosaics.

[59.] A royal chapel built under Roger II, King of Sicily from 1132–40, Capella Palatina is filled with Byzantine mosaics. According to Bonhoeffer's opinion, the mosaics of Monreale stick out unatttractively, especially the Christus Pantocrator in the apse, in comparison with the mosaics in the Capella Palatina.

[60.] On 600 meters of steeply sloping rock on the northern end of the Bay of Palermo.

[61.] In Girgenti are five Doric temples from the 5th and 6th centuries B.C.E.

[62.] Literally "Hiking Birds," this is the name of one of the oldest and best-known parts of the German Youth Movement.

[63.] See below, 1/63:113, the letter to Sabine Bonhoeffer dated April 28, 1924.

We spent three days in Girgenti. Then we took off to Syracuse for a day. We had gradually brought our completely imaginative thoughts about traveling to Africa closer to reality by having even more imaginative conversations. In Palermo we believed that the two of us could hardly manage to stretch our finances to live comfortably in Sicily. Now, however, we had the audacity to invite a very adventurous artisan to travel to Tripoli with us. Our extravagant way of life—eating three times a day—was transformed into eating once or at most twice a day. The inns we stayed in also began to take on a different appearance. So after spending one day in Syracuse, whose location is the most beautiful thing about it, we boarded the ship for Tripoli.

We got the necessary passes with the help of an Italian. So we were able to leave Europe for the first time on the 29th.[64] The voyage was quiet. Klaus, as always, did his duty. I had some pleasant conversations with some Italian soldiers. We also played some music together and sang while someone played a guitar. In this way the voyage passed quickly in spite of a 6-hour wait in Malta where we were not allowed to go ashore. So on May 1, when we raised ourselves up from our pallets, we saw Africa before us illuminated by beautiful sunshine.

Tripoli[65]

Only short comments, otherwise there would be far too many. Immediately upon our arrival, we met a photographer from Stuttgart. We camped out in the best hotel of the city, the "Patria," for 1 mark. Our arrival was reported in the *Corriere di Tripoli*. A walk through the city. Next morning, to the oasis, to the Friday market. Evening: we got to know 2 Austrian soldiers[66] with whom we were now often together. Walks to the sea to swim, to the little mosque, to the desert (by the way, lunch is between 1 and 4 o'clock). Trip to Garian[67]— Gibli[68]—car travel. Greeting in Garian. Bedouins—[. . .][69] sick. Driven away in an officer's car as unwelcome guests.[70]

[64.] April 29, 1924.

[65.] Cf. the letters of Klaus and Dietrich to their parents on May 5th and 9th, 1924 (see below 1/64:113ff. and 1/65:115f.).

[66.] They were from the southern part of Tirol; see below, 1/66:119.

[67.] Garian or Gharyan is a city in northwest Libya one hundred km south of Tripoli in the low Jebel Nefusa mountain range. It lies about 600–850 meters above sea level on a plateau; the desert begins south of this place.

[68.] [The Gibli is a seasonal, hot, sand-bearing wind that blows up from the Jebel in the south of Libya.][WF] Thus, "Coming here from Jebel" means a hot wind from the south.

[69.] Illegible; perhaps "Hommel."

[70.] Tripolitania, today a part of Libya, was conquered by the Italians 1911–12 in a war with Turkey. The hinterland could be forced to submit only after World War I; hence the strong military presence that the brothers observed. They scarcely found themselves in a peaceful hinterland, which may explain the nervous reaction of the military authorities.

Saturday, May 10, in the evening, after many difficulties, departure for Europe.—One no longer dare go to Africa unprepared. The shock is too great and intensifies from day to day, so that you are happy to go back to Europe again.

Calm departure to Syracuse. From there immediately on to *Taormina* [Sicily]. We stayed in an inn in Giardini, and after making the necessary purchases we went up to the Taormina at about 5 o'clock. Around sunset, we arrived at the Greek theater. In front of us, surrounded lightly by fog, Mount Etna. To the right, not very far away, the beautifully formed mountain ranges merge with it. These come up alongside of the Greek theater. The sun set behind them. In the foreground was the Greek theater. It is not the most prominent architectural and cultural artifact but, because it lies in ruins, it had an indescribably beautiful harmonious quality.

For the first time, one was able to breathe freely again. It was as if fetters had been removed from our limbs. We saw European trees again and the richness of the soil. While in Africa, one had truly yearned for nothing as much as to see a beautiful German forest. Although this particular wish had not been fulfilled at all, even the orange and the lemon trees seemed to remind us of home. We sat there near the theater for a long, long time. Again and again, we looked toward the Italian shore, lying in the dusk, which was enveloped in mild hues and rose abruptly out of the sea. The sea was as smooth as glass and flawless. In the distance were a few sailboats. Old Etna, with her many children, was always in front of us. When it was finally night and the stars were out, we went swiftly on the path to Giardini. We went to bed in a strange, happily excited mood. We were home again. If we had to accept everything in Africa without measure, truly without even the possibility to come to terms with it, then we would also be damned to complete passivity. This suddenly changed when we arrived in Europe. We had often tried in vain and had clumsily sought to react correctly to a particular situation in Africa. We were often forced simply to assimilate and perhaps later process the experience. Because of this our affection for and understanding of Europe increased. We reveled with enthusiasm in a landscape that elicited affection for one's native country.

101

In Africa, it was as if enormous amounts of the heaviest materials had been thrown into a completely empty container. This container was not very well constructed and threatened to break open if it were not reinforced. If this were to happen the material would fall into boundless depths, get lost, and cause a fair amount of damage. Now, because this container had been supported by new impressions for a short time at least, one's attention was drawn to other things. During this time, the material in the container could become firm and solidify. Soon, however, real reinforcement through extensive study will be necessary in order to avert the catastrophe, because what one had seen was enormous.

One more day in Taormina. Then a trip to Naples by way of Messina and the magnificent southern Italian west coast. The little town of Scilla[71] built on a cliff projecting out into the ocean was especially beautiful lying in the evening sun.

We got up around 4:30 in the morning and took a little morning walk to *Paestum*. Although the temples in Girgenti hadn't appealed to me very much, the impression these made on me was enormous. In any case, the Poseidon temple[72] made the most lasting impression on me. I sat before it for almost 4 hours. I left it with great difficulty. The sun rose over the mountains and cast its most beautiful morning light on the temple while the grass still glittered with dew. An endless number of birds swarmed around the temple. A great many lizards endeavored to see if the sun were doing its duty. That morning is unforgettable because of its harmonious purity and multifaceted nature. 102

Around 9 o'clock we traveled to Naples on the train. Afternoon, Posilippo. The next day, Pompeii and Vesuvius. The climb up to Vesuvius was difficult and unappealing except for the view and 2 bottles of Lacrimae Christi.[73] At the top, we met Kranz and Heinrichs[74] completely by chance. Vesuvius was in good working order, and now and again it spewed out a bit of lava. There, at the summit, one believes one has been transported back to the time before the creation of the world. The view beneath could be only slightly inferior to the view of paradise.

In the evening, ate supper in a pub in Torre Anunziata[75] (cf. Auerbach's Cellar!). Then return trip to Naples. From there, trip to Rome the next morning.

Rome: Second Stay

I must say that leaving Naples wasn't very difficult, considering that I was traveling toward Rome. I only needed to think about it to ease any sadness I felt about leaving. I couldn't say what it was exactly that drew me so irresistibly. Even if I had said "St. Peter's," I wouldn't be speaking of the church itself. No, it is Rome as a whole that came to be epitomized most clearly by St. Peter's. It is the Rome of antiquity, the Rome of the Middle Ages, and equally the

---

[71.] Tiny fishing village lying at the northern entrance of the strait of Messina. [It is one of the pair of towns Ulysses had such a difficult time getting past – Scylla and Charybdis.] [WF]

[72.] The Temple of Hera II, built around 469 B.C.E. [according to legend by Jason and the Argonauts, was once thought to be the Temple of Poseidon (the Roman God Neptune); indeed Paestum was long known as Poseidonia.] [WF]

[73.] *Lacrimae Christi* is a very sweet, dark-colored Italian wine. [WF]

[74.] Difficult to decipher. Cf. above, 1/31:54, editorial note 6.

[75.] A town approximately twenty km south of Naples. On "Auerbach's Cellar" see Goethe, *Faust*, 128ff.

Rome of the present. Simply stated, it is the fulcrum of European culture and European life. My heart beat perceptibly when I saw the old water conduits accompanying us to the walls of the city for the second time.

After we got off the train, to St. Chiara. No room there. For a few days in a very mediocre hotel near the Pantheon. In the evening, the Pincio district. For me the beginning of a new epoch. For Klaus the end of the first.

103

The 17th,[76] Saturday morning, Pinacoteca, where a *Madonna* by Gentile[77] was highly inspiring. The interpretation is thoroughly original and interesting. Mary is the natural mother of her natural son. She is a carpenter's wife, and the child's expression and costume reflect these circumstances. Then St. Peter's. Klaus went for the last time. When I tried to put myself in his place my spirits underwent a great change and I quickly looked forward to 4 magnificent weeks. Klaus left around 2 o'clock in the afternoon. I looked for lodging and found it with Mrs. Prof. Bigi, Via Quintino Sella 8. Good, inexpensive, and simple.

Sunday the 18th: Morning, Terme museum[78] without much enjoyment. Afternoon: Pincio. Read Kant, then played music with Signora Jocca for several hours: Bach, Brahms, Dohnanyi, Mozart. Evening, went to meet Kranz.

Monday the 19th, Santa Croce, which disappointed me. Studied the Lateran. San Clemente[79] with the lower church. Very interesting. Afternoon, college lecture and worked at home.

Tuesday, St. Maria della Pace.[80] One has to have seen Raphael's Sibyls so that one can appreciate Michaelangelo's all the more. In my opinion they belong to the most beautiful of Raphael's works. St. Maria dell' Anima.[81] The Catholic church even goes so far as to turn ancient statues into statues of saints (Apollo—Sebastian)! The church is not very interesting architecturally. St. Luigi dei Francesi[82] with good paintings (Raphael, Reni). College lecture, etc.

[76.] Cf. below, 1/68–70:120–22, to his parents, Sabine Bonhoeffer, and Julie Bonhoeffer from the middle of May 1924.

[77.] The *Madonna* by Gentile da Fabriano presumably is in the Pinacoteca Vaticana in Rome.

[78.] Presumably the National Museum, *Museo Nazionale delle Terme.*[WF]

[79.] Santa Croce in Gerusalemme, or Holy Cross in Jerusalem, is one of the seven Pilgrim Churches. Exterior walls are from the 4th century. The three-nave Roman basilica was built in 1144 and then renovated in 1743 in the Baroque style. St. Clemente is a basilica built in 1108 on top of a Mithras shrine, with wall paintings from the 8th to the 11th centuries in the underground church.

[80.] "Our Lady of Peace" in Rome was built in 1480; [a side chapel contains a fresco from 1514 by Raphael of the four Sibyls: Luma, Persia, Phrygia and Tibur, each receiving a revelation from an angel.] [WF]

[81.] "Our Lady of the Souls," was built 1500–14; it was earlier the German National Church.

[82.] It was consecrated in 1589 as the French National Church.

Thursday, Galleria Colonna. Beautiful galleries. Leonardo: *Holy Family.* Caravaggio. Bordone: *Sebastian.* Botticelli: *Madonna.* The rest consisted of a lot of boring things and a lot of [Nicolas] Poussin as well. Afternoon, St. Lorenzo Fuori.[83] The most wonderful mosaics in the lower church, not so much because of their subject matter as the skillfulness of their execution.

Wednesday: Campo dei Fiori. Attempted to buy something pretty, but everything exceeded my financial abilities. Not a true Italian market like those, for example, in Palermo or Naples.—Kolleg.[84]

104

Friday,[85] Galleria Doria.[86] Velasquez, Rondinello: *Madonna.* Titian: *Triton* and a great deal of other outstanding works. One of the most diverse galleries in Rome. For example, Claude Lorrain was very well represented. Hardly an inferior picture among them and everything was well chosen.

Afternoon, Caelius[87] with churches. St. Gregorio with 3 side chapels. One thing that is enchantingly beautiful is the *Concert of Angels* by Reni.[88] No one should be allowed to leave Rome without having seen this work. It is absolutely perfect in its design and, without a doubt, ranks among the premier artworks of Rome. Both the busts begun by Michelangelo leave one cold, especially the one of the pope, which is, I think, devoid of any complexity in artistic style or expression. Architecturally it is constructed in the purest basilica style (cf. Sistine Chapel).

The disfigured church of Saints Paolo e Giovanni.[89] Did not see the lower church.

St. Maria Navicella.[90] Architecturally the width of the mosaic arches has an unflattering effect, hardly intentional. I found the mosaics very exceptional, in spite of Burckhardt.[91] Apparently they don't fit into his typological categories. The church as a whole is most charming, and is situated in an

---

[83.] "St. Lawrence Outside the Walls" was founded by Constantine and rebuilt in the 6th and 13th centuries as a patriarchal church.

[84.] Reference unclear: This may be an abbreviation for Kollegium, or College, perhaps referring to a lecture Bonhoeffer attended.[WF]

[85.] Cf. the postcard to his parents of May 21st (see below, 1/71:122) and the letter to Sabine Bonhoeffer of May 22, 1924 (see below, 1/73:123f.).

[86.] In the Palazzo Doria, from the 17th century.

[87.] *Caelius Mons,* or "Coelian Hill," the most southeasterly of the hills of Rome upon which the following churches are found.

[88.] The St. Gregorio Magno church, dedicated to Pope St. Gregory the Great, was founded in 575 and totally renovated in the 17th–18th centuries. [One of the three chapels in the gardens has a painting by Guido Reni in the vault of the apse, *Concert of Angels.*] [WF]

[89.] Santi Giovanni e Paolo, SS. John and Paul on the Coelian Hill, was founded in 400 C.E., and has often been rebuilt; there are very old frescoes in the subterranean church.

[90.] Santa Maria in Domnica, "Our Lady in the House-Church," also known as Santa Maria della Navicella because of its location in the Piazza della Navicella, was built between 817 and 824 C.E.

[91.] Jacob Burckhardt, *The Cicerone, or an Art Guide to Painting in Italy:* "In the following pontifical church, the mosaics become successively primitive and lifeless, until the figures represented are unbelievably deformed."

idyllic spot. Next to it St. Stefano Rotondo[92] an old market building that
serves well as a church. The circular form generally gives the churches a
more intimate character (cf. the baptistery in the Lateran). A disagreement
with the sexton's thieving wife couldn't take away the idyllic atmosphere of
the whole.

105

Saturday the 24th, morning. First to the Quirinal to the legislative celebration.[93] The royal family, ministers—among them also Mussolini—drove
through the city to the Parliament in a festive procession. Without general
enthusiasm, the crowd applauded the king. A monk who had been praying
couldn't finish his prayer when the royal car drove by but began to applaud
with touching enthusiasm.

Then the Vatican. First the Stanzas,[94] which did not fascinate me very
much. Historical painting appears to me to be without style in every respect.
I have to think about this more carefully. Why is it? Then I studied the Sistine Chapel carefully and with increasing enthusiasm. First the frescoes
(Perugino!!),[95] then the paintings on the ceiling in their proper order. But
I was hardly able to move beyond Adam. There is an inexhaustible abundance of ideas in the picture. The figure of God reverberates with colossal
power and tender love, or rather with the divine attributes that supersede
these two human attributes that are often far removed from each another.
Man is about to awake to life for the first time. The meadow sends out shoots
in front of unending mountain ranges, thereby foreshadowing man's later
fate. The painting is very worldly and yet very pure. In short, one can't
express it.

The most impressive painting is probably that of Jonah. One only need
notice the unbelievable art of perspectival shortening.—Enough of this or it
will get too long.

Afternoon, the Vesta temple,[96] with an enchanting baroque well. Behind
it Santa Maria in Cosmedin an attractive old Roman house church. In the

---

[92.] Santo Stefano Rotondo al Celio, "St. Stephen's Rotunda at the Coelian," is a round
church erected 460–80 c.e. over a Mithras shrine. [It is dedicated to St. Stephen of Hungary, formerly to St Stephen the Deacon; it is the Hungarian National Church.] [WF]

[93.] [The Quirinal Palace is the residence of the President and is near the Parliament
buildings] [WF]; presumably Bonhoeffer refers here to the opening day of Parliament.

[94.] The Raphael Stanzas are a series of spectacular frescoed rooms in the Vatican
painted by Raphael and his students.

[95.] Pietro Vannucci, known as Perugino, was among the painters who worked on the
Sistine Chapel frescoes, including "Scenes from the life of Moses," and "Scenes from the life
of Christ," including the famous "Presentation of the keys to St. Peter." [WF]

[96.] The Temple of Vesta, home in mythology of the perpetual fire guarded by the
Vestal Virgins, is on the Forum Romanum, the Roman Forum.

sacristy a beautiful mosaic fragment: *The Three Kings.*[97] Villa Malta[98] with garden and keyhole.

Sunday, Morning, Villa Borghese. Immediately to the Titian: *Sacred and Profane Love.*[99] Attempted for a long time to find the real meaning, without success. Burkhardt can hardly be correct: "Love and Prudishness" (amore profano and sacro!?).[100] In the same gallery, more interesting: El Greco. Then Leonardo, Perugino: *Madonna* and *Saint Sebastian*; Botticelli; perhaps slightly technical and therefore seemingly stilted: Bronzino. At the moment, it gives me great pleasure to try to guess the schools and the individual artists. I believe that gradually I am better able to understand something about the subject than I was before. However, it might be better for a layperson to be completely silent and to leave everything to the artists, because the current art historians really are the worst guides. Even the better ones are awful. This includes Scheffler and Worringer,[101] who arbitrarily interpret, interpret, and further interpret the artworks. There is no criterion for their interpretation and its correctness. Interpreting is generally one of the most difficult problems. Yet, our whole thinking process is regulated by it. We have to interpret and give meaning to things so that we can live and think. All of this is very difficult. When one doesn't have to interpret, one should just leave it alone. I believe that interpretation is not necessary in art. One doesn't need to know whether it is "Gothic" or "primitive," etc., persons who expresses themselves in their art. A work of art viewed with clear intellect and comprehension has its own effect on the unconscious. More interpretation won't lead to a better understanding of the art. One either intuitively sees the right thing or one doesn't. This is what I call an understanding of art. One should work diligently to try to understand the work while looking at it. After that, one gets the absolutely certain feeling, "I have grasped the essence of this work." Intuitive certainty arises on the basis of some unknown procedure. To attempt to put this conclusion into words and thereby to interpret the work is meaningless for anyone else. It doesn't help one person, other people won't need it, and the subject itself gains nothing by it. In this case, regret-

106

[97.] Santa Maria in Cosmedin, "Our Lady in Beauty," was built in the 5th century on the foundation of a temple of Heracles; [the sacristy contains an 8th-century mosaic of the Adoration of the Magi.] [WF]

[98.] Villa that hosts the Grand Priory of Rome, including the Embassy of the Order to the Holy See; the round opening above the keyhole provides a surprising view of the dome of the church of St. Peter.

[99.] This villa in a magnificent park was built in 1605, for the express purpose of displaying the art collection of Cardinal Borghese, the Galleria Borghese, in which this famous 1514 painting by Titian hangs, surrounded by many other well-known works of art.

[100.] See Burckhardt, *Der Cicerone*, 583: "Amor sacro e profano, that is: love and prudishness."

[101.] Karl Scheffler and Wilhelm Worringer were highly influential art critics. See Wilhelm Worringer, *Abstraktion und Einfühlung*.

107

tably, you are dealing with quantities and values that are difficult to measure. Of course, the matter is a long way from being resolved.

Afternoon, Ponte Molle.[102] The bridge is an attractive structure with a friendly, charming view. I spend a lot of time with Maria Weigert. Surprisingly, her idiosyncrasies make her only slightly unpleasant to be with. Moreover, she really seems to understand something about art—or should we say that she really enjoys it? She is a little academic in her way of thinking, and that is boring in the long run.

Monday the 26th, Sant'Ignazio.[103] Similar to Gesù and S.S. Apostoli. Museo Kircheriano.[104] At this point one can't look at things that are outside of one's immediate scope of interest. Here, one always becomes more specialized. At the moment all of my thoughts are focused on early Christian art. This stretches from the catacombs to the mosaics, which I carefully study. Then S. Maria in Via Lata with interesting crypts.[105] Saints Cosma e Damiano with magnificent mosaics and a large lower church.[106] In the afternoon, bought photographs. Finally after three weeks, letters from home with 50 marks from Papa's Geneva trip enclosed. This is very nice, because I don't like to talk about money. It has been a sore spot with me since our trip to Africa.

Tuesday the 27th,[107] Museo Barracco.[108] A truly magnificent collection with only two galleries but exclusively outstanding works. One really can't name one particular work but can study any one of them with pleasure for a long time. Then St. Peter's. Afternoon, St. Pudenziana.[109] Very fine mosaics.

[102.] [This is also known as Pons Mulvius or Ponte Milvio.] [WF]

[103.] [Sant' Ignazio di Loyola a Campo Marzio , "St. Ignatius of Loyola at Campus Martius"] [WF], is a baroque church designed by architect Orazio Grassi and built 1626–50 in honor and in recognition of the sainthood of Ignatius Loyola.

[104.] A collection of Christian archaeology established at the Jesuits' Roman College by Athanasius Kircher S.J. It contained, among other important artifacts, the so-called Spott Crucifix, a graffito that had been discovered on the plaster of a beam in the Pdagogioum on the Palatine, showing a man with a donkey's head, clad in a perizoma (or short loincloth) and fastened to a crux immissa (regular Latin cross). Beginning in 1876 the Kircher collection was associated with the Museum for Folklore and Prehistory; today it is divided among other museums.

[105.] Santa Maria in Via Lata, "Our Lady at Via Lata," where according to tradition St. Paul spent two years living in the crypt while under house arrest awaiting trial. [WF]

[106.] [Santi Cosma e Damiano, dedicated to Saints Cosmas and Damian, physicians and martyrs] [WF], was built in the 6th century; according to Baedeker, the mosaics there are the most beautiful in all of Rome.

[107.] Cf. below, 1/76:176f., to his parents, and 1/72:123, to Hans von Dohnanyi, from the end of May 1924.

[108.] The Barracco Museum that Bonhoeffer visited was demolished in 1938 and rebuilt in its present location; it housed a collection of Egyptian, Greek, and Etruscan art.

[109.] St. Pudentiana, according to legend, named for a probably fictional martyr, is the oldest church in Rome; it houses mosaics from the 5th century. [It is the National Church of the Philippines.] [WF]

Especially pretty from the exterior, built in a very old Roman house. Then Sant'Agnese fuori.[110] In spite of a lot of restoration it gives the impression of being stylistically pure. The catacombs are very interesting. Among other things, a painting of the Madonna without a halo but with a ☧ above her head. Santa Costanza.[111] The round structure is not as architecturally interesting as Santo Stefano Rotondo. But the mosaics are characteristic of the ancient technique in Christian art. Pretty ornaments, but the end of this art form (4th century) is already in evidence.

108

Wednesday the 28th, Santa Paschala,[112] interesting only architecturally. Pillars with arches interspersed between the columns. Mosaics (based on Revelation). Nothing special. Lateran Museum. Only the Christian part, with very interesting pieces. If only I had time to do a lot of work on early Christian art, for history-of-religions knowledge and especially the understanding of intellectual history. It is a striking fact that it seems as if a *completely* new intellectual history started with Christianity from the very beginning without being able to take anything at all from the Greco-Roman culture. What was taken over in art (sarcophagi—catacombs) did not endure. Scala Santa[113] with many believers. Thermal baths of Caracalla.[114] Afternoon, took my leave from San Paolo with various and sundry thoughts. I was unable, as recently when viewing ancient buildings, to enjoy the thermal baths from the perspective of art history. But I enjoyed them from a more sentimental perspective[115] without denying the artistic impression they made on me. Just received a letter from Sabine informing me that money is on the way. In addition, visited Prof. Mingazzini[116] in the evening.

Ascension Day: in the morning to St. Peter's for Mass, at a stone altar without much celebration. Afterwards, the Jubilee Year Bull was read. The dates were set for opening the Porto Santa by the cardinal's secretary of state, in

109

[110.] Sant' Agnese fuori le mura, "St. Agnes Outside the Walls," was founded at a nearby site by Constantia, daughter of Constantine; its mosaics are from the 7th century, when the current building was constructed under Pope Honorius I, and then restored by Pope Hadrian I.

[111.] Saint Constance is the mausoleum for the daughter of Constantine; it has mosaics from the 4th century.

[112.] Bonhoeffer no doubts means Santa Prassede, St. Praxedes, the sister church of Santa Pudenziana, which was built by Pope Hadrian I and then altered by Pope St. Paschal I c. 822 C.E.

[113.] These are the "Holy Stairs" upon which it is said that Christ, crowned with thorns, was led to the praetorium of Pilate in Jerusalem; they are to be climbed only on one's knees. [They consist of twenty-eight marble steps near the Lateran which are said to have been brought to Rome in the early 4th century C.E. by St. Helena, the mother of Emperor Constantine.][WF]

[114.] These were opened by Emperor Caracalla in 216 C.E.

[115.] Cf. Friedrich Schiller, "Concerning Naive and Sentimental Poetry," in his *Complete Works*. Of course, by sentimental literature Schiller did not mean art appreciated from immediate feeling but rather through reflective perception.

[116.] Giovanni Mingazzini.

front of the central door of St. Peters. Afternoon, Santa Maria in Traste-vere[117] with a particularly beautiful Bellini and Perugino. Also nice mosaics from the 12th century and less attractive ones from the 14th. All in all, the structure impresses one as old and not badly renovated.

Baptism in a small sect[118] with good choral music (—St. Cecelia[119] not pretty—). Maybe Protestantism should not have tried to become an estab-lished church; perhaps it should have remained a large sect, which always have an easier time, and so might have avoided the present calamity. A terri-torial church believes that it has the ability to extend, to give everyone some-thing. That Protestantism was able to do this when it began was probably largely due to a political climate no longer present today. The more the polit-ical situation changed, the more Protestantism's ability to captivate the mass-es has dwindled. Now a lot of things are cloaked under the name Protestantism that one should openly and honestly call materialism. The only thing about Protestantism that is still considered valuable and is still taken into account is the possibility of thinking freely. Even this was intend-ed by the Reformers in a completely different sense. Now when the official ties of state and church have been severed, the church is confronted with the truth. For too long it was an asylum for the homeless and a shelter for ill-bred enlightenment. If Protestantism had never become an established church,[120] the situation would be completely different. It would still have a not inconsequential number of enthusiastic adherents. In view of its size, it would hardly be designated as a sect but would represent an unusual phe-nomenon of religious life and serious thoughtful piety. It would therefore be the ideal form of religion, which is sought after in so many ways today. It is not the content of the gospel of the Reformation that repels people so much as the form of the gospel, which one still tries to tie to the state. If it had remained a sect it would have become the church the Reformers intended. Now it can no longer be called that. Perhaps herein lies a way to provide relief for the great difficulty the church finds herself in. The church must begin to limit itself and to make choices in every respect, especially in the matter of its religious educators and materials. In any case she must com-pletely separate herself from the state and maybe even give up the right to provide religious instruction. It wouldn't be long before the people return,

110

[117.] This church was founded in the 3rd century and rebuilt in the 12th century. It is one of the oldest churches in Rome [possibly the first church there where mass was cele-brated openly.] [WF]

[118.] Other details of this event are not given; presumably Bonhoeffer uses the con-cept "sect" in the manner of Troeltsch's *The Social Teaching of the Christian Churches*, rather than in the modern usage of "free church."

[119.] St. Cecilia's, dedicated to the 2nd-century Roman martyr and patron saint of musicians, has often been totally rebuilt. It was founded in Trastevere during the 5th cen-tury, but its mosaics are from the 9th century.

[120.] But cf. also below, 2/9:313f.

because they must have something. They would have rediscovered their need for piety. Could this be a solution? Or not? Have absolutely all alternatives been exhausted? Will everyone soon return to the bosom of the "only fount of salvation" under the guise of brotherhood? I would really like to know.—

The day after tomorrow I will be in an audience with the pope. Tomorrow I am going to Tivoli where I wasn't able to go recently because of bad weather. Only 4 more whole days left here. I can't imagine what it will be like when I have to leave St. Peter's for the last time and see it from the Pincio for the very last time. My Soldo will demonstrate its power in the Fontana Trevi;[121] I believe it will be successful.

Friday. Tivoli, Villa d'Este, Cascata, Villa Adriana.[122]

Saturday, audience with the pope. Great expectations dashed. It was fairly impersonal and coolly celebrative. The pope[123] made a fairly indifferent impression on me. He lacked everything that is indicative of a pope. All grandeur and anything extraordinary was missing. Sad that it had that effect!—Afternoon: Pincio.

Sunday, St. Peter. Celebration of the Constitution.[124] Pontificale[125] at the papal altar. Sistine Chapel. Afternoon St. Peter's again: the great *Te deum.*   111
I had always hoped once again to experience something beautiful in St. Peter's. But I had not even dreamed it would be like this. The choir sang angelically, supernaturally beautifully. The whole congregation sang the antiphon. It made an enormous impression. Once again, at the end of my stay, I saw what Catholicism is, and once again I became truly fond of it.

Monday, the last day in Rome.

Morning, Galleria Corsini[126] and the grottoes of St. Peter's.—Afternoon, walk through the whole city. Then by way of the Pantheon to the Fontana Trevi to pay the Obolus.[127] After that a glass of sweet wine [vino dolce], then to Maria Weigert's. Paid my bills and at the end went to the Pincio. Then home to bed. I must say that my actual parting from Rome was easier

---

[121.] A Soldo is a Vatican (Papal States) copper coin; according to legend, those who throw a coin in the Trevi Fountain will be assured their eventual return to Rome. [WF]

[122.] Tivoli is a city forty km east of Rome. [Nearby, the Villa d'Este is known for its gardens, fountains, and cascades (Cascata)][WF]; and the Villa Adriana is the ruins of the property of Emperor Hadrian, built in the early 2nd century C.E. Cf. also below, 1/77, letter to his parents, May 30, 1924.

[123.] Pius XI, pope from 1922 to 1939.

[124.] This is a national Italian holiday in honor of the Constitution, celebrated on the first Sunday in June.

[125.] The Pontificale Romanum is a liturgical book that contains the rites for various Episcopal functions carried out by a bishop.[WF]

[126.] The Palazzo Corsini, built in the 15th century, houses the Galleria Nazionale d'Arte Antica, National Gallery of Ancient Art.

[127.] Bonhoeffer refers here to throwing his symbolic coin into the Trevi Fountain—an Obolus was an ancient Roman coin, equal to a penny.[WF]

than the anticipation of it was. I was able to do most things without sentimentality. But when I saw St. Peter's for the last time my heart began to ache,
and I quickly got on the streetcar and departed.

Tuesday: Return journey

First to *Siena*. I got to know a nice German banking civil servant on the
train. I arrived around 1:30 at midday. I am living quite luxuriously at the
"Scala."[128] Once in a while, when it happens to be affordable, you can treat
yourself to something like this.

Wednesday:[129] I have probably never known a more charming city than
Siena, as far as the landscape and the inhabitants are concerned. The same
delicate and lively charm that is barely expressed in the paintings of a
Buoninsegna or a Lippi has, on the whole, remained. The city lies in the
most sumptuous surroundings, in hilly country. If you walk on the street or
look out of a window you think you have been transported back several centuries. The city's most characteristic buildings, the tower of the Palazzo
Publico[130] and the cathedral on a hill, can both be seen when you are far
from the city. It is an unusual pleasure to be able to enjoy Gothic architecture, even when it is heavily mixed with Renaissance style.[131] We're going

112   north!—The Campo[132] is a very generously laid-out square. Because it is set
lower, the Palazzo Publico seems very impressive.

The museum is a bit tiring, perhaps because it offers too many duplica-
tions. Nevertheless, the characteristic style of Siena is clear, represented most
clearly by Buoninsegna and Guido da Siena.

The works of Sodoma are outstanding.[133] Good examples of his work are
hanging in Rome, in Santa Maria della Pace, and especially in the Oratorio
Bernardino. Perhaps this museum gives greatest pleasure to the person who
is interested in paintings. This afternoon I took a walk around the charming
environs of the city and was reminded quite often of Württemberg. Like the
people in Württemberg the people here also exhibit a marvelously natural
kindness. For the first time one feels free from the money-grabbing practices

---

[128.] The reference is to lodging associated with Santa Maria della Scala, the huge
medieval hospital complex in Siena.[WF]

[129.] Cf. below, 1/78:128, the postcard to Klaus Bonhoeffer of April 6, 1924.

[130.] Following the architectural design of Pisano, the Palazzo Publico, or Town Hall,
of Siena was built between 1297 and 1310; its Torre del Mangia, or Bell Tower, 102 meters
high, was constructed between 1338 and 1349 by two brothers, Muccio and Francesco di
Rinaldo.

[131.] The Siena Cathedral was originally built in the 12th century c.e. in the
Romanesque style, then transformed in the 13th century into the Italian Gothic style.[WF]

[132.] The Piazza del Campo, Siena's main square, was built on a slope in the form of
a shell and surrounded by secular Gothic buildings at the lower end of the Palazzo Publico, the Town Hall.

[133.] Sodoma was the professional name of Giovanni Bazzi, a painter of the Siena
school.

of the south. The people are so pleased to be greeted with friendliness that they will amiably do small favors for you.

I won't enumerate the particulars of what I have seen, but I found the Palazzo Sarasani, a Renaissance work, very interesting. Tomorrow morning at 8:30 to Florence![134]

58. To His Parents[1]

Dear Parents,

After the 44-hour, yet fabulous trip, we arrived in Rome at 2 o'clock. We had magnificent weather from Innsbruck on. During the stop in Bologna we took a two-hour evening stroll through the city with a Catholic priest.[2] It is spring here. There are green meadows and almond trees. Met Axel. Tomorrow, on Sunday, we'll go to the Colosseum and the Forum. I'll write more soon.

    113

My best to everyone.
Gratefully yours,
Klaus

We were in St. Peter's. It was fabulous.
Yours,
Dietrich

59. To His Parents[1]

April 16, 1924

Dear Parents,

We received your message yesterday. Thank you very much. Everything went very smoothly at customs. They didn't even look at our things. Here things truly get more beautiful every day. I'll have to write to you in detail again soon because there is a great deal to tell you, especially about the distinctive worship services at St. Peter's.[2] Maundy Thursday is tomorrow. It is here one of the most important Holy Days of the church. I intend to go to the Lateran on Friday. It is said that they sing beautifully there. We are on our way to the Far-

---

[134.] Cf. below, 1/79:128, a postcard to his parents, June 6, 1924.

[1.] *NL* A 7/1(21); undated handwritten picture postcard mailed from Rome, showing the Piazza di San Pietro. The date is probably April 5; previously published in *GS* 6:47.
[2.] Cf. above, 1/57:83.

[1.] *NL* A 7/1(22); handwritten picture postcard dated "16.4.24" mailed from Rome showing the Basilica di San Paolo fuori le Mura.
[2.] Cf. above, 1/57:83.

nesina[3] to see the Raphaels that are hanging on our walls at home. Monday we are off to Palermo. We already know where we can stay on our trip.

Best wishes to you from Klaus.
And from your grateful,
Dietrich

60. To Sabine Bonhoeffer[1]

Rome, April 16, 1924

Dear Sabine,

This is just a quick note to tell you that I was able to buy a beautiful guitar with an adjustable bass string for 27 marks. There are 2 available just in case Grete would also like one. If so it would be best to send me the money in stabilized marks.[2] You really are allowed to do this. Send it to Signora Jocca's address, Corso de Italia 29. It probably won't get here before I go to Palermo, and I don't know if I'll still live at this address when I get back. I'll look for other guitars when I get to Sicily. Can you lend me a little bit of money? There are such magnificent photographs and reproductions here. They are very inexpensive, but still too expensive for me to buy. If you could somehow manage it, I would appreciate it very much. Moreover, could you look around and see if you can find a photograph of me, so that I can use it for a museum identification card.

My best wishes to everyone and happy holiday wishes to you.
Yours,
Dietrich

61. To His Parents[1]

Holy Saturday, April 19

Dear Parents,

It is Holy Saturday evening. Klaus has gone for a walk with a classmate whom he met here. Every morning and afternoon since Wednesday I have been either in St. Peter's or in the Lateran, and I have followed and studied

114

[3.] Cf. above, 1/57:90.

[1.] *NL* appendix A 5(4); dated "16.4.1924." Bonhoeffer's handwriting transcribed by Sabine Leibholz.
[2.] Cf. 1/41:64, editorial note 2.

[1.] *NL* A 7/1(23); handwritten letter dated "Stillsonnabend den 19. IV." mailed from Rome on April 19, 1924; previously published in *GS* 6:47ff.

the Missal very carefully. Catholicism first becomes lucid and distinctive when one studies the Missal closely.[2] Some of the texts are biblical and the others can be dated at the latest to the ninth century. The generally dreadful recitation of these texts by the priest and the choir at home leads one to believe that the quality of the texts themselves is equally poor. This is completely wrong. For the most part the texts are wonderfully poetic and lucid. Every text flows from the main theme of the Mass: the sacrificial death and its continuous reenactment in the sacrificial Mass of communion. These concepts are historically very interesting. Now, however, they are being pushed so terribly into symbols by modern Catholic theology that they are almost incomprehensible.[3]

115

The ceremony is always performed with enormous festivity. It certainly gives the impression that the classical tradition has been retained. This afternoon I experienced a further development of this ceremonial aspect at an Armenian-Catholic celebration of the resurrection.[4]

Here they always transpose the events of the following day, in this case Easter, onto the afternoon of the day preceding it. So it is as if they can never surrender themselves to the moment in which the events take place. In this way even Palm Sunday carries with it the attributes of Good Friday. To a certain degree this is due to its ceremonial fixing, but in other ways this constant anticipation corresponds well to the somewhat excited, dramatic, impatient atmosphere of the ceremony.

So the Armenian worship service this afternoon was exclusively comprised of liturgy and symbol. The whole service gave one the impression of watching an oriental, very poetic performance of a fairy tale. The clerical robes worn by the priests were thoroughly Asiatic. The choir had a peculiar way of singing, and the melodies were unusual. The liturgy originated in the 2nd and 3rd centuries. Even though the people perform it with great seriousness and fanaticism, it seems gradually to have become stiff and devoid of new life. Catholicism, as practiced by the Roman church, also seems to be following this path, although they don't yet seem to have arrived at this point. In Catholicism, there are many religious establishments where a vital religious life still plays a part. The confessional is an example of this. The unification of Catholicism and Protestantism is probably impossible, although it would do both parties much good.[5] Catholicism will be able to exist for a long time without Protestantism. The people are still very devoted [to it]. The Protestant church often seems like a small sect when compared to the enormous range of the local festivals. I spend a lot of time with our priest (from

---

[2.] Cf. above, 1/57:91.
[3.] Cf. ibid., page 90–92.
[4.] Cf. ibid., page 92–93.
[5.] Cf. ibid., page 89, 91, 106–7.

116   Bologna) and let him explain many things to me. He will also register me at the monastery of Monte Cassino,[6] where he will go for a few days. The Benedictine monks are very friendly to guests and it will certainly be interesting.

So, the day after tomorrow we go to Palermo, a 26-hour trip. I'm looking forward to it very much. Holy Week, with its many worship services, at which one has to stand for about 4 hours, did make one a little tired. Tomorrow evening we will be at Signora Jocca's.—I learned from Sabine that everything is going well again in Berlin. The next time I'll tell you about something else.

My best regards and wishes for warm Easter weather for you.
Gratefully yours,
Dietrich

62. To His Parents[1]

Dear Parents,

After a beautiful sea voyage from Naples we landed here this morning.[2] The sea nonetheless exacted its tribute, but in a friendly way near the end of the voyage. At the moment we are sitting under a blue sky in a park filled with palm trees. We have a beautiful view of the Mediterranean and Monte Pellegrino. We have received your letter, dear Mama, and we thank you very much. Please don't worry. Everything is really going as smoothly and as wonderfully as could be imagined. The day after tomorrow we'll go to Girgenti, Syracuse, Taormina, and Naples. I have been invited to visit Monte Cassino by my Italian priest. Perhaps, perhaps, I'll still go there for 3 days. Astoundingly, it is not very hot here at all. You are not tempted to buy anything.

117   Best wishes from Klaus and myself.

Gratefully yours,
Dietrich

I am very pleased that the Rüdigers[3] will stay in Berlin.

[6.] The monastery at Monte Cassino, founded in 529 c.e. by Benedict of Nursia, is the mother house of Western monasticism. Bonhoeffer did not visit the monastery. Destroyed in February 1944 by bombs, its rebuilding continued until 1954.

[1.] *NL* A7/1 (24); undated picture postcard from Palermo showing the San Giovanni degli Eremiti, postmarked April 22, 1924; previously published in *GS* 6:49ff.

[2.] Cf. above, 1/57:94.

[3.] Bonhoeffer means the Schleichers.

63. To Sabine Bonhoeffer[1]

Girgenti, April 28, 1924

Dear Sabine,

We haven't even thanked you for your letter. So I am doing it today.

We landed here yesterday morning.[2] We immediately went to the temples that are situated by the sea. In the sunset they looked completely red, although the sky was a magnificent blue. Above a most sumptuous garden filled with fruit trees, colossal cacti are perched on cliffs hanging over the water. A sea, ranging in color from sky- to steel-blue, is always in the immediate background. How sad that we can stay in one place for only 2 days. One could live here a long time. The donkeys, laden with wine and hay, fit nicely into the landscape. People ride on them, and huge herds of goats can always be found alongside them. Best wishes! I'll write more soon. We are now going swimming in the Africanum, with a couple of pleasant travelers whom we have gotten to know on the way here.[3]

Best regards.
Yours,
Dietrich

64. From Klaus Bonhoeffer to His Parents[1]

118

Dear Parents,

We have experienced a lot since my last card from Palermo.[2] Dietrich has, as you know, already written about the magnificent days in Girgenti—at the Greek temples by the sea—and about Syracuse. We made a very sudden decision in Syracuse. A great many Italian troops, with whom we had become friendly on the train, were being transported directly to Tripoli. We sang and played the lute, which belonged to a young German artisan who traveled with us and conversed very well in bad Italian. In this way we got to know an officer who later recognized us on the streets in Syracuse. He told us that he could get us a visa to visit the colonies, and that the ship departed that same evening. Because everyone thought that it would be less expensive in Tripoli than in Sicily, we took the opportunity and traveled over in steerage. A colorful throng was present: military personnel, immigrants, Turks, and Arabs—the liveliest traveling company one could imagine. We were offered sweet-wine [Südwein], cigarettes, etc. The soldiers

---

[1.] *NL* A 5(5); dated "28.4.1924." Bonhoeffer's handwriting transcribed by Sabine Leibholz.

[2.] Cf. above, 1/57:94.

[3.] Ibid.

[1.] *NL* A 7/1(25); undated handwritten letter mailed from Tripoli, c. May 5, 1924.

[2.] Cf. above, 1/57:94–96.

provided us with meat and noodles until I had to throw everything up. Music was played the whole time. Guitars, horns, violins, and song. Although it was not as comfortable as 2nd class, it was certainly 10 times more interesting.

We had an eight-hour stopover in Malta but, because we were Germans, we were unable to go ashore without special permission from the English governor. The Italians were allowed to go ashore without further ado. It is the first time that I have come across hostility toward Germans. In Italy and especially in Sicily you are used to being treated especially well as a German. In Sicily you are practically acclaimed. It is the French who are hated. I was often reminded of Finland, except that the Sicilians are greater pacifists by nature.

Malta is situated magnificently. The city lies high up on a steep cliff. Below, colorful nib-shaped skiffs swarm about, from which one can buy cigarettes, oranges, clothes, parrots, etc. by means of ropes and baskets. Two colossal English warships were docked in the harbor.

The sea voyage didn't do us any harm at all. We are now in Tripoli. A gentleman from Stuttgart whom we got to know when we arrived procured lodgings for us at one of the best hotels for 1 mark.[3]—It is an Arab building, but it is managed in the European manner. Then he showed us the city. It is completely oriental [orientalisch] except for the harbor. Even now it seems like a dream to me when I go out into the street and see Arabs, Bedouins, and Negroes sitting on donkeys in great, picturesque white cloaks or with laden camels. The houses are low and chalk-white. The living quarters open onto the street. The artisans live in certain streets according to their professions. The 10,000 Jews live in a special quarter. They have little in common with our German Jews or the Polish Jews. The streets are narrow in the inner city, unpaved, and very dusty; yet they are not dirty like they are in Italy. It is also a lot quieter.

The Arabs maintain much more decorum on the street than Italians do. They often stride around with solemn gravity. Greetings are exchanged peacefully. Even when they sit together in the evening with a water pipe, you don't hear any shouting. You are allowed in the mosques barefoot, after you have washed your feet. We intend to visit one in the next couple of days. Today we were only in the outermost building, where the homeless tend to sleep—These fellows simply lie on the ground wrapped up in clothes like mummies, in order to protect themselves from the sun. Every three hours a call to prayer rings out from the minaret. A "crier" sings portions of the Koran to the 4 points of the compass. Apparently here in Tripoli, which has been an Italian colony only since 1912, the life of the people is much more primitive and untouched by Europe than in Algeria or Tunisia. The inhabitants are therefore very intimidated. They are afraid of Europeans and make way for them on the streets. Above all, the Negroes are submissive. They are considered the lowest class and are looked down upon by the Arabs. Because every crime against a white person is very severely punished, one supposedly has nothing to fear from anyone. This is true even if one goes out all alone at night to outlying areas. All the same, we naturally avoid doing something like this. Today at sun-

119

[3.] Ibid.

set we stood before the city beside the sea. Forests of date palms grow along the coast there. I am constantly reminded of the stories from the Old Testament. Arabs, Jews, and blacks travel with their camels and donkeys to the cisterns. You are entirely in the Middle East [Morgenland], and nothing reminds you of Europe.

The contrast between Italy and Africa is tremendous. I find it indescribably interesting that I am able to experience Middle Eastern culture right after being in Italy, where I saw European culture in its purest form. I hardly know how to write to you about it, because almost everything is different from what it is at home.

Tomorrow we are going to drive to an oasis with the man from Stuttgart. It lies a few kilometers from the city. On Friday, the caravans from the interior of the country come to the market. We will have to leave at 5 o'clock in the morning because of the heat. At the moment, the heat is very intense because it is summer. When the wind from the sea lets up, it is even hotter. The heat, however, is less bothersome than the brightness. I now wear blue glasses to occasionally rest my eyes and to protect them from the dust. Dietrich is less sensitive.

120

We want to travel back with the boat on May 10. It goes directly to Sicily. We want to avoid going by way of Tunisia, although we are told that there are no objections to Germans going there.

You will be a bit astonished at our undertaking. Considering how things stand, however, we thought that you would agree with our decision. You really don't need to be worried because we are, of course, very careful in everything we do. We know Germans and Italians here. In an emergency one can always turn to the local German Consulate.

We often regret that you can't see all this as well. Karl-Friedrich should by all means also visit. He would surely benefit a great deal from it. I hope that I can purchase some of the local products cheaply and bring some home. Ostrich feathers must be cheap, because every better carriage horse wears one on his head and looks quite festive. In addition, wonderful things made out of precious metals are sold here by weight. I must close, because we are leaving early tomorrow.

To all my best wishes.
Gratefully yours,
Klaus

65. To His Parents[1]

Dear Parents,

The mail boat will not leave until today, so I want to tell you something about the last few days. Early yesterday morning we went to a large market at an oasis near Tripoli. Caravans and other natives from the interior assemble

---

[1.] *NL* A 7/1(25); handwritten at the end of the previous letter on the same sheet of paper.

121   there to sell and trade their wares. It was a colorful throng of peculiar figures. Yet, in comparison to our markets, and in even greater comparison to the Italian markets, trading proceeded with incredible calm and precision. As is apparently characteristic of the Arab traders, they also concealed their transactions from strangers. One hardly ever sees an Arab begging. The Jews are different. They are well respected here and are seen as smart, enterprising traders. Yet they consort with foreigners and are therefore considered to belong to a lower class. Some of the Negroes here are Abyssinian—the soldiers often have very intelligent faces and good physiques. And some who immigrated from the Sudan are incredibly ugly and are treated like cattle. What enrages one the most here is that a people like the Arabs, who have such a well-developed sense of tradition and culture, are to be transformed into slaves. When one sees that the Arabs are treated with great brutality and vulgarity by the Italian soldiers, one can understand their bitterness and callous fear.

The pictures of the market and of our walks to the sea were fabulously beautiful. Outside the city one sees bedouin tents along with their inhabitants, to whose face and form the long white robes lend a brilliant appearance, as is also the case with the Arabs. Because the next mail boat leaves in 8 days at the earliest, we also want to send you a telegram on Friday. Because we don't want our message to be garbled we are sending it in both Italian and German.

My best wishes to all.
Gratefully yours,
Dietrich

Klaus has asked the public prosecutor to excuse his lateness for a few days due to sickness.

122   **66. To His Parents**[1]

Tripoli, Friday, April 9, 1924

Dear Parents,

Well, tomorrow the boat travels back to Syracuse, then to Rome again where we arrive on the 13th. We hope to receive some mail from you in Naples.

Day before yesterday we drove into the interior of the country for 2 days with our acquaintance from Stuttgart. By chance a troop of Italian soldiers

---

[1.] *NL* A 7/1(26); handwritten. Although dated "Freitag den 9.4.24," the correct date is May 9, 1924; previously published in *GS* 6:50ff.

drove with us. They even took us with them in a car a good bit of the way, about 2½ hours, and provided us with lodging. We found ourselves at the end of the earth. The elevation was 600–700 meters.[2] As far as the scenery goes, the mountain range gives the impression of being very peculiar, but extraordinarily beautiful. Because a large troop of Italians chanced to arrive on the same day as we did—I don't know why—great festival performances by the native blacks, Arabs, and bedouins had been planned. Some of the performances involved fabulously clever tricks. The Bedouins' races with their amazing horses were very grand. At furious speeds they readied their rifles, shot, and then, as if it were a game, hurled their rifles into the air and caught them. We took several pictures of this, as well as some of a very amusing Negro dance. As the sun was setting we took a short walk. Several Arabs whom we met on our walk spoke to us. When they discovered that we were Germans they were incredibly friendly. They showed us a lot of things. Moreover, they said that we were the first Germans who had been there, and that was why they were so happy. It gets cold after sunset, especially compared to the temperature during the day, which when the Gibli—the south wind—so hated by the natives, is blowing, has been observed to reach 58° [136° F]. In spite of the terrible heat one doesn't feel ill. The air is very dry, never humid, always windy.

The houses of the natives are noteworthy. They use deep caves as dwellings. A passageway leads about 10 meters deep into the ground until it reaches a big round room about 25 meters in circumference. From this room many passageways in all directions lead to dark individual rooms. Three to four families live in such a cave and, in the Middle Eastern manner, these families are very large and have an endless number of children, women, and servants.

Only a few isolated and amazingly beautiful olive trees grow on the mountains here. Water is brought in from a distant oasis. The southern night sky is truly magnificent. For a short time after sunset it is deep blue, and the way the sharp contours of the mountains are brought into relief against it is beautiful. As soon as the stars appear, the color changes to a wonderful black. The stars flicker and shiver with a completely radiant light. The intense interest in the starry sky is truly fundamental to the Mediterranean. One needs to have been here to truly understand the natives' fear of demons. Life on the street only begins shortly before sunset. The women walk to do the milking, carrying large bowls on their heads. The men and boys ride to the waterholes on donkeys. Caravans set out at this time. From the minarets believers are called to worship. In short, no one is at home anymore. The only exception is the aristocratic Arab woman. She doesn't allow herself to be seen, even at this most beautiful hour of the day. Streets that had glowed in the sun just 2

123

[2.] Cf. above, 1/57:97, editorial note 67.

hours before come alive and become boisterous. The natives protect themselves in their caves against the intense heat and cold, which can reach 0 [32°
F]. After a whole day in the Middle East, you are reminded in an astonishing
way of Old Testament scenes and atmosphere. In general, it seems to me that
there is an immense similarity between Islam and the lifestyle and piety
recorded in the Old Testament. In Islam, everyday life and religion are not
separated at all. Even in the Catholic church they are separated, for the most
part. At home one just goes to church. When one returns a completely different life begins. It is thoroughly different for the Muslims. To a great
degree, this is due to their strong and overt pride in their race. This same
trait is exhibited by the Jews and the Arabs. The Arab stands apart from every
person of a different race as a person stands apart from an animal.
Mohammed is the prophet of the Arabian tribes. This is why the tendency to
propagandize is now totally absent, as in the past when they didn't attempt to
evangelize Christians but simply did away with them as non-Arabs, i.e., unbe-
lievers. In such relationships, the church, of course, plays only one role
among many, whether religious or national. So war is also a service to
Mohammed and Allah.

124

In addition to the daily hours of prayer, "Phantasie"[3] provided for constant excitement from a purely religious point of view. The children and all
the men go to the market, to the tearooms, or stand around on the street.
There they sing in monotone from the Koran accompanied by tam-
bourines—similar to the practice in the Catholic church. Everyone listens
devoutly and gives generously to the collection that follows.

I imagine that it was very similar in ancient Israel where the situation was
surely comparable. Both Islamic and Israelite piety must, of course, be
expressly law-oriented. This is the case because the national and cultic
moments are so heavily mingled that they coalesce, so to speak. It is the only
way that their sharp separation from other races and religions can be
achieved. A religion that would be a world religion, like Christianity or Buddhism, can't be a religion of law at all. In the eyes of an Arab Muslim, a Negro
Muslim is a Negro as before; conversion, strictly speaking, is not possible.

It would really be very interesting to study Islam on its own soil, but it really is very difficult to gain access in some way to the cultic aspects. So today we
were in the Great Mosque for the first time. We were allowed in today only
with the permission of the Kadi.[4]

[3.] "Fantasy" in the Middle East designates artistic performances, festive processions,
and dance accompanied by music; it also describes performances by men on horseback, as
previously described.

[4.] [The Kadi was the local Muslim judge, to whom someone evidently had appealed
for a ruling about whether these foreign tourists would be allowed into this Muslim holy
place.] [WF]

Tomorrow we will to try to get a visa to go ashore at Malta. The ship will dock there for 8 hours. By the way, you are able to get along quite well if you speak Italian, and we usually manage well enough at present. At any rate, for 125 the most part, the natives speak Italian worse than we do, and so we don't have to be embarrassed. One can talk about almost anything to the Italians. If you make a mistake, they correct it very politely; and they flatter you quite dreadfully. They tell you that you speak Italian so very well, and even that you speak better Italian than they do, because you do not speak a dialect as they do. It really is peculiar to observe the relationship of the Italians to the Arabs. The Italian's very nature is anything but imperious, but this same Italian now attempts, often stupidly, tactlessly, and brutally, to inspire respect from the power-starved and stubborn Arab. I think this seems ridiculous to the Arabs as well.

We spent a lot of time with 2 soldiers from Bolzano.[5] They have to do Italian military service and are naturally happy to be able to speak a little German. They both have graduated from Gymnasium and have been here for 2 years. They will probably be discharged soon. Because we got to know them we were able to see many things that we otherwise wouldn't. This evening they invited us to a farewell feast because, as you know, we are leaving tomorrow.

I am very much looking forward to Rome. I know I will be able to understand the lectures, because I noticed that I was able to understand many of the sermons I heard. I'm sure it will be enormously interesting. As soon as I get there I'll visit Pastor Schubert. I wasn't able to see him the last time I was in Rome. I'll ask him to advise me about visits with the Catholic religious.[6]

We have to go. Please give everyone my love, also the Hörnchens.[7] We hope to learn in Naples when the Rüdigers will have their child baptized.[8]

For the last time from Africa, my best wishes to you.

Gratefully yours,
Dietrich

[5.] Bolzano or Bozen is the capital of the South Tirol in northern Italy, near the Austrian border; it is a dual-language region and all the towns have both an Italian and a German name.[WF]

[6.] In Roman Catholicism, 'religious' [Geistliche] is used as a noun to indicate a member of a monastic order, especially a nun or monk; it is not clear whether Bonhoeffer means it in this way here, or more generally to include all sorts of ecclesiastical persons, ordained or not.[WF]

[7.] Richard and Maria Czeppan.

[8.] Baptism of Hans Walter Schleicher, born February 2, 1924. See below, letter 68.

126   **67. To His Parents**[1]

bonhoeffer grunevvald   Berlin
vvangenheimstrasse 14 berlino   *5/11/24 6.30 v*
                                                                  Grunewald
Telegram from: ="="= *berlin fr. tripoli 21 11/10 10 18/35,-*
everything is fine, we are very well – best wishes = "

          68. To His Parents[1]

Dear Parents,
    We landed here yesterday and immediately got our mail. When we went to
our hotel they suddenly claimed that there were no rooms available. So we
had to move into another hotel. Today I finally found lodgings at the home
of a German professor's widow, who is very friendly and attentive: Mrs. Professor Bigi, Via Quintino Sella, angelo Via Flavia. Klaus will surely tell you
everything else. We didn't find out until yesterday that the child's baptism
had taken place on the 16th. Nevertheless we drank "est est est"[2] to the
health of the little one. Hearty greetings to you and to everyone from your
grateful

Dietrich

127   **69. To Sabine Bonhoeffer**[1]

                                                        Rome, May 17, 1924

Dear Sabine,
    Thank you very much for your two letters. I found them waiting for me
when I arrived in Rome. Today I have been widowed. Klaus has gone to

---

    [1.] *NL* A 7/1(27). Dated "11.5.24." A telegram form was used and teletype strips were
pasted onto it. The letters on the teletype strips are in italicized type; previously published
in *GS* 6:54.

    [1.] *NL* A 7,1(28); undated handwritten picture postcard mailed from Rome and show-
ing Il Colosseo, postmarked Rome, May 17, 1924; previously published in *GS* 6:54.
    [2.] According to Italian legend, in the year 1110, Bishop Johann Defuk was on his way
from Ausburg to Rome for the coronation of Henry V as Holy Roman Emperor. He sent his
cupbearer, Martin, ahead with orders to write in chalk on the door of any inn where the
wine was good, the word 'Est', 'It Is'. In Montefiascone, just north of Rome, the wine was so
good that Martin, who was beside himself with enthusiasm, wrote 'Est Est Est!' on the door
of the inn. It is said that the Bishop returned to live in Montefiascone, and eventually was
buried there; so a barrel of wine is poured over his tombstone every year. [WF]

    [1.] *NL* appendix A 5(7); dated "17.Mai 1924." Bonhoeffer's handwriting transcribed by
Sabine Leibholz.

Berlin. One more day and he will be in Tübingen. I just ate a supper of milk, an egg, and whipped cream. It cost 50 pfennigs, but this is a very sumptuous meal. The menu usually consists of pasta asciutta, i.e., macaroni with cheese and tomato. Signora Jocca will go with me tomorrow to buy the guitar. Thank you very much for the money that you sent me. It is difficult with fine things, not only because they are too expensive, but also that I would have bought some things on the spot but didn't because I was worried that you might not like them. If I had had money in Africa I could have brought back fabulous things for 10 marks. But as it was, I couldn't even buy anything for myself while we were there. Instead, Klaus bought something for himself with my money. I wish I could have brought the same thing back for you. At any rate, the next time I see something pretty for 50 lira I'll simply buy it and send it to you. You can then send me 10 marks. It would be even better if you would send me the money beforehand, because I even have to keep a damnably close watch on my spending money. In the morning a glass of milk, at noon *pasta asciutta*, and in the evening bread and cheese. That is my daily ration. As you see, it's too bad but I can't splurge. Could Grete[2] lend me any money? When you write to her maybe you could ask her. Think about it. I don't really need the money but I could use at least 10 marks.

The light just went out in my room. Now I am sitting in a pub drinking coffee. I am not exactly living royally tonight. I am on a dark street and staying in an even darker inn but at least there are no bugs. That is what attracted me to it. Tomorrow an art student I got to know in Sicily is arriving,   128 and he'll share my room. I'm looking forward to it. Besides, he is a very well educated, intelligent person and about the same age as Uncle Bubi.[3] The day after tomorrow I'll move in with a local professor's family. They have taken me in and are very friendly. It is, thank God, very inexpensive. I'll stay there for the foreseeable future.

It is more delightful to return to Rome than it was to arrive here the first time. When Klaus left today and I realized that I would have to take the same painful path in less than 4 weeks, I felt very strange. It is as if I am now completely at home in Rome. It is the most curious city that I know of in this respect. You are here only for a short time and already you are under her spell and can hardly escape. On the other hand, she never stops entertaining you. You think you know everything about her, but on nearly every street corner something new and impressive is waiting. I believe it would be this way even if one stayed here for years. This morning I was in the Vatican gallery where, among others, a picture of C. H.[4] hangs. You really have to come to Rome.

[2.] Margarete von Dohnanyi.
[3.] Benedikt von Hase.
[4.] Unexplained. Perhaps the great-grandfather of Dietrich Bonhoeffer, Carl von Hase.

Yours with my best regards,
Dietrich

I'm adding a card to Aunt Elisabeth to your letter. I've dragged it around with me for a long time. Greet her warmly from Klaus and me.

70. To Julie Bonhoeffer[1]

Dear Grandmama,

Before you move to Berlin I want to send you much love from Rome. I gathered from the letters I received from home that Mama and Christel are with you now. But by the time I get any news it is at least 14 days old.—The time I have spent here has been unbelievably beautiful. It is flying by. In 3 weeks I'll practically be in Berlin again. Klaus will surely have told you everything about Africa. So long! I wish you good fortune and a great deal of courage for you trip.

Best regards.
Gratefully yours,
Dietrich

71. To His Parents[1]

Dear Parents,

It is very nice and neat in my new living quarters, Via Quintino Sella 8. I am able to follow the college classes that I am attending very well and am finding them very interesting. It is too bad that dogmatics is not taught; but that church history is seen from this completely different perspective is very stimulating.[2] I intend to go see the pope[3] on Saturday. I've been to see the Schuberts. I'll write more next time. It is already 11:30.

My best wishes to all.
Gratefully yours,
Dietrich

[1.] *NL* A 7,2(2); undated handwritten picture postcard mailed from Rome and showing the Campidoglio-Palazzo Senatorio, sent during the middle of May 1924.

[1.] *NL* A 7/1(29); undated handwritten picture postcard mailed from Rome showing the Piramide di Caio Cestio, postmarked Rome, May 21, 1924; previously published in *GS* 6:54f.

[2.] Roman Catholic theologians consider it impossible that Bonhoeffer studied at a Catholic school or institution, e.g., Gregorian University. Visiting students were prohibited at theological seminaries and at that time the only accepted language of instruction at any ecclesiastical institution in Rome was Latin. Bonhoeffer talked about how well he could follow the lectures in Italian. There remains only the possibility that he attended a state university.

[3.] The pope at that time was Pius XI (cf. above, 1/57:107).

72. To Hans von Dohnanyi[1[

Dear Hans,

Greetings from Rome and please give this note to Klaus. This letter should not be brought home, because our financial arrangements and debts are discussed in it and I don't know how much Klaus has told them about them. Would you please give it to him as soon as possible, because I am fairly broke at the moment. In 2½ weeks I have to leave this country; it's almost inconceivable. Soon instead of being able to take an evening walk on the Pincio or going to see St. Peter's I'll be able at best to take a walk on the Bismarckallee past the Grunewald church. It has been incredible here. When I realize that I was able to stay down here for almost a quarter of a year, I know I would like to return. Still, I have barely seen anything. When I think back, however, I really have seen an incredible amount, and one has to stop sometime. I don't think anyone could possibly get through with Rome, not even seeing it all, even if they were here a year. How are your exams going? There were times when we felt sorry for you.

My best to Grete.
Yours,
Dietrich

130

73. To Sabine Bonhoeffer[1[

Rome, May 22, 1924

Dear Sabine,

I've looked for a guitar for you every day. Now it looks like I've come across an incredibly fabulous one. It is a new neapolitan one[2] with a bass string that is in good condition. Tomorrow evening I'm going to try it out again. It will, however, probably cost a little more, but I'm sure you won't mind paying a bit more for such an instrument. I envy you unbelievably! Otherwise, as far as scarves go, there doesn't seem to be anything else. I went to a flea market where splendid things were for sale, but everything was very expensive. The inexpensive things are old Italian bowls, vases, and pitchers. Some of the pitchers have a beautiful form and are decorated with very good drawings. Would you possibly like something like that? If so, I can get you something nice for very little money. I haven't heard from home for 14 days.

[1.] *NL* A 7/2(9); undated handwritten letter; on the letter by an unknown hand are scribbled the words, "End of May 1924." Mailed from Rome; previously published in *GS* 6:55.

[1.] *NL* appendix A 5(8); dated "22.5.1924." Bonhoeffer's handwriting transcribed by Sabine Leibholz.

[2.] A flat-top, rounded-back style guitar. [WF]

131   Please write to me soon so that everything doesn't pile up at the end. Via
        Quintia Sella 8 ptr. Professor Bigi.

        Best wishes to Aunt Elisabeth and to you.
        Yours,
        Dietrich

74. From Theodor Pfizer[1]

Tübingen in May 1924

Dear Bonhoeffer,

    I haven't yet thanked you for your card from the Appian Way [Via Appia]. Until now
I didn't have the necessary leisure, but now it is quieter. I like being in Tübingen fairly
well. But I still would rather be in Marburg. At any rate, I hope to be able to come to
Berlin in the winter. I am really looking forward to it and to the thought of seeing you
again. Do you have any idea how much I have to thank you for? I don't believe you can
even imagine how much. I am aware that I often came to you when I was in a bad or a
irrational mood. I more or less cried my heart out to you. That is a weakness of mine.
Nevertheless, you accepted me in the very nicest way. This was true even though you
were closer to other people (Held, Dreier, Weynand, etc.) at the end. I can understand
that very well. At any rate, I now miss you a great deal. I am, after all, fairly alone in
Tübingen at the moment. The only older ones that are still here are candidates who are
taking examinations and they are more or less crumbling behind their books. There is
no one special among the new Foxes (in spite of a good average). The only ones who
remain are my co-Foxes. Every one of them, more or less, goes their own way. I don't
have a very close friend in the fraternity. Does the ideal of friendship that I hope for
exist at all?

    I don't think it is necessary to tell you anything more about me. You are probably
able to discern my mood and perhaps my state of mind from my handwriting.[2] At any
rate, once again I am lacking the tenacity, the well-being, and the χρυσόμετρον.[3] I am
132   fairly scatterbrained in every respect, jumpy and extremely ineffectual. All of this will
surely pass at some point. I am like this only periodically.

    I was deeply concerned about your sister's serious illness, and I hope that by now
she has been feeling better for a while.—Yesterday your grandmother left Tübingen for
good.[4] Now there is nothing left to tie you to Tübingen. I have followed your travels
and excursions with joy, and wholeheartedly wish you good luck in all your undertakings. You have always known how to achieve whatever you set out to do. You will sure-

---

[1.] *NL* C 16(1); handwritten by Theodor Pfizer and dated "im Mai 1924."

[2.] Bonhoeffer had an exceptional ability to interpret handwriting. See *DB-ER* 50; *LPP*
245–46 and 273.

[3.] "The Golden Rule."

[4.] Bonhoeffer's grandmother moved to Berlin (see above, pages 65 and 122).

ly continue to do so in the future. I wonder where these lines will find you. Hopefully they won't arrive too late. Don't forget me altogether.

Yours,
Theodor Pfizer

75. From Richard Czeppan[1]

Berlin-Grunewald, May 23, 1924

Dear Dietrich,

Thank you very much for your postcard from Libya and for sending me your greetings via Klaus. You have certainly been subject to very deep impressions in the last weeks! They have an even more permanent effect when you are still young. You will enjoy recalling your first Italian trip for the rest of your life. The scenes of the first trip will be especially vivid and will be clearly imprinted on your memory.

How long will you stay in Rome? Perhaps I'll be able to come. How expensive is full, or half, room and board for a simple furnished room for approximately 8 days? Could you just ask at the Hotel (Albergo[2]) Piemonte, on the Via Principe Amadeo, which is a side street of the Via Cavour, how much a simple room would be? Without breakfast, which I usually eat in a trattoria—in Rome! The owner of the Albergo Piemonte is named Canapero. I stayed at this hotel in the beginning of July, from the 6th on, in 1907; in July 1911; and at the end of July 1913. It was very well run, as one can easily tell from the hotel books. If Mr. Canapero still owns the hotel please give him my regards. He will, of course, hardly be able to remember me after such a long time.

133

Don't forget to go to Tivoli,[3] the Albano mountains with Lake Nemio and Monte Caro, the Villa Adriana, and the new excavations at Ostia. Are the new excavations at the Forum currently accessible? Fa l'Italia lotto da tì?[4]

When you are relaxing from the many mentally taxing impressions, it might be worthwhile to stroll along the right bank of the Tiber to the Ponte Molle. There is a trattoria with a beautiful shady garden in the Via delle Bottéghe Oscure[5]—a poetic name! One reaches it from the Corso Vittorio Emmanuele, through the Via di San Marco. Several natives recommended this trattoria to me. The food is simple, good, and inexpensive and is frequented for the most part by Italians. One can also eat well at the Piazza San Silvestre, across from the post office. It is frequented mostly by Germans.

How often have you been to the antiquities in the Vatican? How often have you been to the Stanzes? As a theologian, the right side of the Lateran will interest you.[6] I advise

[1.] *NL* C 9(3), handwritten letter dated "23.5.24."
[2.] [Italian: "Hotel"] [WF]
[3.] Cf. above, 1/57:107, editorial note 122.
[4.] "Is Italy becoming a part of you?"
[5.] "Street of the Dark Pub."
[6.] Probably refers to the side aisle with the grave markers of popes, cardinals, and other important persons; there is also a fresco attributed to Giotto.

you to keep a diary, even if it contains only catchwords. It is especially worthwhile if you write down your immediate impressions in short anecdotes. Later on in life you will read it with enjoyment. Notes of this kind, along with pictures that are brought back, aid the memory. How often were you on the Monte Pincio? It was my favorite spot, especially in the evenings. How often have you been to the Villa Medici? I would be very pleased to receive a detailed letter. In addition, could you perhaps use Italian stamps? I would enjoy a variety of newly printed ones in the smaller denominations. I am including a fascinating clipping that you will read with interest. Klaus said that you met these Wandervögel in Girgenti. We were very amused by your experiences in Tripoli. We especially liked the festive reception you received.

Best regards.
Yours,
Richard Czeppan

Best wishes to you from me as well. Hörnchen.[7]
The Garibaldi-Campanile stamps might be inexpensive.

134   **76. To His Parents**[1]

Rome, May 27, 1924

Dear Parents,

Thank you very much for your letter of May 23. I also received Klaus's letter. I thank you kindly, dear Papa, for sending me greetings from Geneva. I was very happy to hear from you. There are so many pleasant things here that are difficult to pass up. The photographs and reproductions are especially tempting.

I also believe, as do you and Uncle Hans, that it would be good to matriculate on June 15 and to attend lectures the last 6–7 weeks. As tempting as it is to remain here, if I were to remain I would ultimately have to spend more and more time in my room. I have reached the point where I need to begin organizing the incredible bulk of stimuli, to pursue the details more thoroughly, and to concentrate on very specialized areas.[2] This would probably not make much sense, because I am still lacking in several general areas. I would like to hear lectures in Berlin on subjects that relate to these specialized areas of interest. I believe that in the long run this would make more sense, although it is to have the object of study close at hand as, of course, one has here. I have noticed so many things in the last few weeks that I would

---

[7.] Handwritten by Maria Czeppan.

[1.] *NL* A 7/1(30); handwritten letter dated "den 27.Mai 1924."; previously published in *GS* 6:56f.

[2.] Cf. above, 1/57:106–7.

like to study more generally. I might not be able to do that here, so I am really looking forward to Berlin.

Every day I visit one of the old basilicas, the domes[3] of which are usually decorated with very interesting mosaics. I visited the catacombs again today, which were especially interesting. It would be highly stimulating to study here for a long time, if only because of the Christian art, which is a wonderful fount of knowledge for dogmatics and the history of religions. This is especially true for this earliest period until the 7th century, after which the   135
mosaic designs were replaced by the Byzantine art.

On my trip home I'd like to stay in Florence, which is on my route, for 2–3 days. Then from Horb[4] to Tübingen for 1–2 days, where I've had repeated invitations. I would then arrive in Berlin on the 14th and be matriculated on the 15th.

Tomorrow I'll go to Tivoli. The day after tomorrow is Ascension Day. There will be a beautiful worship service in St. Peter's. On Friday I finally hope to see the pope. I hope he is well again.

A fond greeting to my brothers and sisters and the Rüdigers.[5] I wish someone would tell me about the baptism. Best wishes also to the Hörnchens.[6] In 3 weeks I can tell you about everything in detail.

Best wishes.
Gratefully yours,
Dietrich

Please ask Klaus to send me the photos from Tivoli as soon as they are developed. I am very anxious to see them, as are many other people.

77. To His Parents[1]

Dear Parents,

I visited Tivoli the whole day today. After two rainy days the weather is magnificent again. At the moment I am waiting for the train to Rome. I am finally going to see the pope tomorrow at midday, around 11:30.[2] By the

---

[3.] Probably refers to the apse, the part of the church where the clergy are seated or the altar is placed.

[4.] [Horb am Neckar, which is 36 km west of Tübingen; two members of Bonhoeffer's Hedgehog fraternity lived there.] [WF]

[5.] Rüdiger and Ursula Schleicher.

[6.] Richard and Maria Czeppan, née Horn.

[1.] *NL* A 7/1(31); undated handwritten picture postcard showing Tivoli-Secatelle, postmarked Rome, May 31, 1924. Cf. above, 1/57:107.

[2.] Cf. above, 1/57:107.

way, I was at the Mingazzinis. I believe I forgot to tell you about it. He wants to write to you himself, dear Papa. I'll write more after the papal audience.

Best regards.
Gratefully yours,
Dietrich

136   **78. To Klaus Bonhoeffer**[1]

Dear Klaus,

Thank you very much for your letter and the enclosures. You will have received my letter in the meantime. I got off the train here on my way to Florence. It is magically beautiful. There are purely preserved early Renaissance churches and palaces.[2] There is hardly a modern house in the whole city. Tomorrow Florence. Monday Milan, etc.

My best to everyone.
Yours,
Dietrich

79. To His Parents[1]

Dear Parents,

I have traveled a good bit of the way home; yet Italy, it seems, is beautiful up until the very last moment. It was magnificent in Siena;[2] but here for the first time the beauty of Italy is simply inexhaustible: the churches, the palaces, the galleries. One simply has to choose, and this is certainly very difficult.

My very best wishes.
Gratefully yours,
Dietrich

[1.] *NL* A 7/2(6); undated handwritten picture postcard showing the Siena-Panorama visto d' St. Domenico, postmarked Siena, June 4, 1924; previously published in *GS* 6:58.
[2.] Cf. above, 1/57:107.

[1.] *NL* A 7/1(32); handwritten picture postcard showing the vista of the Cathedral of Florence from San Lorenzo, postmarked Milan, June 6, 1924; previously published in *GS* 6:58.
[2.] Cf. above, 1/57:108.

D. University Years in Berlin.
June 1924–July 1927

80. To Sabine Bonhoeffer[1]

Berlin-Grunewald, June 1924

Dear Sabine,

Well, I haven't written to you for a fairly long time. The last time I did, I tarried in more beautiful regions; I believe it was Siena. Since then I have been in Florence and Milan and then took the fateful steps over the Italian border. I also stayed in Zurich for a couple of hours and then traveled on to Horb, where two members of the Hedgehog fraternity were waiting to take me on a short excursion into the Black Forest.

I then went home on June 13th to be matriculated and now have that all that behind me. At the moment I am in the middle of work again.[2] I had planned to go to Friedrichsbrunn in August, as you know; but now I'd rather stay here, because I absolutely have to get some work done. It really is too bad that my change in plans has affected your plans. Now you won't be able to take a break. You don't seem to want to go up there with Susi and her friend. I'm still not sure what I'm going to do about going hiking. Held, from Tübingen, made me promise that if I were to go hiking at all I would go with him. He's coming here next semester, and if we were to go hiking he would come to Berlin earlier. Perhaps we'll be able to find something short and pleasant.

Hans-Christoph will not visit us in July but will go to the North Sea instead. Karl-Friedrich traveled to Hamburg today to give a lecture.—Tomorrow we will have an evening of music here. We'll play the *Forellen Quintet*.[3] Two

---

[1.] *NL* appendix A 5(11); dated "Juni 24." Bonhoeffer's handwriting transcribed by Sabine Leibholz.

[2.] See below, Appendix 3, the list of the lectures Bonhoeffer attended.

[3.] Franz Schubert's *Trout Quintet* is often referred to in German as the Forellen Quintet, with referene to "Die Forelle," the art song on which the quintet was based.[WF]

members of the Hedgehog fraternity[4] will play the first violin and cello, Miss Rohloff[5] the viola, Klaus the second cello, and I the piano. We intend to practice regularly during the week.

138

Otherwise, I am very occupied with make up work and other things so that I don't have a chance to practice much. I intend to be a bit more conscientious during vacation. Today is the first time that the temperature is humane—measured by Italian standards, that is. The others, however, are complaining about it quite a bit. I have to go into the city again. Time and paper are at an end. Please give my regards to Aunt Elisabeth. Our parents and siblings send greetings.

Yours,
Dietrich

81. From Wilhelm Dreier[1]

Tübingen, July 24, 1924

Dear Dietrich,

Thank you for your last letter. I regret that I wasn't able to answer until now; I wasn't calm enough before today. First a few news items about the state of things here. Work in preparation for the Hedgehog commemorative celebration is piling up.—This doesn't mean I have to take on any new burdens. The amount of work that the commission is responsible for has decreased. Three mimes, a play, and a Hans-Sachs comedy will be presented. Burger, Kayser,[2] and I composed the mimes, the latter without enthusiasm. Kayser, as xx,[3] is working a lot. As a result he is nervous and not much fun to be with a lot of the time. It is the same with some of the others. Pfizer is in a state of high agitation because he has to decide by noon today if he wants to go with 2 other Tübingen students to the Baltic. This undertaking is organized by the University Group for the German Way.[4] The students will stay with Baltic families from August 10 to October 5. Pfizer will probably go.

Stadelmann[5] passed the first of his oral doctoral examinations. It seems he did well. The second part follows on Saturday. There is a lot of unofficial drinking in the fra-

---

[4.] The identity of these persons is not known.
[5.] Sabine Bonhoeffer's violin teacher.

[1.] *NL* C 11(2); handwritten letter dated "24.7.24" by Wilhelm Dreier, who had become very attached to Bonhoeffer in Tübingen. For the following see Pfizer, *Im Schatten der Zeit*, 76ff.
[2.] Ewald Burger and Wolfgang Kayser were Bonhoeffer's "co-Foxes."
[3.] The three elected representatives of a fraternity, "the ones given charge," place x, xx, and xxx behind their signatures.
[4.] The *Hochschulring Deutscher Art* was one of many private initiatives to help German families in Eastern Europe to preserve their culture after the changes brought about by the Versailles peace treaty.
[5.] Rudolf Stadelmann.

ternity. I have kept myself (Good God the nib! Hopefully, soon a fountain pen) pretty   139
much away from those who do. I am close only to Stadelmann and Maier.[6] (I am also
fairly close to Pfizer, Burger, and Held.) The fox Kordau[7] has handed in his resignation
from the fraternity. It will be approved. (Now I will have to continue like this.)[8] He
declared that he truly does not like the Hedgehog fraternity spirit. Inasmuch as he pursued religious concerns and wanted to pursue practical Christianity, he believed that he
couldn't do that in the fraternity. He had tried and had pretended, but now he wanted
to free himself from this painful compromise. He might join the DCSV[9] later. I was
asked by the fraternity to speak to him. He had said once that he trusted me. He made
quite a good impression on me. You know him, of course. The conversation unnerved
me quite a bit. Kordau had the upper hand in it. He had the courage to be true[10] to
himself, to be an "I" [Ich]. I didn't have that same courage in February. At some point I'll
write to you from Munich about the problems entailed by being an "I."

My parents are in Freudenstadt. A short time ago I was with them in Ulm. There is
a huge contrast between them and me. I don't believe there is a good solution. My work
in law is only average. I have usually received a 3 and a 2 on two of my papers. But is
this a profession that one makes fun of? The rest will become clear in Munich. I finished
Karamazovs.[11] I didn't like the second half of the third book very much. It was too
harsh[12] and too diffuse. One also knows exactly who will say what. At times, I found
the character of Ivan very exciting.[13] Ivan's struggle with himself, with "his bad I [Ich],"
was portrayed in an incredible way. It left me morbid and tense. I would like to write a
lot about the Karamazov, i.e., about Ivan, because his character encompasses everything. But I can't. Try if you can to imagine someone in a wild hubbub of preparations
for the festivities. How can you have any quiet time? At the moment, I am reading something light for relaxation: *David Copperfield.*[14]

Recently Tillich/Marburg, gave a lecture on church and culture.[15] The lecture was
very good and free of clutter. The main topics covered by the lecture were the follow-   140
ing: first, separation of the profane and the sacred. Basic concept: proceed from understanding, (a) meaning in actions (a) (b) belief in meaning (b) (c) world: objective content
of all meaning (1) objective (2) religions: holy. He developed this further. I'm not calm
enough to go into details. He then came to historical development (autonomy, het-

---

[6.] Hermann Maier.

[7.] Difficult to decipher in the original manuscript; The identity of this person is not
known.

[8.] He must now write in pencil.

[9.] *Deutsche Christliche Studentenvereinigung*, German Christian Student Association. See
Kupisch's *Studenten entdecken die Bibel.*

[10.] Difficult to decipher in the original manuscript.

[11.] Fyodor M. Dostoyevsky, *The Brothers Karamazov*, Dreier refers in what follows to Part
2, Book 5, chapters 4ff.

[12.] Difficult to decipher in the original manuscript.

[13.] Difficult to decipher in the original manuscript.

[14.] Charles Dickens, *David Copperfield.*

[15.] Cf. Paul Tillich, "Church and Culture," a lecture delivered to the Tübingen Youth
Group in July 1924.

eronomy, theonomy). At the end of the lecture he addressed the possibility of a revelation that is at the same time beyond the profane and beyond the sacred. It would be a breakthrough that would assist the religions in freeing themselves from themselves. I don't know if you understand this. One can't restate it in such a short amount of space. Even I don't quite understand all of it anymore.

I read with eagerness your reply about faith. I agree with you about most of it. I still am not sure yet if faith is *only* something that is nonexistent, purely negative. Above all, I can't find anything new to say.—At any rate, faith, as you say, is not a work.—On the other hand, it is dubious to assert that the self-revelation of God[16] is out of the question. (This assertion is based on your basic attitude, which I affirm for the most part.) Now, I think that it is completely impossible. I'm not able to cite evidence to counter your statement. But the feeling that it isn't sufficient [. . .].[17] Maybe I'll write more about it. As I have said, at the present I am not calm enough. I'll write later about Bremen. Please write again soon, also about philosophical things!!—And please forgive me if you have to wait for an answer.

Cordially yours,
Wilhelm

Held sends his regards. Kayser sends his regards.
Both [. . .].[18]
Pfizer and Held will get the letters.—The notes [. . .].[19] not found.

141   **82. To Paula Bonhoeffer**[1]

Grunewald, August 5, 1924

Dear Mama,

Thank you very much for your letter, which came yesterday. Early today Karl-Friedrich left. The elder Schleicher returned from England yesterday evening, and Karl-Friedrich was able to get a few extra tips from him. He'll arrive in London tomorrow morning around 7. Since it will be Sunday it probably won't be the most convenient time for an English pastor's family.

All in all, everything here is following its regular routine: Grandmama is well, the Schleichers are looking forward to and preparing for their trip, and Klaus has begun to prepare for his doctoral thesis and is always exhausted after working on it a short time. I don't know if he is looking forward to taking up his official position on the 15th. Sabine and Susi are on vacation, i.e., Sabine is even devoting herself to her violin again. Neither of them, howev-

---

[16.] Difficult to decipher in the original manuscript.
[17.] The line as a whole cannot be deciphered.
[18.] Illegible.
[19.] Illegible.

[1.] *NLA* 7/1 (33); handwritten letter dated "den 5. August 24"; previously published in *GS* 6:91f.

er, can be tempted to go swimming. I nonetheless go swimming every morning for a short time; it is a very pleasant form of bodily exercise. At the moment I am working on a very interesting paper: Max Weber's sociology of religion.[2] I also meet once a week with another theology student. We spend the time reciting church history to each another. After I finish Weber, I intend to read Troeltsch's work on the social teachings of Christian ethics[3] and to work through Husserl.[4] If I have time at the end of vacation, I want to study Schleiermacher thoroughly.[5] In addition, of course, I have to cram in some of the historical and philosophical subjects and take up Hebrew again. All things considered, it will be a very nice vacation in any case.

Every week we have an evening of music, which gives us all great pleasure. I'm sure you are enjoying being so nice and lazy in Kissingen. I hope you are happier about the weather than we are here. It is a bit like fall. It makes you already begin to think ominously of winter. I thought I might go hiking with my Hedgehog fraternity brother, Held. He is coming here for the winter semester and is arriving in the first days of October. I'd also like to go hiking so that I can slim down a bit and better conform to my sisters' perception of beauty. One really can become fairly fat from sitting a lot. Please give Papa my very best wishes, also the Goltzes from us all. My best regards.

142

Gratefully yours,
Dietrich

83. From Wilhelm Dreier[1]

Freudenstadt, August 8, 1924

Dear Dietrich,

[. . .]To address the problem, first I want to restate your solution, in order to guard against misunderstandings. You proceed from the perspective of transcendent cate-

---

[2.] Max Weber's chief published work in this area was his 3-volume, *Gesammelte Aufsätze zur Religionssoziologie*, published in the years following 1920.

[3.] Troeltsch, *The Social Teaching of the Christian Churches*.

[4.] Edmund Husserl's *Ideen zu einer reinen Phänomenologie and phänomenologischen Philosophie: Allgemeine Einführung in die reine Phänomenologie* (*Ideas: General Introduction to Pure Phenomenology*) was in Bonhoeffer's library. [NL 7 A 31]

[5.] In addition to Schleiermacher's *Reden über die Religion (On Religion)* (see above, 1/39:62, editorial note 2), Bonhoeffer owned *Der christliche Glaube (The Christian Faith)*, and *Monologen/Weihnachtsfeier (Soliloquies* and *Christmas Eve)*.

[1.] *NL* C 11(4); handwritten. This is the end of a sixteen-page letter dated "8.8.1924" in which Wilhelm Dreier recounts, in great detail, the anniversary celebration of the founding of the Hedgehog fraternity. He also tells Bonhoeffer about his plans to go against his father's wishes and to give up studying law. The exact background of the theological and epistemological discussion between the friends can no longer be determined.

gories (that is to say = divine). In addition you presuppose that the divine is *the very thing* that can't be defined. Wouldn't that involve a transformation of the divine? From this point of view, in contrast to categorical considerations, all psychological acts[2] appear absolute and therefore logically cohesive.[3] (Each one is a "being.") They are of absolute value. Each works itself out by crossing over into the categorical, according to its nature. (For example, emotion works itself out in the category of religion.) The reverse is not true—that objects have an effect on these[4] absolute values by way of the categories. (They would then induce something [*Auswirken*] and not transform something [*Einwirken*].)

143

Then you assume that belief is connected with its opposite, injustice, or grace with sin, etc. This appears to me not very important and especially not provable. Here logic is at an end.—Some questions about this (I must admit that at first I was completely disconcerted; but now, more clearheaded, I agree with you in a *certain* sense.)

1. Basically, the whole represents a limited view of the relationship to absolute value—to be more precise, to the sphere of the philosophy of religion, i.e., to the *logical sphere*. A view based on feeling would be just as legitimate and perhaps just as correct. This view would be a religious one. Why is the logical view superior to one based on feeling? Both logic and feeling are absolute values. (To be sure, we are not really talking about a logical view but some other view, because the logical view does not work itself out in the categorical sphere as logical(?).)

2. One should not ignore the following question: What or who is God? This question does not directly belong here but only insofar as God (as has already been explained) apparently is connected to this[6] absolute value. This is because of God's indefinable, transcendent categorical character. But all of this is a hypothesis. Couldn't the divine play a part in absolute value? How can this be conceived? This is, however, a speculative view.

3. How can the tripartite division of will/logic/feeling be demonstrated? Is it merely a hypothesis? I tend to see the will as the encompassing thing.

4. I can't challenge your whole solution. At first I was a bit unwilling to accept it, but

---

[2.] Difficult to decipher.

[3.] Difficult to decipher.

[4.] Difficult to decipher; probably replaces "our."

[5.] Illegible.

[6.] Difficult to decipher in the original manuscript; probably replaces "our."

now I am less so. I still don't know of a way to live according to this solution. To a certain extent, living according to it will be very lamentable (please forgive this; I don't know anything better at the moment). We can know so very little. This stimulates me very much, and I have a very strong desire to pursue this trajectory, although the ultimate is always an assumption, a belief. This is incidental.—First one has to be content   144
with the as-if.—But I have to think about it further.

5. Is God's existence absolutely necessary for our, *your* solution? It almost seems to be. If it were not, then the transcendental category would not be possible; cf. 2.

By the way, did you not already answer my questions 1 and 2 to a certain degree when you added that in a "generally valid religious sense" one has to accept "grace" as the most comprehensive of absolute values? Is this correct? At this point I really wanted to say something more about your remark about "freedom"—also in a critical vein. Yet for once you have not come to a final conclusion about it. Now I have to finish this letter. If I don't, it can't be mailed. The problem has fascinated me intensely. I was very happy to be able to work on something philosophical, if only for a short time. Write again *soon*, because of the other matter as well. Well, please forgive this shamelessly long, and perhaps—especially in the last part—silly letter. Hopefully you won't get too bored.

My parents and siblings send their regards.
Yours in friendship,
Wilhelm Dreier

84. To His Parents[1]

Grunewald, August 20, 1924

Dear Parents,

A letter to Sabine and the money for Christel just arrived. Up until now we've arranged it so that we play music as a quartet every week. Sabine hasn't wanted to join us yet, because she feels that she has fallen behind in her technique. She does intend to play a piece with us the next time. Beginning the week after next she really has to play with us regularly, because the members of the Hedgehog fraternity will be gone then—Christel was in a cheerful mood when she and Hans came home on Sunday evening. Hans went on to Hamburg the next morning. They brought us a big, wonderful honeycomb.—Klaus spends most mornings in his office. He brings his files home   145
with him. But he is still stressed out. He sleeps fairly long in the afternoon. As a result he doesn't go to bed until very late and has to leave the house early in the morning. On Monday he'll be at a trial by jury. The Schleichers will travel on Sunday. It seems that Rüdiger did not discover anything new in

---

[1.] *NL* A 7/1 (34); dated "den 20. August 24." Previously published in *GS* 6:92.

Stuttgart.—We often hear from Karl-Friedrich. It seems that he really likes the British Museum. Sabine has begun to practice the violin again in the evening. She also draws and reads. Susi is going to school again and corresponds almost daily with her friends in Switzerland. On her birthday, if the weather gets better, we'll take a trip on a steamship to Peacock Island [Pfaueninsel]. Otherwise we'll go see something nice. After all, none of her friends are here and she doesn't care much about music and things like that.—We'll celebrate Grandmama tomorrow. This evening is Hanni Delbrück's[2] wedding-eve party [Polterabend]. None of us will go.

I am still reading Max Weber. Regrettably, one can't sit in the garden at all now; it has become fairly cool since the last storm, and the sky alternates between clear and rainy. Because of this we are probably in for a mild autumn. The weather does not often tempt you to go swimming. Nevertheless, I intend to go again. After a few days of not going, I immediately notice a big difference. You easily get tired when you don't exercise at all.

I'm sorry to say that my Hedgehog fraternity brother[3] from Munich is still very sick. He has had to be tapped again and again. His temperature oscillates between a high fever and a low temperature of 35.6 [96° F]. He has been sick now for 4 months.

Best wishes from Grandmama and everyone.

Gratefully yours,
Dietrich
The maids were extremely delighted by the postcards you sent, dear Mama.

146   **85. From Theodor Pfizer**[1]

Gülzow in Pomerania, August 21, 1924

Dear Bonhoeffer,

My "official" thank-you—addressed to your grandmother—has no doubt already arrived in Berlin. I also want to thank you again for the 2 wonderful days, which were very meaningful to me. Time and again I enjoyed talking to learned and sensible people. Perhaps this is an instinctive need that compensates for a certain "lack" on my part. I

[2.] Johanna Bräuer, née Delbrück, called Hanni, married Dr. Ernst Bräuer. [In Germany it is customary to have a loud party on the eve of a wedding, *Polterabend.* The guests bring pieces of old crockery and tableware, which they throw against a wall or any other designated place in front of the bride and groom. The theory is that *Scherben bringen Glück,* i.e., potsherds will bring the newly wedded couple good luck.][PDM]

[3.] The identity of this person is not known.

[1.] *NL* C 16(3); handwritten letter dated "21. August 24" mailed from Gülzow near Greifenberg in Pomerania. [Pomerania, formerly a province of pre-war Prussia, after World War II became part of North Poland and North Germany.][WF]

experienced this in the most gratifying way during the hours I spent at your house. To be sure, it is once again entirely clear to my consciousness—without value judgments or making comparisons, note well—that all my boorish feelings have no meaning. I have to learn to think rationally. You are entirely right when you say that one should not divide people into 2 classes, i.e., the emotionally driven and the intellectually driven. I am also not a *purely* emotionally driven person at all. But it is useless and senseless to refuse to give account of certain things just because you "feel" them. I know definitely that sensitive[2] people have this advantage: they see and understand what others are blind to. However, I won't forget and overlook the danger that such a person is always faced with. On the one hand, they are overly sensitive; on the other, they are vague, disingenuous, and unclear about everything. I must learn more about this. I believe that I can do it. I can't believe that nature is so strong that it has given us prescribed lines. Associating with the type of person that you are can only be helpful to me. And I hope that in the coming winter there will be time for both of us to meet. In addition I will have to plow through my law books.

Did I leave my slippers at your house? Please save them for me so that I can pick them up in the winter. And now, off to my beloved dreamland.

Yours,
Theodor Pfizer[3]

86. To His Parents[1]

147

Flensburg, the 30th

Dear Parents,

Shortly before our departure we completely changed our plans. Instead of hiking in the heathland, we decided to hike to Schleswig-Holstein.[2] First we traveled to Lübeck. There I met an acquaintance from Italy on the street. He had previously hiked through Schleswig-Holstein and was able to give us more precise information. We walked via Timmendorf in the direction of Kiel, via Ploen, and through the remarkably beautiful area bordering the sea. Then we arrived in Kiel. From there we hiked into the Dithmarschen area.

[2.] The German text reads *sensible* [*sic*]; it should say *sensibel,* sensitive. [WF]

[3.] Theodor Pfizer was on a trip organized by the *Hochschulring Deutscher Art,* the University Group for the German Way, to visit German families who lived in the Baltic countries; he went to Dorpat and Narwa [in Estonia] and Riga [in Latvia], among others (see above, 1/81:130).

[1.] *NL* A 7/1(35); handwritten letter dated "den 30." postmarked September 30, 1924, from Flensburg, a city in Schleswig-Holstein. Previously published in *GS* 6:92f. Bonhoeffer traveled through Schleswig-Holstein with Robert Held. See above, 1/56:80, editorial note 2.

[2.] A state in northwest Germany, between the Elbe River and the Danish border. [WF]

We hiked there for quite some time. You can walk for quite a distance on a seemingly endless country road through completely flat, verdant, wet meadowland. One seldom sees either a meadow or a birch thicket. Many seagulls fly over from the sea. There is just nothing but an endless plain that dissolves into the horizon. The country has many large farmsteads. All in all the landscape looks like I imagine Holland to be. It is much more desolate, lonesome, and monotonous to wander over than the heath. There are no colors to enliven the landscape. Until now we have had almost entirely a magnificent blue sky. Everything is going well as far as money is concerned. With everything included, we only need approximately 1 mark or 1.2 marks a day. Youth hostels are almost everywhere, we cook with alcohol, and we get a lot of things from the farmers for free or for very little money. Because of this we can spend more money on travel. Tomorrow, we'll travel from Flensburg to the North Sea. We'll hike in the area at low tide on a small island where we have been invited to visit by a farmer. From there we'll set sail to Sylt.[3] It will certainly be astoundingly beautiful.

Flensburg is a marvelously beautiful ancient city situated on the Fjord.[4] We took a small detour to reach it. It is very charming, friendly, and completely different from Husum,[5] for example. The inhabitants are as obliging and helpful here as they were there. They have probably not yet been overrun by travelers [Wandervögeln].

148   I have to stop; this page is at an end. I am tired and our pea and sausage soup is ready. Please give my love to Grandmama. I thank Sabine warmly for the coat. I'll write her soon.

Best regards,
Gratefully yours,
Dietrich

87. To Richard Czeppan[1]

Dear Richard,

Yesterday we left Flensburg and headed for the North Sea. Tomorrow morning we will take a 3-hour hike along the sand dunes toward the little

---

[3.] Sylt is the largest of the North Frisian Islands in the North Sea off the coast of Schleswig-Holstein.[WF]

[4.] Flensburg is Germany's northernmost city, located on the Flensburg Fjord, an arm of the Baltic Sea, at the Danish border.[WF]

[5.] Husum is a North Sea port town across the Schleswig-Holstein peninsula west from Flensburg.[WF]

[1.] *NL* A 7/2(7); undated handwritten picture postcard of the Northgate in Flensburg; thought to have been mailed from Husum, postmarked October 4, 1924 (see *GS* 6:94).

island of Langeneß, where we'll stay 2 days; then we'll go to Sylt. The weather has been magnificent up until now. The Swiss region of Holstein was especially beautiful.

My regards to your wife and my best to you.
Yours,
Dietrich

88. To His Parents[1]

[. . .] sitting on the bridge. Then we began from the beginning, "Won't you take us with you?" This time the answer was, "No, we don't have any room." We asked again after 10 minutes had passed. They both disappeared into the boat. We waited again. It was our last chance to get to Sylt. Soon, both of them came back up and we called over for the last time. We told them that we might pay them. After a short while the answer came. "Come on over!" When he saw that we didn't have a boat he finally decided to row over. We assumed he had come over to strike a bargain with us. When he arrived, he simply said in a very friendly tone, "You don't need to pay anything. I only ask that you bring me something to smoke." We quickly bought some cigarettes. An hour later we climbed aboard the boat. We set sail under a wonderful sun with very little wind. Because of this, we naturally did not reach our destination on the same day. We dropped the anchor at night. On the next morning there was a stiff wind and we made wonderful progress. Suddenly, there was a gentle jolt. We were stuck in the sand. For an hour we tried in vain to get free. The tide was going out and we had to stay there. Luckily, we were only 2 kilometers away from Sylt so we were able to walk across the sandbars at low tide. We arrived at the farthest eastern point of Sylt. I wasn't able to find out when the others eventually were able to get there. That same day we walked farther toward the ocean. There was an incredibly, astonishingly beautiful sunset over the dunes. The ocean was in the background, and it looked like an enormous piece of metal. Yesterday and today we walked almost completely around the island. A strong wind, a stormy ocean, and a lot of rain accompanied us. These were three extremely glorious days.

Today, we are sailing on a steamship to Helgoland, and tomorrow we'll go on to Cuxhaven[2] (it is too bad the connections are so poor). On Monday

149

[1.] *NL* A 7/2(7); undated handwritten fragment of a letter written around October 10, 1924, and mailed from Sylt or Lesum, where Bonhoeffer and Held visited Wilhelm Dreier's parents; previously published in *GS* 6:94f.

[2.] Helgoland is another North Sea island south of Sylt; it is west of the port town of Cuxhaven, on the Schleswig-Holstein mainland.[WF]

the 13th I intend to be back in Berlin again. My money has lasted quite well. We were often able to get milk and things like that from the farmers for free. They often have so much that it just seems absurd to them if anyone offers to pay them for it. On the whole, people are enormously friendly here. We never had problems with staying with the farmers and were often served supper and breakfast as if it were a matter of course. The only thing that cost a lot of money was the railway trip. We got half-price tickets for the steamboat trip at a youth hostel. You usually have to stay at the hostel for 3 days to get the half-price tickets, but we couldn't because the hostel was full. So they let us buy the tickets at half price without our having to ask for the price reduction.

My regard to Grandmama as well as my siblings.
And my warmest regards to you.
Gratefully yours,
Dietrich

17:19 **88a. To Kurt Rohrer**[1]

Dear Mr. Rohrer,

Robert Held[2] gave me the task of finding you a room for the winter. Although no message had come from you to Held about your arrival, etc., which we were actually expecting, I hope that you have not found a room in some other way. I have looked for one for you today and intend to rent one of the possibilities tomorrow. I will send the address to you so you can have your suitcases brought there, if that is what you would like to do. The room will then be available from the 15th on so that you can come at any time. Robert will probably not come back before the 17th–18th. I'm writing you already today so that you will know what is going on in any case, even if I can rent the room only the day after tomorrow.[3] If you need anything else, I'll be glad to help you. (Grunewald, Wangenheimstr. 14.)

All my best.
Yours,
D. Bonhoeffer

[1.] *NL* Rohrer; this is an undated handwritten postcard stamped October 14, 1924, Berlin-Grunewald. "Addressed to Theological Student Mr. Rohrer, Stuttgart Kronenstrasse 48." Previously unpublished, this letter first appeared in DBW 17:19, on which this translation is based.

[2.] Robert Held was a university friend of Bonhoeffer's from Tübingen; e.g., see above, page 80.

[3.] There was an urgency in the matter because of the beginning of the semester.

89. From Robert Held[1]   150

Dear Dietrich,

Your letter just arrived at a time when my eagerness to work is no greater than yours is. Hence the prompt answer. Answering promptly is usually not my strong suit.

I will begin by giving you a short overview of my experiences.[2] First we were in Bethel, as you know. Then we went to Essen and entered a completely different atmosphere: Chamber of Commerce, the Krupps factory and grounds. Finally, in the evening we went to the astoundingly beautiful Ruhr. Bochum: the Bochum Organization (a Stinnes company)[3] and a school for miners. Duisburg-Ruhrort: the Schiffer Church, Rhine harbor. Ruhrort is the largest European inland port; it boasts a greater number of reshipments than Hamburg. The coal shipments to satisfy the reparations agreement are collected here. We visited the Institution for Public Welfare. On the last day we visited the Gute-Hoffnings foundry at Oberhausen (a Haniel company).[4] There we got the best glimpse into the refinement of coal and metal. We learned about the process of turning the raw ore and coal into the finished product and the by-products.

At this point the trip organized by the university was over. I visited a textile factory in Barmen on my own as well. People generally work from 6 A.M. until 6 P.M., 10 hours a day. Underground in the mines they work 8 hours a day. Wages are 24–50 marks a week.

This was my first impression of the Ruhr region. Here people work harder than anywhere else in the country. But then, only a few people have created this success. They hold and expand everything. 80% of the coal and steel production is in the hands of 9 companies. In 1890 Essen had 60,000 inhabitants. If 10 times that many live there today, then, viewed from outside, it is due solely to the Krupps factory. It is precisely here, as nowhere else in the "democratic age," that the importance and power of the individual can be clearly seen. Spengler[5] comes to mind. In spite of their wealth, none of the owners of the companies in the whole Ruhr area is the least bit snobbish. To be sure, such snobbishness is exhibited by those who profit indirectly from this work. These   151
people live in Cologne, Frankfurt, and Berlin. With respect to these entrepreneurs one must think of *Max Weber.*[6] Their god is the factory and the power that can be achieved through the factory. In this situation our theologians are confronted with the following alarming question: What kind of peculiar piety is this? Isn't something missing in these people's lives? It occurred to me that this question has even deeper roots, as I became better acquainted with the workers. The contrast became very blatant for us, because

---

[1.] *NL* C 15(4); handwritten and dated "23.III.25".

[2.] Cf. below, editorial note 8.

[3.] Refers to Hugo Stinnes.

[4.] Refers to Franz Haniel.

[5.] This most likely refers to Oswald Spengler, *The Decline of the West*, N.B. volume 2, chapter 5, "The Shape of Economic Life."

[6.] Cf. Weber, *The Protestant Ethic and the Spirit of Capitalism.*

we came from Bethel. Already in Bethel we had asked whether it would be better not to let the most unhappy of these creatures live and suffer.[7] This question is based on the principle on which the Ruhr industry is built. Its rationality would also walk over these corpses. Surely every new development has to walk over corpses; but is the manner in which it is done here really necessary? How wide is the gap is between the two worlds became clear to me for the first time in this way. Yet we are materially dependent on the one, chained to it, and are still drawn to the other through more than mere tradition.

And now what is new, at least for me: I didn't know until now that the "World of Love" ["Welt der Liebe"][8] had so many supporters in worker circles. The Quakers' ideas are especially widespread—especially in the textile region. All of this has become so awkward[9] and confused. But so many people are interested in it that it had to express itself somehow. I also found all of this confirmed when I visited the Rhine. I met two merchants—without Schiller collars[10]—in a youth hostel in Frankfurt. They had given up their professions and were traveling around the countryside. Naturally they were vegetarians. They intend to continue traveling until they can establish a community based on love in another country. The whole movement, however, is not so cowardly. It believes that it can even introduce love instead of self-interest to industry and advocate—to express it colloquially—a spiritual socialism. Neither of these words is ever mentioned by them. The word spiritual is not used—I can't blame them. We got to know a pastor from the Ruhr region, the director of the youth homes in Essen. He defended the 10-hour workday "on divine grounds." The workers are so tired when

152

[7.] Cf., for example, Binding and Hoche, *Die Freigabe der Vernichtung lebensunwerten Lebens: Ihr Maß und ihre Form.*

[8.] The "World of Love" was a contemporary Christian movement. Robert Held wrote to the compilers of the German edition of *DBW* 9, in a letter dated July 9, 1985, that the trip was an educational trip sponsored by the Office for Social Affairs at the University of Berlin. He wrote, "I took similar trips that were sponsored by this office to Upper Silesia and southern Germany. I told Dietrich Bonhoeffer about these only verbally." He wrote the following about the "World of Love": "I was accepted into these circles in Barmen because an aunt of mine came out of the circle of Blumhardt (Bad Boll). She was also a social worker for the homesteading movement. These circles correspond somewhat to our Hahn communities. I also heard Silvio Gesell speak to these circles. The lecture was very well attended. He was the progenitor of an ethically based theory on the abandonment of money. Today I would not consider it a widespread movement." The Hahn'sche Gemeinschaft, Hahn Community, was one group within a broad pietistic movement mainly in Württemberg, originating in the early 19th century. This was a lay movement, strongly represented among farmers and working-class people who were not content with the normal pastor's preaching and came together for Bible study and prayer. [The Blumhardt reference is to the movement of spiritual awakening in the late 19th century in the Black Forest region of Germany led by Johann Christoph Blumhardt and his son Christoph Friedrich Blumhardt; they opened and led a retreat center at Bad Boll in southern Germany until the death of the son in 1919.] [WF]

[9.] Difficult to decipher in the original manuscript.

[10.] The Schillerkragen was a mark of young men belonging to the youth movement, or *Jugendbewegung*. These two merchants obviously were wearing ties, and stood out as unusual among men their age.

they get home at night that they don't get into any trouble!—They don't use the word socialism either. The people don't express themselves in a long-winded way at all. But the ever-recurring basic concept—often in connection with Oppenheimer[11]—is that the acquisition of land and soil is robbery ("political accumulation," not original). Therefore the people are mainly supporters of the settlement idea. In addition, they assert that neither the rent charged for the land nor the interest on the capital has been earned. The movement is composed of socialists, Christian Unionists, friends of nature, and very many people from the Youth Movement. This is their goal. They want to return to practical (!) work. I spoke to you about this once before. In addition, many teachers and pastors belong to the movement. This is also an attempt to emerge out of the schism and to bring the material side and the other side together. The movement's influence on the workers can also be explained, because the meaning of the material side is fully known. But the significance of its rationality, which is often unknown to them, is that no factory could exist without them. Then thoughts of freedom generally play with: Nobody should. . . . [12] Finally, equality plays a part. This is yet again a picture of inner disunity.

Enough of that. You may be smirking, but the situation has to be taken more seriously.

It was also wonderful on the Rhine. I have made a firm decision to come back in the summer. In Frankfurt I was admitted to the bank and stock market operation centers through my friend from school. I was also able to attend the Frankfurt newspaper's adult education classes and see Hellpach.[13]

I have to add something about the industrial region. There are fabulous new buildings there. You have never seen anything equal to them in Berlin. Among them are the new stock exchange in Essen, Krupps' new mechanized workshop, [Masons'] Lodge House, Gute-Hoffnung foundry, Wilhelm-Marx-House in Düsseldorf, and Stumm's[14] company house. Every one of these buildings attests technical and economic skill. It would be a mistake not to call these buildings art. Although the architectural styles are brutal, they are not more brutal than our time. I'll bring several pictures with me when I come to Berlin.   153

You asked about my work. I should actually be working on criminal law. My inclination to do this is minimal, all the more understandable because Max Weber's work (his *Sociological Essays*, 1924) is lying in front of me.[15] I have begun to study Gandhi,[16] and I would also like to read Cassel[17] and Oppenheimer. I also willingly took part—horri-

[11.] See Franz Oppenheimer, *Die Siedlungsgenossenschaft.*

[12.] "This means working for someone else, 'being a slave'" (from a letter of Dr. Robert Held dated October 11, 1985).

[13.] Willy Hellpach.

[14.] Karl Ferdinand Stumm.

[15.] Max Weber, *Gesammelte Aufsätze zur Sozial- und Wirtschaftsgeschichte.*

[16.] Cf. Gandhi, *Die Botschaft des Mahatma Gandhi.* Cf. also *DB-ER* 105.

[17.] Gustav Cassel.

ble dictu—in a very interesting recruitment trip.[18] Several people whom we met are considered possibilities. It might interest you to know that Udo Weynand's brother is coming to Tübingen in the summer. By the way, I found a letter from Mrs. Weynand waiting for me when I arrived home.

I don't have any further complicated plans for vacation. If I discover I want to go skiing for a few days, I'll go.

I am really very happy that you are staying in Berlin. That way I won't be so completely alone after all. Fauser[19] won't be coming, and at this time Pfizer doesn't know what he'll do. This time, however, I definitely want to visit Naumburg on the trip up.

There is a student conference[20] April 24–29 in Spandau. Will you be going? I doubt I will be there that early.

I have not written such a long letter for a long time.

Completely exhausted, I remain yours,
Robert Held

17:20   **89a. To Walter Dreß**[1]

Dear Walter Dreß,[2]

Many thanks for your card. I wish you a quiet vacation, which you seem to have needed.—Holl is presenting a seminar on Luther's 1542 work, "Exem-

---

[18.] This recruitment trip, in German *Keilausflug*, was undertaken for the purpose of recruiting new members for the fraternity.

[19.] "Fauser was an enthusiastic member of the class-conscious society. We [Held and Bonhoeffer] often had discussions with him" (from Held; see above, page 143, editorial note 11).

[20.] In the letter dated July 9, 1985, Dr. Held remembers, "The conference in Spandau mentioned in the letter no doubt goes back to Siegmund-Schultze. Dietrich Bonhoeffer introduced me to him and his social study group in northern Berlin. To be sure, Siegmund-Schultze's social study group was in eastern Berlin (see, e.g., Erich Gramm, 'Die Soziale Arbeitsgemeinschaft Berlin-Ost')."

[1.] *Nachlaß Dreß*; property of Andreas and Heidi Dreß, Bielefeld, Germany. Undated handwritten postcard postmarked May 19, 1925, Berlin-Wilmersdorf. Addressed to Mr. Walter Dreß, Theology Student, Bockswiese-Hahnenklee, c/o Miss Weber, Waldheimat, Harz. From D. Bonhoeffer, Grunewald, Wangenheimstr. 14. First published in *Zeitschrift für Neuere Theologiegeschichte/Journal for the History of Modern Theology* 4 (1997): 270; also in *DBW* 17, 20, transcribed by Eberhard Bethge, on which this translation is based. Hahnenklee-Bockwiese near Goslar was a frequently visited favorite vacation spot of the Dreß family.

[2.] On the friendship between Bonhoeffer and his brother-in-law Walter Dreß, see Dreß, "Weg und Zeugnis Dietrich Bonhoeffers," in *Evangelisches Erbe und Weltoffenheit*, 107–15, and "Dietrich Bonhoeffer in Tübingen," pages 151–74. See also *DB-ER*, passim, and Reinhart Staats, "Dietrich Bonhoeffers Abschied von der Berliner 'Wintertheologie'," *Zeitschrift für Neuere Theologiegeschichte/Journal for the History of Modern Theology* 1 (1994): 180–82.

pel, einen rechten, christlichen Bischof zu weihen."[3] The lectures are interested solely in the church-historical aspects of the subject and are not very stimulating. I have to submit a paper about "Luther's Feelings About His Work"[4] from 1540 and on, on June 8th. Do you know anything of any importance about this subject? Further—do you know anything about Luther's opinion of history? It would be *very* important to find something out *soon*. Did Luther develop an *independent* dualistic view of history, or did this only *arise* from his recognition of having found grace and of his calling?[5] Is there a philosophy of history in the scholastic tradition, a dualistic one? Do you think Luther's view is dualistic? I would be very grateful for a speedy reply.—Seeberg's seminar, "The Word of God." You were able to avoid presenting a paper because of your absence. Harnack is reading Tertullian.[6] Other than that nothing is going on. I have a great deal to do at the moment. A paper on "Historical and Pneumatic Exegesis"[7] for Seeberg interests me very much, but I don't have to finish until the end of July. Relax,[8] and don't return too quickly to this site of lamentation; and please write to answer my questions soon.

My best regards.
Your,
Dietrich Bonhoeffer

89b. To Walter Dreß[1]   17:21

Dear Walter Dreß,

I tried to telephone you several times, because I haven't heard from you. Today, however, I received the laconic message that I wouldn't be able to reach you until after Pentecost. Since I am leaving today, I beg you to please

---

[3.] "Exempel, einen rechten, christlichen Bischof zu weihen" (*WA* 53) ["The Problem of Installing a True Christian Bishop"]. The list of lectures Bonhoeffer attended can be found below, Appendix 3:584f.

[4.] See below, pages 257–84.

[5.] See below, pages 263–65.

[6.] Concerning Seeberg's and Harnack's seminars, see below, Appendix 3:584–86.

[7.] Cf. below, pages 285–89.

[8.] The phrase "write soon" is crossed out.

[1.] *NL* Walter Dreß; property of Andreas and Heidi Dreß, Bielefeld, Germany. Undated handwritten postcard postmarked Berlin-Grunewald May 30, 1925. Addressed to Mr. Walter Dreß, Theology Student, Lichterfelde Ost, Hindenburgdamm 11. The street name Hindenburgdamm 11 is crossed out by an unknown hand and replaced by Marthastr. 7. First published in *Zeitschrift für Neuere Theologiegeschichte/Journal for the History of Modern Theology* 4 (1997): 270ff., transcribed by Eberhard Bethge. Also published in *DBW* 17:21, on which this translation is based.

write and tell me if any particular formalities are necessary for the paper I'm writing for Holl[2] and anything else that would be useful to know for it. It has to be turned in on July 8. In addition, where does the saying "the servant should not know his master's secrets"[3] come from? How long is the average seminar paper? If you can think of anything else that would relate to my subject, please write me and please write soon: *Friedrichsbrunn*, Eastern Harz Mountains (near Suderode). I have finished gathering material and have completed a portion of the paper, but I still have to slave over it quite a bit. The first time I had it 3/4 finished I crossed it all out and started over. I'm really not satisfied with it. Therefore write soon!

Yours,
Dietrich Bonhoeffer

154   **90. To His Parents**[1]

Lesum, August 25, 1925

Dear Parents,

I have been here near Bremen since Sunday. Actually, I wanted to leave Hamburg a day earlier than I did. Hans[2] didn't have any free time until Saturday, so he wanted me to stay a day longer. I certainly did have a very nice time, and I especially liked their apartment. Christel told me that in your last telephone conversation you had said that you would leave on Monday and that the Schleichers would leave on Sunday. I really wanted to return home on the Saturday before you leave, but I don't believe that it would be polite to leave here earlier than planned without a very good reason. I especially wanted to find out from you, dear Papa, how I should manage this situation with Seeberg.[3] Should I somehow refer to your conversation with him? Does he want to talk with me some more about my future work or about my report?[4] Could you please leave me a message with Grandmama or one of the other children and tell me what your thoughts are on the subject? I

[2.] Cf. below, pages 257–84, Bonhoeffer's essay, "Luther's Views of His Work."

[3.] Luther: "A servant should not know the secrets of his master but only what the master commands," from circular letter to the Christians at Antwerp, *WA* 18:550, 18. Quoted by Holl, *Gesammelte Aufsätze* 1, *Luther*, 52, note 3 (Holl gives an incorrect page number).

[1.] *NL* A 9/1(6); handwritten letter dated "den 25. August 25." Previously published in *GS* 6:95f. Lesum was the community where the Dreier family lived, twenty-five km northwest of Bremen on the Weser River.

[2.] He is speaking of a visit with Christine (Christel) and Hans von Dohnanyi.

[3.] Reinhold Seeberg was Professor of Systematic Theology in Berlin. In the summer semester of 1925 Dietrich Bonhoeffer attended one of his seminars.

[4.] Refers to Bonhoeffer's oral report and paper, "Report on the Historical and Pneumatological Interpretation of Scripture," see below, pages 285–89; cf. *DB-ER* 79.

probably won't see you until September unless I can leave here early. Please thank Grandmama warmly for me for her long letter. I'll write to her soon. Best regards to you and to everyone else.

Gratefully yours,
Dietrich

91. From Karl Bonhoeffer[1]

Grunewald, August 30, 1925

Dear Dietrich,

As far as Seeberg is concerned, when he suggested that you visit him sometime, he no doubt did not intend to have a renewed discussion of your report in his class. He wanted instead to have a general discussion concerning systematic theology or history and your particular preference for one or the other. If you are not sure you want to do advanced academic work under him, I would do the following: I would tell him that you are not sure whether you want to stay in Berlin or to study abroad for another semester.

At any rate, I believe that a visit with him would be very advantageous for you. You could get to know him better. It's too bad that we won't be able to see you. Now it will probably be 8 weeks before we see each other again.

My best regards,

Your Father

Seeberg is probably still traveling. You can certainly inquire by telephone.

92. From Paula Bonhoeffer[1]

August 31, 1925

Dear Dietrich,

You should at least find a letter from me immediately upon your arrival home. It has often distressed me recently that I have not written to you at all. I was also so sorry that you were not here with us on Sunday. I could have sent you a telegram somehow, but I thought that you wanted to spend 14 days there. I didn't want to cut your vacation short.—Hopefully, you'll return home from your vacation fresh and invigorated. Papa has left behind a letter for you. I keep wondering whether you shouldn't write a

[1.] *NL* A 9/2(1); handwritten letter dated "30.8.25," previously published in *GS* 6:96.

[1.] *NL* A 9/2(2); handwritten letter dated "31.8.25" mailed from Berlin-Grunewald; previously published in *GS* 6:96f.

155

history of doctrine thesis under Holl.[2]—You can certainly habilitate later with a systematic thesis when Seeberg is gone.—Rethink this. I'm writing in the train. That is why my handwriting looks like it does.—I have been reading a collection of lectures given by Troeltsch[3] and find them very interesting. Can you send me the same Barth[4] book to Kissingen that you sent to Uncle Hans?[5] It is as if a whirlwind blew through my mind yesterday. Ursel's future worries me a great deal.—Susi will be a bit lonely now. Take care of her a little. Sing with her in the evenings or take a little walk with her.— The next few days will still be fairly stressful. We will then, hopefully, have an uninterrupted stay in Kissingen.—Take care and give my best wishes to everyone at home.

From your,
Mother

156   **93. To His Parents**[1]

Grunewald, September 21, 1925

Dear Parents,

Seeberg returned to Berlin in the time between my last letter and this one. I had left a message for him that I had returned to Berlin. When he received my message, he telephoned me and asked me to accompany him to the train station at 7 A.M. He was going to be in Berlin only for one day. In the meantime I had thought about the subject and had come to the conclusion that it really doesn't make sense to go to Holl or to Harnack[2] to write my thesis. Seeberg wouldn't be at all opposed to a thesis on the history of doctrine. So it doesn't matter if I write it under one or the other; since I believe that Seeberg, on the whole, is sympathetic, I'll stay with him in any case. I proposed a subject to him that is half-historical and half-systematic. He readily agreed

---

[2.] Karl Holl, for whose seminars Bonhoeffer wrote two papers about Luther; see below, pages 257f., and 325ff.

[3.] This probably refers to Ernst Troeltsch, *Der Historismus und seine Überwindung.*

[4.] Barth, *The Word of God and the Word of Man.*

[5.] Hans von Hase.

[1.] *NL* A 9/1(7); handwritten letter dated "den 21.9.25"; previously published in *GS* 6:97f.

[2.] When this was written in 1925, Adolf von Harnack was retired. For three semesters Bonhoeffer attended one of his private seminars and wrote a paper on 1 Clement (see below, pages 216ff.). For Harnack's 75th birthday Bonhoeffer put together a collection of contributions by the participants of the seminar. It was entitled "'Joy' in Early Christianity: Commemorative Paper for Adolf von Harnack" (below, pages 370ff.). After Harnack's death, it was Bonhoeffer who gave a talk in the name of the students at the memorial service at the Harnack-Haus (Cf. *DB-ER* 67–68 and 138–39). See in addition, Zahn-Harnack, *Adolf von Harnack*, 174.

with it. It relates to the subject of religious community.[3] I told you that I was interested in this subject one evening a while ago. I have to do all sorts of historical work now, which won't do me any harm. At any rate, the thesis seems to interest Seeberg quite a bit. He said he had waited a long time for someone to work on this subject. It was very nice, he said, that I had come up with the idea myself. Then he referred to your conversation with him, dear Papa, without mentioning it specifically. He said that everything would certainly go very well. He had already seen that from my work in the past![4] When I laughed a little he repeated it again! In this way I settled the thing with him, and I believe that it is very good like this. Now there is still one difficulty that I have to overcome, which I really would like to do in order to begin promptly with the thesis. I need a few books that, in Seeberg's opinion, I will use continuously. Checking them out of the library isn't a possibility, because they are usually very hard to get. And my allowance isn't large enough to cover their cost. I could buy the most important ones, Hegel, Spencer, and Max Weber,[5] for 25–30 marks. Can I get them? During the day I work, practice, read, and take a lot of walks. Yesterday, Grandmama, Susi, and I went to see *Die Fledermaus*. Grandmama said, however, that she never thought that at 80 she would still go to see such an "indecent piece." The Delbrück[s] want to give us a final answer to my request. As soon as we can, we'll write to you in Kissingen.

157

Best wishes from everyone.
Including your grateful,
Dietrich

[3.] Cf. *Predigten—Auslegungen—Meditationen*, 1:165f.

[4.] Bonhoeffer refers to the "Report on the Historical and Pneumatological Interpretation of Scripture," which he wrote for Seeberg's seminar in the summer semester of 1925 (below, pages 285f.).

[5.] At that time Bonhoeffer owned G. W. F. Hegel's *Der Begriff der Religion*, Pt. 1 of *Vorlesungen über die Philosophie der Religion* (Vol. 12 of *Sämtliche Werke*, edited by Georg Lasson), which had just been published that year. Later, he acquired four additional volumes in Lasson's edition: 1 (*Erste Druckschriften*), 2 (*Phänomenologie des Geistes*), 13 (*Die bestimmte Religion*, Pt. 2 of *Vorlesungen über die Philosophie der Religion*), and 14 (*Die absolute Religion*, Pt. 3 of *Vorlesungen über die Philosophie der Religion*). In 1925 he acquired Max Weber's *Gesammelte Aufsätze zur Religionssoziologie*, volumes 2 and 3. Herbert Spencer was an English philosopher who saw evolution as the unifying principle of all the sciences; it is not known which of Spencer's books Bonhoeffer had in mind here.

93a. To Walter Dreß[1]

Dear Walter Dreß,

17:22
    You haven't responded at all. Are you sick? I had hoped to find you in town yesterday, but you weren't in the library. I'll be in town Saturday morning, and I'd like to meet you in the theology section of the National Library at around 11:30. If you aren't going to be there, please call me Saturday morning, because I have to be out of town on Thursday and Friday. When you call, tell me when we can meet on Monday.

Best regards,
Dietrich Bonhoeffer

93b. To Walter Dreß[1]

Dear Walter Dreß,

    Do you know when the *first* date for the Hebrew exam[2] this semester is? I would like to know for my cousin.[3] Please be so good as to call me on the telephone to let me know.
    Many thanks.

Yours,
Dietrich Bonhoeffer

    [1.] *NL* Walter Dreß; property of Andreas and Heidi Dreß, Bielefeld, Germany. Undated handwritten postcard, postmarked Berlin-Grunewald October 29, 1925. Addressed to Mr. Walter Dreß, Theology Student, at the Wolffs', Lichterfelde–West, Marthastr. 7. First publication: *Zeitschrift für Neuere Theologiegeschichte / Journal for the History of Modern Theology* 4 (1997): 271. Transcribed by Eberhard Bethge. Also published in *DBW* 17:19, on which this translation is based.

    [1.] *NL* Walter Dreß, property of Andreas and Heidi Dreß, Bielefeld. Undated handwritten postcard postmarked Berlin-Grunewald October 31, 1925. Addressed to Mr. Walter Dreß, Theology Student, at the Wolffs', Lichterfelde–West, Marthastr. 7. First publication: *Zeitschrift für Neuere Theologiegeschichte / Journal for the History of Modern Theology* 4 (1997):272. Transcribed by Eberhard Bethge. Also published in DBW 17:22, on which this translation is based.

    [2.] Hebrew exam taken by all theology students.

    [3.] Hans Christoph von Hase, cf. below, page 164.

94. From Richard Widmann[1]

Nufringen, near Herrenberg, November 17, 1925

Dear Mr. Bonhoeffer,

Thank you for not requiring an apology for my long silence.

My vacation is over and I am again a parish pastor. You can imagine the rest. And, in addition, you just don't want to translate this theological text.

I could tell you a lot about my work in Bethel,[2] which was only practical. I believe such work is necessary, even though it seems hopeless at first. The spiritual atmosphere of the brothers, sisters, house fathers, and pastors is, I admit, that of the famous second generation. One feeds on the inheritance of old Bodelschwingh.[3]

My doctoral work is at a total standstill.[4] Maybe I'll make some progress on it in the near future.

Your licentiate work, however, can have all sorts of consequences that are of pressing importance at the present time. See Althaus and his "living congregation." See Barth's lecture in Duisburg-Meiderich (newest issue of *Zwischen den Zeiten*); see Kierkegaard's *Attack*; see the newest "movement" in the youth movement. Everything calls for "covenant," "society," and "community."[5] See the Bavarian Concordat![6]

I would be very grateful to you if you could get Barth's *Dogmatics*.[7] I would work through it as quickly as possible. Perhaps you'll write to me again sometime. Maybe then my answer will be better than it was today.

It is almost midnight.

Cordially yours,
Richard Widmann

158

[1.] *NL C* 14(1); handwritten letter dated "17.11.25" mailed from Nufringen, a village two km north of Herrenberg. Richard Widmann was a friend of Paul Schempp's and Hermann Diem's; like them he sought to position his thinking in line with the theology of the Reformation and Karl Barth. Cf. *DB-ER* 82, 92–94.

[2.] Widmann added a period of study in Bethel after he had spent a semester in Berlin, where he had met Bonhoeffer in a seminar led by Holl.

[3.] Friedrich von Bodelschwingh, founder of the Bethel Institute for epileptics, alcoholics, and the homeless.

[4.] Widman was working on Pascal, perhaps with Karl Müller in Tübingen, but later abandoned his doctoral study.

[5.] Cf. Paul Althaus, *Das Erlebnis der Kirche*; Karl Barth, "The Desirability and Possibility of a Universal Reformed Creed," in *Theology and Church; Shorter Writings, 1920–1928*; Søren Kierkegaard, *Attack upon Christendom* (a German-language abridgement entitled *Der Augenblick* [The Instant] was owned by Bonhoeffer). In the fall of 1925 a conference for young theologians on the "renewal of the church through the spirit of the youth movement" took place in Hoheneck, Bavaria. Cf. Korn, ed., *Die Jugendbewegungen*, 240.

[6.] On March 29, 1924, a concordat was signed between the State of Bavaria and the Apostolic Nuncio, Eugenio Pacelli, the future Pope Pius XII. The text, legal assessment, opinions, and occasionally very critical reactions to this treaty, among these the opinion of Prof. Gerhard Anschütz, are found in his "Die Bayrischen Kirchenverträge von 1925."

[7.] See below, 1/95:154, editorial note 7.

94a. To Walter Dreß[1]

Dear Walter Dreß,

    After waiting for you twice in vain, I fear that you must have gotten sick. Let me hear from you soon to know what the problem is. Rößler[2] also sends his regards. At the moment, I am sitting in Mahling's[3] class again for the first time. I just happened to meet him with Sellin in front of the University and had to greet him. I have no idea what he is talking about. I think he's lecturing about something quite nice. Holl was very nice. In Seeberg's class, a twenty-year-old[4] reported on problems in marriage. Afterwards there was a report about socialism.—Confirmation—Bucer[5]—Bohemian brothers[6]—Caspari[7]—Erasmus' Commentary on Matthew[8]—Baptismal promise.—I just picked that up. 1539 Church Order from Kassel[9] (better Rippgener[10])—The Ziegenhain Resolutions.[11] Now I have to work through Heußi.[12]

17:23

Best regards,
Dietrich Bonhoeffer

    [1.] *NL* Walter Dreß; property of Andreas and Heidi Dreß, Bielefeld. Undated handwritten postcard postmarked Berlin-Grunewald February 8, 1926. Addressed to Mr. Walter Dreß, Theology Student, at the Wolffs', Lichterfelde–West, Marthastr. 7. First publication: *Zeitschrift für Neuere Theologiegeschichte / Journal for the History of Modern Theology* 4 (1997): 272. Transcribed by Eberhard Bethge. Also published in *DBW* 17:22–23, on which this translation is based.

    [2.] Helmuth Rößler was a student friend of Dietrich Bonhoeffer. See below, pages 169f. and 439.

    [3.] With reference to the Berlin theologians named in this letter, Mahling, Sellin, Holl, Seeberg, see below, Appendix 3:585–86, the list of lectures that Bonhoeffer attended in winter semester of 1925–26; also see below, pages 215–441, the papers that were written by Bonhoeffer during this time. Bonhoeffer's papers written directly afterwards for Mahling and Sellin are found below, pages 470–75 and pages 420–36.

    [4.] Illegible. It might also read "twenty-five-year-old."

    [5.] Martin Bucer (1491–1551), reformer at Strassburg.

    [6.] A reform movement within the Hussite movement that originated about 1453.

    [7.] Walter Caspari, *Die evangelische Konfirmation, vornehmlich in der lutherischen Kirche.*

    [8.] See Desiderius Erasmus, *Paraphrasis in Evangelium Matthaei.*

    [9.] Martin Bucer, *Ordenung der Kirchenübung. Für die Christen zu Cassel.*

    [10.] Difficult to decipher.

    [11.] Martin Bucer, *Ordenung der Christlichen Kirchenzucht. Für die Kirchen in Fürstenthumb Hessen* (the so-called Ziegenhain Resolutions) also included an order of confirmation. All of the authors mentioned here obviously relate to Mahling's lectures on practical theology.

    [12.] Heußi, *Kompendium der Kirchengeschichte.*

95. From Richard Widmann[1]   159

Nufringen (Württemberg), February 25, 1926

Dear Mr. Bonhoeffer,

I am finally writing a letter to you. I hope that I don't have to apologize too much. Perhaps you know how much I regret our silence. But you are bogged down in work and so am I. Also many things take place for me that don't relate directly to work. In such a village as this, you live so closely with so many people that you meet people every day who are personally important. I am irrepressibly attracted by the big city; the pace of village life is oppressively slow. The rigid social structure burdens one. You are "the pastor" wherever you go. You are taboo, separated from the "people" and critically watched. Every awkward move insults those who are not "gentlemen." At the same time it gives them a certain malicious pleasure. ("Even you are no better than we!") I feel incredibly ridiculous when I pay attention to it. However, you are an even more ridiculous figure if you ignore these social barriers.

My work on Pascal is at a complete standstill. I wanted to abandon it. I wrote to Holl to ask if he would take me on as a licentiate. (I believe I wrote to you about it.) He advised against it for several reasons, which I had to accept. So I remain with Pascal. At this time I am writing a long report about Stockholm.[2] It is, however, very critical. The more one occupies oneself with the subject, the more doubtful it becomes. (The subject would be less doubtful if it didn't strive to be more than an international alliance to promote ethical culture. It does, however, strive to be more! One truly wants to build the kingdom of God!!) You asked me for a contribution[3] for your work on the "Holy Spirit in the Disputations."[4] I simply didn't have the time to do it. As far as I can   160
remember, my search wouldn't have had any great results for you either. If you would send me the paper, I would like to read it.

How successful was the Harnack seminar about the *City of God* [civitas dei]? The concept of predestination? Visibility and obscurity of the church (as a community of saints)?! These same problems will certainly have given you trouble in your paper on "Church and Eschatology."[5] Barth's "correction" to the Reformed doctrines of both predestination and eschatology reflects a basic dialectical relationship between time

---

[1.] *NL* C 14(2); handwritten letter dated "25.2.26."

[2.] Widmann traveled to the Stockholm World Conference for Practical Christianity, August 19–30, 1925, as the correspondent for Stuttgart newspapers, among them the *Schwäbischer Merkur* [Swabian Mercury]; he also wrote a theological assessment for theological friends (cf. *DB-ER* 72).

[3.] Widmann bought the Weimar edition of Luther's works (*WA*) on credit. Volume 39, with the "Disputations," had just been published. By "contribution" Widmann means excerpts from the *WA* that he made and sent to his friends; apparently Bonhoeffer knew of this and had already profited from them.

[4.] See below, "Luther's Views of the Holy Spirit according to the Disputations of 1535–1545," pages 325–70.

[5.] See below, "Paper on the Church and Eschatology," pages 310–24.

and eternity! "The moment"[6] will probably be right. I am still working through Barth's *Dogmatics* II.[7] I am pleased that some things are said better and more clearly here than in *The Epistle to the Romans.* The problems seem to me to be even more clearly outlined and more carefully defined than they are in *The Epistle to the Romans.* Because Barth proceeds more systematically, things obtain their proper place within the thought processes and therefore receive no more nor less importance than is their due. In *The Epistle to the Romans* there is a lot of sensationalism and journalism. The *Dogmatics* is more objective. I can't give either one precedence over the other. You once protested[8] that you regretted the slavery that Barth has fallen into in this *Dogmatics*—that he timidly guards himself against walking in the footsteps of the old dogmaticians.[9] I don't think the reactionary gesture is misplaced. First of all, for him it is certainly only a question of trying to establish a connection to the past. Perhaps he is not merely trying to establish a connection but also to seek strength and encourage motivation and fruitful thoughts. One doesn't shake a dogmatics like this out of one's shirtsleeve. Barth is cleaning the manure out of an Augean Stable.[10] He will be genuinely grateful for his orthodox supporters. I certainly also believe, however, that a dogmatics that manages to exist without these reactionary crutches and seeks connection with the future is just as necessary. In its formulations ("because it will certainly mainly be a question of these formulations")[11] *The Epistle to the Romans* is certainly much less reactionary. In this regard the *Dogmatics* is a step backward. Perhaps the next time Barth will take two steps forward. This, I hope, will occur when his *Dogmatics* has accomplished its "tactical purpose." At that point it will not be a question of its depending upon the old ones as much.

161

Hopefully by this sermon you will be inclined to continue our dialogue.

By the way, I thank you for your two postcards and send you best regards in happy anticipation of your answer.

Yours,
Richard Widmann

[6.] Barth, *The Epistle to the Romans*, 346f. (predestination), 237 (eschatology) and 109ff. (moment).

[7.] This was based on notes of Barth's lectures in Göttingen during the summer semester of 1925 on the doctrine of reconciliation.

[8.] This refers to comments made during their studies in Berlin in the summer semester of 1925.

[9.] Bonhoeffer's statement and Widmann's theological analysis that follows demonstrate how the young "Barthians" critically pursued Barth's approach in his *Christian Dogmatics.* Bethge points to this moment as the starting point in Bonhoeffer's critical appreciation of Barth's theology (*DB-ER* 75–77). Later Bonhoeffer was to speak of "a positivism of revelation" as a weakness in Barth's theology (e.g., *LPP*, 286 and 325ff.).

[10.] The reference is to the mythic Augeas, king of Elis, whose stable contained 3,000 oxen, and had not been cleaned for 30 years; Hercules cleansed it in a single day. [WF]

[11.] The quote is from one of Bonhoeffer's lost letters.

96. From Richard Widmann[1]

Nufringen, March 13, 1926

Dear Mr. Bonhoeffer,

Your letter, for which I thank you very much, is filled with questions. I'll try to answer some of them briefly. Today is Saturday and I'm using a break in the preparation for Sunday to write letters.

I definitely believe that one can discuss everything with children. By all means read Dostoyevsky sometime on this point. (Read Zossima's talks in the *The Brothers Karamazov* and the confessions of Prince Myshkin about his experiences with children in *The Idiot*.)[2] I am acquainted with Kutter's picture book.[3] I am, however, careful about following it. I believe that I am a very bad pedagogue. I never come to the point of a "religious conversation," but I know that there is a very good possibility that I might have one. One only has to guard oneself from giving too much of an answer. Sometimes one has to let "I don't know" be the answer. My method: the highest possible verbatim retelling of the contents of the story. Then I take a thought and hammer it in. I use drastic subjects, caricatures, examples, comparisons, and conversations to do this. I keep everything as short as possible. If possible, nothing is repeated. I am always the leader of the children's worship service. I therefore always talk to about 100 children at a time. This is a barrier to "religious conversation." For the most part I am also very tired from the preceding sermon. The children from the village are naturally not nearly as lively, inquisitive, or fluent, etc., as those in Berlin. I avoid anything that is sentimental (pious leaflets). Sentimentality is not childlike. Be as objective as possible! Just the stories (examples) without the famous touching ending, without the pragmatic aspects of dramas and novels. I don't think it is suspicious if one has "success" with the children, provided that they are children. The threshold should often be set very low. But you will soon notice whether it is an unhealthy "success." The [...][4] expresses itself in children more directly than it does in adults.—I would not take any children from another group.[5] I believe one has to work against oneself for the principle of the thing. Moreover, a terrible disturbance would certainly erupt among the children. This is terribly dangerous.

I will probably be able to send you the manuscript of my report[6] in the near future.—By the way, I am now beginning to work on my Pascal paper again.—And by

162

[1.] *NL* C 14(3); handwritten and dated "13.III.26."

[2.] See Dostoyevsky, *The Brothers Karamazov*, 337ff., especially 375ff., and *The Idiot*, 87ff., especially 87.

[3.] Hermann Kutter, *Das Bilderbuch Gottes*.

[4.] Illegible.

[5.] Bonhoeffer asked Widmann if he should agree to take children from a children's worship led by someone else into his own. See below, Part 3, for examples of Bonhoeffer's sermons in children's worship services.

[6.] Cf. above, 1/95:153, editorial note 2.

the way, I would be very grateful if you would send me Barth's main precepts.[7]—Have you read the new issue of *Zwischen den Zeiten* (1926:2)? The foreword to the 5th edition of *The Epistle to the Romans*[8] is printed in it. Especially interesting are lines 1ff. of page 101, among others (lines 5–12 from the top!!!). So after all that, he doesn't take the "two steps forward"! It is regrettable. With this, my fate as a pastor is practically sealed.

Now I'll address briefly the most important thing for today! You indeed write that I am not cut out to live in a village. But "ultimately it isn't determined by that!" Very true—and yet false! The church as it is today is based on two classes, the middle class and the farmers, the people of the land. This has consequences for dogmatics and ethics. I belong neither to the middle class nor to the people of the country. Instead, I belong to the intellectual world (to use a phrase!). The intellectual world doesn't sit in church and of necessity has no confessional position. As meaningless as this may be for the problem of the church, the sociological limitation of the church really has the greatest significance for me. I stand in another world than the one in which my listeners stand or can ever stand. The world to which I direct my talk and out of which I speak does not go to church. It would not be the worst thing (in fact, again meaningless) if I were to deny my past and like Barth become reactionary, out of necessity. One does not believe one has the strength "blow by blow to say and to do what would have to be said and done"[9] in order to open the portals of the church to the intellectual world.—Still I don't want to deny my past. I have already seen that it doesn't help to stuff the sermon full of psychology in order to make it understandable to my listeners. My listeners, though, sense this other world and they reject me for it. For an intellectual pastor there is nothing left to do but either emphatically renounce his former world or leave his office, unless he can become a university professor. The sermon is, after all, a dialogue. But a dialogue between an intellectual and a middle-class person or a farmer is not possible. Neither one understands the other anymore. As an intellectual pastor I am condemned to tragic solitude. Barth's theology, as presented in *The Epistle to the Romans*, has grown in the soil of the modern world. It is inappropriate for the pulpit of a church of the middle class and farmers. Barth's theology has very definite sociological prerequisites. They are not determinative for the church of today. Barth remained in the church and became reactionary. This is how the problem is posed today. For the time being, I'll wait and allow myself time to think. What do you say about this proposition? For once, take the church as a sociological reality seriously and draw the consequences from it. Once again the future is dark, unsteady, and uncertain for me.

Enough!

Cordially yours,
Richard Widmann

[7.] Cf. ibid., editorial note 7.

[8.] See Barth, *Romans*, 23: "Should this more favorable explanation of the 'success' of my book also be justified, then, whatever can be rightly said to the contrary, it does mark the moment when a breach, however small, has been made in the inner and outer afflictions of Protestantism."

[9.] Ibid.

1/96a and 1/96b. To Walter Dreß[1]

אֹהֵב שָׁלוֹם לְךָ אֵיךְ אַתָּה
הֲלַקְנָה אֶל־הַגְּרוּן
וְלֵךְ הַיָּמִים אַחֲרֵי מָחָר אֲנִי
בְּבַיִת מָתַי יָכַלְתָּ תֵלְפְנִיְרֶה
נִי קֵל דָּבַרְתִּי עַתָּה כְּעִבְרִי
שָׁלוֹם לְךָ
[2]דְיֶתְרִיח בנהֶפֶּר

96b. To Walter Dreß[1]　　　　　　　　　　　　　　　　　　17:24

Dear Walter Dreß,

A small change. Can't you go to the doctor in the morning and travel earlier with the D 132[2] from Charlottenburg? You'll have four hours to wait in Stendal if you take this train. If this is too early for you, you could also make your connection in Stendal by taking the passenger train at 4:30 in the afternoon. Please call me tomorrow on Sunday around 1–2 o'clock and tell me whether you are taking this train. We'd perfer it. Dreier is arranging lodging in Lüneburg. I've written him already.[3]

[1.] *NL* Walter Dreß; property of Andreas and Heidi Dreß, Bielefeld, Germany. Undated handwritten postcard with text in Hebrew; postmarked Berlin-Grunewald, March 15, 1926. Addressed to Theology Student Walter Dreß, Lichterfelde West, Marthastr. 7. First published in *Zeitschrift für Neuere Theologiegeschichte / Journal for the History of Modern Theology* 4 (1997): 273. Transcribed by theology students at Kiel. Also published in *DBW* 17:23, on which this translation is based.

[2.] "Friend, Peace be with you. How are you? Would you like to go to the Grunewald together? I'll be at home day after tomorrow. You can call me then. I'm speaking like a Hebrew. Peace be with you. Dietrich Bonhoeffer." By הֲלַקְנָה is probably meant הֲלַכְנוּ in which the ה interrogativum has been put at the end. The verb forms in the perfect tense are to be understood as present. Textual criticism by Dr. Georg Wasmuth, Kiel.

[1.] *NL* Walter Dreß; property of Andreas and Heidi Dreß, Bielefeld. Undated handwritten postcard, postmarked Berlin-Halensee, April 17, 1926 and stamped express mail, to which is added by hand pneumatic post. Addressed to Mr. Walter Dreß, Theology Student, Lichterfelde-West, Zehlendorfestr. 12. Handwritten: Sender Bonhoeffer, Grunewald, Wangenheimstr. 14. First published in *Zeitschrift für Neuere Theologiegeschichte / Journal for the History of Modern Theology* 4 (1997): 273. Transcribed by Eberhard Bethge. Also published in *DBW* 17: 24, on which this translation is based.

[2.] Number of an express train.

[3.] Dietrich and Susanne Bonhoeffer, Ilse and Walter Dreß, as well as Grethe von Dohnanyi and Wilhelm Dreier traveled together to heaths of Lüneburg during their vacation in 1926. This was a very popular holiday resort in the lowlands of northern Germany.

Please call tomorrow between 1 and 2 and let me know. If you don't, I'll have to telegraph Dreier and tell him it's off!

Yours,
Dietrich Bonhoeffer
Pflzbg 26 16[4]

97. From Richard Widmann[1]

Nufringen, April 29, 1926

Dear Mr. Bonhoeffer,

I let your letter lie around for some time, just as I have let my thoughts lie around for some time. I believe I wrote you already that I am inclined to wait a year before I decide one way or another. I really accept the rebuke that I have drawn "nondialectical consequences"[2] from Barth's work. It is this rebuke that I had already considered for the most part. But, I believe that the church does not merely have a dialectic that springs out of its uniqueness as the "church," but also a dialectic that arises out of its sociological reality. The question is simply, can at some point this sociological dialectic become so critical that even the theological dialectic cannot be of any assistance? I readily admit that my line of questioning moves on a secondary, tertiary, etc., plane. "In the end, nothing will depend on it."[3]

But what if "in the end" penultimate and ante-penultimate things do make a difference? At some point they can amass so much importance that, in spite of everything, they can cause a vocational existence to fall apart. Or do you mean that only "last things," "things in the end," can force one to make a decision?[4] If I had to decide to leave this pastorate, I would not do it triumphantly. It would not be as if by chance I alone had understood Barth's theology and had accepted the consequences of it better than had Barth himself. It would rather be that, in spite of everything, Barth's concern had become too difficult for me. Whether I would have more success or satisfaction among intellectuals than I do among farmers is, I hope, not a criterion for me. It is not a matter of my personal pleasure but something else. I also don't believe, as Althaus does, that I am confusing the "experience of the church"[5] with belief in the

164

[4.] "Pfalzburg 26 16" was the telephone number of Prof. Dr. Karl and Mrs. Paula Bonhoeffer.

[1.] *NL* C 14(4); handwritten dated "29.IV.26"; also previously published in part in *DB-ER* 93.

[2.] Quote from Bonhoeffer's letter.

[3.] Quote from Bonhoeffer's letter.

[4.] The two young theologians have been discussing Barth's interpretation of eschatology. Cf. Barth, *Romans*, "If Christianity be not altogether thoroughgoing eschatology, there remains in it no relationship whatever with Christ" (314). Cf. *DB-ER* 94 and *E* (*DBW* 6):137–217: "The ultimate and penultimate things."

[5.] Althaus, *Das Erlebnis der Kirche*, "The experience of the one holy church" (22).

church. If I do flee, I hope that I am not fleeing from the church or even renouncing belief in the Protestant church. Instead I hope I am fleeing because I know that it is outside of my power to be all things to all people. The weak person still has to take a stand for weal or woe, even if he understands that in the end nothing comes of it.

The first thought in Barth's preface to the 5th edition[6] encourages me, moreover, to identify my problem with those who listen to me. The "other" (the farmer and the middle-class person) makes known to me most unsympathetically the limited nature of my theology and my preaching style. Limited, precisely because of historical-psychological factors. This disturbance[7] has certainly been to my benefit. In my case, the fact that "all flesh is grass"[8] is certainly authenticated by my brilliant failure.

A comforting prospect has, however, opened itself up at the end of this somewhat   165
rough path. It is that this insight could lead to a somewhat better understanding of the subject in question. Perhaps—perhaps—you will be able to say the same thing on another level without confusing the plane on which you move, where you are and become, with the subject itself. One thing is necessary for this. One has to be seriously concerned about other people (forgive [. . .]).[9]

The second problem is that it is evident in these passages that the conversation is about the church as a "homogeneous subject," as you had previously expressed it. The subject of growth is specified in several passages as the σῶμα τοῦ Χριστοῦ, which I translate as "Christ himself." I do this with reference to Barth's interpretation of the σῶμα τοῦ ἀνθρώπου.[10] This is precisely the human being himself, which "I" am. But Christ himself is the crucified and resurrected Christ! Consequently, the church is not merely the "representation of Christ" but Christ himself! Therefore, you are altogether one in Christ (Gal. 3:28). Compare this with the Pauline concepts of living *with* and dying *with*, etc. This certainly is not supposed to be primarily understood as *imitatio Christi* in which the "I" establishes this "being together with" itself. Instead it is a relationship that has already been established *imitatio passiva!* Christ becomes "I" and "I" become Christ (cf. Luther). To be sure, no identity takes place. Creator and creature remain distinct. Still, Christ = *communio sanctorum* = the one. One single comparison can be established. It is the solidarity of the children of Adam! Adam = *communio peccatorum* = the one (cf. Rom. 5). Christ himself (the body, the church) increases where Christ rules. It increases where Christ is the beginning and the end, etc. "He must increase, but I, etc." (John 3:30).

[6.] See Barth, *Romans*, ". . . and are my readers also deceived in supposing a thing to be relevant today which was in fact relevant only for Paul and Luther and Calvin? Have they been presented with what is really no more than a rehash, resurrected out of Nietzsche and Kierkegaard and Cohen?" (22).

[7.] Cf. Barth, *Romans*, 461. The catchword *Störung*, disturbance, refers to the title under which the chapters on ethics in the *Romans* are subsumed (cf. 424).

[8.] Isa. 40:6 (RSV); Barth, *Romans*, 22.

[9.] Illegible.

[10.] The Greek reads "body of Christ" and "body of humankind"; cf. Barth, *Romans*, 31–32. On the following comments of Widmann see Bonhoeffer's resumption of this topic in *SC* (*DBWE* 1):127, 165–92.

Further determinations according to Barth's *Dogmatics* II: To believe in the visibility of the church in spite of the invisible nature of the church (Christ himself) is the first stipulation. To believe in its invisibility in spite of its visibility is the second stipulation. ... The visible *church* is present *only* where the *invisible* church is present; and the *invisible* church is *only* present where the visible church is present. ... The church seen as a "religious association" is certainly unmistakable: church of the Antichrist, synagogue of Satan, etc. Barth goes this far.

166

The visible church is crucial when ethics are considered. At this point, however, the invisible church is made manifest. Nowhere other than in the visible church does the invisible church, Christ himself, confront us. In this way, it is Christ himself who confronts us in the individuals who are baptized and in the regulations of the church. (These regulations are represented by the offices of the church.) It is Christ himself who calls us to true service (cf. Barth on 1 Cor. 12-14).[11] The decisive ethical condition, therefore, is love (cf. 1 Cor. 12-14, Eph. 4:7-16). I am held in this obedient service by an individual, by one link in the chain. Through this link I am subject to the sovereignty of Christ. Therefore it can be said that the body of Christ is given unity by the mere presence of the other when he calls me to serve as the other. The body of Christ is not scattered, because his sovereignty is not impugned. This is how I exegete the difficult passage Eph. 4:16, πᾶν τὸ σῶμᾰ ["from whom the whole body"] up to ἐπι-χορηγίας ["with which it is equipped"] as well as Col. 2:19. Here several things must be said about the "You" [Du]. (By the way, Gogarten[12] says several good things about it in his epilogue to *On Free Will*, which he edited.)—Incidentally, I see the difference between the concept "You" and the concept of individuality in the fact that the "You" is a reflexive condition but the concept of individuality is an immediate condition. The "You" is surrendered; individuality is the given.

I can't say much about your difficulties concerning the children's worship service, because I don't know the situation well enough. I have written enough for now. Another time I'll write more.

Please make sure to give me more details about the conclusions that you've reached as a result of your work! Maybe the above will stimulate you to do so. My wife asked me to thank you for your friendly concern and to send you her regards.

Best regards
Yours,
Richard Widmann

[11.] Barth, *The Resurrection of the Dead*, 69ff.

[12.] See Gogarten's "Nachwort" to Martin Luther, *Vom Unfreien Willen*. Concerning Bonhoeffer's understanding of the I-You relationship, cf. *SC* (*DBWE* 1):44–57.

97a. To Walter Dreß[1]

Dear Walter Dreß,

Something incredibly stupid has happened. My sister[2] told us yesterday that you wanted to come by today and say, "Thank you." My mother told the maids not to show anyone in other than "Mr. Dreß." Naturally these pearls of maids didn't understand; and so the unhappy event happened that you were sent away. None of us was at home. My Father was upstairs in bed and my mother was with him. She learned about the mistake only after it was too late to do anything about it. Ergo nostra culpa.[3] Please forgive us! Odi profanum vulgus (ancillas!)[4] My sister thanks you for the generous return of the exquisite gloves.

17:25

Best regards
Dietrich Bonhoeffer

97b. To Walter Dreß[1]

[June 17, 1926][2]

Dear Walter,

This is sent with cordial greetings and best wishes for tomorrow from my sister[3] and me.

Yours,
Dietrich

[1.] *NL* Walter Dreß; property of Andreas and Heidi Dreß, Bielefeld, Germany. Undated handwritten postcard postmarked Berlin–Grunewald, May 16, 1926, 12 o'clock, and stamped express mail. Addressed to Mr. Walter Dreß, Senior Theology Student, Lichterfelde West, Zehlendorfestr. 12. First published in *Zeitschrift für Neuere Theologiegeschichte / Journal for the History of Modern Theology* 4 (1997):274. Transcribed by Eberhard Bethge. Also published in *DBW* 17:24–25, on which this translation is based.

[2.] Susanne Bonhoeffer, later married to Walter Dreß.

[3.] "It is therefore our fault."

[4.] "I despise the uneducated throng and I keep them at a distance." Bonhoeffer quotes the beginning of a famous Horace ode (3.1) and adds in Latin (maids!)." [Bonhoeffer wrote an essay for school in 1923 on Catullus and Horace; see below, pages 198–214.] [PDM]

[1.] *NL* Walter Dreß. Property of Andreas and Heidi Dreß. Bielefeld, Germany. This undated handwritten piece of paper might have been placed in a birthday gift for Walter Dreß. First published in *Zeitschrift für Neuere Theologiegeschichte / Journal for the History of Modern Theology* 4 (1997):274. Transcribed by Eberhard Bethge. Also published in *DBW* 17:25, on which this translation is based.

[2.] The date is inferred. Walter Dreß was born on June 18, 1904.

[3.] Susanne Bonhoeffer.

97c. To Margarethe Dreß[1]

My very highly esteemed Mrs. Dreß,

17:26   I'm sure you know that Walter's greatest secret wish[2] is to own Hauck, *Kirchengeschichte Deutschlands*, 5 volumes. This should be considered only in case there is a chance to get it from a secondhand bookshop. (De Gruyter would be the best, since they also search for books. The work is fairly expensive. It could cost as much as 100 marks.) Then Zündel, *Jesus* (8 marks); I don't know whether or not he recently bought Ritschl, *Rechtfertigung und Versöhnung*. If he hasn't I'm sure he would be happy to get it (3 volumes, only from secondhand shops, around 20 marks). I'm also not sure about Althaus, *Die letzte Dinge*. He was *very* interested in it a little while ago, but he might have already bought it (but I don't think so) (12 marks). Also Hirsch, *Idealismus und Christentum* (12 marks). It would be best to get these at Grote (Hegelplatz) after you make sure you can exchange them if you'd like. I'm sure he doesn't have Zündel and Hirsch. Finally *Missale Romanum*,[3] the little Padua altar edition (between 12 and 20 marks), which can be purchased at Herder. Dilthey, *Weltanschauung und Analyse des mittelalterlichen Menschen.* Overbeck, *Christlichkeit der Religion*[4] (this is the approximate title), from the same author, *Anfänge der Scholastik.*[5]

Most respectfully I remain your most devoted
Dietrich Bonhoeffer.

[1.] *NL* Walter Dreß; handwritten card, dated July 8, 1926. Property of Andreas and Heidi Dreß, Bielefeld, Germany. Recipient was Mrs. Margarethe Dreß, née Voigt, Walter Dreß's mother. First publication *Zeitschrift für Neuere Theologiegeschichte / Journal for the History of Modern Theology* 4 (1997): 274ff. Transcribed by Eberhard Bethge. Also published in *DBW* 17:25–25, on which this translation is based.

[2.] This letter is in answer to a question about a fitting present for the young theologian Walter Dreß. It is not known if a special occasion initiated the query.

[3.] Since his first visit to Rome, Dietrich Bonhoeffer loved the texts of the Roman Missal. Cf. below, page 166.

[4.] The correct titles are Dilthey, *Weltanschauung und Analyse des Menschen seit Renaissance und Reformation* and Overbeck, *Über die Christlichkeit unserer heutigen Theologie.* [Bonhoeffer was later to study Dilthey and Overbeck in his lectures on "Die Geschichte der systematischen Theologie des 20. Jahrhunderts," given in the winter semester 1931–32, cf. *DBW* 11 (2/3):139ff., and to read the Dilthey volume during his time in prison, *DB-ER*, 855 and 944.] [PDM]

[5.] The list of books in this letter, especially Hauck's *Kirchengeschichte*, reflects Walter Dreß's initial, but not yet fully developed interest in church history. Moreover, the titles listed were of interest to both theologians.

97d. Paula Bonhoeffer to Walter and Ilse Dreß[1]

Grunewald

Professor and Mrs. Bonhoeffer request the honor of Mr. Dreß and Miss Dreß's[2] presence on Sunday the 11th of July for supper in the garden at 7 o'clock.

Tel. Pfbg 26 16

97e. To Walter Dreß[1]

Dear Walter Dreß:

I'm sorry to tell you and your sister that we have to cancel tomorrow's event.[2] My young nephew,[3] who has been visiting us for the past few days, is sick, and my Father is not well. Would it be possible to reschedule for the 25th of this month at the same time?

Best wishes!
Dietrich Bonhoeffer

[1.] *NL* Walter Dreß; property of Andreas and Heidi Dreß, Bielefeld, Germany. Undated handwritten postcard, written by Mrs. Paula Bonhoeffer. Postmarked Berlin-Charlottenburg, 7-8-26. Addressed to Mr. and Miss Dreß, Lichterfelde, Zehlendorferstr. 12. First published in *Zeitschrift für Neuere Theologiegeschichte / Journal for the History of Modern Theology* 4 (1997): 275. Transcribed by Eberhard Bethge. Also published in *DBW* 17:27, on which this translation is based.

[2.] Ilse Dreß, Walter Dreß's sister.

[1.] *NL* Walter Dreß; property of Andreas and Heidi Dreß, Bielefeld, Germany. Undated handwritten postcard postmarked Berlin-Lichterfelde 7-10-26, and stamped "express mail." Address: To Mr. Walter Dreß, Senior Theology Student, Lichterfelde West, Zehlendorferstr. 12. First publication: *Zeitschrift für Neuere Theologiegeschichte / Journal for the History of Modern Theology* 4 (1997): 275. Transcribed by Eberhard Bethge. Also published in *DBW* 17:27, on which this translation is based.

[2.] Cf. above, 1/97d, postcard dated July 8, 1926.

[3.] Hans Walter Schleicher.

17:28   **97f. To Walter Dreß**[1]

Dear Walter,

Having fled from Heussi and Sellin[2] in a state of great unhappiness, I dispatch my longing thoughts to your desk, on which I imagine seeing both heavy tomes resplendently displayed and open.[3] Otherwise it isn't bad here, although it is snowing today.

Warmly yours,
Dietrich B.

Cordial greetings, Hans Christoph v. Hase.[4]

167   **98. To Susanne Bonhoeffer**[1]

Dear Suse,

This afternoon my visit here will be over. Early this morning we were still able to take a nice steamboat ride. Thus far we've encountered lemon trees, forests of olive trees, and cypresses that circle the sea, which was often as blue as the beautiful evening sky and as clear as glass. You were able to see the fish and sea flora that were far beneath the surface. Yesterday evening we went sailing in beautiful stormy weather. The whole sea bore little crests of foam and tossed the ship around quite a bit. Give my love to Mother and Father. Best wishes.

Yours,
Dietrich

[1.] *NL* Walter Dreß; property of Andreas and Heidi Dreß, Bielefeld, Germany. Undated handwritten picture postcard of Compitello in the Dolomites and the northern Fassa valley, with the Langkofel group of mountains in the background. Postmarked Trento, August 3, 1926. Addressed to Mr. Walter Dreß, Senior Theology Student, Berlin-Lichterfelde, Zehlendorferstr. 10 or 12. First publication: *Zeitschrift für Neuere Theologiegeschichte / Journal for the History of Modern Theology* 4 (1997):276. Transcribed by Eberhard Bethge. Also published in *DBW* 17:28, on which this translation is based.

[2.] Bonhoeffer used Heussi, *Kompendium der Kirchengeschichte*, and Sellin, *Einleitung in das Alte Testament (Introduction to the Old Testament)* to prepare for the first theological exams.

[3.] The sentence is meant to be taken ironically.

[4.] This line is written in the hand of Hans Christoph von Hase, Bonhoeffer's cousin.

[1.] *NL* A 9/1(12); undated handwritten picture postcard of the Gardasee showing Malcesine, with a view of the northwest. Postmarked August 19, 1926. Bonhoeffer traveled with Karl-Friedrich Bonhoeffer and Robert Held to the Gardasee, the Dolomites, and Venice.

99. From Paula Bonhoeffer[1]

August 26, 1926

Dear Dietrich,

By now you will be in Berlin again, and your fine trip will seem to have taken place long ago. I find that it always goes by so fast, sadly! I was always so happy to receive your good news. Yet one thing made me uncomfortable: you never gave me an address where you could have been reached in the event that it would have been necessary to do so. Once again I am sitting here in the wind and the rain in a wicker-basket beach chair. You will see the spots on the piece of paper. The weather is so fickle that in a quarter of an hour the sun could be shining again. The wind always blows in from the west and whips up the waves beautifully. Susi and Papa are also enjoying it very much.

Today, Rudi and his wife[2] left. We actually liked her quite a lot, but she is definitely   168
too old for him. We intend to leave here on Saturday the 4th, spend the night in Hamburg,[3] and travel on to Berlin on Sunday with the express train.

Susi wants to be there for the children's worship service. She will leave on Saturday and travel all the way through without stopping so she can be at the train station at 11 o'clock. Do you think this is necessary?

I really hope that she has had a nice time here. Apparently Papa is very comfortable here.

How is your tennis game progressing? Could you reserve the courts for me twice in September? I thought that Susi, you, Hanna Cauer,[4] and perhaps the man who wrote to you could play.

The wind is blowing so strongly that one can hardly write. Therefore I will end my letter and send greetings to everyone!

Yours,
Mother

[1.] *NL* C 1(9); handwritten letter dated "den 26.8.26" mailed from Kampen on Sylt Island, where his parents were spending their summer vacation with Susanne.

[2.] Married couple, Rudi Hirtle and his wife. During his early school years, Rudi, together with the Bonhoeffer sons, received his education from Paula Bonhoeffer.

[3.] At that time Hamburg was the home of Christine and Hans von Dohnanyi.

[4.] A distant relative; she became a painter and sculptor.

99a. To Walter Dreß[1]

Dear Walter,

I had already supposed that your paper wouldn't let you go.[2] But nothing is gained by stringing it out too long. That is why term-paper deadlines are so helpful. Moreover one runs the risk of robbing the paper of its internal cohesiveness. So finish it up.

The size of my Roman Missal[3] is 17 x 26 cm, and it costs 38 marks, if one were to get it here. In that case, it is worth your while to order it. So get 75 lire soon so that we can get moving.

17:29   Will you also be at Diestel's[4] on Wednesday the 20th? I won't be there, since I am planning to take my paper[5] with me when I go to the Harz Mountains with my parents from Sunday until Thursday. Please stop by before then!

What was embarrassing about Ruber's sermon?[6]

Do you know anything about Greßman's seminar? I naturally would like to be enrolled in the course in which one has to do the least and can be absent the most. When you can, please find out about it for me.

As far as I know, one doesn't learn anything about the grade one received on one's licentiate paper before the examination. However, Stolzenburg[7] is always a good source.

I'm almost through with Budde-Hollenberg.[8]

It's very difficult for me to actually begin writing my paper, and I always cross out whatever I've written.—So, phone me soon!

Best wishes.
Yours,
Dietrich B.

[1.] *NL* Walter Dreß; property of Andreas and Heidi Dreß, Bielefeld, Germany. Undated handwritten postcard postmarked Berlin–Grunewald, October 12, 1926. Addressed to Mr. Walter Dreß, Senior Theology Student, Berlin-Lichterfelde-West, Zehlendorferstr. 12. First published in *Zeitschrift für Neuere Theologiegeschichte / Journal for the History of Modern Theology*4 (1997): 276ff. Transcribed by Eberhard Bethge. Also published in DBW 17:28, on which this translation is based.

[2.] In the fall of 1926 Walter Dreß wrote his dissertation, *Die Mystik des Marsilio Ficino.*

[3.] Cf. above, 1/97c:162 , letter to Margarethe Dreß.

[4.] Superintendent Max Diestel was a member of the examination committee and occasionally invited examination candidates to his home for an evening of discussion. See below, page 178, editorial note 1.

[5.] This refers to Bonhoeffer's doctoral dissertation *Sanctorum Communio.*

[6.] Nothing is known either about the person or the incident.

[7.] Hugo Greßman and Arnold Stolzenberg were members of the Theological Faculty of Berlin University.

[8.] Hollenberg-Budde, *Hebräisches Schulbuch.*

99b. To Walter Dreß[1]   17:49

Dear Walter,

Here is what I know:[2]

1. Cyril's 23 catechetical lessons[3] for the φωτιζόμενοι (competentes)[4]
    and for the νεοφώτιστοι [νεόφυτοι] (catec[heses].)
    mystagogicae[5]
    Following this *probably* (?) the division into the mature
    catechetical students and the "neophyte" catechetical students (?).[6]
2. Form for blessing or consecration: "Take the Holy Spirit, the refuge and
    protection against everything that is evil . . . (a few words are missing
    here) from the merciful hand of God, the Father, the Son, and the Holy
    Spirit."
    (Spener:[7] "Bring head and heart with you")
    confirmandi through the local church, not confirmantes.[8]
    Bucer's 1539 Church Order from Cassel![9]
    I missed the classes on ordination and on education in the Middle Ages.
3. For Sellin: Isaiah 26, Daniel 12. Resurrection.
    Psalms 16, 46, 73 including immortality.

[1.] *NL* Walter Dreß; property of Andreas and Heidi Dreß, Bielefeld, Germany. Undated handwritten postcard postmarked Berlin-Wilmersdorf January 28, 1927, Addressed to Mr. Walter Dreß, Senior Theology. First published in *Zeitschrift für Neuere Theologiegeschichte / Journal for the History of Modern Theology* 4 (1997): 277ff. Transcribed by Eberhard Bethge. Also published in DBW 17:49–50, on which this translation is based.

[2.] In the following Dietrich Bonhoeffer gives advice for preparing for the theological exams. Points (1) and (2) refer to Prof. Mahling's lectures on practical theology. See above, 1/94a:152, postcard of February 8, 1926.

[3.] Cyril of Jerusalem, *Catecheses*. [The introductory discourse, or Procatechesis, outlines the significance of the rite of initiation into Christian community. This is followed by eighteen catechetical discourses (i–xviii) for use during Lent by the *competentes*, those who have completed a first stage of preparation and now are officially seeking baptism; these are preparatory teachings for those not yet admitted into the full community of the church. Then come five "Catecheses Mystagogic" (xix–xxiii), which were used during Easter week to further teach those who have just been baptized; they are for the initiated, and are intended to lift the veil of secrecy more completely.] [WF]

[4.] Greek: "The enlightened ones." [These are the *competentes*, those competent to seek baptism.] [WF]

[5.] Greek: "The newly enlightened (reborn) mystagogical catechists." [These persons have been baptized at the Easter Vigil and now can be taught fully the mysteries of the faith.] [WF] Note: The parentheses and square brackets above are reproduced as they appear in Bonhoeffer's letter.

[6.] Both question marks are from Bonhoeffer.

[7.] Philipp Jakob Spener, leading exponent and author of Lutheran pietism.

[8.] *Confirmandi* refers to the confirmands, those who are confirmed, and *confirmantes* to those who confirm them.

[9.] On Martin Bucer and the church order of Kassel see above, 1/94a:152.

Job no resurrection! Read the portion on Job in Sellin's *Introduction*[10] thoroughly! Hosea 6:6; 1 Samuel 15:22; Micah 6:8.

17:50　　　Prehistory of the Israelites. Genesis 14!

4. For Seeberg:[11] overview of modern history of dogmatics, according to the table of contents. (Biedermann, Thomasius, Frank, *v. Hofmann*).[12] stranger foreigner.

Do you know the difference between גֵּר and נָכְרִי?

If I think of anything else, I'll write to you.

ὀλιγόντε φιλόντε,[13]

Yours,

Dietrich

Sellin: Patriarchs and Prophets. Basic history.

99c. To Walter Dreß[1]

Dear Walter,

How far have your plans to go to Bockswiese[2] progressed? I'm making the following suggestion on the advice of my parents. We could go to our house in Friedrichsbrunn where we could get more rest and be able to divide our time up etc. as we please. I would take my paper with me.[3] If you're sure all the peace and quiet wouldn't bore you, it would be very nice if you would come with me. The only thing that you would need to bring would be sheets and pillowcases, because we can't get at ours very easily.

[10.] On Ernst Sellin see his *Introduction to the Old Testament*. Cf. above, 1/97:158f.

[11.] On Reinhold Seeberg see above, 1/90:146, editorial note 3.

[12.] Hans Biedermann, Gottfried Thomasius, Hermann Reinhold von Frank, and Johann Christian Konrad von Hofmann all were representatives of the Erlangen School to which Reinhold Seeberg also was connected.

[13.] "Short and good."

[1.] *NL* Walter Dreß; property of Andreas and Heidi Dreß, Bielefeld, Germany. Undated handwritten postcard postmarked Berlin–Wilmersdorf, March 17, 1927, and stamped "express mail." Addressed to Mr. Lic. Walter Dreß, Lichterfelde-West, Zehlendorferstr. 12. At the top of the card are notes made in pencil with two train connections: "6:55 Halberstadt 10:14 Thale 11:33" and alternative connections: "[6:55] Magdeburg 9: 24/32 Suderode 11:31 Quedinburg 11:31." At the bottom of the card is written: "Calvin NT." First published in *Zeitschrift für Neuere Theologiegeschichte / Journal for the History of Modern Theology* 4 (1997): 278. Transcribed by Eberhard Bethge. Also published in *DBW* 17:50–51, on which this translation is based.

[2.] Cf. above, 1/89a: 144, editorial note 1, the postcard of May 19, 1925. Walter Dreß obviously planned to take a vacation there.

[3.] The manuscript of Bonhoeffer's dissertation.

I tried without success to reach you. Today at 9 A.M. no one was there. Please, if at all possible, give me your answer *by calling me direct.* My parents 15:51 are leaving tomorrow and might have to put a few things in order.

My best,
Dietrich

100. To His Parents[1]

March 22, 1927

Dear Parents,

Today at noon the temperature was reminiscent of the temperatures in Rome. It is very remarkable that at certain times the temperature can carry a particular fragrance with it. Endless memories associated with the warmer climate suddenly arise. I hope that you will not be pestered in this manner by memories of Berlin while you are in Rome. Beginning tomorrow evening, I can actually follow your journey fairly accurately from a distance. The night trip through Italy will (hopefully!) be less romantic for you than it was for us. However, during the time you are in Rome, hardly a day will pass when I will 169 not also stroll on the streets to St. Peter's and St. Paolo, take a ride on the Appian Way or a walk through the Forum on the Palatine. I can still do it so well. It is as if I had done it just a few weeks ago.

Everything is going well here. Karl-Friedrich has received an invitation for this evening, as have the Schleichers. Grandmama is listening to the radio with little Hans.[2] Klaus has gone for a walk with Justus. Lilo,[3] who was recently at a revue with Karl-Friedrich, Klaus, and the Delbrücks, is out most of the time. Grandmama is comfortably at home again. She is very cheerful and in a good mood. Most evenings she is either entertained by the radio or by someone reading aloud to her. She is very grateful for your suggestion to use your room, dear Mama, when it gets too loud for her in her room. I believe, though, that she will hardly make use of it. Lilo likes to be here. She is always content and amiable. Yesterday was a hard day for Klaus, and tomorrow will be another one.

By the way, I offered to let Mr. Rößler[4] stay at Friedrichsbrunn for a few (5) days. He is the theology student with whom I played tennis in the summer. He was at the Delbrücks' fairly often. He has now completed his theological examination and wanted very much to take a short vacation with me.

[1.] *NL* A 9/1 (9); handwritten letter dated "den 22.3.27" mailed from Berlin-Grunewald.
[2.] Hans Christoph von Hase.
[3.] Lilo Anschütz.
[4.] Helmuth Rößler.

He definitely wants to bring his own things, especially since he discovered that Dreß[5] had already been invited. I hope that this will be all right with you. Nothing will be more complicated because of it. Either we'll need to sleep on the sofa or put another bed in the room. If we move a bed we will definitely move it back. Hopefully, you, dear Mama, will not worry unnecessarily about it. If you were going to, it would have been foolish of me to make the arrangements that I have. I want to end the letter. It is 11:30. I sincerely wish you a truly beautiful time in Rome.

Gratefully yours,
Dietrich

I'll send you the letter to the famigliara del papa.[6] As you know, you will need it only when you return.

101. From Susanne Bonhoeffer[1]

Heidelberg, March 24, 1927

Dear Dietrich,

I only want to tell you quickly that you really don't need to worry about the Easter hike with Max and Jörg.[2] I am going to go to Geneva for a month. Mama just wrote me from Rome that I had been invited to go there for April and May. I will, however, be there only from April 12 until May 12. I don't want to miss the whole spring in Berlin, and they all speak French there. That is still a very nice amount of time. The Forrels[3] speak German well, but they always speak French with each other. Three children, ages 13, 9, and 7, are also at home. Only the oldest speaks a little German. So, I can learn a great deal of French.

Yesterday I arrived here from Munich. Lola[4] is really very nice and touchingly attentive to Lothar.[5] He got on my nerves a bit with his incessant talk about drops of blood, the battle for souls, divine will, and similar things. But he is a touchingly concerned cousin. When he saw that it was pointless, he gave up trying to convert me. In return,

---

[5.] Walter Dreß, married to Susanne Bonhoeffer.

[6.] The identity of this person is not known; perhaps he meant the *famiglia pontificia*, who is responsible for the audiences in the Vatican, among other things.

[1.] *NL* C 7/1: handwritten. The original letter dated "den 24.3.27" remains in the possession of Susanne Dreß. Susanne Bonhoeffer was visiting the Anschütz family in Heidelberg at this time.

[2.] Max Delbrück and Jörg Schleicher.

[3.] Dr. Forel, a psychiatrist and director of the sanatorium La Materie near Nyon.

[4.] Lola Bonhoeffer.

[5.] Lothar Bonhoeffer.

he wanted to. But he is a touchingly concerned cousin. When he saw that it was point-less, he gave up trying to convert me. In return, he wanted to know what my philoso-phy of life was, as well as that of my siblings'. Other than that, I enjoyed Munich very much. By the way, one can buy roasted chestnuts on every street corner in Munich. They are absurdly inexpensive. If you had written me and told me whether you really had gone up to the cottage, I would have sent you a 10-pound bag.

Hans-Christoph just wrote me that he really doesn't want to take a trip with Max.   171
I was not aware that they didn't like each other. He said that Max and Anneliese[6] expected too much. I think that it is strange, especially in Anneliese's case. Could his parents be against it because they are anti-Semitic? Now, however, it's over. Hans-Christoph is angry because you did not go hiking with him and Dreier. When will you actually hand in your thesis?[7] I will certainly be there again in the middle of May.

Until then, best wishes.
Yours,
Suse

102. To Karl Bonhoeffer[1]

Friedrichsbrunn, March 26, 1927

Dear Papa,

Although you are probably taking a walk under flowering trees and through the most magnificent flower gardens on your birthday,[2] may the snowdrops, liverwort, anemone, and daphnes (I believe at least that there are some) bring you springtime greetings from here in Friedrichsbrunn. Spring is already marching headlong into the birch groves near Treseburg and along Bergratmüller's pond. You probably have never celebrated your birth-day in as summerlike a manner as you are today. I hope this is the case, at any rate. I can't imagine that it is very difficult to celebrate a birthday in Rome. In the morning and in the evening I would be on the Pinceo. At noon, I would be in St. Peter's and the Vatican. Finally I would sit in a nice trattoria Trevi Fountain and drink Est Est Est.[3]

So, I wish you a happy birthday, especially since you are in Rome on this day. I believe that one could never forget such a birthday. And my greatest wish is, first, that everything you encounter is as beautiful as it can be. I also   172

[6.] Anneliese Schnurmann (see *DB-ER* 229–31).

[7.] This refers to Bonhoeffer's dissertation *Sanctorum Communio*.

[1.] *NL* Appendix A 9; handwritten. The original letter dated "den 26.3.27" remains in possession of Susanne Dreß.

[2.] March 31, 1868.

[3.] For the background of this Roman drinking toast, see above, 1/68:120, editorial note 2.

wish that from now on you won't see another cloud in the sky, never feel a drop of rain, see as many beautiful things as possible, soak up so many new impressions that you can feast on them for a long time. Finally, I hope that you come home after Easter very refreshed and can only think of the time you'll be able to travel back again.

In spite of our unexpected arrival, we found everything up here in perfect order. There was one thing, to be sure, that was strange. Is it true that you gave orders to take down the table and the stairs to the veranda in the winter so that they don't rot? I don't quite believe it. Both are missing. If it is a lie, it would be a pretty big effrontery to rip out the stairway from the house. In addition, our neighbor Steffen has asked if we could cut down the firs at the entrance drive and plant little ones. He doesn't get any light in the rooms on his first floor and has to turn on his lights during the day. I have no doubt that we should grant his request. Besides, little firs that would cover up the ugly garden fence would also be prettier. Would you please write and send me information on both of these things?—We will be in Berlin beginning on Saturday.

Our housekeeping is going along fairly well. Although it doesn't keep us from taking walks, it does keep us from doing our work. Moreover, it is so very beautiful here that I don't really know if I would rather be in Italy. The weather is tolerable yet changeable. Other than a fairly stormy wind, everything is so quiet that we are both enthralled. My best wishes to Mama and to you.

Gratefully yours,
Dietrich

Highly esteemed Mr. Privy Councilor,[4]

From the wonderful springtime air of the forests of Friedrichsbrunn, I take the liberty to send you best wishes on your birthday. With the entreaty to be commended to your highly esteemed wife, I remain your gratefully devoted

Walter Dreß

[4.] Handwritten by Walter Dreß on the same paper as the previous letter of Bonhoeffer.

102a. To Walter Dreß[1]

Dear Walter,

Since I have tried several times to reach you without success by telephone and assume that it will be just as futile this noon, I want with this card to thank you very much for your invitation. We[2] would love to come—that is, unless something unforeseen interferes, but I'll tell you about that when I see you. Please tell your mother that we thank her from our hearts, and that we send her our devoted respects.

Cordially yours
Dietrich

102b. To Walter Dreß[1]

Dear Walter,

Can you tell me where I can find Luther's statement to the people of Wittenberg: "The summons of death comes to us all, and no one can die for another,"[2] etc.? Did Holl[3] quote it? I would be very grateful if you could tell me for sure by tomorrow.

In addition, can one speak of the reality of reconciliation in Christ in con-   17:52
trast to its actualization through the Holy Spirit? In any case isn't reconciliation through Christ potential!?[4] Please think about it.

Thanks and greetings
Dictrich.

[1.] *NL* Walter Dreß; property of Andreas and Heidi Dreß, Bielefeld, Germany. Undated handwritten postcard offering an aerial view of the Charlottenburg Palace in Berlin. Postmarked Berlin–Grunewald June 11, 1927. Addressed to Mr. Lic. Dreß, Lichterfelde-West, Zehlendorferstr. 12. First published in *Zeitschrift für Neuere Theologiegeschichte / Journal for the History of Modern Theology* 4 (1997): 279. Transcribed by Eberhard Bethge. Also published in *DBW* 17:51, on which this translation is based.

[2.] Probably refers to Dietrich Bonhoeffer and his sister Susanne.

[1.] *NL* Walter Dreß; property of Andreas and Heidi Dreß, Bielefeld, Germany. Handwritten postcard postmarked Berlin-Charlottenburg, June 16, 1927. Addressed to Mr. Lic. Dreß, Lichterfelde-West, Zehlendorferstr. 12. First published in *Zeitschrift für Neuere Theologiegeschichte / Journal for the History of Modern Theology* 4 (1997): 279. Transcribed by Eberhard Bethge. Also published in *DBW* 17:51–52, on which this translation is based.

[2.] The Luther quotation is from "The First Sermon: Invocavit Sunday," March 9, 1522 (*WA* 10:3 [*LW* 51:70]); Bonhoeffer quotes this passage in *Sanctorum Communio* and again in *Life Together*.

[3.] On Karl Holl, cf. above, page 148, editorial note 2.

[4.] Cf. Bonhoeffer's dissertation, *Sanctorum Communio*, concerning the theological problems discussed here (*SC* [*DBWE* 1]:145–61).

E. Graduation with a Doctoral Degree and First Theological Examinations. July 1927–January 1928

103. To the Theological Faculty[1]

I request of the highly esteemed theological faculty of Berlin to be admitted to the Licentiate Doctoral Examinations. I do so by submitting my doctoral dissertation entitled *Sanctorum Communio: eine dogmatsche Untersuchung* and my documents.

I request to be examined by the gentlemen Privy councilor R. Seeberg
Privy councilor Deissmann
Privy councilor Mahling
Privy councilor Sellin
Professor Lietzmann[2]

Dietrich Bonhoeffer

The dissertation and final school report were returned.[3]

[1.] *NL* A 17/4; July 1927; typed transcript from the files of the Friedrich-Wilhelm University of Berlin concerning graduations. Located in the archive of the Humboldt University of Berlin, Berlin 1927–29, Part 1, volume 11, 42a. Transcript provided by Christfried Berger.

[2.] Adolf Deißmann was for many years the Chair of the German Section of the World Alliance for Promoting International Friendship through the Churches. Bonhoeffer was to become its Youth Secretary in 1931 (see *DB-ER* 72 and 190–93). The other examiners were Reinhold Seeberg, Friedrich Mahling, Ernst Sellin, and Hans Lietzmann.

[3.] Handwritten postscript by Bonhoeffer.

104. Curriculum Vitae[1]

I, Dietrich Bonhoeffer, was born on February 4, 1906, in Breslau as the son of University Professor of Psychiatry Karl Bonhoeffer and his wife, Paula, née von Hase. Due to my father's appointment we moved to Berlin in March 1912. I attended the Friedrich Werder'sche Gymnasium from Michaelmas 1913 until Easter 1919. Subsequent to transferring to the Grunewald Gymnasium, I passed the Abitur examinations there in Easter 1923. I studied Protestant theology in Tübingen for my first two semesters. I attended the University of Berlin[2] from the summer semester of 1924 until the summer semester of 1927. Throughout this time, I attended the church history seminar of Prof. von Harnack for three semesters, the church history seminar of Prof. Holl for two semesters, the New Testament seminar of Dr. Bertram and Prof. Deissmann for two semesters, the homiletics seminar of Prof. Mahling once, the catechetical seminar of Prof. Mahling twice, the Old Testament seminar of Prof. Sellin for one semester, the introductory seminar of Prof. Seeberg once, and the systematic theology seminar of Prof. Seeberg regularly since the summer of 1925.

105. Reinhold Seeberg's Evaluation of Bonhoeffer's Dissertation[1]

Dietrich Bonhoeffer, *"Sanctorum Communio: Eine dogmatische Untersuchung."* 354 pp.

The intention of this work is to study from every perspective the internal coherence of the concept of the church on the basis of recent sociological research. The very detailed table of contents informs one sufficiently about the content of the work. A reproduction of the particulars is therefore superfluous.

From beginning to end the arrangement is in accordance with its purpose. First, the author treats recent methods of the sociological sciences. In doing so he arrives at clear results: social philosophy concerns itself with the sociality of the human spirit. Sociology is the science of the structure of human communities. Now, however, because *Christianity* presupposes a particular *concept of personhood*, this is first investigated by means of an ongoing interchange with idealism, examined for its sociological usefulness.—On the basis of the presuppositions gained, the author then addresses the problem of sociology in the *understanding* [Verstand]. That means he concerns himself with the nature of human community, grounded upon the human essence of personality and society (vis-à-vis a community based upon the will). In the end he proposes a typology of

---

[1.] *NL* A 17/4; July 1927; typed copy from the doctoral graduation files (see above, 1/103:174, editorial note 1). Part 1, volume 11, 42b. Copied by Christfried Berger.

[2.] On the following see below, pages 584ff.

[1.] *NL* A 17/4; July 1927; copy from the University doctoral graduation files, Part 1, volume 11, pages 42e (front and back) and 42f (front and back). Transcription by Ilse Tödt and C.-J. Kaltenborn. Cf. above, 1/103:174, editorial note 1.

human communities (community as a system of intellect, society as a rational system of purpose; added to that—according to the varying degrees of volitional strength—the formation of authority, as well as the volitional support of the masses; objective spirit).—The relationship in-itself of wills existing in community and society is, however, undermined by the egoism of the *state of sin*, as demonstrated in detail.—Further, it is concerned with the *church* as the *sanctorum communio*, which restores the community established in human personality and sociality and realizes itself in opposition to the corruption caused by everyone's sinful egotism. In this part, which encompasses more than half of the work, exhaustive investigations into the nature of the church are undertaken. It examines the church's relationship to Christ and to the Holy Spirit and the specific form of the Christian community. The author seeks to discover the latter in a thorough elevation of the concept of community and society as a love-based community of the Holy Spirit. The results attained are then examined in terms of the empirical form of the church with its objective spirit, in relationship to the Holy Spirit, universal priesthood and office, word and sacrament, cult, social problems, and eschatology, among others.

The author is not only well oriented in the theological field but also thoroughly acquainted with sociology. He is decidedly gifted in systematic thinking, as demonstrated by the dialectic in the structure of his work both in general and in particular. He seeks to discover his way on his own. He is always prepared for intelligent discussion of other opinions. Even if one does not share his opinions, one will readily acknowledge the scientific interest and the energy of the argumentation. Characteristic of the position of the author is his strong emphasis on the principles of Christian ethics, which always serve as the starting point. From here he struggles in various ways against the worldview of "idealism." The strong skepticism reminds one of Heim. Here and there one finds allusions to Barth, as the terminology (call [an-rufen], answer [ant-worten]) demonstrates. Yet these influences are neutralized by others and do not determine the author's thought formation. The presentation as a whole is very intelligent, even if the too strict systematic[2] approach carries with it occasional repetitions. The dialectical arguments of the author are not always convincing. So perhaps is the odd argument that an "I" can arrive at knowledge of a "You" only through a detour by way of God. Accordingly I do not wish to subscribe to everything that the author deduces dialectically concerning the structure of the empirical church, e.g., whether the category of "society" really forms a necessary extension of the category of "community" within the church. For the rest, it is exactly in this context that these splendid observations are pronounced. The author could have left out the historical "excursus," pages 112ff.,[3] because it brings forth nothing new. So also the critical comments concerning church praxis or the joyous hope in reference to the proletariat as well as the low estimation of the middle class are superfluous, because they do not follow from the principles of the work but involve only subjective value judgments. Finally one cannot always agree with the author's criticism of others (e.g., Troeltsch!).

[2.] The German word for occasionally, "bisweilen," is struck out here.
[3.] See *SC* (*DBWE* 1):96–97.

Nonetheless, all of these insufficiencies are common in every youthful work. They are only the converse of the many good qualities of the work: its enthusiasm for Christianity, the precise systematics in the method of the entire study, the inner concentration on his task, the ingenious particularity of his view, and his critical ability to cope with other views. On the whole, the work can be characterized as a very satisfactory model of serious[4] academic erudition.

Consequently I *move* that the honorable faculty *accept* this as licentiate work, and suggest as its evaluation the *grade* I/II.

R. Seeberg.

Agreed.

	Sellin 7/20.	von Harnack 7/19.
"	Mahling 7/21.	Richter 7/7.
"	Ltz 7/24.	Schwartz 7/28.
"	D 7/25	7/29 Mi.
"	E. Seeberg 7/27	St. 7/28[5]

17:52

105a. To Walter Dreß[1]

Dear Walter,

Thank you so much for taking care of it. It's good that T.[2] didn't write directly to the consistory. I haven't turned anything in yet.[3] I arrived here by ship via Helgoland after taking breaks in Düsseldorf, Cologne, Elberfeld, and Bremen.[4] The weather turned horrible today.

With great respect.
Your servant,[5]
Dietrich Bonhoeffer

[4.] Difficult to decipher in the original manuscript; perhaps it is "first."

[5.] The following abbreviations refer to certain professors. Ltz refers to Lietzmann, D to Deißmann, Mi to Wilhelm Michaelis, and St to Arnold Stolzenberg. The other professors who signed Reinhold Seeburg's letter of approval for Bonhoeffer's dissertation were Erich Seeberg, Julius Richter, and apparently Paul Schwartz.

[1.] *NL* Walter Dreß; property of Andreas and Heidi Dreß, Bielefeld, Germany. Undated handwritten postcard showing a photo of a "group of villagers from List," on the island of Sylt. Postmarked Kampen Sylt, August 9, 1927, 20–21. Addressed to Mr. Lic. Dreß, Lichterfelde-West, Zehlendorferstr. 12. First published in *Zeitschrift für Neuere Theologiegeschichte / Journal for the History of Modern Theology* 4 (1997):280. Transcribed by Eberhard Bethge. Also published in *DBW* 17:52, on which this translation is based.

[2.] Unknown.

[3.] Refers to the application to take the First Theological Exams (see below, 1/106:178).

[4.] This may refer to a visit with his parents, who were vacationing with Bonhoeffer's sister, Susanne, in Kampen (see above, 1/98:164).

[5.] This exaggeratedly polite salutation is obviously meant to be taken ironically.

177   **106. Formal Request to be Admitted to the First Theological Examination**[1]

Berlin-Grunewald, September 13, 1927

Wangenheimstr. 14

Re: Petition to be admitted to the first
    theological examination
    I petition the Evangelical Church Council of Mark Brandenburg to be
admitted to the first examination on the basis of the appended documents.
    At the same time I request to be allowed to submit a work with the title
"*Sanctorum Communio: eine dogmatische Untersuchung*," which I have completed
and which has already been submitted to the Theological Faculty of the University of Berlin and has been accepted by them as a Licentiate thesis instead
of the academic examination.

Dietrich Bonhoeffer

To the
Evangelical Church Council
of Mark Brandenburg, Berlin Section,
Berlin, S.W. 68
via the Superintendent
of Berlin-Lichterfelde

178   **107. List of Documents Appended to the Petition**[1]

Summary
of the documents appended to the petition of September 13, 1927.

1. Curriculum Vitae
2. Baptismal certificate
3. Certificate of Confirmation
4. Matriculation certificate from the University of Berlin
5. Certificate attesting to attendance at the lectures on church music

---

[1.] *NL* D 11(3); typed, dated "den 3.9.1927," Bonhoeffer's personal file at the Protestant Church Council of the Province Brandenburg, no. 3. Under the sender is an entry:
"*4631/8 enclosure+.*" On the border is written, "*birth certificate absent: final report card see enclo-
sure. + -7/1 Ang. bes.*" [*Ang. bes.* probably means "Angestellter bestellt" or "sent for by an official."] [PDM] Above the address is the stamp of the date of entry: "Office of the
Superintendent, First District of the Diocese of Kölln, 9/13 1927, record book no. *2235;
Diestel.*" Handwritten entries are cursive. Max Diestel was superintendent of the Diocese of
Cologne I, to which the Grunewald parish belonged.

[1.] *NL* D 11(4); typed. Personal file, number 4 (see above on this page, editorial note 1).

6. Certificate attesting to participation in the life of the church and worship and attesting to participation in the children's worship service.

7. Certificate from the Theological Faculty of Berlin attesting to their acceptance of the licentiate work that was submitted.

The last report card from school is at this time among the papers that I submitted to the Theological Faculty of Berlin in order to be awarded the licentiate degree.

108. Curriculum Vitae[1]

I, Dietrich Bonhoeffer, was born on Febraury 4, 1906, in Breslau as the son of the Venerable Tenured Professor of Psychiatry at the University of Breslau, Karl Bonhoeffer, and his wife, Paula, née von Hase. We moved to Berlin at Easter 1912 because my father was called to the local university. I attended the Friedrich-Werder Gymnasium from the fall of 1913 until Easter 1919. From Easter 1919 on, I attended the Grunewald Gymnasium. There I passed the final examinations, including Hebrew. I went to Tübingen to study Protestant Theology for my first and second semester. I studied in Berlin from my third semester on, and in my 6th semester, following a quarter year of special studies in Rome, I began my licentiate work on the topic of the *sanctorum communio* as a dogmatic and sociological problem under Mr. Privy Councillor Seeberg. I finished this paper in July 1927 and submitted it to the Theological Faculty of Berlin. It was accepted by them on August 1, 1927.

179

109. Certificate Attesting to Participation in the Life of the Church[1]

Herewith it is certified that theological candidate Mr. Dietrich Bonhoeffer, from Berlin-Grunewald, has taken part in the worship life of our congregation including the celebration of the Holy Eucharist. In addition he served as an assistant in the children's worship service with constant faithfulness and devotion. He also temporarily stood in for the coordinator of the children's worship service.

Karl Meumann[2]
Pastor

[1.] *NL* D (11)5; handwritten. Without signature. Personal file, number 5 (see above, 1/106:178, editorial note 1).

[1.] *NL* D (11)8; typed personal file, number 8; cf. *DB-ER* 91–92 (and see above, 1/106:178, editorial note 1).

[2.] Karl Meumann was the Assistant Pastor to the Grunewald church; next to his signature is the stamp of the Grunewald parish.

110. To the Consistory[1]

Berlin-Grunewald, Wangenheimstr. 14

November 8, 1927

Herewith, I submit for the first theological examination a sermon on Luke 9:51-56 with a preceding meditation and disposition and a catechetical lesson on Matt. 8:5-13.

180   I certify that I completed both papers independently using the literature cited below. For the exegetical work on the texts I used commentaries of Hollzmann, Lietzmann (Matthew by Klostermann, Luke by Klostermann-Greßmann), Johannes Weiß, Theodor Zahn. In addition, for the catechetical lesson, I used Zündel, *Jesus*, Bultmann, *Jesus*, and a sermon by Luther on Matt. 8:1-13 (from *70 Predigten Luthers*, edited by von Planck—Calwer Verlagsverein).[2]

111. Karl Bonhoeffer to Reinhold Seeberg[1]

December 5, 1927

Most esteemed Mr. Seeberg,

My son Dietrich tells me that you would like a statement from me to the effect that I would pay for the publication of his licentiate thesis if it could not, for whatever reason, appear in your series. I gladly agree to this and want to use this opportunity at the conclusion of his period of study to thank you cordially for the sympathetic regard that you showed him. With best wishes, I remain your very devoted

Bonhoeffer

[1.] *NL* D 11(15); handwritten personal file, number 15 dated "den 8.XI.27"; see above, 1/106:178, editorial note 1. On September 27, 1927, Bonhoeffer received from Superintendent Diestal the biblical texts for the examination's sermon and catechetical lesson. He had six weeks to work on them. On the upper border on the right is the date of entry stamp of the consistory.

[2.] To the left under the text one finds this date-of-entry stamp: "Office of the Superintendent, First District of the Diocese of Kölln, November 8, 1927, entry no. 4741, Diestal." In the list of reference works used by Bonhoeffer for the sermon, "Hollzmann" probably refers to Heinrich J. Holtzmann, *Die Synoptiker. Die Apostelgeschichte*. The exact commentary he used by Hans Lietzmann is not known. In addition he used Erich Klostermann, *Das Matthäusevangelium*; Klostermann and Greßmann, "Das Lukasevangelium"; Johannes Weiß, "Das Lukas-Evangelium" and *Die Predigt Jesu vom Reiche Gottes*; Theodor Zahn, *Das Evangelium des Lucas*. And in preparing for the catechetical lesson, Bonhoeffer used Friedrich Zündel, *Jesus in Bildern aus seinem Leben*; Rudolf Bultmann, *Jesus*; and a sermon by Martin Luther on Matt. 8:1-13 from *Siebenzig Predigten*.

[1.] From the Federal Archive in Koblenz, literary archive of Reinhold Seeberg, item no. 60. The letter is handwritten and dated "5. Dezember 27." On the top right of the document is printed the number 31. It was mailed to the University in Berlin.

112. To the Consistory[1]

Berlin-Grunewald, Wangenheimstr. 14,[2] December 7, 1927

Concerning the first theological examinations.
Herewith, I submit to the Protestant Church Council of Mark Brandenburg, Berlin Section, the requested licentiate thesis and at the same time the certificate attesting to the positive outcome of the oral examination.

Dietrich Bonhoeffer

To the Protestant Church Council
of Mark Brandenburg, Berlin Section[3]

113. Doctoral Diploma[1]

QVOD FELIX FAVSTVMQVE SIT

VNIVERSITATIS LITTERARIAE FRIDERICAE
GVILELMAE

BEROLINENSIS

RECTORE MAGNIFICO

EDUARD NORDEN

THEOLOGIAE ET PHILOSOPHIAE DOCTORE IN HAC VNI-
VERSITATE PROFESSORE PVBLICO ORDINARIO A CONSI-
LIIS REGIMINIS INTIMIS INSTITVTI ANTIQVITATIS STVDIIS
COLENDIS DESTINATI DIRECTORE ACADEMIAE SCIEN-   182
TIATVM BORVSSICAE SOCIO ORDINARIO SOCIETATIS

[1.] *NL* D 11(31); handwritten and dated "den 7.XII.27"; personal file, number 31 (see above, 1/106:178, editorial note 1).
[2.] Above the sender one finds the date-of-entry stamp: "VII. Protestant Consistory, Berlin—9th Dec. 1927"; next to this is handwritten: "5764/1 File A – Vol. [licentiate thesis] Dibelius" [difficult to decipher in the original manuscript].
[3.] Difficult to decipher in the original manuscript: "H. Lecturer [. . .] the licentiate thesis is not in VII. VII 8/2." On the border is written "Berlin, February 13, 1928. The work is returned to the candidate after perusal on the basis of passing his exam. To the files. Coulon 13/2."

[1.] *NL* Appendix A 17/3; engraved diploma found in the archive of Humboldt University.

LITTERAIAE GOTTINGENSIS ET ACADEMIAE VINDOBO-
NENSIS SOCIO EPISTVLARI ORDINIS AQVILAE RVBRE IN
QVARTA CLASSE COMMENDATORE

EX DECRETO ORDINIS THEOLOGORVM SVMME VENE-
RANDI PROMOTOR LEGITIME CONSTITVTVS

IOHANNES LIETZMANN

SS. THEOLOGIAE DOCTOR ET IN HAC VNIVERSITATE
PROFESSOR PVBLICVS ORDINARIVS SEMINARIORVM AD
PROMOVENDVM HISTORIAE ECCLESIASTICAE NEC NON
ARTIS CHRISTIANAE STVDIVM INSTITVTORVM DIREC-
TOR ACADEMIAE SCIENTIARVM BORVSSICAE SOCIVS OR
DINARIVS SOCIETATIS LITTERARIAE GOTTINGENSIS SO-
CIVS EPISTVLARIS

ORDINIS THEOLOGORVM H.T.DECANVS

VIRO CLARISSIMO

D I E T R I C H B O N H O E F F E R
SILESIO

POSTQVAM DISSERTATIONEM LINGVA GERMANICA
SCRIPTAM CVIVUS TITVLVS EST

"SANCTORVM COMMVNIO, EINE DOGMATISCHE
UNTERSUCHUNG"

EXHIBVIT
EXAMEN RIGOROSVM SVMMA CVM LAVDE[2] SVSTINVIT ET
THESES PVBLICE DEFENDIT[3]

S.S. THEOLOGIAE LICENTIATI

HONORES ET PRIVILEGIA

183   DIE XVII.M. DECEMBRIS A. MCMXXVII

[2.] Of the 12 doctoral graduates of the year 1927 at the University of Berlin, Bonhoeffer was the only one to receive the distinction of summa cum laude.

[3.] See below, pages 439ff.

HONORES ET PRIVILEGIA[4] RITE CONTVLIT

COLLATAQVE PVBLICL HOC DIPLOMATE THEOLO-
GORVM ORDINIS OBSIGNATIONE COMPROBATO
DECLARAVIT

L S[5]

Berolini
typis expressit Aemilivs Ebering[6]

114. Certificate of the First Theological Examination[1]   184

The results of the first theological examination for theology student
Lic. Dietrich Bonhoeffer

born in *Breslau*	*February 4, 1906*
examined in Berlin	*January 14–17, 1928*

1. German Language	*Passed*
2. Exegesis of the O.T.	*Good*
3. Exegesis of the N.T.	*Sufficient*

[4.] The words "Honores et privilegia" are inadvertently printed twice.

[5.] Abbreviation for "Locus sigilli." These Latin words indicate the place on the diploma where the the original seal is to be imprinted.

[6.] "May it be of good fortune and favorable. Under the auspices of the Rector of Friedrich-Wilhelm University, Berlin, Doctor of Theology and Philosophy, appointed tenured Professor of this University, his magnificence, Privy Councillor Eduard Norden, Director of the Institute for Archaeology, appointed member in full standing of the Prussian Academy of Sciences, corresponding member of the Göttingen Society of Sciences and the Academy of Vienna, Member of the Order of the Red Eagle, Fourth Class on the decision of the highly esteemed theological faculty, according to the proper order, appointed for the undertaking of awarding doctoral degrees, Johannes Lietzmann, Doctor of Sacred Theology and appointed tenured Professor of this University, Director of the Seminar for Church History and the Institutes for Christian Art, appointed member of the Prussian Academy of Sciences, corresponding member of the Göttingen Society of Sciences, currently Dean of the Theological Faculty, has celebratively awarded the outstanding Mr. Dietrich Bonhoeffer of Silesia, after he submitted a dissertation in the German language with the title: '*Sanctorum Communio: eine dogmatische Untersuchung*' and after he passed the doctoral exams with the highest praise and publicly defended his thesis, the rights and privileges of a licentiate of Sacred Theology, on December 17, 1927, and has made this known by granting this official diploma imprinted with the seal of the theological faculty.—Place for the Seal—Printed in Berlin by Emil Ebering."

[1.] *NL* D 11(29); form with handwritten entries (cursive). Personal file, number 29; see above, 1/106:178, editorial note 1; previously published in *NL* A 6/7.

4. Church History and History of Dogma	*Sufficient*
5. Dogmatics and Symbolism	*Sufficient*
6. Ethics	*Good*
7. Practical Theology	*Sufficient*
8. Philosophy	*Good*
9. Quality of the academic papers submitted for the examination	1) *Replaced by the licentiate thesis* 2)
10. Quality of the papers submitted for grades	Old Testament: *Good*[2] New Testament: *Sufficient*[3] Church History: – Dogmatics: *Sufficient*[4] Ethics: –
11. The sermon submitted for the examination	*Passed*[5]
12. The catechetical paper submitted for the examination:	*Passed*[6]
13. Special Remarks:	The candidate has to apply to take the second examination no earlier than *July 17, 1929* and no later than *January 17, 1932*.
14. Final Grade:	*Sufficient*

D. Vits D. Fischer Coulon
D. Mahling D. Sellin Fahland[7]

[2.] See *NL* D 11(27).

[3.] See *NL* D 11(26).

[4.] See below, pages 441ff.

[5.] See below, pages 540ff.

[6.] See *NL* D 11(20/21) = *NL* A 14/5.

[7.] The examination committee consisted of: (1) representatives of the consistory. They were Dr. Ernst Vits, bishop of Neumark and Niederlausitz; Dr. Alfred Fischer, member of the consistory; Pastor Albert Coulon, clergy inspector, member of the consistory and pastor of the French Hospital Church in Berlin-Niederschoenhausen; (2) two representatives of the Theological Faculty of the University of Berlin: Privy Councillor of the Consistory and Prof. Friedrich Mahling; High Councillor of the Consistory and Prof. Ernst Sellin; (3) the commissioners of the Provincial Synod: Dr. Gotthelf Bronisch, superintendent in Züllichau; Gustav Posth, pastor in Stolpe; and Paul Fahland, pastor in Berlin-Lichtenberg, probably as an alternate.

Examination paper of candidate *Dietrich Bonhoeffer* submitted for the First Theological Examination[8]

This is a work that, in spite of several—some of them considerable—external and internal shortcomings, on the whole truly merits acceptance, indeed, even a certain recognition, because it presents gratifying evidence of intensive thought and of thoroughgoing effort to comprehend the text from every perspective. It gives evidence of a serious struggle to utilize these points of view and groups of thoughts in a fruitful homiletical manner. To be sure, the author, who can be trusted to develop himself enthusiastically, will still have several things to take account of and to learn before he can truly compose a well-rounded sermon.

Externally: He should take greater care with respect to punctuation, grammar, and the choice of individual expressions (why, e.g. always "Samaritaner" instead of "Samariter"?). He should take special care to clarify and polish his style of writing, which fairly often displays pomposity, exaggeration, and clumsiness. He has not yet attained noble naturalness.

Internally: He should conceive of and construct a sermon as a uniformly laid out and developed, analytical, synthetic work of art. The theme of the submitted sermon is variegated, and there is no central unit. As a result, the sermon itself is also missing the tight unity that would in itself have brought pleasing brevity.

Critical details, of which fairly many could be listed here, have not been enumerated.

The author, who certainly follows a strong desire to master his subject, is advised to diligently study model sermons (Dryander, Conrad,[9] Althaus, etc.). He is advised to guard against broad presentations and forced or contrived trains of thought (cf. the exposition on "the people of the church" in the sermon under discussion). He is advised to cultivate a straightforward noble simplicity in attempting to grasp the most important aspect at hand (in the text under discussion, "The Christian before locked doors").

    186

The intellectual energy that the sermon attests to will certainly, step by step, enable the author to achieve the goal of becoming a capable preacher.

Passed.

Züllichau November 26, 1927   *Sup. Dr. Bronish*

Evaluation of the *catechetical lesson.*

Examination submitted by the candidate *Dietrich Bonhoeffer* for the first theological examination[10]

The candidate does not cite any literature that he studied prior to writing his paper. Apparently he didn't use any. The didactic as well as the methodical aspects of the catechetical lesson reveal considerable deficiencies. Before presenting the lesson to the children he should

---

[8.] *NL* D 11 (18); form with handwritten entries; copy from *NL* A 6/7.

[9.] Ernst von Dryander and Paul Conrad.

[10.] *NL* D 11(22): form with handwritten cursive entries; copy from *NL* A 6/7.

have elaborated his main points. Then he wouldn't have had to read the text twice(!). There are few places in which he links the new material to something that the children are already acquainted with. The children are not given the chance to summarize the new material. This would have given him proof that the children had understood what had been presented to them. The application will not touch the children's hearts. The whole lesson is really nothing more than an exposition of the text. It is often so patently dogmatic that the children would be bored. The answers the children give, in the formulation at hand, show that the teacher is not aware of what he can expect 14–15-year-old boys to know, even if they attend an advanced secondary school. Much of what the religious instructor teaches them in a long-winded, didactic exposition could much more easily have been developed by asking questions. [I am referring to the comments made in the composition.][11]

Acknowledgments like "right," "yes," "surely," etc., should be avoided if at all possible. The critique of the text from the Gospel of Luke does not belong in the lesson. This is especially true as that text is not under consideration. Does the candidate really believe the words, "And when he speaks, it happens" were spoken by Jesus?!!

Only with regard to the unmistakable diligence that was applied in composing the paper and with the expectation that the candidate will put forth effort seriously to study the catechetical and psychological side of a lesson can the paper be considered good enough to obtain a passing grade.

Posth November 30, 1927

Evaluation of the sermon[12]

1. Presence:	Good
2. Memorized:	Good
3. Voice:	Pleasant modulation in tone of voice
4. Expression:	Good
5. Gestures:	Dignified: varied from animated to calm.
6. Comments:	The sermon was preached with great assurance and vitality at the evening worship service in the Hochmeister Church in Halensee on January 8, 1928.

Evaluation of the catechetical lesson

1. Bearing of the teacher:	Good
2. Understanding of the material:	Very Good
3. Ability to ask questions:	Still very clumsy
4. Ability to respond to the children's questions:	Good

[11.] The square brackets are in the manuscript.
[12.] *NL* D 11(19), form with handwritten entries; copy from *NL* A 6/7.

5. Discipline:	*Good*
6. Comments:	*Bonhoeffer teaches with a great deal of liveliness. He captivates the children. The catechetical lesson was taught on January 11, 1928, for the Confirmation Class of the congregation of the church in Grunewald.*

[Seal of the Superintendent][13]   *Diestel*

115. Certificate Attesting to Bonhoeffer's Inclusion in the List of Candidates Approved for Ordination[1]

188

[Official Stamp and Seal][2]   No. 2a

Permission has been granted to the theological student Mr. *Licentiate Dietrich Bonhoeffer,* born in *Breslau on 4 February 1906,* to perform official religious duties with the exception of administering the sacraments (including hearing confession), performing marriages and confirmations, because he has passed the first theological examination with a grade of *"Sufficient."* The privileges accorded him are stated in the church canon law, established on August 15, 1898. A current certificate, which he must show to the superintendent of any diocese in which he resides, has been stamped with our seal.

Herewith, he is charged to observe the regulations detailed in the church canon laws established on July 1, 1899, and the regulations contained in them concerning the further preparation for the ecclesiastical office and the supervision and guidance of the candidate.

Berlin, the 17th of January 1928
(Seal)
Dr. Dibelius[3]

(Handwritten mark)

[13.] Handwritten entry: "1/17/1928, log, no. 175."

[1.] *NL* A 6(7); form with handwritten entries (cursive); copy from *NL* D 11(30).
[2.] Imprint of stamp: "Protestant Church Council of the Province Brandenburg." On the stamp is handwritten: "Berlin, 2/6/1928, K VII No. 5957."
[3.] Bishop Otto Dibelius of Berlin-Brandenburg.

189   **116. From the Consistory**[1]

Protestant Consistory   Berlin SW 68,   *January 28*
of Mark Brandenburg   Lindenstr. 14   *1928*
K. VII, No. 5959

You are given the certificate prepared for you due to the results of the first theological examination. You are also given a copy of the examination proceedings with reference to the requirements of the church canon laws that are referred to in the certificate. Report to us immediately, and to the Superintendent under whose auspices you stand, whenever you change your occupation or residence.

For your personal information we are also sending you a copy of the detailed evaluations of the papers you submitted, the sermon you preached, *and the catechetical lesson* you taught.

Dibelius[2]

Office of the Superintendent, First District of the Diocese of Kölln
Telephone number: Lichterfelde 476, Dahlemerstr. 87
Berlin-Lichterfelde, February 8, 1928, log, no. *440*[3]

Diestel[4]

To
the Theological Candidate
Mr. *Licentiate Dietrich Bonhoeffer*
of
Berlin-Grunewald
Wangenheimstr. 14

[1.] *NL* A 6(7); typed form with typed entries (cursive) dated "den 28. January 1928." Copy from *NL* D 11(30).
[2.] Handwritten.
[3.] Stamps with handwritten entries.
[4.] Handwritten.

PART 2
Writings, Presentations, Notes

A. Papers from Secondary School Years.
February 1920–January 1923

---

1. Paper on Germany's Situation before the First World War[1]

Germany's Situation before the World War

In order to be able even to address this subject [. . .],[2] we must first divide it into two areas:[3] Germany's foreign policy and Germany's domestic policy. If we start by looking at the former, then the following picture of Germany in relationship to the other countries of Europe emerges. In 1905

[1.] *NL* A 5, 1; handwritten. On the notebook's cover is written "Report: Germany's Situation before the World War. Dietrich Bonhoeffer." On the first page to the right is the date, "February 1920." The report received many correction notes, but it has neither a grade nor a teacher's signature. In February 1920, at the age of fourteen, Bonhoeffer was in the lower Second Form. Graduation took place at Easter. For this report Bonhoeffer used Egelhaaf, *Geschichte der neuesten Zeit*, the chapter on "The German-French treaty concerning Morocco 1911: Germany 1912–1913" (632ff.). German-English naval negotiations (see below, 2/1:000ff.) could not yet be discussed by Egelhaaf, because the details were kept secret by the German government until 1916. Bonhoeffer used another source, unknown to us, for this information. At points he quotes it word for word. The choice of the topic, the Moroccan crisis and the German negotiations concerning the fleets, demonstrates that Bonhoeffer saw the confrontation between Great Britain and the German Empire as the main cause of World War I; this was not at all the generally held opinion at that time. Whether it was the teacher who guided the teenage student in that direction or his neighbor Hans Delbrück can no longer be ascertained. Delbrück was a member of a German Academic Commission that at Versailles wanted to refute the position that Germany alone was solely responsible for World War I. After Versailles, Delbrück continued to discuss this with English scholars; cf. Delbrück and Headlam-Morley, *Deutsch-Englische Schuld-diskussion*.
[2.] Illegible.
[3.] The instructor deleted the beginning of the sentence and incorporated Bonhoeffer's title: "In order even to be able to address Germany's situation before the World War, we must first divide it into two areas."

194 agreement with France about Morocco was reached in the so-called Algeciras Act. This specified that the Sultanate of Morocco was independent of any country. At the same time, it ensured the normal commercial activities of foreign countries. This act, however, was barely in effect for one year.[4] One day the Moors stoned the French doctor Mauchamp, who had raised the French flag above his house. Shortly afterward they killed some Italian and Spanish residents. In retaliation for Mauchamp's murder, France occupied the city of Oujda.[5] On the 7th of August, Casablanca was reduced to ruins, which destroyed a great deal of European property. Soon afterward, the French landed among[6] the surrounding tribes with 3,500 troops, and fierce fighting began. Nevertheless, after a very serious incident in Casablanca, the Algeciras Act was renewed. Just, the German Consul, attempted to board three deserters who were German officers onto a German ship, but they were captured by the French. They were taken away, but not without violence. This led to conflict, because each maintained that the other was at fault. The French claimed that Just had attempted to assist Swiss and Austrian[7] deserters [. . .].[8] This could easily have escalated into war. Germany would have had to oppose England, France, and Russia by itself because Austria was preoccupied with the Balkans. The party seeking peace, however, gained the upper hand, and the situation was handed over to the court in The Hague. France and Germany promised to work with each other under the same conditions as before.

This time peace lasted only two years.[9] Then the population around Fez staged a revolt, which the Sultan could not suppress without help. The opportunity was seized by Minister Monis, who had taken Briand's place, to administer a decisive blow. This was done in spite of the vocal warnings of the English press, the enormous, widely reported agitation in Spain, and the

195 attack of the Social Democrat Jaurès on the government, which, he said, "was acting in the service of profiteers." Monis ordered 21,000 men, under the command of von Moinier, to advance and occupy Fez in March 1911. Germany thought this action had gone too far and dispatched the gunboat "Panther" to Agadir, "in order to secure the property of the German firms."[10] This ship naturally created a great sensation. Because it needed spare parts, it was later replaced by the cruisers "Berlin" and "Eber." Although the intention of this move was, as declared, to indicate[11] that Ger-

---

[4.] On the following, see Egelhaaf, *Geschichte*, 632.
[5.] The correct spelling in German is Udschda, not Uschda.
[6.] The instructor replaced this with "near."
[7.] Egelhaaf, *Geschichte*, 635.
[8.] Illegible.
[9.] Egelhaaf, *Geschichte*, 635.
[10.] Quoted from Egelhaaf, *Geschichte*, 636.
[11.] The German word *Fingerweis* was replaced by the instructor with *Fingerzeig*. [Translated literally into English these terms are virtually indistinguishable in meaning.] [PDM]

many continued to be involved, it was interpreted by the foreign press as a threat of war. Throughout Germany it was feared that aggressive intentions[12] were at the heart of this so-called 'Panther pounce', even though an atmosphere of peace prevailed almost everywhere. England believed that if an agreement between France and Germany were to take place, France should hand over all of the Congo to Germany, to compensate them for Morocco. France would then be offered parts of Togo and Cameroon. Lloyd George addressed this issue in the lower house of Parliament. He said, "If a position should be forced upon us in which peace can only be achieved through our abandoning the position that we have achieved through heroic efforts, or by allowing an action to take place in which the vital interests of our people would be threatened, as if we had no importance among the nations, then we would not be able to accept this."[13] Once again[14] we see that, in the event of a German-French war,[15] England was not likely to come to our aid. Shortly thereafter, Cambon came to Kiderlen,[16] and negotiations took place concerning the Moroccan question. In the end, the following terms were agreed upon: Morocco was ceded to France and, in return, Germany was granted security for its economic interests[17] in Morocco and   196
territorial compensation in the French Congo. All institutions—such as the law courts, financial entities, the economy, military, etc.—were placed under the French protectorate. In return, France recognized the right of all nations to trade freely in Morocco. Germany had an interest in the national bank, and gained approximately 233,000 square kilometers. Germany received 275,000 square kilometers of the Congo. In this way, it gained its longed-for access to the Congo River, the second largest river in Africa. In return, Germany handed over an area of 12,000 square kilometers to France, so that the area it had secured was approximately as large as Prussia without Silesia and Eastern Prussia. In France as well as in Germany, however, this treaty was seen as quite unfavorable. In France, on the one hand, the people were enraged that they had allowed a country like the Congo to be taken away from them without resistance. Many in Germany, on the other hand, saw the ceding of Morocco as a severe moral defeat. The emperor said he sought to "always hold our interests high in his land." Now the opposite had occurred. Nonetheless, as a result of the treaty, the relationship between France and Germany was fairly well settled. While this conflict was still going on,[18] Italy made its presence felt in its colonies, Tripoli and Cyrenaica. It announced

---

[12.] The instructor adds "of the government."
[13.] Cited from Egelhaaf, *Geschichte,* 637.
[14.] Deleted by the instructor.
[15.] Deleted by the instructor.
[16.] Egelhaaf, *Geschichte,* 641f.
[17.] The word "interests" was probably added by the instructor.
[18.] For the following, cf. Egelhaaf, *Geschichte,* 651.

that it would occupy these Turkish provinces. Complications ensued between Turkey and us that, however, did not damage our relationship. Italy also recognized the loyal attitude of the Germans, and it seemed that Italy would become more closely allied with us at the same time as it was withdrawing more and more from England and France. It also seemed that, after the war was settled, England's policy of encirclement, put into effect after the death of Edward VIII,[19] slowly lost its force. In this way, the war had the effect of bringing Italy closer to its allied partners and alienating it from other nations.

197   Now we come to our major competitor at that time, England. England saw that we had developed quite rapidly. It no doubt noticed that we intended to expand our naval power and with it our commercial interests [. . .].[20] Consequently, it opposed us. England quietly made advances toward us, which quickly proved futile. Then it tried to draw Italy, Russia, and Japan, as well as France, into its circle and thereby formed a kind of coalition. England still had its special relationship with Japan, established by the Ten Year [Treaty][21] of August 12, 1902. This stipulated that each nation would come to the aid of the other in the event of war. It was also agreed that, with the assistance of the other partner, Japan could move the borders of Korea, which had become important to it during the Sino-Russian war, and England could change the borders of India. Thus began England's encirclement policy. When we, for our part, attempted to get equal treatment, England rejected our proposal. Nevertheless, in England, the party advocating freedom soon had gained the upper hand. Grey's laws were revised, and at one point an English newspaper declared, "We have come to the point where we always see Germany, as Germany always sees England, from a position of mistrust and hostility." From that point on, our relationship improved. Both[22] countries quickly enlarged their navies. However, England stated[23] that if Germany were willing[24] to establish a peaceful relationship it had to "recognize English superiority on the sea." No enlargement of the navy was to take place. Indeed, it was possible that the navy might be reduced in size. In return, England would not oppose our colonial expansion. No war would take place between the two nations. At the same time, England requested a rapprochement on both sides. On this occasion,[25] England sent its acting

---

[19.] Replaced with "7" by the instructor.

[20.] Illegible; replaced by the instructor with "in an untrustworthy manner."

[21.] The instructor adds "treaty."

[22.] "From that point on. . . . Both" is replaced by the instructor with "It seemed as if an improvement had occurred in our relationship. However, both. . . ."

[23.] The words "However, . . . stated" are replaced by the instructor with "England formulated a statement."

[24.] Added by the instructor.

[25.] Replaced by the instructor with "negotiation."

Minister of War, Haldane, to Berlin. Haldane's demands primarily focused on the several battleships [that][26] we again wanted to build. England   198 requested that new construction of ships cease during the following year and that construction of the battleships be restricted to one ship a year during the years 1913, 1916, and 1919. Bethmann's formal declaration read as follows:[27] Should one of the highly esteemed treaty partners be drawn into a war with one or more powers, then the other treaty partner should at least maintain benevolent neutrality with respect to the treaty partner involved in the war. The partner should try with all its power to attempt to contain the conflict.

On the other side, Haldane proposed this formulation: Neither of the powers will attack or make preparations to attack the other without provocation. Neither will it take part in an offensive against the other that would result in an attack on the other, or participate with any other power in planning a military or maritime offensive intended to lead to an attack. Haldane repeatedly emphasized that closer ties between England and Germany must not be allowed to damage the English-French relationship. At one point, he related his concern to Bethmann that such a treaty might imply that we might attack France unprovoked. The rest of the treaty dealt with colonial issues. Haldane offered extensive aid for Germany's project of the Baghdad railroad. In addition to possessing Southwest Africa and acquiring Portuguese Angola, he also wanted us to relinquish Zanzibar and Pemba. When Haldane returned, all of England's leaders expressed satisfaction. The press was the only entity that repeatedly stressed England's absolute loyalty to its friendship with France as the prerequisite to all other relationships. In[28] England, however, little emphasis was placed on the battleships. Much more weight was placed on the naval crews.

After much vacillation, Grey made this final formal announcement:[29]   Because both powers desire to guarantee peace and friendship with each   199 other, England declares that it will make no unprovoked attack on Germany and will refrain from an aggressive political stance against Germany. No treaty specifies or foresees an attack on any alliance in which England is currently vested. Neither will England enter into a compact that has such an attack as its aim.

Since this proposal did not assure us of England's position in the event, for example, of a Franco-Russian offensive, we insisted on the addition, "should Germany be forced into a war." Grey, however, out of fear of harm-

---

[26.] Added by the instructor.

[27.] For the following cf. Ernst Graf zu Reventlow, *Politische Vorgeschichte*, 249ff. Bonhoeffer obviously did not use this volume.

[28.] "Bei" was replaced by the instructor with "in."

[29.] In the manuscript a new paragraph begins here.

ing England's relationships to other nations, flatly rejected this. Therefore, the stalemate of 1909 was resumed. Consequently, England concluded a maritime agreement with France, according to which France was responsible for defending the Mediterranean, and England was responsible for defending the North Coast.[30] In order to secure its position with Russia, England concluded an additional maritime compact with Russia. Russia, therefore, expected English ships to assist them in invading Pomerania. These, however, were not granted. England naturally attempted to conceal these agreements and now[31] sought new allies. There was no question that war was imminent, and this war broke out in 1914.

Let us now turn to the domestic political situation.[32] In spite of the repeated attempts by Bethmann to establish new voting rights, the proposal was constantly rejected. He was, however, able to get the so-called national insurance regulatory law passed. Accident, medical, old age, and disability insurance were funded[33] and widows and orphans received a small subsidy. The medical benefit for the better-paid workers was raised by 50 pfennigs. In 1907 the total price of[34] these insurance policies was 859.5 million marks. This amount was covered, in part, by the subsequent[35] taxes. During the summer of 1909 von Sydow worked on plans to control the financial crisis. He arrived essentially at seven points.[36]

200

1.) The empire will take over the buying and selling of brandy. Revenue: 100 million marks.

2.) The brewing tax will be raised 2 marks per hectoliter. 100 million marks.

3.) A factory tax will be added to tobacco. 77 million marks.

4.) A tax of more than one mark on domestic and foreign wine: 20 million marks.

5.) Tax on gas and electricity: 50 million marks.

6.) Tax on newspaper advertisements and posters: 33 million marks.

7.) A gradually increasing tax on estates over 20,000 marks not regulated by a will: 83 million marks.

This accounted for 475 million marks, which were intended for[37] the above-mentioned social assistance programs and our naval fleet. Finally conversations revolved around something other than our nation's impending

---

[30.] The instructor added "of France."

[31.] Replaced by the instructor with "further."

[32.] The instructor added "briefly."

[33.] The words "the so-called . . . funded" are corrected to read "in order further to continue the social legislation begun by Bismarck and to extend the accident, medical, old age, and disability insurance coverage."

[34.] Replaced by the instructor with "The total expenses for."

[35.] Replaced by the instructor with "still to be agreed upon."

[36.] Altered by the instructor to read "There are, essentially, seven points."

[37.] The instructor added "the."

bankruptcy. There was, altogether, brilliant commercial progress on taxes.[38] A spirit of invention was fostered. For example,[39] Zeppelin, industry, and agriculture blossomed. Yet[40] there was in Germany a certain amount of peevishness against the empire. Thus there was a strong demand for parliamentary participation in the government's business.[41] Riots also took place during wage negotiations. The luxury in which the upper classes lived incited the lower classes—and yet there was everywhere a great disinterest in politics.[42] In spite of this,[43] during the elections,[44] special-interest issues took center stage almost to the exclusion of anything else. The conservatives focused on agriculture, and the national-liberal tendencies favored large-scale industry. Even so, the Social Democrats were at a disadvantage. Nevertheless, the military was constantly being enlarged, and more and more ships were being built. After all, the navy had become Germany's favorite child and since then it has become a favorite of ours.[45]

201

[38.] The words "altogether" and "on taxes" are replaced by the instructor with "In fact at that time there was."

[39.] The words "fostered. For example," are replaced by the instructor with "had increased; one thinks of."

[40.] The words "Yet . . . there was," are replaced by the instructor with "But it did not correspond to their political interests, there was."

[41.] This sentence was replaced by the instructor with "The parliament demanded to participate in the business dealings of the government."

[42.] The two previous sentences are deleted by the instructor.

[43.] The phrase "In spite of this" is replaced by the instructor with "And yet."

[44.] The instructor added "and in the parliament."

[45.] The last page of Bonhoeffer's manuscript is missing. The following page contains a cleanly written version of a correction, written on the side of the page. It is not in Bonhoeffer's hand. It replaces the final passage of the report ("Even so, the Social Democrats . . . since then it has become a favorite of ours") with "the tendencies of the broad-minded were with trade. The Social Democrats [in the final version changed to 'socialists'] attempted to raise the position of the proletariat. A unifying, mutual interest was missing. Even the military and the navy, which represented the power and the defense of Germany, could only be [here ends the correction; the final version continues with] strengthened in spite of extensive fighting between the political parties. This was the situation when war broke out in the year 1914."

2. Matriculation Essay on Catullus and Horace[1]

Catullus and Horace as Lyric Poets

202

The task of characterizing and comparing the two great ancient Roman lyric poets is best approached with great caution. Even if we valiantly attempt to be objective, in truth we can only offer subjective opinions. This is especially true if we discuss their merits and not merely compare them philologically.[2] The main task of this paper focuses on discussing their merits. We must seek to understand what these poets continue to mean for us today and not just what they meant in the past.

First, I intend to discuss briefly the circumstances of the poets' lives and then characterize them with broad strokes. In order to address the actual task, I will subsequently define lyric poetry, turn to the lyric experience,[3] and then investigate their work[4] with the goal of discovering its content and form. I will conclude the paper with a study of their poetry. Finally, I shall briefly present my own opinion on the subject.[5]

Horace was born in Venusia in southern Italy.[6] His father was a libertinus[7] who had been so successful that he could send his son to one of the better schools in Rome. He raised him simply and kept everything common away from him. At twenty-two, Horace was recruited into Octavian's army. He held the rank of a tribunus militum,[8] a position[9] for which he was not at all prepared.

[1.] *NL* A 5, 2; handwritten. The work is filled with many comments and notes, some of which are documented here, by Walther Kranz, as indicated in the editorial notes below with his surname. Date of the corrections is January 2, 1923 (cf. *DB-ER* 30). It can no longer be determined which sources Bonhoeffer used as a basis for this paper. As secondary literature it is fairly certain that he used Schanz, *Geschichte der römischen Literatur.* English translations, unless otherwise noted, are from Catullus, *The Poems of Catullus,* and Horace, *The Complete Odes and Epodes,* with citations using the standard numbering system of these editions.

[2.] Kranz: "κρίσις is a legitimate component of philology."

[3.] Kranz: "phrasing is unsuccessful."

[4.] Kranz: "Too arrogant."

[5.] Kranz: "One cannot say that this arrangement is very adroit. Because the author first wants to treat generalities and then specifics, he has to anticipate some (unproved!) conclusions. This, at least, is how it appears finally in the execution of the paper."

[6.] Walther Kranz: "One would expect that one would begin with Catullus! See the paper title."

[7.] A freed slave.

[8.] A staff officer of a legion. [Octavian later became Emperor Augustus, the first emperor of Rome, 27 B.C.E.–14 C.E.] [PDM]

[9.] Kranz: "He volunteered, but in the army of Brutus and Cassius!"

At approximately the same time, Horace became acquainted with Maece-nas.[10] Supported entirely by his friends, he lived the contemplative life of a poet in the city or on his country estate. His works are the four books called *Carmina*, a book of *Iambi*, his *Sermones, Epistulae*, and other small works.[11] Here we are interested only in the *Carmina*, i.e., the lyric poems. As we will soon see, one portion of the book contains pure sentimental poetry while another contains contemplative poetry. Several citations will enable us to understand him better at a later point.[12]

Catullus grew up under different circumstances. He was born the son of   203 a wealthy, aristocratic family in Lombardy. He was sent early to the best edu-cational institutions. We wonder whether Celtic blood flowed through his veins, because his whole manner of poetry and living was[13] not Roman. His main work is the *Nugae*.[14] He also composed poetry on request.[15] Exam-ples of this are a marriage poem and several epic tales.

The titles of the books alone can tell us a great deal about the character of the poets. Horace calls his poetry *Carmina*, which originally meant "epi-grammatic poetry," i.e., celebrative poems. Catullus calls his *Nugae*, which means "little nothings" or "small things." Horace certainly was the stalwart[16] Roman and Catullus was the high-spirited Lombard.

The individuality of their styles is clear from their external circumstances. Let us choose but one passage, e.g., the one from Horace,

pretius vives, Licini[17]

that represents the "aurea mediocritas."[18] He who is accustomed to a well-balanced, simple life does not care for emotional upheavals.[19] Everything happens in a certain contemplative manner. Catullus oscillates from one extreme to the other:

[10.] Kranz: "This event is added quite clumsily." Maecenas was a Roman statesman and patron of literature. He was a close friend of Octavian.[PDM]

[11.] *Carmina* (poems, songs) = Odes; *Iambi* = Epodes; *Sermones* = Satires; *Epistulae* = Let-ters (in verse).[PDM]

[12.] Kranz: "Phrasing is unsuccessful."

[13.] Kranz : replaces with "almost seemed to be."

[14.] *Nugae* = 'practical jokes', 'flirtations'. Kranz: "Catullus may have judged differently."

[15.] Kranz replaced "on request" with "larger works."

[16.] Kranz: "self-assured."

[17.] "The proper course in life Licinius." Kranz amends "pretius" to "rectius." The word "pretius" is translated literally "more worthwhile," "more valuable."

[18.] "The golden mean." Kranz adds: "It is not very skillful, at this point, to use the lyric poems of both poets to characterize their styles. This should occur only later."

[19.] Kranz: "These are generalities that would have been better presented later as *results*, as they in fact later reappear."

odi et amo.[20]

He hates and loves. Everything is movement and temperament.[21] With Horace it is calmness and clarity. This contrasts with Catullus's utter lack of a sense of humor. He is merely ironic.[22] One only needs to remember the

disertissime Romuli nepotum.[23]

204   Disdain and ridicule are present in the ponderous, unromantic sentence structure, with its heavily charged superlatives and the pompous, festive style that accompanies them. The poem contains the sharpest irony and is satire in its purest form. No trace of good-natured humor is evident. Catullus always[24] stands right in the midst of a situation. Horace is able to rise above it with a certain smile, a certain humor. He likes his fellow citizens and takes pleasure in their frailties without, however, ridiculing them.[25] This is a vast difference between the men. Catullus transforms everything into passion, i.e., he places it within the emotional realm. In Horace, everything follows the contemplative path. One is revolutionary;[26] the other is conservative. This pattern of thought leads us directly to the next point: the definition of lyric poetry and its application[27] to the works of our poets. I define lyric poetry as the rendering of one's own voice in as perfected and stylized an expression as possible.[28] Any kind of mood can be expressed, even a philosophical one. Thus we can create a scale with sentimental poetry[29] on one extreme. Slow gradations lead to pure contemplative poetry. There are, of course, no representatives of the extremes themselves, but several poets, including Catullus and Horace, correspond closely to them. Thus we see[30] that great differences [exist][31] between the two. Indeed, these are so great that they presuppose completely different types of souls. Everything else that we observe below can be directly related to this difference.

According to this premise,[32] these poets' concepts of experience and their views of the world, as reflected in their lyric poetry, diverge widely. The following observation illustrates the main difference between the two. Horace and Catullus naturally respond to the world very differently. (And

---

[20.] "I hate and I love."
[21.] Kranz: "Good."
[22.] Kranz: "Good."
[23.] "Silver-tongued among the grandsons of Romulus."
[24.] Kranz: "This really should not be concluded from a single illustration."
[25.] Kranz replaces this phrase with "hardly, at all, in later years."
[26.] Kranz: "is very unexpected."
[27.] Kranz: "Phrasing is unsuccessful."
[28.] Kranz: "Good."
[29.] Kranz: "An audacious image, but one understands what the author means."
[30.] Walther Kranz replaces with "We will see."
[31.] Completed by Kranz.
[32.] Kranz: "Clumsy."

here we see where the basic differences lead.[33] They remain intact, even 205
though one hardly recognizes them.) For one poet all space is illuminated by
the same light. He assumes a vantage point that is external to this space. His
task is to focus on a particular prominent subject, and he assimilates many
less important subjects to it.[34] In the eyes of the poet these minor points
often supersede the primary ones and force them to the background. We can
barely pick them out.[35] This is the process, one of selecting and combining
points[36] that are similar to the original experience. The other poet sees
himself in the midst of a vital part of life that is suddenly illumined. He limits himself to this small part, absorbing it fully and creatively. An inner meld-
ing takes place between the subject and the poet. It is clear that this poet
does not speak of a subject isolated from the whole.[37] Instead, he expresses the result of his soul's relationship with the external object. The first poet
is Horace; the second poet is Catullus. Therefore,[38] the "I" dominates in the
first poet's work, and the "object" dominates in the second poet's work.
Horace expresses emotions[39] about the world, while Catullus expresses the
emotions of the world, as they are bound up in his own emotions.[40]

Neither poet stands in an evolutionary or comparative relationship to the
other.[41] Instead, both stand at contiguous poles and are equally valuable.
Their completely different ways of thinking and processing an experience
rest further on the different ways each assimilates primitive experience.
Horace sorts things out, places them alongside each other, brings them
together, compares them.[42] In short, it is the manner of a philosopher or a
historian.[43] All this belongs to his imaginative thinking, which characterizes 206
his primary poetic trait[44] as intuitive in method. He creates pictorial impres-

---

[33.] Kranz: "Can."

[34.] Kranz: "The image is not well chosen, the spatial perspective is somewhat odd."

[35.] Kranz: "Thus not understandable."

[36.] Kranz underlines the words "one of" and puts an exclamation mark in the margin
beside them.

[37.] Kranz replaces the phrase "a subject isolated from the whole" with "a subject in
contrast to the whole."

[38.] This sentence is deleted by Kranz. In the margin he wrote, "*So*, in *this* simple
phrase the truth comes out."

[39.] Kranz replaced with "thoughts."

[40.] The phrase "the emotions of the world" is replaced by Kranz with "presents a particular experience that, however, has been resolved into a mood."

[41.] Kranz: "Phrasing unsuccessful."

[42.] Kranz: "Good."

[43.] The phrase "a philosopher or a historian" is replaced by Kranz with "spectator."

[44.] The phrase "All this . . . trait," is replaced by Kranz with "All of this, however,
shapes his—actually original truly poetic—power."

sions out of an abundance of images.[45] Naturally, one cannot discover whether he is driven by an intention to discover such impressions or if the process proceeds in the opposite direction. This is immaterial. The impression, with its drastic character, is present. To a certain extent, his poems are like paintings. They do not effect depth.[46] They leave an impression because of their richness and splendid breadth. This is the antithesis of Catullus's poetry.

Catullus does not think in a perceptual manner at all. If one wanted to draw a parallel between his work and the fine arts, then one would draw a parallel with sculpture.[47] His works leave a deep impression.[48] Life presents itself to him in segments and he delves into them fully. He assimilates himself into them and binds them to himself. This is the reason why his poems do not leave an impression of broad richness, but instead of deep "simplicity."

Catullus relates everything to a single experience, and reflects only upon it. We often find more detailed explanations or hints of later developments in Horace's works. It is difficult to say how often we find unnecessarily[49] long and expansive illustrations and comparisons. In

Maecenas atavis . . .[50]

he offers eight complete illustrations of the one idea of his poetic realm! We never find anything like this in the nugae. Whether it is a poem about the Lesbia episode or a poem about nature, his work always focuses on one subject matter. Offering an example to illustrate this would be trivial. Thus, Horace's reflective method[51] has the effect of relegating experience to the
207   backdrop of a stage.[52] This backdrop, however, is so hidden by the actors[53] that one doesn't know where and in which relationship one stands to it. Briefly stated, the background, which gave rise to his work, always remains obscure. This is true even when this background is not always essential. It is naturally not at all necessary to uncover the experience that gave rise to the

---

[45.] Kranz: "And the power of portraying the events."

[46.] Kranz puts " They do not affect one deeply" in parentheses and comments, "Does not fit."

[47.] Kranz: "Does not fit at all; doesn't it [sculpture] present something that is quite 'perceptual'?"

[48.] The sentence "His works leave a deep impression" is replaced by Kranz with "The effect of his work reaches much more into the depths of experience."

[49.] Deleted by Kranz. In the margin referring to this he writes: "The author is not supposed to evaluate until later."

[50.] "Maecenas, descended from olden kings."

[51.] Kranz replaces with "manner."

[52.] Kranz: "Good."

[53.] Kranz: "This description does not fit *theater* at all well."

mood of the poem in order to understand the poem. It simply makes understanding the mood of the poem easier. If the mood of the poem is unintelligible it can be explained by the experience that occasioned it.[54] It must always be emphasized that experience is not essential for Horace.[55] One may not and cannot fail to understand this point. Catullus's emotive method of understanding a situation allows one easily to uncover the experience, at least as it is mirrored in his soul. It is essential for his poetic expression. Catullus's poem must be written down immediately following the experience. The poem is a necessary and immediate sequel to the experience. This is true because the poet no longer has a reference point as soon as the experience and its consummation are over. Horace can find this reference point in his comprehensive worldview, with its multitude of analogies.[56] Horace can create poetry at any time.[57] He has a grasp of the necessary material and intentionally delays completing the final draft[58] of his poem for a long time. So one might place the phrase, "nonum per annum prematur,"[59] from his own book as a motto above his *Carmina.*[60] We are able to recognize the most distinctive characteristics[61] of the two poets from these observations.[62] Horace is, in essence, a poet who wrote descriptive, interpretive, and finally contemplative lyrics. Only seldom does his poetry contain passionate lyrics. Catullus is the exact opposite. In the blink of an eye he throws verses on paper; soon afterward they could be forgotten. One can't imagine him as a philosopher.

Let us now move from generalities to particular illustrations.[63] Let us begin with Catullus.

No doubt the most beautiful and famous of his poems are his "Lesbia Songs."[64] When he was twenty-six years old,[65] he became acquainted with a woman who was several years older than he. She was from the Clodian fam-

208

[54.] Kranz: "Unclear."

[55.] Kranz: "Right."

[56.] Kranz: "Unclearly expressed."

[57.] Kranz: "What an exaggeration! What is meant is: 'One could imagine that'."

[58.] Replaced by Kranz with "formulations."

[59.] Kranz replaces the Latin 'per' with 'in'. See "and keep it back till the ninth year" (*Ars Poetica*, 388; Loeb 483). [The actual phrase in Horace reads, "nonumque prematur in annum."] [CG]

[60.] Kranz: "Good."

[61.] Kranz: "Expressions."

[62.] On the following characterization of Horace and Catullus, cf. Schanz, *Geschichte*, 2:170 and 1:78.

[63.] Kranz: "See the comment above. Only the opposite path, to proceed inductively, not deductively, would have been *scholarly.*"

[64.] Cf. Schanz, *Geschichte*, 1:78.

[65.] Kranz: "Very doubtful." Bonhoeffer uses the chronology of Schanz, *Geschichte*, 1:62.

ily. From what we can infer from other reports, she was a completely morally depraved woman.[66] She was, however, especially beautiful and gifted. Catullus was filled with burning passion for her, and his most beautiful poems were written for her.[67] We can discern a distinct evolution in this series of poems. We can see the beginning of the passion in the trans[lation][68] of the sapphic ode[69] with its strange, unusual ending. Here, in essence, the feeling of uncertainty dominates. The poet does not yet know where his passion will lead him, but he suspects that something powerful—indeed, something almost bordering on a catastrophe—awaits him. We can recognize the sudden emotional change simply from the external structure of the poem. He interprets, and suddenly he shudders at the thought of a catastrophe. Under the influence of this sentiment, he quickly writes the final words.[70] One of the most beautiful songs of Catullus,

vivamus mea Lesbia atque amemus . . . (12),[71]

demonstrates the enormous growing intensity of his passion, until he approaches madness. The poem is held within the bounds of the former until line 6. But then, he is seized suddenly by confusion and a fear that his passion might end. The final lines are composed while he is in this emotional state. The poem is written in ecstasy, shortly before or after a happy hour of love. Perhaps only a very short time afterwards he wrote the song

209

quaeris, quot mihi basiationes . . . (7).[72]

Here he calls himself vaesanus Catullus.[73] His passion begins to consume him. What he expected did happen. The affair ended in catastrophe, in a break between Lesbia and him. His magnificent two-verse poems were composed during this period. One of them,

odi et amo . . . (87),[74]

[66.] Cf. Schanz, *Geschichte,* 1:67.

[67.] Kranz underlines the word "for" and puts a question mark beside it in the margin.

[68.] Completed by Kranz.

[69.] The phrase "sapphic ode" is dotted with exclamation marks. *Carmen* 51 is intended; cf. Schanz, *Geschichte,* 1:75f.

[70.] Kranz: "otium Catulle, tibi molestum est" ("Idleness, Catullus, does you harm," 51.13).

[71.] "Lesbia, let us live and let us love." The correct reference is 5.1.

[72.] "You ask [Lesbia] how many of [your] kisses will [satisfy] me . . ." (7.1).

[73.] Read "vesanus Catullus" ("obsessed Catullus"); cf. 7.10.

[74.] The correct reference is 85. [English: "I hate and I love."] [PDM]

has become world famous. It expresses deeply and movingly the emotional tension and exhaustion resulting from this separation and the ensuing disintegration of his entire inner life. The poet finds himself trapped by these powers. He does not desire it; and yet, for all that, he must desire it. The same struggle is fought in (8)

> miser Catulle, desinas ineptire[75]

until victory is won. Once again [he recalls] their wonderful times together.[76] He begins with the song,

> fulsere quondam candidi tibi soles,[77]

and ends this paragraph with the same,

> fulsere vere candidi tibi soles. . . .[78]

But now he does not want to continue. He calls himself powerless, and says courageously:

> obstinata mente perfer, obdura,
> vale puella—iam Catullus obdurat.[79]

Again suffering overwhelms him in the final two lines, but he is able to close with a firm

> at tu, Catulle, destinatus obdura.[80]

This ends the Lesbia episode. The only thing that remains is the final prayer to the gods for purification from the illness of passion (c. 76). Shortly thereafter the poet may have died. We don't know the particulars. We only know that he died while he was still a very young man. Did he commit suicide or did his passion physically exhaust him? Who can tell? At any rate, this episode was the high point[81] of his life. Through it he demonstrated his power in all

210

[75.] "Break off, fallen Catullus, time to cut losses" (8.1)

[76.] Kranz: "Sentence structure unclear." [The suggested emendation of the German editor is in square brackets.] [PDM]

[77.] "Bright days shone once" (8.3).

[78.] "Bright days shone on both of you" (8.8).

[79.] "A clean break hard against the past. Not again, Lesbia. No more. Catullus is clear" (8.11f.).

[80.] "Enough. Break. Catullus. Against the past" (8.19).

[81.] Kranz: "Then it really was more than just an episode."

its sovereign greatness.[82] All people can restrain their passion and shut themselves off from it,[83] but to struggle through all that is beautiful and terrifying and not be afraid takes an enormous amount of emotional power. At the end of this struggle Catullus had mastered it and was victorious. He appears so great to us because we can see this in all his poems. He was not crushed by his passion. Yet he fell as the victor, not as the vanquished. As he saw that everything was collapsing about him he found the path to his gods, and they had to listen him:[84]

> o, di, reddite mi hoc pro pietate mea.[85]

He also found solace, as did another poet who, with poetic artistry, wrote the following verses:

> And when the man is struck dumb in his agony,
> then a god gives the power to describe how he suffers.[86]

His poetry truly is the purest poetry of experience, that is, the purest passionate poetry.[87] In addition to these Lesbia songs, Catullus also wrote songs about nature, traveling, and friendship. Any material he takes up is filled with the poet's soul. So that,

> iam ver egelidos refert tepores. . . .[88]

Something completely new and original is given birth. At every point an element of nature that was previously conceived of as lifeless is elevated to the place of the subject.[89] This enlivens all language. The event is brought to life. Nature is personified.[90] Volemus is the only poem where individuality shines through. It is worth noting, however, that the "I" never does. Thus nature is always the actor. In regard to Catullus's poems, one could also

211

[82.] Kranz: "But maybe he truly *died* because of it."

[83.] Kranz: "That is a *big* mistake; that can also require an enormous spiritual effort."

[84.] Kranz: "But we don't get the impression that they heard him!"

[85.] Cf. 76.26: "that the gods cure me of this disease and, as I once was whole, make me now whole again."

[86.] Catchphrase from an elegy of Goethe in "Trilogie der Leidenschaft," *Werke* 1:381; cf. also *Torquato Tasso*, act 5, scene 5.

[87.] The sentence "His poetry . . . passionate poetry" is put in brackets by Kranz.

[88.] "Now spring bursts with warm airs" (46.1).

[89.] Kranz: "Remains unintelligible, because the author does not *analyze* the poem."

[90.] Kranz: "Weak as well as wrong."

write[91] that they are "fragments of a long confession."[92] According to Goethe's categories, all of his works are episodic poems.[93] The opposite is true for Horace.

Hardly any of his poems emerge[94] from the moment. He ridicules every one of his small love affairs a little. One time he speaks of the "dulce loquens Lalage."[95] In short,[96] one does not get the impression that any of his many love affairs has affected him very much. Can anyone get a clear picture of any of the many women who play a role in his life? The only exception may be the person of Lydia in

> donec gratus eram tibi. . . .[97]

We get to know her as a soft but very determined woman.[98] Catullus would never have been capable of such a fine portrayal with so few words.[99] He could not have put himself into someone else's soul.

As we have previously mentioned, Horace is rarely completely captivated by experience in a poem. It is always the emotions emerging from an experience that he addresses. He distances himself from material through reflection, whereas Catullus unites with the material through his emotional penetration of it. Most of the time Horace presents some meager experience and develops a maxim from it. This could be the situation of the poem entitled:

> tu ne quaesieris . . . (1.11).[100]

Horace's lover spoke lightly about the possibility of separation in the near future during a casual conversation. The poet recalls the conversation and attaches to it the thoughts found in lines 6–12. Often we cannot reconstruct any particular experiences, as in

> Aequam memento rebus in arduis servare mentem. . . .[101]

[91.] Kranz: "Is a bit abrupt."
[92.] Goethe, *The Autobiography of Johann Wolfgang Goethe*, Part 2, Book 7, 304–5.
[93.] Cf. Schanz, *Geschichte*, 1:70.
[94.] Kranz: "So it *seems*."
[95.] "Lalage's sweet talk" (cf. 1.22.23f.).
[96.] Kranz: "*Too* short."
[97.] "When I was dear to you" (3.9.1).
[98.] Kranz: "Not enough!"
[99.] Kranz: "Good."
[100.] "Do not inquire" (1.11.1).
[101.] "Be sure to retain an equable mind in vexation" (2.3.1f.).

212   The experience has become a concealed[102] backdrop. The thoughts are pursued very clearly and in great detail, but the temperament is missing. Emotion is there but spirited sentimentality is not. He did, however, write other poems. They will deservedly remain eternal.[103] It is hard to believe that the same artist wrote such divergent works of art as the dreamy symposium ode,[104] the dry poem of dedication written for Maecenas,[105] the poem for the celebration at the well,[106] or, to name another political poem,

nunc est bibendum. . . .[107]

Here, for the first time, we recognize what is actually missing in the other poems, and what elevates Catullus's poems. It is movement. Catullus's poems are movement. Horace's poems stand still.[108] It is precisely this richness of movement that gives us pleasure in the above-mentioned poet's work. What kind of movement do we feel in

nunc est bibendum . . . (1.37)?

The news of Cleopatra's death is received with the greatest euphoria. This mood, however, is restrained or transformed into a feeling of awe mingled with rage at the thought of this woman's nature. This woman has degraded Roman men! Again this mood gives way to the next, one of profound ridicule and disdain at the thought of Caesar, who frightens her away like a "dove or a rabbit." This malicious pleasure then shifts suddenly, yet psychologically very understandably into the opposite mood. Sympathy and admiration are felt in tandem at the thought of a weak woman sought after by Caesar. The sentiment begins with the words "fatale monstrum,"[109] and these feelings are heightened by the thought of her courageous death. The poem is full of enthusiasm for her and ends with the words,

213   saevis Liburnis scilicet invidens
privata deduci superbo

[102.] "Concealed" is put in brackets by Kranz; cf. above, editorial note 53.

[103.] Kranz: "Clumsy, that the critique is brought in here again; it ruins the objective presentation."

[104.] Kranz: "1.38?" Cf. Below, 2/2:209, where Bonhoeffer says about this poem, "The poet is lying outdoors . . . holding a symposium."

[105.] 1.1.

[106.] 3.18.

[107.] "Now it is time to drink" (1.37.1).

[108.] Kranz: "Good."

[109.] The phrase "The sentiment . . . monstrum" is replaced by Kranz with "which in the words 'fatale monstrum' ["curs'd monster" (1.37.21)] shows itself for the first time."

non humilis, mulier, triumpho.[110]

With every word we feel here the poet's ardent gasp for breath. Any carefully thought out arrangement is entirely missing. Living is everything.

The mood in

Persicos odi, puer, apparatus . . . ,[111]

is very different, yet strikingly similar. The poet is lying outdoors underneath
a grape arbor holding a symposium. He is completely surrounded by nature.
Nothing abstract disturbs us. The words

rosa, quo locorum sera moretur . . .[112]

allow a glimmer of the personification of nature's processes,[113] how[114]
only

spargit agrestis tibi silva frondes. . . .[115]

The plants live. They live for the people. They feel and experience with us.
This is incredibly novel. It is, however, a completely different relationship to
nature than we find in Catullus when he writes,

iam ver egilidos refert tepores.[116]

Here everything pulsates.[117] Catullus does not speak to himself in his poetry. Instead, nature speaks. In short, Catullus retreats into nature.[118] Horace
always holds himself apart from nature. He never speaks with a second person. This reflects an enormous difference. In "Rosa, quo locorum,"[119]
nature truly does become personified, yet the poet sees nature as a living
being in relationship to himself. The duality remains. Catullus dissolves into
nature and becomes one with it.

[110.] "She was no docile woman but truly scorned to be taken away in her enemy's
ships, deposed, to an overweening triumph" (1.37.30–32).

[111.] "Persian elegance, my lad, I hate" (1.38.1); *Horace: The Odes and Epodes,* 103.

[112.] "Where the last rose is blowing" (1.38.3f.).

[113.] The words "glimmer . . . processes" are replaced by Kranz with "a sympathy for
the process of nature is sensed."

[114.] Here Bonhoeffer wrote *die,* 'the', when he probably meant *wie,* 'how'.

[115.] "The rural forest sheds its leaves for you" (3.18.14).

[116.] Cf. editorial note 89.

[117.] Kranz: "Unclear!"

[118.] Kranz: "This is incorrect. Here the relationship is more likely the opposite."

[119.] Cf. above, editorial note 112.

214   One can see similarities to this in the Faunus song (3.18) and the poem
for spring (3.13). There is only one more poem that fits this type which must
definitely be considered. It is the (3.30)

Exegi monumentum, aere perennius.[120]

The monumental effect of the Latin language is demonstrated in this poem,
as is the might of the entire ancient Roman world that Horace understood so
well. The image,

dum [. . .] scandet cum tacita virgine pontifex,[121]

describes eternal Rome and holy Rome as one and the same entity. The
entire poem is a song of praise for "Roma aeterna." It would be vanity if such
a poem were overly absorbed in self-reflection.[122] Here none is perceptible.
The poem represents acknowledgment by the free Romans of their enormous well-deserved power in Augustus's empire.

Following this glance at the content of the poetry, we must now focus on
form. The particular art forms and styles represented by Catullus and
Horace can be discovered from several typical examples.[123] Let us begin
with Horace by observing several texts from the "Odes to Rome." Their language presents us with a cohesion and a richness of images that cannot be
found anywhere else in all of Roman literature. Let us single out Part 1,
lines 14–16:

aequa lege Necessitas
sortitur insignis et imos,
omne capax movet urna nomen.[124]

Necessitas is personified, perhaps as a woman. She is conceived of as someone who churns the huge urn containing each person's fate. Playfully, but
with an impartial justice, which stipulates that everyone will have a turn, this
or that destiny pops up. It can be the fate of the poor or the rich man. Per-
215   haps the example from 1.4 is even better,

[120.] "I have achieved a monument more lasting than bronze . . ." (1.30.1).
[121.] Read, "dum Capitolinum scandet . . . ;" "while Pontiff and Vestal shall climb the
Capitol Hill . . ." (3.30.8f.).
[122.] Kranz: "Unclear."
[123.] The words "art forms and styles" are placed by Kranz in square brackets and
replaced with "thought formations."
[124.] "But with impartial justice Necessity chooses from high and low, the capacious
urn shuffles every name" (3.1.14–16).

> pallida Mors aequo pulsat pede pauporum tabernas,
> regumque turris.[125]

It is incorrect to translate this, "knocks without distinction," i.e., when one renders "aequo" as "without distinction." Something very special is meant by "impartially." Death's knock does not sound any different on the door of the poor person than on the palace of the rich person.[126] Death does not knock more quietly here, nor more softly. In the "pallida Mors," we believe we can already see our Death, before whose ghastly knock everything must give way. We have to interpret a single verse of Horace with many words.[127]

In both examples one sees the high art of condensing achieved by Horace. Therefore, we find so many pregnant expressions in his work as well as the quote that is still known by everyone today.[128] Even though they are short,[129] the images are drastically clear. A colossal self-discipline and rigor is inherent in Horace's art that Catullus never could have achieved. Catullus's goal is to become intoxicated by his feelings. Horace's goal is to force them into the limitations of classical thought.[130] Horace's words, such as

> dulce et decorum est pro patria mori,[131]

are eternal. The harmony of thought and word in some phrases is incredibly meaningful and unique.[132] Innumerable other similar quotations [could be][133] cited. Among others is Horace's well-known, two-word maxim,

> carpe diem.[134]

Catullus condenses his thoughts as well, but only seldom and unconsciously. 216
What he condenses are only his own personal sentiments, not maxims. One of the best examples of this is,

> Odi et amo, quare id faciam fortasse requiris,
> nescio sed fieri sentio et excrucior.[135]

[125.] "Pallid Death kicks impartially at the doors of hovels and mansions" (1.4.13f.).
[126.] Kranz: "Good."
[127.] Kranz: "One would have to do a lot more."
[128.] The phrase "quote . . . today" is changed by Kranz to "words that today are well known to everyone as quotations."
[129.] Kranz: "Expression is not well chosen."
[130.] The sentence "Horace's . . . thought" is changed by Kranz to "Horace wants to capture them within specific limitations."
[131.] "It is sweet and proper to die for one's country . . ." (3.2.13).
[132.] Kranz: "Good."
[133.] Inserted by Kranz.
[134.] "Seize the day" (1.11.8).
[135.] "I hate and I love. And if you ask me how, I do not know: I only feel it, and I'm torn in two" (85.1).

Catullus believed that this only related to himself. He didn't consider that this is a basic principle of all action—yes, even the entirety of life.[136]

Only very seldom do we find images in Catullus. They only serve as comparisons as in (lines 3 and 7),

quaeris, quot mihi basiationes. . . .[137]

Unlike Horace's poetry, they do not express an action.[138] Instead, they are brought in casually, so they also do not represent anything in particular. Let us now take a moment to compare Horace's dedicatory poem for Maecenas with Catullus's dedicatory poem for Cornelius Nepos. This will enable us, once again, to examine their particular features in the broadest terms. One is written in heavy monumental Aesculapian and the other in dainty, light, almost French-like Alexandrine verses.[139] It is interesting to compare them further in respect to[140] their final verses. It almost seems like a caricature. How great the difference is in which each celebrate their fame as poets! Horace has pathetic fantasies about his poet's crown. He sees himself carried away to Jupiter. His thoughts are with the stars. He calls out to the muses not to abandon him. In contrast, Catullus asks the muse very humbly, almost jokingly,[141] to let his work endure for at least a century.

If we acknowledge that one poet puts emphasis on the wealth of images, i.e., on explanation and brevity,[142] and the other is indifferent to all of this, replacing it all with a wealth of emotion, then we may turn to the composition of the individual songs. Thus far, our discussion has led to the following: in Horace's poems, the subject matter is ordered prior to the act of poetic composition. In the "Odes to Rome" we can reconstruct the development precisely. It must necessarily have been established beforehand. This is the case, for example, in 3.2, the subject of the "vir Romanus" that is treated

217

[136.] Kranz: "It is neither. The author means that one could give this thought a general setting."

[137.] Cf. above, editorial note 72.

[138.] Kranz: "Not sharp enough."

[139.] Replaced by Kranz with "hendecasyllabic." [Aesculapian meter is found in the lyric verse of Greek drama. It is associated often with the work of Sappho. Alexandrine verse is characterized by artifice, an over emphasis on beauty, and an elaboration of form. Catullus is thought to have been strongly influenced by the Greek school of Alexandrine poetry.] [PDM]

[140.] Kranz: "Expression is not well chosen."

[141.] Kranz: "He naturally *means* the same as Horace does."

[142.] Kranz: "Certainly not only! Clumsy!"

a. in war
b. in the res publica
c. as a personality.[143]

Such an arrangement cannot have arisen on the spur of the moment. The masterpiece of the composition, however, is (3.9)

donec gratus eram tibi. . . .[144]

It is one of the rare cases where Horace's method of polishing and going into extreme detail does not irritate but rather elevates.[145] In each pair of alternate stanzas the poet and the lover answer each other. The first verse always matches the second, except that the lover always manages to outdo the poet.

Catullus must have polished his poems, but it is not noticeable. Everything seems to have been composed effortlessly. Because of this, his lyric composition is completely different. The arrangement arises as the poetry is composed. The order arises naturally. Horace's order is weighed carefully.[146] The familiar contrast that we have observed from the beginning can be found again and again. It is the contrast between feeling and contemplation—or whatever else one wants to call it. No matter how hard we try to discover deep, shared characteristics of both men, our attempt is doomed to failure. Both simply are typical representatives of different epochs,[147] which are unconnected[148] to each other.[149] Both have given us new ideas, each in a different way. Horace hoped to educate the people with his poetry. He yearned for the return of the "virtus Romana."[150] He praises Rome's lost importance and power and sees it returning. Catullus writes because he must. Perhaps his poems were known among his circle of friends, but the poet never expected that they would extend beyond this circle to our time.[151] He did not advance theories of state,[152] nor did he contemplate educating his people. That was very far from his intentions. He lived only for himself and was then destroyed. Horace lived for his people and the future.

218

[143.] Kranz: "Does not quite hit the mark."
[144.] Cf. above, editorial note 97.
[145.] Kranz: "Good."
[146.] Kranz: "This is always the case with a *disposition!*"
[147.] Kranz: "This appears very unexpectedly."
[148.] Kranz: "Does not fit."
[149.] Kranz: "This is also demonstrated in their verses."
[150.] "Roman virtue."
[151.] Kranz: "Is not true for his *entire* work."
[152.] Kranz: "Did Horace do it?"

I want to offer briefly my own personal opinion. If I were to give one of the poets precedence over the other, I would, without a doubt, choose Catullus. On a purely emotional level,[153] I find contemplative poetry like Horace's to be an absurdity and an attempt at cultivating later culture. Reflections have never conquered the world, but emotions have. The most impressive[154] thoughts fade away, but great emotions are eternal.[155]

[153.] The phrase "purely emotional level" is placed in brackets by Kranz.

[154.] Changed by Kranz to read "The greatest."

[155.] Kranz: "As correct as the first thought is, that is how incorrect (and juvenile) the second one is. Emotion is 'noise and smoke'. Art remains forever. Art, however, can also reflect the character of eternity. And it is an eternal *truth*!" Above in the margin is the final assessment of the teacher: "This industrious work shows clearly the mistakes and the excellent aspects of a beginner's work. The arrangement is not especially well done; the expression is often very poor—it is full of spirit, good ideas, and singularly pleasing points. What is most valuable about it, however, is that it shows that the author can address a very difficult subject with enthusiasm and seriousness and bring his work to completion—even if he chose the paper's topic himself. Quod felix faustumque sit! ["May it be fortunate and favorable!"] February 1, 1923 Kranz. [In the German education system, topics for papers are often chosen by the teachers and not the students.][PDM]

B. Papers Reflecting
Theological Orientation.
1925

3. Two Notes on Schleiermacher's *On Religion*[1]   219

If everything is true, then the concept of falseness is abolished; as a result, so too is the concept of truth, i.e., all attributes disappear into infinity. It becomes only existence without determination or[2] the existence of the universally valid value.[3]

Abolishes individual determination in favor of the existential assertion.

[1.] *NL* A 5, 3; handwritten; published in *DB-ER* 55. The first note was discovered on a small piece of paper placed in Bonhoeffer's copy of F. D. E. Schleiermacher's *On Religion: Speeches to its Cultured Despisers*, between pages 68 and 69 in the German original, the Pünjer edition of the *Reden über die Religion*. It refers to a sentence that he had underlined, "In its immediate relation to the infinite, all stand together in their original genuine connection, all is one and all is true" (*On Religion*, 55). In addition, a cross is placed at a point in the text that refers to the second note, which is found handwritten at the bottom of page 68 of Bonhoeffer's copy. The date of both notes is uncertain. It is also uncertain whether they were written at the same time, although it is clear that the note on the piece of paper refers to the note on the page. Bonhoeffer's study of *On Religion* is mentioned in a letter of August 16, 1923 (cf. above, 1/39:62); cf. also the letter of August 5, 1924 (cf. above, 1/82:133).

[2.] Difficult to decipher.

[3.] Difficult to decipher; perhaps also "of the word."

220 **4. Seminar Paper on 1 Clement**[1]

The Jewish Element in First Clement:
Its Content and Relationship to the Whole Letter

This investigation will be focused by the following question: which elements of this letter could have been written by a Hellenistic Jew, and how are these related to the entirety of the letter? We understand such elements to be words, sentences, concepts, images, etc., that are characteristic of Jewish
221 speech patterns, writings, thought, concepts, etc., and are present in one or more Jewish texts. In such an investigation, all questions about the way in which the texts were transmitted, etc., naturally fall by the wayside. They would not touch on the essence of our question, which focuses on the problem: what is the importance of Hellenistic and Palestinian Judaism for the Christian church-community in Rome and, on a larger scale, for the early Christian 'church' as a whole? In the final analysis, the question is: has Christianity fulfilled the law, or has it superseded it? Clearly, in order somehow to achieve our goal and principal aim, we cannot be content with merely isolating the Jewish element. Instead, we must follow this investigation with a comparison of the inner relationship of the Jewish element to the whole let-

---

[1.] *NL* A 11, 1; typwritten; first published in *GS* 5:17–63. The handwritten title page contains the following text: "The Jewish Element in 1 Clement: Its Content and Relation to the Whole Letter. Dietrich Bonhoeffer, Winter Semester 1924–25." The seminar paper was written for Adolf von Harnack, who evaluated it; see below, Appendix 3, page 585. Cf. also *LPP* 126 and *DB-ER* 78. In addition see Agnes von Zahn-Harnack's *Adolf von Harnack*, 436. As the source for the text of 1 Clement, Bonhoeffer used Gebhardt and Harnack, *Patrum Apostolicorum Opera*, I/1: *Clementis Romani ad Corinthios quae dicuntur epistulae*. In addition, he certainly used the Clement editions of J. B. Lightfoot and Rudolf Knopf. For the history of the concepts, he relied heavily on the German edition of Hermann Cremer's *Biblico-theological Lexicon of New Testament Greek*. He also consulted the monograph of Wilhelm Bousset, *Die Religion des Judentums*. The rest of the secondary literature is less significant; see Bonhoeffer's bibliography, below, 2/4:256, and editorial note 279. His inconsistent and sometimes inaccurate citations in the body of his text are reproduced here unchanged. However, "Cl" and "1 Cl" always refer to 1 Clement, "C" to chapters within it ("Ma." is his abbreviation for Maccabees). The German translation of Clement used by Bonhoeffer was Knopf, "Der Erste Clemensbrief"; the English translation of passages from 1 Clement is that of Cyril C. Richardson in *Early Christian Fathers*, citations being given by chapter and verse. Bonhoeffer's numerous Philo quotations that are embedded in the text have various citations: the chapter numbers are from the 1828 Richter edition of Philo's works, the paragraph numbers are from the Cohn-Wendland edition, and/or the page number is from the Mangey edition; in the editorial notes of the German edition these citations are presented in a consistent manner according to the editions of Cohn and Mangey. In this volume the works of Philo are cited with the same numeration as Cohn in the German editorial notes, and with added reference to the Loeb Classical Library edition, cited as Loeb. Citation of classical Greek and Roman authors is by the standard numeration system as used, for example, in the Loeb editions; normally the volume and page number in the Loeb edition of the writings of the particular author are also given. Bonhoeffer's omissions that cannot be identified are designated in the text as follows: [. . .]. Missing or false citations are identified in the editorial notes or are corrected.

ter. Before doing this we will attempt to gain a clear understanding of the kind of life and teaching which characterizes the whole letter. In order to describe the systematic path of the investigation, some of the results that are gleaned must be presented at the beginning of this investigation. These, it must be explicitly emphasized, are results and not premises. After we have separated the Jewish elements from the whole and have completed our investigation of the remainder of the letter, we will find that a uniquely Christian life and discipline has not been achieved, even though the remainder of the letter does distinguish itself substantially from the Jewish elements and has its own character. Indeed, the Christian life is dependent on the stream of Jewish life, which we have separated from it. This means that a substantial portion of the Jewish intellectual heritage converges with the Christian intellectual heritage. As we begin this process of isolation, a third independent element emerges. It is the Greco-Roman spirit.

This third stream of thought works in two very different ways. We will see that everything in this stream that had the capacity to invigorate[2] had already been used by the powerful currents of Judaism (especially the Hellenistic branch) to form fresh, decisive thoughts. This stream of thought was transmitted in such a way that a second positive outcome accompanied the first. Better said, this stream formed the undercurrent of 1 Clement's entire world and gave it direction. We will establish that the truly formative, moving factors were Christian and Jewish; while the Greco-Roman factor should be regarded as the one that gave direction[3] to Clement's world.

First, we will investigate the Jewish element and its content. All of Jewish literature composed up until the end of the first century after Christ must be used as primary sources for discerning Jewish elements or Jewish-Hellenistic elements. Then we will focus on the writings that we can be certain Clement used and the literature he cited. This list includes the Old Testament books of the Pentateuch, Josh., 1 Sam., 1 Kings, 2 Chron., Pss., Job, Isa., Jer., Ezek., Dan., Mal., Hab., and the Apocryphal books Wisd. of Sol., Prov., Jth., Est., and Sir. We cannot establish with certainty which of the Pseudepigrapha Clement was acquainted with. The New Testament books cited[4] are 1 Cor., Rom., Heb., and Eph. In addition, he used sayings of Jesus that originated in an oral tradition or another tradition that has not been preserved. Because the parallels from Matt. and Luke cannot form the tradition for the sayings' wording,[5] it is highly improbable that a man of Clement's stature would cite

222

[2.] The phrase "that . . . invigorate" is underlined with a curved line by Harnack.

[3.] The word "direction" is underlined with a curved line by Harnack; who comments in the margin: "The expression 'direction' can be misunderstood, but it is not wrong. The Judeo-Christian stream flows through the Greco-Roman landscape. It is, therefore, guided in its direction by it and also receives elements and color from the riverbanks."

[4.] Harnack adds, "or clearly used."

[5.] Changed by Harnack to "be the sources of the tradition for the wording."

the sayings of Jesus from memory so poorly. The fact that such a tradition existed will be dealt with below in another context. In addition, there are five citations whose origins we cannot establish. Whether one of these (17:6) is from the *Assumption of Moses* and another from the *Apocalypse*[6] *of Elijah* (34:8) cannot be determined. Clement's curious connection to Philo will also be discussed below. Here we have Clement's direct sources before us. We are not putting forth the hypothesis that the author was [not][7] familiar with considerably more literature than he cited. This is even probable. It seems that he was directly or indirectly familiar with some rabbinical traditions. Where else could these remarkable stories possibly originate? C. 11:2 tells us of Lot's wife who was transformed into a pillar of salt that supposedly still exists today (cf. Josephus, *Ant.*11.1.4,[8] who also gives the same information); and C. 31:3 tells us that Isaac voluntarily went up to be sacrificed (*fragm. melitonis*, Josephus, *Ant.*1. 14.4),[9] by mixing together Genesis 22:7 and Isa. 53:7, and the account in C. 43 (cf. Philo, *de Abrah.* 32, p. 26, and Josephus 4.4.2).[10] We will now cease this line of inquiry in order to focus on our subject.

It is important to draw attention to the phenomenon that Wendland[1] summarizes this way: "It is because of the paucity of extant profane literature that we often find parallels for ancient Christian literature in Jewish Hellenism, which might not involve anything specifically Jewish." This realization leads us to understand the entire intellectual situation of that time, namely, to gain insight into the pervasive intellectual syncretism of which Jewish Hellenism is a symptom.[12] The east and the west had come into the closest contact. Although the former was politically humbled and abased, an unstoppable, powerful intellectual current flowed from it. The latter had to

---

1. *Hellenistische Kultur*, 119.[11]

[6.] 'Pseudepigrapha' is non-canonical literature originating in the century before and after Christ. It was originally Jewish, and then became influenced by Christianity, more (as in the *Apocalypse of Elijah*) or less (as in the *Assumption of Moses*).

[7.] Addition of the German editor.

[8.] The correct reference is Josephus, *Jewish Antiquities* 1.11.4 (Loeb 4:101). Bonhoeffer's incorrect citation is based on Gebhardt and Harnack, *Clementis Romani*, 25, footnote 2.

[9.] Cf. Melito, *Fragments* 9. The correct reference is Josephus, *Antiquities* 1.13.4. Both citations, including the incorrect Josephus citation, are found in Gebhardt and Harnack, *Clementis Romani* 51, footnote 3.

[10.] The German edition corrects Bonhoeffer's Philo citation to *De Vita Mosis*, 2 [3], 175–80; however, this has to do with Aaron, not Isaac. The correct reference is to *De Abrahamo*, XXXII.167–76 (Loeb 6:85–89). The second citation refers to Josephus, *Antiquities* 4.4.2 (Loeb 4:507f.). [CG]

[11.] Bonhoeffer's quotation from Wendland is not exact in every word, but the meaning is essentially the same. [CG]

[12.] Harnack replaces, "for which . . . symptom," with, "which especially comes to the fore in Jewish Hellenism."

recognize this in order to absorb quickly the east into itself. This intellectual current was fundamentally religious in nature. Greek philosophy, Platonic and Stoic (as united in Posidonius)[13] in particular, reacted to the Jewish world of ideas that had spread over the whole Roman Empire like powerful propaganda. Judaism's political position in the Diaspora forced it to become cosmopolitan. This setting favored the mission of early Christianity. The new cosmopolitan Jewish Hellenism was centered in Alexandria. It was there that, among many others, the Wisdom of Solomon and 4 Maccabees were written and there, in approximately A.D. 50, that Philo encapsulated in himself the entire movement.

A Jewish community of more than 8,000 had lived in Rome, the capital of the empire, since the days of Cicero, as he, Horace, Tacitus, Suetonius et al. inform us about it.[14] The fact that Caesar protected the community and that it was allowed to sing songs of mourning during his funerary procession[15] demonstrates the community's not inconsiderable significance.[16]

The influence of Greek philosophy not only expanded to the intellectual world of Rome but was well known in all of the centers of the empire. In Rome, the most stringent ethical—even ascetic—principles were advocated. An example of this is setting aside a room for the poor in the palaces of noble patricians. From about the time of Cicero onward, one found oneself rooted in purified religious and moral views. There was, however, a lack of a concept of a historical revelation of God and a cosmology (on both, see below). The fact that early Christianity was able to provide both was decisive for its development.[17] Oriental mystery cults could be found everywhere. In short, the intellectuals of the time were caught up in a movement of great spiritual and intellectual transformation. With Wendland we can no doubt assert that much of what we will later confirm as having its origins in Hellenistic Judaism could just as easily have been found in other intellectual currents if more of them had been handed down to us.[18]

We begin the enumeration of the Jewish components in 1 Cl. with a formal borrowing from the Old Testament. The Old Testament is Holy Scripture κατ'ἐξοχήν[19] for all of Judaism. It was the most ancient scripture, in

224

225

[13.] On this see Wendland, *Die hellenistich-römische Kultur in ihren Beziehungen zu Judentum und Christentum*, 29–30.

[14.] See, e.g., Cicero, "Pro Flacco," in *The Speeches*, 67–69 (Loeb 10:437–41); Horace, *Satires*, 1.5.100 and 1.9.67ff. (Loeb, *Satires*, 73 and 111); Tacitus, *Annals* 2.85 (Loeb 3:515); Suetonius, *Lives of the Caesars*, on Julius Caesar 1.84 (Loeb 1:143f.) and on Tiberius 3.36 (Loeb 1:363f.). The number of 8,000 Roman Jews is taken from Josephus, *Antiquities* 17.11.1 (Loeb 8:511). On this cf. also Bousset, *Die Religion des Judentums*, 70.

[15.] Cf. Suetonius, *The Lives of the Caesars*, on Julius Caesar 1.84 (Loeb 1:145).

[16.] Harnack: "Paragraph!" In the original there is merely a dash at this point.

[17.] Cf. Harnack, *History of Dogma* 1:125, footnote 1.

[18.] Harnack: "Style!"

[19.] "Par excellence."

addition to being the wisest and the most untouchable. Whoever ordered their lives according to its precepts could be certain of attaining eternal salvation. This understanding of the Old Testament, a necessary development in view of the political and religious attitude, was common in Palestinian as well as Hellenistic Judaism. It was practically identical with the view held in early Christianity. There is indeed only one new trait in comparison with Palestinian Judaism: a little of the fear and awe of the holy texts had been lost. They were viewed from a position of superiority. It should not seem odd if we find more than one hundred citations of Old Testament texts or allusions to Old Testament stories in 1 Cl. I prefer to see Clement's view fundamentally represented by a quote, ἐγκεκύφατε εἰς τὰς ἱερὰς γραφάς, τὰς ἀληθεῖς, τὰς διὰ τοῦ πνεύματος τοῦ ἁγίου. ἐπίστασθε, ὅτι οὐδὲν ἄδικον οὐδὲ παραπεποιημένον γέγραπται ἐν αὐταῖς[20] (C. 45:2f.). One could apply this statement to everything that Clement teaches us about the Old Testament. For Clement the Old Testament was the book that had contributed greatly to his own Christian faith and to his conversion to Christianity. We will have to keep this feature[21] in mind throughout our entire investigation. One symptom of this, even though it is a purely extrinsic one, is the citation formulas that we find in Clement.[22] Most of the Old Testament citations are introduced with an ordinary γέγραπται[23] (4:1; 14:4; 17:3; 29:2; and so on). This is evidence of the self-evidence of citation from the Old Testament (it was also read in congregational worship). Then there is the neutral λέγει ἡ γραφή[24] (34:6 et al.). This phrase sounds very Christian, yet it is witnessed already in Jewish usage. The form that appears more often is λέγει τὸ πνεῦμα τὸ ἅγιον[25] (C. 13:1; 16:2) and φησὶν ὁ ἅγιος λόγος[26] (13:3; 56:3). These are formulas that Philo frequently used [and that] also appear in Hebrews. The very modest sounding phrase λέγει που[27] (15:2; 21:2; 26:2; etc.) comes from this expression. This expression is used to indicate that the place where the ἅγιος λόγος or the πνεῦμα speaks is quite unimportant. This method of citation can be found in Heb. 2:6; 4:6, and often in Philo: *De plant.* 21 (1:342), *De ebriet.* 14 (1:365).[28] These formulas, therefore, tell us two things: (1) There really is only *one* book, after all,

226

[20.] "You have studied the Holy Scripture, which contains the truth and is inspired by the Holy Spirit. You realize that there is nothing wrong or misleading written in it" (1 Clem. 45:2f.).

[21.] The words "this feature" are underlined by Harnack with a curved line.

[22.] On the following see the manner in which the citations from 1 Clement are noted in Gebhardt and Harnack, 9, footnote 1.

[23.] "It is written."

[24.] "The Scriptures say."

[25.] "The Holy Spirit says."

[26.] "So says the Holy Word."

[27.] "That means somewhere."

[28.] Philo, *De Plantatione*, 90 (Loeb 3:259), and *De Ebrietate*, 61 (Loeb 3:347f.).

that one cites. (2) This book was written by the Holy Spirit or the λόγος. It is from these basic assumptions that the strangeness and inconsistencies of Philo's system arise and his method of interpretation necessarily follows. On the one hand, once the scripture is thought to be inspired, the text cannot be touched and contradictions within scripture are unthinkable. On the other hand, since a deeply intelligent scribe would be confronted with a profusion of contradictions, the principle of arbitrary combinations and amplification of the text through imaginative speculation arose. This is the principle that came to be expressed in the Halakah and the Haggadah.[29] It did not originate, as one might expect, in Hellenistic Judaism. The definitive counterproof is provided by the books of Chronicles, which arose in the Palestinian community. They represent a historically haggadic amplification of the books of Kings and Samuel. But beside these historical haggadoth there also existed the widely influential free religious haggadoth. Even though the former was, to a certain extent, bound to the text, the latter spilled over into boundless speculation and corresponded to the ongoing further amplification of the law through halakic interpretation. In the New Testament we already find several highly measured examples of this second kind of haggadic interpretation: Matt. 22:31f.; Rom. 10:6; 1 Cor. 9:9; Gal. 3:16; 4:22f. and others. The principle behind them is to relate the sacred text to new perspectives in any way possible and then to set forth and allegorize its whole meaning and significance expressly for that situation. The very modest beginning of this can be found in 1 Cl., but the sharpest consequences of this movement were drawn by the Epistle of Barnabas,[30] which attempted to deny the Jews the Old Testament altogether. To be sure, Clement uses the haggadic mode of interpretation very infrequently. It is in his writings, however, that one first recognizes that this apologetic principle of late Judaism conceals within itself the seed of a self-destructive weapon that could emerge full-blown at any time.

227

In Clement C. 12 we see haggadic interpretation in its purest form when Clement uses the crimson cord that Rahab is instructed to hang from her house—as a sign that she should be spared and through which she is saved—as an allusion to the λύτρωσις διὰ τοῦ αἵματος τοῦ κυρίου.[31] Here, the haggadah is used to proclaim Christian messianic proof from prophecy. In the final analysis, haggadic interpretation is found throughout the entire letter. Lipsius comments on the letter to the Hebrews with the words, "Ipsa lex Mosaica umbra est futurorum bonorum."[32] The typology seen in Hebrews

---

[29.] Halakah is the body of Jewish oral law concerning daily life and customs, formulated by scribes. Haggadah is interpretation of the extralegal parts of the Holy Scriptures.

[30.] "The Epistle of Barnabas" is propaganda in the form of a letter. It is aimed at non-Jewish Christians living in the first half of the second century.

[31.] "Redemption through the blood of the Lord" (1 Clem. 12:7).

[32.] "The Mosaic law is a shadow of future good." Lipsius, *De Clementis Romani epistula*, 49.

10:1; 8:2; 8:5 is nothing other than an inversion and continuation of the Jewish haggadah used by Philo and others. We also find portions of historical haggadoth in our letter. When we read, for example, that Isaac went willingly to be sacrificed γινώσκων τὸ μέλλον,[33] this is a motif that has arisen from a combination of Gen. 22:7 and Isa. 53:7 that is found already in the haggadic exposition of Josephus, *Ant.* 1.14.4 and 13.3, and in the *Fragments of Melito.*[34] 2 We can also turn to the story from Num. 17, preserved in Philo and elaborated upon in C. 43.[36] Even more important, these haggadic embellishments on historical texts are significant cases of exposition, which begin with Rahab and which attempt somehow to derive the gospel and the Christian church-community and its worship from the Old Testament.

228

The principle, however, is not one of causal connection. Instead, it is a paradigmatic usage of a given divine revelation. A pronouncement made by the πνεῦμα ἅγιον in the Old Testament is related to every conceivable setting, and the current situation is said to result from an Old Testament prototype. One did not shrink from distorting the sacred text in order to have a "sacred prototype." The daring—and no doubt conscious—distortion of the citation from Isaiah used to justify the office of episcopate and diaconate (C. 42) comes to mind. The word ἄρχοντες is unscrupulously replaced with ἐπίσκοποι,[37] a term that was never used in the technical sense in the[38] Diaspora. For cultic worship the synagogue example as decreed in Leviticus suggests itself. Here, no causal connection to the Old Testament is established either. Instead the connection is paradigmatic and points ahead. In 41:4 ὅσῳ πλείονος κατηξιώθημεν γνώσεως, τοσούτῳ μᾶλλον ὑποκείμεθα κινδύνῳ[39] we find an extraordinary mention of divine priesthood (Num. 17) with haggadic embellishment and a maxim for scriptural research. Scriptural interpretation is gnosis, not simply reception.[40] It is work on the sacred text that seeks to elucidate and uncover its "true meaning." Indeed, the entire Christian church-community is already seen as being present in

---

2. [and] the content apparently altered for the messianic proof.[35]

[33.] "Fully realizing what was going to happen" (1 Clem. 31:3).
[34.] The motive of the obedient sacrifice of Isaac is found in Josephus, *Antiquities* 1.13.4 (Loeb 4:115f.), and in the *Fragments of Melito* 9; with reference to these two texts, see above, 2/4:000, editorial note 10.
[35.] Handwritten addition by Bonhoeffer.
[36.] See above, editorial note 11.
[37.] "Ruler," "bishops"; cf. 1 Clem. 42:5. Regarding Bonhoeffer's judgment, cf. Gebhardt and Harnack, 69, footnote 5. [The citation is from Isa. 60:17.][PDM]
[38.] Harnack adds "Jewish."
[39.] "The more knowledge we are given, the greater risks we run" (1 Clem. 41:4).
[40.] Harnack replaces *Übernehmung*, 'reception', with *Übernahme*, 'taking over'.

the Old Testament via Deut. 32:8f.; 4:34; 14:2; Num. 18:97.[41] This is why Christians are able to speak of πατὴρ ἡμῶν Ιακώβ,[42] etc. The pious people of the Old Testament are prototypes for and ancestors of the Christians (30:7; 31:7; 60:4; 62:2). In 62:2 they are the πατέρες προδεδηλωμένοι;[43] on πρόδηλον[44] cf. 12:7; 40:1. Out of this concept that the divine paradigm was unique to the Old Testament appropriately emerged the idea that prophecy was a gift attributable to everyone for whom the Old Testament was inspired[45] (cf. 43). These include Moses and οἱ λοιποὶ προφῆται,[46] whose only true function was to relate the divine witness to Mosaic law. In this way, Rahab is also considered a prophet (12:8), as is Isaac (31) and also the 12 (or 2?) apostles (45:1). The πνεῦμα ἅγιον and Christ speak in the Old Testament. What is already there at work is Christian. In this way Paul's entire historical problem is solved. Anything that existed and was believed to be exemplary was considered Christian, or at any rate, pointed to Christianity. Clement does not make an exact distinction. In particular, it is not really clear what significance he actually attributed to Christ. To clarify, I want to repeat: The direct interpretation of the Old Testament was not primarily haggadic but, in the ordinary sense, parenetic, even though the view of the Old Testament as a whole can be traced back to haggadic methodology. We will address the christological ideas below. In this context, the only thing that interests us is the principle of interpretation. It is enough to draw attention to the common methodology that the early Christian writer appropriated from the Judaism of late antiquity.

Thus especially two formal parallels are found in the way in which 1 Cl. and Hellenistic Judaism cited and interpreted the Old Testament. We will join this with our comments on the manner in which the Old Testament style of writing was appropriated. We are primarily referring to the Psalms whose style is frequently imitated.[47] Instead of subordinating, one appropriated. Parallelismus membrorum is used in particularly significant places. The most characteristic example is certainly C. 27:4 to 28:4, and portions from the great prayer in C. 59ff. However, true grammatical Hebrew terms are also present (21:9; 61:1). When Clement says in C. 6:1, τούτοις τοῖς ἀνδράσιν . . . συνηθροίσθη πολὺ πλῆθος . . . ,[48] it is obviously a translation of the

229

230

[41.] The correct reference is Num. 18:27 (cited in 1 Clem. 29:3).

[42.] "Our father Jacob" (cf. 1 Clem. 4:8).

[43.] "Are the Fathers previously revealed." Bonhoeffer wants to understand the phrase in this sense, anyway; Knopf and others translate this "the previously mentioned Fathers."

[44.] "Foreshowing."

[45.] The words "for whom the Old Testament was inspired" are crossed through with wavy lines by Harnack.

[46.] "And the other prophets" (1 Clem. 43:1).

[47.] Cf. Harnack, *Der erste Klemensbrief,* 56f. Characteristic of Hebrew poetry is the "parallelismus membrorum," the formal parallelism of a number of verse segments.

[48.] "To these men . . . was joined a great multitude . . ." (1 Clem. 6:1).

Hebrew וַיֵּאָסֶף אֶל־.[49] The same is true of the frequently used expression κληρονομέω when referring to divine promises, 10:2; 45:8, among others, translated from נחלה[50] cf. Heb. 6:12; 11:9; Gal. 3:29; Num. 18:20; 34:2; 1 Sam. 26:19; Ps. 37:18; Jub. 32:19.

One can imagine that the language of the Old Testament must have made a great impression on the Greeks schooled in rhetoric. This was one of the main reasons that the Psalms were so highly valued. Tatian first uses Old Testament linguistic form in his confessions (*Or.* 29)[3] when he recounts the various reasons that convinced him to value this "barbaric book" above all others. In Wisd. of Sol., we have a nice parallel for the above-mentioned observation of Clement's writing. Wisd. of Sol. was written in Alexandria by a Jew (between 100 and 50 B.C.E.) who knew the Greek language very well. It consciously imitates the style of the Psalms with parallelismus membrorum etc. The formulas used for salutations and doxologies in 1 Clement are also derived from Jewish usage. It is striking that Clement, whose mastery of Greek extended to its rhetorical craft, should write correct Hebraisms (cf. C. 1 and especially the rhyme in C. 30:1). However, this is certainly no proof to establish that the author was of Jewish origin. To a large extent it is the disagreeable mixture of Greek rhetorical style and a Hebraizing tendency that displeases us and makes us uncomfortable with the style of the letter.[52] This, however, is characteristic of all Hellenistic-Jewish literature.

This concludes what needed to be said concerning the formal connections (if one can make this distinction) between Jewish and early Christian literature, especially in respect to 1 Clement. We will now address a much more important and interesting aspect of our topic: the concepts that have been appropriated by Clement from Judaism and the parallels that can be found between 1 Cl. and Judaism.

Jesus placed people in a new relationship to God. יהוה צבאות had become πατήρ. The slave to the law had become a child of God the Father.[53] This new message about the relationship between God, the Father and human beings, God's children, was intended for the world. First, we will see what happened to this message.

231

---

3. Harnack, *Mission and Expansion.*[51]

[49.] "To be gathered to."

[50.] Both words mean "to inherit."

[51.] Harnack, *Mission and Expansion,* 1:281, where Tatian, *Oratio ad Graecos* 29, is cited.

[52.] Both of Bonhoeffer's theses, (1) that the style of 1 Clement is not proof of the Jewish origin of its composer and (2) his judgment of its style, are based on Harnack, *Der erste Klemensbrief,* 57. A different opinion is held by Gundert; cf. "Der erste Brief des Clemens Romanus an der Corinther," 651f.

[53.] "Yahweh Sabaoth had become Father." In making this connection, Bonhoeffer identifies himself with the central thesis of Adolf von Harnack's famous lecture from the turn of the century on the nature of Christianity. Cf. Harnack, *What Is Christianity?* 40ff., especially 44.

In 1 Cl., on one hand, the designation of God as πατήρ appears six times (7:4; 19:2; 23:1; 29:1; 35:3; 56:6).[54] In only one of these does it have a specifically Christian meaning (29:1). On the other hand, there are many times where God is designated as δεσπότης (occurs more than 20 times), κύριος, κτίστης (3 times), and δημιουργός 5 times (20:11; 26:1; 33:2; 35:3; 59:2)."[55] If we search the Old Testament and the New Testament for these expressions, we find that the word δεσπότης never occurs in Paul. In Luke 2:29 and Acts 4:24 we find that the word occurs characteristically in the prayers of Jewish Christians[56] who had just recently converted to Christianity. The first time it is spoken by Simeon, and the second time by the community in Jerusalem after the healing miracles of[57] Peter and John. It then occurs in 2 Pet. 2:1; Jude v. 4, Ἰησοῦς Χριστὸς δεσπότης καὶ κύριος;[58] and Rev. 6:10, which, as Vischer[59] has shown, is certainly a Christian revision of a Jewish apocalypse. Jude and 2 Pet. were written by a Jewish Christian. In the Septuagint, δεσπότης is a translation of אֲדוֹנָא or (וֹהִים)אֵל[60] and is quite often seen in connection with κύριος (cf. Judges 5:20; Job 5:8; Sir. 23:1, 36:1; Wisd. of Sol. 6:7, 8:3, 11:26; 2, 3, 4 Macc.; Prov.; generally found more often in the later literature). Κύριος, insofar as it designates God, is the most common translation in the LXX of אֱלוֹהִים, אֲדוֹנָא, יהוה. Philo says of the relationship of κύριος to δεσπότης in *Quis Rerum Divinarum Heres* 6: συνώνυμα ταῦτα εἶναι λέγεται.[61] In the New Testament, the designation of God as κύριος recedes and is primarily used of Christ. The same is true of 1 Cl., where both usages are found (1:1; 12:7; 16:2; 20:1; etc; but 2:9; 16:3; 22:1; etc.).

The designation of God as κτίστης is not very common in the Old Testament. There it is primarily used in late Old Testament literature (cf. Judg. 9:22; 2 Sam. 22:32—LXX misunderstood the Hebrew text—Sir. 24:8; 2 Macc. 1:24; 7:23; 4 Macc. 5:25; 11:5). In the New Testament, it occurs only in 1 Pet. 4:19. The designation is not uncommon in Josephus. We only find δημιουργός once in the Old Testament (2 Macc. 4:11). The expression originates from Platonic philosophy. It is very common with the Neoplatonic philosophers and would have come to Clement through a detour by way of Josephus and Philo, who uses the term frequently.

[54.] The correct reference is 56:16; see also 8:3 and 62:2.

[55.] "Ruler," "Lord," "Creator," "Demiurge."

[56.] Originally, "Jews." This was altered in Bonhoeffer's handwriting to "Jewish Christians."

[57.] The phrases "community in Jerusalem" and "healing miracles" were added by hand to his illegible typed text.

[58.] "Ruler and Lord Jesus Christ."

[59.] Corrected by Bonhoeffer from "Fischer." Vischer, *Die Offenbarung des Johannes,* is intended; compare also Harnack's epilogue to Vischer's study, as well as Harnack's *History of Dogma* 1:100f., footnote 2.

[60.] Old Testament terms for God (El[ohim], Adonai).

[61.] The words κύριος and δεσπότης, 'Lord' and 'Master', "are said to be synonyms" (Philo, *Quis Rerum Divinarum Heres,* 22 ; Loeb 4:295).

232

233

Tatian (*De orat.* 29) joins 1 Cl. in attesting that the concept of God as κτίστης τοῦ συμπάντος κόσμου,[62] or as δημιοῦργος were very important to gentile Christianity (cf. Harnack).[63] The Greeks had before them in the Old Testament a distinctive[64] cosmogony and cosmology whose creator and constructor was God (cf. 1 Cl. C. 20, which is completely permeated by Greek conceptions; see below).

Next, we find numerous epithets and predicates attributed to God. Here we find ourselves at the point where Clement's world of ideas was the richest and most inexhaustible. But we are also confronted with excessive bad taste. One must refer to it as such, when Clement speaks of the γλυκύτης τοῦ ποι-ήσαντος ἡμᾶς.[65] It is almost impossible to list all the names Clement finds for God. We will limit ourselves to a characteristic selection.

Παντοκράτωρ[66] (cf. 2:3; 32:4; 56:6; 60:4; 62:2) is the LXX translation of יהוה צבאות or צבאות אלהי יהוה, or יהוה, or cf. Job שַׁדַּי.[67] It is very common in the LXX. In the New Testament, 2 Cor. 6:18 can clearly be designated as a translation. Otherwise, characteristically enough, it is found in Rev. 1:8; 4:8; 11:17; 15:3; 16:7; 21:22. A few predicates follow that probably have their origin in Greek philosophy and, as far as I know, are not attested in Jewish writings. In late Jewish literature we often find the concept of God as εὐεργέτης, εὐερ-γετικός[68] (59:3; 20:11; 23:1. LXX: Esth. 8:13; Wis. of Sol. 19:14; 2 Macc. 4:2; 3 Macc. 3:19; Wisd. of Sol. 7:22; Ps. 103. In the New Testament it is found only in Luke 22:25).⁴

---

4. The New Testament speaks of the εὐεργεσίαι of God several times. Then par-ticularly Philo, cf. *De spec. leg.* 1:209; Seneca, *Ep.* 95; *De benef.* 2.29[69] bases this expres-sion on another plane,[70] for we wish especially to expound upon the technical names of God (1 Cl. 19:2; 21:1; 38:3; etc.).[71]

[62.] "The creator of the entire cosmos."
[63.] Cf. above, editorial note 51.
[64.] Underlined by Harnack, who put question marks in the margin. Cf. on this also above, editorial note 17.
[65.] "The sweetness of our Maker" (1 Clem. 14:3; trans. altered).
[66.] "Ruler of all." [The citations following the Greek word in the text are to 1Clement; so are those below following εὐεργετικός and Πανάγιος and those in the following para-graph beginning "We find predicates. . . ."] [PDM]
[67.] Old Testament names for God (Yahweh Sebaoth, Yahweh Elohe Sebaoth, Shad-dai).
[68.] "Benefactor," "beneficent."
[69.] Regarding "the beneficent acts of God," see Philo, *De Specialibus Legibus,* 1.209 (Loeb 7:219); for Seneca, see *Epistulae morales* 95.49 (Loeb 3:89) and also *De beneficiis,* 2.29.3, in *Moral Essays* (Loeb 3:109). The three references are found in Knopf's "Der erste Clemensbrief," 75. However, the Philo references do not speak of the "beneficent acts of God," as Bonhoeffer implies, but rather of God as the benefactor.
[70.] Uncertain transcription.
[71.] Bonhoeffer adds note 4 by hand in the margin.

Πανάγιος[72] 35:3; 58:1 can be found only in 4 Macc. 7:4; 14:7. In the   234
New Testament the word is missing completely. It probably has its origins in
Greek thought[5] and later became a central cultic expression in the Greek
church.

On ὕψιστος cf. Sirach.[74]

We find predicates like ἀόργητος (19:3), ἐμπεριέχων (28:4), and ἄρχε-
γονον ὄνομα[75] in Greek philosophy. [ἀόργητος][76] was first used by Aristotle, *Eth. Nic.* 2:7. It was then used by Epictetus, *Diss.* 3.20.9; 3.18.16
εὐσταθῶς,[77] Marcus Aurelius 1.1, i.e., an expression from Stoic philosophy.
ἐμπεριέχων is a characteristic designation for the Stoic world-soul. Lightfoot
mentions Aristotle *De mund.* 6 and other later Christian citations for ἀρχέ-
γονος.[78] Compare LXX: 2 Macc. 14:35; 3 Macc. 2:9 for ἀπροσδεής,[79]
which, to be sure, occurs in Clement only once (52:1). I mention these designations because I think that they are illustrative of Clement's conception of
God (see below). ἐλεήμων, ἔλεος, οἰκτίρμων, οἰκτιρμός[80] (9:1, 18:2, 22:8,
28:1, 50:2, 56:5; 23:1, 60:1; 9:1; 18:2; 20:1; 56:1)[81] is a series of terms repeated so unbelievably often in late Judaism.[82] The more casuistically the lives   235
of the pious were constricted, the greater the increasingly repetitive, desper-
ate, and implausible-sounding entreaties for compassion and pity became.
These pleas were naturally connected with the expectation of judgment

---

5. Knopf, *Kommentar zum I. Clemensbrief.*[73]

[72.] "All-holy."

[73.] Cf. Knopf, "Der Erste Clemensbrief," 105.

[74.] "Most High." The reference to Sirach is found in Wrede, *Untersuchungen zum
Ersten Klemensbriefe,* 63, footnote 2.

[75.] "Gracious" (literally: "free from anger"), "the one who encompasses all" (literally:
"the original name"). Cf. 1 Clem. 59:3, the only place where this word occurs in 1 Clement,
according to the translation of Knopf, [". . . daß wir auf deinen] Namen [hoffen], der
[allem Geshaffenen] das Leben gab."] "Your name, the source of all creation."

[76.] Elaboration by the editor: the following references are all found in Lightfoot, *The
Apostolic Fathers* 1/2:69, footnote 21: Aristotle, *Nicomachean Ethics* 2.7, 1108a 8; Epictetus, *Discourses* 3.20.9; the correct reference is 3.18.6 (here in connection with εὐστασθῶς"; Loeb
2:115); Marcus Aurelius, *Communings* 1.1 (Loeb page 3).

[77.] "Calm."

[78.] Cf. Lightfoot, *The Apostolic Fathers* 1/2:172, footnote 1. Lightfoot verified the word
ἀρχαιόγονος ("primordial") with a reference to Pseudo-Aristotle, *De mundo* 6 (399 a 26).
See "On the Universe," in *The Complete Works of Aristotle,* 1:637.

[79.] "Without need," "self-sufficient."

[80.] "Compassionate," "pitying," "pity," "sympathetic," "sympathy."

[81.] From the list of occurrences of these four terms, Bonhoeffer mistakenly left out
the one occurrence of ἐλεήμων (1 Clem. 60: 1). The groups of citations are separated by
semicolons; the first group refers to ἔλεος, the second to οἰκτίρμων, and the third and
fourth to οἰκτιρμός (the correct reference is not 20:1 but 20:11).

[82.] Harnack: "style." Compare here, and with the following as well, Bousset, *Die Religion des Judentums,* 357–74.

(cf. 1 Clem. 28:1). The same can be said for the entire book of 2 Esdras, where we find countless variations of this one distinct plea. In the Old Testament this frequent plea is based on a completely different foundation. It is found frequently and was taken over by late Judaism. We will discuss this in more detail when we discuss the concept of δικαιοσύνη[83] (cf. Exod. 34:6; Pss. 77:38; 85:15; 102:8; Sir. 2:11; among others). In the New Testament we primarily find the concept in Paul (Rom. 12:1; 2 Cor. 1:3; Phil. 2:1; Col. 3:12), then Heb. 10:28, then only in Luke 6:36 and in Jas. 5:12—in a very Jewish-sounding sentence. At any rate, the concept plays a lesser role in the proclamation of Jesus and Paul than it does in Clement. In Clement, these concepts correlate to δεσπότης, παντοκράτωρ, ὁσιώτατον τῆς μεγαλσύνης ὄνομα (cf. 58:1), ὕψιστος, πανάγιος, ἀπροσδεής, βασιλεὺς ἐπουράνιος τῶν αἰώνων, etc.[84] The ἀγάπη[85] of God for humanity is seldom mentioned—as far as I can see, only twice, in C. 49. We will see below that a completely different motif takes its place in Clement. This is the "grace of election" (see below). If one wanted to cite a portion of 1 Clement that demonstrates a characteristic Jewish compilation of almost all of the above-mentioned appellations for God, then one would cite the long concluding prayer in C. 59ff. Lightfoot has tried to compare this prayer with the *Shemone 'Esre* by removing all of the Christian portions and enabling it to accommodate almost all of the *Eighteen Benedictions*.[86] We do not need to address detailed questions concerning the prayer.

236   Let us now proceed to the human dimension, which corresponds to these concepts of God. This single stern monotheistic God, who embodied power and grandeur, was already contrasted in the Old Testament, as well as in several Hellenistic cultures,[6] with the δοῦλος.[88] This expression, however, only appears once in the entire letter (60:2) (the word δουλεύειν[89] appears twice). In 1 Clement it appears in a context which, if not taken directly from the Old Testament, at least approximates it very closely (LXX: Num. 14:18). When Lightfoot says, "The idea of subjection to God is thus very prominent

---

6. Reitzenstein, *Hellenistic Mystery-religions*, excursus on κάτοχος.[87]

[83.] "Justice," "righteousness."
[84.] "Lord," "Ruler of all," "the Holiest Name of Eminence," "Most High," "All-Holy One," "self-sufficient," "Heavenly King of the Aeons."
[85.] "Love."
[86.] The *Shemone Esre* (*Eighteen Benedictions*) is a central prayer of Jewish worship. It is prayed three times daily and consists of eighteen blessings and petitions. On his comparison with 1 Clement chapter 59ff., cf. Lightfoot, *The Apostolic Fathers* 1/1:393–96.
[87.] Cf. Reitzenstein, *Hellenistic Mystery-Religions*, 38–39.
[88.] "Servant," "slave."
[89.] "To serve."

in Clement . . . ,"[90] he can only deduce this from the constantly repeated concept of δεσπότης. One can hardly overlook the fact that the concept of δοῦλος, which appears so often in Paul and the Old Testament, is shoved into the background (Rom. 1:1; Phil. 1:1; Gal. 1:10; Col. 4:12). Now, even if the expression is common only in Jude, 1 and 2 Pet. [and] Rev., and does not appear in the Pastoral Letters (whether Clement knew them is left aside) and Heb. (which he demonstrably used), it can be seen as representative. The Pastorals and Hebrews reflect a conceptual world very similar to Clement's. It almost seems as if there was here a shared aversion to this term and that it attained full value only later, with Hermas and Cyprian,[91] in gentile Christianity. I am certainly not in the least ready to fashion a theory from this, for the argument e silentio is tricky. But it is naturally something completely different when a Roman chooses the self-designation δοῦλος than when a Roman is constantly confronted with the terms ὑπακοή, φόβος θεοῦ, ταπεινοφροσύνη.[92] These are not moments that are conducive to humility. Similar terms in 1 Clement for δοῦλος are:

237

1. λειτουργία,[93] the LXX translation of עֲבוֹדָה—priestly service at a holy place; the word is also translated by ἐργασία, δουλεία, λατρεία[94] (on λειτουργία, -γέω, -γός[95] cf. 9:4, 20:10, 40:2, 5, 41:1, 44:2, 6; 9:2, 32:2, 43:4, 44:3; 8:1, 36:3, 41:2; 34:5 in reference to angels who serve the Lord, cf. Philo, *De virt.* 74, p. 387).[96]

2. θεράπων[97] 4:12, 43:1, 51:3, 15,[98] 53:2 is used only by Moses, in Exod. 4:10, 14:31; Num. 12:7, 8 etc. (Heb. 3:5; Barn. 14:4).

3. The important religious and ethical terms that have been listed above. We will now investigate the extent to which these can be characterized as being Jewish in origin.

ὑπακοή is one of the main religious concepts in Judaism. In 1 Cl. we find it in the following passages: 9:3, 10:2, 7, 19:1, 63:1; ὑπήκοος: 10:1, 13:3, 14:1, 60:4, 63:2; ὑπακούω:[99] 7:6, 9:1, 39:7, 57:4, 58:1. This is a total of fifteen occurrences. Almost all are used in a parenetic context. "Religion for late

---

[90.] Cf. Lightfoot, *The Apostolic Fathers* 1/2:37, footnote 7: "The idea of *subjection* to God is thus very prominent in Clement, while the idea of *sonship*, on which the apostolic writers dwell so emphatically, is kept in the background."

[91.] For Hermas and Cyprian, see index of names.

[92.] "Obedience," "fear of God," "humility."

[93.] "Service." On the following see Cremer, *Lexicon*, 762.

[94.] "Occupation," "service," "worship (of God)."

[95.] "Service," "to serve," "servant."

[96.] Philo, *De Virtutibus*, 74 (Loeb 8:207).

[97.] "Servant."

[98.] The correct reference is 51:3, 5. ["Barn." means the Epistle of Barnabas.] [CG]

[99.] "Obedience," "obedient," "to obey." Cf. on the following Cremer, *Lexicon*, 83.

Judaism is equal to obedience," said Bousset.[7] Thus, it is hardly necessary to give more exact particulars. Oddly, we find the concept in the LXX only in 2 Sam. 22:36 (the word cannot be found in classical Greek). The verb ὑπακούειν is primarily the translation of שמע[101] but not very[102] often does it occur. This does not, however, impact Bousset's assertion, because Torah-true morality is inherent in obedience.

This concept of obedience frequently occurs in the New Testament. The primary difference between the concept as it appears in the New Testament and Old Testament is that obedience to the law became "the obedience of faith."[103] A Christian's obedience, which consisted of subjection to the divine will, was derived from the concept of obedience as the fulfillment of the law, which consisted of individual deeds of obedience. Our main goal, as mentioned above, is to list the inventory of Jewish elements present. Everything fundamental will follow later. Here we only intend to gather the material with which we will work later. Another concept is embedded within ὑπακοή. It is the φόβος τοῦ Θεοῦ (21:6, 7; 23:1; 2:8; 3:4; 19:1; etc.).[104] Along with the term ὑπακοή this term forms the religious basis of late Judaism. One only need look at Prov., Eccl., Sir., as well as the prophetic books. This concept is central (cf. Sir. 1:11, 18, 26, 27, 30; 2:10. . . . Prov. 1:7, 29; 2:5; 8:13; 9:10; Ps. 33:18; Isa. 12:2; Jer. 30:10 in connection with ἔλεος).[105] In the New Testament the term fades into the background. It is found scarcely twenty times (in classical Greek: Plutarch, *De superst.* 11: θάρσος τὰ θεῖα σώφροσιν βροτῶν φόβος δὲ ἄφροσιν καὶ ἀχαρίστοις καὶ ἀνοήτοις. . . .[106] On the whole, this is not the common opinion).

If φόβος θεοῦ is a central religious concept in Judaism, it follows that one gladly takes on every chastisement that is sent from God. Yes, the παιδεία

---

7. Bousset, *Religion des Judentums,* 1:111.[100]

[100.] Cf. Bousset, *Die Religion des Judentums,* 111, footnotes 1 and 353. Bousset writes on page 111, "Religion is ὑπακοή" and on page 353, "According to the concept of early Judaism religion is obedience (ὑπακοή)."
[101.] "To hear."
[102.] Bonhoeffer added by hand: "but not very."
[103.] See Bousset, *Die Religion des Judentums,* 111, footnote 1: "Paul speaks after his conversion enthusiastically of ὑπακοή πίστεως [the obedience of faith]."
[104.] "Fear of God." On the following, cf. Cremer, *Lexicon,* 898ff.
[105.] "Mercy."
[106.] This citation is not found in the place Bonhoeffer notes. The correct reference is Plutarch, *Moralia,* 34A (Loeb *Moralia* 1:178), "Quomodo adolescens poetas audire debeat," 12 ("How the Young Man Should Study Poetry"). It reads, Θάρσος τὰ θεῖα τοῖσι σώφροσιν βροτῶν, φόβος δὲ τοῖς ἄφροσι καὶ ἀνοήτοις καὶ ἀχαρίστοις. ("God's doings make the wise to feel assured, but they do make the silly and foolish and ungrateful to feel afraid"). Bonhoeffer cites from Cremer's *Lexicon,* 899, taking from Cremer a mistaken reference.

238

θεοῦ = יהוה מוּסַר[107] is seen as being granted only to special, favored believers (35:8, especially 56:2ff., 62:3), because "the Lord reproves the one he   239
loves" (Prov. 3:12). Μακάριος ὁ ἄνθροπος ὃν ἤλεγξεν ὁ κύριος[108] (Job 5:17ff.). Παιδεία is the prerequisite[109] for true piety. Thus, one should pass on the παιδεία τοῦ" φόβου τοῦ θεοῦ or παιδεία ἐν Χριστῷ[110] (21:6, 7) to one's children. We find the same connection between φόβος and παιδεία in Prov. 16:4 as well as in Sir. 1:27: σοφία καὶ παιδεία φόβος κυρίου[111] (comp. also Prov. 1:2, 7, 29, 3:11; etc.; *Sir. Prol.* 3; 1:20 . . .). Παιδεία always has the meaning of "discipline," "chastisement," never merely "teaching, lesson." In the New Testament, the term is found only in Heb. 12:5, 7, 11; Eph. 6:4; 2 Tim. 3:16.

According to Jewish practical wisdom a third term belongs with παιδεία and φόβος mentioned above, namely, σοφία.[8] To be sure, the term does not occur in this context, but we find a similar concept in Clement, which can be accounted for by the free flow of ideas. For Ben Sira's school and proverbial wisdom, wisdom was second only to discipline as a prerequisite for φόβος τοῦ Θεοῦ. Thus, our parenesis also says that it is folly to oppose the will of God. Therefore, an ignorant person can never truly attain the fear of God (cf. 39:1).

If these are the religious consequences of the concept of φόβος Θεοῦ, then ethical activity consists in individual good deeds, each of which is a deed of ὑπακοή. (I am not offering here a systematic Jewish theology, but only an approximate arrangement.) We will be able to prove that these thoughts (see below) in 1 Clement are very similar to Jewish thought. Yet the   240
most important element would be missed if we merely persisted in this comparison. For the Jew, every "good deed" must be a glorification of δικαιοσύνη.[113] In discovering this, we have come upon a term that could lead us farther along an alternate path than we intend to go at this time. Here we intend to investigate Jewish ethical beliefs that are present in Clement's thought.

---

8. That here we have the concept σοφία in a truly natural, nonphilosophical use is clear. Concerning hypostasis, see below, page 235.[112]

[107.] "Discipline (training, upbringing) of God"—"discipline of Yahweh." Cf. also Cremer, *Lexicon*, 814f.

[108.] "Happy is the one whom God reproves." Bonhoeffer's references, Prov. 3:12 and Job 5:17, are cited in 1 Clem. 56:4, 6.

[109.] "Prerequisite" was marked with wavy lines by Harnack.

[110.] "The discipline of the fear of God," "the discipline in Christ." The correct reference is 1 Clem. 21:6, 8.

[111.] "For the fear of the Lord is wisdom and discipline, fidelity, and humility are his delight" (*Sir.* 1:27).

[112.] Bonhoeffer added note 8 by hand in the margin.

[113.] "Justice," "righteousness."

Holy Scripture is written by God, and thus it is the embodiment of God's will. It is the κανών, plumb line of life (7:2, 41:1). The Jew has innumerable expressions for this "walking in accordance with the law," etc. Several of these were firmly established in the mind of the writer of 1 Cl. Off and on, correctly or in modified form, he slips them into his ethical teaching:[114] 1:3: ἐν τοῖς νομίμοις τοῦ Θεοῦ (τῶν προσταγμάτων 40:4) πορεύεσθαι[115] from Lev. 18:3, 20:25; Jer. 26:4; Ezek. 5:6; 1 Clem. 2:8: write my commandments ἐπὶ τὰ πλάτη τῆς καρδίας αὐτῶν. . . .[116] Prov. 7:3, 3:4: διὰ τοῦτο . . .[117] Isa. 3:5. Without direct parallels: 13:1: ποιήσωμεν τὸ γεγραμμένον.[118] 7:3: τὶ τερπνόν[119] 1 Tim. 2:3, 5:4. Νόμος[120] occurs in 1 Cl. only once (1:3), and there it does not refer to the Mosaic law.

241

The more Palestinian Judaism lost of its national character, the more casuistic its ethics were naturally forced to become if it still wanted to assert itself at all. That meant that the most meticulous determination of an individual's life before God had to replace the more generous determination of the community of all believers.[121] However, the more casuistic the ethics became, the more narrow [and][122] superficial and, to the same degree, the more rigorous it became. Inward collapse was being prepared by this rigorous superficiality. This necessarily grew out of the discrepancy of a religious structure that was unmistakably rigid and spiritually destitute. It was both casuistically constricted into the smallest detail as well as anxious. (We can find many instances of this in the Catholic church.) God was no longer the one who was

---

[114.] Bonhoeffer added the following, up to the end of this paragraph, by hand.

[115.] "Walked in God's laws." See 1 Clem.1:3. Bonhoeffer is following the text of Lightfoot, *The Apostolic Fathers* 1/2:10, and not that of Gebhardt and Harnack 4 (cf. editorial note 120 below). Cf. footnote 5 of Lightfoot. It is from Lightfoot that he took his LXX references.

[116.] Instead of αὐτων the correct word is ὑμων. English: "on the tablets of your heart" (1 Clem. 2:8).

[117.] The complete Greek text of 1 Clem. 3:4 is: Διὰ τοῦτο πόρρω ἀπέστη ἡ δικαιοσύνη καὶ εἰρήνη, ἐν τῷ ἀπολιπεῖν ἕκαστον τὸν φόβον τοῦ θεοῦ καὶ ἐν τῇ πίστει αὐτοῦ ἀμβλυωπῆσαι, μηδὲ ἐν τοῖς νομίμοις τῶν προσταγμάτων αὐτοῦ πορεύεσθαι μηδὲ πολιτεύεσθαι κατὰ τὸ καθῆκον τῷ Χριστῷ, ἀλλὰ ἕκαστον βαδίζειν κατὰ τὰς ἐπιθυμίας τῆς καρδίας αὐτοῦ τῆς πονηρᾶς, ζῆλον ἄδικον καὶ ἀσεβῆ ἀνειληφότας, δι' οὗ καὶ θάνατος εἰσῆλθεν εἰς τὸν κόσμον. "For this reason righteousness and peace are far from you, since each has abandoned the fear of God and grown purblind in his faith, and ceased to walk by the rules of his precepts or to behave in a way worthy of Christ. Rather does each follow the lusts of his evil heart, by reviving that wicked and unholy rivalry, by which, indeed, 'death came into the world'."

[118.] "Let us do that which is written" (1 Clem. 13:1).

[119.] The complete Greek text of 1 Clem. 7:3 is: καὶ ἴδωμεν τί καλὸν καὶ τί τερπνὸν καὶ τί προσδοκτὸν ἐνώπιον τοῦ ποιήσαντος ἡμᾶς. "Let us note what is good, what is pleasing and acceptable to him who made us."

[120.] "Law"; see 1 Clem.1:3. Here Bonhoeffer is following the text of Gebhardt and Harnack, 4. Cf. above, editorial note 115.

[121.] Compare this and the following with Bousset, *Die Religion des Judentums*, 103ff.

[122.] Added by Harnack.

seen to combine mercy and justice as God did in the Old Testament.[123] Instead, God was the severest, the most demanding judge. For late Judaism this meant the "most just" judge who, "without regard to the person, rewards everyone with what they deserve" (Sir. 16:12,14; Prov. 24:12).[124] We get the most painful impression from 2 Esdras, or Jub. 5:14, 33:18, and others. People perform "righteous" works out of their own power, and God, the judge, rewards or damns each person "according to their merit." Individuals plead for mercy and tremble more at the prospect of being damned than they believe in the fulfillment of their acceptable prayer. This was the situation that Jesus and Paul encountered. Paul took the decisive step of stripping away the perception that people could be righteous in relationship to God. Only God is righteous, and it is owing to God's mercy that a person becomes submissive and comes to faith and through this now becomes—logic cannot grasp it—righteous. This means that an individual becomes righteous before God only as a result of God's gift. One must take this history of the problem into account when discussing 1 Cl. Only then can one understand the unhesitating way Clement says that the pious person "performs righteousness." Next, however, we must recall that the concept of δικαιοσύνη carried an incredibly large breadth of meaning. Almost all specifically moral acts could be called righteous, whether small or great (cf. C. 48). It is partially due to Hellenistic Judaism that the specific Jewishness of the law is relegated to the background, behind general moral-humane teachings. This breadth of meaning is foreign to Palestinian Judaism. The fearful anxiety about mercy gave way to an odd firmly rooted certainty of election, on the basis of which a person "can act with righteousness" (cf. 31:2). Clement's perception of the unity of works-righteousness and obedience runs parallel to the Jewish idea and is contrary to Paul's perception, for whom faith and obedience coincide. It is impossible as well as unnecessary to list in detail what "doing righteousness" meant in the Jewish context. In addition to all moral acts, ceremonial acts are subsumed under this concept. We learn from the exceedingly pointed remark in C. 41 that the latter was not meaningless for Clement. He states there that all who fail in their cultic duty deserve the death penalty.

242

This general discussion was necessary in order to place the above-mentioned Jewish world of ideas into a comprehensive worldview. Naturally, we still cannot discuss our letter systematically, because the whole fundamental circle of Clement's world of ideas is still missing. It does not at all fit into the scholastic outline of belief, obedience, and justification, from whose inter-

---

[123.] Bonhoeffer added "as God did in the Old Testament" by hand.

[124.] This phrase used by Bonhoeffer (cf. perhaps 1 Pet. 1:17) is not a direct quote, but rather a freely composed synopsis of statements from *Sir.* 16, Prov. 24 and Jub. 5 and 33. Cf. in reference to this and the following Bousset, *Die Religion des Judentums*, 351ff., especially 360f., where these references are noted.

relationship it was thought that any individual's Christianity could be regulated and arranged. Before we treat this specifically Christian aspect, we must bring to a close what still has to be said about the Jewish element.

First, we need to investigate briefly the eschatological element, i.e., to investigate the question of judgment, reward, and hope in Jewish piety. It is remarkable—or perhaps not remarkable at all—that pious individuals caught up in dogmatic casuistry fill with the whole ardor of their souls the only way that was left to meet their spiritual needs. This liberated sphere was the sphere of eschatological-apocalyptic hope. There were no dogmas for this hope, and therefore no limits. This gave rise to the truly immense collection of apocryphal apocalyptic literature, from which Clement cites sparingly. This literature accompanied the Greek Old Testament, as several others, now included in the canon, had done before. The conceptions of judgment are diverse and the fears and hopes boundless. With Clement the thought of judgment, along with all eschatological hope, recedes altogether into the background. He apparently puts forth the view that only evil will undergo judgment (9:2, 21:1, 28:1, 11:1, 18:5). To be sure, he believes that reward for moral behavior still stands within an eschatological context, but all the gruesome details are missing. Chapter 11:1 and 13:2 are typical passages. One is able to see from the striking tradition of the sayings of Jesus, in which the ὡς-οὕτως first[125] became -ἵνα,[126] that Clement values the idea. Because ὡς-οὕτως is present in the other sayings, one certainly should not place great importance on the repeated ἵνα, other than recalling the observation that Clement was not able to express fine-tuned nuances. Clement does not have much to say about promise and never mentions its content. The place where the pious will abide is ἅγιος τόπος or χῶρος εὐσεβῶν.[127] These are very obscure half-Jewish and half-Hellenistic thoughts. We will come to understand later why Clement expressed himself in this way.

Up to this point, we have primarily addressed elements of Old Testament and Palestinian-Jewish thought that are found in 1 Clement. We will now investigate those elements that bear the marks of a mixture of Greek and Jewish spirit, setting aside even the preliminary questions.

[125.] Bonhoeffer added the word "first" by hand.

[126.] Bonhoeffer is referring to a list of sayings of Jesus cited in 1 Clem. 13:2: Οὕτως γὰρ εἶπεν·᾽Ελεᾶτε ἵνα ἐλεηθῆτε, ἀφίετε ἵνα ἀφεθῇ ὑμῖν· ὡς ποιεῖτε, οὕτω ποιηθήσεται ὑμῖν· ὡς δίδοτε, οὕτως δοθήσεται ὑμῖν· ὡς κρείνετε, οὕτως κριθήσεσθε, ὡς χρηστεύεσθε, οὕτως χρηστευθήσεται ὑμῖν· ᾧ μέτρῳ μετρεῖτε, ἐν αὐτῷ μετρηθήσεται ὑμῖν. "For this is what he said: 'Show mercy, and you may be shown mercy. Forgive, that you may be forgiven. As you behave to others, so they will behave to you. As you give, so will you get. As you judge, so will you be judged. As you show kindness, so will you receive kindness. The measure you give will be the measure you get'."

[127.] "The holy place" (1 Clem. 5:7), "the place of the pious" (1 Clem. 50:3).

In the Hellenistic-Jewish period, it was a firmly held theory that everything considered important to people could be hypostasized[128] and therefore considered to be preexistent. This striking tendency can initially be explained as a mixture of abstract Greek philosophical thought with the realistic kind of Jewish thought that could be impacted only by actual events. Plato's ideal-absolute construction[129] was thereby robbed of some of its transcendence and to it was ascribed both eternal life and concrete effects in reality. In this way terms like σοφία, πνεῦμα, λόγος[130] became understood as realities and each was accorded its concrete sphere. We have a vestige of this late Jewish way of thinking in our letter. (If we see that preexistence was even attributed to the apostles in a slightly later period, then we can see how far esotericism reached.) If the concept of σοφία had already been hypostasized in Prov. (cf. 8:1, 8:22, 3:19; Job 28:23), then this concept achieved its high point in Wisd. of Sol., where it was seen as a mediator between the people and God (cf. Wisd. of Sol. 10). In Sir. (cf. 17:11, 1:26, 15:1, 19:20, 45:5) and Wisd. of Sol. 7:22, the concept of σοφία borders on the Stoic concept of the world soul. A very poor reflection of this has been preserved in 1 Cl. where the book of Proverbs is called πανάρετος Σοφία[131] in 57:3 and 58:1. This is a later, fairly common expression that stems from Prov. 8:22. The πνεῦμα ἅγιον—רוח קדש יהוה[132] plays a larger role as God's revelatory principle. It is hypostasized in Ps. 51:13; Isa. 63:10; Dan. 4:5, 4:6, 4:15, 5:11; Wisd. of Sol. 1:5, 9:17; Jub. 1:2; Psalms of Solomon 17:37; Ascension of Isaiah 5:14; and Philo. It speaks already through persons in the Old Testament (see above; cf. 1 Cl. 8:1, 13:1, 16:2, 22:1, 45:2). Indeed, it is operative in Clement himself (63:3). The loosely quoted[133] sayings of Jesus must necessarily be interpreted from the assumption that the Holy Spirit continued to speak through early Christian authors (cf. C. 47). If the Spirit is still at work, then what is the purpose of established tradition? This is one of the last vestiges of the "epoch of enthusiasm." (We also often found in Hebrews the idea that the Holy Spirit speaks from the Old Testament. In Clement it also appears as the "power of God" 21:2, 28,[134] as the Christian "Holy Spirit" 42:3, 46:6, 58:2; as the animating spirit of human life 18:10, 52:4, 59:3.)

245

[128.] That is, understood as self-subsistent being (hypostasis).

[129.] Bonhoeffer added "Plato's" by hand.

[130.] "Wisdom," "spirit," "Word."

[131.] "All-ruling wisdom." On hypostasization in the book of Proverbs, cf. Lightfoot, *The Apostolic Fathers*, 1/2:166f., footnote 8; cf. also Bousset, *Die Religion des Judentums*, 336ff.

[132.] "Holy Spirit," "the Holy Spirit of Yahweh." It is not found in this form in the Old Testament. The references that Bonhoeffer uses (*Jub.* 1:21 is correct instead of *Jub.* 1:2) are found (up until Pss. Sol.) in Bousset, *Die Religion des Judentums*, 343; on the Spirit as principle of revelation, cf. Cremer, *Lexicon*, 507–8.

[133.] Harnack: "But is it a loose quote?"

[134.] Citations are not verifiable.

In Hellenistic Judaism the concept of the Logos allows us to observe very interesting cases of hypostasizing and ideas of preexistence. For the most part, scholars have strictly denied that Clement was at all influenced by the logos doctrine and especially by Philo.[135] First, let us make some comparisons. It is beyond doubt that, according to 1 Cl., Christ was preexistent (this concept is clearly presupposed in 16:2. The same is true for 22:1, 38:3 προε-τοιμάσας τὰς εὐεργεσίας αὐτοῦ πρὶν ἡμᾶς γεννηθῆναι.[136] At the very least one cannot doubt that redemption through Christ belongs to this εὐερ-γεσίαι). If the concept of preexistence can be established in Clement, then one can also ask whether the Christ presented in Clement carries traits of the

246   philosophical Logos. We read in Cl. C. 16:1: τὸ σκῆπτρον (τῆς μεγαλωσύνης?) τοῦ θεοῦ[137] and in C. 27 ἐν λόγῳ τῆς μεγαλωσύνης αὐ-τοῦ[138] that he created everything. The active power of God was already clearly postulated in the expression σκῆπτρον. Here the term "Logos" expressly occurs (cf. Heb. 1:2, δι' οὗ καὶ ἐποίησεν τοὺς αἰῶνας,[139] and with it a concept that is fundamental for Philo (cf. *De spec. leg.* 1.81),[140] *De migr. Abr.* 6,[141] *Sap.* 9.1; *De sacr. Ab. et Caini* 8, διὰ ῥήματος [. . .] δι' οὗ καὶ ὁ σύμ-πας κόσμος ἐδημιουργεῖτο . . . ";[142] *Sap.* 9.1, ὁ ποιήσας τὰ πάντα ἐν λόγῳ σου. . . ."[143] In 36:2, with glaring omissions and some variations, Clement cites Heb. 1:3. This indicates that it was a phrase that Clement had in memory and suited his Christology, and that he took over perhaps completely unaware that it was from Hebrews. We can compare with Philo, *De opif. m.* 51, πᾶς ἄνθροπος κατὰ μεστὴν διάνοιαν ᾠκείωται θείῳ λόγῳ τῆς μακαρίας φύσεως ἐκμαγεῖον ἢ ἀπαύγασμα γεγονώς,[144] then 1 Cl. 33:4 τῆς ἐαυτους

[135.] By "logos doctrine" is meant a concept of the Logos developed by Philo as an intelligible entity (hypostasis) by blending Platonic-Stoic world reason and the divine creative word (Gen. 1). The early Christian Apologists of the second century connected this with the concept of the preexistent nature of Christ. Harnack, Knopf, and others deny that this identification of the Logos and Christ was already present in 1 Clement. Cf. Gebhardt and Harnack 47, footnote 4, and Knopf, "Der Erste Clemensbrief," 91, footnote 4.

[136.] "[Brought us into his world] . . . and the preparations he so generously made before we were born" (1 Clem. 38:3).

[137.] "The scepter (of the majesty?) of God"; the correct reference is 1 Clem. 16:2. Bonhoeffer is following the textual edition of Lightfoot, *The Apostolic Fathers* 1/2:57, who considers the Greek τῆς μεγαλωσύνης doubtful and sets it in parentheses.

[138.] "By his majestic word" (1 Clem. 27:4).

[139.] "Through whom he also created the worlds" (Heb. 1:2).

[140.] Philo, *De Specialibus Legibus*, 1.81 (Loeb 7:147).

[141.] Philo, *De Migratione Abrahami*, 6 (Loeb 4:135).

[142.] "Through that Word by which the whole universe was formed." Philo, *De Sacrificiis Abelis et Caini* 8 (Loeb 2:101).

[143.] "Who have made all things by your word" (*Sap.* 9:1).

[144.] The Greek text reads, πας ἄνθρωπος κατὰ μὲν τὴν διάνοιαν ᾠκείωται λόγῳ θείῳ. . . . "Every man, in respect of his mind, is allied to the divine Reason . . ." (Philo, *De Opificio Mundi,* 146 (Loeb 1:115).

εἰκόνος χαρακτῆρα[145] (Dorner already suspected this referred to Christ),[146] Heb. 1:3, and Philo, *De confus. ling.* 20 (1:419) εἰκὼν θεοῦ— λόγος ἱερώτατος[147] and *De plantat.* 5 (1:337) εἶπε αὐτὴν (τὴν ψυχὴν) [...] τυπωθεῖσαν σφραγίδι θεοῦ, ἧς ὁ χαρακτήρ ἐστιν ἀίδιος λόγος. . . .[148]   247
Here, as in 1 Cl., the human being is created according to the Logos. This is further confirmed by the following verse. Here are words that we find first in Philo and then in our letter: 36:2 ἐνοπτρίξεσθαι—*Leg. All.* 3.33;[149] 41:2 μωμοσκοπεῖν—*De agricult.* 29 (1:23);[9] [151] *De Jos.* 7.34 τὸ κοινωφελές;[152] *Leg. All.* 1.18; Epictetus, *Diss.* 3.20.[153] We observe the concept of the high priestly Logos as Hebrews found it in Philo: 1 Cl.36;[154] Philo, *Quod deus immut.* 134 (p.292); *De gig.* 52; *De migr. Abr.* 102, 452; *Test. Levi* 18.[155] We find expressions like ὄμματα ψυχῆς[156] (19:3) and ὀφθαλμοι; τῆς καρδίας[157] (36:1) in the Hellenistic mystery cults (ἀθάνατα ὄμματα)[158] and in Philo

9. Formed according to the similar sounding Hebrew word םוּם.[150]

[145.] "Did he form in the likeness of his own image by his sacred and faultless hands" (1 Clem. 33: 4).
[146.] Cf. Dorner, *History of the Development of the Doctrine of the Person of Christ*, 100.
[147.] "The image of God," "the most holy Word." Cf. Philo, *De Confusione Linguarum*, 97 (Loeb 4:63). [The Greek actually reads "his image," not "the image of God."][CG]
[148.] Moses regarded the soul as "signed and impressed by the seal of God, the stamp of which is the eternal Word [logos]." The correct reference is Philo, *De Plantatione*, 18 (Loeb 3:223). Either Bonhoeffer (or his source) has shortened or changed the Philo text. It reads in the original: εἶπεν αὐτὴν τοῦ θείου καὶ ἀοράτου πνεύματος ἐκείνου δόκιμον εἶναι νόμισα σημειωθὲν καὶ τυπωθὲν σφραγίδι θεοῦ, ἧς ὁ χαρακτήρ ἐστιν ἀίδιος λόγος. Of the soul Moses "averred it to be a genuine coinage of that dread Spirit, the Divine and Invisible One, signed and impressed by the seal of God, the stamp of which is the Eternal Word."
[149.] "[Was] reflected in a mirror." Cf. 1 Clem. 36:2. Philo, *Legem Allegoriae*, 3.101 (Loeb 1:369). The reference to Philo (there κατοπτρίζεσθαι has the same meaning) is from Lightfoot, *The Apostolic Fathers* 1/2:111, footnote 15.
[150.] "Imperfect, impure." Bonhoeffer's note 9 is a handwritten addition.
[151.] "Careful examination." Its literal meaning is "examine for impurity." Cf. 1 Clem. 41:2. The correct reference is Philo, *De Agricultura*, 130 (Loeb 3:175). The comment about Philo and the reference to the similiar sounding Hebrew word (cf. Bonhoeffer's note 9) are found in Lightfoot, *The Apostolic Fathers* 1/2:126f., footnote 3, and in Knopf's "Der Erste Clemensbrief," 115, footnote 2.
[152.] "The common good." See 1 Clem. 48:6, Philo, *De Iosepho*, 34 (Loeb 6:159). The comment about Philo is in Knopf's "Der Erste Clemensbrief," 125, footnote 6.
[153.] Because the evidentiary term has mistakenly been left out, these references— Philo, *Legum Allegoriae*, 1.59–62 (Loeb 1:185–87) and Epictetus, *Discourses*, 3.20 (Loeb 2:117–23)—cannot be verified.
[154.] 1 Clement 36:1 is meant.
[155.] Philo, *Quod Deus sit Immutabilis*, 134 (Loeb 3:77); Philo *De Gigantibus*, 52 (Loeb 2:471); Philo, *De Migratione Abrahami*, 102 (Loeb 4:191); *Testament of Levi*, ch. 18.
[156.] "The eyes of our soul" (1 Clem. 19:3).
[157.] "The eyes of our hearts." The correct reference is 1 Clem. 36:2.
[158.] "Immortal eyes." Bonhoeffer cites Dieterich, *Eine Mithrasliturgie*, 4.

(*De Abr.* 12.19 ὅρασις ἡ μὲν δι᾽ ὀφθαλμῶν—ἡ δὲ διὰ τοῦ τῆς ψυχῆς ὄμματος[159] 24:1).[160] We are reminded of similarities in the way in which Clement, Hebrews, and Philo cited their sources, mentioned above. Clement and Philo relate the same traditions about the patriarchs of the Old Testament and their epitheta ornantia[161] (cf. 9:3, the juxtaposition of Enoch and Noah, Heb. 11:5, 11:7. Philo, *De Abr.* (M 2:3)[162] (cf. Sir. 44:16f.), Noah as a preacher in Philo, *De congr. erud. grat.* 17 (M 1:532f.); Josephus, *Ant.* 1.3;[163] C. 43: Moses πιστὸς θεράπων ἐν ὅλῳ τῷ οἴκῳ;[164] Heb. 3:2, 5 (Num. 12:7); *Leg. Alleg.* 3.81 [1:132].[165] The example of Lot's wife being changed into a pillar of salt which still exists today is found in Wisd. of Sol. 10:7; Philo, *De vita Mose* (M 2:161); Josephus,[166] and others). We recall the haggadic interpretation used by Philo, which extends to his comprehensive interpretation of the Old Testament and its gnosis. This method of interpretation was not unique to him. Finally, we must ask if all of these common themes could merely be coincidental.

In addition, the term συνείδησις,[167] which can be found as early as Paul's writings, originated with Philo and his school. Paul uses the expression 23 times. It does not appear in the Gospels. In the LXX it is only used in Wisd. of Sol. 17:10 where it has the meaning of "conscience." Philo prefers τὸ συνειδός[168] (*De spec. leg.* 1.235, 4.6, 40; and Josephus,[169] among others;

[159.] "Seeing through the eyes," "seeing through the eye of the soul." The correct reference is Philo, *De Abrahamo,* 57 (Loeb 6:33). In the second part of this citation Bonhoeffer unites two phrases; cf. Philo, *De Abrahamo,* 57 (Loeb 6:33), διὰ του της ψυχης ἡγεμονικου, 'through the leading part of the soul', and *De Abrahamo,* 58 (Loeb 6:33), τὸ της ψυξης ὄμμα, 'through the eye of the soul'.

[160.] The correct ordering of the reference cannot be determined.

[161.] "Honorific epithets."

[162.] Philo, *De Abrahamo,*17ff. (Loeb 6:13ff.) is concerned with Enoch and, linked with this, Philo, *De Abrahamo,* 27ff. (Loeb 6:17ff.) with Noah. [Here Bonhoeffer cites Mangey.][CG]

[163.] Philo, *De Congressu quaerendae Eruditionis gratia,* 90 (Loeb 4:503), Josephus, *Antiquities,* 1.3.1 (Loeb 4:33f.). Philo definitely does not introduce Noah as a preacher, but as the first just person recorded in holy scripture.

[164.] "A faithful servant in all his house" (1 Clem. 43:1).

[165.] Philo, *Legem Allegoriae,* 3.228 (Loeb 1:457).

[166.] Philo, *De Vita Mosis,* 2 [3].171 (Mangey 1:61), Josephus, *Antiquities,* 1.11.4 (Loeb 4:101). Cf. above, 2/4:218.

[167.] "Consciousness," "conscience." Cf. on the following Cremer, *Lexicon,* 233ff., especially 234f.

[168.] "Consciousness," "conscience."

[169.] Philo, *De Specialibus Legibus,* 1:235 (Loeb 7:237); Philo, *De Specialibus Legibus,* 4.6 (Loeb 8:11) and 4.40 (Loeb 8:33) The three Philo references are found in the German edition of Cremer's *Biblico-theological Lexicon;* see *Wörterbuch,* 396, where one finds a list of references to Josephus as well: "Contra Apionem," 2.30.2 (Loeb 1:303); *The Jewish War* 1.23.3 and 2.20.7 (Loeb 2:213f. and 2:545f.); *Antiquities,* 13,11.3, 16.4.2 (Loeb 7:385f. and 8:247f.).

in our letter: 1:3, 2:4, 34:7, 41:1, 45:7). The doctrine of παλιγγενεσία[170] is
Pythagorean in origin. It is then handed down from the neo-Pythagoreans to
the Stoics (cf. M. Aurelius 11.1. ἔτι δὲ περιέρχεται ψυχὴ τὸν ὅλον κόσμον[. . .] εἰς τὴν ἀπειρίαν τοῦ αἰῶνος ἐκτείνεται καὶ τὴν περιοδικὴν
παλιγγενεσίαν τῶν ὅλων ἐμπεριλαμβάνει;[171] cf. Titus 3:5). This word has
also found its way into the mystery cults (cf. Dieterich, *Mithrasliturgie,* p.
176).[172] Philo borrowed the word from there and uses it often (cf. *De aetern.
mundi* 47: καὶ μὴν οἵ γε τὰς ἐκπυρώσεις καὶ τὰς παλιγγενεσίας εἰσηγού-
ʹμενοι τοῦ κόσμου νομίζουσιν . . . ;[173] these were rejected. In addition, one
finds the word relating to life after death: *De cherub.* (M 1:159); *De vita Mos.* (M
2:144) about the future epochs of the world;[174] in the LXX cf. Job 14:14).

On the question whether everything that has been mentioned could be
merely coincidental agreements, I decisively maintain that Clement
undoubtedly knew Philonic ideas. It is an open question how this may have
occurred. (He might have taken the Greek philosophical terminology from
such circles.) He came upon these thoughts in Hebrews and used them for
his letter. A direct influence (from the study of writings) can hardly be
demonstrated—certainly not from the above-mentioned parallels. Nevertheless, the connections are striking and prove that Clement was familiar
with Jewish-Hellenistic thought.

For the time being, we will end our attempt to isolate the Jewish element.
In doing so, we are fully aware that we could have addressed many more
details, but they are not very significant for the systematic relationships we
have tried to establish. Several important results will come to light below.

To summarize briefly, we have gained the following insights: early Christianity held in common with Judaism (Palestinian and Hellenistic):

(1)   its entire attitude toward the Old Testament,

a. with regard to the idea of its origin (πνεῦμα ἅγιον)
b. to its importance

[170.] "Rebirth," i.e., the doctrine of the periodic renewal of the world. For the following Bonhoeffer supports himself by the work of Knopf, "Der Erste Clemensbrief," 58f., footnote 4, and Cremer, *Lexicon,* 238f.

[171.] "Further it [i.e., the soul] traverses the whole universe, (. . .) and it extends itself
into the infinity of time, and embraces and comprehends the periodical renovation of all
things . . ." (Marcus Aurelius, *Communings,* 11.1; Loeb page 293). Bonhoeffer is citing from
Knopf, "Der erste Clemensbrief," 58, footnote 4, and adds ψυχή (soul) to the beginning of
the citation.

[172.] Cf. Dieterich, *Eine Mithrasliturgie,* 175f. Dieterich refers to Cremer, *Lexicon,* 150.

[173.] "And, moreover, those persons who allege conflagrations and regenerations of
the world, think and confess [that] . . ." (Philo, *De Aeternitate Mundi,* 47; Loeb 9:217). Here
Bonhoeffer cites Knopf, "Der Erste Clemensbrief," 58, footnote 4.

[174.] Philo, *De Cherubim,* 114 (Loeb 2:75–77), Philo, *De Vita Mosis,* 2:65 (Loeb 6:481).
Cf. Cremer, *Lexicon,* 151. For the complete reference see the German edition, *Wörterbuch,*
239.

c. to the haggadic method of interpretation

d. its imitation of biblical language

Through the haggadic interpretation, Christians demonstrate: (1) their awareness of being a new people [Geschlecht], (2) their ecclesial institutions, and (3) their doctrines (see above).

(2)   the Jewish names for God,[175]

(3)   the primary terms related to Jewish doctrines concerning human religious and ethical behavior,

(4)   the Hellenistic doctrines of hypostasis and preexistence, with all their consequences.

We will have gained nothing by this knowledge, however, if we do not at the same time consider what Christianity added to the mix and how the whole construct of Jewish teaching received a completely new substructure and superstructure. It is necessary to understand a phenomenon without which we could gain nothing: How did a gentile Christian like Clement come to understand himself as a new creation [Kreatur], which saw itself in distinction from Gentiles and Jews as a "third kind,"[176] and eclipsed them? If it were truly the case that nothing other[177] than the Jewish element was present with several added Christian ingredients, then interpreting this phenomenon would be impossible. At this point, Clement's motive was fundamentally different from Paul's. For Paul, the fundamental bases of Christianity were, first, Christ's appearance on the Damascus road and, second, sacramental[178] redemption through Christ's death. For Clement, Christianity's basis included:

First, the historical message that God had sent a man, who revealed the will of God anew, and with this established a new basis for a moral and religious life that consisted of the incomprehensible fact of election. It is clear that the cleft, which also runs through the entire Pauline teaching, has not

251

[175.] Deleted: "with the addition of a few Christian predicates."

[176.] Harnack, *Mission and Expansion*, 240–78. [Translation altered. James Moffat's translation of Harnack's *Geschlecht, Volk,* and *genus* with 'race' anachronistically projects a pernicious modern category into the self-consciousness of early Christianity, and also into the relationship of Jews and Gentiles. Harnack did not use the word *Rasse* in his excursus. He pointed out that the phrase "*genus tertium*" derived originally from Christians themselves, and meant "third category of human beings" vis à vis pagans and Jews; they also called themselves "new people."] [CG]

[177.] Bonhoeffer adds by hand, "i.e., more."

[178.] Harnack underlines "sacramental," puts a question mark in the margin, and comments: "NB: I would at least speak not only of 'sacramental' redemption in Paul; it is connected much more with redemption by faith and forgiveness." Bonhoeffer's capsule characterization of Pauline theology is an attempt to conflate (1) the image of Paul, based on the "Damascus experience," sketched by his Berlin professor Adolf Deißmann (*Paul,* especially pages 97–115) with (2) the depiction of Paul by Wilhelm Bousset (*Kyrios Christos,* 153ff.), which brings the cultic-sacramental "Christ mysticism" to the fore.

been bridged. Seen psychologically, the moral imperative directed at people must precede and continue to be a part of election[179] and cannot be united with the indicative of revelation (see below).

Clement's second theme is the historical fact of the church-community, which is the immediate consequence of the divine will and is seen as the ἐκκλησία τοῦ θεοῦ.[180] Everyone is united in a fellowship. The work within this and beyond this (1:2) is Christianity. Moralism that could no longer be considered "enthusiastic" developed in this church-community. In the entire letter there is no mention of speaking in tongues, demons, etc. Indeed, we have a picture that we could recognize in a Calvinist community. Everything characteristic of the latter we find in 1 Clement: rigorous seriousness paired with consciousness of election and the understanding of moral action as verification.

The entire didactic character of 1 Cl. is built on this foundation. He is purely practical. Theoretical interests, if I may put it this way, play only a historical role for him, even as Paul and Hebrews were strongly influenced by such. We must therefore view the entire letter from these perspectives. This method will lead us to a more satisfactory result than we can attain by using systematic-theological methods. By doing this we can observe the entire substructure of the Jewish element that we demonstrated above. Soon we must explicate this more exactly. We will clarify briefly the picture of the Christian church-community by means of several representative terms and concepts.

252

1. ἐκκλησία, from the Jewish קְהָל (translated in this way by the LXX), arose from the Palestinian communities instead of עֵדָה = συναγωγή.[181] Using the word ἐκκλησία was especially propitious, because a special value was placed upon it already in gentile Greco-Roman culture.

2. ἀδελφότης (2:4) was unknown in secular Greek. In 4 Maccabees it designates siblings. In the sense used here it can be found only in 1 Pet. 2:17, 5:19. Ἀδελφοί in the Old Testament (LXX): a neighbor is an ἀδελφός—אָח[182] in Gen. 9:5; LXX: Gen. 43:33. In secular Greek, it is used as an expression for close friends. In the sense of Christian community of mutual love, it can be found in Matt. 23:8; Acts 22:5; Paul: Tim.; 1. Cl. 1:1, 1:7,[183] 13:1, 14:1, 16:17, 33:1, 37:1, 41:4, 43:4, 45:5, 52:1, 62:1.

[179.] In the original German text we find the word *Erwähnung*, 'mention'. Harnack places a question mark over this word and changes it to *Erwählung*, 'election'. [This may have been a typographical error.] [PDM]

[180.] "Church of God."

[181.] "Ecclesia (church, church-community, congregation) from the Jewish qahal (gathering of the people) . . . instead of edah (worship community) = synagogue." Cf. Cremer, *Lexicon*, 332ff.

[182.] "Brotherhood," "brothers," "brothers," "neighbor" [Hebrew, ach]. Cf. on the following references (not 1 Pet. 5:19 but 1 Pet. 5:9); Cremer, *Lexicon*, 66ff.

[183.] The correct reference is 1 Clem. 4:7.

3. ἐκλεκτοί 1 Cl., introductory salutation: ἡγιασμένοι 2:4, 6:1, 46:3, 4, 8, 49:5, 50:7, 58:2, 59:2; ἐκλογή[184] 29:1 (cf. below for the Old Testament viewpoint).[185]

These are the main designations of Christians. One could claim that it is possible to develop Clement's entire view of Christianity from these three terms. The ἐκκλησία is a supra-terrestrial institution that is the product of divine will and is only "living as a foreigner" on this earth. (For παροικοῦσα, παροικέω:[186] LXX: Ps. 119:54, 120:5; Wisd. of Sol. 19:10. New Testament: 1 Pet. 1:17/1:1/. Philo, *De Cherub.* 120 ἕκαστος ἡμῶν ὥσπερ εἰς καινὴν πόλιν ἀφῖκται τὸν κόσμον ἧς πρὸ γενέσεως οὐ μετεῖχε καὶ ἀφικόμενος παροικεῖ μέχρις ἂν τὸν ἀποπεμφθέντα τοῦ βίου χρόνον διαντλήσῃ.[187] Also compare Gen. 23:4 and its haggadic interpretation in Chron.)[188]

Ἐκλεκτός: An individual is called by God through Christ to this institution. Both terms are thought of from the divine perspective. Ἀδελφότης is the earthly, empirical community of life and love of those who are called. They remain successors to the life of Christ while striving toward universality. This is the empirical result of divine will. If we valiantly attempt to relate this chain of thought to the real circumstances of life, then we have the Roman Christian concept of church-community before us. It is distinguished from the Jewish concept (1) by the new moral formation of life based on the message of God's new election; (2) by Christ as the ultimate proclaimer, the goal of world history (here the concepts become confused), through which we are elected (see below); and (3) by the awareness of being a "church-community" striving toward universality, with the secure feeling that one is bound together with God and Christ through the Holy Spirit.

If we here speak always of the focus of the Christian view of life as being the consciousness of election—in part of the individual and in part of the whole church-community—then we must be very clear about the fact that being "the holy people of Yahweh" stood objectively in the foreground of ancient Judaism, but no longer in late Judaism (cf. 1 Cl. 55:5ff., 59:4, 64, etc.). When, however, Judaism entered the Diaspora, the content of this kind of thought was lost, even though, to be sure, it was all the more often repeated.

[184.] "The elect" (the references that belong to this term follow ἡγιασμένοι), "the sanctified" (1 Clem., Introduction); "chosen" (1 Clem. 29:1).

[185.] The parenthesis is a handwritten addition by Bonhoeffer.

[186.] "[The church] living as exiles [Rome or Corinth]." Cf. the Introduction of 1 Clement on the notion of "living in exile." On the following references see Cremer, *Lexicon*, 795f.

[187.] With this citation, Bonhoeffer made several errors. Cf. Cremer, *Lexicon*, 795. The Greek text reads, ἕκαστος γάρ ἡμῶν ὥσπερ εἰς ξένην πόλιν ἀφῖκται τόνδε τὸν κόσμον . . . and μέχρις ἄν τὸν ἀπονεμηθέντα του βίου χρόνον διαντλήσῃ. "Then every one of us similarly has arrived as if in a foreign city, of which one had no part before birth; and after one's arrival, one lives there as an outsider, until one's allotted lifetime has ended."

[188.] Cf. 1 Chron. 29:15.

However, we have seen—and indeed will see again—that for Christians three thoughts were inseparably connected with the word ἐκλογή and other words. The first is "Jesus Christ," the second, a completely new moral way of life, and third, a new attitude toward the world. [For Christians the world was only a temporary resting place],[189] and, with that, also a new perception of the heavenly sphere,[190] where the Christian's true home is.

From this point on, everything that has been said above is given a different orientation. The foundation on which everything is based is the θέλημα, βούλημα τοῦ παντοκράτορος δεσπότου.[191] It is now clear why in our letter we find these descriptions of God much more frequently than we do that of a loving father. So it is not a deficit in childlike trust that is expressed here.[10] Instead, it is the need to meet the one whose will determines everything, "whose breath is in us and, when he wants to, he will take it away," the one whom "the throng of angels serve" with humility.[193] We are justified only through God's will (32:2), not through our own works, piety, or through anything our most ardent and faithful heart desires. When ἀλλὰ διὰ τῆς πίστεως[194] follows this statement, then it is as if we stand with Paul, who views faith, submission, and justification together. Here we only have one formula before us, which, however, is not as empty as one might think. Yet this principle cannot be viewed as being the center of Clement's thought. What is meant is clear: it is intended to be a repetition of what was said before, by means of a Pauline statement. That a person's faith is the most essential and basic thing that the θέλημα τοῦ παντοκράτορος can direct toward itself is generally Christian; it is also systematically contradictory. If we read, for example, in C. 12 about Rahab that διὰ φιλοζενίας καὶ πίστεως ἐσώθη[195] (the juxtaposition "is to coordinate the root of the plant with one of the flowers," Lightfoot, 1:396)[196] and in 31:1 similarly [about] Abraham,[197] then we can understand what Clement means by πίστις. It is evident that he

255

---

10. This can be proved not least by his position on election and on Christ and his church.[192]

[189.] Square brackets are from Bonhoeffer.

[190.] Bonhoeffer adds "also" by hand.

[191.] "The will, the intention of the almighty Lord."

[192.] Bonhoeffer adds note 10 by hand.

[193.] Cf. 1 Clem. 21:9 and 34:5f.

[194.] "But through faith" (1 Clem. 32:4)

[195.] 1 Clem. 12:1 reads, διὰ πίστιν καὶ φιλοξενίαν ἐσώθη ʽΡαὰβ ἡ πόρνη. "Because of her faith and hospitality Rahab the harlot was saved."

[196.] Lightfoot, *The Apostolic Fathers* 1/1:397.

[197.] According to 1 Clem. 31:2, Abraham was blessed, "because he acted in righteousness and truth, prompted by faith" (δικαιοσύνην καὶ ἀλήθειαν διὰ πίστεως ποιήσας); on the other hand, 1 Clem. 10:7 speaks of Abraham's "faith"' (πίστιν) and "hospitality" (φιλοξενία).

elevates faith above the other "virtues," but yet as one of them, considered—so to speak—as a "work." Yet, in spite of this, I am not attempting to ascribe a theory of works-righteousness to Clement. Someone who no longer views the theological-historical relationship between Jews and Christians as a problem would also consider the other central contrast, law and faith, to be invalid. It is quite improper to attribute to Clement the "systematics" of such problems. It is certainly the case that "good works" are evidence of God's election. They are, indeed, absolutely necessary. Everything depends on the willingness to do them, not on the works themselves (cf. C. 34:2)! It almost seems like faith in the law. Yet a considerably different picture results when we contrast it with Clement's answer to the question posed in Rom. 6:1. In C. 33:1 he answers it with "May the Lord never permit this to happen," i.e., whether or not God allows us to do good or evil, everything is in God's hands. One could also turn to C. 50:2, "Who is able to possess it save those to whom God has given the privelege?" or to C. 51:3ff., where one finds the theory of hardening, or C. 34, which speaks of the election of the holy people. An essential contribution to this picture is made by his view of a "good work." It is clear from 33:1 that a "good work" is not understood as a commendable achievement. In this passage creation is conceived of and described as God's ἔργον ἀγαθόν and ὑπόγραμμος.[198] We find the emphasis placed on good works as the individual's κόσμος[199] twice in a row. In the same way, the expression in 30:3, ἔργοις δικαιούμενοι καὶ μὴ λόγοις,[200] should be taken only in a nonsystematic way. He merely emphasizes the precedence that a good work has over a lot of talk. This is a parallel to chapter 38—the σοφὸς should prove themselves μὴ ἐν λόγοις, ἀλλ'ἐν ἔργοις ἀγαθοῖς[201]—and to Rom. 2:20. In Clement, the δικαιοῦσθαι[202] should not be taken in the strict sense of justification. One should compare the many synonyms of this one term: μεγαλύνεσθαι, δοξάζεσθαι, σῴζεσθαι.[203] All only have one meaning, and that is "to be chosen by God" and therefore "to be able to stand before God."

Finally, I would like to introduce the terms χάρισμα and χάρις.[204] All Christians hold their offices by grace. To try to reach beyond this is sin (C. 38 and C. 37). God's own χάρις is not a frequently recurring term, to be sure. Yet, if joined with the passages about election, this complex comprises no

---

[198.] "Good deed" (1 Clem. 33:1) and "as an example." The correct reference is 1 Clem. 33:8.

[199.] "Adornment." See 1 Clem. 33:7.

[200.] ["We should be . . .] justified by our deeds, not by words" (1 Clem. 30:3).

[201.] "The wise man must show his wisdom not in words but in good deeds" (1 Clem. 38:2).

[202.] "To be justified," "to be righteous."

[203.] "To be exalted," "to be glorified," "to be saved."

[204.] "The gift of grace," "grace."

small portion of the letter. (In the LXX χάρις can mean "attraction," "favor"; in Philo it means "the goodness of the creator," but it first became a term for grace in Paul.)

In Clement we find an attitude that would not seem at all noteworthy if one did not approach it directly from a Pauline perspective, but it is thoroughly understandable from the perspective of our initial position. Morality stands at the forefront of this attitude, and it finds[205] a new religious foundation in the fact of election. Everything else is subordinated to it. Clement does not have much more in common with Paul. We will see the primary reason for this below.

Almost everything that we have excerpted above as being taken from the Old Testament fits well into the framework of the new consciousness. Several specifically Christian terms, which morally surpass the Jewish ones, accompany those mentioned above. There are primarily two terms, which, although they are already present in Judaism, play a subordinate role   257
there:[206]

In Judaism no religious and moral attitude encompasses all of life. For every individual case there is prescribed a specific position. (At times these are ethically very valuable, at others less so.) The synthesis, however, has been lost. (A rare exception is this statement from Rabbi Hillel, "Whatever you would not that someone do to you, do not do to your neighbor. This is the whole teaching, the rest is commentary." One could also mention Rabbi Akiba's statement, where he wrote the following as the guiding principle for the whole law, "You should love your neighbor as yourself!"[207] We do not need to discuss the moral loftiness of these "all-encompassing life principles.") For Clement there is in Christianity an overall attitude that determines religious and moral life. It is ταπεινοφροσύνη.[208] It is not enough to translate this term as "humility." It is in any case not only humility with respect to God but also in relation to people and the world (cf. C. 2:1, 13:13,[209] 17:2, 30:3, 30:8, 38:2). The best example of ταπεινοφροσύνη is Christ himself (cf. 16). ὑπακοή is only one element of ταπεινοφροσύνη (13:3) and represents an attitude towards one's environment (2:1). Ταπεινοφροσύνη is, first, pious self-knowledge seen from the perspective of the glaring contradiction between one's own nothingness and the gift of

---

[205.] Replaced by Harnack with "lays."

[206.] One actually expects the two terms—ταπειοφροσύνη (humility) and ἀγάπη (love)—to follow the colon that ends this paragraph in the original. Bonhoeffer, however, does not introduce them until later; see below, 2/4:245 and 2/4:246.

[207.] The saying of Rabbi Hillel (ca. 20 B.C.E.–C.E. 15) is in the BabylonianTalmud, *Shabbat* 31a (page 1:140); that of Rabbi Akiba (ca. 50/55–135 C.E.) concerning Lev. 19:18 can be found in the Midrash *Sifra*.

[208.] See editorial note 206.

[209.] The correct reference is 1 Clem. 13:1, 3.

258

grace God has given one. Second, it is the moral way of life that flows from this knowledge. The Greeks characteristically did not develop this notion in this way; instead, they conceived of ταπεινοφροσύνη as slavish degrading of individuals (Epictetus 3.28; Plato, *Leg.* 4.716A).[210] Even Philo understood the term in this way. This understanding is foreign to the Old Testament. The term is only present in a few passages, which seem to approximate the Christian sense of the word. They are Job 22:23; Ps. 50:19; Isa. 58:3; Sir. 7:12, 31:8. Yet, here also the concept is limited to one's relationship to God. Almost everything we said about the Jewish ethic belongs to Clement's concept of ταπεινοφροσύνη. Here, as well, one absolutely should not schematize. There are certainly also passages where ταπεινοφροσυνη is not stressed to this extent. Yet, all in all, one can say that, for Clement, it is a prerequisite for ὑπακοή, φόβος θεοῦ, παιδεία.[211] It is a distinctive feature of Clement that he deeply comprehends and exhausts each worthy term, and that such a concept is rarely left a mere formulation. We seldom find unqualified trivialities in his writing, although on the surface he usually juxtaposes terms. We cannot discover a thorough classification system anywhere. One has to rely on one's historical-theological sense in order to understand what was important to him.

A second term that was completely regenerated in the Christian ethic is ἀγάπη.[212] This word, which is almost completely foreign to profane Greek, came to mean in the LXX self-giving and merciful love. It is often found together with ἔλεος (Jer. 2:2).[213] In a completely different sphere, the concept is elevated in the New Testament by three things: first, ἀγάπη is an imitation of the divine; second, ἀγάπη has become a duty; and third, this duty to love is extended unto a universal. If ταπεινοφροσύνη emphasizes the human aspect, then ἀγάπη emphasizes the initial effect of imitating the divine. [The fact that ἀγάπη leads to the forgiveness of sins (50:5) is, on one hand, the aftereffect of the Jewish commandment to give alms. On the other hand, it is a very weak indication of the Catholic sacrament of penance as the repeatable forgiveness of sins.][214]

[210.] At this point and in the following Bonhoeffer follows Cremer, *Lexicon*, 541, 882, thereby, however, making several errors. First, the citation from Epictetus can be found in his *Discourses* 3.24.56 (Loeb 2:203). Second, in the passage from Plato the word ταπεινός 'humble', is simply not used in the sense of slavish degradation. See instead Plato, *Laws* 5.728 E or 6.774 C. Finally, instead of the *Sirach* reference cited by Bonhoeffer see Sir. 7:17, 3:18.

[211.] "Obedience," "fear of God," "discipline."

[212.] Cf. editorial note 206. For the following see Cremer, *Lexicon*, 13ff.

[213.] "Mercy."

[214.] Square brackets are Bonhoeffer's.

From the Jewish perspective, we can only contrast this thought with the famous saying of Ben Sira or the above-mentioned saying of Rabbi Hillel.[215]   259 We acknowledge the incredible chasm.

In order to achieve our goal of gaining an overall view of the specifically Christian way of life by relating concepts to one another, etc., we will add a few more terms. These are more typical than pivotal. (We used the same technique above to attempt to gain a perspective on the Jewish view of life.)

We saw above that in our letter πίστις is not something that is on God's side, as it is with Paul. Instead, it is closer to being similar to a "work." Like everything pertaining to God's will, however, it is the first human prerequisite to a religious and ethical Christian attitude. Clement did not worry about the systematic relationship of ταπεινοφροσύνη and πίστις. The fact that humility cannot exist without faith, nor faith without humility,[216] is a paradox.[217] However, that humility is the first duty is all that he saw clearly, and thus there is an unsystematic juxtaposition. What is significant for us is that πίστις is much more important here than it is in the Old Testament, even though in principle it is not used differently (only this point is relevant in this context). (In the LXX, πίστις is never used to refer to the relationship of people to God.) For Clement εὐσέβεια and πεποίθησις[218] are forms of πίστις. For the Greeks εὐσέβεια and σωφροσύνη[219] (cf. Xenophon, *Mem.* 4.3.2)[220] are thought of as a unified whole and mean the "thoughtful carrying out of human possibilities." In the same way εὐσέβεια and δικαιοσύνη are thought of as a unity (Plato, *Deff.* 412 E[221]) [11] so that δικαιοσύνη can be seen as σωφροσύνη.[223] Compare Titus 2:12 and 1 Clem. 1:2. (Compare also   260 Cicero's phrase in *De nat. deor.* 2.61.153 "Pietas cui coniuncta justitia est reliquaeque virtutes.")[224] We might translate this word as "pious timidity." In

---

11. Nägelsbach, *Nachhomerische Theologie.*[222]

[215.] It cannot be determined which "famous saying of Ben Sira" Bonhoeffer means. But see Bousset, *Die Religion des Judentums,* 112 for the passages cited from *Wisdom of Ben-Sira.* See above 2/4:245 above concerning Rabbi Hillel.

[216.] Replaces the handwritten word "obedience."

[217.] Harnack underlines "paradox" and puts a question mark in the margin.

[218.] "Piety," "confidence," "trust." The following, including the quotations from koiné Greek and the reference to secondary literature, is taken from Cremer, *Lexicon,* 830ff.

[219.] "Reasonableness" and "degree."

[220.] Xenophon, *Memorabilia,* 4, 3, 1–2 (Loeb 4:297ff.).

[221.] Plato, "Definitiones," *Complete Works,* 412 E.

[222.] Nägelsbach, *Die nachhomerische Theologie,* 191–227 (on εὐσέβεια) and 227–318 (on σωφροσύνη and δικαιοσύνη); concerning the relationship between εὐσέβεια and σωφροσύνη see especially 229f.

[223.] Ibid., 237f.

[224.] "Piety with its comrades justice and the rest of the virtues." Cicero, *De natura deorum,* 2, 61, 153 (Loeb 19:271).

the LXX it is found only in Prov. 1:7, and Isa. 11:2, 33:6, as the translation of יִרְאַה יהוה [225] which is usually translated by the word φόβος. The term is more frequent in Macc., Wisd. of Sol., and Sir. In Josephus the term has become central.[12] In Pauline and Lutheran piety the concept has no meaning at all. Although it is also seldom used in Clement, it does, in my opinion, fit well with the character of the letter. Πεποίθησις extends to ἐπαγγελίαι,[227] and is "the side of faith directed to the promise"[13] (2:3, 26:1, 31:3, 35:2, 45:8). It has no specific Christian meaning (see above). No trace of Greek influence can be seen in Clement's concept of ἀλήθεια. As in the LXX, its meaning always is "truthfulness" (cf. 19:2, 23:5, 31:2, 35:1, 35:5, 47:3, 60:2, 4, 62:2, 63:1).

μετάνοια [229] was central to Jesus' proclamation of forgiveness of sins and the kingdom of God. For Paul this concept is probably already united with the sacrament of baptism (Rom. 2:4) and included in the act of justifying grace. In our letter (7:4ff., 8:1ff., 57:1, 62:2), the term does not play a leading role. On one hand, it is less important than the concept of election and, on the other hand, it is insignificant as a purely ethical concept. It is, therefore, seldom used in parenesis. In any case, in 62:2 it is classified among the (admittedly rather arbitrarily constructed) central concepts of Christian parenesis (ὑπακοή, ταπεινοφροσύνη are missing). The word has its prehistory in the Apocrypha. It does not appear in the LXX. (Prov. 14:15 is based on a misunderstood Hebrew text.) Apocrypha: Sir. 44:15; Wisd. of Sol. 12:10; Dan.[230] Pseudepigrapha: Ps. Arist. 188; Test. XII Patr.: Rub. 1, Jud. 15.[231] Orac. Sib. 1.129, 168. More often in Philo: *Quod det. potr. ius.* 96 (M 1:210);

261

---

12. Schlatter, "Wie sprach Josephus von Gott?"[226]
13. Albrecht Ritschl, *Entstehung der altkatholischen Kirche*, 380ff.[228]

[225.] "The fear of Yahweh."
[226.] Adolf Schlatter, "Wie sprach Josephus von Gott?" 76.
[227.] "Confidence," "promises."
[228.] The correct reference is Ritschl, *Die Entstehung der altkatholischen Kirche*, 282f. Bonhoeffer certainly misunderstood Ritschl. The sentence that Bonhoeffer cites reads in the original, "The certainty of divine promises (πεποίθησις) is clearly understood as an element of faith, but when Clement relates justification to faith, it is not, as in the letter to the Hebrews, faith as directed toward the promise of God that is prominent, but rather obedience."
[229.] "Repentance." Cf. Cremer, *Lexicon*, 441, 792f.
[230.] Susanna is meant. [This is chapter 13 of the Greek version of Daniel.] [CG]
[231.] In his Pseudepigrapha references, by "Ps. Arist. 188" Bonhoeffer apparently means "Ep. Arist.," the Letter of Aristeas, which in 188 refers to repentance; the references to the *Testaments of the Twelve Patriarchs* are to *T. Rub.*1 and *T. Jud.* 15. [CG]

De monarch. 58 (M 2:220).[232] [14] In ἐγκράτεια[236] we also find expressed in our letter a characteristic of that entire period (30:3; 35:1).[237] It is found in Roman and Greek philosophical education as well as in their ascetic practices and also in sects that emerged among the Jews.

Finally, the significant concept of παρρησία (34:1, 35:1) should be mentioned. It is insignificant in the construction and doctrines of the letter,[238] yet very significant as an indication of early Christianity's impressions of a worthy life. Such "honesty," namely, in relationship to God, could only arise from the certain consciousness of election, from the certainty that God personally had offered salvation. It is the conclusion of the Pauline "Rejoice, and again I say to you, rejoice. . . ."[239] It is the last reflection of the joy of the gospel and of Christ, which waned so soon behind the rigorous seriousness of a moral way of life in the interest of the church as institution. It documents most clearly and emotionally the difference between Jewish casuistry and the gospel message.

262

We now come to the final section, the doctrine of Christ. We saw above that Jesus speaks from the Old Testament. He is preexistent. To this we add the paradigmatic, exemplary significance of his life, death, and work (cf. C. 16:17). Since we find only paradigmatic themes in Clement, the christological formulas appear systematically unconnected. However, it would be false to conclude that such a Christology has no special interest in the person of Jesus Christ or that it was inconsequential. Clement certainly never posits a

---

14. For Jesus μετάνοια was directly connected to the ἄφεσις ἁμαρτιῶν;[233] corresponding to the fading of the first term in our letter, the second also lost central significance. We have the term ἄφεσις still in 50:5 and here in context with the work of love (!). Otherwise we find the idea that God is reconciled through repentance (7:2, 48:1), that love redeems sin (50:2; etc.). Yes, we must remember: the called Christian does not sin out of free will, and in this perspective we can see a totally pious consequence of the belief in election, from which the "forgiveness of sin could disappear into the background."[234] In the LXX the expression is not found, but cf. Philo: ἐδικαίωσεν[. . .]ὁ ἱερὸς λόγος τῷ τοῦ θεοῦ βωμῷ δι' οὗ πάντων ἁμαρτημάτων καὶ παρανοημάτων ἀπολύσεις γενέσθαι καὶ παντελεῖς ἀφέσεις[235]

[232.] Philo, *Quod Deterius Potiori insidiari solet*, 96 (Loeb 2:267); Philo, *De Specialibus Legibus*, 1, 58 ("De monarchia," Loeb 7:133).

[233.] "Forgiveness of sins."

[234.] The reference is missing; cf., however, Seeberg, *Textbook*, 1:56ff., 75ff., especially 76.

[235.] Read γίνονται instead of γενέσθαι at the end of the citation. "The holy word, therefore, thought good that the altar of God, by which is given absolution and complete remission of all sins and transgressions. . . ." See Philo, *De Specialibus Legibus*, 1.215 (M 2:244; Loeb 7:223).

[236.] "Restraint," "self-control."

[237.] The correct reference is 1 Clem. 35:2.

[238.] In the original, "concepts."

[239.] Phil. 4:4.

πίστις εἰς Χριστόν.[240] The profound impression that the Lord's suffering left on Clement can be seen simply from the fact that we repeatedly find passages in which the suffering and the blood of Christ are specifically mentioned. This almost always occurs in connection with a christological formula. Only in C. 2 is it mentioned without being connected to a christological statement. Here, at the beginning of a description of the ideal Christian community, it is stated that "his sufferings" were held "before the eyes of the Corinthians."[241] Here we have Clement's characteristic pattern before us. It is not the formula that is central to his statements about the blood and the death of the Lord. Instead, most importantly, it is the fact that he repeatedly cites suffering and death[242] and, within the citation, that which precedes them. We will analyze a typical form: 7:4: ἀτενίσωμεν εἰς τὸ αἷμα τοῦ Χριστοῦ καὶ γνῶμεν, ὡς ἔστιν τίμιον τῷ θεῷ τῷ πατρὶ αὐτοῦ.[243] This is the real motive for Clement: gazing at and pondering the preciousness of this blood. Διὰ τὴν ἡμετέραν σωτηρίαν ἐκχυθέν[244] is the Pauline formula that was handed down and used in the church-community but had long since ceased to be understood as Paul intended. Originally, σωτηρία certainly consisted of the fact that he παντὶ τῷ κόσμῳ μετανοίας χάριν ἐπήνεγκεν,[245] which God had already announced to humanity through Noah, Jonah, and others (on μετανοίας τόπος see Wisd. of Sol. 12:10; Heb. 12:17, ἐν γενεᾷ καὶ γενεᾷ,[246] and Esth. 9:23). Here the historical character of Christ's act is obvious, although the fact that Christ brought "the whole world" the gift does not replace the principal difference between Paul and Clement (cf. 12:7, 21:6, 49:6, 55:1 also relates to the death of Christ). One does not quite understand why, according to Clement, it is only through the death of Christ that the σωτηρία, or λύτρωσις,[247] is granted us. It can only be understood psychologically that, for Clement, Christ's greatest act of love was that he allowed himself to be nailed to the cross. To this Clement adds the Pauline doctrine of the cross as the λύτρωσις. Clement wants to retain this formula, but he fills it with a completely different content, because he believes that Christ's death is merely the perfection of his life's work. Even though Christ's death is the goal of everything that preceded it, Christ's deeds are seen as belonging to the same typology as those of the pious people of the Old Tes-

263

[240.] "Faith in Christ."

[241.] Cf. 1 Clem. 2:1.

[242.] The phrase "suffering and death" is handwritten and replaces words that have become illegible in Bonhoeffer's typewritten text.

[243.] "Let us fix our gaze on the blood of Christ, and let us know that it is precious to his Father."

[244.] "Poured out for our salvation" (1 Clem. 7:4).

[245.] "Brought the grace of repentance to the whole world" (1 Clem. 7:4).

[246.] "Place of repentance," "from generation to generation."

[247.] "Salvation," "rescue."

tament and the pious pagans (for Clement, this does not prejudice the Christianness of the Old Testament), as also is Christ's death (cf. 36:1, 59:3). Yet, it is not systematic when Clement states in C. 32:41, 46:6, 50:7, 64 etc. that an individual is elected by God through Christ, who is the divine revealer and the one to whom the whole of the Old Testament already points. Through his life's work, he offers us such an excellent example that God has elected those who follow him by giving them τοῖς ἐφοδίοις Χριστοῦ.[248]

It is no accident that the application of the concept of the high priest to Jesus is not associated with his death, because only the sacramental Jewish understanding of sacrificial death could have been employed here. Could it be a coincidence that only one passage points to Christ's sonship, 7:4? (For in 36:4 the word υἱός anticipates the subsequent citation, and certainly the παῖς ἠγαπημένος[249] is taken from Isa.) 264

The significance of Christ's resurrection diminishes with that of his death. His resurrection makes it probable, as do many other signs (from nature, Greek mythology, etc.), that at some time we too will be resurrected. An inner relationship between his death, resurrection, and ourselves, however, does not exist. The often-repeated formula ἐν Χριστῷ[250] has neither mystical nor sacramental meaning. Instead, it is intended to express something like: "in the sense of Jesus. . . ."[251]

This decidedly natural understanding of the life and death of the Lord only seemingly contradicts the notion of his transcendence. It is chiefly provoked by the historical fact of the emergence of a church, with which Christ was still somehow thought to be connected, and whose head he was supposed to be; i.e., through consciousness of election through him; this notion was always immanent in Jesus' proclamation as Clement conceived it. This is supported by Paul and Hellenistic Judaism (see above). In this way, Christ and the ecclesia are identified with each other (we learned about their double character, to be sure, above). Christ is the head, and all of us are the members (C. 46; 1 Cor. 12; Eph.). The Holy Spirit is the bond that is established between Christ and us, the divine power that speaks from all the pious.

If, on the one hand, Christ was understood as being completely transcendent, then, on the other hand, one hoped for the imminent parousia (23:5). This, of course, corresponds to the designation ἐκκλησία παροικοῦσα.[252] As we already saw above, the eschatological ideas attached to the coming of Christ are pale in comparison to Jewish apocalyptic literature or the apoca-

---

[248.] "The rations of Christ" (1 Clem. 2:1). This refers to the spiritual gifts that Christ gives for daily life. In referring to this passage Bonhoeffer follows a textual variant suggested by Knopf, "Der Erste Clemensbrief," 45.

[249.] "Son" (1 Clem. 36:4); "beloved child," "beloved Son" (1 Clem. 59:2, 3).

[250.] "In Christ."

[251.] See above, 2/4:240 and editorial note 178.

[252.] Cf. editorial note 186.

265   lyptic material in the Gospels. One hoped for a resurrection. From time to
         time the promise is mentioned (27:1, 35:3 and many others). Clement, how-
         ever, answers the question as to how and when this will all take place with a
         characteristically deflected answer. "If we such and such . . . , then we will
         know" (35). In Clement, βασιλεία[253] is a concept that has not yet been
         understood. It is mentioned twice (42:3, 50:3), the first time in the apostle's
         announcement that the βασιλεία *will* come (!), and the other time without
         any concrete perception at all. The fact that the thought of the βασιλεία
         θεοῦ (οὐρανῶν)[254] is based on a Jewish concept is well known (Wisd. of Sol.
         6:5, 10:10; Tob. 1:3; Ps. Sol. 17:4; 1 Enoch. 84:2; Jub. 12:19, Berak. 2:2, 2:5,
         Gamaliel.[255] Here βασιλεία was understood as God's rule in the present,
         but there are also messianic passages in rabbinic literature). Clement did not
         understand this term nor any other eschatological ideas of Jewish origin.
         They were too materialistic and realistic for him. We spoke above about his
         concept of judgment. We find one apocalyptic and apocryphal citation in an
         eschatological context (23:3). In 45:8 he refers to a Book of Life, a specifi-
         cally Jewish concept.
              But after all this, is it not completely clear that Clement *must* think in this
         way? Where could he have accommodated eschatology? For him the last
         things were no longer the last things. Instead, they were foreseen a long time
         ago. What could the believer, who already here had assurance of election,
         still hope for? For the believer, of course, everything was already in place. Yes,
         the believer already had the ζωὴ ἐν ἀθανασίᾳ, δικαιοσύνη, ἀλήθεια, πίστις,
266   ἐγκράτεια, ἀθάνατος γνῶσις.[256] These were blessings that the pious Jewish
         person hoped to receive only in eternity. The Christian who belonged to the
         elect had already attained everything in the present.[257]
              Let us briefly pull together the work that has been done. The Jewish ele-
         ments in 1 Cl. point in two directions: first, they point to the pure Jewish
         piety that is preserved for us primarily in the Old Testament and, then, to
         Hellenistic Judaism. As we saw above, the content of the former reaches out
         into the ethical and religious realm. The content of the latter extends only
         into the speculative realm. (The only specifically religious concept that can
         have originated from Hellenistic Judaism, as far as I can tell, is εὐσέβεια.
         Expressions like ἀθανασία, γνῶσις, δημιουργός, etc., have their origins in

         [253.] "Kingdom."
         [254.] "Kingdom of God (of heaven)." The following citations in the text can be found
         in Cremer, *Lexicon*, 136.
         [255.] The second of the citations mentioned by Bonhoeffer from the Mishnah tractate
         Berakot refers to a saying attributed to Gamaliel.
         [256.] "Life with immortality," "righteousness," "truth," "faith," "self-control." This list of
         terms can be found in 1 Clem. 35:2, and "immortal knowledge" in 1 Clem. 36:2.
         [257.] Harnack marked the sentences, "What could . . . in the present," with a wavy line
         in the margin and wrote: "If this really is true, it is conceived too triumphalistically."

philosophy.) We find every one of the purely Jewish compositional motifs refined by Christianity, while the Hellenistic Jewish motifs are practically unaltered. Most are preserved in a faded form. The refinement by specifically Christian interpretation is represented (1) by religious thoughts of God's election through Christ, with the consequences (and all of the lack of consequences!) of the new establishment of a moral way of life, and (2) by the introduction of new religious and ethical concepts, i.e., the re-creation of old religious and ethical concepts (ἐκκλησία, ἀδελφός, ταπεινοφροσύνη ...) resulting from the above-mentioned way of life. The specifically christological element does not, in principle, refine the Jewish concept of divine revelation in the Old Testament.[258] Instead, it does so only gradually, through the "historical" understanding of the work of Christ. The notion that the Old Testament is a Christian document is also not in principle a refinement. Instead, it is only an inversion[259] of a Jewish-Hellenistic concept. In spite of all the Christian refinement of Jewish thoughts, we must definitely hold to the belief that Clement's Christianity needs these Jewish ideas as material. It is especially true that it would not have had life at all without the Old Testament. Wrede calls Clement's Christianity Bible Christianity.[15] This is hardly too strong an expression, but we must guard against confusing this phrase   267 with "legalistic Christianity."[261] The specifically Christian element forbids this. The Bible as divine revelation and as reference to Christ, however, does not contradict this at all.

We would be finished, if one circumstance did not detain us. It is the question about the remarkable transformation of the concept of Christology along with the concept of justification that is connected with it. How did it happen that the person of Christ was forced from the centrally significant role in religious and salvation history to become the object of religious contemplation? How is it that Christ was reduced from the position he occupied in Paul, which was the intersection of the divine and human planes, to a religious-heroic model? As such he became one paradigm among many others who were, to be sure, of lesser significance. In my opinion there is only one satisfactory explanation. It consists in the introduction of an element to which we have already referred in the course of this paper. It is the Greco-Roman element, which in the final instance relegates all else to a secondary

---

15. Wrede, *Untersuchungen zum 1. Clemensbrief.*[260]

[258.] "The specifically . . . in the Old Testament" is handwritten and replaces "The christological element supersedes the Jewish element."

[259.] The word "inversion" is underlined with a wavy line by Harnack.

[260.] Wrede, *Untersuchungen*, 107.

[261.] Seeberg, *Textbook*, 1:80, speaks of a religion of the law. [For the complete reference see the German edition, *Lehrbuch der Dogmengeschichte*, 1:180.] [PDM]

position.[262] We have to allow the following idea to sink in. The young seedling of a new Christian type of life sprouted from Roman ground. With this insight all the veils fall away. The individual, educated in Greco-Roman culture, who stands behind our letter grew up under the influence of all the powers mentioned at the beginning of this paper. With a deep sense of responsibility that being a citizen of the world entails, he emerged, on the one hand, with the high self-consciousness of the civis Romanus,[263] and, on the other, with the knowledge of necessary subordination under the whole of the res publica. Both of these are complexes that in our letter prevail in a religiously modified form. The former finds itself in (1) the self-evident manner of the demand for an ethical rigorism and (2) the caring actions for other congregations (that have some of the "pacification" (pacare) of Caesar). This occurs in complete subordination to a higher will, which can exist in the divine sphere, as well as in the church-community (cf. 44:3, 54:2). It is just as self-evident. Σωφροσύνη, φρόνησις, δικαιοσύνη, ἀνδρία[264] are the cardinal virtues of the Stoics. When these terms are filled with new meaning they can be considered characteristic of our letter. (One can see from Wisd. of Sol. 8:7 that these concepts were already taken up by Hellenistic Judaism.) Words from Seneca, like "unum bonum est, quod beatae vitae causa et firmamentum est, sibi fidere," or "turpe est etiam nunc deos fatigare; quid votis opus est? fac te ipse felicem,"[265] and so on, were, to be sure, materially meaningless for our author. The sentiment, however, that such a phrase could build upon, was alive and present. Thus, we cannot be explicit enough about the kind of apparently paradoxically configured soil early Christianity took root in, with Rome as the center of its work. If we have seen this clearly, then it becomes obvious to us that several things that were imported across the sea from the east resonated and echoed differently in the church-community. What could possibly have been offered to Christianity on such soil? It was nothing other than the yearned-for divine revelation, which had become history in Jesus' message. It brought with it a solution to the Romans' innumerable and unresolved problems. It is not our intent here to investigate the extent to which Christianity later used this position to benefit the city of Rome.

268

[262.] Harnack has underlined the phrase "the final instance . . . secondary position" and notes, "This is overstated; see my remarks concerning page [2/4:]217."

[263.] "Of the Roman citizen."

[264.] "Reasonableness," "understanding," "righteousness, justification," "bravery."

[265.] "There is only one good, the cause and the support of a happy life—trust in oneself," and "It is base for a man who has already traveled the whole round of highest honors to be still importuning the gods. What need is there of vows? Make yourself happy. . . ." Seneca, *Ad Lucilium epistulae morales*, 31. 3 and 5 (Loeb *Epistles* 34:223 and 225).

It was impossible[266] to expect Romans to place a sacramental idea, which had its eastern origin tattooed on its forehead, at the center of their new 269 practical ethical-religious proclamation (cf. also 4 Ma. 6:28). Everything that was connected with the meaning of the sacrificial death "for all people," and with it to the person of Jesus Christ as the center of salvation history, must be relegated to the margins in favor of the ideas of election through Christ and the Christian ethical way of life that was founded upon it. Terms like μετάνοια, ἄφεσις ἁμαρτιῶν[267] were treated in the same way as the problem of salvation history, which is not preserved in a Pauline sense. All substantive and effective sacramental concepts were reduced to paradigmatic historical concepts.

It does not lie within the subject matter to demonstrate more accurately how all these ideas were modified and made acceptable to Roman thought. Yet we already see from our letter how quickly the Jewish and the Hellenistic cosmologies were amalgamated [(cf. 20). It was only the Greek influence in Clement that used the concept of 'cosmos' as opposed to chaos in order to understand the creation story and the contemplation of created matter. Expressions from Stoic philosophy—διοίκησις, ἀόργητος, λόγοι ἀστέρ-ων[268]—accompany those from the sacred scripture (cf. Sir. 16:18, 28:3, 59:3; Job 28:25, Jer. 18:14 ἄβυσσοι, תהום.)[269] Ideas about the ocean, as in 33:3, are typically Hellenistic.[270]] In addition, we see how Roman organization and the institutions of the synagogue (cf. 40:41) shared common ground. One can recognize that the gesture of prayer described in in 29:1 can be Jewish as well as Greek. This can be seen from (1) the examples of praying figures in catacomb art, αἴρειν χεῖρας[271] (this terminus technicus means to pray), and (2) from the Jewish נשא כפים[272] in Ps. 28:2 and Lam. 2:19. One can recognize how the understanding of paradise and the Christian life to come was mingled with the Greek mythological conception of the Isle of the Blessed (50:3, 5:4, 44:5; C. 25). We have already mentioned the Greek names for God that were transmitted through Judaism. This is typical[273] of nonreligious statements as well. Among them is the characteristic Roman form for self- 270 ostracizing that is used in chapter 54 (cf. Cicero, *Pr. Mil.* 83).[274] Images from the arena clarify the manner of Christian life (5:19). The reference to

---

[266.] The word "impossible" is replaced by Harnack with "at the time it was very difficult."

[267.] See 2/4:248.

[268.] "Direction" (1 Clem. 20:1), "free from anger" (1 Clem. 19:3), "words of stars" (?).

[269.] "Abyss," "chaos" (Hebrew: *tehom*).

[270.] The square brackets are Bonhoeffer's.

[271.] Literally: "to raise one's hands." These figures in art from late antiquity have their hands raised in prayer.

[272.] "To raise one's hands."

[273.] For the following cf. Harnack, "Der erste Klemensbrief," 58f.

[274.] The correct reference is Cicero, "Pro Milone," 93 (Loeb 14:111).

"our military" is intended as an educational example for the Christian church-community. Finally, stylistic Greek can be seen in the diction of the letter (cf. the captationes benevolentiae, C. 1, C. 2, C. 53:1). Yet, all of these are trivial in comparison to what was said above.[275]

We will break off and conclude:

We have to regard the structure of the Greco-Roman spirit as the decisive directing factor.[276] It was not fruitful in a religious sense. It united the currents of Christian and Jewish thought and directed them along paths upon which later the Catholic church traveled further.[277] The fact that the fundamental stock of the religious conceptual world of Greek origin was brought to Christianity from Hellenistic Judaism is demonstrated above. With this we have arrived at the assertion with which we set out, and whose correctness we had hoped to present in the preceding pages.[278]

271   Literature cited:[279] W. Bousset, *Religion des Judentums*; Cremer, *Biblico-theological Lexicon*; Gundert, *1 Clemensbrief*; von Harnack, *Kommentar zum 1. Clemensbrief*, *History of Dogma*; *Mission and Expansion of Christianity*; Lightfoot, *Commentary on the Epistle of St. Clement*; Diestel, *Das Alte Testament in der christlichen Urkirche*; Lemme, *1 Clemensbrief und Judenchristentum in der Urkirche*; Lipsius, *epistola Clement I*; Pfleiderer, *Lectures on the Influence of the Apostle Paul*; Reitzenstein, *Hellenistic Mystery-Religions*; Ritschl, *Entstehung der altkatholischen Kirche*; Siegfried, *Philo von Alexandrien . . .* ; Wendland, *Hellenistische Kultur*; Wrede, *Untersuchungen zum 1. Clemensbrief*; and Kautsch's Apocryphal texts; Wendland and Cohn's edition of Philo.

[275.] Harnack: "NB: The *Greco-Roman world* of the author of this letter had not yet imposed upon his consciousness that religion is *practical* and not speculative. There are striking proofs, (1) that he (C. 62) sees the religious arena in the 6 points πίστις [faith], μετάνοια [repentance], ἀγάπη [love], ἐγκράτεια [self-control], σωφροσύνη [reason], μακροθυμία [generosity]; (2) that he is not speculatively pursuing either a theology or a Christology, so does not consider such contemplation when talking about πίστις. This must be strongly emphasized."

[276.] Harnack: "Here the position of this phrase cannot be misunderstood because the following sentence curtails it further." Cf. above, 2/4:217 and editorial note 3.

[277.] Cf. Harnack, "Der erste Klemensbrief," 54f.

[278.] The final evaluation by Harnack: "February 2, 1925. As regards the layout and execution as well as the completeness and correctness of the viewpoint and the diligence that was applied: *very good*. Were the paper thoroughly reworked and polished and the Greco-Roman element more carefully developed (which was not required by the subject), the paper would represent a real advance in the analysis and the historical understanding of the letter. v. Harnack."

[279.] The complete details of the following books can be found in the volume bibliography below, pages 595ff. "Cremer, *Lexicon*" refers to Hermann Cremer, *Biblical-theological Lexicon of New Testament Greek*. By "von Harnack: *Kommentar*" Bonhoeffer refers to the scholarly apparatus of the Clement edition of Gebhardt and Harnack. Bonhoeffer did not list here Adolf von Harnack's "Der erste Klemensbrief" nor Rudolf Knopf's "Der erste Klemensbrief."

5. Seminar Paper on Luther's Feelings about His Work[1]

Luther's Feelings about His Work as Expressed in the Final Years
of His Life Based on His Correspondence of 1540–1546.

One can classify people according to the perspectives listed below. The
first type of person—and these are in the majority—live out their years. If
they should engage in retrospection they see a series of events, bound and
linked together accidentally, that dominate their past. Others have a life his-   272
tory. This means that they have lived and experienced with conviction and a
sense of direction. Looking back, they see a history that defines the center of
their lives. The third type, however, is the person of history. Their lives rise
and fall with their work, i.e., as their life affects and is intended to affect history. If they complete their work, then their goal in life is complete. These
are people with a concrete calling. Among them, religious individuals are
unique. They experience a philosophical, metaphysical unity of their work
with themselves and with the rest of the world. All of their thoughts and
actions are aligned with their work, as they feel it should be. This is more true
of them than it is of other individuals of history. Now, if these individuals look
back on their work at the end of their lives and ask how their work should
have turned out and how it developed, then they review their entire lives.
This is true because their work can no longer be separated from themselves,
in spite of all attempted conscious objectification carried out by all masters.
This is especially true for Luther, who attempts to do this to a great extent.
Through his reviewing of his life we are enabled to see the conclusion he
drew about himself.

When we try to understand the psychology of the older Luther, we must
draw a sharp distinction between (1) what became his permanent conviction
through his continually reviving religious experience in the years after he dis-

---

[1.] *NL* A 11, 2; handwritten, previously published in *GS* 5:64–95. The title page contains, in addition to the title given here, "Enders-Kawerau Volumes 12–18," and below this
is written: "Dietrich Bonhoeffer, summer semester 1925, June 8 [replaced 'May']." For
this paper, written for Karl Holl's seminar, Bonhoeffer used as his source for Luther's correspondence *Dr. Martin Luthers Briefwechsel*, edited with commentary by Enders. Here the
source is cited as follows: Enders, volume number, letter number. Cf. further Holl, "Martin Luther on Luther." Bonhoeffer modernized and transformed some of the original
language of Luther's letters; he also altered the capitalization. Such changes from the
original text are not as a rule individually noted. Bonhoeffer's unnoted omissions are
bracketed thus: [. . .] and, as far as they are necessary for understanding the text, are
given in the editorial notes in an English translation, also in square brackets. References
that Bonhoeffer did not provide are also provided in the editorial notes, usually in connection with the translation. Bonhoeffer's erroneous references are also provided. The
published English translations are from *Luther's Works*, volume 50, and *The Letters of Martin Luther*, edited by Margaret Currie (hereafter *Letters*); otherwise they were made directly from the Latin.

273   covered the gospel and (2) his constantly varying opinions about these experiences. These were not a result of inner experience but were tied to arbitrary and accidental external events. In the latter case, these experiences
were based on certain psychological fundamentals. For Luther, these religious experiences have bearing on his own religious assessment of his work
and of himself within it. They therefore need essentially to reflect Luther's
strength and the thoughts that led to the completion of his work. These
would include his certainty of having found a gracious God and the conviction that his calling gave him the authority that permitted and required him
to oppose a thousand-year-old tradition. His augmentation of these thoughts
and his being almost completely freed from the spiritual assaults of the early
years[2] essentially led to the constant flow of observations, evaluations, and
feelings held by the elderly Luther concerning his work.

Reformation thought cannot be seen as the basis for these ideas, which
are more varied and, seen from a religious standpoint, consist of accidental
opinions. Instead, they are the thoughts of Luther, the man. At sixty he had
aged greatly, was extremely ill, was worn down by work, and longed for death.
His very wish for peace could not be granted, because he was needed as a
powerful worker and a person of authority. With him were connected all the
large and small events of the time and the internal and external problems
with which the work of the Reformation had to contend.

Luther began to confront death during the first years of the Reformation,
from about 1524–25 onward. He was weakened by serious illness. He believed
death was imminent when, as a powerful outward witness to his faith, he married. In the year 1537 this illness took on a life-threatening dimension. He was
tormented by it from that time until his death, and it had a lasting effect on
his physical strength. (One recalls the frequent fainting spell during his ser-

274   mons and at lectures.) It must also have left a lasting mark on his psyche.

Luther's temperament was easily excitable and sensitive from his youth
onward. He reacted with egregious impulsiveness to minor things and was
always easily excited. This temperament stayed with him. During his development, his shy reclusiveness and timidity was forced to give way to greater
self-assurance and composure. He reacted to both pleasant and unpleasant
events, which were unimportant within the scheme of things, with the full
strength of his emotions.[1] This constant tremendous use of energy also

---

1. Cruziger writes (*Corpus Reformatorum* 5:13), . . . non diu est, cum levicula re
offensus sed conceptis suspicionibus, quas saepe multas ac diu secum alit tacite, credo
adversus nos omnes . . .[3]

[2.] Holl: "Will the spiritual assaults [Anfechtungen] gradually cease?" Cf. Holl, "Martin Luther on Luther," 11.
[3.] "It was not long ago, [because he could,] that when he had been hurt by a matter
of little consequence he nevertheless harbored suspicious conjectures, which he often had

sapped his strength. Years before his death he yearned for that "blessed little hour."[4]

We must be clear that the proposed differentiation between religious experience and changing, non-religiously motivated feelings cannot be strictly upheld in life. This is especially true if the representation is essentially one of images and not analytically circumscribed. This differentiation, however, can be of specific theological interest and important for the structure of psychology. In the main, it can lead us to understanding and to the differentiation between the essential and the nonessential.

In the letters Luther wrote during the final years of his life, he makes few comments about the beginnings of his work, and these were mostly kept as brief and clear as possible. Nevertheless, we can discern many important things from the few comments that we have.   275

Two impressions move the elderly Luther deeply when he looks back on what now stands before him as a completed lifework and contemplates the difficult hours of its birth. The first is the feeling of being propelled by a higher power out of the deep darkness in which he found himself at that time, toward the light and toward a task. This was a task for which his own strength and insight would not have sufficed, and in which he was led even though he was able to have only the vaguest idea of what would come of it. The second, however, is the impression that the path on which divine guidance had placed him was not straight and untroubled but instead was steep, stormy, and difficult to follow. In this manner, an enormous lifework was laid out, before which the elderly Luther still stands with astonished eyes, an astonishment he never forgot on this path.

What is the importance of such a feeling, and what does it mean in a larger context? "God began the matter without our strength and understanding."[2] Out of deep darkness and into God's wonderful light[3] God called the reformer, and this means to be called into the service of the gospel.[4] Yet, because this service was divine, it was difficult, entailed pure

---

2. Enders 14:3016.

3. 15,3282: . . . qui ex tantis tenebris me vocavit in admirabile lumen suum . . .[5]

4. Cf., for example, 16:3483 ministerium evangelii.[6]

---

in large number and nursed silently, I believe, against all of us [that he could only be mollified and kept from leaving the church and university and going away with a great deal of energy with pleas and tears from everyone.]" Holl: "Is this pertinent or merely the judgment of servants (gossip)?" The cited text comes from a letter from Caspar Cruciger to Melanchthon written on February 15, 1544.

[4.] Cf. perhaps: Enders 14:3160 (July 13, 1542) or *Letters*, 439 (March 30, 1544). [Luther's German phrase "seliges Stündlein" refers to the peaceful end of life.] [PDM]

[5.] Enders 15:3282 reads, "who has called me out of such darkness into his wonderful light." Cf. 1 Pet. 2:9.

[6.] "Service to the gospel."

unending effort, struggle, and suffering. His church afforded[7] him "many and much."[5] "What one begins in the name of God can be accomplished only through difficulty, earnest prayer, and much suffering."[6] In a letter of comfort, Luther writes that he experienced greater suffering than death.[7] Because he now serves God's command, God works through him. These are certainly only two different expressions with the same significance, whether Luther says, God, whom we serve as servants, or who works in us.[8] God works in and through us, i.e., the work that 'we' do is God's work. Our work is not our work, our preaching is not ours.[9] Amidst the many intense death and life conflicts, we leave our human words behind,[10] because God desires to speak through us. Therefore, it is no longer Luther who speaks. Instead, anyone who hears him hears God, "because I do not want to speak my own, but God's word."[11] Yet Luther cannot escape the doubt that necessarily surfaces. At this point, the tension can be felt that dominates Luther's entire life, and always becomes evident when he speaks of his lifework. How can he, the peccator pessimus,[12] proclaim God's word? All of Luther's comments intersect at this point when he confronts his divine task head-on. It is exactly here that the two basic religious moods separate from each other: (1) his personal inadequacy in relationship to the office and the randomness and replaceability of his existence and (2) the awareness of absolute, obligating election to proclaim the divine word and the divine power of his

276

277

---

5. 16:3481.

6. Enders 14:3153.

7. 16:3459; cf. for these citations 16:3502: . . . in principio causae, cum solus sudarem in sustinenda furia papae.[8]

8. 16:3429: [Deus] cui servimus, hoc est, qui in nobis operatur.[9]

9. 14:3048: . . . qui nostra verba putant esse nostra, id est humana.[10]

10. . . . quod Evangelium, quod confessi sunt, pro verbo humano habeant, cum nos omnes verbum humanum tot agonibus exploserimus . . .[11]

11. I don't want to. . . [see above]. . .whoever hears me, hears God, 14:3125; cf. also 13:2960: because whether we are too unimportant or unworthy of the cause, it is truly so good and certain that it must be considered God's own cause and not our own. If God were to forget God's own cause they will certainly come to realize this—the longer, the more. Therefore we should be comforted and courageous.

[7.] I.e., "cost."

[8.] Enders 16:3502 reads, "at the beginning of the cause, when I alone sweated when enduring the fury of the pope."

[9.] Enders 16:3429 reads, "[God] whom we serve, i.e., works within us."

[10.] Enders 14:3048 reads, "[People] who believe that our words [are only] our words, that is [only] human [words]."

[11.] Enders 14:3048 reads, "[The rumor will be disseminated] that they hold the gospel that they have confessed to be human words, while all of us have expelled the human word through so many battles."

[12.] Enders 14:3013 reads, "the worst sinner"; cf. 1 Tim. 1:15 and *SC* (*DBWE* 1):116.

sermon. Both moods are honestly and earnestly present to the same degree.[13]

Luther believed he was the worst of all sinners[12] and felt truly unworthy of the great proclamation. Nevertheless, no one would ever be worthy of the task of proclaiming God's word. It is too great even for the angels.[13] If one were to follow this premise, then Christ could never be proclaimed on this earth.[14]

It was for this reason that God elected him, the sinner, to this high office. "In this way God's word is entrusted to me, a poor sinner, and I have been commanded to preach it. I can boast of this with a good conscience and must accept the responsibility for it."[15] And what he would find impossible God could not find pleasant.[16] He is a creature who has been created in this manner and, as such, is an instrument in the hand of the master.[17] He is nothing without the master's guidance, and his glory is entirely merged in that of God's. He can only boast or allow himself to be boasted about on the master's behalf. "With God's help" he was able to bring "his poor service to the point that the Christian church can have a pure Scripture, clear under-   278

---

12. 14:3012: peccator pessimus.[14]

13. 15:3301: Nam quis ipse est idioneus satis? ait Paulus (2 Cor. 3:5). Verbum est Dei, Sacramenta sunt Dei, ut angeli sese non dignos hoc officio existiment . . .[15]; cf. 16:3517: Filium Dei nobiscum . . . loqui per Spiritum Suum sicut cum Apostolis locutus est[16] etc.

14. 15:3335.[17]

15. 15:3361.

16. 14:3162.

17. For 'organon' cf. 15:3376 and often. In addition to the self-designation of organon Dei,[18] Luther likes to use the term larva Dei;[19] cf. 14:3099: Oportet enim ecclesiam in mundo apparere. Sed apparere non potest nisi in larva, persona, testa . . . ac tales larvae sunt [. . .] Lutherus, Amsdorffius. . . .[20]

[13.] On the following compare Holl's comments on Luther's "consciousness of being an instrument." See Holl, "Martin Luther on Luther," 19ff.; see also Dudzus (ed.), *Bonhoeffer for a New Generation*, 106 on being a servant of God.

[14.] See above, editorial note 12.

[15.] Enders 15:3301 reads, "For who is sufficient in themselves? says Paul (2 Cor. 3:5). The word is God's, the sacraments are God's so that the angels don't consider themselves to be worthy to perform this service." The biblical reference is added by Bonhoeffer.

[16.] The correct reference is Enders 16:3516, which reads "that the Son of God with us . . . speaks through his spirit, as he spoke with the apostles," etc.

[17.] The correct reference is Enders 15:3334.

[18.] "God's instrument."

[19.] "God's mouthpiece." [The meaning of *larva* here is like *persona*, 'theatrical mask'; see the following editorial note.] [CG]

[20.] Enders 14:3099: "Because the church is evident in the world. But it is only evident as a mouthpiece, a mask, a vessel . . . and such mouthpieces are [. . .] Luther, Amsdorff." Cf. also 2 Cor. 4:7.

standing, and be able correctly to administer the sacrament and all worship services . . . so that at one point the church and true Christians will testify that I have done this (because they are God's gifts, not the work of me or anyone). . . ."[18] Truly if one is able to glorify God, then this also means that one should do so.[19]

This leads to the realization that whenever Luther focuses on his work, he is consciously aware of an absolute division between his person and his work. This means that he simultaneously experiences the devastating self-condemnation of a sinning, confessing person and the elated feeling of a preacher called by God; they exist together and do not cancel each other out. Nothing would be more presumptuous than to fuse the two together, to allow the sharp boundary to become blurred.

His person is sinful, but his work is untouched by this. Indeed, it only becomes truly exalted by this division. In this manner the success of God's cause is completely independent of his person. He writes to Katie that she should not worry in God's stead, "as if he were not all powerful. Could he not have created ten Doctor Martins if the old one was drowned?"[20] Luther admits that one could with good reason attack his person as imperfect and sinful, but to believe that this has even touched the cause that he pursued (better: pursued him!) would be very wrong. It was the predisposition of the pope and his supporters, which allowed them to rant against Luther's human weaknesses, to bypass the true issue and to think that they had thereby eliminated the problem.[21] Luther considers it a special achievement to make this differentiation in all religious matters. He believes his heart is configured in such a way that he "could not be an enemy or antagonist of any person on earth."[22] Luther does not attack the person of his archenemy, the organum Sathanae Albert of Mainz.[23] He says that he does not for one hour wish his calculus[24] on him, and it causes him pain to see this one run toward hell so

279

---

18. 14:3197.
19. This reminds one of the words that Luther is supposed to have spoken at Magdalene's death: "In the last thousand years, God has given no bishop such great gifts as he has given to me, for one should boast of God's gifts."[21]
20. 17:3614.
21. 13:2832: . . . Sic enim hactenus fuit totius papae mos et ingenium, in personam meam furere, praeterita causa, quam agerem. . . .[22]
22. 16:3492.

[21.] *WA TR* 5:190 (no. 5494); *LW* 54:430. [Magdalene was Luther's daughter.] [CG]
[22.] Enders 13:2832 reads, "Because such was the custom and the mind-set of whole papacy, to rage against my person and looking away from the cause that I am carrying on."
[23.] Albrecht von Mainz, a powerful opponent of the Reformation, was called by Luther and others "Organum Satanae singularissimum" ("unique instrument of Satan)." See Enders 15:3224.
[24.] "Kidney stone."

quickly, "although I make furious onslaughts on him (sc. as the organum Sathanae)."[25]

It could be that here Luther did not know himself well enough to see that he was not always able to operate on the basis of this strict differentiation. Instead, his temperament often plays tricks on him. But when this occurred, it was also the sinful individual who was at work and not the one who had received God's commission to proclaim and defend God's gospel. Therefore, Luther did not feel his gospel was directed against human nature; instead, it was directed against demonic inclinations.

The entire history of the world is to be seen under the aspect of this battle between gospel and devil. This was especially true in this final crisis that had emerged as the gospel was proclaimed anew, i.e., in Luther's work. Here person and work must also be seen as thoroughly distinct. The forces which stand inimically opposed to each other in this battle are in no way person and person, but are instead God and Satan. One is very much mistaken if one sees the matter at hand as a worldly, human one, "in which one can with human reason mediate and master, give and take,"[23] because "it is a matter in which God and the devil themselves, with angels on both sides, take part."[26] An individual may certainly give advice on human situations and conflicts and can understand them and give aid. This can be understood as "mediating and mastering with reason."[27] It is completely different in relationship to divine matters. Here a person cannot and should not understand or seek to gain insight, because it is not a person's affairs that are being negotiated, but God's. Here a person can do no more and no less than obey and serve.[24] (Deus cui servimus, hoc est, qui in nobis operatur;

280

---

23. 13:2970.

24. 14:3099: Si in nostro consilio esset, quid aut quantum per nos Deus facere vellet, nihil omnino per nos faceret, scilicet subito perturbaremus eius consilium, ostendentes ei finem formamque efficientem, longitudinem, latitudinem, profunditatem, id est nostram illam sapientissimam carnis sapientiam, qua impeditus cogeretur nos dimittere in desideriis cordis nostri . . . nec sapientius quicquam agamus, quam dum stultissime videmur nobis agere. . . . Contra numquam peius agimus, quam dum nobis videmur intelligere, quid et quantum agamus, quia tunc fieri vix, imo non potest, quin nobis aliquantulum placeamus in nostro facto . . . nec adeo pure Deum solum glorificemus. . . .[28]

[25.] Bonhoeffer cites Enders 16:3492; the parentheses are from Enders; see editorial note 23.

[26.] Enders 13:2970.

[27.] Ibid.

[28.] 14:3099: "If we could decide about what or how much God wanted to do through us, then he would do nothing at all through us. It goes without saying that we would immediately ruin God's plan, because we would show God the goal and the form, length, breadth, depth, i.e., the forms of our all-knowing fleshly wisdom, through which God would be hindered and be forced to leave us alone with our hearts' desires. . . . [Now the follow-

see above).[29] There is nothing that is at the same time so foolish and so presumptuous as to force oneself into the divine plans,[25] because through our own foolishness we would destroy our own path toward the goal by immediately confusing God's intentions. We would charge God with all sorts of human hesitations, i.e., "that wisdom of the flesh which is so superior."[30] God would have to let us have our own heart's desires and plans and let us find satisfaction in them. Now, through God's benevolence, something completely different has occurred. The more we want to comprehend and understand what is actually being accomplished through us, the more foolish and wicked we are. The more foolish and incomprehensible our own actions appear to us, the more judiciously we act. This intellectual reticence is based upon the notion that it is almost unavoidable that, when an individual's achievement (i.e., God's action through the individual) is shown to be judicious, then the person will feel a little pride because of what is accomplished and therefore will not give God alone the glory. Ultimately, such a person will feel more than a mere instrument in the hand of the master.[26]

In this way, all the important events in history are humanly incomprehensible insofar as they originate with God, and the individual is therefore organum Dei or Sathanae in the truest sense. Hence the situation that has arisen as a result of the strife surrounding the newly proclaimed gospel is not "quaedam comoedia inter homines, cum res declaret, esse tragoediam inter Deum et Sathanam, ubi res Sathanae florent, Dei autem sordent. Sed catastrophe erit, ut solet ab initio, et liberabit nos quoque ipse poeta huius tragoediae omnipotens."[31] [27] Are we standing here before a dualistic understanding of history, a conflict between the God of light and of the

---

25. See footnote 24.
26. Cf. 13:2995: . . . in order that we don't become proud or brag about ourselves as if we had really done something in such things that belong to the exalted divine majesty. . . .
27. 13:2971.

ing is true of God's goodness, . . .] that we can never behave in any way that is more wise than the times we think that we are behaving completely foolishly. . . . On the other hand, we never behave in a worse way than when we think we understand what and how much we do; because then it is barely possible—yes, it is impossible—not to try to please [ourselves] a little . . . and therefore not to glorify God alone."

[29.] Enders 16:3429. See above, Bonhoeffer's footnote 8.

[30.] Bonhoeffer's translation of "illam sapientissimam carnis sapientiam." See Enders 14:3099; cf. Bonhoeffer's footnote 24.

[31.] Enders 13:2971: "a kind of comedy among humans, while the facts of the matter make clear that it is a tragedy between God and Satan, where Satan's cause blossoms but God's lies in the dirt. But a reversal will occur, as it always has from the beginning, and the author of this tragedy, the Almighty, will also free us."

darkness, or are we confronted with a superstition of Luther that arises from the medieval belief in demons and the devil? We believe that one option is as erroneous as the other. In reality, it is God who allows Satan to exist in the world as God's competitor. The final result will be that God's cause will win the day. As we shall see, Luther himself is uncertain whether this will happen in this world or the next. Conversely, for Luther the devil is not merely a demon of superstition. Instead, especially in his religious world, the devil is a mighty power, who stands in God's way and in the way of God's work. The devil wants to overthrow God and God's work. Like God the devil has worldly devices. The problems arising from this thought process do not concern us here.

Now, if all of world history occurs under the circumstances described, what does Luther see as his contribution to his life's work? After all, we saw above that the elderly Luther found both experiences coexisting side by side when he reviewed his work. On the one hand, he saw evidences of divine guidance and, on the other, he saw evidences of the fact that he did not spend his life idly. This corresponds to the sense of responsibility that Luther strongly feels for his life's work. We will soon understand the conditions under which this realization occurred. 282

Luther could condense the content of his enormous life's work into three areas, each of which has different characteristics. They are spiritual assault, prayer, and sermon. In Luther's opinion these are the three things essential for his work and for those who adhere to it. Luther experienced more than enough spiritual assaults in the cloister and in the initial years of his public work. The older he grew, however, the more confident and constant his belief became,[32] and spiritual assaults began to decrease. When his belief in the beginning of his cause faltered momentarily, then the enormous construct that he had erected on this foundation also began to falter. This is the reason he felt such relentless agony when he perceived that the entire weight of the Reformation movement and the responsibility for it rested upon his soul. Shortly after he nailed the theses on the door, he wrote in a letter[28] dated September 17, 1521[34] that he had already been assailed by such

---

28. Enders 1:1261, 71.[33]

[32.] Holl marks this sentence on the side of the page with a vertical mark and makes the following note: "Cf. Luther's *Table Talk*." Cf. Bonhoeffer's footnote 29 and Holl, "Luthers Urteile über sich selbst," 383 note 1. [This note is only partly reproduced in the English translation, "Martin Luther on Luther," page 31, endnote 5.][CG]

[33.] The correct reference is Enders 1:52. The incorrect citation is due in part to Holl, "Luthers Urteile über sich selbst," 383 note 1, where one reads "Enders I [page] 126, [letter no.] 71." [The English translation omits the Enders citation.][CG]

[34.] Incorrect dating from Bonhoeffer. This refers to a letter written on November 11, 1517; see Enders 1:52.

thoughts. Later, the memory of the elderly Luther relegates the date of these doubts to a psychologically more unlikely time.[29] The faster and more eagerly the new proclamation was accepted, the more the attacks receded into the background. We hear very little about them in the letters from the final years of Luther's life. He had succeeded in more evenly distributing his soul's burden and in casting the burden of the responsibility for his actions and their consequences on God. He also began to realize that it was God's cause and that God controlled it. Even during this brief period, he did this without losing the utterly exacting earnestness of his belief in his cause and in himself. On the contrary, one can say that his judgment increases in certainty, i.e., relentlessness and rigor, to the same extent as his spiritual assaults decrease. There is still a great deal to add to this below.

There were, of course, times when the elderly Luther also experienced spiritual assault. (These have nothing to do with the feelings of depression that we will discuss below.) During such times he privately asked himself about the reason for the workings of this world. He could not discover it. During such difficult hours God came to his aid and advised him to be patient with the events and consoled him with "mitte vadere, sicut vadit."[35] [30] Now, we would be mistaken if we believed that Luther ignored such spiritual assaults. They had been present since the beginning of time when the woman's seed and the snake's seed began to be locked in battle.[31] The human being,[38] however, would prevail, because "the human being would crush its [the snake's] head."[39] According to Luther, spiritual assaults are the Protestant Christian's lifeblood. It is the basis of their superiority

29. *WA.T* 1:61, 30, and often.

30. Cf. 16:3555:[36] It is truly a difficult temptation that opposes providence: "But on the other hand we must know that we have been forbidden to know such things and have to accept it. Because whatever God wishes to keep secret, we should not want to know. Because this is the apple that Adam and Eve ate, which caused their death and the death of all of their children; since they wanted to know what they were not supposed to know. . . ."

31. 16:3394: Aliter non habet nec habere potest ecclesia Dei vera. Solatium est autem nostrum, quod victoria semper est penes conterentem contra mordentem, sicut scriptum est: ipsum conteret caput tuum.[37]

[35.] "Let it go, as it is going!" This is a frequently cited maxim of Luther, also found with the addition: "quia vult vadere, sicut vadit," "because it wants to go the way it is going." Cf. Enders 14:3108, 14:3120, 14:3192; 15:3202; 16:3409, 16:3429.

[36.] The correct reference is Enders 16:3554.

[37.] Enders 16:3394: "The church does not and cannot have God's truth any other way. However, it is our comfort that the victory always falls to those who trample the attackers [with their feet], as it is written, 'He will crush your head'." Cf. Gen. 3:17 in the Vulgate.

[38.] Holl underlines "the human being" and comments in the margin, "Christ!"

[39.] Bonhoeffer's translation of "ipsum conteret caput tuum." See Enders 16:3394; cf. Bonhoeffer's note 31.

over the demonic, i.e. papal, Christians. One should only think, Luther says, of how self-confident, lazy, pleasure-seeking, i.e., papal Christians would become if such a constant training in faith did not exist.[32]

When he suffers spiritual assaults, Luther always flees to prayer. He knows "that it pleases God and will be heard in its time."[33] In prayer, Christian duty is renewed. Anything that Christians can do, either for themselves or for others, can be done through prayer. It is the "sola omnipotens imperatrix in rebus humanis."[41] [34] There is hardly one letter written during Luther's final years in which he does not stipulate that prayer is a faithful Christian's duty. He especially recommends prayer in worship services to his theological friends. Personally he was only able to continue his work "by means of toil, serious prayer, and a great deal of suffering."[35] When Luther heard that Duke Maurice of Saxony[42] had declared war, he writes indignantly and confidently, "I will speak against him to a Lord who is man enough for him and who for his anger certainly sits at the right hand of God."[36] Here, in prayer, a concrete achievement is accomplished for his cause. It is reported that he often prayed for three hours[43] during the time of the day best suited for work. He attempted to free his conscience entirely from the oppressive feeling of ineffectiveness through prayer and preaching. "Without stopping and unimpeded,"[37] he intends to pray and preach as long as he is still alive, and he advises his supporters to do the same. Prayer and the "dear word of God" are "the two inexpressible jewels that the devil, the Turk and the pope [. . .] don't have." Because of this, they are much poorer and more wretched than any beggar on earth.[38] Therefore, Luther regards his service as a preacher to be the second thing that he owes to his cause and for which he is responsible. "The office of preacher, the office of pastor, and the gospel are not ours nor any person's, not even an angel's. Instead, they belong solely to God our Lord. . . ."[39] This means that it is a divine task that he must fulfill. We don't

285

---

32. 14:3111.
33. 15:3883.[40]
34. 13:2841.
35. 14:3153.
36. 14:3131.
37. 15:3249.
38. 15:3883.[44]
39. 15:3240.

[40.] The correct reference is Enders 15:3383.

[41.] See Enders 13:2841: "This alone is the only sovereign of human affairs." See *Letters,* 384f. [trans. altered].

[42.] Maurice, Duke of Saxony, supported the political breakthrough of the Reformation. Cf. *WA.B* 10:3739.

[43.] According to Veit Dietrich in a letter to Melanchthon written on July 30, 1530 (*Corpus Reformatorum* 2:159).

[44.] The correct reference is Enders 15:3383.

need to go into more detail here, because we addressed some of this above and still must address other aspects below. Still it is interesting to note that Luther does not expand his post as a preacher beyond the required scope. He writes in detail to Count von Mansfeld on the subject of their dispute, "not in order to judge, I cannot and should not do that . . . ," but in order to preach and to warn.[45] To judge falls to God. Here again, we have the opportunity to observe the sensitivity with which Luther confidently circumnavigates all the possible barriers of self-conceit.

With this we have learned the particulars on which Luther's sense of responsibility toward his work is anchored and where his main life's work, with which he was charged until the end, lies. The Holy Spirit really did not need us for the accomplishment of its plans. If, however, by grace the Holy Spirit once desired us, then it would not call in vain. Instead, the Holy Spirit would command loyal service to the gospel.[40] This service consists of prayer and preaching.

Even though Luther in the course of the Reformation's expansion had found it possible to cast his "historical worries" on the Lord (the phrase he used so often when counseling), he continued to feel fully responsible, as we have discussed above. He boasted about his responsibilities with a "good conscience," because they came from God, and God had to accept the responsibility for them.[46] Seen from this standpoint, the Christian church becomes Luther's church. We hardly need to reiterate that everything he could do for his church, through prayer and preaching, naturally came from God in the final instance.[41]

Because he feels that the condition of his church is his responsibility, he feels duty-bound to fight against encroachments on her territory. It is from this standpoint that his declaration about the decision to battle the lawyers must be seen. "These would have been happy guests in my churches, and I would have had to be responsible before God, that these money-changers and dove-sellers had obviously made such a den of murderers out of *my*[48] churches."[42] Luther had achieved as much as was possible for him to achieve through preaching and prayer. On the whole Luther knew that he had done

---

40. 15:3376.
41. Cf. above, page 260. Enders 15:3883.[47]
42. 16:3481.

[45.] See Enders 16:3568. The Counts of Mansfeld are Albrecht, Johann Georg, and Philipp. Counts Johann Georg and Philipp were nephews of Count Albrecht. Cf. *WA.B* 10:3760 and 3724.
[46.] Enders 15:3361. Cf. above, 2/5:261.
[47.] The correct reference is Enders 15:3383.
[48.] Bonhoeffer's emphasis.

everything that he was commissioned to do with all his might and to the best of his ability.[43]

At this point, it would be incorrect to say that he had Pharisaic tendencies. This is a feeling that appeared in the course of time, due to purely human comparisons. It does not, however, impinge upon his feeling "pessimus peccator"[50] in relationship to God. In the same vein, when the elector did something that did not please him, Luther writes to him:[51] "Your excellency must take responsibility; I am excused."[44] With this, he limits his responsibility to the area of his direct influence. He comforts a friend, who is grieving because his mother refuses to profess the new faith, with the statement, "Pray unceasingly for her et satisfecisti."[52] [45] With this statement, Luther advises him to cast his troubles upon the Lord and not to allow himself to succumb to concerns that would go beyond his responsibility. There is, without a doubt, a certain severity in these words. Yet one must understand them as something without which Luther's personality and his work might have been in tatters. On the one hand, the spiritual anchoring of his faith contributed to this severity. On the other hand, in the course of his lifetime Luther had to set an immovable barrier between what individuals can (and should) do for their fellow human beings and where they are freed from their duties and the responsibilities that accompany them. One is always acquitted of responsibility when one hands the further course of the matter over to God's hands and will.

Luther realized that he was forced to compromise in the world. In the beginning one is astounded when one reads in his work of someone being relatively superior to someone else. He says that the saints really are correct (sicut decet et oportet)[53] if they speak of their way of life and their deeds as being without blemish, if only before God they could rely on nothing but his

287

---

43. Vixi et quem cursum dederat Deus, ipse peregi;[49] 13:2979.
44. 13:3115.
45. 14:3111.

[49.] The English translation of Enders 13:2979 reads, "I have lived and I myself have followed to the end the path of my life which God had given me."

[50.] See editorial note 12.

[51.] The letter cited by Bonhoeffer was not addressed to the elector, but to Counts Philipp and Johann Georg von Mansfeld. Cf. editorial note 45.

[52.] "Ora pro ea indesinenter, et satisfecisti," "Pray unceasingly for her and you have done enough"; see Enders 14:3111. Luther's friend in this case is Anton Lauterbach.

[53.] "As is seemly and decent." See Enders 15:3379, cited in Bonhoeffer's footnote 46.

288

mercy.[46] One would be correct if one were to surmise he thought something similar of a Protestant's ability to serve as an example.

For the time being, whatever individuals are able to do and not to do (sc. with God's help!) now stands in relationship to the consilium Dei imperscrutabile, (sc. quod) nos ferre [. . .] adorare decet non explorare aut indignare.[55] [47] This means that they must be seen in relation to the one for whom we should exist only as an instrument and not as ourselves anymore. The tragedy between God and Satan is played out without our assistance.[56]

The battle that has now openly broken out between God and Satan had already been prophesied by the prophet Daniel. This was perceived as a comfort so that the faithful knew which side to ally themselves with. It also serves as proof that, in spite of the detestable nature of the schisms, the "division" that will take place at the end of the world "is very pleasing to God,"[48] because it truly leads from the devil to God.

Once again, however, we face the question we saw Luther struggle with above. Keeping this in mind, what is the true meaning of the thousand-year-old Christian tradition? Does it stem wholly from the devil? If it stems from God, on whose authority can a person ignore it or even destroy it? In this instance, how is Luther's work judged when viewed against the course of the history preceding it? What position can Luther's work assume in history?

On this point, we find that Luther's statements seem oddly contradictory. We saw how his spiritual assaults in the early years of the Reformation always questioned his authority to oppose tradition. His answer was an appeal to the traditional divine command. In this way, he truly succeeded in breaking with tradition with a good conscience. To a great extent, the penetrating power of

---

46. 15:3379: Nam etsi vitam et opera sua iudicent coram hominibus irreprehensibilia esse (sicut decet et oportet) tamen coram Deo nituntur sola misericordia et bonitate eius tacitis meritis et in vulneribus Christi. . . .[54]

47. 14:3048.

48. 12:2816. The citation could possibly come from Luther, even though the document might possibly have been written by Melanchthon, although this itself is very questionable.

[54.] Enders 15:3379: "Therefore, even if they were to represent their lives and their works as without blemish before their fellow human beings, (as is seemly and decent), nevertheless, when they stand before God, they rely exclusively on God's compassion and God's goodness and are silent about their merits and [hope] to be found in the wounds of Christ [just as those doves are found in the openings of the cliffs (the cliff, in this case, is Christ)]." Holl: "He is speaking of Paul!"

[55.] Enders 14:3048: "the inscrutable counsel of God, (which) it behooves us to endure [and] worship, [but] not to explore or to become indignant because of it."

[56.] Cf. above, 2/5:264 and editorial note 31.

Reformation thought had lain in this fact. But now severe consequences resulted from its proclamation. Should Luther's work be considered to be so superior to history that none of Protestantism's prototypes taken from Christianity's history can be at all meaningful? Here Luther answers that, in fact, the faith as proclaimed by him is not dependent upon historical corroboration, nor does it have anything to do with it. This means that everyone's own faith in the word must be sufficient for them to do battle against the gates of hell.[49] Once again, however, Luther understands the necessity of compromising with the natural order. He understands that even when the spirit is willing, the weak flesh needs to have support[57] to be successful in battle. This support of the weak is the example given by many who were before him and who stood with him on the word of God, i.e., tradition. The strong individual (cf. Rom. 14) does not need history. Luther himself was victorious without it. It should not, however, be taken away from the weak, who need it to strengthen their faith. Luther was convinced that these things are only of minor importance to God. The fact that Luther also set limits on this point was in the interest of the cause and of true neighborly love. Those who wanted to wait for the council's universal decision before openly defending the cause of which they were inwardly convinced seemed to Luther to be consigned to hell. A weak faith should be strengthened, but a cowardly one should be damned.[50] Now, however, Luther was not as consistent as one should expect in regard to himself. After all, it is as certain that personal faith in the word exists independent of historical corroboration as it is that such faith had already been evidenced long ago in history. It had been attested to and had only been sullied and obscured and distorted through time. Therefore, Luther's doctrine is only "purified Catholic" doctrine. He apparently called his church the "true catholic" church.[58] It is Luther's categorical wish not to have his work seen as something completely new or at all sensational. This powerful need to find a way to reclaim tradition in a different manner, after radically rejecting it, is characteristic of the position that Luther assigns himself within his work. It is inadequate, because it is a tautology, to refer here to the so-called need for authority. It attests to an emotional state that we intend to analyze. We must recall how Luther feared[59] that he and his name could possibly be seen as something independent and

289

290

---

49. Cf. 15:3379.
50. 14:3085.

[57.] See Matt. 26:41.
[58.] Cf. Enders 13:2892a.
[59.] Holl: "To a greater extent it is the concept of God which is at stake here! Could God have abandoned the church for so long?"

novel.[51] It was apparently not enough for him that this had not occurred; for him, his feelings of fear were based on the fact that it could have occurred.

When the final great renunciation of the devil and the turn toward God had finally become necessary and had been accomplished, then Luther saw exploiting this opportunity to advocate more self-serving schisms[52] as abominable. Thus, in the ordination certificate, Luther usually emphasized that the ordinand should "relate the Christian [. . .] doctrine well, while at the same time being an enemy of all sects. . . ."[53] This example testifies that the inner enemy is worse than the outer enemy.[54] Luther further states that the ordinand must confess pure evangelical doctrine, which the church in one spirit unanimously upholds and confesses with Christ's catholic church. The ordinand must be repelled by the opinions that are erroneous according to the judgment of Christ's catholic church.[55] Everyone who strays willfully from the true catholic church does so out of self-serving motives, i.e., disobedience against God. Luther writes to a pastor who is celebrating communion in a way that seems to be influenced by Zwingli, and he asks, "Why don't you follow the example of the other churches? Why do you want to stand alone and be seen as a new and dangerous ringleader?"[56]

We have also traced the authoritarian attitude found in Luther's work to the idea that an individual should only be an instrument but in fact always desires to be more. Now, if all individuals chose the correct path, then their triumph and, to an even greater degree God's triumph, is certain. No matter what happens in this world, the final victory is as certain as the fact that God is taking part in the battle.

291

---

51. Cf. also *WA* 8:685; *LW* 45:70-71:[60] "What is Luther? After all, the teaching is not mine. Neither was I crucified for anyone, . . . I neither am nor want to be anyone's master . . ."; but compare 'Lutherani' 18:3769 and 15:3224.

52. 16:3502 on Zwinglians and other sacramentarian movements.

53. 13:2907.

54. For example, 13:2970 and often. Beatus vir, qui non abiit in consilio Sacramentariorum, nec stetit in via Cinglianorum nec sedet in consilio Tigurinorum 17:3600.[61]

55. 15:3265; cf. also 18:3771.

56. 15:3285.

[60.] *LW* 45:51ff., "A Sincere Admonition by Martin Luther to All Christians to Guard against Insurrection and Rebellion," 1522. Cf. Holl, "Martin Luther on Luther," 20. The note alludes to John 7:16 and 1 Cor. 1:13.

[61.] The correct reference is Enders 17:3602: "Blessed is the person who has not been led astray by the advice of the sacramentalists and has not remained on the path of the followers of Zwingli and does not sit in the council of the Zürichers." Instead of "in consilio Tigurinorum" Enders reads, "in cathedra Tigurinorum" ("on the seat of the Zürichers"). Cf. Ps. 1:1.

Here lies the point at which Luther's emotions rise and fall in a powerful rhythm. Here they rise in triumphant jubilation and fall again with intensifying world-weariness. It is at this point that his entire temperament is invested in his cause, reaches its fullest development, and can be examined with the greatest clarity. It is here that the elderly Luther's often-cited "pessimism" and his prophetic triumphant attitude originate. Here is the point at which Luther's humanity becomes recognizable in all its weaknesses and strengths. It is also the point at which the important and unimportant events of the world are echoed in the Reformer's mood and where they attain meaning. Here we must let ourselves be influenced thoroughly and precisely by what we said at the beginning about the psychology of the aging Luther. If what we previously treated was primarily Luther's prevailing mood that arose from the Reformer's religious experience and growth, then it served as the basis for everything else and was to a great extent a consistent character trait. In this context the idea of the final battle and the following Judgment Day affects Luther's mood by pure chance and is the result of fleeting mood swings.

When Luther observed the many deplorable consequences of his reforming work, he became certain[62] that the end time had arrived and that the final battle, foretold by the prophets, Jesus, and Paul, had come. Satan was raising himself up with terrible power against God for the last time. Judgment Day was at hand. In 1541, using a chronological table of history, Luther reckoned that half of the prophesied world history was soon over. In the same way that Christ spent only one and a half days in the grave instead of three, the history of the world would also be shortened by half.[63]

In this great battle, Luther was certain of two things. First, in spite of everything, it was God's word that had come into the world; and second, those who aligned themselves with it would certainly be victorious and triumph on Judgment Day. To be sure, what these people had to suffer and to fight for in the world until that day arrived was uncertain. This, however, was not in the least important. Every misfortune suffered in the world certainly carries with it eternal glory and pleases God.[57] Humanity possesses prayer

292

---

57. 15:3288: Miseria est, in qua vivis; sed ea coniuncta est cum gloria aeterna beneplacito Dei. . . .[64]

[62.] Holl: "Much more! as soon as it became clear to him that the pope was the 'Antichrist'."

[63.] Between 1536 and 1540 Luther put together a historical table which at first he used for his own studies. This was published in 1541. This table takes the duration of eras and numbers of years from the Bible and points to the upcoming end of the world. Cf. *WA* 53:1ff., especially 171, *Supputatio annorum mundi*, 1541–45.

[64.] Enders 15:3288: "It is misery in which you live, but it is connected to what is pleasing to God, together with eternal glory."

and "God's precious word." What would be gained is so great "that it [humanity]" should "properly and willingly see and suffer temporal evil."[58] The only reason humanity lives in misery on this earth is so that it can recognize how much greater the misery is from which Christ has delivered it.[59] Therefore, humanity should accept whatever it confronts,[60] because the world is temporal, transitory, and will soon have reached its end. The world is old, and godlessness and hedonism have increased[61] as it has aged. The world raves in folly as the elderly do when dying. Soon the world will cease to exist.[62] Luther is certain that the world is on the verge of collapse.[63] Valeat, perdatur mundus.[67] [64] We now need to investigate these convictions in greater depth.

In the year 1541 the Turks once again crossed their borders,[68] and the Christians marched against them in battle. Luther anticipates the battle with great concern,[65] because it seems to him as if the Christians were tempting God, "that we send ten thousand against twenty, yes even fifty thousand and we, truly burdened with sins and unrepentant, especially the king and the papists, will have hands full of innocent blood. These cannot be the people through whom God is made known or would perform wonders or great things."[66] Every defeat confirms to him that this was frivolous; everything is a prelude to Judgment Day. The Turks are the rod of wrath with which God repays us for our sins.[67] Everyone is sinful and should understand that they

---

58. 15:3883.[65]

59. 15:3311.

60. Laetandum et ferendum est omne, quod acciderit.[66]

61. 12:2823.

62. 15:3378.

63. 14:3120.

64. 14:3108.

65. Luther's hymn "Lord keep us in your Word and curb the murdering of the pope and the Turks" was written in this year.[69]

66. 14:3036.

67. Cf. 3316 [70] and 14:3036.

[65.] The correct reference is Enders 15:3383.

[66.] Enders 15:3288: "One must be cheerful and bear everything that happens to one."

[67.] Enders 14:3108: "Away with the world, let it succumb."

[68.] In the late summer of 1541 the Turks under Suleiman I occupied Hungary and put it under the administrative control of the Ottoman Empire. This led Luther to write, "Appeal for prayer against the Turks"; see *WA* 51:585, *LW* 43:219–41; and *WA.B* 9:3653.

[69.] *WA* 35:467f. See *Lutheran Book of Worship* No. 230, "Lord keep us steadfast in your word," and *Evangelisches Kirchengesangbuch* 142; cf. *WA* 35:235ff. Luther gave it the superscript, "A children's song which can be sung in opposition to the two arch-enemies of Christ and Christ's holy church, the pope and the Turks, etc." [See also Bonheoffer's footnote 68 below.] [CG]

[70.] Enders 15:3316 is intended.

are justly punished at the hands of the Turks.[68] No one wants to admit that they are guilty and sinful.[69] Even the Protestants live in a sinful body, but they are still free of the innocent blood[70] with which the papists are stained. Indeed, what is most terrible is that these knowingly sin against the recognized truth.[71] The world is foolish. It believes that it can carry the church with its own strength, but the exact opposite is true.[72]

294

However, it does not only look so frightening in the enemy's camp as one begins to hear of rumors of war in one's own camp. Tactical moves, personal battles are in full swing. All his life Luther had been unable to achieve a good relationship with the princely and royal classes. Both wanted to force the church to serve them, just as (sub nostro tempore—sub papa!)[73] the pope had previously wanted the world to be in his.[73] With this, however, selfish interests came in play. This contradicted Paul's words in Rom. 14:23: "Whatever does not proceed from faith is sin." People scorn peace and seek their own righteousness. Luther responds to this by saying, "We can be blessed without our own righteousness, but without peace we cannot be Christians, quia Christus est pax. . . .[75] What one cannot settle without disturbing the peace, one should wind up in a ball until God personally unwinds it."[74] It is such disturbers of the peace who, "for the sake of their honor (dung, I say) distress the whole church."[75] Therefore, unity in one's

---

68. 14:3036: "If anyone wants to go to war against the Turks, he should before all else think about the fact that the Turks are God's rod and anger at the world and especially at the Christians, whom God wishes to punish . . . ; we should be worthy, we who are being punished by the Turks. . . ."

69. See footnote 68; 14:3164.

70. 13:2841: . . . miseri peccatores, tamen puri sumus a sanguine. . . .[71]

71. 12:2815.

72. 14:3112: Sic mundus nescit se stare viribus alienis, i.e., Ecclesiae, et putat, Ecclesiam stare viribus suis, i.e., mundi.[72]

73. 15:3329: sub papa miscuit ecclesiam politiae (sc. Sathanus), sub nostro tempore vult miscere politiam ecclesiae. . . .[74]

74. 16:3408.

75. See footnote 74.

[71.] Enders 13:2841: "[Although we] poor sinners [also live in sinful flesh], yet we remain unstained by blood."

[72.] Enders 14:3112: "And so the world does not know that she is supported by an outside force, i.e. the church, and believes that the church is supported by means of its, i.e. the world's, power."

[73.] Enders 15:3329: "in *our* time—as in the pope's time." Cf. Bonhoeffer's note 73. Bonhoeffer's exclamation point.

[74.] Enders 15:3329: "Under the pope he (sc. Satan) meddles in the church with politics. Now he wants to meddle in politics with the church." The words in parentheses are Bonhoeffer's.

[75.] Enders 16:3408: "because Christ is peace."

own camp—because all of the former is written to oppose this—is the first requirement.[76]

295

If, as we saw, Luther had become "objectively" free from responsibility— in truth, he would have found it intolerable—such disunity affected him deeply in his role as counselor and preacher. He attempted to heal the breach with exhortations ranging from curses to pleas. One should be unified in support of the church against the enemy. Abandoning the church during her time of greatest need would be tantamount to showing disdain for the holiest institution, which is so tormented and exhausted and has truly been crucified with her bridegroom.[77] The worldly battles within Protestantism were compounded by the sectarians, immoral behavior at the university, the dishonesty and unloving nature of his own supporters,[78] and finally by the unpleasantness that Luther experienced in his own family. This leads Luther to cry out in anguish: "The strokes of fate press upon us like our sins. We rage against each other in fury." God's wrath is even greater than the faithful believe it is and penance can be found nowhere.[79] "Wonders occur and we don't see them; that is how blind our reason is."[80] Germany was once

---

76. The Protestant may only resort to weapons when attacked and in self-defense. If God wants to change something in the world with war, "then God will provide its beginning telling us that we have to defend ourselves and should not be in a hurry to do so." A sentence follows that in its profundity almost encompasses the whole wisdom of the Lutheran way of life: "A Christian's wisdom and strength is not to rush toward a certain profession but to hold quietly onto faith and await the appointed time. Human fear hurries and exhausts itself" (16:3418). Longanimitate nobis opus est, brevianimitate nihil efficimus (16:3472).[76]

77. 14:3155: [Ecclesia] quam deserere nisi sacrilegi non possumus, sic vexatam, agitatam, fessam, laborantem, fatiscentem, languentem et cum Sponso suo crucifixam.[77]

78. Cf. 14:3164.

79. 14:3146.

80. 17:3596;[78] cf. 14:3133: Germania obsurduit, caeca est, [. . .] ut spem contra spem [. . .] habere non liceat.[79]

[76.] Enders 16:3472: "We need patience. We won't be able to accomplish anything through impatience."

[77.] The correct reference is Enders 14:3154: "[The church] whom we can abandon only sacreligiously [needs you and people like you] because she is so tortured, agitated, exhausted, suffering, weary, enervated, and crucified with her Bridegroom."

[78.] Bonhoeffer's German rendering of "Nos videmus et habemus hodie mirabilia, nec tamen credimus nec miramur. Adeo ratio est caeca et insensata" Enders 17:3596 translates: "We see and experience wonders today, yet we do not believe in them nor are we astounded by them. This is how blind and unperceiving reason is."

[79.] The translation of Bonhoeffer's German rendering of the quotation from Enders 14:3133 reads: "Germany has become deaf, it is blind [and has a clogged heart] so that [we] cannot have hope against hope." Cf. Rom. 4:18. Bonhoeffer is responsible for the omissions.

alive and will never again be what it was. In former times the world was a bet- 296
ter place, but that time is gone forever and what remains is nothing more
than a diluvium malorum.[81] Luther believed he had seen the best of what he
was meant to see.[82] At this point in his life he believed that he either had
never known the world or that a new world is born every night when he is
asleep, because unbelievable things were occurring.[83]

In all of this, one thing is certain. The day is coming soon, finis, finis, finis
instat![81] [84] For the Lord himself has prophesied that it would be this way.[85]
Luther speaks of three great challenges that the true church must withstand.[86] They are tyrants, heresy, and the unbridled desires of the lawless,
godless life, "as if we were full and had a satiety of the word of God, because
it was really unnecessary any more, when the enemy had been conquered."[84] These are the temptations against the Father, the Son, and the
Holy Spirit. Tyrants and heresy are not dangerous and are soon conquered.
But an unrelenting fight is waged against the third of these challenges,
against the ridiculers and scorners, who say "nullus est Deus";[85] and it is
these people who are in the majority.

Should people at this point resign themselves completely to a world whose
"greatest number abuse the gospel and hold it in contempt"?[87]

The comforting phrase that Luther had made his own as a result of confronting troublesome controversies was mitte vadere, sicut vadit.[86] It means, 297
resign yourself to the world. Do not be anxious about the world, and do not
hold out any hopes for it. Moreover, another kind of belief about security in

---

81. 15:3254: In hoc seculo quaecunque bona futura sperata sunt, ea fuerunt et
transierunt. Nihil restat nisi diluvium malorum, quod coepit et operatur.[80]

82. 15:3383: "I have seen the best I shall ever see upon the earth, for it looks as if
evil times are at hand."

83. 15:3300.

84. 15:3272[82] (cf. 3328[83] and others).

85. 15:3271.

86. 14:3048.

87. 16:3482.

[80.] Enders 15:3254: "In this age is what one always hoped to have as future good is
over and past. Nothing remains outside of the flood of evils, which already have begun and
continue on."

[81.] Enders 15:3277: "The end, the end, the end stands before us."

[82.] The correct reference is Enders 15:3277.

[83.] The reference is incorrect; probably Enders 15:3378 is meant.

[84.] English translation of Bonhoeffer's rendering of the following Latin, Enders
14:3048: "ut qui sumus et fastidio habemus verbum, quo iam non sit opus, cum hostes victi
sint."

[85.] Enders 14:3048: "There is no God." Cf. Ps. 14:1.

[86.] Cf. editorial note 35.

God necessarily arose from this belief. It advised resignation to the world. It arose from the feeling that one had done all in one's power to do what God had commanded. This feeling of certainty is found during the phases that we can designate as depressive. In Luther this is a purely personal feeling. It does not express itself in loud triumphant cheers of victory but in a few inner words that attest to a peace with God that is not disturbed in spite of all the evil. During these moods Luther looks with uncommon sorrow upon the frenzy within his own camp. He cannot bring himself to have a general feeling of hope. When his moods are optimistically charged, his focus centers mainly on the external world, which attacks the gospel. In this way the feeling that we will come to understand under the concept of "being chosen" comes to the fore.

First we will talk about the state of Luther's deeply pessimistic feelings. In the process we will observe that such an emotional state corresponds to a strong, inward, personal certainty of salvation. His letter of warning to the people of Wittenberg[88] is indicative of this. For nearly thirty years, he and many others with him preached the gospel to them, and now, at the end of his life, he discovers that "it has never been worse than it is now."[87] This would be awful to hear before God and the world. It would greatly sadden both the Holy Spirit and him, and would certainly be a sign that "this city deserved a special curse like Chorazin, Bethsaida, and Capernaum." They would barely escape from the flood, and it was not his fault.[88] In spite of all skepticism about the world, one cannot find the slightest personal scruple in such expressions. In their emotive content, they are not unlike asking why he should continue to waste his powers on those who had been rejected.[89] Let it happen as it wants to, because it truly will happen as it wants to.[90] Volenti non fit iniuria.[90]

Luther knows well that this should not provoke him to lay his hands in his lap. Instead one should "do what is commanded according to your calling and leave the rest to God."[91] Nevertheless, he interprets this completely

298

---

88. 14:3106.
89. 14:3120: Quare nos [. . .] maceremur et conficiemur propter perditos, perituros et perdendos? Volenti non fit iniuria.[89] cf. 14:3108; 15:3203 and others.
90. See footnote 89.
91. 16:3477.

[87.] Enders 14:3106.
[88.] Ibid.
[89.] The Latin text reads, "conficiamur." Enders 14:3120 reads: "Why should we [uselessly] destroy ourselves and die on account of men, who are [already] ruined, who will perish, and must perish? Whoever wishes this receives their just due."
[90.] Cf. editorial note 35.

in accord with his varying mood. On the pessimistic side, he drew the external consequence in a letter to Katie on the 28th of July 1545. In it he tells of his decision to allow Wittenberg to take care of itself and to step back from his worries for his cause.[91] It would be a mistake to infer from such an intention, as from other pessimistic sayings of Luther, that in the end he had begun to regret his work and planned to abandon it. One look at both of his final letters to Katie, written shortly before his death, proves that this proposition of slowly growing doubt and regret is completely baseless.[92] We must also challenge the notion that Luther ever doubted his work, even during the times when he was depressed. If we have demonstrated that Luther never lost the certainty that his cause was God's cause, then it would be nonsense to imagine that he doubted the work that had been accomplished. On the contrary, he always found support for this conviction. It guided him on uneven roads to a final majestic triumph. To regret God's cause is insanity. Therefore, we must understand the decision expressed in the letter merely as an intense expression of his frequent depression. It testifies to the fact that, although his belief in this world is completely lost, his belief in God's guidance is unshakable. In this way, what is evident in this letter is the mood of an individual who feels personally unfortunate.[93] This mood does not in the least impact his work. In such time of tristitia,[94] Luther writes phrases like, "obmutescere cogimur, et sinimus Sathanae suam voluntatem, Deo permittente, super ingratos et superbos habere";[95] 92 or he speaks of being useless to his cause93 and yet feels almost suffocated by

299

92. 13:2884.

93. . . . peto ut Deus . . . iubeat deponere tabernaculum meum (2 Pet. 1:4) hoc inutile, emeritum [. . .] exhaustum. Nullius enim usus esse me satis video.[96] 13:2917.

[91.] Enders 16:3549. The reference is found on Bonhoeffer's page at the bottom. A corresponding footnote number, however, is lacking in the text. Luther stayed in Zeitz from July 25, 1545. From here he wrote his wife that he did not wish to return to Wittenberg due to the immorality found there. On August 18, 1545, Luther nonetheless returned to Wittenberg and ordered ordinances against the existing immorality.

[92.] Cf. Enders 17:3614 dated February 7, 1546 (*LW* 50:301ff.), and Enders 17:3616 dated February 10, 1546 (*LW* 50:305ff.).

[93.] The letter to Luther's wife dated July 28, 1545, mentioned in editorial note 91, is meant; cf. *LW* 50:273ff.

[94.] "Sadness."

[95.] Enders 13:2884: "We are forced to remain silent and leave it to Satan, when God permits, to have his will over the thankless and proud."

[96.] The correct reference is Enders 13:2947: "I plead that the dear God would smite me with illness [instead of you], and command me to lay aside this weary, worn-out frame, which can henceforth benefit no one" (*Letters,* 396; cf. 395f.).

300

his work.[94] He sees battles, which hardly amount to anything in relationship to the enormous battles of the past, and sees them as the largest battles that he has ever had to fight.[95] During these times, his illness bothers him more than usual, and he yearns for death. In this way he begins to be consumed by doubt whether there will be a favorable end to the tragedy or comedy, however one wants to refer to it, in this world.[101]

On one occasion Luther's depression resulted from a relatively insignificant external occurrence (like his flight from Wittenberg due to the immorality of the city, something that he had been aware of for a long time).[102] Often, however, his moods were due to problems within Protestantism. On another occasion, no recognizable reason can be found. Thus, one can conclude that such a condition does not have an indispensable external cause, is recurrent, and is purely psychologically determined. In the letters that witness to such moods we never encounter those tremendous rages of hatred that we are familiar with from other letters. They are reserved, oppressed, and very personal. Moods like this, however, never touch the inner-religious side of Luther. They have nothing to do with the violent storms of perturbation that always lead to optimistic phases. In contrast to the depressed moods his optimistic moods become more infrequent in his final years. (Luther might have called such a mood a perturbation of tristitia acedia.)[103] In spite of the most emphatic pessimism about the world, his characteristic inner-religious certainty remains intact—a fact we can't forget.

---

94. 15:3603: Dies breves . . . tardant opus;[97] 17:3601: Quasi nihil [. . .] egerim, scripserim, dixerim, fecerim, ita obruor scribendis, dicendis . . . rebus.[98] 15:3202:[99] "Would you, however, help us to carry the cross, as we indeed have to bear everywhere, suffer, and work in all sorts of affairs of almost everyone."

95. 15:3367: Ego tibi fateor in hoc anno novo sic me esse acceptum, ut in vita mea et in tota causa Evangelii nunquam fuerim perturbatior . . . than in the battle with the lawyers.[100]

[97.] The correct reference is Enders 17:3603: "The short days [i.e., in January] . . . slow down [my] work."

[98.] The correct reference is Enders 17:3602: "It looks as if I had neither written nor done anything heretofore, so overburdened am I now with writing and talking" (*Letters*, 468).

[99.] The correct reference is Enders 15:3207.

[100.] Enders 15:3367: "but I may tell you that never in my life have I had more worry in connection with the gospel than in the year upon which we have entered" (*Letters*, 437). Bonhoeffer refers to *WA.B* 19:524, note 5 for his translation; he adds, "in conflict with the lawyers." See *Letters*, 436f.

[101.] Cf. above, 2/5:264f..

[102.] Cf. above, 2/5:279 and editorial note 91.

[103.] "Sadness, depression."

A sudden change, following such moods, is characterized by psychological expressions quite contrary to those just mentioned. These stand psychologically at the heart of Luther's moods. In them he views the current state of the church as certainly not completely ruined but something that gives rise to worthy hope. But even when such feelings tend to be optimistic, the full force of hate and hope does not flow from them but rather a placid, joyous confidence in victory. "Even if we are pinched by it at first, so at length we shall conquer with him."[96] Thus, unlike his intense moods, these moods do not offset all his feelings of resistance. This means he can stand against worldly resistance almost in an emotionless way. Here the perspective is much more objective. Luther looks to the future of his cause as well as his own future with a secure, serene composure. His personal letters in particular reflect this type of mood.

One thinks of both of the last letters to Katie, "Leave me in peace with your worrying. I have someone who is better able to worry about me than you and all the angels. He lies in a manger and hangs on a virgin's breasts. But at the same time he sits at the right hand of the all powerful Father. . . ."[97] "Pray, and let God worry. It has not been commanded that you or I need to worry about me or yourself."[98] Here as well the personal certainty about God is dominant.

Luther intends to leave behind a church that blossoms due to its pure and clear doctrine. It will grow daily, due to the care of good shepherds.[99] He looks with satisfaction at the new generation of young theologians.[100] He perceives also that he, in his own person, is seen as authoritative and has a certain prominence. As a veteran in Christ he must introduce and educate the young.[101] From this perspective, he speaks with a certain pride about his almost overwhelming work.

One aspect of Luther's surging temperament is revealed when he loses this calm, serene mood due to a relatively insignificant annoyance and erupts in appalling hatred against the pope and the Turks, etc.[102] It sometimes sur-

---

96. 13:2960.

97. 17:3614.

98. 17:3616.

99. 15:3284 and 3282: Caeterum et ecclesiae nostrae tranquillae sunt, quia doctrina, sincerus usus sacramentum, docti et fideles ubique pastores. . . .[104]

100. 16:3495: "Wir haben gottlob wol Vorrat an jungen Theologen. . . ." ("Thank God we have a good supply of young theologians. . .").

101. 15:3376.

102. For a variety of reasons, one cannot assume much that is certain with regard to chronology, manner, and sequence of opinions from the letters.

[104.] Read with Enders *pura*, 'pure' instead of *quia*, 'because'. Enders15:3282: "By the way, our churches are calm; everywhere [you find] pure doctrine, correct administration of the sacraments, and educated and faithful pastors."

302   prises him.[103] After he is satisfied by such outbursts, the triumphal song of the chosen one follows. Luther counts all the Protestants as belonging to those who have not separated themselves willfully from the Protestant church through strife. Thus, during these moods the internal problems of Protestantism cannot spoil anything, because they are not differentiated from the external problems. In several writings one is brought surprisingly close to the world of the ancient psalms of revenge.[104] The wild hustle and bustle of the world is painted scornfully in the most violent colors. Then, however, a reversal takes place, "Sathan pergit esse Sathan,"[107] or, "quid est mundus,"[108] or something similar, and the description of the wrath on the day of judgment begins. Luther thanks God for having chosen certain people,[105] "and even if they should burn us all to ashes, they will burn in the fires of hell under our feet for eternity, amen."[106] "The sun of the pious ones shines and burns without being able to be extinguished. Clouds and air turbulence are unimportant to us, because they are over soon. The sun, however, remains eternal."[107]

God fights for the gospel, and gradually, step by step, God descends from the throne to the anticipated trial.[108] We can sleep because God fights for us.

303   We, however, should not rest, but should run toward Satan in order to engage Satan in battle.[109] We should not wait until Satan has attacked our herd but should drive Satan away with a stick, as we would a wolf.[110] The peo-

---

103. 17:3602: Iratus enim sum in ista bruta plus, quam deceat tantum me theologum et senem.[105]

104. Compare the psalms at the chronological end of his writings, e.g., "Against Hans Worst."[106]

105. 14:3133, 15:3347 and often.

106. 13:2919; cf. 15:3302; 13:2966: Reges manebimus subiectis inimicis sub pedibus nostris, amen.[109]

107. 14:3081: Sol noster inextinguibiliter lucet et ardet ut nihil faciant nubes et caligo aeris . . . peribunt iam cito. Sol manebit in aeternum.[110]

108. 13:2976.

109. 17:3601.[111]

110. 14:3019.

[105.] Enders 17:3602: "For I am more indignant at the senseless asses than is seemly for such a theologian as I am to be, and an old man to boot" (*Letters,* 469; cf. 468f.).

[106.] *WA* 51:565ff.; *LW* 41:252ff., "Against Hanswurst."

[107.] Enders 15:3329: "Satan continues to be Satan."

[108.] Enders 16:3429: "What is the world!"

[109.] Enders 13:2966: "We will remain kings, after our enemies are thrown under our feet. Amen."

[110.] Enders 14:3081: "Our sun shines and burns without ceasing, so that the clouds and the dark fog can do nothing . . . ; they will soon be destroyed. The sun will remain unto eternity." Enders has *enim,* 'for', instead of Bonhoeffer's *iam,* 'already'.

[111.] The correct reference is Enders 17:3603.

ple of Atlantis, saviors, conquerers of the world, of the devil and hell, are those who believe this to be true.[111] The angels and all of God's creation give them their blessing. The pope will grieve and tremble with the monsters of Satan. The gates of hell quake.[112] No one need fear. We will conquer and live, even though we are sinners.[113] Yea, God upholds this generation of humans only because of the gospel.[114] Christ is the conqueror of the world, and through him so is the one who believes.[115] God promises magnificent things as a sign of the day of judgment.[116] Yea, those who believe are the last trumpet sound that prepares Christ's return.[117] God may give one the ability to overcome evil through good, to remain victorious, not to flee from evil, but instead to see through Satan's intrigues.[118] Luther wants to have patience with people, because it horrifies him "that everywhere in the Scripture the thorns are threatened by fire."[119] Never show Satan that you are sad or oppressed. Instead show yourself to be confident and joyous, because you are able to crucify Satan through joy![120] O Deus conserva nobis haec gaudia, imo hanc gloriam tuam![116] 121

In psychology it is assumed that the concepts with which it works cannot be logically limited. Instead they are given a certain amount of leeway. In this way, insofar as its boundaries are fluid, the psychological scheme that we use lags behind reality, because we are dealing with living creatures. Only a few letters of Luther express this in its purest form. We present some of them in this study as paradigmatic. In most of Luther's letters one can argue convincingly on both sides of the psychological scale. Should the letter be placed under the heading of the calm and serene Luther or should it be placed under the heading of the intense Luther? In order to make a judgment, one studies the piece of writing in question, at the same time attempting to be

304

---

111. 14:3012.[112]
112. 16:3517.[113]
113. 13:2881.
114. 13:2920.
115. See footnote 113.
116. 14:3178.
117. [. . .][114]
118. 15:3228.
119. 17:3612.[115]
120. 15:3332.
121. 16:3575.

[112.] The correct reference is Enders 14:3112.
[113.] The correct reference is Enders 16:3516.
[114.] The reference is lacking in Bonhoeffer's text. See Enders 16:3497.
[115.] See Luther's letter to his wife, February 6, 1546, *LW* 50:300.
[116.] Enders 16:3575: "O God, preserve for us these joys, indeed, this is your glory."

completely objective and to use one's ability to make a match. On this basis a decision can be made.

In order to further this study, it would be necessary to take the very concrete relationships mentioned above and investigate their paradigmatic significance as the basis for understanding the psychological structure with which the elderly Luther approached his work. In order to support the investigation by concrete examples, one would have to investigate Luther's stance as regards the emperor, the barons of the country, the nobles, the pope, his friends, the nation, and many individual historical events.

Luther fundamentally rejected the possibility of a reunion with Catholicism based on eschatological concepts. When the Parliament at Regensburg[117] sought to broker an agreement, Luther faced a difficult dilemma. He would rather "take the cause to himself and stand alone as he did in the beginning" than make peace without God. "Instead of that, one would rather endure all strife."[122] As we saw more than once above, Luther considered peace to be better than anything else in the world. He truly desired "that Germany would truly be of one heart and mind and have a lasting good peace and law."[123] Because of this the tragedy of his life, that he disrupted the peace (which was no peace) and had to bring the sword, can be keenly felt. Luther no longer believed in unity in this world. Peace is divine, "quia Christus est pax."[118] But in order to arrive at divine peace, you must pass through the world with the sword of the divine word. Herein lies the paradox of the work of the Reformation, which Luther no doubt recognized. Because it was of God, he agreed with it as far as he was able.[119]

305

---

122. 13:2970.
123. 16:3479.

[117.] The Conference of Regensburg (Ratisbon), which took place from April 5 to July 29, 1541, belongs to a series of efforts in 1540–41, in the face of the danger of the Turks, to settle religious strife through conversations. Luther rejected the basis of the conversation, the so-called "Book of Regensburg." See *WA.B* 9:3637 and 3650 (see *LW* 50:190, note 16; *LW* 50:230, note 24). The conference ratified the Nuremburg Religious Peace until a general council or a new conference could take place.

[118.] Enders 16:3408: "because Christ is peace." Cf. above, 2/5:275, editorial note [75].
[119.] Grade for the paper: "Very good (I) Holl."

6. Paper on the Historical and Pneumatological Interpretation of Scripture[1]

Can One Distinguish between a Historical and a Pneumatological Interpretation of Scripture, and How Does Dogmatics Relate to This Question?

Christian religion stands or falls with the belief in a historical and perceptibly real divine revelation,[2] a revelation that those who have eyes to see can see and those who have ears to hear can hear. Consequently, in its 306 innermost nature, it raises the question we take up here, namely, the relationship of history and the Spirit. With respect to the Bible this question refers to the letter and the Spirit, scripture and revelation, and human word and God's word.[3] Methodologically we should not proceed historically but philosophically.[4]

The Bible, translated quite simply "the ultimate book," narrates the most significant of events. They are more than just "accidental truths of history," and do not intend to be "eternal truths of reason," as rationalism wanted to see it.[5] Certainly, one cannot prevent someone from considering this book as one book among others. Indeed, we all do this, for ordinary human beings wrote it. But it is the historian[6] who expressly approaches the Bible with this sole presupposition that it is one book among others that has nonetheless gained a unique and incomparable significance above others. The 2000-year

---

[1.] *NLA* 11, 3. Typescript. The title page of the paper, presented to Seeberg's seminar on systematic theology, included, in addition to the title, the following: "Dietrich Bonhoeffer, summer semester 1925. Report for July 31." For contents and literature used see below, 2/6:299. Seeberg, who evaluated the paper, gave the presentation a passing grade of satisfactory, the lowest grade Bonhoeffer received for his work in systematic theology. In this report Bonhoeffer discussed dialectical theology's understanding of Scripture and Karl Holl's interpretation of Luther's hermeneutics. Cf. Thurneysen, "Schrift und Offenbarung," in *Anfänge der dialektische Theologie*, 247ff.; Barth, "Menschenwort und Gotteswort in der christlichen Predigt," in *Zwischen den Zeiten* 3/2 (1925) 119ff.; "Das Schriftprinzip der reformierten Kirche," in *Zwischen den Zeiten* 3/3 (1925) 215ff.; Holl, "Luther und die Schwärmer," as well as "Luthers Bedeutung für den Fortschritt der Auslegungskunst"; both essays are in Holl's *Luther*, 420ff. and 544ff., the second being a debate with Dilthey's article, "The Rise of Hermeneutics."

[2.] Concerning this sentence, which was later to be very important to Bonhoeffer (for example, *AB* (*DBWE* 2): 72f.), cf. Kaftan, *Dogmatik*, 37. Bonhoeffer rejected the distinction between 'historical revelation' and 'inspiration' found in Girgensohn, "Die Inspiration der Heiligen Schrift," 121ff., 161ff., and 225ff. and Seeberg, *Revelation and Inspiration*; see below, 2/6:287f.

[3.] Concerning "letter and Spirit," cf. Holl, *Luther*, 557–58. Concerning Thurneysen, "Schrift und Offenbarung," and Barth, "Menschenwort und Gotteswort," see the essays listed by these authors in the first editorial note. See also *SC* (*DBWE* 1):231–36, in particular footnote 102.

[4.] Seeberg struck out "philosophically."

[5.] Cf. Lessing, "On the Proof of the Spirit and Power," in *Theological Writings*, 53: "Accidental truths of history can never become the proof of necessary truths of reason." On this cf. Thurneysen, "Schrift und Offenbarung," 14.

[6.] Seeberg adds: "*as* historians."

history of the Christian religion rests on this book as the foundation for this approach. Without a doubt it is one writing among others—and one of extraordinary historical significance. It is no wonder that historical criticism found here its first and most enduring issue; no wonder that it here learned sharply to refine its best tools.

Its general principles are based on a scientific-mechanistic worldview. Its epistemological methods are, for that reason, those of the natural sciences.[7] Every dogmatic connection is eliminated. This is the basic pillar upon which all historical research is built and must be built. Its knowledge should be attainable for every reasonable person by separating, in principle,[8] the knowing subject and known object. Like science, it should be "universally valid."[9] The growing interest in psychology, which brings with it new theories on the nature of understanding alien emotional life, could not bring about a decisive turning point in the understanding of the Bible.[10] (One should mention in passing that when seen in relationship to the mechanistic method this is a powerful positive step beyond historical[11] knowledge as such.)

Regarding the form of the Bible, with this approach the concept of the canon disintegrates and becomes meaningless.[12] Textual and literary criticism are applied to the Bible. The sources are distinguished, and the methods of the history of religions and form criticism fragment the larger and even the remaining short textual units into little pieces. After this total disintegration of the texts, historical criticism leaves the field of battle. Debris and fragments are left behind. Its work is apparently finished.[13]

The content of the Bible is leveled and made to match contemporary history. Parallels to the miracle stories are found. Yes, even the person of Jesus is stripped not only of the divine but also of human majesty. He disappears unrecognizably[14] among various rabbis, teachers of wisdom, and religious

---

[7.] Seeberg has added in the margin question marks, lines, and the words, "Yes, historical methods." Bonhoeffer's formulation corresponds to the positivistic conception of history, which Ernst Bernheim describes and attacks in his *Lehrbuch der historischen Methode*, 101. This book was known to Bonhoeffer, but he did not seriously study it. In contrast, Karl Groos, whose lectures Bonhoeffer attended in Tübingen (*DB-ER* 55), saw strong parallels between science and history. See Groos, *Naturgesetze und historische Gesetze*, especially 21; and Bernheim, *Lehrbuch*, 121.

[8.] Seeberg: "How can one know that?"

[9.] Cf. Girgensohn,"Die Inspiration des Heiligen Schrift," 227–28.

[10.] Cf. Thurneysen, "Schrift und Offenbarung," 12.

[11.] Underlined by Seeberg.

[12.] Seeberg: "But history created it, certainly!" A different opinion is expressed by Thurneysen in "Offenbarung und Geschichte," 17ff.

[13.] Seeberg: "But it is only preliminary work for history." In addition, this sentence is marked with lines in the margins. Cf. against this opinion Thurneysen in "Schrift und Offenbarung," 24, who speaks of "fragments" and "field of ruins."

[14.] Seeberg: "That is certainly pessimism." Cf. Seeberg, *Die Kirche Deutschlands*, 307, where he writes, "We believe in the divinity of Christ in its specific and ancient sense, not

visionaries [Schwärmer]. To be sure, even the critically reflective historian recognizes[15] that this book is concerned with unique and extraordinarily profound things, that here one catches sight of things of enormous significance. But if one did not, one would truly be an unsound historian, just as unsound a historian as if one believed that one could use such statements to prove that the Bible is God's word. One begins to see (recall Dibelius)[16] that a certain final principle lies behind the synoptic tradition in spite of its fragmentation,[17] as both Albert Schweitzer and Overbeck recognized.[18] Yet our historical investigation stops here, and its work is completed.[19] We will now continue our investigation.

First, we will compare unrelated types of pneumatological interpretation. Only one of these will pose a problem for us.

The first statement of spiritual interpretation [Pneumatik] is that the Bible is not only a word about God but God's word itself. In some way the decisive concept of revelation must be introduced here. When revelation is found, the extraordinary enters and its power is self-evident. The past is made present or—better—the contemporaneity and trans-temporality of God's word are recognized.[20]

Let us review for a moment. Due to lack of insight into the relationship of revelation and scripture, nothing perplexed the early church more than the creation of the canon. With subjectively similar justification, orthodoxy and heresy quoted revealed passages in the discussion until the catholic   309 church established a standard external to the Bible. This rule became the standard by which all catholic Christians were—and still are—supposed to interpret scripture.[1] This was the regula fidei, i.e., the tradition, i.e., ultimately, the church.

---

1. This process is presented by Tertullian in *De praescriptione haereticorum.* Cf. also the Catholic Perrone: "Ecclesiae magisterio subordinata est scriptura et traditio," Book 3, §3.[21]

because it is 'prescribed', but because our modern methodological consideration of history and religious psychological analysis leads us to this result." Against this see Thurneysen, "Schrift und Offenbarung," 23ff.

[15.] Seeberg: "He recognizes a historical context."

[16.] Cf. Martin Dibelius, *From Tradition to Gospel,* his 1919 work on form criticism.

[17.] Seeberg: "content."

[18.] Thurneysen called Albert Schweitzer and Franz Overbeck destroyers and conquerers of the liberal picture of Jesus. Cf. Thurneysen, "Schrift und Offenbarung," 18, 25, and 28f.; the reference to Dibelius is found on page 24.

[19.] Seeberg: "No!"

[20.] On the concept of 'contemporaneousness', cf. Thurneysen, "Schrift und Offenbarung," 26ff., esp. 28 note 10, where there are more references to Kierkegaard, *Philosophical Fragments,* Chapter Four, "The Situation of the Contemporary Follower"; cf. 68ff.

[21.] Tertullian, "The Prescription against Heretics," *Ante-Nicene Fathers* 3:243–65 (*PL* 2:9ff.). See Giovanni Perrone, *Praelectiones Theologicae,* vol. 3, § 3: "Scripture and tradition

This step was the first, most decisive, and yet most thorough misunderstanding of the concept of revelation. In principle, all attempts to objectify and to tie down revelation as scripture follow from this misunderstanding.[22] This includes attempting to grab hold of revelation in scripture by applying humanly introduced means external to scripture. This method was implemented by the mystics, the Anabaptists, and other groups up to and including the establishment of Orthodoxy. All seek to bring an external standard to bear upon scripture, which is used to locate and interpret positive revelation within scripture. One cannot find such a standard within the Bible itself. For the mystics and Anabaptists this might be found in the free spiritual experience that is considered to be barely subordinate to scripture.[2] For the orthodox, it might be the principle of verbal inspiration; other groups would employ other approaches.[24] In every case these methods sought to locate and to objectify revelation from outside of scripture and thereby to separate the source of truth and its verification.[25] The difficulties that arise out of this for the necessity and significance of scripture are generally overlooked. (1) Does God actually impart personal revelation so that what God once clearly stated can still be confirmed? An example would be the Anabaptists' spiritual experience. It ought to be confirmation enough that God speaks. "Deus solus de se doneus testis est in suo sermone" (Calvin).[26] Is a double revelation needed? (2) Do incorrect consequences result for interpretation? When hermeneutical standards external to scripture are brought to bear, then abuses are unavoidable. In order to force the text, particular methods that permitted an incredible breadth of interpretation were in use for a considerable period of time. The method of allegorical interpretation completely ignored historical reality. It used speculative and rationalistic methods that could read into the text whatever one wished. Its history is as old as our chronology. Protests against its arbitrariness rang out again and again.[27]

310

---

2. "Der Sohn Gottis hat gesagt, die Schrifft gibt gezeugnis da sagen die Schriftgelehrten, si gibt den Glauben" (Munzer).[23]

---

are subsumed under the teaching office of the church." Both references are found in Karl August von Hase, *Handbuch der protestantischen Polemik*, 69–70 (Tertullian) and 82, note 33 (Perrone).

[22.] Seeberg: "Good." Cf. Barth, "Menschenwort und Gotteswort," 125: "by interpreting it [the word of God] as a public, direct matter, demonstrable from paper."

[23.] "The Son of God has said that Scripture gives witness, while the scribes say that it gives faith." Cited according to Holl, *Luther*, 432, note 1.

[24.] Compare with Barth, "Menschenwort und Gotteswort," 125.

[25.] So, e.g., Ihmels, *Centralfragen der Dogmatik*, 64ff., who attacked Julius Kaftan with a polemic.

[26.] "God alone is a fit witness of himself in his Word." See Calvin, *Institutes* (1.7.4), 79. Bonhoeffer cites Thurneysen, "Schrift und Offenbarung," 254.

[27.] Dilthey, "Development of Hermeneutics," 252.

Even the history of philosophy's much more profound typological treatment of the Bible[28] led to exaggerations.

The doctrine of the fourfold sense of scripture was authorized by the Catholic church in order[29] to be able to satisfy its demands on the Bible. This is a principle that may be easier to justify sociologically than dogmatically. With it progress was certainly made with respect to detailed exegesis, but this is not significant for our principal question. Whether it is the enthusiasts' principle of spirit or the psychological understanding of liberalism, in every case we find a humanization, i.e., a superficial reduction, of the concept of revelation. The divine was conceived in terms of the human in that a strict distinction was not made; the old maxim finitum incapax infiniti was forgotten.[30]

An energetic counterblow had to take place for independence in the sense of the deepening of the concept of revelation in relation to scripture.

Revelation for us can be found only in scripture. To the question why revelation is to be found precisely here the answer must simply be that this is where God speaks and this is where it pleases God to be personally revealed.[31] Luther says, "If God gives me wooden apples and tells me to take and eat, I should not ask why."[32] God's will cannot be given a basis but only experienced and proclaimed. Revelation is confirmed in scripture. Scripture uses the term "witnessed."[33] Scripture itself belongs to a great complex of revelation as a *document that gives witness*. For us, it is its only remnant.[34] Consequently, scripture is not revelation. If it were, one would once again objectify scripture by rational means. *Scripture* is not experienced as revelation, but the matter that it deals with.[35] One can discover nothing a priori except that revelation is present where individuals hear it, where the human word becomes God's word, and where time becomes eternity. The single claim the scripture makes is that if it is to be understood it must be understood in the spirit of revelation. Where does this spirit come from? The paradoxical

311

[28.] Seeberg adds question marks.

[29.] The original has *in*, which Seeberg changed to *um*, 'in order'.

[30.] "The finite is incapable of the infinite." This Reformed maxim is intended to emphasize the transcendence of God. It is directed at the Lutheran maxim, *finitum capax infiniti*, 'the finite is capable of the infinite', which has in mind the becoming human of God in Jesus Christ.

[31.] Cf. Barth, "Menschenwort und Gotteswort," 124: "the Bible is God's Word . . . because it pleased God to speak to us through the Bible."

[32.] This citation is found in Barth, "Menschenwort und Gotteswort," 124. It reads, "Wenn der Herr mir Holzöpfel fürleite und hieße es mich nehmen und essen, sollt ich nit fragen: warum?" Cf. Bullinger's report on the religious language at Marburg given in 1529, found in Huldrych Zwingli, *Werke*, 2/3, 48.

[33.] Cf. Barth, "Das Schriftprinzip," 218 and Thurneysen, "Schrift und Offenbarung," 15.

[34.] Cf. Kaftan, *Dogmatik*, 44 and 53.

[35.] Cf. Holl, *Luther*, 548.

answer: it comes from scripture itself.[36] We stand, therefore, before a circle.[37] If we wish to understand and preserve the concept of revelation, one assertion cannot be true but both are necessary. There is only one revelation.

312   A multiplication of revelations would amount to the humanization of revelation, and so revelation must be understood from itself.

This problem of consistent spiritual interpretation is one that the exegetes of the Catholic church and of the Anabaptists do not acknowledge. They both bring arbitrary standards external to scripture to bear on scripture. The *principle of interpretation* must derive from an already-understood scripture. Does God truly speak in scripture in such a way that only God and not humans can hear?[38] The Spirit comes from the word and the word comes from the Spirit.[39]

Is there a solution, or are we, along with the concept of revelation, plummeting further and further into darkness as we search for light and enlightenment? The solution lies in the fact God opens human eyes to receive revelation in certain indescribable and undetermined moments and words. The object of understanding creates for its subject the means of recognizing in the act of knowledge.[40] The object must become subject. God becomes the Holy Spirit.[41]

This certainly occurs in the act which theologians might call "inspiration."[42] In this concept one can see an actual commingling of both apparently circular assertions. Theological methodology cannot describe this in any other way than as successive and reciprocally consecutive. Only in this way can one speak of an objective, i.e., necessary *plainly literal*, understanding of scripture.[43] This is true only when one considers the subject not externally but internally. Luther writes, "scriptura sacra est sui ipsius inter-

313   pretes."[44] Like can be understood only by like. God can be understood only

---

[36.] Seeberg: "in the Spirit at work in scripture." In reference to this cf. Holl, *Luther,* 547. When Thurneysen criticized Holl in "Schrift und Offenbarung," 26, for equating the spiritually effected conception of the sense of scripture with the psychological response, he overlooks the fact the Holl certainly does say elsewhere that Luther could understand that only the Spirit from God is the Spirit whose work is the Holy Scriptures. See Holl, *Luther,* 558 and 555. It is exactly on these texts in Holl's work that the young Bonhoeffer relies.

[37.] Cf. Holl, *Luther,* 567.

[38.] Seeberg: "If God allows him to hear, he can hear." Cf. Thurneysen, "Schrift und Offenbarung," 12f.

[39.] Cf. Holl, *Luther,* 557f.

[40.] Seeberg underlines the word "subject" and notes in the margin, "good."

[41.] Seeberg underlines the words, "the object must . . . Holy Spirit," and places in the text a question mark with the note, "He is already subject—neither does he become the Holy Spirit first here."

[42.] Seeberg underlines the words "theologians" and "might" and notes, "Is that the real 'inspiration'?"

[43.] Cf. Holl, *Luther,* 551.

[44.] "Holy scripture is its own interpreter." *WA* 7:97, 20ff., "Assertio omnium articulorum."

by God.[45] From this it can be concluded that the concept of revelation that emerges is to be conceived not substantially, but rather functionally.[46] One does not encounter a being in scripture, but rather a judgment or God's will.

For this new way of knowledge (in cognitione sita est fides, Calvin, *Institutes* 3.2.2),[47] the implementation of historical temporality into contemporary existence, of the past into the present, is applied to the Bible.[48] Directly associated with this is the fact that spiritual exegesis can relate the circumstances of the past and the present only if they exist in the same "dialectical" relationship. This is the only way, for example, that Karl Barth can justify as a completely literal translation his rendering of the Pauline "Israel" in Romans 9–11 as "church."[49]

Let us also consider the issue of the so-called intuitive historical understanding. To be sure, it is difficult to interpret Goethe's lyrical poetry or ancient Indian Vedic poetry.[50] The process here is different. It is to be understood in purely psychological terms and in terms of a reaching outward and a returning from the alien "I" to the self. This is a persistent, never completely possible advance toward the object.[51] The final renunciation of the "I" in the understanding can never be perfected in this way. Even the most ingenious interpreter understands things from the "I." Faith, which is itself God's will, understands things from the subject matter itself. Faith, in particular, must not leave out what historical and psychological exegesis *must* leave out. Everything depends on the final renunciation of the "I." Here it is necessary to fend off another misunderstanding. Spiritual understanding is not to be identified with the a priori judgment of, for example, mathematical axioms. A divinely created a priori mental structure must be assumed[52] here, which in spiritual understanding has to be created by God himself. God

314

[45.] That like can be known only by like is a formula found in Aristotle's philosophy. Cf. Aristotle, *Metaphysics* (1000 b5), in *The Complete Works of Aristotle*, 1580. It was taken up by dialectical theology and related to the knowledge of God. Cf. especially Barth, "Das Schriftprinzip," 220 and Thurneysen, "Schrift und Offenbarung," 12.

[46.] Seeberg: "Good."

[47.] "Faith rests upon knowledge." Cited according to Thurneysen, "Schrift und Offenbarung," 11.

[48.] Seeberg notes: "Or an object to an objective force." Cf. Thurneysen, "Schrift und Offenbarung," 26–27.

[49.] Seeberg puts a question mark against this. See Barth, *Romans*, 330ff.

[50.] Thurneysen, "Schrift und Offenbarung," 19 and Barth, "Menschenwort und Gotteswort," 124.

[51.] Cf. Holl, *Luther*, 568: "Interpretation is never anything other than a constant leaping over and under one's own alien ego, from word to the subject matter and from subject matter to word." Holl, who is criticized here by Bonhoeffer, depends completely on Dilthey, "Development of Hermeneutics," 259: "So all understanding always remains relative and can never be completed."

[52.] Seeberg: "Or [uncertain reading] already created and now set in motion." Cf. also Thurneysen, "Schrift und Offenbarung."

can be understood only from God's Spirit. This understanding is then a most remarkable experience, not an a priori one.[53] It is only here that illumination can be achieved, without which *all* this is *nothing.* Sine spiritus illuminatione verbo nihil agitur, Calvin's *Institutes* 3.2.33.[54] Through this unique understanding, "inspiration" is received by the believer.[55] Thus the believer comes to understand the category[56] of revelation and uses it as the foundation for all further interpretation. Here we recall Augustine. "You would not seek me if you had not already found me."[57] To be sure, this does not nullify the fact that we always need the Spirit anew. We receive it to the same extent as we find Christ, just as we must always be renewed through God's will.

How does the Bible, as a historical literary classic, offer itself to this type of spiritual understanding? Now that we have understood the principles of historical-critical and pneumatological exegesis, we can address this question

315 of how they relate to each other (the terminology originates with Beck).[58] The question now centers on the relationship of the Spirit to the letter and of revelation to the written word.[59]

Here we can, I believe, gain some important information from the analysis of the term "word."

On its dialectical side, a word is the finite and verbal form of an entity that, out of the infinitude of living things, occurs for the communication of the same. It occurs as a fragment of a whole that can never be completely represented. On the one hand, it is something that is finished and complete and is dead at the moment of conception.[60] On the other hand, however, it is something that is open, unfinished, and alive. On the one hand, it is entity.[61] On the other hand, it is power, life, and volition. But, of course, not

---

[53.] Seeberg puts a question mark in the margin.

[54.] "Without the enlightenment of the Spirit the word can do nothing." Bonhoeffer cites this according to Thurneysen, "Schrift und Offenbarung," 10.

[55.] Seeberg, *Revelation and Inspiration,* 59ff.

[56.] Seeberg underlines the word "category" and marks it with a question mark. Cf. Barth, "Menschenwort und Gotteswort," 122 and 125.

[57.] Bonhoeffer falsely attributes this citation to Augustine. It comes from Pascal. In the original it reads: "tu ne me chercherais pas, si tu ne m'avais trouvé." See Pascal, *Pensées,* 336 (Brunschvicg 553). The English translation reads, "You would not be seeking me if you had not found me." Pascal's thought is based upon a passage in Bernard of Clairvaux, *On Loving God,* 24f. The mistaken reference to Augustine is probably based upon a misreading by Przywara, "Metaphysik und Religion," 134 and 136.

[58.] Cf. Beck, *Einleitung in das System der christlichen Lehre,* 261ff. See also Girgensohn, "Die Inspiration der Heiligen Schrift," 123.

[59.] With this formula, Bonhoeffer refers to Holl, *Luther,* 557f. With the following linguistic philosophical remark, he attempts to avoid the religious-psychological tendencies of Holl.

[60.] Seeberg puts a question mark in the margin and remarks, "Is being dead?"

[61.] Seeberg underlines the word "entity."

every word conceals eternity within it. This is true only of the word that has its origins in eternity. We can express this also in other ways. It belongs to the nature of the word that it expresses an *objective relationship* but not necessarily a *spiritual relationship*. The objective relationship is that part of the word that leads to an immediate a priori understanding. In this way, it is the *prerequisite* for the historical and psychological as well as the spiritual understanding and interpretation. At this point, we can already recognize that the historical and the spiritual do not relate to each other as cause and effect.[62] Instead, they both have a common presupposition and only diverge later on.

In the Bible, we have the designation of Christ as the "Word of God" (John 1:1; Heb. 1:2). From God's perspective, for whom the terms "God spoke" and "it became so" are identical, Christ is the speaker and the doer of the word. Jesus existed in history. He was in the past and is not contemporaneous. Christ is the one who is born out of eternity through the Spirit of God. He is always living and present. In order, however, to be comprehended as Spirit, he must appear in verbal form. Jesus is one of the endless possibilities of God. Christ is the Spirit in personal form. If Christ is understood from the perspective of Jesus, then the past becomes present. This does not occur as a particular entity, a doctrine or a miracle, but rather through the particular as totality. The totality of Christ can be understood through one word. In this manner, every word is infinitely deep. It is not, however, flesh and blood that reveal the human Christ to be the Son of God. Instead it is the Spirit of the Father through[63] the Holy Spirit.[64]

Scripture is to be understood and interpreted on the basis of pneumatological interpretation in the sense that it was written by those to whom the Spirit had disclosed that revelation could be found precisely in this historical person, Jesus—fully human, appearing completely in the framework of ordinary events. Therefore, the biblical authors do not interest us as individuals but instead as apostles, prophets, and persons inspired by God. That is, it is not Paul whom we hear speaking but God. It is not we who hear but again it is God who hears in us.[65] Still, the Bible remains a paradox.[66] It will always remain the words individuals spoke to one person or to another. In order to transmit this realization they needed the proclaimed word, first as "good tidings and report," as Luther said,[67] and then as a written

316

[62.] Seeberg underlines "cause and effect."

[63.] Seeberg underlines and puts question marks in the margin.

[64.] Allusion to Matt. 16:17. The biblical reference is found in Thurneysen, "Schrift und Offenbarung," 25.

[65.] Seeberg underlines "God hears with us" and notes, "then we will not hear." Cf. above, 2/6:290 and editorial note 38.

[66.] Seeberg underlines and writes in the margin, "Why?"

[67.] Cf. "Preface to the New Testament," *LW* 35:358. Bonhoeffer is citing Holl, *Luther*, 562.

record.[3] Each of these written words of the Spirit, which mediate the understanding of the facts, is an incarnate image of the person of Jesus Christ himself. These are contained in a fully historical, insignificant, and unimposing husk, but behind that there is the other, what "inculcates Christ,"[69] where Christ is truly alive and present. For Catholics this occurs in the sacrifice of the Mass. In the word Christ is present—not as a substance, however, but as revelation, judgment, and will.

Such a view of the relationship between the letter and the Spirit, scripture and revelation, paves the way for a completely proper incorporation of historical exegesis into the general area of interpretation. We must say a priori that it is unacceptable for a pneumatological, faith-based interpretation to be dependent on historical methods of reading scripture with their shifting results. The difficulty rises from the fact that belief cannot free itself from the ὁ λόγος σάρξ ἐγένετο,[70] nor does it want to. On the other hand, the historian's sense of truth cannot tolerate any patronizing by foreign methods. None of us can return to a pre-critical time.[4] Both methods are used side by side by any pneumatological interpreter.[5]

Now, historical criticism is properly limited when it is placed in relationship to the pneumatological method. For a long time, liberal dogmatics was founded upon the leftovers of historical criticism. One was comforted by the thought that in the final analysis it really could not become dangerous.[72] We have seen above where the historical-critical method can and must necessarily lead[73] and—of course, not simply because of this negative reason—how it must follow another path.

For both the historical and the pneumatological methods the Bible is, first of all, writing, text, and the words of human beings. Both examine each con-

---

3. Luther thinks that "it is not all in line with the New Testament to write books on Christian doctrine." *EA* X, 388.[68]

4. We cannot agree with Perrone's statement: "Debet (the critique) esse modesta ac sobria, ita ut non refragetur communi patrum sensui ecclesiae iudicio . . . ," vol. 3, § 468.[71]

5. One thinks particularly of Calvin.

[68.] Bonhoeffer here cites the Erlangen edition of Luther's *Werke*, 10:388.[CG]

[69.] Cf. "Preface to the Epistles of St. James and St. Jude. (1545)," *WA.DB* 7:384, 27, 29; *LW* 35:396. See also Seeberg, *Revelation and Inspiration*, 20f. and Barth, "Das Schriftprinzip," 223.

[70.] "The Word became flesh" (John 1:14).

[71.] "It [the critique] must remain measured and reserved, so that it does not contradict the common understanding of the church fathers and the judgment of the church." Perrone, *Praelectiones Theologicae*, 3, § 468; Bonhoeffer most likely cites from Hase, *Handbuch der protestantischen Polemik*, 82, footnote 32.

[72.] Seeberg must have felt directly attacked by this.

[73.] Seeberg marks this with a question mark.

text of meaning for its pure, external relationship to reality, i.e., its literal meaning. If there are problems here, then, after a precise reading of the manuscript's text, textual criticism plays a role. After the original text has been established, each of them goes its own way. If the contents are being examined, then the tradition at hand will be interpreted. We must pay attention to this. An examination of the *contents* can never be anything other than an *interpretation* of the tradition.

We will leave aside the consequences for a moment and turn to the analysis of the *form* of the tradition, which is sharply separated in principle from the results. That is, we remind ourselves of the field of ruins described above, bestowed on us by the critic.[74] Insofar as the conclusions are true,[75] they are *fully* recognized by pneumatological interpretation. Only when we are looking at these ruins do we see something else as well, something that holds everything together as a whole. To put it more precisely, it is not we who see, but instead our eyes are opened for us so that we can see what has been hidden, namely, the revelation to which the texts lay claim. The question of *genesis* can never touch the other question—of the thing itself.[76] Therefore, there is no difficulty whatsoever in combining the two methods.

At first glance, it seems more difficult to take a position on the critique of the contents. We may not forbid the historical method to search for the actual events that lie behind the text and to examine them as sources. It must, however, investigate the uniqueness of the tradition, which is essentially not historical but cultic. If the results happen to be negative and even the person of Jesus slips out of[77] reliable hands and disappears into the darkness, then one can assert that the pneumatological method seems to be completely at an end. We counter this statement: (1) If one remembers what was established above, observing the content is interpreting the tradition. In our case this means that the person of Jesus in the Holy Scriptures can, at most, be *interpreted* as a free composition of the author. A conclusion regarding historicity is disallowed in principle.[78] (2) Completely immersing oneself in the contemporary period in order to attain a pure historical perspective is symptomatic of the Christian concept of revelation. The God who entered history made God unrecognizable[79] to the children of the world, from the manger to the cross. In extreme cases, the critic can contest the image of Jesus as a leader or a religious genius but never as *God's Son*.[80] (3) It can be

318

319

[74.] Underlined by Seeberg. Cf. 2/6:286 above, and editorial note 13.

[75.] Underlined by Seeberg; cf. Thurneysen, "Schrift und Offenbarung," 19f.

[76.] Cf. Thurneysen, "Schrift und Offenbarung," 20.

[77.] Seeberg adds question marks.

[78.] Seeberg: "What kind of principle is that?"

[79.] Seeberg: "Is that revelation?" Cf. Seeberg, *Revelation and Inspiration*, 43ff. Here Bonhoeffer follows Barth, "Menschenwort und Gotteswort," 120f.

[80.] Seeberg: "What does that mean?"

positively stated that the pneumatological interpretation has its own plausibility for comprehending actual historical events. Because God speaks to people by means of the *authentic witness* of historical revelation[81] through the Bible, God must personally also have spoken in historical events. This is, of course true only of important historical events that are embedded in faith, such as those of the prophets and the historical person of Jesus Christ and his death on the cross for us. Individual accounts like the miracle stories, etc., are naturally not included here. Instead, they are included only insofar as the totality of faith directly depends on the factual truth of the historical events.

I intentionally did not include the "historical fact" of the resurrection. In my opinion, given all that has been said, it is senseless and clumsy to construe it as a naked historical fact. God wished to become manifest *in history*.[82] The resurrection takes place within the realm of faith and revelation.[83] All other interpretations seek to remove the decisive characteristic of *God within history*.[84] In respect to the question of miracles, we can say with certainty that the laws of nature are not absolutely valid. They are, instead, statements about experience. However, to conclude from this that miracles are not breakthroughs but are instead unknown forms of the laws of nature is also historically incorrect. We must accept them for what they claim to be in the Bible—true miracles.[85] Neither history nor spiritual interpretation can give us information about the facticity of particular miracles. This is true because belief in Jesus Christ and historical revelation is not linked to the veracity of

this or that miracle. Therefore, our concern with pneumatological interpretation is not, "Did the miracle in fact take place?" but rather, "What role does it play in the context of witness to revelation?" This is the case throughout. Scripture is only a *source* for history. For spiritual interpretation, scripture is a *witness*.[86] In the final instance, this is based on the assertion that the inspiration of the biblical authors can never extend to the events. Instead, it can only extend to interpretation and knowledge. The question concerning the spiritual meaning of miracles and their ability to contain meaning, in spite of the complete immersing of the divine in history, belongs to exegesis itself.

Therefore, it is within this framework that historical criticism is put into play. The resulting tension is the necessary characteristic of pneumatological interpretation. At one point it is absolutely necessary that the noncontem-

---

[81.] Cf. Kaftan, *Dogmatik*, 44.

[82.] Seeberg marks the sentence, "God wished . . . *in history*," in the margin.

[83.] Seeberg: "So then it is *historical!*"

[84.] Seeberg: "So!" Cf. also Barth, "Das Schriftprinzip," 225, 227, and 241.

[85.] Seeberg underlines "true miracles," and comments in the margin, "What does this mean?" Cf. Seeberg, *Revelation and Inspiration*, 44f., and Bonhoeffer's reflection on this idea in *LPP* 285.

[86.] Cf. Barth, "Das Schriftprinzip," 226.

poraneous, the historical, and the contingent be known and recognized. At the same time, however, the contemporaneous always emerges as the essential element. With this tension we find ourselves with our interpretation in exactly the same place as the writers of the Holy Scriptures themselves (cf. Luke 1:1ff.).[87] It is absolutely necessary that we assure ourselves of the fallibility of these texts so that we can recognize the miracle that we really do hear God's words in human words.

The interpretation of the Synoptic Gospels has been compared to crossing a river on a thousand blocks of ice.[6] One has to get across, but one cannot stop at any one point. One has to keep the whole picture in view. Yet we can be comforted by someone to whom we seldom go for advice. We have a model in the same tradition, who is a greater interpreter than we are. It is the apostle Paul himself.[7]

The standard that must be preserved in the exegesis of scripture is handed to us along with the word that is the revelation and foundation of the Bible. This standard is taken from the Bible itself and is, as Luther noted, "what drives toward Christ." What the content of revelation does not have is not canonical.[8]

321

However, as far as the pneumatological method is concerned, the canon comprises only the highly striking evidence of the deep insight by which the significant writings were chosen from the great amount of literature of that time. Conversely, the canon can never be a proof of revelation. In principle, it must be acknowledged as open.

In principle, the Old Testament does not have a different status from the New Testament, although the Old Testament relates to the New as promise does to fulfillment, and Law does to Gospel. In both, the word of God is heard. "The same yesterday as today" (Barth).[91]

Christian dogmatics, which has divine revelation in history as its subject matter, must hold upright the characteristic relationship of revelation and scripture as the representation of the entire complex of revelatory experience. If the spiritual elements were to be suppressed, then dogmatics would become the presentation of New Testament piety. If the historical-critical

---

6. Thurneysen, "Schrift und Offenbarung," 1924.[88]

7. Cf. EA 63, 115, "Preface to the Letter of James." [89]

8. Hereby we are criticizing Calvin's Reformed principle of Scripture and its repristination by Barth, which places the concept of the canon above Luther's individual statement. We know that Luther is taking a very bold step, but we also know that it is in the interest of Protestant faith for us to take it with him.[90]

[87.] Cf. Thurneysen, "Schrift und Offenbarung," 26.
[88.] Ibid., 28.
[89.] Luther, *Werke* (Erlangen edition), 63:115.[CG]
[90.] Cf. Barth, "Das Schriftprinzip," 221ff. esp. 223.
[91.] Ibid., 224.

method—not the historically factual element, which can never be suppressed—were to be suppressed, then it would take away some of the clarity of the concept of revelation. In principle, however, such a suppression would not necessarily change anything. The category of dogmatics is solely and alone the λόγος τοῦ θεοῦ,[92] insofar as it is in the proper sense "theology." Revelation is the source of truth for dogmatics at the same time as it is the confirmation of dogmatics. As the word of God, it has normative character.

The empirical representation of religion in the form of the church and congregation has the λόγος τοῦ θεοῦ as its source of truth and its norm. There is no independent[93] church-community or church, as there is in Catholicism.[9] The sermon is the gift of grace for the proclamation of what has been made known.[10] Ἀνάγκη γάρ μοι ἐπίκειται οὐαὶ γάρ μοί ἐστιν ἐὰν μὴ εὐαγγελίζωμαι, 1 Cor. 9:16,[95] cf. *WA* 53:252.[96]

Its fate is the fate of interpretation and the fate of the scripture itself. It is the attempt to speak God's word with human words. This attempt will never go beyond the stage of experiment if God does not assent to it. Here we are at the very end, the most profound point. It lies buried in everything that had been said before. Every attempt at pneumatological interpretation is a prayer, a plea for the Holy Spirit,[97] who alone determines, according to its pleasure, the hearing and understanding without which the most spiritual exegesis will come to naught. Scriptural understanding, interpretation, preaching, i.e., the knowledge of God begins and ends with the plea: "Veni creator spiritus."[98]

322

---

9. The famous objection of Bellarmine, in "de verbo Dei," that the Reformers are dependent upon tradition simply through the reference to the Bible is blatant sophistry.[94]

10. Cf. Jer. 20:9; Amos 3:8.

[92.] "The Word of God."

[93.] Seeberg: "In reference to what?"

[94.] Bellarmine, *De verbo Dei*, Book 4, Chapter Three, and following, in *Opera Omnia*, 1:197–204.

[95.] "And woe to me if I do not proclaim the gospel" (1 Cor. 9:16). With εὐαγγελίζωμαι Bonhoeffer is offering another variant of the text, which has been replaced by εὐαγγελίσωμαι in *Novum Testamentum Graece*, ed. Nestle, since the 11th edition of 1920.

[96.] Luther, "Exempel, einen rechten christlichen Bischof zu weihen," 1542.

[97.] Seeberg: "Only?" Bonhoeffer here follows Barth, "Menschenwort und Gotteswort," 139–40.

[98.] "Come, Creator Spirit," the beginning of an early Christian hymn written for Pentecost by Hrabanus Maurus (d. 856). Cited according to Barth, "Das Schriftprinzip," 233.

Literature used in preparing the paper[99]

Karl Barth, Prefaces to the *Epistle to the Romans*; Bengel, *Gnomon*; Bernheim, *Lehrbuch der geschichtlichen Methode*;[100] Dilthey, *Sigwart-Festschrift*; Girgensohn, Inspiration, *PastBl.* 67.3; Heim, *Leitfaden der Dogmatik*; Holl, *Luther*; Ihmels, *Centralfragen*; Kaftan, *Dogmatik* and "Zur Dogmatik"; Kropatschek, *Geschichte des Lutherischen Schriftprinzips*; Luther, "On Translating. An Open Letter"; Seeberg, *Inspiration and Revelation*; Seeberg, *Geschichte der Kirche im 19. Jahrhundert*, pp. 352ff.; Schlatter, *Das christliche Dogma*; *Zwischen den Zeiten*, nos. 6, 10, 11.[101]

323

Contents

Introduction: Outline of the Problem.
I.   Historical Interpretation: methods and application
     used in reference to the NT
II. Pneumatological Interpretation
     a.   Interpretation through an abbreviation of the concept
          of revelation.—Faulty separation of Scripture and
          revelation. Therefore bringing extra-biblical
          standards to bear on interpretation
     b.   Scripture and revelation separated.—Interpretation
          according to the circular argument: God can be
          conceived only through God.—Its solution through
          "inspiration."—Inspiration, historical intuition,
          and mathematical evidence.
III. Relationship of historical interpretation to
     pneumatological interpretation—Object-related,
     Spirit-related—Jesus Christ as the
     Word.—Independent character of both methods.—
     The historical method discerns the proper limitations
     through the spiritual.—Scripture as source and
     witness.—Toward an interpretation of the synoptic

[99.] Cf. the complete publication details of books used by Bonhoeffer in the volume bibliography, below, pages 595ff. The three issues of *Zwischen den Zeiten* are those mentioned in editorial note 1 of this paper, above 2/6:285, containing the articles of Thurneysen and Barth.

[100.] Alfred Feder, not Ernst Bernheim, was the author of the book with this title; its third edition was published in 1924, the year before Bonhoeffer wrote this paper (previous editions had the title *Lehrbuch der historischen Methodik*, which was almost identical to Bernheim's). Cf. above, 2/6:286, editorial note 7; it is possible that Bonhoeffer knew the Feder book as well as the Bernheim. [CG]

[101.] Final grade: "Satisfactory Seeberg, July 31, 1925."

writers.—The critical standard of interpretation,
What Christianity does. Contra Calvin—Barth.—
The Canon,—OT and NT.
IV. Dogmatics and our problem.—Congregation.—
Sermon.—Conclusion.

324   **7. Note on Luther's Lectures on the Letter to the Romans**[1]

Theological logic intends to set itself free from psychologism.[2] It does not
speak of sin and revelation as contents of consciousness. Instead, it speaks of
them as realities of revelation: acknowledgment of what is spoken in revelation and by the authorities.
Believe in sin. Rom. 11. p. 69[3]   Continuation.

[1.] *NL* Appendix A 20 (b), handwritten. In Bonhoeffer's copy of Johannes Ficker, ed.,
Luthers Vorlesung über den Römerbrief, 1908, were found three handwritten notes on paper
with mostly very short remarks. This is the one longer text, which clarifies Bonhoeffer's
reception of Luther. It was found in volume 2 between pages 68 and 69. Thesis 8 of Bonhoeffer's graduation (licentiate) theses presupposes this remark (cf. below, 2/16:440). The
exact date of this remark is unknown. Due to the closeness of its content to the topic of
Bonhoeffer's paper on the interpretation of Scripture, it is placed here. The more immediate context within the book where the note was found involves four corollaries to Rom.
3:5, of which the second takes up the words from Rom. 3:4: "Stands as written": "Et ita Deus
per suum exire nos facit ad nos ipsos introire et per sui cognitionem infert nobis et nostri
cognitionem. Quia nisi Deus ita prius exiret et verax fieri quereret in nobis, nos non pos-
semus introire ad nos et mendaces ac iniusti fieri. Non enim potuit homo ex se ipso scire,
quod talis esset coram Deo, nisi ipse Deus hoc ipsum revelaret." See Ficker, *Luthers Vorlesung*, 67. The English translation reads, "And so God effects through his departure [from
himself] that we return to ourselves, and thereby, in order that we know him, he brings us
knowledge of ourselves. For if God did not first depart [from himself] and truly desire to
be in us, we could not arrive at ourselves and would become liars and unrighteous. For
human beings cannot know from themselves that they are created before God, if it were not
revealed to them by God."
[2.] The concept of "psychologism" is directed against the doctrine of the religious a
priori developed by Ernst Troeltsch; cf. his *Psychologie und Erkenntnistheorie*. There it is connected to Kant. The doctrine of religion "is to seek the a priori law of consciousness, which
expresses itself in the actuality of religious life and holds the last achievable scientific foundation for the attainment of the truth-content of religion in this law of consciousness. It is
therewith also a medium of critical refinement and progress for the natural development
of psychological religion." Troeltsch, *Psychologie*, 27; cf. also 35, where Troeltsch introduces
the concept of the "religious a priori."
[3.] In the Luther volume there follows, at the place cited in editorial note 1 from the
Romans lectures (Ficker, *Luthers Vorlesung*, 67f.), the following citations from scripture:
Rom. 11:34, 1 Cor. 3:18; Luke 1:51; Ps. 51:5ff.; Ps. 32:5f.; 1 John 1:8ff. In one of the following corollaries it says, "Etsi nos nullum peccatum in nobis agnoscamus, credere tamen
oportet, quod sumus peccatores." "Even if we know no sin in us, we must still believe that
we are sinners." The last two lines of Bonhoeffer's note refer to this.

8. Paper on Reason and Revelation[1] 325

Reason and Revelation in Early Lutheran Dogmatics

If Christian dogmatics keeps in mind the principles on which it is based, then it will necessarily understand itself as a structure erected upon an understanding of the principles of revelation and reason as its epistemological sources. Their relationship to each other can certainly be varied. As I see it, every conceivable combination of the concepts "reason and revelation" or "philosophy and theology" has appeared in the course of the history of theology, from the radical proscription of all rational knowledge with respect to a transcendent authority, from the most blunt rejection of the possibility of Christian philosophy, to the identification of revelation and the immanent ethic of reason, from the credo, quia absurdum,[2] to Fichte's *Critique of All Revelation* and Kant's *Religion within.* . . .[3]

In the beginning of our investigation of the use of reason in early Lutheran[4] theology, we will proceed from the evidence that we can extract from the prescriptions in the Formula of Concord. At the very beginning we read the words, "credimus confitemur et docemus unicam regulam et normam, 326 secundum quam omnia dogmata omnes[que] Doctores aestimari et judicari oporteat nullam omnino aliam esse, quam Prophetica et Apostolica scripta cum veteris tum Novi Testamenti."[5] Here we find stated that, like all other disciplines, theology has a principle and a norm upon which all its scholarly work is based. This norm is the Holy Scripture. Now we would like to know something more precise about this procedure in relationship to scripture. It is here that the question about the use of reason should come to the fore, but nothing further is said. If we bring to bear other passages in which the ratio humana is discussed, then at one point we hear that this ratio humana in

---

[1.] *NL* A, 1. Handwritten presentation for the seminar of Stolzenburg (cf. the course list, Appendix 3 below, page 585). Underneath the title is found in Bonhoeffer's handwriting, "Report for November 10, 1925. Dietrich Bonhoeffer." There are no footnotes by Bonhoeffer or corrections by the reader. See, however, 2/8:309, editorial note 80. The theme is connected to the paper on scriptural interpretation (cf. above, 2/6:285ff.), and does not belong to the works he wrote in preparation for his dissertation. Bonhoeffer used for this work Troeltsch, *Vernunft und Offenbarung bei Johann Gerhard und Melanchthon,* and Karl von Hase, *Hutterus redivivus.*

[2.] "I believe because it is absurd." Cf. Hase, *Hutterus redivivus,* 58, and Barth, *Romans,* 112. The citation is attributed by Hase and others to Tertullian, but cannot be found in his work. A similar statement by Tertullian is found in "On the Flesh of Christ," chapter 5, page 525.

[3.] Fichte, *Attempt at a Critique of All Revelation;* Kant, *Religion within the Limits of Reason Alone.*

[4.] Replaces: "Protestant scholasticism."

[5.] "We believe, teach, and confess that the only rule and guiding principle according to which all teachings and teachers are to be evaluated and judged are the prophetic and apostolic writings of the Old and New Testaments alone . . ." (*The Book of Concord,* 486).

rebus spiritualibus prorsus est caeca,[6] that it is venefica,[7] larva Diaboli.[8] It has to "close its eyes and simply believe the word of the apostles."[9] It is corrupted and therefore insufficient and inadequate. It cannot grasp the truths of revelation. Because its ability to discern knowledge is weak, due to the fact that "it knows only a little about God and the law, it can never grasp the gospel of the Son of God and eternal salvation, comprehend it, believe it, and consider it true."[10] Consequently, reason *has* its own—albeit minimal— ability of itself to know something about God and the law. Therefore, in addition to the knowledge of faith that proceeds from the "Scriptures as norm and rule"[11] and relates all statements to them, there is an independent rational knowledge, which, however, is very weak. We are unable to extract much more from the formula present in the *Book of Concord* in answer to our question. Yet, one could maintain that here everything has already been said that is later further developed systematically by the scholastics and that had, shortly before, been developed by Melanchthon.[12] J. Gerhard is the first person who asks himself the pointed question about the way reason is used in theology. In his loci he arrives at the doctrine of a triplex usus philosophiae.[13] We will base our discussion of the problem on this and see how it is developed prior to and within the tradition of early Lutheran scholasticism.

327

The proper and *singular* principle of theology remains inspired Scripture.[14] [Here we have a completely nondialectical understanding of the idea of revelation, different from Luther's idea.][15] Since the time of Aristotle, every discipline had the duty to identify its epistemological sources through the principle of self-evidence.[16] Theology submitted to this requirement by developing the doctrine of the efficacia Spiritus Sancti in cordibus.[17] However, if this proof is acknowledged to possess methodolog-

---

[6.] "That human reason and understanding are absolutely blind in spiritual matters" (cf. *Book of Concord*, 491.2, 545.9, 546.12–13, 545.9; and further Hase, *Hutterus redivivus,* 58, footnote 3).

[7.] "Sorceress," "witch"; cf. Formula of Concord, Solid Declaration 8.41 (*Book of Concord*, 623.41).

[8.] "The devil's mask," ibid., 623.40. Cf. also the essay on "Luther's Feelings about His Work," above, 2/5:000, editorial note 78.

[9.] Formula of Concord, Solid Declaration 11 (*Book of Concord*, 645.27).

[10.] Bonhoeffer translated the Latin text freely, abbreviating its content. Cf. Formula of Concord, Solid Declaration 2 (*Book of Concord*, 545.9–15).

[11.] Cf. editorial note 5.

[12.] Like Troeltsch, Bonhoeffer treated first Gerhard and then Melanchthon; cf. Troeltsch, *Vernunft und Offenbarung,* 6f.

[13.] "Threefold use of philosophy"; cf. Troeltsch, *Vernunft und Offenbarung,* 7.

[14.] Bonhoeffer probably has in mind here Gerhard, *Loci theologici,* 1:5a (§19); otherwise he cites Gerhard following Troeltsch or Hase's compendium.

[15.] The square brackets stem from Bonhoeffer.

[16.] Troeltsch, *Vernunft und Offenbarung,* 17.

[17.] "The effectiveness of the Holy Spirit in the heart" (ibid., 18).

ical rigor, then theology, because of its comprehensive and certain knowledge, eo ipso had sovereignty over the imperfect disciplines based upon reason. The use that theology made of the complete fabric of the philosophical disciplines has, since Gerhard, been designated as usus organicus.[18] This necessarily falls into two sub-disciplines, each of which must serve theology: the instrumental and the material. The most important thing about the usus organicus, however, is that here the philosophical material as such is brought to bear only when it is organically connected with theology as a scholarly discipline and stands completely in the service of theology.[19]

Since the time of Aristotle an added resource was indispensable in order to make possible the "acroamatic,"[20] as Aristotle expressed it, i.e., the academic structure of a discipline. This resource was formal scholastic logic, or exact methodological procedure. Although grammar and rhetoric belong to the instrumental disciplines and are necessary, the scholarly character of a work is based solely on formal logic.[21] This is indispensable, in order to clarify the simplest notions of faith. Sohnius believed that he had to apologize for discussing theology in a methodical-logical manner. At a later date Hollatz opined, "certe non brutis, sed hominibus sana ratione utentibus, Deus aeternae salutis sapientiam in suo verbo revelavit."[22] In its formal usage, reason was never attacked, even by the harshest despisers of reason. Tertullian did not, nor did Luther, who instead demanded in Worms, "nisi convictus fuero testimoniis scripturarum aut ratione evidente."[23] Luther also wanted his statements to be shown to be materially contrary to scripture or formally illogical before he would retract them. We will, however, see later that Luther here could be referring only to the formal use of reason. This is what he meant by his seemingly contradictory words against reason.

328

[18.] "The organic use," i.e., the use as "instrument," Troeltsch, *Vernunft und Offenbarung*, 7.

[19.] Troeltsch, *Vernunft und Offenbarung*, 8.

[20.] Ibid., 47. The acroamatic method was originally the lecture, which was heard primarily by students. [An acroamatic doctrine is one that is orally transmitted. Bonhoeffer is using the term in a modern sense, i.e., as a doctrine ready to be taught.] [PDM]

[21.] Ibid., 48.

[22.] "Certainly, God revealed the wisdom of eternal savlation in his Word not to brute beasts, but rather to human beings, who use sound reasoning." (Schmid, *Die Dogmatik der evangelisch-lutherischen Kirche*, 12.) [The English translation, *The Doctrinal Theology of the Evangelical Lutheran Church*, differs significantly from the seventh German edition of 1893 familiar to Bonhoeffer.] [PDM] The remark inserted by Bonhoeffer concerning Georg Sohnius is meant in opposition to the mistaken interpretation of Hans Emil Weber, *Der Einfluß der protestantischen Schulphilosophie*, 19–20.

[23.] "Unless I am convinced by the testimony of the Scriptures or by clear reason"; see "Luther at the Diet of Worms," *WA* 7:838, *LW* 32:113; cf. Hase, *Hutterus redivivus*, 59, footnote 5.

However, during the time of early Lutheran scholasticism, things were not going well for logic and methodology. They held on to the well-worn doctrines of concept, judgment, and conclusion. They were, however, unable to find a way to unify in principle the material of theology with a logical method.[24] It is true that they possessed Melanchthon's humanistic methodus particularis of the loci with its pattern of questioning, "an sit, quid sit, causae, cognata, oppugnantia."[25] A further differentiation was easy to find here, but the methodus universalis was missing. Through Giacomo Zabarella this need was met by means of the differentiation of synthetic and analytic method, assigning theology to the latter.[26] Only gradually was the turn[27] toward the analytical practical method[28] completed. Without exception, however, this occurred only in Lutheran theology and in contrast to Reformed theology. This was done by taking into account even the seemingly external contradictions. Dogmatics moved from its place at the head of all disciplines, where Melanchthon had placed it, down to the practical disciplines, such as medicine and cooking, as Troeltsch expressed it.[29] Logic became completely free from rhetoric. It now schematized material according to its own laws, without the least ability to make the material correspond to it.[30] In the exact logical process one found the truth claim of the clarified statements substantiated. The scholarly ideal at first was a constantly renewable differentiation into the individual loci. It then became an attempt to achieve unity through compartmentalization. As far as I know, they did not realize that the material treated by such a forceful logical method undergoes changes.

Alongside this use in theology of the instrumental philosophical discipline stands the material discipline [Realdisziplin].[31] This relates essentially to material explanations, concrete explanations of terms that belong to both theology as well as philosophy, like terra, caelum, *locus* (ubiquity), and then to res politicae, etc.[32] The phrase about philosophy being the ancilla theologiae[33] refers substantially to its service in material explanation. At any

---

[24.] Troeltsch, *Vernunft und Offenbarung,* 48–49.

[25.] Ibid., 49 and 52. Here one finds "pugnantia" instead of "oppugnantia." The citation reads, "If there is what there is, causes, relations, and correspondences."

[26.] See Zabarella, *De methodis libri quatuor;* cf. Troeltsch, *Vernunft und Offenbarung,* 49f.

[27.] Deleted, "from the synthetic."

[28.] Hase, *Hutterus redivivus,* 33, footnote 6.

[29.] Troeltsch, *Vernunft und Offenbarung,* 50.

[30.] Ibid., 49, footnote 6.

[31.] Cf. ibid., 50f.

[32.] "Earth, heaven, place (ubiquity), then politics, etc." Ubiquity characterizes the doctrine developed by Luther, in connection with the doctrine of the communication of attributes (communicatio idiomatum) between the divine and the human natures of Christ, that the human nature of Christ is omnipresent. This is an important concept for Luther's doctrine of the Lord's Supper.

[33.] "Handmaid of theology."

rate Calov[34] and others point to this. It is self-evident that philosophical argumentation must join the theological in the service of material explanation. If this were not the case, it would be guilty of μετάβασις εἰς ἄλλο γένος,[35] a phrase that was constantly in use at the time. With this phrase, everything that is problematical is addressed, e.g., the difficult question of the quaestiones mixtae,[36] i.e., what happens when a theological and a philosophical term are connected in a statement. Here a critical danger threatened theology. Yet one said, if philosophy wanted to argue from itself at this point, then this would be μετάβασις εἰς ἄλλο γένος. A famous dispute related to this was the Lutheran doctrine of the ubiquity of the body of Christ.[37] Theology is authorized to immediately reject any philosophical argument. In academic form, this claim of authority sounds like this: the medius terminus,[38] which is the deciding factor in the conclusio,[39] belongs to theology in the final procedure. With this the question is settled in the interest of theology. The question about universality is addressed by forcing in the theological concept of θεάνθρωπος[40] as a terminus medius, and with this the theological and philosophical concepts are conjoined in the conclusion in the interest of theology. In this way, every attack by reason was, in principle, repulsed from the beginning. There was nothing that could not be proved.[41] But is not the validity of the law of reason, the dictum concerning contradiction, abolished if body and non-locality are wedded by ubiquity? Gerhard answers, No, it is not abolished in the sphere of revelation, but it cannot be used for dogma! Merely because something is stated in scripture means that its consistency is vouched for. There are no contradictions in dogma, even though our reason may understand so little of it. One recognized early on that it is exactly here that one finds the weak point in Gerhard's doctrine of the usus organicus. To assert a valid and an invalid law of reason at the same time is clearly nonsense.[42] At any rate, it is significant that, with claims of authority and violation of logic, theology suppressed the rational knowledge that was becoming hazardous to it. Theology laid claim to the position of reason by means of the appearance of scholarship but also

331

[34.] Unclear if Bonhoeffer's intended reference is to Abraham Calov or Georg Calixt.

[35.] "Transformation to another type, to a foreign genus." According to Aristotelian logic, this is a proof of error. In the text Bonhoeffer strongly emphasized this concept, which was used very often by Troeltsch (cf. *Vernunft und Offenbarung*, 3, footnote 2; elsewhere, 22, 23, 55, and 90).

[36.] "Mixed questions" (Troeltsch, *Vernunft und Offenbarung*, 23).

[37.] Ibid., footnote 32.

[38.] "Middle term."

[39.] "Conclusion."

[40.] "Divine-human."

[41.] Troeltsch, *Vernunft und Offenbarung*, 24.

[42.] Ibid., 24f.

with a true belief in it. Positive influence on the content of faith became impossible in the usus organicus of reason.[43]

If in this exposition philosophy has been seen essentially as a discipline assisting theology, the second question addresses the constructive function of reason for "natural theology,"[44] which is the usus catasceuasticus.[45] As far as I see, the solution to this question is the remarkable combination of humanistic and Reformed ideals that is characteristic of Orthodoxy.[46] Particularly noteworthy is the fact that reason and revelation, as independent sources corresponding to the Aristotelian requirement of self-evidence, lie in two toto coelo[47] different spheres of the human capability for obtaining knowledge. The first relates to the natural life and the knowledge of religious things, insofar as they are accessible to natural thought. The second relates to transrational divine mysteries that can never be grasped by reason.[48] The main endeavor of Catholic scholasticism was to establish a relationship between two deeply separated areas. Melanchthon,[49] and with him the[50] early Lutheran scholastics, find their solution to the problem of natural theology in a predecessor, Thomas Aquinas.[51] This problem became critical for the first time when, with the entrance of Aristotle, the question was posed concerning the relationship of the knowledge of truth to Christian knowledge from revelation. Later, after nominalism, it reawoke in humanism and its goal of toleration. The ancient Greeks could not possibly have been totally mistaken. Here a scriptural passage, Rom. 1:19, was especially taken into consideration.

One proceeded from the concept of the single and unified highest truth.[52] In this way, revelation cannot be contrary to reason. Instead it must transcend reason. This is affirmed in a sentence from late Protestant scholasticism, philosophia est scientia veritatis ac sicut verum vero non contradicit, ita veritas philosophiae theologicam non impugnat (Hollatz).[53] Consequently, rational knowledge also carries with it the character of truth, even if

332

[43.] Ibid., 46f.

[44.] Replaces the phrase "the constructive use of reason."

[45.] "Use [of reason] to confirm [the revealed truth]." Troeltsch, *Vernunft und Offenbarung*, 99. [The word *catasceuasticus*, 'constructive', is a Greek term from Aristotle and retained in Latin spelling by the Roman and medieval logicians. It refers to the confirmation of an initial assumption, as against *anasceuastieus*, which refers to refutation.][CG]

[46.] Ibid., 64f.

[47.] "Worlds apart."

[48.] Troeltsch, *Vernunft und Offenbarung*, 15.

[49.] Cf. ibid., 70.

[50.] The words "with him the" replace the word "his."

[51.] See below, 2/8:308. Bonhoeffer appears to ignore Troeltsch, *Vernunft und Offenbarung*, 21, footnotes 1 and 95!

[52.] Cf. ibid., 17.

[53.] "Philosophy is a science of the truth, and since one truth cannot contradict another truth, so the truth of philosophy does not conflict with theological truth" (Hollatz, *Examen theologicum acroamaticum*, 32).

it has been weakened by the status corruptionis.[54] In this way, reason can prove the existence of God. The deus uni-trinus,[55] however, can be grasped only by belief in revelation. Such examples are plentiful. Now there are two types of rational knowledge. One type comes to a person through the external observation of nature by the well-known via eminentia, negationis, causalitatis.[56] The second type exists in notitia insita, innata, congenita.[57] On this basis, the individual has an a priori intuitive insight. An example of this is the doctrine of divine things. Because of the fall, however, this knowledge has been destroyed. Only a small remnant remains. What had earlier been a natural understanding was now a mystery beyond the natural.

In this way, the natural knowledge of reason can only be recognized if and insofar as it is present in scripture. In the doctrines of faith there are articuli puri and mixti.[58] The first belong only to the sphere of revelation. The last are also approachable via the natural knowledge of reason, but are always justified only through the witness of scripture. Melanchthon transferred his thought about lex and evangelium[59] onto this fundamental split between reason and revelation. The lumen naturale,[60] the point where contact between the spheres of revelation and reason is made,[61] even allow the pagans to have an understanding, albeit dim, of the lex naturae (cf. Rom. 2:15).[62] This lex naturalis is joined by the lex moralis in the Decalogue.[63] Both, however, stand together. They are only differentiated quantitatively as rational knowledge (lex naturale = lex divina!) and are contrasted to absolutely suprarational revelation in the gospel.[64] Thus the contrast between reason and revelation is sharpened and becomes the contrast between law and gospel and the contrast between iustitia propria and iustitia aliena.[65] Since, however, preaching the gospel cannot take place without the law, a bridge now spans the divide.[66] The distinction between the laws

333

[54.] "State of Corruption."

[55.] "Triune God."

[56.] "Way of eminence [eminentiae], negation, and causation."

[57.] "Implanted, innate, inborn knowledge."

[58.] "Pure and mixed articles."

[59.] Troeltsch, *Vernunft und Offenbarung*, 160 and 138. For the following cf. Melanchthon, "De lege naturae," in *Loci praecipui theologici*, (*Corpus Reformatorum* 21:711–16).

[60.] "Natural light."

[61.] Troeltsch, *Vernunft und Offenbarung*, 100.

[62.] Ibid., 154.

[63.] Ibid., 155.

[64.] "Natural law = divine law" (ibid., 125, 144f., 160, 163, and 192).

[65.] "One's own righteousness and foreign righteousness." Cf. Troeltsch, *Vernunft und Offenbarung*, 130f. ["Own righteousness" means righteousness achieved by one's own action; "foreign righteousness" is righteousness conferred by another, namely God.] [PDM]

[66.] Ibid., 160f.

is the accomplishment of Melanchthon and Orthodoxy. Luther, according to Holl,[67] never brought this to a conclusion. Instead, he always saw the law as a unified whole in contradiction to the gospel. This included all laws from the law of nature to the law in the Sermon on the Mount. Luther's position on natural reason wavers. On the whole, though, he opposes it sharply.[68] Therefore, the picture of two separate stories of a house built one on top of the other necessarily arises when one views early Lutheranism's full understanding. In this schema, the second only adds something to the first. Gratia naturam non tollit sed perficit![69] This thought reminds us of Thomas even in its details.[70] Collisions between both spheres[71] cannot take place. All seeming contradictions result from μετάβασς εἰς ἄλλο γένος.[72] The virgin birth can easily be considered unthinkable from the perspective of rational knowledge. Rational knowledge, however, cannot claim to have[73] a voice in matters of revelation.[74] So it was precisely the fact that reason and revelation were so sharply and radically differentiated in their original state that enabled them to be unified in the highest *single* truth. Hollatz was the first to give precision to these thoughts in this strict form, but they are merely consistent conclusions. We do not need to address the usus anasceuasticus,[75] which only discusses the polemical use of the first and second usus.

Looking back at the whole presentation so far, it can be seen that historically and genetically there are two streams that flow alongside each other and must be distinguished: Lutheran biblicism and humanism.[76] The man who combined both was Melanchthon, the praeceptor Germaniae.[77] Yet a contradiction lies at the basis of his great system. One could not omit the claim that scripture was the sole authority and recognize only the usus organicus. One also wanted to secure a place for rational knowledge within the system

[67.] Holl, *Luther*, 247; cf. *E* 303ff., especially 307f.

[68.] Cf. Troeltsch, *Vernunft und Offenbarung*, 190.

[69.] "Grace does not abolish nature, but perfects it."

[70.] The statement cited is found for the first time in Bonaventure's commentary on the *Sentences* of Peter Lombard (II *Sent.* D. 9 question 9 ad 2). In Thomas it receives foundational significance and is found often in his writings, first in his commentary on the *Sentences* in II *Sent.* 9.1.8 ad 3 (Thomas Aquinas, *Opera Omnia* 1:152), and in III *Sent.* 24.1.3. (ibid., 1:349); later in *De veritate*, question 14, article 9 ad 8 (ibid., 3:97 and in *Truth*, 2:248–9), and question 27, article 6 ad 3 (*Opera Omnia* 3:172), and finally in the *Summa theologiae*, I, question 2, article 2 ad 1 (*Opera Omnia* 2:187; *Summa theologiae*, 2:11). Cf. also above, editorial note 51.

[71.] Cf. editorial note 48.

[72.] Cf. editorial note 35.

[73.] Read, "require."

[74.] Cf. Hase, *Hutterus redivivus*, 61, footnote 15.

[75.] "Use [of reason] to refutation [of the arguments against the revealed truth]." Troeltsch, *Vernunft und Offenbarung*, 99, note 1.

[76.] Ibid., 64f.

[77.] "The teacher of Germany" (ibid., 56).

of doctrine and therefore used the usus catasceuasticus. The later theologians tried to reconcile both through the articuli mixti. But it is precisely at this point of tension that the uniqueness of the principal doctrine of early Lutheranism lies. Troeltsch demonstrated Melanchthon's all-encompassing influence on the whole of orthodoxy's construction of a system.[78] The formation of an independent church in 1526 resulted in the need for a new dogmatics. It could be built only upon the broad basis of the general education system of secondary schools and universities. The dualism between natural and supranatural knowledge should be represented, and yet without disturbing their unity. The entire further scholastic development is based on this foundation, in which logical ossification like a change in method could change nothing.[79] When religious life was devastated in the Thirty Years War, pietism demonstrated that it was weak and sectarian. In its stead, fresh authoritative rational knowledge invaded from abroad. This was the path that late scholasticism consequently traveled—the way to rationalism.

335

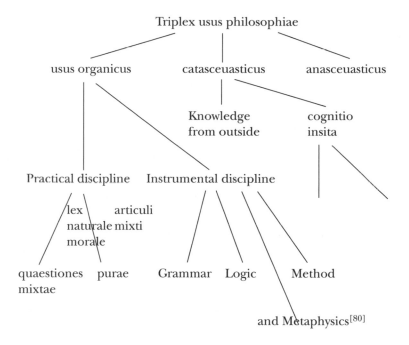

[78.] Cf. ibid., 65ff. and 144ff.

[79.] Ibid., 210.

[80.] The word "metaphysics" has probably been penciled in by Stolzenburg, not by Bonhoeffer.

C. Papers on the Third Article in the Field of Bonhoeffer's Dissertation. January–November 1926

9. Paper on Church and Eschatology[1]

Church and Eschatology
(or Church and the Kingdom of God)

After having examined the concept of the empirical church more closely in the previous hour, today we focus our sights in the opposite direction, as we attempt to uncover the connection between the church and its eschatological component, the kingdom of God.

It is always a sign of religious strength and true integrity when eschatology becomes a topic of theology. When this happens, one does not just fill up a few pages, a little shamefacedly, out of a sense of duty, as is so often seen in nineteenth-century theology; but instead, following the example of the Reformers, one truly recognizes eschatology as the end and goal to which

---

[1.] *NL* A 12, 2; typed. Paper written for a seminar with Seeberg, who evaluated the paper on January 22, 1926 (see below, Appendix 3, page 585). There are two versions of this text. One is the original, corrected by Seeberg (ms. 1) and the other is Bonhoeffer's carbon copy (ms. 2). Both versions have Bonhoeffer's handwritten corrections. Ms. 1 is printed here. Divergences from ms. 2 are noted in the editorial notes. This is the first paper written for Seeberg after he had taken on Bonhoeffer as a doctoral candidate (see above, 1/93:148f., Bonhoeffer's letter of September 21, 1925, to his parents). Like the following papers, it serves as a preparatory work for his dissertation. See *SC* (*DBWE* 1):282–88. It has been concluded that for the first portion of the paper Bonhoeffer used Seeberg, *Christliche Dogmatik*, 2:319–53 (§37 and §38), and Johannes Weiß, *Jesus' Proclamation of the Kingdom of God*, 81–105. For the second part Bonhoeffer used Emanuel Hirsch, *Die Reich-Gottes-Begriffe des neueren europäischen Denkens*, 12ff.

everything must be related. It will soon be demonstrated that by eschatology we are not referring to fantasy-filled enthusiasm and apocalyptic curiosity. The Reformers considered that, without eschatology, the doctrine of justifi- 337 cation was stunted. The person who is justified is iustus nondum in re sed in spe.[2] Due to human sinfulness, the status gratiae[3] must be raised [aufgehoben] to the status perfectionis.[4] "Faith is the assurance of things hoped for."[5] Eschatology was therefore not mythology or something similar; instead it necessarily emerged as a goal from the human experience of the divine. In a doctrinal investigation of an eschatological concept, we need not take up all New Testament apocalyptic developments but instead we single out in systematic order prototypes that are significant for the faith. The central concept of all Christian eschatology throughout the ages is the early Christian concept of the kingdom of God. This concept can be found in personal eschatology. Nonetheless, fundamentally, it presupposes that social and historical elements act as complements within human experience.[6] This means that it is not so much the faithful individual who is the partner or counterpart of the concept of the kingdom of God, but more so the concepts of church, then nation [Staat], humanity, and all of history.[7] Most distinctly, however, we see the kingdom of God in relation to the phenomenon of the church, wherein the relationship exists. Our inquiry concerns the type of relationship this is. First, we want to understand the concept of the kingdom of God and the concept of the church.

It is well known that the New Testament's eschatological concept of the kingdom of God is not developed in only one way. The description of the kingdom of God is approached from many different angles. Observed systematically, we can see in the New Testament two or three forms of the concept of the kingdom of God. We must emphasize, however, that underlying the clearly distinct forms that we have found there is a central, cohesive idea 338 concerning the true nature of the kingdom. The kingdom of God is a spiritual [geistig pneumatisch] reality in which the sovereign will of the Father, the redeeming and judging will of the Son, and the love-forming will of the Holy Spirit for the spiritual community of the kingdom's children have been truly realized in complete unity in authoritative, singular effectiveness. Thus, this realm guides the world to its goal.[8] The kingdom of God therefore is a

---

[2.] "Righteous not in reality, but in hope." Cf. Luther's Galatians commentary, *WA* 2:495.1; *LW* 27:227: "Omnis qui credit in Christum, iustus est, nondum plene in re sed in spe." "Everyone who believes in Christ is righteous, not fully in point of fact, but in hope."

[3.] "State of grace."

[4.] "State of perfection."

[5.] Heb. 11:1.

[6.] Cf. Seeberg, *Dogmatik*, 1:505ff.

[7.] Ritschl, *The Christian Doctrine of Justification and Reconciliation*, 3:577f.

[8.] Bonhoeffer's exposition is based on Seeberg, *Dogmatik*, 2:334–5. In the latter, however, Bonhoeffer's words "the Son's will of judgment" are missing.

community of redeemed persons. Membership is comprised only of those elected by God. This results in obedient submission to the sovereignty of God.[9] The historical realization of this election occurs in Christ and his continued spiritual work. The binding of the members in love occurs in the work of the Holy Spirit.

All of the common and essential concepts concerning the kingdom of God found in the New Testament fit into this general form. The larger problem, and with it the multifaceted nature of the conceptions of the kingdom of God, is due to the position of this spiritual-eternal entity that is necessary for it to be temporally present. Here we are referring again to the twofold or threefold conception of the kingdom of God found in the New Testament.

On one hand, the kingdom of God is conceived as being present. Satan's power is limited by the coming of the kingdom of God. Εἰ δὲ ἐν πνεύματι θεοῦ ἐγὼ ἐκβάλλω τὰ δαιμόνια, ἄρα ἔφθασεν ἐφ' ὑμᾶς ἡ βασιλεία τοῦ θεοῦ, Matt. 12:18,[10] or Luke 10:18: Εθεώρουν τὸν σατανᾶν ὡς ἀστραπὴν πεσόντα ἐκ τοῦ οὐρανοῦ.[11] Luke 17:21.[12]

Or, as in the message to John:

Τυφλοὶ ἀναβλέπουσιν καὶ χωλοὶ περιπατοῦσιν, λεπροὶ καθαρίζονται καὶ κωφοὶ ἀκούουσιν, καὶ νεκροὶ ἐγείρονται καὶ πτωχοὶ εὐαγγελίζονται,[13] which certainly means that Satan's kingdom has finally been demolished by Jesus. God's kingdom has attained its fullest reality, and people seize upon it with violence. Matt. 11:11.[14] These statements differentiate themselves in nuance from the parables[15] of Matthew 13 and parallels. In them, indeed, the kingdom of God is conceived as already present. Yet it will only be revealed after it has developed from this seed throughout history, so that its fulfillment will not occur until the end of time. It is here that we find the plea for the kingdom to come:[16] ἐλθάτω ἡ βασιλεία σου.[17] These words stand in striking contrast to others, like those in the apocalyptic speeches of Mark 13 and parallels. The kingdom of God will break in unexpectedly upon sleepers like a thief in the night. A divine show of force will suddenly end the world, and the Son will descend on the clouds, intent on judgment. Jesus awaits this time in the very near future, ἀμὴν λέγω ὑμῖν ὅτι εἰσίν τινες ὧδε

339

[9.] Cf. Ritschl, *Justification and Reconciliation*, 2:29–30.

[10.] "But if it is by the Spirit of God that I cast out demons then the kingdom of God has come to you" (the correct reference is Matt. 12:28).

[11.] "I watched Satan fall from heaven like a flash of lightning."

[12.] Luke 17:21 added—by Seeberg?

[13.] "The blind receive their sight, the lame walk, the lepers are cleansed, the deaf hear, the dead are raised, and the poor have good news brought to them" (Matt. 11:5).

[14.] The correct reference is Matt. 11:12-13. Cf. Weiß, *Jesus' Proclamation*, 83.

[15.] Bonhoeffer added the words "from the parables," by hand.

[16.] Seeberg put a question mark in the margin.

[17.] "Your kingdom come" (Matt. 6:10).

τῶν ἑστηκότων οἵτινες οὐ μὴ γεύσωνται θανάτου ἕως ἂν ἴδωσιν τήν βασιλείαν τοῦ θεοῦ ἐληλυθυῖαν ἐν δυνάμει.[18]

Therefore at one point the kingdom of God is present now, be it in its full reality or merely as a bud and seed. At another point, it is found in the future as the referent of the fulfillment at the last days. How can these opposing positions be reconciled?

We answer, "Where Christ is, there his kingdom must also necessarily be and consequently be present." This refers both to Christ's life on this earth as well as to his continued spiritual work.[19] Applied, however, to the course of history, this only means the beginning of the kingdom, which is active in history and is consummated at the end, i.e., beyond history. As a spiritual entity, the kingdom, seen from above,[20] is there, but those who will share the kingdom will assemble over time. The content and extent of the kingdom are foreseen in election and therefore are complete in every instance. In our eyes, however, the course of time cannot be pushed out of mind. The kingdom of God thus expresses the kingdom that is at work[21] on earth as it is perfected in eternity. Consequently the kingdom of God, insofar as it develops and grows here on earth, is an eschatological concept in the same way as the kingdom that has been fulfilled in eternity, because it is the same thing. It is the corollary of God's sovereignty here as there. Eschatology is not a temporal concept; it is supra-temporal. We will find more about this below. Here the same tension exists that we find in the contrast between Johannine and Pauline theology,[22] as in the *possession* of eternal life through faith and the effort to attain the *goal* that has been set or, as in the Augustinian paradox, "You would not seek me if you had not already found me."[23]

In theological terms, every gift of God is at the same time a task,[24] just as the reverse is true that every task presupposes a gift. To the extent that the kingdom of God is temporal, it must work itself out in time. This means: it is made visible at some fortuitous place in history through the task of proclaiming the kingdom of God and the forgiveness of sins. This occurs in the empirical church, the so-called ecclesia militans.[25] In this way, we are deliberately directed from the kingdom of God to the empirical church. What follows from this may now be very clearly determined. The empirical form of

340

[18.] "Truly I tell you, there are some standing here who will not taste death until they see that the kingdom of God has come with power" (Mark 9:1).

[19.] Bonhoeffer later added this sentence by hand.

[20.] Seeberg underlined the phrase, "seen from above."

[21.] Seeberg: "developing." Against this cf. Weiß, *Jesus' Proclamation*, 81ff. Weiß talks of an "antithesis to the 'theories of evolution'."

[22.] Concerning this see Bonhoeffer's essay on John and Paul, below, 2/13:395–404.

[23.] Bonhoeffer mistakenly attributed a quotation from Pascal to Augustine (see above, 2/6:292, editorial note 57).

[24.] Ritschl, *Justification and Reconciliation*, 3:31 and 3:34.

[25.] "Church militant."

the church is intended as the instrument of the kingdom of God with the word of God as its weapon in battle.[26] The word of God, however, is only a temporal, clear expression for the supra-temporality of election, of judgment.[27] The word continually cuts an unseen incision through the middle of the whole empirical church—calling to some, hardening others. Thereby it presupposes judgment and grace, whose unveiling and perfection can be known only on the judgment day.[1] In this way, through the empirical church, it procures vital new members. The goal of the church is the expansion of the kingdom of God, the gathering and maintenance of old and new members, whom Christ redeemed. The church-community [Gemeinde] that had previously been elected and constituted by God in history therefore has the same goal as the kingdom of God. It also has the same relationship to its members, because the kingdom of God, like the church, is ultimately based on God's decision to elect. Therefore the church is essentially the entity that has been predetermined by the Father in eternal election, the church-community of believers that has been established by the saving action of Christ in history as the spiritual body of the spiritual head. It is kept active by the Holy Spirit by means of living, community-building love. As such she is una, one as the Lord is one, sancta, holy because the Holy Spirit is at work in her, and catholica, catholic because she is dispersed throughout the world wherever the word of God is proclaimed. As such, she is the church-community of those who pray for each other [füreinander Bittenden] and of the believers, who are invariably penitent sinners and are continuously being judged and justified anew. In contrast to the empirical church, this invisible church is not bound to any other social relationships. The bond is purely spiritual.

If we compare this definition of the church to the earlier definition of the kingdom of God, we can recognize the essential identity of both as far as their content is concerned. The only thing that differentiates the two is that the church is restricted to a portion of history, whereas the kingdom of God encompasses the entire unfolding of the world. This parallels the relationship of the Son to the Father. In this way, pronouncements about the salvation of the Old Testament patriarchs as well as belief in the salvation of people who have never been touched by revelation are subsumed under the concept of the kingdom of God—not the church. The identity of both concepts is expressed, for example, in Eph. 5:5, where the kingdom of God and the kingdom of Christ are used interchangeably.

---

1. *WA* 3:24.[28]

[26.] Seeberg underlined and commented in the margin, "Why in battle?"
[27.] Seeberg underlined and put a question mark in the margin.
[28.] *First Lectures on the Psalms, LW* 10:23f. Cf. Holl, *Luther*, 293–94 and 294 footnote 1.

Therefore, we understand the kingdom of God and the essential church, the so-called invisible church, as being conceptually identical in purpose and constitution, and as temporally identical entities. The church-community that constitutes itself in time has two reasons to accept the fact that it may have to harbor non-elect members. First, experience shows us that there is no empirical group that does not find "fellow travelers" among its members. Second, it nonetheless lies in the nature of things that, through divine election by the word, these cannot be outwardly recognized and cannot be humanly judged. From this it follows that the difference between true and false members does not lie in the sinlessness of the one and the sinfulness of the other but in the fact that the elect are in status gratiae and the lost are in status corruptionis.[29] The external circumference of the empirical church therefore is larger than the circumference of the essential church, i.e., also the development of the kingdom of God for the time being.

The concept of the church, however, is not split into two parts. Instead its unity is seen (1) by the unity of purpose and (2) by the unity of power that holds the invisible and the visible church[30] together.[31] How does the church reconcile itself to the fact that the non-elect are among its members? We can answer that the empirical church is the place where salvation is offered to everyone. Whether or not this comes to fruition is in God's hands. Those for whom this does occur are members of the supra-empirical church. But if salvation is offered to everyone in the church, then the goal of both— the empirical and the supra-empirical—is the same, namely, salvation. The power that holds both of them together is the word, proclaimed and offered to all, and the sacrament.[32]

To use an image, the empirical church is nothing other than the door and the signpost[33] to the hereafter of the invisible church. It is a window through which the kingdom of God should always be visible. In the sacred story it appears as the person of John the Baptist, and woe unto them when they cover up the door and cloud the glass by making John into Christ.

343

Now, can such a church be an object of faith? Yes, because faith in the church only relates to the effect of the word of God and the Spirit in her, i.e., to the promise of Isa. 55:11. It also relates, therefore, to the fact that in this empirically dispersed community there is a unifying bond, i.e., certainly of the invisible in the visible church, but even in the visible. It follows from this that there must be in every empirical church a piece of the invisible church,

[29.] "State of grace" and "state of corruption."

[30.] The handwritten addition by Bonhoeffer, "invisible . . . church," replaces "it."

[31.] In the original, the order of numbers (1) and (2) is altered by Bonhoeffer. The text has been modified to reflect these changes.

[32.] The sentence is a handwritten addition by Bonhoeffer.

[33.] Seeberg adds, "page 314 instrument!" [This refers to Bonhoeffer's statement above, 2/9:314, that the empirical church is an 'instrument' of the kingdom of God.] [CG]

i.e., again, that the empirical church can never be characterized as the only way that can make blessed.[34]

When we speak of working for and building the kingdom of God, we must be clear that it is not we who are building but it is God through us or, more precisely, through the word that we speak about God. The kingdom cannot be built even through the best ethical behavior.[35] If we believe we are building the kingdom of God, we are in great danger of confusing the kingdom of God with a human organization. We thereby put ourselves outside the door of the church.[36] This is and will remain the fate of great attempts to build the kingdom of God on earth.

Paul took up Jesus' proclamation of the kingdom of God, combining it with the Jewish idea of the people of Yahweh, and transformed it into the idea of the church. He does not differentiate between the essential and the empirical church; kingdom and church are for Jesus and Paul completely unalloyed, purely holy spiritual entities. In this way, the concept of the kingdom of God retreats, and the more powerful concept of the kingdom of Christ advances; i.e., the church according to Paul's understanding presents no essential difference from Jesus' ideas. Nevertheless, in the New Testament we already see an inversion of a thought that could become dangerous.[37] When Jesus speaks in John 3, Ἀμὴν ἀμὴν λέγω σοι, ἐὰν μή τις γεννηθῇ ἐξ ὕδατος καὶ πνεύματος, οὐ δύναται εἰσελθεῖν εἰς τὴν βασιλείαν τῶν οὐρανῶν,[38] entering the kingdom of God is identified with baptism, i.e., it is the precursor to the later Catholic idea.[39] A second thought that matches this idea is expressed in Matthew 13. Here the kingdom of God in the world has become mixed, in which wheat and weeds grow together in a field; fresh and decaying fish are in a net; and elect and non-elect are together.[40] Here in this world one dare not separate them for fear that one might pull out the wheat with the weeds. That will wait until the day of judgment. In spite of this disordered situation, the whole is called the kingdom of God (an

344

[34.] Seeberg underlined the word "way" and wrote in the margin, "But it still is door and signpost." See above, 2/9:315.

[35.] Seeberg: "Yes, but God is active in such ethical behavior!"

[36.] Seeberg: "But this is something different! We certainly should *do* something!" Cf. Barth, *Romans*, 431ff.; also Bonhoeffer's sermon on Ps. 127:1 (below, 3:5:470ff.) and his children's address on the Decalogue (below, 3/2:456ff.).

[37.] Seeberg placed a question mark here.

[38.] "Very truly, I tell you, no one can enter the kingdom of God without being born of water and Spirit" (John 3:5). Bonhoeffer cites a variant given in Nestle, *Novum Testamentum Graece*.

[39.] Seeberg adds, "But birth takes place ἐκ πνεύματος [by the Spirit]."

[40.] Matt. 13:24-30 and 47-50. Cf. Seeberg, *Dogmatik*, 1:345.

unusual way to refer to this concept).[2] We have remarked above that here we are discussing the Roman Catholic identification of the kingdom of God and the empirical church.[42] If one believes, however, that the kingdom of God is embodied[43] in the empirical church, then all[44] external forms are immediately sanctioned, stabilized, and holy in themselves. Only the one   345
who enters through these historical forms in the historical church can be or become a member of the kingdom of God.[45] This is the first significant historical attempt to solve the problem[46] of the kingdom of God and church. It had slowly and almost imperceptibly developed from the earliest form of Christianity. The church was not content to be door and signpost; it built a palace where it would have free space.[47] The issue of how the question of predestination was incorporated, which threatened[48] to demolish the whole edifice, can be laid aside. The kingdom of God on earth is realized in the organized church as regnum externum[49] and is brought to perfection in eternity. Here it is militant, there triumphant. This is the ancient and the new Catholic doctrine of the church.[50]

Attacks from the most divergent sides have been leveled against the Catholic identification of the kingdom of God and the church. The sect sees the basic evil in the fact that obviously unworthy people are counted as belonging to the holy church. It therefore attempts, by insisting on absolute holiness in life, to place before the world a visible community of the elect.[51] It thereby comes into conflict with the divine commandment not to differentiate between weeds and wheat in this world and, with this, becomes disobedient and thereby not a holy church.[52] Luther's view of this matter is

---

2. Following everything that has been said, one can assume that Jesus did not lay a great deal of weight on the designation of the kingdom of God. For him the important thing was describing the intermingled situation; the rest presupposes the church-community experience of the empirical church.[41]

[41.] This note is a handwritten addition by Bonhoeffer.
[42.] Seeberg queries with a question mark.
[43.] Seeberg underlines the word and writes in the margin, "Where do you find that?"
[44.] Seeberg underlines the word and writes in the margin, "which?"
[45.] The word "can" is underlined by Seeberg, who wrote in the margin, "Are forms other than the historical at his disposal? It became Catholic only as a result of legalism."
[46.] Seeberg underlined, and put a question mark in the margin.
[47.] The words, "free space," are underlined by Seeberg who wrote in the margin: "What does this mean?"
[48.] Ernst Troeltsch, *The Social Teaching of the Christian Churches*, 73ff.
[49.] "External kingdom."
[50.] Seeberg comments, "law! gratia infusa ['infused grace']!" "Infused grace" is the grace of God that is given to people through God's love, with whose help they can do good works by themselves. This concept was rejected by Luther.
[51.] Bonhoeffer orients his thinking according to Troeltsch, *Social Teaching*, 328ff.
[52.] This sentence is added later by Bonhoeffer.

346

essentially that elaborated earlier and need not be repeated here. In pietism one attempted once more to understand the basic relationship between the kingdom of God and church according to Luther. It so emphasized the church as the instrument and builder of the kingdom of God, however, that it could not avoid sectarian consequences. The secularization of the idea of the kingdom of God leads on a path from Rousseau to Saint-Simon, Marx, and Tolstoy up to our current Religious Socialists and to a large segment of our Youth Movement [Jugendbewegung].[53] Saint-Simon said everything fundamental. The aspect of the perfected kingdom of God was stricken from the Protestant sermon, just as was the concept of church. What remained was the kingdom of God that was supposed to be erected on Christian brotherly love in order to remedy social abuses. All of humanity was intended to be incorporated into an enormous organization led by their spiritual leader in Rome, their center.[54] This fantastic organizational concept was taken up by Marx[55] and Comte. It then diminished in Tolstoy and our Religious Socialists. These confined themselves to seeing the kingdom of God realized in the idea of brotherly love and in this way hoped for its arrival. Here everything related to the church falls away.[56]

The critique of this thought process is evident in what has been said above. The kingdom of God is simply never actualized here on earth, in the sense that one could say that it is here or there; it can be more powerful in times of terrible social need than in times of social contentment.

At a completely different trajectory in intellectual history, the concept of the kingdom of God is developed into a distinctive form, namely, in the philosophy of German idealism from Leibniz to Kant.[57] Here again, as in Luther, it receives a purely spiritual stamp in that it is understood as a community of spiritually and ethically liberated personalities. However, everything that emerged in Luther from contact with God emerged for idealism from human spiritual abilities. Concepts like sin and election were nonexistent. What did an entity like the church mean in this context? Therefore, here as well, we see a secularization of the concept of the kingdom of God,

347

[53.] In the following, Bonhoeffer relies upon Hirsch, *Die Reich-Gottes-Begriffe*, 12ff. See, on the philosophers of the Enlightenment: pages 12–16 in reference to Jean-Jacques Rousseau; pages 16–18 in reference to Claude Henri de Rouvroy, Count of Saint-Simon, a representative of utopian socialism; pages 18–19 in reference to Karl Marx; page 19 in reference to Leo Tolstoy; pages 19–20 in reference to 'Religious Socialists', beginning with the theologians Hermann Kutter and Leonhard Ragaz, mostly confined to Switzerland; page 19 in reference to Auguste Comte, a Saint-Simon scholar, founder of positivism and of modern sociology.

[54.] Seeberg underlines the word "Rome"; cf. Hirsch, *Die Reich-Gottes-Begriffe*, 18.

[55.] Seeberg underlines and puts an exclamation mark in the margin.

[56.] Seeberg writes: "Compare, however, the critique of the writer on page 316f."

[57.] Concerning Leibniz and Kant, see Hirsch, *Die Reich-Gottes-Begriffe*, 20ff.

even if it is on a more intellectual level. The fact that idealism understood the concept of church so poorly also derives from the fact that, although the concept of the spiritual [geistig] personality was clearly understood, the concept of the community remained completely ignored and had to be reintroduced in the romantic era in the theology of Schleiermacher.[58] If, however, the ideas of election and community are missing, so are the central components of the idea of the church but also the Christian concept of the kingdom of God. It is lost and replaced by the general concept of the rational spirit. In this way, all these attempts prove to be inadequate for solving the problem in a Christian sense. In denigrating the concept of church, one becomes disobedient to God's will. In arbitrarily making visible the kingdom of God on earth, one confuses it with human accomplishments. God's will and work simply may not be made into a concrete thing in an ecclesial or social[59] organization, or in a club of moralists.

We must glance at idealism's very significant philosophy of history. We will then have the opportunity to describe the Christian understanding of the kingdom of God and of the church throughout all of history until its "end."

In idealism, since Leibniz, history is presented as a constant evolution in human perception and morality, which finds its goal in the kingdom of God on earth. Through gradual progress evil is removed from the earth. All of humankind will find itself united in the kingdom of God. The history of the world is at the same time the history of the kingdom of God. The church will merge into the world of morality. Opposed to this stands the Protestant understanding of the passage of history and the fate of the kingdom of God in history. It sees an evil religious indifference in the idealistic construct. The parable from Matthew 13 of the weeds and the wheat gives expression to the thought that the path of history is not unilinear but twofold. These two courses do not simply run parallel but rather are in constant friction, tension, and conflict. Now this battle does not end in the eventual conversion of everyone to the good. Instead, the good and the sinful both grow increasingly powerful—intensively as well as extensively—until the final judgment separates them through judgment and grace. For the Christian faith, idealism's framework shatters especially upon the thought that God became human: the necessity of sin must be timeless, not something that would eventually disappear. Otherwise the death on the cross would have been for nothing. In the second place, it fails simply because of the historical facts of destruction and violence, the complete moral disintegration of elevated cultures, the power of egoism, the unhappy course of innumerable grand undertakings, all of which progressive optimism is able to ignore in silence.

348

[58.] Seeberg puts the phrase, "in the theology of Schleiermacher," in parentheses and writes in the margin, "questionable."

[59.] Seeberg adds, "or state."

Here Christian faith sees the weeds in the field. Certainly, progress cannot be denied if one wants to talk about technological and scientific discoveries as such. Yet in the most decisive questions one moment is like another. There really are times of acute morality and self-evaluation, of the soul coming to itself, as Hegel had hoped. However, the greater the knowledge is, the greater the sin. Wheat and weeds remain in the field. Who may decide between good and evil? We do not have any criteria; the "winnowing" (judging and separating) is up to God. To use the powerful measuring stick of the kingdom of God, which is at our disposal, remains an undertaking of greatest danger; and yet every true discourse about church history must attempt it. At every moment the judgment of God is present in history through the word of God. "Every age is in direct relationship with God";[60] and this also means every moment. Every moment is the end of history, and yet it is not the end, because the end will occur only when "death is swallowed up in victory."[61] Christian mythology expresses this in the image of a temporal end that follows a final battle against the Antichrist. Here we cannot speak in any other way than in the language of myth. The result is that the Christian concept of history is dualistic. God's kingdom does not grow organically before our eyes; instead, evil will always rise again. Just as it does in the life of an individual, its development proceeds in bits.[3]

349

In this world, the church does not dissolve into the concepts of culture and state. Instead, the church is the actual place where struggles take place and from where power and all other life relationships radiate. In the midst of this world the empirical church is the sole signpost pointing beyond this world toward the kingdom of God.[63] The church fulfills her mission and fights with word and sacrament. Through them God establishes the kingdom.

The church will take a double position in relationship to the bustle of the world. On the one hand, its members are asked to be the leaven of the whole. They are to speak with every person as if each stood in God's grace. Yet, to no less degree, in service to God, they are to proclaim judgment and to remain awake. The church should not shut itself off from the state and culture. Yet

---

3. Examples that speak against this, like the 'seed growing by itself' or the 'four soils', address the process of organic growth from God's perspective.[62]

[60.] Bonhoeffer cites a statement written by Ranke aimed at Hegel that in its entirety reads, "I, however, claim, that every epoch is immediately present before God, and its value is not found in that which proceeds from it but instead in its existence as such, in its immediate self." Leopold von Ranke, "On Progress in History," 53. This citation is found in Barth, *Romans*, 95.

[61.] 1 Cor. 15:55.

[62.] Bonhoeffer added by hand footnote 3. Cf. Mark 4:1ff. and 26ff.

[63.] Seeberg: "Instrument would be better."

certainly it will not dissolve into them (this contra Rothe).[64] It will see in the concept of the state "the kingdom of God on the left hand." It will certainly not be fully developed in the actual practice of the state, which is a support for the weak intended and established by God.[65] Therefore, the members of the church will not refuse their service to the actually existing state. The statement in Revelation about the greatest of all states as designating a satanic kingdom of the world refers only to one side of the issue. The world exists for the sake of the invisible church, not the other way around. Sic mundus nescit se stare in viribus alienis, id est ecclesiae, et putat ecclesiam stare viribus suis, id est mundi.[66] The church will never take the fatal step that "everything that exists is sin."[67] Instead, it will know how to differentiate between creation and human distortion and thereby sharpen its sight. This means that the church is destined to remain both positive and negative, to bind and to loose, to bring faith and hardening into being. It will be unable to do one without the other. All details must here remain to the side. That the history of the empirical church is not identical with the kingdom of God,[68] and why this is so, need not be enlarged upon following the discussion above.

What we have to say about the state of fulfillment of the kingdom of God and the church does not offer anything new as far as content is concerned.[69] We saw earlier that the ideas about the end of time and fulfillment only hide a line of thought that we cannot follow through to its conclusion. This is the idea that fulfillment is a nontemporal concept and that, therefore, every moment in time in which God's word is active shines into eternity. Fulfillment is always present where God is. It can be seen in the struggle as well as in the triumphant church. Facta dicit, quae tamen fienda patit, quia semper ecclesia est militans *et triumphans* in hac vita. WA 3:85[70] Now we can speak of this

350

351

[64.] Rothe saw the church as a stage in the development of the kingdom of God, that would at some point be replaced by the perfect religious and moral human community. See Rothe, *Theologische Ethik*, vols. 1–5.

[65.] Cf. Holl, *Luther*, 255.

[66.] "So the world does not know that it has existence because of foreign powers, i.e. those of the church; and the world believes that the church has existence because of its powers, i.e. the world" (*WA Br* 10:5, 31ff.).

[67.] Cf. Barth, *Romans*, 478.

[68.] Seeberg underlines the word "identical" and adds in the margin, "But, certainly, in relationship!"

[69.] The words, "does not . . . concerned," are handwritten by Bonhoeffer. In ms. 2 he wrote instead, "is nothing new according to its content."

[70.] Read: "Facta dicit, que tamen fienda petit. . . ." "He considers something as having already occurred that obviously, for all that, must still occur, because in this life the church is always both equipped for battle *and triumphant* at the same time" (Luther, *WA* 3:85, 26). Bonhoeffer cites Holl, *Luther*, 297, footnote 7, where the emphasis can be found. The text, which follows the Luther citation ("Now we can . . . face to face," ending on 2/9:323) is an addition that was written by Bonhoeffer on a separate sheet of paper. In ms. 1, a handwritten note is in the margin, "See additional page." The first two sentences of the

fulfillment only as a monumental event that will take place in the future. Yet we must be clear about the meaning of this future. It is also clear that we have already heard the most important things below.[71] They need only to be systematically ordered. We saw above that the "end of history" must contain within it a colossal dualism, an irreconcilable rift between the kingdoms of God and Satan. If the antichrist is present, then the day of judgment will not be far off. It is that which, through the word of God and the proclamation in the church, invisibly directs our eyes and becomes grace, enlightens, and perfects. It will clearly say, "to the right" and "go into the joy of your Lord," as well as a clear "to the left."[72] In this way the power of death is finally defeated, and death is swallowed up in victory.[73] This is the necessary consequence of the concept of church. In this the church preaches the word, it expresses judgment and grace and remains fast in a dualism, because through the church, in her word, God speaks eternal judgment.[74]

Certainly we must not deny that other Christian considerations contradict this one or, better, lead to a more superordinate view of an ἀποκατάστασις πάντων[75] in the New Testament. The fact that this perspective must ultimately not contradict the Christian concept of God is admitted. This is true

352

because all created spirits must return to their Creator Spirit,[76] and yet as those who stand in the church we cannot commit ourselves to this. The danger[77] is near, and great, that we might forget the seriousness of judgment and, together with it, the seriousness of grace. Certainly, if the church wants to be serious about predestination, it must recognize that there is election outside of its word,[78] in the same way that we recognized above the faithful believers of the Old Testament. From this follows, as we already mentioned, that the kingdom of God extends beyond the church. The church, however, does not have the courage to take a further step here in the sense of ἀποκατάστασις, or it would betray its essence. With that, she would risk vanishing.[79] In the final judgment, the invisible church will be removed from

---

addition are present on Bonhoeffer's carbon copy handwritten in the margin. The remainder is missing from that place.

[71.] Seeberg writes, "above?"

[72.] Cf. Matt. 25:21, 23, 33.

[73.] Cf. 1 Cor. 15:15.

[74.] Seeberg: "To be sure, for this temporal development."

[75.] "Restoration of everything." According to this doctrine, rejected by the church, at the end of the Last Judgment no one would be damned forever, but all people would return to God. In reference to this see Bonhoeffer's essay on early Lutheran eschatology, below, 2/12:385ff., especially 392f.

[76.] One finds in the original "admitted." The phrase "because . . . must return," is an addition made later by Bonhoeffer.

[77.] Seeberg underlines the word "danger" and comments in the margin, "Yes, but it can be worked against."

[78.] Seeberg: "Well!"

[79.] Seeberg has added a question mark.

the visible church and be transferred from the status gratiae into a status perfectionis. Whether this process is sudden or gradual cannot be decided. The
New Testament favors the former view. Also, due to our time bound conceptual possibilities, the difficulty of whether or not the deceased members of
the invisible church remain as such or if they immediately enter the state of
fulfillment cannot be eliminated. "Now we see in a mirror, dimly, but then we
shall see face to face."[80] The invisible church will be transplanted from the
status gratiae into the status perfectionis, i.e., into sinlessness and salvation.
It will be freed from the world of impurity and struggle after overcoming the
last enemy, death, through resurrection. Hope will lead to fulfillment; tena-
cious faith will lead to vision; everything that has been begun and hinted at
will be fulfilled. Paul summarizes all of this in the thought that at the end
Christ will subjugate his kingdom, i.e., the holy church, to his Father so that
God will be all in all. 1 Cor. 15:28.[81]

The empirical church must collapse. In the New Jerusalem, there will be
no church (Rev. 21:22). The visible church and the world will be united in a   353
great synthesis. Καὶ ναὸν οὐκ εἶδον ἐν αὐτῇ, ὁ γὰρ κύριος ὁ θεὸς ὁ παντοκράτωρ ναὸς αὐτῆς ἐστιν, καὶ τὸ ἀρνίον. Rev. 21:22[82]

Conclusion: The kingdom of God is, on one side, complete, and on the
other side, a growing earth-bound kingdom burdened by sin.[83] As far as
content is concerned, the concept of the kingdom of God is identical with
the concept of church,[84] because the powers that constituted it and the goal
are the same. Whereas the church exists within history, the kingdom of God,
which encompasses the whole of the church, exists beyond history. Whereas
the sinful church incorporates false members within it, the kingdom of God
is free of these.[85] The empirical church is an essential and necessary
embodiment of the essential church. It is never its own goal, always only a
gate and a signpost.[86] The church struggles, gathers, and preaches grace
and judgment through the power of the word of God. Through the concept
of the kingdom of God, we obtain a Christian interpretation of history that
stands in contrast to that of philosophical idealism. The kingdom of God, as

---

[80.] 1 Cor. 13:12. This is the end of the addition mentioned in editorial note 70.

[81.] Deleted sentence: "Whether or not one is supposed to imagine that in the end all
spirits subjugate themselves to God will not be discussed here."

[82.] "I saw no temple in the city, for its temple is the Lord God the Almighty and the
Lamb" (Rev. 21:22). In Bonhoeffer's carbon copy, i.e., ms. 2, the Greek citation is missing.
Instead, we find the sentence, "What kind this will be, who will be able to say?"

[83.] Seeberg notes, "Not very well expressed! Compare page 319, line 26!" Cf. above,
2/9:319.

[84.] Seeberg comments: "But see page 315f." Cf. above, 2/9:315f.

[85.] Seeberg underlines the words "sinful church" and "free" and writes in the margin,
"The sinners are not therefore 'false'!"

[86.] Seeberg: "But gate and signpost are clearer to grasp than 'embodiment'
[Darstellung]."

a community of persons elected by God, can never be identical with the state. Thus, the church can never dissolve into it. A false expansion of the belief in the kingdom of God results in an antichurch stance. Because the empirical church is acknowledged to be founded and willed by God and Christ, one must reject disobedience and pride.[87] Fulfillment is not a concept that is set in time but beyond time. At the final judgment the separation between the wheat and the weeds will free the church from its false components and the church will move from the status gratiae into the status perfectionis, dissolving into the fulfilled kingdom of God.[88]

354

Overview of the Contents[89]

Eschatology according to the Reformers. A few remarks about the concept of eschatology.—The kingdom of God as the central concept. In the New Testament. Definition of content: election, redemption, holy community. Kingdom of God and time: the present, developing and fulfilled kingdom. Concerning the concept of eschatology in relationship to the concept of time. Kingdom of God as gift and task at the same time: possession and hope.—The empirical form of the kingdom of God and the essential church. Identity of the purpose and the nature of the kingdom of God and[90] the church. Differentiation within history.—The empirical church—Unity between the empirical and the invisible church. Relationship between the empirical church and the kingdom of God as the invisible church.—On the possibility of building the kingdom through the church.—Historically and systematically important attempts to find a solution to the kingdom of God and the church: Catholicism, sects, socialism, and idealism.—Course of history, kingdom of God, church, Christian understanding presented through a critique of the idealistic philosophy of religion.—World, kingdom of God, and church.—Fulfillment: on the concept of fulfillment and the end of history.—Dualism, Antichrist, judgment.—Concept of the church and of the final judgment.—Church and ἀποκατάστασις—Church in status perfectionis—Church in the whole of the perfected kingdom of God, 1 Cor. 15:28—The "New Jerusalem," the great synthesis.—Conclusion.[91]

[87.] Seeberg: "Eschatology is missing."

[88.] Grade: "Good, Seeberg, January 22, 1926."

[89.] The overview of the contents is handwritten on two smaller pages.

[90.] Deleted: "essential."

[91.] Marked with "L" for Luther on an additional piece of paper in ms. 2 is the following handwritten sentence by Bonhoeffer: "That is, that it may prevail among us and with us, so that we may be a part of those among whom his name is hallowed and his kingdom flourishes." This is a citation from Martin Luther's interpretation of the Lord's Prayer in the Large Catechism, *The Book of Concord*, 446. It is possible that the citation on 2/9:313 was supposed to follow after "be reconciled?" There one finds a mark in the copy indicating that something should be added; or perhaps on 2/9:312 something should be added after the sentence ending "this general form," where in the copy we find an "L."

10. Seminar Paper on the Holy Spirit according to Luther[1]

Luther's Views of the Holy Spirit
according to the *Disputationen* of 1535–1545 edited by Drews

In the disputations Luther preferred to speak about pressing questions that seemed to him to be of theological significance. Let us remember that the essential intent of a disputation was that it should be an academic exercise for the young generation. It was important to provide them with complete clarity on the fundamental questions of the Lutheran understanding of
the gospel. In addition, if one remembers the attacks that the antinomians waged against Luther's understanding of law and gospel in the years of our disputations, and that the aging Luther was singularly and personally interested in the subject that comprised the beginning of his lifework, then it is no wonder that the greatest portion of the disputations deal with the problem of justification, law and gospel, faith and love. It is certainly true that they also speak about scripture, church, the Trinity, Christology, etc. However, Luther does not seem to have been greatly interested in these questions. This is the case even though several dimensions of the Lutheran system become more

---

[1.] *NL* A 11, 5; handwritten. Previously published in Christian Gremmels, ed., *Bonhoeffer und Luther: Zur Sozialgestalt des Luthertums in der Moderne*, 186–232. The title page contains, in addition to the title given here, "February 22, 1926—Dietrich Bonhoeffer." In Bonhoeffer's literary estate are thirty-two pages of material, almost exclusively filled with Latin citations, that pertain to this text (*NL* A 11, 5). The paper was written for Holl's seminar "Luther and the Holy Spirit" held in the winter semester of 1925–26. Holl evaluated the paper. See *Bonhoeffer und Luther*, 188 and below, Appendix 3, page 585. Holl allowed his students to do research on various writings of Luther for a lecture on this subject, which he planned to give before the Luther Society on September 26, 1926. See Emanuel Hirsch, in Walter Bodenstein, *Die Theologie Karl Holls*, Appendix 1, 322. In this appendix Hirsch has published some of Holl's notes that he discovered. They are based in part on the papers that the students prepared. It is certain that the notes, which are published there under the title "7 Disputations," are based on Bonhoeffer's paper (343–34); see below the editorial notes 22, 55, 101, 167, 181, and 207. Bonhoeffer then used the material again for his dissertation. See *SC* (*DBWE* 1): 173–74, footnote 35; 232, footnote 101; 234, footnote 105; and 289, footnote 148. In this paper Bonhoeffer discusses Martin Luther's disputations of 1535–45 held at the University of Wittenberg as found in the edition of Paul Drews. [English translations of some of the Drews's collection are found in "Theses concerning Faith and Law," *LW* 34:105–32, and "The Disputation concerning Justification," *LW* 34:145–96.][PDM] Bonhoeffer used the following secondary literature: two essays by Holl: (1) *What Did Luther Understand by Religion?* and (2) "Der Neubau der Sittlichkeit." Both essays are in Holl, *Luther*, 1ff. and 155ff., respectively. Every reference is cited following Bonhoeffer's form. Departures from the original are noted in the editorial notes, except for mere capitalization. Bonhoeffer usually writes 'Spiritus Sanctus' ['Holy Spirit'] differently from Drews. The citations that are missing in Bonhoeffer's work are supplied in the editorial notes, usually in connection with a translation. Incorrect citations are corrected in the same place. Omissions that are not indicated by Bonhoeffer are indicated by [. . .] and, as far as they are necessary for understanding the text, they are noted in the editorial notes or are placed in brackets in the translation.

distinct than before, especially those concerning the question about the councils and with them the related concepts of the meaning of the word. In addition, during the debate Luther seizes the opportunity to speak most of all when considering the former problems. However, because Luther had delved into these problems and considered their final consequences and deepest foundations before the beginning of the disputations, their further development within these is inconsiderable and unimportant.

The disputations are, for the most part, extant in two or more copies. This assures us that their literary tradition is so solid that we can confidently consider the work to be a source for Luther's views. For the most part it does not give Luther's stated opinion verbatim; yet to a certain degree it distinctly represents Luther's language style as we know it from the letters and writing of the time. As far as is possible in the decisive points of our presentation, we will refer only to the responses[2] that were clearly uttered by Luther. It will be our intention without prejudice to report the facts that the disputations demonstrate concerning Luther's views of the Holy Spirit.

357 For Luther the starting point for the problem of the Spirit, and therefore also the point at which the decisive question concerning its meaning and its certainty must be raised, lies at a completely different place than it does for Catholic scholasticism. For the latter, the actual decisive starting point of the problem of the Spirit lies in the question raised by metaphysics concerning the Trinity. Consequently, a Catholic doctrine about the Holy Spirit would be situated here. From here one can derive the relation of the Spirit as a Trinitarian person to the Spirit active on earth. One would almost like to say that it is done deductively. In a very weakened and fleeting form without content, one has then finally traced the Spirit down to humanity. The value of doing this is purely theological and systematic. An interest in individual religiosity is absent. Luther bypasses the whole development of dogma that took place in the Middle Ages and arrives at early Christianity and the Pauline view of the Spirit for his completely different starting point for this problem. Experience-of-conscience and faith are understood by him as belonging together in essence, and with this the justification of a purely metaphysical doctrinal thought process is brought into question. The question of truth is no longer intellectualized. Instead, it is answered from the perspective of human "experience." (Granted, "experience" here means something completely different from what the nineteenth century meant!) Thus, the thought process of Luther runs exactly opposite to that of scholasticism: from the problem of Spirit and humanity, the means of grace and so on, up to, finally, the Trinity.

Human beings have their first experience with the Spirit in the fear of judgment, with the recognition of their own sinfulness and guilt, with enormous convulsions of conscience, with the complete destruction of the former morality, and in despair with themselves and with God. This experience

---

[2.] Latin *responsiones*, 'answers', in other words, the arguments and conclusion that rebut an opponent's objections to the fundamental thesis of a disputation.

is called forth by the law.[3] Prior to the law everything was calm and good. There "was" no sin; humanity lived completely in security and protection.[1] It is not the case that they had not heard the law[2] but that it did not touch them. It was completely external, cold, dead. It was not the case that they perhaps lived "immorally." No, they held to that which was commanded and did it. Only the motive was external. Behaving like this was the thing to do, etc. . . . Then it awakened in humankind. That is, the words remained the same, but they now received a completely different force and emphasis. Humankind, which formerly felt compelled to take great pains[3] not to commit adultery and not to covet (and these were those who took the matter most seriously), now heard the same law spoken: ego spiritualis sum.[7] This means: I seek a pure and spiritual heart; one satisfies me only with joyful service and a spirit that has been renewed by the Holy Spirit.[4] Then suddenly the depth and the magnitude of the law and its relentless seriousness become evident to humans, and with this recognition they see at the same

358

359

---

1. 456: Et qui securus est, non habet legem. Et certe securitas est absque et ante legem, sed veniente lege cessat securitas et ducit nos in cognitionem nostri.[4]

2. Sine lege esse est idem dicere, quod securum esse ut fuerunt isti aliquando securi, sed usque ad illam horam, in qua erumpit et reviviscit lex.[5] 476

3. 182: Lex mandat et *extorquet* opera. . . .[6]

4. 386: lex seipsam damnat, est spiritualis[8]. . . . Et spiritualiter intellecta damnat illam carnalem et externam iustitiam legis, quam . . . in hypocrisi praestitimus corde impuro et repugnante, imo aliud conante, quam quod foris praestiterat homo invitus et coactus vel poenarum timore vel amore laudum et gloriae. . . . Hic itaque accedit lex illa spiritualis, ut [9] Paulus ait, et iudicat illam carnalem [. . .][10] iustitiam vi extortam a lege[11]. . . . quasi dicat lex: Ego spiritualis sum, hoc est, cor purum et spirituale requiro, non satisfit mihi nisi hilari corde et spiritu per spiritum sanctum renovato; . . . lex est spiritualis[12] et vult a spiritu impleri.[13]

[3.] Cf. Holl, *What Did Luther Understand by Religion?* 48ff.

[4.] Drews, 456, reads, "And whoever is secure has no law. And certainly, security is far from the law and precedes this but, when the law comes, security disappears and [the law] leads us to self-knowledge." [Where Bonhoeffer's footnotes consist solely of one or more digits without any quoted text (as in footnotes 8, 17, 24, and often), these are references to page numbers in the Drews edition of Luther's disputations.] [PDM]

[5.] Drews, 476, reads, "To be without the law: this means the same as being secure, so just as these were once secure, but [only] until the hour in which the law breaks through and lives. . . ." In Drews one finds *est* and *quod* in square brackets.

[6.] Drews, 182, reads, "The law commands and *extorts* works" (Bonhoeffer's emphasis).

[7.] "I am spiritual." See Bonhoeffer's footnote 4. Cf. Rom. 7:14.

[8.] In Drews, "Lex seipsam damnat, est enim spiritualis." "The law condemns itself, [because] it is spiritual" (see editorial note 13).

[9.] Replaces: "hoc."

[10.] Omitted in the manuscript, "seu (externam)."

[11.] The following is found in Drews, 388.

[12.] In Drews: "Lex spiritualis est."

[13.] Drews, 386, reads, "The law condemns itself, [because] it is spiritual. . . . And [the law,] which is recognized by spiritual means, condemns the fleshly and external justice of the

time the lack of prospects for fulfilling the law. Thus the law, the holy and good law, came into being. It began to become forcefully active. It spoke very directly to humankind, very simply and clearly with its tenfold "you shall" and "you shall not." People will do anything, but they must see that they cannot, that they cannot even *want* to. Commandments can only be "obeyed" in following the will of the commander. However, individuals have *their* will and not God's will. With this recognition, human beings place the whole weight of their sinfulness on their hearts, and they truly feel for the first time what conscience is. The next consequence, however, is that they grumble against their strict Lord; they rebel. Humans, who before the law so peacefully knew how to handle "their" God, become rebellious. They feel their conscience sharply confronted and are terrified, as by an enemy. They begin to hate God, to slander,[5] to curse, to doubt not only themselves, but also God; and so they sin against the first commandment.[6]

In evil confusion they flee from God, "since the world is becoming too narrow for them,"[7] and break down as if they were dead from the terrible burden. This is the first part of the enormous process in which God and the individual become active, and which should lead to forgiveness and healing. What, however, is its meaning in the trans-psychological, objective sphere of events, that is, from God's perspective? In the experience described, Luther does not see any inner surging of emotion of a humble heart. Instead, he saw the true confrontation between God and the human being. For Luther the subjective process was actually objectively grounded. He derives certainty concerning this from the radical character of experience that can never be grasped in purely psychological terms. Because of his experiences in court,

360

---

5. 471: ibi necesse est, ut desperem, ut incipiam odisse et blasphemare Deum, qui ita inique videatur mecum agere.[14]

6. Desperatio de nobis ipsis optima est et Deo placet. At de Deo desperare est summum flagitium et peccatum contra primum praeceptum. . . .[15] 482

7. [. . .]\[16]

law, which . . . we fulfill with hypocrisy with impure and unwilling hearts, yes, even with a heart that attempts to do something other than what the person fulfills outwardly, unwilling and forced or out of fear of punishment or out of love of praises and honor. . . . To this the spiritual law is added, as Paul says, and judges the fleshly [or (external)] justice that has been forcibly extorted by the law. (388:) . . . as if the law were to say: I am spiritual, i.e., I seek a pure and spiritual heart. One satisfies me only with a joyful heart and a spirit that has been renewed by the Holy Spirit; . . . the law is spiritual and wants to be fulfilled by the spirit."

[14.] Drews, 471, reads, "Then I would have to despair, so that I would begin to hate and blaspheme God, who seems to act so unjustly towards me."

[15.] Drews, 482, reads, "To despair of ourselves is very good and pleases God. But to despair of God is the greatest wickedness and is a sin against the first commandment."

[16.] This citation is missing in Bonhoeffer's paper. Cf. the quote from Drews, 382, which reads, "Talis enim est doctrina legis, ut, si vere tangat cor, wo wirt einen die weite welt zu enge." "Because such is the teaching of the law, that when it truly touches the heart the wide world becomes too narrow."

Luther must have observed a vast difference from what scholasticism had proposed—and even more the mystics and the monks.[17] All of them also knew methods and ways to reach a heart broken and overwhelmed by remorse; and these methods were cruel and hard. One desired truly to humble oneself before God, as a sinful individual should. However, it was the case that one *wanted* and one did not *have* to. In the ascetic humiliation of the mystics, etc., the human will was always ultimately at work. It contained the thought that one could please God with such humility and with this added a measure of self-satisfaction and delight in pain to the certainty of truly being able to stand completely alone before God's court of judgment. This was due to the faulty differentiation between subjective and objective will. A human court of judgment was simply not God's court of judgment. Luther experienced the verdict of judgment, which came to him through the law, in a completely different way. He experienced it as something that ran totally counter to one's will, as something that wanted to destroy even his innermost being, as something against which resistance could not help. The condition into which human beings would be brought could not be claimed to have any worth before God in itself. Its essence lay in the fact that the person would be overcome by God and, indeed, *morally* overcome through the word in the conscience. Not only did some "numinous" force bring terror,[18] but the individual would also be morally broken by the personal will of God, who had laid a simple, clear requirement on each person. It was due to this requirement that human beings were broken. Luther calls this peronal will the Holy Spirit "in its majesty."[8] Although this is "not a proper expression,"[9] for one usually characterizes the action of the Holy Spirit in different terms, Luther actually intends nonetheless to claim that the Holy Spirit functions not only as "gift" but also as Deus, as majesty. In this way the Spirit convicts human beings of sinfulness and causes their hearts and consciences to fear. Thus the one who convicts is God, who has created everything,[10] and whose finger wrote the law on the stone tablets of Moses. As such, the Holy Spirit is

361

---

8. Cf. 151, 268, 294, 298, and often; cf. also footnotes 9 and 10 below.

9. 294: quamquam iste sermo, legem sine Spiritu Sancto non arguere peccata, improprius [. . .]. Nam vocamus Spiritum Sanctum plerumque, eum, quem nobis Christus a patre misit donum. . . .[19]

10. 268 (Spiritus Sanctus), qui et Deus creator omnium est legem suo digito scripsit in tabulas lapideas. . . .Distinguimus igitur de Spiritu Sancto, et de Deo in sua divina natura et substantia, et nobis dato. . . . Sic Spiritus Sanctus, quando scribit

[17.] Deleted: "In the ascetic mortifications of the mystics."

[18.] Contrary to Rudolf Otto; cf. *The Idea of the Holy*, 116ff.

[19.] Drews, 294, reads: "that way of expressing yourself, namely, that the law without the Holy Spirit does not uncover sins, [is] improper. For we call the Holy Spirit mainly that person whom Christ offered us as a gift from the Father."

our enemy,[11] to the same extent as God has true divine nature and majesty. The Holy Spirit cannot but crush and destroy us.[12] "not our bodies but rather our hearts."[13] For Luther, the Holy Spirit and God accord in his view of the maiestas. He can replace one with the other. Whether the Holy Spirit as God, or God personally, holds court in the law is essentially the same for him.[14] The most formal precise expression is no doubt, "God through the Holy Spirit,"[15] in which it is precisely asserted that God as agent can only ever be the Holy Spirit. We can grasp the concept of maiestas Spiritus Sancti or Dei in its main points here. Power and holiness are united in majesty in equal parts—power in that God demonstrates himself to be absolutely superior to humanity, and holiness in that God is a specific personal moral will who breaks whatever opposes God. (We will hear more below about the power to sanctify.) Therefore, maiestas is not taboo. It is not an amorphous, somehow capricious sanctification of a terrifying force. Instead, it is an effective moral will with all its consequences. A force that can only terrify and destroy and also annihilate me like an object has no meaning for Luther. That would be like death, something that does not affect my inner being. It would truly only affect my feelings of fear, but not my heart, my conscience.

---

digito suo legem in tabulas Mosis lapideas, est in maiestate sua ac certe arguit peccata et terret corda.[20]

11. . . . Deus in natura et maiestate sua est adversarius noster, exigit legem et minatur transgressoribus mortem . . . 268.[21]

12. ubi igitur nudus Deus in maiestate loquitur, ibi tantum terret et occidit, 296 and often. Add to footnote 12: 416: Spiritus sanctus . . . quando in hac maiestate sua ut Deus revelat legem, non potest non occidere et vehementer terrere.[22]

13. 176: Deus conterit nos, concutit corda, non carnem. . . .[23]

14. Cf. footnote 10, 268.

15. 53: Deus occidit hominem per revelationem peccati per Spiritum Sanctum. . . .[24]

[20.] Drews, 268, reads, "(the Holy Spirit), who is God, the creator of all things, and who wrote the law with his finger on stone tablets. . . . Therefore, we differentiate with the Holy Spirit, *on the one hand*, between God in God's divine nature and substance, and *on the other hand*, that which was given to us. . . . So, the Holy Spirit *in his majesty*, when he wrote with his finger on Moses' stone tablets, lays sins bare and *terrifies hearts*." Bonhoeffer's emphases.

[21.] Drews, 268, reads, "God, in his nature and majesty, is our enemy, he insists on the law and threatens those who disobey it with death."

[22.] Drews, 296, reads, "where, therefore, God speaks in his unveiled majesty, there he only terrifies and kills." Drews, 416: "the Holy Spirit . . . , when he in his majesty as God reveals the law, can only kill and terrify greatly." The words, "Add to footnote 12 . . . terrere," are inserted later by Bonhoeffer in the margin. Like Bonhoeffer, Holl collates citations from Drews, 268, 296, and 416 (see Bodenstein, *Die Theologie Karl Holls*, 344); these are the same citations that Bonhoeffer lists in his notes 10–12.

[23.] Drews, 176, reads, "God makes us contrite, and he strikes the heart, not the flesh." [Cf. *LW* 34:172.] [PDM]

[24.] Drews, 53, reads, "God kills the person, in that he reveals sin through the Holy Spirit."

A force, however, which as a morally superior person annihilates my "moral person"—that certainly means something. Indeed, it means everything, because only it truly annihilates *me*.

The requirements of the Holy Spirit [are] articulated in the law. This is not a gift[16] but the word and command of the eternal, all-powerful God in divine majesty. As such the word regnum Dei efficax et potens in cordibus nostris.[26] [17] This law is the absolute requirement that the Holy Spirit makes of human beings, [and] as such it is just, good, and holy.[18] Now, Spirit and law are not related in such a way that where the law is the Spirit is as well. This means that the Holy Spirit is not somehow substantially inherent in the law. On the contrary, the Spirit is an active force and blows and operates where it wills.[19] It moves the hearts it wills to move.[20] To be sure, when the law operates, it is moved by the Spirit; and where it is understood, there the divine will moves the human will.[21] If the human being could activate the law, then the *human being* and not the Spirit would speak against the human in the court of judgment.

363

---

16. 268: Sine isto spiritu sancto, qui donum est, arguit lex peccatum, quia lex non est donum, sed Dei aeterni et omnipotenti verbum, qui est ignis conscientiis. . . .[25]

17. 242.

18. 123: Bona enim est lex. . . .122.[27] 136: Est iusta, bona, sancta. . . .[28]

19. 286: et Spiritus Sanctus efficax est et spirat et operatur, ubi vult. 53: Spiritus Sanctus ubi vult spirat. . . .733, Th. 27: ipseque novit horas et momenta, quibus corda tangi oportet.[29]

20. 294: Nemo intelligit legem, nisi tangatur sensu et vi eius in corde. Is autem tactus seu sensus legis est divinus. Ergo lex sine Spiritu Sancto non arguet peccata. . . .[30]

21. 338, Th. 37: Sed et hoc falsum est, quod sine spiritu sancto arguat lex peccatum, cum lex sit scripta digito Dei.[31]

[25.] Drews, 268, reads, "Without the Holy Spirit, who is gift, the law exposes sin, because the law is not a gift, but rather the word of the eternal and all-powerful God, who is a fire to consciences."

[26.] Drews, 242, reads, "the rule of God, which is active and powerful in our hearts."

[27.] "Then the law is good." The Latin text offered by Drews reads, "Bona quidem est lex." ["The law is indeed good."] And, "Necessaria est lex, quia est bona." ["Necessary is the law, because it is good."] See as well, Drews, 122, "Necessaria est lex bona et sancta et iusta." ["The good, holy, and just law is necessary."] Cf. Rom. 7:12.

[28.] Drews, 136, reads, "It [i.e., the law of God] is just, good, holy."

[29.] Drews, 286, reads, "and the Holy Spirit is effective, blows, and is active where it wills." Drews, 853, reads, "the Holy Spirit blows where it wishes." Drews, 733, Th. 27, reads, "and it knows the hour and moment when it must touch the heart" (cf. John 3:8).

[30.] Drews, 294, reads, "No one knows the law, if they are not touched by its feeling and power. The touch and feeling of the law is divine. Therefore the law without the Holy Spirit will not expose sins."

[31.] Drews, 388, Th. 37, reads, "But also this is false, that without the Holy Spirit the law exposes sins, because the law is written with the finger of God."

At first, all persons find the law within themselves. It is, to be sure, written
364   on the heart of every person since Adam.[22] There is no doubt. No persons
        are so abhorrent that they would not know that they have to honor and love
        God.[23] Therefore, in every person there lives a conscience, although it may
        be weak, formed by the law. It is a moral law and so a consciousness of guilt.
        But, because it is based in the human conscience, this law cannot be the cer-
        emonial law, which only reflects the particular characteristics of a particular
        people.[24] These notitiae communes[34] have been forgotten through the
        flesh, the devil, and the world, or, at any rate, they have been obscured.[25]
        Thus it was necessary for the second giving of the law by Moses to recall what
        had been forgotten and to show us "what we were and what we are."[26] Yet, the
365   Mosaic giving of the law was not an absolute necessity for humanity, because

---

22. 312: Nihilominus [. . .] habuit naturae legem insculptam cordi, ut omnes
homines. 462 . . . leges has nobiscum in mundum attulimus. . . .[32] Cf. 622 and often.

23. 378: A condito mundo decalogus fuit inscriptus omnium hominum mentibus, . . . Nam nulla natio unquam sub sole tam crudelis aut barbara fuit ac inhu-
mana, quin senserit Deum colendum, diligendum esse. . . . 337, [Th.] 38: Omnis
veritas, ubicunque est, a Spiritu Sancto est. . . .[33]

24. 461/62.

25. 467: Adest enim nostra caro, diabolus et mundus, qui diversum suadent et
legem Dei in mentibus scriptam obscurant.[35]

26. 382: Nam etiamsi tollas has literas: 'lex'. . .tamen manet chirographum inustum
cordibus nostris, quod nos damnat et exercet.[36]

[32.] Drews, 312, reads, "Nonetheless he had [. . .] the law of nature *implanted in his
heart*, as have all people." Drews, 462 reads, "these laws were brought into the world with
us." Bonhoeffer's emphasis. Cf. Rom. 2:14f.

[33.] Drews, 378, reads, "From the beginning of the world the Decalogue was implanted in the understanding of all humans, . . . then no people ever under the sun were ever so
horrific or barbaric or inhuman, that they did not sense that God should be honored and
loved." The correct reference is 338, Th. 38, which reads, "All truth, wherever it is, is from
the Holy Spirit." The last citation is in the manuscript on the margins of the page next to
Bonhoeffer's note 25. According to its subject matter, however, it belongs to footnote 23.

[34.] "Universal concepts."

[35.] Drews, 467, reads, "Then it is because our flesh, the devil, and the world advise the
weak, and the law, which is implanted in our understanding, is obscured."

[36.] Drews, 382, reads, "Then one may set aside also the letters [of this word]: 'law', . . .
there remains nonetheless the writing burned into our hearts that condemns and plagues
us." Instead of the citations mistakenly given by Bonhoeffer, cf. here Drews, 461, "Sed quia
homo in peccatum lapsus ac paulatim hominibus magis ac magis a Deo declinantibus et
neglecto Deo in peius ruentibus, donec fere tota obliterata et obscurata est, coactus est
Deus a novo nobis, ne prorsus suam legem oblivisceremur, metam proponere, ut sic recor-
daremur saltem, qui iam antea fuerimus et qui iam simus." "But because human beings
have fallen into sin, and turned even more from God, ignore God, and descend into even
greater corruption, until it [i.e., the law] is almost forgotten and has vanished, God is
forced anew to set before us a goal even further away from us, so that we do not totally forget the law, so that at least we remember who we once were and who we now are."

the essentials of moral understanding remained with them. One only needs to think of the patriarchs.[27] Consequently, the natural law and the Mosaic law are identical in content. If the Holy Spirit wrote the Mosaic law (see above), then the natural law must also be[28] written by the Holy Spirit as creator of all things (see above). In this way, the law is holy, just, and good. The conscience, however, is too weak to be able to understand the whole intention of the law by itself. One need not even speak of its ability to muster the power to fulfill the law, if the Holy Spirit had not personally stepped in anew and made its requirements clear and plain to the conscience. Thus conscience is especially not something like God's voice in humanity as though, if conscience were silent, then God had nothing to say. Instead only in the conscience awakened by the Spirit does humanity feel the Holy Spirit, i.e., only when the person feels judged and destroyed by conscience is the Holy Spirit active and present. Thus the conscience becomes the place where the Holy Spirit is truly *experienced* by humanity. Therefore, not every conscience is the voice of the Holy Spirit, but the voice of the Holy Spirit is *felt* only in the conscience.

If the Holy Spirit brings the conscience to life, then there *necessarily* arises the experience described above. Why is this? The law, holy and good, which at first only wants to be fulfilled, makes this inexorably clear to humanity and shows humanity "what it is," and convicts it of its sinfulness.[29] Now the Holy Spirit wants the person to experience self-despair,[30] but with this the individual necessarily also loses trust in God and despairs of God. In this way humanity sins the most grievous sin and has been driven to it by the law! So

366

---

27. Cf. 462.

28. 348.

29. (Lex) ... ostendit naturam peccatricem esse, et prohibendo exercet peccatum. [. . .] Nam si taceret et quiesceret, homines suaviter viverent, non sic irascerentur Deo nec sic peccarent nec sic abundaret peccatum . . . diximus,[37] legem non esse effectivam causam peccati, sed ostensivam, non auctricem, sed monstrativam istius tam perversae et corruptae naturae hominis.[38] 470 and often.

30. 482: Lex non vult, ut desperes de Deo, sed magis agnito peccato de te ipso....[39]

[37.] Drews reads *delictum*, 'offense', instead of *peccatum*, 'sin', and then proceeds, *Iam diximus* . . . , 'We have already said. . .'.

[38.] Drews, 470, reads, "(The law) ... demonstrates that nature is sinful, and through prohibitions it excites sins. [. . .] For if it were silent and calm human beings would live a pleasant life. Humans would not to such a degree be angry and sin against God, and sins would not be so richly present. We have already said: the law is not the effective cause of sin, but rather it exposes it. It does not cause it, rather it demonstrates how degenerate and corrupt human nature is." The parentheses around *Lex*, "the law," are Bonhoeffer's.

[39.] Drews, 482, reads, "The law does not wish that you despair of God but much rather, through the knowledge of sin, of yourself."

also the[40] law in fact *engenders* sin and is nevertheless holy, good, and the word of the majestic Spirit. Now, has the Holy Spirit become the originator of sin? No, because sin is the fruit of corrupted human nature.[31] Thus, through the action of the Holy Spirit, the law creates qua Deus not only the recognition of sin, but sin itself (this, however, through humankind!), flight from God, and blasphemy.[32] It reveals the wrath of God and is punished by death.[33] This is no simile, but it touches upon the subject itself. The person who curses and hates God has in fact died a spiritual death. Indeed, if God were to show someone the complete violence of guilt caused by humankind and what it means not to love and fear God, the person who saw that would also have to die a physical death.[34] That person would see the whole wrath of the majestic God, and no one can endure that.[35] The attitude of the soul, to which[44] the human being is forced through the law, is contritio,[45] which is itself death and grumbling[36] against God. Hate, fleeing from God, and blasphemy are certainly not *my* work but the work of the law.[37] Because the one whose conscience is dead cannot hate God and blaspheme against God (known only as *his or her own* God!), that also is action that proceeds only from the Holy Spirit. This is certainly never directly so, but instead works through human corruption. Therefore, the causa effectiva[47] lies with me, as does the guilt. The holy work, however, lies with the Holy Spirit.

---

31. Cf. 470ff.

32. 53: Omnis contritus horret et timet Deum et fugit, nec fert eius iudicium et iram. Est igitur contritio non meum opus, sed opus legis Dei, odium, fuga a Deo, blasphemia Dei. . . .[41]

33. Tamen is eius (legis) proprius effectus est, ut reos faciat et humiliet homines ac iram Dei ostendat.[42]

34. 471.

35. 705: David and Nathan; cf. 624: Ex hac cognitione erit perpetua poena.[43]

36. Nam contritio est ipsa mors et murmuratio contra Deum.[46]

37. See footnote 32.

[40.] Deleted: "holy."

[41.] Drews, 53, reads, "Wholly contrite, he is terrified and flees the wrath of God. Contrition, then, is not our work, but the work of God's law, which begets hatred of God, flight from God." [Cf. *LW* 34:172.] [PDM]

[42.] Drews, 282, reads, "Yet its [i.e., the law's] particular effectiveness is that it makes people guilty and humiliates them and makes plain the anger of God." The addition is from Bonhoeffer.

[43.] Drews, 624, reads, "From this knowledge everlasting punishment arises."

[44.] The words "the attitude of the soul, to which . . ." replace "The point to which. . . ."

[45.] "Contrition."

[46.] Drews, 196, reads, "Then contrition is itself death and grumbling against God."

[47.] "Effective cause."

With this understanding of contritio, Luther absolutely opposes monasticism, etc. Monasticism believed first that it could reject this overwhelming remorse. Luther answers, "conterente Deo conterimur."[38] Because contrition occurs only through the recognition of sin, recognition of sin only through the law, the law only through the Spirit, therefore contritio can only occur through the Spirit. If this were not the case, it would change from a passio[39] to an actio.[49] The other view, that one could earn anything with such contritio, is even more absurd. What kind of claim can a person who flees from God and hates God possibly have on God?[40] Here we recognize very clearly the firm establishment by Luther of the question of certainty in contrast to monasticism.

368

Result: this encounter with the law creates recognition of sin, sin, and rage. God, however, who through the Holy Spirit has so moved people in their consciences and allowed them to flee from shame like Adam, transforms the contritio that leads to despair into evangelica desperatio.[51] [41] Wherever this part has not come to pass there is eternal despair. God grasps humankind from its contrite and yet sinful struggle and has mercy upon it, in that God says to the individual, "You will not die."[42] In these words of compassion God gives the person forgiveness of sins and faith, i.e., the Holy Spirit. God does not do this because of the deeper contrition of one compared with another. Instead, contritio remains opus legis.[52] It remains sin. The contrition of Peter and that of Judas are differentiated only in the fact that[53] it is said about Peter, "and the Lord looked at him,"[54] and it does not say this about Judas.[43] At one moment, therefore, death is the beginning of the law and, at the other, it is its end, totally according to the will of God.

---

38. 176: Nos non possumus nos conterere, ut docebant monachi, sed conterente Deo conterimur.[48]

39. 54:176f.

40. 54: Quid quaeso meretur homo, qui sic est in fuga et in odio habet Deum et non potest audire Deum, repellit Deum. . . .[50]

41. 352.

42. 705, and often.

43. 324; cf. 122f.

[48.] Drews, 176, reads, "We are unable to make contrition ourselves, as the monks taught, but rather we are contrite because God causes our contrition."

[49.] "From a suffering to an action." [Suffering, as effect, is contrasted with action.] [CG]

[50.] The correct reference, Drews 53f., reads, "What, I ask, does a man merit, who flees from and hates God, and *cannot hear God,* and repels God." [Cf. *LW* 34:172.] [PDM] Bonhoeffer's emphasis.

[51.] "Evangelical despair."

[52.] "Contrition remains the work of the law."

[53.] Deleted: "God."

[54.] See Luke 22:61.

In our eyes there is no direct path from the wrath of God to grace. Here we see only a rupture.

Contrition is the action of the Holy Spirit, and yet the Spirit is not given to all who are contrite.[44] Why not? The reason has not been revealed and is known only to God. The Holy Spirit blows where it wills.[56] Luther in the disputations touches only very seldom on the question of predestination. When he does, he does so only briefly. He explains it as a mystery for us. We will come across it when we discuss sin against the Spirit. Contrition (contritio) is never at all[45] a reason for God's grace, and justification is never a consequence of contrition.[46] Instead the reason for God's grace is only God himself, and justification is only the consequence of grace.

Thus something completely new and unexpected occurs when God grasps the sinner and gives the sinner the Spirit. Yet it is not so completely new, because it certainly was God's wrath that the person felt. It was certainly not artificial self-annihilation. Instead, it is holy self-recognition. It must be illuminated through the Holy Spirit for it to be seen. Only the lex spiritualiter intellecta[59] has revealed the unattainable nature of its requirements. Seen from this perspective, the picture looks very different. The Holy Spirit in its majesty kills humanity, but because it is the *Holy* Spirit, it cannot allow humanity to perish. It takes the burden from the person who is buried under its weight and brings comfort.[47] The person believes in the fact that it has been removed and gains the evangelica desperatio.[48] Because the person believes, hatred against God turns to love. In this way the human being can fulfill the law and be justified and sanctified before God. This is the second part of the action of the Holy Spirit in the human person.[61]

---

44. 480: At non omnibus contritis datur Spiritus Sanctus. Cur sic et non aliter? Respondeo: Hoc nobis non est revelatum, sed reliquendum iudicio Dei.[55]

45. 53: Contritio non est causa iustificationis, sed Spiritus Sanctus ubi vult spirat, et Deus quos vult iustificat. . . .[57]

46. Iustificatio quidem sequitur ad contritionem, non ut effectus contritionis, sed gratiae. . . .[58] 284.

47. Consolatur, sanctificat et vivificat;[60] 416 and often.

48. 352; cf. 779.

[55.] The correct reference, Drews 481, reads, "But not all contrition is given by the Holy Spirit. Why [is it] so and not otherwise? I answer: this is not revealed to us, but rather it must be left to the judgment of God." Holl takes over Bonheoffer's incorrect page reference; see Bodenstein, *Die Theologie Karl Holls*, 344.

[56.] John 3:8; cf. above, 2/10:331.

[57.] Drews, 53, reads, "Contrition is not the cause, but the Holy Spirit, who breathes where it wills, [. . .] and God justifies whom he wishes."

[58.] Drews, 284, reads, "Justification follows from contrition, not as a result of the contrition, but rather [as an effect] of grace."

[59.] "The spiritually known law."

[60.] Drews, 416, reads, "He comforts, sanctifies, and gives life."

[61.] There is no paragraph break here in the manuscript.

¶God desires the sinner. How can the human being grasp this? The human being can hear and understand it intellectually, because it is certainly said in words. However, the human being can grasp it and relate to it only through a means that is analogous to the divine will. Like can only be known by like. This would be an instrument that the human being could never acquire independently, precisely because humanity is unacquainted with it. It must therefore be personally created by God; and it is created through the Holy Spirit, which is given to us as a gift (donum) "in" faith. In faith God, who through the Spirit as maiestas destroys us through the law, gives us the Spirit as a gift.[49] Luther often says that the Holy Spirit gives us faith;[50] in this way he can equate fides and Spiritus Sanctus.[51] The object of faith, however, is God, not God's absolute being, because this cannot be conceived (if the Holy Spirit is donum!), but gift and ability, and that means Christ. Thus Luther says once, "Christ is ours[66] through faith." This means Christ has been brought to us as a gift through the Holy Spirit.[52] [67] In faith, which is

371

---

49. 414: fides . . . impetrat et affert secum Spiritum Sanctum. . . .[62] Compare with this expression especially that which follows concerning word and spirit, and the following citations. 302: Deinde concipimus per fidem Spiritum Sanctum. . . .[63]

50. 9, Th. 1: Fides hic vera et donum illud Spiritus Sancti intelligi debet. Page 10, Th. 15: Hanc fidem Paulus praedicat, quam Spiritus Sanctus ad vocem evangelii in cordibus audientium donat et servat. 36, [Th.]28: Sed fides, quae ex auditu Christi nobis per Spiritum Sanctum infunditur, ipsa comprehendit Christum. 224: Dicimus, quod fides sit forma et actus primus ipsius Spiritus Sancti operatione. . . . 396: (Spiritus Sanctus) qui datus est in corda nostra, in quo clamamus: Abba pater.[64] and often.

51. 326: Itaque Spiritus Sanctus seu fides semper inculcat legem. . . .[65]

52. See footnotes 53 and 54. What is said here can be fully understood only together with the understanding of the word and Spirit, pages 359f.

[62.] Drews, 414, reads, "faith . . . obtains and *brings with it* the Holy Spirit."

[63.] Drews, 302, reads, "Then we receive through faith the Holy Spirit." The reference point and the citation are added by Bonhoeffer in the margin.

[64.] Drews, 9, Th. 1, reads, "True faith must here be understood as true and a gift of the Holy Spirit." [Cf. *LW* 34:109.] [PDM] Drews, 10, Th. 15, reads, "Paul preaches this faith, which the Holy Spirit gives and keeps in the hearts of those who heed the voice of the gospel." [Cf. *LW* 34:110.] [PDM] Drews, 36, Th. 28, reads, "But faith itself, which is poured into us from hearing about Christ by the Holy Spirit, comprehends Christ." [Cf. *LW* 34:153.] [PDM] Drews, 224, reads, "We say faith is the form and the first reality [i.e., love] on the basis of the work of the Holy Spirit." Drews, 396, reads, "(The Holy Spirit), who is given in our hearts and by which we call out, Abba, Father." The second reference, Drews, 10, Th.15, is added in the margin by Bonhoeffer, and the words added in parentheses to the last citation stem from Bonhoeffer.

[65.] Drews, 326, reads "Thereby the *Holy Spirit or faith* constantly imprints the law." Bonhoeffer's emphasis.

[66.] Deleted: "From the Holy Spirit."

[67.] Deleted: "But then: Christ earns for us the Holy Spirit, and this insofar as the content of faith and its gift as such are the same."

the action of the Holy Spirit, we grasp the pro nobis[68] of his death and his resurrection. We not only see the historical events objectively;[53] we recognize that he died for our sins and was raised for our justification. In that we grasp this, we possess Christ as a gift.[54] Christ is in us through the fact that the Holy Spirit is in us. Because, however, Christ has earned this Spirit for us,[55] we can say that in faith, that is, in the Spirit who is acting in us, Christ being always attendant, Christ is in us in the same way as our faith is in us, that he is in us, lives, is raised, etc.[56] So, faith from the Spirit, Christ in faith, Spirit from Christ, and therefore in faith Christ gives the Spirit. This is the essential interrelationship. If I begin with the perspective of faith, then faith grasps

372

---

53. 10, Th 12: Haec est autem fides apprehensiva (ut dicimus) Christi, pro peccati nostris morientis, et pro iustitia nostra resurgentis.[69] Th. 13: Hoc est quod non tantum audiat res a Judaeis et Pilato in Christo configendo gestas, vel resurgente narratas.[70] 11, [Th.] 34: Illud pro Me, seu Pro Nobis, si creditur, facit istam veram fidem et secernit ab omni alia fide, quae res tantum gestas audit.[71]

54. Ita Christus nobis proponitur ut donum seu sacramentum et exemplum. . . .[72] 392; cf. 425, Th. 50 and 60.

55. Christus [. . .] per hoc, quod legi sua sponte se subiecit et omnes eius maledictiones pertulit, emeruit credentibus in se spiritum. . . .[73] 262; cf. 272. 435: (Christus) solus [. . .] conscientiam [. . .] consolari vult, dare ad hoc spiritum sanctum, qui satis ornat suos.[74] Cf. 294: Spiritus Sanctus [. . .] quem nobis Christus a patre misit donum.[75]

56. 424, Th. 37: Christus nondum est in suis fidelibus perfecte suscitatus, imo coepit in eis, ut primitiae, suscitari a morte.[76] Cf. 117, Th. 34.

[68.] "For us."

[69.] Drews, 10, Th. 12, reads, "Moreover, this faith, as we put it, apprehends Christ, who died for our sins and arose again for our justification." [Cf. thesis 12, *LW* 34:110.] [PDM]

[70.] Read from Drews, 10, Th. 13, "Hoc est, quae non tantum audiat rex a Judaeis et Pilato in Christo crucifigendo, gestas, vel de resurgente narratas." "That is, a faith which not only hears the things done by the Jews, and Pilate in crucifying Christ, or narrated about the resurrection." [Cf. thesis 13, *LW* 34:110.] [PDM]

[71.] The correct reference, Drews, 11, Th. 24, reads, "Accordingly, that 'for me' or 'for us,' if it is believed, creates that true faith and distinguishes it from all other faith, which merely hears the things done." [Cf. thesis 24, *LW* 34:111.] [PDM]

[72.] The Latin text reads, "Ita Christus proponitur nobis." Drews, 392, reads, "So Christ is placed before our eyes as *a gift or a sacrament or an example.* Bonhoeffer's emphasis.

[73.] The Latin text reads, "Christus tamen per hoc." Drews, 262, reads, "[Yet] Christ has thereby, in that he freely submitted his will to the law and bore all of its slander, earned the Spirit for all who believed in him."

[74.] "(Christ) alone [. . .] wishes [. . .] to console the conscience and thereby give the Holy Spirit, which is adequately equipped for his own." The addition of "(Christ)" is Bonhoeffer's.

[75.] Drews, 294 reads, "(The Holy Spirit) which is sent to us by Christ as a gift from the Father." Bonhoeffer adds "Spiritus Sanctus" in his footnote.

[76.] Drews 424, Th. 37: "Christ has not yet been totally resurrected in his believers, nay, he has [only] begun to be resurrected from death as the firstfruits."

Christ and God and receives the Holy Spirit therefrom. If I speak about the event from God's perspective, then through the merit of Christ I [attain][77] faith through the Holy Spirit. With this difference in view, however, the petitio principii of the inner state of affairs is not and cannot be solved. Luther likes to clothe the events in time. It often appears that Luther even wanted to place the reception and action of the Spirit only after faith[57] with sanctificatio.[79] With this, however, Luther only wanted to point to the main tendency of the Holy Spirit, namely, to be efficax,[80] and that is precisely to sanctify. After all that has been said, another interpretation seems to me to be impossible. Up until now, we have seen often that faith cannot be simply a constant form of the reception of divine gifts. Instead, in faith the action of the Spirit's form and content cannot be differentiated. The Holy Spirit is precisely power and gift at the same time. In faith the Holy Spirit creates a "holy circle"[81] from God through Christ to faith, all three of whom belong immediately together and can be grasped only through each other. Only in faith, i.e., through the Holy Spirit, can God be grasped and be owned through Christ. The inability to prove this reality includes the necessity of a petitio principii. This somewhat difficult dialectic grew for Luther immediately out of the experience of faith. He could say at the same time, "I believe, I have the Holy Spirit, I have Christ." The psychologically motivated differentiation between the Holy Spirit in me and Christ in me, attested in other writings, can scarcely be found without prejudice in the doctrinal statements. Only the expression "God in us" is consciously avoided, due to understandable reticence.[58]

373

---

57. 280: *Insuper* dat Spiritum Sanctum, ut incipiamus hic implere legem. 272: *Deinde* affert Spiritum Sanctum . . . ut voluptatem habeant in lege domini. 786, Th. 39; 356; and often 400: Posita fide (through or after?) datur Spiritus Sanctus.[78]

58. 150: Deus [. . .] manet in nobis charismatibus et donis. . . .154: Deus operatur adhuc in nobis. . . . 228: Deus movet ipse nos in cordibus nostris. . . .[82]

[77.] German editor's addition.

[78.] Drews, 280, reads, "*Then* he gives the Holy Spirit, that by which we fulfill the law." Drews, 272, reads, "*Afterwards* he grants the Holy Spirit . . . , upon which they have their pleasure in the law of the Lord." Drews, 400, reads, "Through (or: after) the granting of faith the Holy Spirit is given." The emphases, as well as the addition *legem* in the first citation and the remark in parentheses in the last citation, are Bonhoeffer's.

[79.] "Sanctification."

[80.] "Effective."

[81.] Concerning "holy circle" see above, 2/6:289ff., especially page 291f.; and Holl, *Luther*, 566–7.

[82.] Drews, 150, reads, "God (. . .) remains in us through spiritual graces and gifts." Drews, 154 reads, "God works in us even today." Drews, 228 reads, "(God) moves us in our hearts." The addition "Deus" in the last citation is from Bonhoeffer.

374

Now if it is part of faith that only Christ gives the Spirit and Christ can only be grasped in the Spirit, then Luther surely knows the dangers[59] to which the monks, the mystics—yes even, according to his own words, for a short time he himself—were subject. It is exactly the same danger to which the followers of Müntzer and the Anabaptists subjected themselves when they neglected Christ by extolling themselves for possessing their own revelation of the Spirit. They believed they could associate with an unveiled God. They are certainly going in the wrong direction, because wherever God speaks in divine *unveiled* majesty the only thing God can do is destroy. Here ecstatic excitement is of no use in approaching God. Instead, only reflection upon the word from Christ helps, through which God has given us the Spirit, and that means the possibility of associating with God. The gift of the Spirit is only there where there is revelation; and the Holy Spirit in the human person leads only to the place where revelation is, to Christ. Also those who believe that they can ferret out God's

---

59. 294: Periculosum est, sine Christo mediatore nudam divinitatem velle humana ratione scrutari et apprehendere . . . et ut hoc periculum evitemus, donatum est nobis verbum incarnatum. . . . Qui relicto illo filio suas cogitationes et speculationes sequitur, maiestate Dei obruitur et desperat. . . . Dionysios Areopagita, monks, Luther himself! . . . non tamen sine magno meo damno![83] Easdem stultitias sparserunt in vulgus Muntzerus et Anabaptistae, qui remoto Christo iactitabant, se habere revelationes, cum nudo Deo agere et loqui. . . .Ubi igitur nudus Deus in maiestate loquitur, ibi tantum terret et occidit. Deut. 18. Deus pater mandavit, ne tales raptus (namely, these dervishes!) [. . .][84] sed filium in quo omnes thesauri [. . .] reconditi sunt.[85]

[83.] The following is found in Drews, 296.

[84.] Bonhoeffer's ellipsis; add *audiamus.*

[85.] Drews, 294, reads, "It is dangerous without Christ as mediator to desire to seek and grasp with human reason unveiled divinity. . . . To avoid this danger, the word that became flesh is given to us. . . . Whoever follows his own reflections and considerations having set aside Christ will be destroyed and confused by the majesty of God (Dionysius the Areopagite, monks, Luther himself!) not however without the greatest personal damage!" Drews, 296, reads, "The same foolishness was passed on to the people by Müntzer and the Anabaptists, who boasted that without Christ they had revelations, contact with the unveiled God, and conversations (with him). . . . Where God speaks unveiled in his majesty, God only terrifies and kills. (Deut. 18). . . . God the Father commands that we [should not listen] to such reports of being enraptured (namely, the dervishes!), but rather to the Son in whom all treasures are found." The section, "Dionysius . . . Luther himself!" and the remark "(namely, these dervishes!)" are Bonhoeffer's additions. The reference to "Deut. 18" is found in Drews in a sentence not cited by Bonhoeffer.

mysteries miss their goal. What God has not revealed to us we should not attempt to grasp.[60] Christ is the mediator, "that is voluntas revelata."[87]

Yet there is the working of the Spirit external to faith in Christ.[61] This working corresponds to the designation of the Spirit as the creator omnium[89] (see above), because it refers to the conservatio[90] of the evil ones as well—certainly not because the Spirit hinders them from the good but because it also preserves them as wicked. It does this not for their sake but rather for the service they do for the community. (More on this in greater detail below.)

Thus the Holy Spirit *in me,* Christ *in me, I* believe! It is of critical importance to preserve this "in me." *My* sin called forth God's wrath. The Holy Spirit annihilated *me.* Therefore *I* must be helped. My guilt must be blotted out. What confronts this is the fact that the *Holy Spirit* is in me, and it must always remain subject, or especially in faith as donum, because it established the holy circle. The Holy Spirit, who must always remain solely effective, is in me. It is of critical importance that both things are a reality. Because if the Holy Spirit is not solely effective, then it is certainly not the Holy Spirit; and then I likewise do not *believe.* If I am not the subject of faith, what is the meaning of the conversation about my faith? Luther dug more deeply into this problem than did the whole of Catholic scholasticism. It concerned the *salvation of the sinner.* The sinful self [Ich] could not remain together with the Spirit. It had to be transformed. In contrast, the essence of sinfulness lies not in works but in unholy convictions. It is here that the *Holy Spirit* must become active. In faith the Holy Spirit creates a new person,[62] a new self, a new will,

---

60. 190: In eo, quod revelavit nobis, consistendum est; quod non revelavit non debemus requirere. [. . .] Extra et supra verbum inquirere et investigare Deum, est admodum periculosum. Ipse Deus vult omnia facere propter Christum in redemptione et iustificatione hominum. This is voluntas revelata.[86]

61. Etsi spiritus seu dona eius donari et adesse possunt absque [. . .] Christi et charitate.[88] 730, Th 7. See below, "Spirit and Theology."

62. 182: Lex mandat et extorquet opera, fides autem facit personam, et hanc condit, parat ad opera bona. 184: Paulus [. . .] dicit, quod persona sit facta per fidem a Deo, qui regenerat nos fide in verbo et usu sacramentorum mediante Spiritu Sancto. . . . 21: Rex vero credit ei et fit nova persona. 270: Christus [. . .] dat voluntatem ut . . .[91] and often; cf. 302.

[86.] Drews, 190, reads, "One must stick to what one uncovers; one may not research what one does not uncover. [. . .] To seek God beyond and above the word is very dangerous. God wishes to do everything for the sake of Christ by the redemption and the justification of humanity. This is the revealed will."

[87.] See Bonhoeffer's footnote 60.

[88.] The Latin text reads, *absque fide Christi.* Drews, 730, reads, "Even if the Spirit or his gifts can be given and be present apart from [faith in] Christ and love [to him]."

[89.] "Creator of all."

[90.] "Preservation."

[91.] Drews, 182, reads, "the law commands and forces works, faith creates the person and establishes these [and] prepares them for good works." Drews, 184, reads, "Paul [. . .]

376   a new heart, who truly and personally desires what the Spirit desires. Faith is
           "to become transformed," not externally but instead inwardly, in the self.[63]
           Now freedom and action are no longer opposed to each other. Instead, they
           are the same *thing* seen from two perspectives. It is truly the *Holy Spirit* who
           gives to the human being; and it is truly the *human being* to whom the Holy
           Spirit is given.
               Here we have found the part of Luther's thought that supplements his con-
           cept of the holy. If we became acquainted above with the destructive moral
           force of the Spirit's maiestas, here we have another function of the Holy Spir-
           it. The Spirit cannot allow sinful persons to die but instead receives them, jus-
           tifies and sanctifies them by making itself a gift, and in this way also sanctifies
           concrete humanity. This is not a capricious action of the Holy Spirit, but
           instead it accompanies faith. In the pro nobis of faith, the Spirit changes the
           whole path of humanity. Hate disappears on its own through the relationship
           of Christ's work for me. Contrition, thankfulness, and love are the necessary
           consequences of faith. A new problem arises immediately. Show me such a
           person, who has been newly created by the Spirit! Luther[64] answers, "I cannot,
           because that person is hidden from this world and is dead to it. The Christian
377   who is justified in God's eyes is thus invisible to human eyes. That person is
           buried with Christ, dead to sin, law, and death, hidden from this world, alive
           in a heavenly life. This is the Christianus reputative iustus, sanctus sub alis gal-

           ───────────

           63. Cf. page 341.
           64. 450-51: christianus est persona, quae iam sepulta est cum Christo in morte eius,
           mortuus peccato, legi morti. . . . Sed hoc ipsum non cernitur, sed est absconditum in
           mundo, non apparet, non occurrit in oculos nostros. . . . Ipse enim non est in prae-
           senti saeculo, non vivit, mortuus est, versatur in alia vita longe supra hac posita,
           coelesti . . . hic vivit christianus reputative iustus, sanctus sub alis gallinae suae. Sed e
           contra christianus in quantum miles et in militia versatur, hic etiam . . . sentit et
           expetit quotidie militiam suam.[92] Cf. 452. 176: Alius et novus homo est ac vere cae-
           lestis et divinus, ut angeli . . .[93] Cf. 144.

           says that the person is created through faith by God, who renews us by means of the Holy
           Spirit through faith in the word and in the use of the sacraments." Drews, 21, reads, "The
           king believes in him and becomes a new person." Drews, 270, reads, "Christ [. . .] gives the
           will with which. . . ."
               [92.] Drews, 450f., reads, "The Christian is a person who is buried with Christ in his
           death, dead to sin, law, and death . . . yet even this is not known but is hidden in the world,
           does not appear, does not come before our eyes. . . . Then he is not in this world, does not
           live, is dead, dwells in another life that is far above ours in a heavenly [life] . . . here lives the
           Christian justified through imputation, holy under the wings of his hen. But insofar as the
           Christian is a soldier and is involved in conflict, . . . he senses his battle here and yearns daily
           for it." The end of the citation reads in Drews, 451, "et expetit quotidie militiam carnis suae
           et huic nimium vivit, ut et divus Paulus conqueritur Roma. 7: Carne vivo legi peccati." "And
           yearns daily for the battle with his flesh and lives too much for this, as also the divine Paul
           complains in Romans 7, with my flesh I am a slave to the law of sin" (see Rom. 7:25).
               [93.] The correct reference, Drews, 178, reads, "He is a different and new human being,
           truly heavenly and divine, like the angels."

linae suae."[94] This person—one can use Karl Barth's[65] expression here—is the "invisible [. . .] *new* subject of the person who stands and exists upright before God, [. . .] who can be comprehended and understood [. . .] only as not given." Only in this way can it be said that the Christian can no longer sin.[66] Therefore it is after all not the Holy Spirit in *me* but instead a second self that has been separated off, and this one lives in heaven far away from here. It is a "heavenly double"[95] of my earthly self! But this should just not be. I am truly the one over there and exist as the same person here. It is one and the same subject from different perspectives. The human, the one who before God's eyes (reputante Deo)[67] *is* already justified through faith, is declared to be justified on the strength of it. It corresponds to the Spirit's holiness also to sanctify the human being in this world of sin per effectum,[96] to allow the human being to *feel*[68] the beginning of new life, i.e., to extend its action from the perceptible into the imperceptible.[97]

378

Spirit and faith are not poured out[69] substantially, quiescently into us. Instead faith is active and alive[70] and must always be effective. Therefore, belonging to the Holy Spirit, the former is a gift according to its content (see above). Yet Luther does not simply want to designate it as such,[71] because a gift seems to him to be something completed, finished, substantial, and the

---

65. *Romans*, 158 [trans. altered].

66. 429-30; page 28, Th. 29.

67. Cf. 354; 356; 50; 44; 292.

68. See footnote 64.

69. Fides infusa, quam adversarii ita appellant, non est donum Dei, sed est plane figmentum.[98] 745

70. Fides est vivax quiddam et operosum, nunquam quiescens neque cessans. 188; 222: [. . .] ipsa fides sit operosum quiddamm . . .[99] and often.

71. 150: Sic habemus (Spiritum Sanctum) non tanquam donum, vel effectum, sed tanquam efficientem.[100] Cf. 116, [Th.] 39![101]

[94.] Cf. Bonhoeffer's footnote 64.

[95.] On the concept of a "heavenly double," cf. *AB* (*DBWE* 2):99. See the letter to Rüdiger Schleicher, April 8, 1936 (*GS* 3:29; *DBW* 14:147), and *Testament to Freedom*, 450.

[96.] "Through effect."

[97.] Holl: "The other way around!?"

[98.] Drews, 745, reads, "Infused faith, as the opponents call it, is not a gift of God but rather completely a delusion."

[99.] Drews, 188, reads, "Faith is something alive and effective, never calm and moribund." The correct reference is Drews, 224, which reads, "[and because] the faith is itself something effective."

[100.] Drews, 150, reads, "So we have (the Holy Spirit) not as a gift or as an effect but rather as an agent." Bonhoeffer's addition (*Spiritum Sanctum*) replaces Drews *eum*, 'him'.

[101.] Footnote 71 is added by Bonhoeffer in the margin. On how Bonhoeffer cites Holl, see Bodenstein, *Die Theologie Karl Holls*, 344, in reference to Drews, 150, and also to Drews, 116, Th. 39.

Holy Spirit is action, not effect. It is true that in its whole[72] being, the Holy Spirit is in us through word and sacrament. It is true in the same way that Jesus was on this earth, but his being is precisely power and gift at the same time (see above). As such it now also makes the human being, who is justified reputante Deo, into a completely new person.[73] From the voluntary form[104] of the concept of Spirit follows an active forming of a relationship between humanity and Spirit. The concrete person, however, stands in the midst of the sinful world. Thus the Holy Spirit is a force that has to fight for the human being. Yet how can this be? Does the Holy Spirit really have to fight like every other will when it comes to us? Is it not impious to believe of the all-powerful will of God that there would also be opposition to it? Here lies the great problem of every voluntaristic concept of God's will. Luther's ingenious solution differentiates between justification, seen from God's perspective as already complete, and sanctification by the work of the Holy Spirit,[105] which began in tempore and resulted from declared righteousness. Therefore, if the Holy Spirit stands fighting in the world, then the Spirit's extra worldly victory is already assured. There, where it is, the victory "is" already won. With this, to be sure, the Holy Spirit's characteristic as a fighter is not weakened. Instead, it is made only more clear. The fact that the final paradox cannot be solved here is due to our concept of will and to our capacity of perception, which certainly can think only in terms of the relationship between subject and object.

If Luther asks himself positively where this gift and the action of faith are demonstrated in new life, then undoubtedly for him the fulfillment of the law in love would be the first fruit of the Spirit. He can also say that it is a new obedience,[74] which the law had sought in vain.[75] At the point at which the Holy Spirit allowed the human being to break, the Holy Spirit must begin to

---

72. 151: Sicut pater fuit praesens et coram loquens, cum baptizaretur filius Iesus Christus in Iordane, sicut filius dominus et servator noster adfuit σωματικῶς,".... ιτα [...] nunc revera adest et operatur in nobis per verbum et sacramenta Spiritus Sanctus.... [102]

73. Cf. 74: Haec purgatio est initium novae creaturae.... [103] 145; 13, [Th.] 68 in *LW* 34:113.

74. 698: Oportet ... etiam novam obedientiam in nobis inchoari.[106]

75. 290.

[102.] Drews, 151, reads, "As the Father was present and spoke before all eyes, as his son Jesus Christ was baptized in the Jordan, [and] as the Son, our Lord and Savior, was present in bodily form, ... so now is the Holy Spirit present and active in us through word and sacrament."

[103.] Drews, 74, reads, "The purification is the beginning of the new *creation*" (Bonhoeffer's emphasis).

[104.] Cf. *NRS* 361ff., especially 369; *SC* (*DBWE* 1):49, editorial note 53; see also Holl, *What Did Luther Understand by Religion?* 62ff.

[105.] Cf. Holl, *Luther*, 219ff.

[106.] Drews, 697f., reads, "A new obedience must ... begin also in us."

construct anew. This is the case because the grace of the Spirit does not consist in the fact that the Spirit allows some of its requirements to be removed. (If it were otherwise, the old human being would not have had to be annihilated!) Instead, it exists in the fact that the Spirit's coming creates a human being who can fulfill what is supposed to be done. It exists so that the person once again becomes the image of God.[76] [108] When people recognize the unimaginable gift[77] that they have received in the Holy Spirit, they will be thankful toward God, will love God, and will call upon God. Further, from the person there flow for God's sake love[78] towards neighbor, moderation, freedom, generosity, and many more things. This means, therefore, a new morality. These consequences are just as necessary as that a good tree produces good fruit,[79] or as that 3 + 7 equals 10. It is so necessary that when the fruit is missing one can conclude with certainty that the right Spirit was missing.[80] The law is no longer outside the human person but lies in the new person as a force within. In the same way, the Holy Spirit no longer stands in majesty in opposition to the person, but instead has entered into the person. With this, morality is the law of oneself [autonom], i.e., truly spiritual. The spiritual human being, i.e., the truly moral human person, is free from the law and lives from himself, from his spirit. This person creates in spirit in that

380

---

76. 730, Th. 5: Qui veterem hominem cum suis concupiscentiis et crucifigit et renovat ad imaginem Dei[107]

77. Christus donat Spiritum Sanctum, ut [. . .] incipiant [. . .] agnoscere hoc immensum, incomprehensibile et ineffabile donum ac pro eo gratias agere Deo, diligere, colere, invocare Deum, expectare ab eo omnia[109] Cf. 151 and 228. 272: Quantum igitur spiritus est in nobis tantum etiam delectationis in lege.[110]

78. 151: Cum infundit nobis fidem, spem, charitatem, modestiam, libertatem, beneficientiam, longanimitatem. . . .[111]

79. 11, [Th.] 34: Fatemur opera bona fidem sequi debere, imo non debere, sed sponte sequi, sicut arbor bona non debet bonos fructus facere, sed sponte facit.[112] Cf. 116, Th. 21.

80. 730, [Th.] 8 and often.

[107.] Drews, 739, Th. 5, reads, "This crucifies the old person with his desires and renews him according to the image of God."

[108.] Deleted: "We knew that these."

[109.] Drews, 284, reads, "(Christ) gives the (Holy) Spirit, upon which [. . .] they begin [. . .] to know and to thank God for this immeasurable, incomprehensible, and ineffable gift, to love God, to honor, to call upon, and expect everything from him." *Christus* and *Sanctum* are added by Bonhoeffer.

[110.] "(272:) To the same extent that the Spirit is in us, so is our joy in the law."

[111.] Read with Drews *beneficentiam.* "(151:) When he infuses faith, hope, love, humility, freedom, charity, long-suffering. . . ."

[112.] "(11, Th. 34:) We confess that good works should follow faith, no, not only should, but do follow spontaneously, just as a good tree produces good fruit, not from obligation, but freely." [Cf. *LW* 34:111.] [PDM] Cf. Matt. 7:17-18.

381   he acts, and thus is creative. Enveloped[81] in the love of the new person, the
      Holy Spirit, or faith, is effective. It is not, however, that love is a quality of the
      Holy Spirit. Here one also sees Luther again opposing the concept of sub-
      stance.[114] The new person does not need a Decalogue.[115] Indeed, the new
      person could create new decalogues, which would be clearer than that of
      Moses.[82] If I have to do without Christ *or* the law, then it is truly better if it is
      the law,[83] because if I possess the Spirit, then I have in me the fulfilled law and
      the power to fulfill it further.[84] Thus the new person creates in himself the
      rules for his action from the knowledge of the determined will of God. The
      last requirement is necessary. The Holy Spirit, however, procures this knowl-
      edge for the human person, who can now also *judge*[85] from the Spirit and be
      lord over all things. Next to creative morality, therefore, stands critical judg-
      ment. Through faith, the ability to judge is given another direction, i.e., of
382   course, only through faith. But it is not as if reason becomes enlightened
      about metaphysical knowledge. Instead the ability to judge is a moral one and
      has as its standard the word or, as the case may be, the Spirit (see below). The
      knowledge of our hearts is not enough; it leads us into error.[86] From the new

---

81. 150: Errat magister sententiarum, cum dicit, quod ipsa caritas sit qualitas [. . .]
Spiritus Sancti, nisi dicat, quod Spiritus sanctus involutus in caritate operetur in
nobis.[113]

82. 12, Th. 53: Imo novos decalogos faciemus, sicut Paulus facit per omnes episto-
las, et Petrus, maxime Christus in evangelio. [Th.] 54: Et hi decalogi clariores sunt,
quam Mosi decalogus. . . .[116]

83. Si utrum sit amittendum, Christus vel lex, lex est amittenda, non Christus. [12,
Th.] 51.[117]

84. [12, Th.] 52 Habito enim Christo facile condemus leges, et omnia recte iudi-
cabimus.[118]

85. 12, [Th.] 52, 56.

86. 678: Si iudicatione cordis iudicamus, tum erramus, sed per verbum et sacramenta iudicemus.[119]

[113.] Drews, 150, reads, "The Master of Sentences is in error when he says that love itself
is a quality [. . .] of the Holy Spirit, unless he means that the Holy Spirit wrapped up in love
works in us." The name, Master of Sentences, refers to the scholastic theologian Peter Lombard. Luther is referring to Lombard's *Sententiae in IV libris distinctae* (1.I, dist. 17B).

[114.] Cf. above, editorial note 104.

[115.] Cf. Holl, *Luther*, 223; and also *GS* 5:165, *NRS* 43, and *E* 249.

[116.] Drews, 12, Th. 53, reads, "Indeed, we would make new decalogues, as Paul does
in all the epistles, and Peter, but above all Christ in the gospel." [Cf. thesis 53, *LW* 34:112.]
[PDM] Drews, 12, Th. 54, reads, "And these decalogues are clearer than the Decalogue of
Moses." [Cf. thesis 54, *LW* 34:112–13.][PDM]

[117.] Drews, 12, Th. 51, reads, "If one of them had to be parted with, Christ or the law,
the law would have to be let go, not Christ." [Cf. thesis 51, *LW* 34:112.][PDM]

[118.] Drews, 12, Th. 52, reads, "For if we have Christ, we can easily establish laws and
we shall judge all things rightly." [Cf. thesis 52, *LW* 34:112.][PDM]

[119.] Drews, 678, reads, "When we judge according to the judgment of the heart we
err; we should instead judge by the word and the sacraments."

ability to judge we are also enabled correctly to judge ourselves. Thus the Christian is judge over all things and can only be judged by God.

In this absolute freedom from the law, the Christian *fulfills* the law in faith. Now should all Christians really attempt to create the norms for their actions? Certainly, the law is where God's will is. If the Holy Spirit leads one to adultery, then adultery [is] a law like every other.[87] The Lord has complete power over the law. (Luther seems to approach the thoughts of Duns Scotus. What for Luther is an unavoidable consequence, however, is a principle for Duns.) Therefore the strong Christian is fundamentally free, but who can consider themselves so strong? That the strong have received their power entirely for the community will be seen below in greater detail. Again, when God gives himself to human beings, can God give one person more and the other person less? Is God not an undivided God? How can God or the Holy Spirit be thought of as *divided*? Here Luther answers[88] that the question is not about the Spirit in its essentia and natura, but about the ministerium Spiritus Sancti.[122] Through this it is revera[123] in the human being and yet diversely. We answer the question about the more or less with another statement from Luther,[89] which asserts that faith may be weak but may never be uncertain. It belongs to the essence of faith, as the action of the Holy Spirit and as possessing God, to be certain of this possession and with this the gospel; thus, the possession of the Spirit in faith, who alone justifies, is equal and complete in everyone. Weakness and strength, less or more, relate to the effective capacity to develop; and this is different in people with equal *certainty* of faith. It is foolish to discuss a whole or divided Spirit, because where I have the Holy Spirit at all, there I also have the Spirit in its infiniteness.

What now follows for preaching the law for those who are "not strong" and perfect Christians? Is it superfluous, just as it is superfluous to command numbers that $7 + 3 = 10$? What is the point of the law for the free Christian?

383

---

87. Dominus leges potest dispensare cum quibus et quomodo ipse vult; eius voluntas est lex. Cum igitur approbante Spiritu Sancto dixerunt plures uxores, non peccaverunt . . . ; si iuberet adulterari, tum esset lex.[120] 622.

88. Cf. 150, argum. et R.[121]

89. 473: fides potest esse infirma, sed non incerta aut dubia. . . .[124]

[120.] The correct reference is Drews, 622 and 624, which reads, "The Lord can administer the law with whom and in what manner he himself wills; his will is law. If with the agreement of the Holy Spirit they married many women, they did not sin . . . ; if he should command one to commit adultery then that would be law."

[121.] The correct reference is Drews, 148 and 150, *argumentum et Responsio,* 'argument and answer'.

[122.] The question is not about "the Spirit in its essence and nature, but the ministry of the Holy Spirit."

[123.] "Really."

[124.] "(473:) The faith can be weak, but not uncertain or doubting. . . ." Instead of *aut,* 'or', Drews reads *et,* 'and'.

Then further, why could not the person have been given the power to fulfill the law through the Spirit in the beginning? Why was it necessary to proceed through this death, which the Spiritus Sanctus in sua maiestate[125] prepared? We will first answer the second question. The human being was so caught up in sin that, when the Spirit came as comforter, the Spirit was not even recognized or felt.[90] If the *person* is to be helped and not just receive a habitus[127] magically infused, then the person's own heart must be shaken through the violent recognition of human sinfulness. With this the person recognizes the need for help. Thus, [the] double action of the Spirit cannot be separated. It is true that the Spirit is not given through the law. Yet[91] through the law the Holy Spirit prepares for itself the "material" with which it can later work, namely, humble and broken hearts. Therefore, without the preaching of the law the Spirit also could not have been distributed. Because of the arrival of the gospel, the law, to be sure, becomes the pedagogue for Christ. It becomes the finger of John the Baptist which proclaims, "Behold the Lamb of God," as Luther likes to express himself.[92] The law was never an end in itself. The

384

---

90. 416: Spiritus Sanctus, ut esset consolator et sanctificator, factus est etiam donum. Sed quia sumus in peccatis, rei aeternae mortis et irae, non statim possumus eum sentire, neque consolationem eius agnoscere. Ideo necesse est, etc. . . .[126]

91. Lex quidem non dat Spiritum Sanctum, ut per evangelium, sed interim per legem praeparatur Spiritui Sancto materia, in qua postea suam vim et potestatem ostendere potest, videlicet, in pauperes, afflictos, contritos . . . nec per evangelium datur Spiritus Sanctus, nisi prius praeparata fuerit per legem materia. . . .[128] 480

92. 370: Now hear tuum officium, non diaboli aut latronis, sed paedagogi, . . . Lex enim per sese tantum potest terrores incutere et deducere ad inferos. Sed deinde venit evangelium et aufert cuspidem legi et facit ex ea paedagogum. Atque ita debet lex per evangelium interpretar i. . . oportet, ut accedat ministerium Spiritus, evangelium id est, seu digitus Ioannis, qui dicat: Ecce agnus Dei, non morieris.[129]

[125.] "The Holy Spirit in its majesty."

[126.] Drews, 416, reads, "The Holy Spirit was also made a gift, in order to comfort and to sanctify. But because we are in sin and are subject to eternal death and wrath, *we cannot feel it immediately* and also cannot recognize his comfort. Therefore it is necessary, etc." Bonhoeffer's emphasis.

[127.] "A disposition," "an attitude."

[128.] Drews, 481 (the correct reference), reads, "Although it is true that the law does not give the Holy Spirit as it is given through the gospel, instead, for a time, through the law, the Holy Spirit prepares the material in which it will later demonstrate its power and might, that is to say, the poor, the afflicted, the contrite . . . and the Holy Spirit is not given through the gospel, if the material has not been earlier prepared through the law. . . ." Instead of *potestam*, 'power', Drews has *virtutem*, 'strength'.

[129.] Drews, 370 and 372 (the correct references), read, "Here, listen to your duty, not the duty of the devil or the robber but the duty of the teacher. On its own accord, the law can only terrify and lead to hell. But then the gospel arrives and takes the thorn out of the law and makes the law a teacher. For this reason the law must be interpreted by the gospel . . . the ministry of the Spirit, which is the gospel, must be added or the finger of John, which proclaims: See, the lamb of God, you will not die." See John 1:29. For the finger of John the Baptist, see Barth, "Menschenwort und Gotteswort in der christlichen Predigt,"

patriarchs of the Old Testament always found the righteousness of faith in the promissio Christi.[130] [93] Now, does the Holy Spirit preserve its own action in this way? No, because the direction of the law's intent was the same holy intent as is present in the gospel. Only the form has changed (see above). The law has not been abolished by the gospel because it is useless; instead the law is "well preserved"[131] in the gospel. Where there is no law, there is no sin. Where there is no sin, there is no forgiveness. Where there is no forgiveness, Christ came into the world and died in vain. Therefore, gospel and law, as the two actions of the Holy Spirit, cannot be and cannot be allowed to be separated, just as repentance and forgiveness cannot be separated.[94] Where the law cannot be understood, there its fulfillment is without an object. Yes, to discard the law means crucifying Christ for a second time.[95] Very well, in its place the law is holy, just, and good.[134] Does it, however, still have a place in the Christian life? In the gospel the law is 'suspended' ['aufgehoben'] in a double sense. Does the believer still need the law? Every person who is imputatively iustus, remains per effectum a sinner[135] in spite of salvation. Concerning those who are carried by the Holy Spirit into the kingdom of God Luther says, "the feet still hang back."[96] As certain as the individual is righteous before God, so certain is it that the individual is still a sinner in this world. As certain as it is that the Spirit is in the individual, that is how certain it is that the flesh is still in the individual. A terrible struggle between the two giants rages in humanity. Death itself and the death of Christ wrestle with each other. But Christ calls out, "I am the death of death, the hell of hell, the devil of the devil, don't be afraid; I have been victorious!"[97]

385

---

93. Cf. 686, Th. 1-7.

94. Lex et evangelium non possunt nec debent separari, sicut nec poenitentia et remissio peccatorum . . . nec impletio quid sit intelligi potest, nisi intelligatur quid sit lex, . . .[132] 332.

95. 458: Nam qui legem reiiciunt, non minus sunt crucifixores Christi.[133]

96. 480.

97. 348.

130, and "Biblical Questions, Insights and Vistas," in *The Word of God and The Word of Man,* 66ff., 75ff., and 84.

[130.] "The promise of Christ."

[131.] Cf. Rom. 7:6, καταργεῖν. Concerning καταργεῖν see also Rom. 3:31 and Barth, *The Epistle to the Romans,* 91ff.

[132.] Drews, 332, reads, "Law and gospel cannot and must not be separated from one another, just as contrition and forgiveness of sins cannot be. . . . One cannot understand what fulfillment is if one does not understand what law is."

[133.] Drews, 458, reads "Then those who reject the law are nonetheless crucifiers of Christ."

[134.] See Rom. 7:12.

[135.] "Righteous through imputation," "through action a sinner."

386   Therefore, the Spirit certainly created a new person, but the will is not a
substance,[136] i.e., something that cannot be supplanted, that has been firmly infused. Instead it is a living force and, consistent with the nature of a
power, it has a power to oppose. This opposition is strong even in renewed
humanity.[98] Here Luther is unconcerned about the extent to which the unity
of both wills—namely, the will renewed by God and the sinful will—can be
perceived psychologically in a person. He is much more sensitive to their ethical unity and his responsibility for both. Thus the ethical problem is also
undiminished and serious for the new person. The Holy Spirit must struggle,
because people cannot, as long as they live, *cease* to sin.[99] We can always only
forge a beginning of a new life,[100] then, however, always repent anew because
we see that we cannot remain without it. But the meaning of evangelical
repentance lies in the fact that when Christians fall into sin through the
power of Satan, they cannot despair because of this. Instead, due to their
humility, the Christian truly glorifies God, experiences childlike, not servile,
fear,[101] and realizes the forgiveness of sins through faith, i.e., through the
action of the Holy Spirit.[102] Original sin remains in us despite baptism and
387   justification. We are pronounced guilty of sin and God's wrath.[103] Day after

98. 145: Nostra enim voluntas non potest hic esse neque fieri perfecta, non potest
implere legem et congruere cum voluntate divina, sicut erit in coelis post hanc
vitam.[137]

99. Antequam sepeliamur, non possumus non peccare etiam sancti.[138] 445.

100. 145: Sumus tantum primitiae creationis, tantum primitias Spiritus accipimus
et habemus in hac vita. . . .[139] Cf. 431, 144.

101. Cf. also p. 362.

102. P. 302.

103. 64: Peccatum originis. . .quoddam ingenitum malum, [. . .] quod nos reos
facit peccati et mortis aeternae. . .et manet in nobis etiam post baptismum repug-
natque legi Dei et Spiritui Sancto. 369: Imperfecta impletio legis est, quando Spiritus
Sanctus incipit formaliter implere legem in nobis, seu quando per Spiritum Sanctum
nos incipimus implere legem.[140]

[136.] Cf. above, editorial note 104.

[137.] Drews, 145, reads, "Because our will cannot be perfect here and cannot become
perfect, it cannot fulfill the law and be in accord with the divine will, as will be the case in
heaven after this life."

[138.] Drews, 445, reads, "Prior to being buried we cannot help but sin, even as saints."

[139.] Drews, 145, reads, "Just as we are the first fruits of creation, in the same manner
we have received and in this life have the first fruits of the Spirit" (cf. Rom. 8:23).

[140.] Drews, 64, reads, "Original sin . . . is to a certain extent an evil with which one is
born, [. . .] which imprisons us in sin and eternal death, . . . and it remains in us after baptism and opposes God's law and the Holy Spirit." Drews, 369, reads, "The fulfillment of the
law is imperfect, when the Holy Spirit [first] begins, in its likeness, to fulfill the law in us,
or when we begin to fulfill the law through the Holy Spirit." The second citation was written in the margin by Bonhoeffer.

day we must be newly purified[104] and reborn. Therefore day after day the Spirit must come in us. Such rebirth is always only the beginning, which will soon be choked by sin again. Certainly, the final victory of the Spirit is assured. Christ always calls anew to human beings, "ego vici."[142] The Holy Spirit remains with humanity.[105] It is unlike an artist who creates a work of art and then goes away. Instead the Spirit remains, is always there, supports, and keeps us, "because the Spirit has to remain always with us and be as if mending an old, bad fur." Yet with sins that are too foul we can chase even the Spirit away.[106] This expression naturally does not suggest a superior power of sin over the Spirit—because God can also give faith to the recalcitrant![107]—but here the donum perseverantiae,[145] which is not guaranteed by the concept of predestination, has been given a new interpretation in the sphere of ethics and guilt. The saying, however, also means a distinct turning against the Catholic view that the justified person falls from the state of grace with every sin and reenters it only though the sacrament. For Luther the sinful person is precisely in his sinfulness in a state of grace.

388

Luther's view of the sin against the Holy Spirit also belongs in this context. Actually for Luther every sin is a sin against the Spirit. In reference to the saying of Jesus, however, for him it consists of a state of final doubt and final arrogance,[108] thus conscious rejection of the revelation given by God in gospel and law. Here again the concept of predestination is transformed. So "it was the case that we wantonly chased the Spirit from us."[147] Thus the

---

104. 145: Imo nos quotidie purgari per verbum et sacramenta, mittente Deo in corda nostra Spiritum suum Sanctum, qui de die in diem nos mundat. . . .[141]

105. 150: Nam opera Spiritus Sancti non sunt sicut artificis, qui perfecta creatura abeat. . . .151: Sed semper adest nobis fulcit et conservat nos. As he always has there. . . . It would be as if we willingly chased him away with our sins.[143]

106. See footnote 105.

107. Fides [. . .] datur . . . etiam contraluctanti, si Deus voluerit.[144] 43.

108. 350: Finalis praesumptio et finalis dubitatio utraque est peccatum in spiritum sanctum.[146]

[141.] Drews, 145, reads, "Moreover, [we say] that we are purified daily through the sacraments, as God sends the Holy Spirit into our hearts which purifies us from day to day."

[142.] "I have conquered." Cf. above, 2/10:349 and Bonhoeffer's footnote 97.

[143.] Drews, 150, reads, "Then the works of the Holy Spirit are unlike those of an artist, who completes a creation and leaves it." Drews, 151, reads, "Rather he is always near us, strengthening and preserving us." The first German sentence immediately joined to the Latin citation finds its completion above in the text. The second sentence reads in Drews, "It would be then that we ourselves could chase it away mischievously with our sins."

[144.] Drews, 43, reads, "The faith [. . .] is . . . also given to the recalcitrant, if God wills it."

[145.] Latin, "gift of perseverance."

[146.] Drews, 350, reads, "Final presumption and final doubt are both sins against the Holy Spirit."

[147.] Cf. above, footnote 105 and editorial note 143.

Holy Spirit is with us and is given to us daily in repentance; this is no contradiction. Thus it certainly does not free us from emotional disturbances and sensuality,[109] but it gives us the strength to overcome[110] them. The Spirit gives me the strength to hate evil, because evil is evil.[111] However, the Spirit creates in me an ever-deepening recognition of sins the more it grows in me[112] and, with it, new desperatio, repentance, as well as tristitia. This is why the pious mourn more about their sins than they rejoice in the gifts of God. Herein lies the actual point at which even the most pious also have to contend, because tristitia is sin, and the more one tries to overcome it with the spirit [Geist] the more it returns.

Especially this mistrust and doubting of God is a sin against the first commandment[113] and a most serious crime. If the gospel came precisely to make God's will clear for humankind,[114] then doubt is the work of the law,[115]

---

109. Cf. 436-37.

110. 454: Ora, ut audiam te, et faciam, ut possis. . . .[148]

111. 358: Spiritus [. . .], quo recepto incipio ex animo odisse omne, quod offendit eius nomen,[149] and often.

112. 330: Ideoque etiam mittitur Spiritus Sanctus, qui ubi occupaverit totum hominem, subinde magis ac magis innotescunt peccata. . . .[150]

113. 482: De Deo desperare est summum flagitium et peccatum contra primum praeceptum. . . .[151]

114. 240: Et totum evangelium nihil aliud agit, quam ut nos de voluntate Dei certificet.[152]

115. 657: Dubitatio manet in sanctis et renatis et viget in illis, etsi non semper, tamen per intervalla. Est autem dubitatio opus legis. . . . Pugnant autem haec duo acerrime inter se, certitudo et dubitatio . . . etsi dubitatio maior appareat, tamen cooperante Spiritu Sancto debilitatur per certitudinem . . . ut semper superet certitudo remurmurante dubitatione.[153]

[148.] Drews, 454, reads, "Pray, that I may hear you, and I will make it possible that you can."

[149.] Drews, 356 and 358 (the correct reference), reads, "The [Holy] Spirit, whom I have received, whom I begin to hate with all my heart, whose name I insult by this."

[150.] Drews, 330, reads, "And therefore the Holy Spirit has also been sent, and as soon as it has empowered the whole person, immediately the sins become more and more apparent."

[151.] Drews, 482, reads, "To doubt God's existence is the greatest baseness there is and a sin against the first commandment."

[152.] Drews, 240, reads, "The purpose of the entire gospel is none other than to assure us of the will of God."

[153.] Drews, 657, reads, "The saints and those who are born again continue to doubt and to doubt strongly, and though they do not always doubt they do so on occasion. Doubt, however, is a work of the law. . . . Both, however, battle very strongly with each other, that is, certainty and doubt. . . . Even when doubt seems to be greater, it nevertheless is weakened by the help of the Holy Spirit . . . , so that certainty always conquers, while doubt grumbles against it." Bonhoeffer reversed the order of the last two sentences when he cited them.

which, although this is not always the case, does afflict human beings at intervals. Yet, for all that, finally the Holy Spirit is victorious in us and the certitudo remurmurante dubio.[154]

Luther can also turn the thought around. As terrible as the battle between Spirit and sin may be, thank God that the Spirit is there. Were it not, then the danger would be great that one would also have lost Christ with the Spirit.[116]   390

Now the meaning of the law for Christians is clear. Insofar as Christians are spirit, they are free and the law is 'suspended'.[156] Insofar as they are sinners, it is in effect and it leads by[117] admonition as mortificatio iustificatoris[157] to repentance, until the spirit of the law is completely dissolved into the gospel, until God's wrath has completely turned to grace. This, however, will not occur here but in the hereafter. Here, as we have often seen, we view the movement of the Holy Spirit persistently driving beyond itself toward an eschatology. Some day the ministerium Spiritus Sancti[158] will no longer[118] exist, when faith has become sight,[119] and when we will be able to endure the sight of the Holy Spirit unveiled in glory.[120] At that moment our sight will be completely pure, and our heart will be completely new.[121] Where the law is

---

116. 431: Nisi essent christianis tales luctationes, pugnae, cruces et tribulationes, periculum esset, ne Christum prorsus perderent et amitterent.[155]

117. 271, 402, 326, and often.

118. 116, Th. 24: Cessabit enim tunc et ipsa fides, reputatio Dei et remissio peccatorum, cum univero spiritus ministerio. cf 128; cf. 737. 116 [Th.] 26: Lex ipsa cessabit et evacuabitur cum omni scientia et prophetia et tota scriptura.[159]

119. See footnote 118.

120. 128: Spiritus Sanctus revelabitur tunc, et quod est sensibile, externum, corporale, illud cessabit. Iam videtur Spiritus Sanctus quodam medio . . . sed illic eum videbimus in sua gloria. . . .[160]

121. 151: Videbimus eum, sicut est, et feremus suam maiestatem. Nam tum oculi nostri erunt purgati et cor nostrum innovatum.[161]

[154.] "Certainty, while doubt grumbles against it." Cf. the end of footnote 115.

[155.] Drews, 431, reads, "If Christians did not have such confrontations and fights, crosses and tribulations, then the danger would arise that they would completely lose and reject Christ."

[156.] Cf. editorial note 131.

[157.] "The justifier who kills."

[158.] "Ministry of the Holy Spirit."

[159.] Drews, 116, Th. 24, reads, "Because, at that point, faith itself, reflection upon God, and the forgiveness of sins will cease along with the ministry of the Spirit." Drews, 116, Th. 26, reads, "The law itself will cease to exist along with all learning and prophecy and the whole scripture."

[160.] Drews, 128, reads, "The Holy Spirit will be revealed at that time, and whatever is able to be perceived by the senses, be it external and corporal, will cease. Now the Holy Spirit [seems to be] mediated to a certain extent . . . , but there we will see it in all its glory."

[161.] Drews, 151, reads, "We will see it as it is and bear its majesty. Because, at that time, our eyes will be cleansed and our hearts renewed."

391   not only fulfilled reputative in faith, but formaliter[162] in love, then the
Holy Spirit will have purified us to such an extent at the final judgment day
that we will be able truly to stand upright before God.[122] A doctrine of the
Holy Spirit that does not include eschatology would have its head broken
off. It would make no sense.

Now with great intensity, at the end of this long interconnected train of
thought, the question previously raised during the discussion of the Holy
Spirit's action in the law is raised again. This is the question of certainty.
How do I come to affirm that the Holy Spirit is within me? Indeed, how dare
I presume that it is precisely my faith that has been brought by the Holy
Spirit? Is that not, perhaps, horrible blasphemy? This means that the question we are facing is the question of the certainty of justification, including
the question of the possession of the Spirit.[164] It is clear that here the
problem is more difficult than it was above. There Luther had at his disposal the subjective proof of experience from the conscience. The individual
had factually died, not voluntarily but necessarily. Something had
approached from outside, had overpowered and morally broken the person. Was experience here just as clear as it was in the indwelling of the Spirit? Does it not lie too close, so that with an illusion one could coax oneself
from the fatal position into which the law had led? Certainly the individual
cannot tell whether innermost motives have truly changed, but God searches hearts. On what basis, however, should a person recognize that it is really not the individual but instead the Holy Spirit that works in the person,
that the individual really has faith, and that means that one is justified
before God?

Here conscience also fails, indeed, even the 'good' conscience in Chris-
392   tians;[123] but is a good conscience not a genuinely ambiguous phenomenon?
Certainly it remains the basis for everything that follows but it might not yet
be able to 'feel' faith.

---

122. Donec vere et prorsus purgetur (sc. peccatum) . . . quod fit in ultimo iudicio.[163] 61.
123. 439: Certe omnes christiani habent bonam conscientiam. . . .[165]

[162.] The meaning of the two Latin words is "not only through imputation in faith, but
in its form. . . ."
[163.] Drews, 61, reads, "Until it (namely, sin) will truly and completely be purged . . .
which occurs at the last judgment." The addition in parentheses is Bonhoeffer's.
[164.] The sentence was added by Bonhoeffer in the margin.
[165.] Drews, 439, reads, "It is certain that all Christians have a good conscience."

At first Luther answers simply that works should testify to you that you have really become another person, and that you truly believe,[124] because only true faith is active in love. This others will recognize in you and you will recognize in yourself that you are a child of God. This thought was developed later especially by Puritanism.[125] To be sure, Luther forcefully rejected the first objection that was made. Given the person's middle position between sin and Spirit, one questioned[126] how certainty over one of the two could ever arise. Luther gave the simple answer that it was not the case that the person does not exist perhaps in sin and perhaps in grace, but exists very definitely in both, as true as it is that the Holy Spirit came to sinful humanity to purify it. One has to make this clear in order to become certain; and every individual[127] ought to do this. If people do not do this, they raise themselves against God's glory. But Luther himself saw that his argument concerning the certainty of possessing the Spirit could not be supported in this manner, for two reasons. (1) Because iustitia externa[169] certainly still exists,[128] there are people who can speak as if they had the Spirit, and it is certain that they do not. (2) How can human beings reason nonetheless from their works, to which some imperfection and impurity always adheres, to an active faith created by

393

---

124. Christus requirit bona opera . . . ut nos et alii certificemur istis bonis operibus, nos certe credere.[166] 194: Est verum, opera certificant nos et testantur coram hominibus et fratribus et [. . .] coram nobis ipsis, quod vere credimus et sumus filii Dei . . . ;[167] cf. 214; 230f.

125. Taken up by Luther in the sentence that we "must make our call certain through works." From 2 Pet. 1:10; cf. 744. Cf. also 44.

126. 473: quia certissimum est, nos esse partim iustos, partim peccatores, . . . et si quis ignorat nec videt peccatum in se, consulat suum ipsius cor et conscientiam.[168]

127. Cf. 240; 742.

128. 502: Longe aliter est credere in filium Dei, habere et exspectare vitam aeternam, quam esse castum coniugare, honeste vivere . . . ;[170] cf. 436.

[166.] Drews, 204, reads, "(Christ requires good works) . . . , so that we and others achieve certainty through them that we believe without a doubt." The phrase in parentheses is added by Bonhoeffer.

[167.] Drews, 194, reads, "It is true; works give us certainty and witness to individuals and brothers and [. . .] ourselves that we truly believe and are children of God." Holl connects Drews 204 with 194, as does Bonhoeffer; see Bodenstein, *Die Theologie Karl Holls*, 344.

[168.] Read "et si quis ignorabat hoc neque videt." Drews, 473, reads, "because it is *completely certain* that we are partially justified and partially sinners, . . . and if anyone does not know this and does not see the sin anymore, then they should consult their own heart and conscience" (Bonhoeffer's emphasis).

[169.] "External justice."

[170.] The Latin text in Drews reads, "Sed longe aliud." Drews, 502, reads, "It is something completely different to believe in the Son of God, to have eternal life and to expect it than to live a chaste life, to marry, to live honestly."

the Holy Spirit? Luther answers[129] that the one who truly believes has the strength to believe that impure, imperfect works also please God and are pure and perfect before God. In this way individuals will attain certainty through their works. That means that *insofar as individuals have faith* they will attain certainty through their works, through which faith is initially *intended to be made certain.* We are clearly facing a petitio principii, but an unavoidable one. Faith can become certain only from faith. The possession of the Holy Spirit can become certain only in that one believes the Holy Spirit, and that means precisely that one "has it." Like can be understood only by like. God is because I believe God, and I believe God because God is. I have the Spirit because I have faith in the Spirit, and because I have the Holy Spirit I believe in the Spirit.[130] In this circle all thoughts of faith necessarily move. If they step out of it, then a circle never existed. That means faith and the Holy Spirit never existed there. Thus it remains a practical piece of advice from Luther that one should judge oneself and derive certainty from one's works. This advice is of great importance, but it takes something that in itself is a correct conclusion—if there are no works, then there is no faith—and turns it around, making it dogmatically unacceptable. Luther recognized this himself and therefore delved into the profoundest depths of the problem.

Everything that has been presented prior to this, insofar as it was not present earlier, is essentially knowledge that resulted from the antinomian battle. That means that it arose in the problem of law and gospel. In this connection, however, we have allowed one problem to be completely ignored, which in its context is inseparable from what we said above concerning the origin of faith. It is only for clarity that we take it up at this point. It is the question of the efficacy of the Spirit through the word.

---

129. 230: Respondeo . . . quod iusti et credentes habent hoc propter[171] misericordiam apud Deum, ut sciant sua opera placere, etiam quando sint impura, immunda et imperfecta. . . . Per se sunt quidem incerta, mala et impia, secundum gratiam sunt pia, bona, iusta, sancta . . . confirmant fidem nostram, et certificant nos, quod vere credimus. . . [172]

130. 360: Habemus [. . .] certum testimonium Spiritus Sancti in cordibus nostris, quod propter Christum certo sint nobis condonata peccata. . . . Hic reipsa et in me ipso experior Spiritum Sanctum habitare in corde meo et efficacem esse.[173] The testimonium Spiritus Sancti necessarily precedes.

[171.] Instead of this Drews reads, *per*, 'through'.

[172.] Drews, 230, reads, "I answer . . . that the righteous and the faithful have this because of God's compassion, so that they know that their works find favor even when they are impure, dirty, and imperfect. . . . It is true that in themselves they are uncertain, wicked, and impious, but due to grace they are pious, good, righteous, holy, . . . they strengthen our faith and assure us that we truly believe."

[173.] Drews, 360, reads, "[. . .] we have a certain *witness* from the Holy Spirit in our hearts that our sins have been forgiven for Christ's sake . . . here *I experience* with certainty, *in myself as well*, that the Holy Spirit lives and works in my heart." Bonhoeffer's emphasis.

We heard that through Christ the Holy Spirit has been gained for humanity, or that faith through the Holy Spirit grasps Christ. Now this does not occur directly through some kind of special outpouring of the Holy Spirit. Instead the Holy Spirit speaks—as impossible as this may seem—through the same word that we use daily.[131] There exists for the transmission of spiritual things precisely just this one medium of the word, which is suitable to the human capacity to understand. Because the Holy Spirit does not want to facilitate aesthetic emotion but instead a clear knowledge of God, it enters into this word. The Spirit veils itself in it,[132] because we cannot endure its unveiled appearance. The Spirit accommodates itself to *our* ability to grasp, and thus remains the Holy Spirit.[133] The Spirit must hide in earthly forms in order to be revealed to earthly beings. The Spirit is in truth [revera] in the word and, according to the content, the word is the word of the Holy Spirit as God, or the word of the Spirit that gives itself as a gift. Therefore the word is not always a gift; but at any rate it is the word of the Holy Spirit and regnum Dei efficax.[177] The paradox of this state of affairs must be mirrored in its effect upon humanity. If the Holy Spirit speaks through the word, then it is clearly not the word itself. Instead, it precisely only works through it.[134] Second, notwithstanding, the word is the origin of faith,[135] since it is only through faith that the Holy Spirit functions. How can I grasp the Holy Spirit's word? To be sure, the word has been so made that it is adequate to me; and its content is also to be understood intellectually. Nonetheless, its power that relates its content to me is hidden. Consequently, the only thing that remains for the Spirit is to establish this relationship. In order to obtain this

357

---

131. 128: Audimus enim (sc. Spiritum Sanctum) in voce humana in verbo.[174]

132. 151: Revera adest [. . .] Spiritus Sanctus, suis involucris tectus et vestibus, ut possit capi ab hac valetudinaria, infirma et leprosa natura ac intelligi a nobis. 150: Non tangit eos sua essentia, quia involutus est, quasi in aenigmate. . . .[175]

133. 480: Verum est, Deus dat Spiritum Sanctum propter verbum auditum datum seu praedicatum mundo per Christum.[176]

134. per [178] . . . 151, 145, 610.

135. 242: Verbum est causa fidei, hoc est certum, . . .[179]

[174.] Drews, 128, reads, "Because we hear it (namely, the Holy Spirit) in human voice in the Word" (Bonhoeffer's addition in parentheses).

[175.] Drews, 151, reads, "In truth [. . .] the Holy Spirit is present, clothed in its veils and robes, so that it can be understood by this sick, weak, and leprous nature and recognized by us." Drews, 150, reads, "Its essence does not touch them, because it is veiled, as in a riddle."

[176.] Drews, 480, reads, "It is true, God gives the Holy Spirit, in that the word is heard that was given and proclaimed to the world through Christ."

[177.] "The effective reign of God."

[178.] "By."

[179.] Drews, 242, reads, "The word is the cause of faith, that is certain."

396

relationship, I need the Spirit.[136] This Spirit, however, only comes to us from the word, and it was indeed for this purpose that the Spirit formed an alliance with the word. This means that, in order to receive faith from the word, I need the spiritual understanding[181] of the word. This spiritual understanding, however, can only originate from the word. Therefore, faith arises only from the spiritually understood word. This, however, assumes faith. Spirit out of faith, faith out of Spirit. Again we stand before a circle and again we were very intentionally led to it. When we look more closely, we see it is always the same holy circle that we encounter in the profoundest depths. Like can be understood only by like. God only through the Spirit, hearing the word or 'receiving faith' cannot be one's own deed, instead it can only be the effect of the Spirit (passio).[137] Through faith God creates in the human person an organ through which God can be grasped. God is, at the same time, the subject and the object of faith, and yet in full freedom the person believes in saying yes and no. Woe betide[183] the person who says no; for that person there is no forgiveness or excuse. There is no difference with the sacrament. Here also the Spirit works through external signs,[138] and here also only in that the Spirit simultaneously creates faith. Thus even children have received from God the necessary faith

---

136. 100, Th. 10: Sed Spiritu Sancto inspirantur homines Dei, ut interpretentur scripturas non propria interpretatione.[180]

137. 242: Auditus (verbi sc.) autem est passio et materia iustificationis.[182]

138. 131: Nunc . . . in baptismo, in voce humana videmus et audimus Spiritum Sanctum. . . . Sic Spiritus Sanctus nos per illa externa, quibus nos lactat et invitat, ad aeterna, coelestia [. . .] invisibilia, quae captum nostrum excedunt, ducit. 151: operatur in nobis per verbum et sacramenta Spiritus Sanctus. . . .[184]

[180.] Drews, 100, Th. 10, reads, "But, through the Holy Spirit, the people of God are inspired not to interpret the Scriptures with their own interpretation" (cf. 2 Tim. 3:16).

[181.] Holl: "What does spiritual understanding mean?" Cf. Holl (cited in Bodenstein, *Die Theologie Karl Holls*, 344): "What does *spiritual understanding* mean? *Personal* relationship, a relationship to *conscience.*" See also Holl, *Luther*, 556ff. Here and in the following Bonhoeffer takes up theses of dialectical theology. Cf. above, Bonhoeffer's essay on the historical and spiritual interpretation of scripture, pages 2/6:285f. and especially page 290f.

[182.] Drews, 242, reads, "Hearing (namely, the Word) is, however, passive and the material of justification." Bonhoeffer's addition in parentheses.

[183.] In Bonhoeffer's manuscript there is a footnote number at this point but the note itself is missing.

[184.] The correct references, to Drews, 129 and 131, read, "Now . . . in baptism [and] in the human voice, we see and hear the Holy Spirit. . . . By these the Holy Spirit guides us through these outward things, by which it entices and invites to the eternal, heavenly, and invisible realm which exceeds our capabilities to understand." Drews, 151, reads, "The Holy Spirit works in us through the word and the sacraments."

for the sacrament of baptism.[139] Here no deeper problems are found for the   397
Holy Spirit.

¶Here, then, is the doctrinal solution to the problem of word and Spirit in
Luther's thought. Dilthey has provided the psychological interpretation of
the process of intellectual understanding.[186] It is not of interest here in the
discussion of Luther's view of the Holy Spirit.[140]

In addressing the problem of word and Spirit, we have the key to the
problem of scripture before us. The meaning of scripture is a gift of the
Spirit and of faith, that is, therefore, the gift of Christ. We receive Christ,
however, only from scripture. Thus this remains, on the one hand, always
the ultimate measuring stick and plumb line. Nevertheless, dialectically
turned around, Luther[141] asks, "If we have the Spirit through Christ, why do
we need Scripture?" "If the opponents adduce Scripture against Christ, then
we advance Christ against Scripture,"[188] "thus we have the Lord, they have
the slaves."[142] Christ is the meaning and the criterion of Scripture, the
whole of Scripture and, therefore, also of the law. In him we have the light
with which we illuminate the Old Testament.[143] If I know that I have Christ   398
and the Spirit, then I am the lord of Scripture, because then I indeed have
the creative power from the Spirit in me from which I "can create a new

---

139. 94: Deus aeque potest infundere fidem infantibus atque aliis;[185] cf. 745.

140. It now becomes clear to us to what extent the question of the spirit of judgment can be answered only from conscience, which, in turn, after having received the
Spirit, can be answered only from faith. In the latter, the word of Christ is understood
by faith, which is the real basis for recognizing the possession of the Spirit.

141. 12, [Th.] 49: Quod si adversarii scripturam urserint contra Christum, urge-
mus Christum contra scripturam.[187]

142. 12,[Th.] 50: Nos dominum habemus, illi servos, nos caput, illi pedes seu mem-
bra, quibus caput oportet dominari et praeferri.[189]

143. 714: Nos habemus novum testamentum, lucernam illuminandi veteris
testamenti.[190]

[185.] Drews, 94, reads, "God can pour faith into children in the same way as God
pours faith into other people."

[186.] Bonhoeffer here refers to Dilthey, "The Rise of Hermeneutics," 246ff. Cf. also *AB*
(*DBWE* 2):54–55, 127–28.

[187.] Drews, 12, Th. 49, reads, "When, however, the adversaries attack Christ with
scripture, we will attack scripture with Christ."

[188.] This represents Bonhoeffer's translation of the disputation thesis that is presented in his footnote 141. In the manuscript, his footnote 142 was placed incorrectly and
belongs to the citation immediately following it.

[189.] Drews, 12, Th. 50, reads, "We have the Lord, they have the slaves, we have the
head, they have the feet or the members which the head dominates and which must be preferred to them."

[190.] Drews, 714, reads, "We have the New Testament, the light which illuminates the
Old Testament."

Decalogue."[191] Thus, in the final instance, we find that scripture is its own measuring stick; from scripture concerning scripture. With this the canon's authority totters. No single letter, like the letter of James, can have such authority that one might reject the doctrina fidei on its account.[144] Therefore, truly there is no verbal inspiration. Instead, we have in principle an open canon according to the measure of the Spirit.

Now how has God taken care that the Holy Spirit's word remains preserved for the world and is always carried further and disseminated? This is taken care of in the existence of the church, in the ministerium verbi,[193] [145] to which it is bound. Now, however, it must be concrete persons by whom this word is repeated. Here a difficult problem emerges. How can the word, which is spoken of in the Bible 'of' the Holy Spirit (i.e., about the Spirit as subject and object), how can such a word be repeated by human mouths without being blasphemed against or even becoming completely dead and ineffective? Here we encounter the emergence of the problem of the 'theologian' and 'theology' in the most precise meaning of the word, as the individual who reflects upon God and speaks, and especially the problem of the preacher.[195] How are preaching and theology possible as talk about God, faith, grace, Spirit, etc.? Let us begin by asking what it is, in general, that induces me to preach, i.e., to attempt to send forth the Spirit through my word. It is that it pleased God, especially in the service in word and sacrament, to bestow the Spirit and allow it to grow.[146] Therefore, preaching is duty, the theologian has a 'calling'. Certainly only those who possess the Spir-

399

---

144. 714: Non est tanta eius autoritas, ut propterea doctrina fidei relinquatur et discedatur ab autoritate relinquorum, apostolorum et totius scripturae. . . . One word is not so important for the Spiritui Sancto.[192]

145. 680: Verum est, ecclesia est alligata ad ministerium, ad evangelium. . . . Verbum that acts.[194]

146. 115, [Th.] 10: Placuit enim Deo per ministerium verbi et sacramenti Spiritum distribui et augeri. 266: Evangelium praedicare debemus. . . .[196]

[191.] Bonhoeffer's translation of Drews 12, Th. 53. Cf. above, 2/10:346 and footnote 82.

[192.] Drews, 714f. (the correct reference), reads, "His [namely, the letter of James's] authority is not so great that one would reject the teachings of the faith because of it and would be allowed to distance oneself from the authority of the other Apostles and all of scripture. A single word is not so important to the Holy Spirit."

[193.] "Service of the word."

[194.] Drews, 680, reads, "It is true: the church is built for service and the gospel. . . . The word: that is what does it."

[195.] On the problem of the theologian as preacher see Barth, "Menschenwort und Gotteswort," 119ff., esp. 139f.

[196.] Drews, 115, Th. 10, reads, "Because it was pleasing to God that the Spirit would be divided and made greater through service to the word and in the sacrament. Drews, 266, reads, "We must proclaim the gospel."

it themselves[147] can speak *about these things*; i.e., others can *speak* about these things, but they won't touch the subject. God desires this, and it must be sufficient for me to desire this as well.[148] Yes, truly "*I* want to inspire followers to impart the Holy Spirit,"[149] an undertaking that justifies itself only because God wants it and I must want it. Thus the preacher is the servant of God's word.[150] Preachers are given the assignment and carry it out as best they can. Another train of thought follows from this one in Luther. It is that God bestows spiritual gifts also on unworthy people for the good of the congregation. The gifts of God are not bound to persons but work of themselves.[202] Thus Judas Iscariot also *did* proclaim God's eternal word.[151] The sacraments can also be correctly administered by someone possessing a dead

400

---

147. 620: "De fide, de gratia nemo potest docere sine Spiritu" and R.[197]

148. 318: Deus sic statuit convertere homines. . . .[198]

149. 410: I want to make followers myself et Spiritum Sanctum dare, sed tamen per verbum.[199]

150. 318: Nos ministri sumus, non domini, qui docere et simul corda movere possint.[200] Cf. "ministerium."[201]

151. 689, [Th.] 41: Non est negandum, miracula fieri posse per impios in fide mortua, praesertim si sunt in officio vel coetu ecclesiastico; [Th.] 42: Sicut verbum et sacramentum id est, vita aeterna,[203] quae superant omnia miracula, etiam per Iudam Scharioth conferuntur. [Th.] 44: Ita Paulus 1. Cor 13 privatim ipsis nihil prodesse dicit, qui fide sua etiam montes transferant.[204] Cf. 730, Th. 9-12.

[197.] The complete Latin text including the "R" (= response) in Drews, page 620, is as follows: "Aliud contra 7. De fide, de gratia nemo potest docere sine Spiritu. Antinomi docent de fide, de gratia. Ergo habent Spiritum, et per consequens non sunt fratres diaboli. R. ad maiorem: Si intelligitur de fide vero sensu, tunc maior est vera, sed diabolus potest sic docere sine vero sensu. Ex hoc praecepto manifestum est, ipsos non habere verum sensum: Non assumes nomen Domini in vanum. Etiamsi scriptura per se vera est, tamen illi falso scriptura utuntur." "The following is against 7. No one can teach about faith and grace without the Holy Spirit. The antinomians teach about faith and grace. Therefore they possess the Holy Spirit and are therefore not brothers of the devil. Answer to the preceding sentence: If one gains enlightenment about faith with true understanding, then the preceding sentence is true but the devil can also teach without true understanding. On the basis of this commandment, it is evident that they do not possess true understanding: You shall not take the name of the Lord in vain. Even if the scripture is true in itself, they, however, use the scripture incorrectly." On the 'commandment', see Exod. 20:7.

[198.] Drews, 318, reads, "In this way God *decided* to convert humanity" (Bonhoeffer's emphasis).

[199.] Drews, 410, reads, "I would also like to teach students and to give the Holy Spirit, but only through the word."

[200.] Instead of "possint" Drews has "possimus." Drews, 318, reads, "We are servants, not lords, who can teach and move hearts at the same time."

[201.] The Latin *verbi*, 'of the word', is deleted.

[202.] Holl put a question mark in the margin.

[203.] The Latin text in Drews reads, "sacramentum et verbum (id est, vita aeterna)."

[204.] Drews, 689, Th. 41, reads, "The fact cannot be denied that the godless can also perform miracles when their faith is dead, when they are in an office or in the community

faith. Indeed, a miracle can even be performed.[152] An unbeliever could possibly do greater things in public than a pious, private individual. Yet 'faith' that leads to miracles is not a saving faith but is meant to be of use only to the congregation. It is certainly such a faith that is referred to in 1 Cor. 13. The people who are talented in this direction have been blessed with a singular trust[153] through which they can perform their miracles and deeds. Such gifts are distributed also to pagans. How much more will God bring about great things among God's people through the pious and the impious. Yet God will only do this for the good of the church-community. Thus, a personal action of the Holy Spirit for the church is assumed independently of its effect in creating faith. The gifts of the strong must also be related to the church-community in this manner. Luther certainly recognizes that miracles also occur outside of the life of the church-community.[154] This, though, causes him little concern. He never thought highly of any particular miracle because, for him, the actual[155] mira-

401

---

152. Cf. footnote 151.

153. 731, [Th.] 23: Fidem hanc publicae utilitatis similem esse dicerem motibus illis, quibus heroici homines excitantur. [Th.] 24: Necesse est, heroicos viros fiducia quadam singulari excitari, si quid magnum et memorabile sunt facturi. [Th.] 29: Etiam in gentibus ingratis dispersit semper excellentia dona et miraculis similia. [Th.] 30: Quanto magis populo suo tam per pios, quam per impios magna facere et donare potest. [Th.] 31: Igitur divisiones gratiarum, ministeriorum, operationum gratuita et publica dona sunt, quibus ecclesiae utilitati servitur.[205]

154. 689, [Th.] 41: *praesertim* si sunt in officio. . . .[206]

155. 730, [Th.] 16: Nam peccatum, mundum, diabolum vincere longe maius est, quam montes transferre. [Th.] 17: Imo Deum et proximum gratuito et perseveranter diligere, hoc est plane mortuos suscitare.[207]

---

of the church." Th. 42 reads, "just as word and sacrament, i.e., eternal life, which is greater than all miracles, is even transmitted by Judas Iscariot." Th. 44 reads, "Thus Paul says in 1 Cor. 13 that it does not personally benefit those who can move mountains with the power of their faith."

[205.] Drews, 731, Th. 23, reads, "I would say that this faith, in regard to its public use, resembles that motivation by which heroic people are motivated." Th. 24 reads, "At the same time, heroic people must be motivated by a unique assurance if they want to do something important and memorable." Th. 29 reads, "Even among the pagans, who are without grace, God always distributed outstanding gifts and items akin to miracles." Th. 30 reads, "How much more can God do great deeds among God's people and give them gifts through the pious and the godless." Th. 31 reads, "The distribution of the gifts of grace, the ministries, and the activities are therefore free and public gifts that serve the needs of the church."

[206.] Drews, 689, Th. 41, reads, "*particularly because* they are in office" (Bonhoeffer's emphasis).

[207.] Drews, 730, Th. 16, reads, "Because conquering sin, the world, and the devil is much more difficult than moving mountains." Drews, 731, Th. 17, reads, "No, it is much more that loving God and your neighbor continually and without hope of repayment obviously means raising the dead." In Bodenstein's *Die Theologie Karl Holls*, 344, Holl connects Drews, 689, Th. 41, and 730f., Th. 16 and 17, in the same way that Bonhoeffer did.

cle takes place where faith is at work in humanity, where the battle and the victory of love takes place in humanity. To love God and neighbor freely and persistently is the true resurrection.

Now back. Preaching is an office [Amt], and in this office we are not given a promissio Spiritus Sancti in individuo,[208] as the apostles were.[156] Because we hold the office we are not different people from what we were before. Yet the promise of Isaiah 55 stands behind our commission.[209] Whether or not it is proved to be authentic through us is not in our hands. The purpose of preaching is to give the Spirit. The word of the preacher either makes an impact or it does not, but it cannot move hearts like the Spirit.[157] If it does make an impact—very well, then it is not *his* word.[158] If it does not make an impact, well then, it just remains a human word about God, not God's word 'from' God.[159] I will never be able to convert through the power of *my* sermon unless the Spirit comes and makes *my* word into *the Spirit's* word.[160] At times the same words may actively impart the Spirit and yet at other times remain empty. One can conclude further that all attempts may fail; even citing the Bible doesn't help. This is not the way to capture the Spirit! Thus the word of people who possess the Spirit does not *impart the Spirit* on its own. Here the Holy Spirit must always join it anew, analogous to the action of the Spirit within the church-community, described above.

Now, how must we view theology, seen as an academic endeavor that indeed does not impart the Spirit but instead intends merely to reflect upon and repeat what is said in the Bible? The prerequisite for doing such work is the unconditional—not, as it is with the preacher, the conditional—possession of the Spirit.[161] Only in this way will the theologian be able to present an

402

---

156. Cf. 104, and see below.

157. 318. See footnote 150.

158. 733, [Th.] 25: Non enim nos sumus, qui loquimur, sed qui gratuito omnia donat, ipse omnia gratuito per nos facit et loquitur.[210]

159. See footnote 158. 266: Neminem virtute meae praedictionis converto nisi Deus adsit et suo spiritu cooperetur. . . . 318: Tangit, quos tangit, nihil possumus amplius. . . .[211]

160. See footnote 159.

161. 620, 7.[212] See above, pages 360f.

[208.] Latin, "promise of the Holy Spirit for the individual."

[209.] Cf. especially Isa. 55:11.

[210.] Drews, 733, Th. 25, reads, "Because it is not we who are speaking but the one who gives everything without thought of repayment and who causes everything to happen through us without repayment and who speaks through us."

[211.] Drews, 266, reads, "I do not convert anyone through the power of my preaching if God is not present working through the Holy Spirit." Drews, 318, reads, "God touches those whom God touches. We can do no more. . . ."

[212.] The citation refers to the discussion "Aliud contra 7" in Drews, 620. Cf. editorial note 197 above.

403

exegesis that is not the theologian's own.[162] If this is the case, however, everything that the theologian says about such matters will be true, because the Holy Spirit has arranged that the individual who possesses the Holy Spirit— better whom the Spirit possesses—can even say something that is logically false and yet obviously true.[163] Theological thoughts are superior to philosophical deductions and are not affected by these,[164] but they are bound by the formulas that the Holy Spirit has given and prescribed.[165] Thus theology must be cautious about what it says; it should reject those things that exceed reason and should repeat the formulations that the Holy Spirit has given and through which the Holy Spirit supports theology. These formulations must be completely adhered to, and "whoever does not want to is a heretic."[166] Yet, in the final instance, where the heart does not err the tongue cannot err either. The Holy Spirit forgives us our stammering.[167] Thus, in the final instance, the paradoxical phrases used by Augustine and others are not 'wrong'. But, out of love for the weak, who could be led astray by such phras-

---

162. Cf. 100, Th. 10.

163. 589, Th. 61: tanta est simplicitas et bonitas Spiritus Sancti, ut homines sui dum falsa loquuntur (grammatice), vera loquuntur sensu. Cf. [Th.] 62; [Th.] 63: Hic potest dici: Si mentiris, etiam quod verum dicis, mentiris, e contra, si verum dicis, etiam quod falso dicis, verum dicis.[213]

164. 50: theologia spiritualis, quam philosophi non intelligunt. . . .[214]

165. 596: Praescribuntur enim ibi nobis a Spiritu Sancto formulae; in illa nube ambulemus. . . . Spiritus Sanctus habet suam grammaticam . . . eloquentia est restringenda et manedum est in formulis praescriptis Spiritus Sancti. Non exeamus absque ulla necessitate, quia res est ineffabilis et incomprehensibilis.[215]

166. 777.

167. 603: Non errante corde non errat lingua, balbutiam nostram condonat nobis Spiritus Sanctus.[216]

[213.] Drews, 589, Th. 61, reads, "So great is the simplicity and goodness of the Holy Spirit that people who belong to the Holy Spirit speak truly even when (grammatically) they speak incorrectly." Th. 63 reads, "Here one can say: If one lies, then one also lies when one tells the truth, and conversely, if one tells the truth then one also tells the truth when one speaks falsely."

[214.] Drews, 50, reads, "the spiritual theology which the philosophers do not understand."

[215.] Drews, 596, reads, "Because the formulas have been prescribed for us by the Holy Spirit. We should walk in that cloud. . . . The Holy Spirit has its own grammar. . . . Eloquence should be limited and one must remain within the prescribed formulae of the Holy Spirit. We should not move away from them without necessity because the subject is ineffable and incomprehensible."

[216.] Drews, 603, reads, "Where the heart is true the tongue may also not be mistaken. The Holy Spirit forgives our stammering."

es (!), we should be careful with such paradoxes, even if we who are strong   404
in spirit can bear them.[168]

These problems concerning 'theologians' arise for Luther directly from
the stewardship of the word by the church and the dispensation of the Spirit. Yet the church, whose duty it is to administer the word, is itself established
by the Spirit active in the word, insofar as our having one and the same
Christ is the creation of the word.[169] With this the reciprocal instructive
exchange between the members takes place through communal faith transmitted by the word, i.e., it is through the content of faith in the communal
possession of the Spirit that the church becomes a community. If the Spirit
were not active through the word, then the element that builds community
would fall away. This word is the mediator between the invisible holy church,
in which only the Spirit is active, and the visible church. The true spiritual
church must necessarily be veiled. It is in the world, and yet not itself a part
of the world.[170] It is in persons, and yet is not identical to these persons. This
means it is hidden and can be recognized only through spiritual faith; i.e.,   405
the Holy Spirit has to reveal it.[171] Therefore the credo ecclesiam.[221]

Through the problem of the council that emerged following 1534, the
question that Luther answered in the disputation at Leipzig became acute

---

168. 603: Oportet nos retinere formulas a Spiritu Sancto praescriptas, praesertim
apud infirmos; apud fortes christianos nihil nocet, quomodo loquaris, sicut apud
me . . . ; apud docendos (!) est abstinendum.[217] Cf. 597.

169. Per Spiritum Sanctum in verbo omnes habebimus unum et eundem Christum, quem invicem alter alterum docebimus.[218]

170. 656: Necesse est, ecclesiam esse involutam in carne, sed non est caro neque
secundum carnem vivit, sic etiam ecclesia exsistit in mundo, sed non est ipse mundus
neque secundum mundum vivit, est in persona etc. . . .[219]

171. 85: Ecclesia non videtur oculis carnis, sed fidei. Ideo dicimus: "Credo ecclesiam. . . ." Cf. 86. 642: Talis congregatio ecclesia, quam, nisi Spiritus Sanctus revelaver-
it, non possumus eam comprehendere. . . .[220]

[217.] Drews, 630, reads, "We must retain the prescribed formulas given by the Holy
Spirit, especially with the weak. With strong Christians it doesn't matter how one talks, [for
example], with me . . . ; with those who need to be taught (!), one has to be reticent." The
exclamation mark was added by Bonhoeffer.

[218.] Drews, 410, reads, "Through the Holy Spirit we all will have one and the same
Christ in the word, whom we will teach, one to the other."

[219.] Drews, 656, reads, "It is necessary that the church is veiled in the flesh, but the
church is not flesh and does not live according to the flesh. In the same way, the church is
in the world, but is itself not the world and does not live according to the world. The
church is in the person, etc."

[220.] Drews, 85, reads, "The church is not seen with the eyes of flesh but with the eyes
of faith. That is why we say, "I believe in the church." Drews, 642, reads, "The church is the
kind of community that we could not comprehend if the Holy Spirit had not revealed it."

[221.] "I believe in the church."

again.[222] It concerned the relationship between the council and the church, and the council and word and Holy Spirit. The Catholic councils made the claim that they possessed the Holy Spirit. Luther maintains that a council only stands [under][223] the Holy Spirit when its basis is the apostolic word and not its own reflections, for the authority of the apostles is superseded only by Christ's.[172] Only they possess the promissio Spiritus Sancti in specie et in individuo[225] as a part of their office. Their followers do not have this. Through a specific divine decree, they have been made our teachers.[173] Such a decree does not relate to us, and therefore we, not the apostles, can err. Thus every visible commission of the church like a council can always only be a representative[174] of the infallible spiritual church. If it is more, then it happens by chance (fit casu), i.e., then the Holy Spirit is active and not the power of the council. As error and sin are present in the council, an individual with great spiritual insight into Scripture may[175] contradict the whole council, as history has certainly often demonstrated. In addition, this results

406

---

172. 100, Th. 1: Nulla autoritas post Christum est apostolis et prophetis aequanda. Th. 3: Apostoli certam (non in specie solum, sed individuo quoque) promissionem Spiritus Sancti habuerunt. [Th.] 5: Nulli successores in individuo promissionem Spiritus Sancti habuerunt. Cf. 104. 101, [Th.]18: Congregari facile est, sed in Spiritu Sancto congregari non possunt, nisi apostolorum fundamentum secuti non suas cogitationes, sed fidei analogiam tractarint[224]

173. 12, Th. 59: Non enim sumus omnes apostoli, qui certo Dei decreto nobis sunt infallibiles doctores missi. [Th.] 60: Ideo non illi, sed nos, cum sine decreto tali simus, errare possumus et labi in fide.[226]

174. 101, [Th.] 19-23.

175. 101, [Th.] 26: Et ipsimet dicunt, quod unus homo potest toti concilio contradicere, si meliorem rationem aut scripturam habuerit.[227]

[222.] For the Disputation of Leipzig (June 27–July 16, 1519) see *WA* 2:160–61.

[223.] The bracketed word was added by the German editor at Eberhard Bethge's suggestion.

[224.] Drews, 100, Th. 1, reads, "After Christ, no other authority can be considered equal to the authority of the apostles and the prophets." Th. 3 reads, "The apostles were given a certain promise by the Holy Spirit (not only the apostles as a whole, but each one individually)." Drews, Th. 5, reads, "None of the followers owned the promise of the Holy Spirit for themselves personally." Drews, 101, Th. 18, reads, "To congregate is easy, but they [namely, the participants in the council] cannot congregate in the Holy Spirit unless they have followed what the apostles have laid down and have not reflected on their own thoughts but the agreement of their faith [with the faith of the apostles.]"

[225.] "The promise of the Holy Spirit for everyone and for each individual." Cf. footnote 172.

[226.] Drews, 12, Th. 59, reads, "Since none of us is an apostle who has been sent as an infallible teacher by a certain decree of God." Th. 60 reads, "Because of this they cannot err, instead it is [only] we who can err and fail in faith, because we were not given such a decree."

[227.] Drews, 101, Th. 26, reads, "They themselves say that an individual can contradict an entire council if such persons have better insight or have scripture on their side."

in the recognition that apostolic succession in the church cannot occur through a person, as it does in Catholicism. Instead "the gospel should be the succession."[176]

The church is only there where the word is.[177] In the Catholic church, however, the gospel has been concealed by human perspectives, and so it is doubtful whether the Spirit is at work in the Catholic church at all. Luther apparently supports this in his reflection on Isaiah 55. Even under poor bishops the "church" has always existed.[178] Wherever the word was, through it the Spirit is effective, and there is the church. We should not live in fear of poor pastors and should not rely too highly on good ones.[179] Our faith is not built upon people, but upon the gospel.

407

With this we have concluded our overview of Luther's perspective on the work of the Holy Spirit in the individual believer, in the word, in the theologian, in the church, and in the council, i.e., here in the world.

What follows is the section on the doctrine of the Holy Spirit, strongly influenced by Catholic scholasticism, which Luther encountered. Luther spent a great deal of time working through this concept in the disputations, albeit for another reason than the scholastic scholars did. This reason was the doctrine of the Trinity. Where the scholastics speculated metaphysically and psychologically, Luther had a completely different interest. Precisely at this point he wanted to reveal the decisive inaccessibility and hiddenness of the Christian religion. He is tireless in his attempts to demonstrate that the dialectical rules fail and must become silent when confronted with this problem.[231] Here one must simply accept and believe. What would belief mean

---

176. 672.

177. 672: Ubi est verbum, ibi est ecclesia.[228] That is right.

178. 662: In ecclesia papistarum mansit vera scriptura et conservat est ipse mirabili Dei consilio. Mansit baptismus, sacramentum altaris, absolutio conservata divino miraculo . . . ;[229] cf. 105.

179. 105: Non igitur terreri debemus a facie malorum pontificum nec confidere in bonos pontifices. Deus non vult fidem nostram in hominem constitui aut aedificari. . . .[230]

[228.] Drews, 672, reads, "Where the word is, there is the church." [In the following sentence Bonhoeffer reports Luther's view of the Catholic church of his own time.] [PDM]

[229.] Drews, 662, reads, "In the papist church, true scripture has remained intact and is preserved through the wonderful decision of God."

[230.] Drews, 105 reads, "We must not allow ourselves to be frightened by the sight of bad popes, neither should we trust in good popes. God does not want us to base our faith or build our faith upon individuals." Bonhoeffer translates *pontifex* in the text with 'pastor'.

[231.] In the manuscript, the footnote text that correlates with this note number is missing. Cf., for example, Drews, 751 and 810.

if one were able to understand it rationally?[180] Consequently Luther does not want to pose a solution to the problem but only repeats the necessary dogmatic assertions from scripture, which have been prescribed by the Holy Spirit: one God,[181] but in this unity of substance three distinct persons[182] and each of these three persons is the whole Godhead.[183] The Son does not have a temporal origin but originates in divinity, and Father and Son are the origin of the Holy Spirit;[184] however this origin is not temporal. The Holy Spirit proceeded from both in eternity in eternal procession.[185] Here the numbers one, two, and three do not retain their accustomed meaning.[186] In this case, one can only think of them in relationship to each other.[187] All three persons have the same attributes and still one ascribes to the Holy Spirit, for example, the attributes of goodness and vivificatio,[233] even though the Trinity participates in this work.[188] In the work of the Son, it is only the Son who became human and died.[189] Yet God, Spirit, and Son are one persona incarnata and impassibilis.[234] However, when the Godhead of Christ died, the Father and the Son had to die.[190] One could continue in this vein. These paradoxical questions and solutions of the 'immanent Trinity' interested Luther only under the aspect of their incomprehensibility. As far as content is concerned, his doctrine of the economic Trinity is based on a grand concept. God the Father, in God's majesty, sends the Son and the Holy Spirit as gifts (in the larger meaning of the word!). Their efficacy, however, comes to an end with the end of the world, because in the status perfectionis[235] we no longer need the word or the sacrament (see above). Therefore we will not need Christ and the gifts of the Spirit, as these have allowed us to be pure before God. This is where everything leads that we have presented above in detail, and what can be proved from the passages cited above.[236]

---

180. 601: Incomprehensibilia esse credimus, si comprehendi possint, non opus esset credere.[232]

181. 785, [Th.]7.

182. 601.

183. 785, [Th.] 9.

184. 789.

185. 898.

186. 799.

187. 834, [Th.] 12-16.

188. 834, [Th.]10; see [Th.] 8.

189. 601.

190. 777.

[232.] Drews, 601, reads, "We believe that this is incomprehensible; if it could be comprehended, then faith would be unnecessary."

[233.] "Making alive."

[234.] One person "incarnate and impassible."

[235.] "State of perfection."

[236.] Final grade: "Good" (I–II), Holl."

Contents[237]

Introduction: Content and the Value of the Disputations

1. Law and Spirit

The origin of the problem of the Spirit in scholasticism and in Luther.—The experience of the Spirit in the law—Spirit and conscience. The objective meaning of the experience of the Spirit and the certainty of this experience—Mysticism and Luther—The Holy Spirit as maiestas. Concept of the maiestas Dei.[238] The concept of holiness.—Spirit and law—Holy Spirit, law, and sin—Contritio as opus legis[239] and the Holy Spirit.

2. Grace and the Spirit

Spirit as donum.[240]—Faith and the Holy Spirit. The circle.—Faith, Christ, Holy Spirit, and their inseparability; faith as a gift, the Holy Spirit as a gift, Christ as a gift, etc.—Faith or the Holy Spirit; Christ and God.—The question concerning the subject of faith. The hope of the nova persona.[241] Holy Spirit and the human being in this freedom and sole efficacy—The hidden person of faith and the Spirit, the imputatio[242]—The visible person of faith and the Spirit—The problem of the militant Spirit and its solution.—The gifts of the Spirit—Faith and Love—Freedom from law through the Spirit of the fulfillment of the law—"Beyond the law"? The strong—The more and less of the Spirit—The sinful Christian and the law—Law and gospel and the Holy Spirit in both—Flesh and Spirit; the ethical person—Daily repentance and the daily renewed possession of the Spirit. The donum perseverantiae,[243] predestination and sin against the Spirit—Spiritual assaults [Anfechtungen], their double character. The drive [of the] doctrine of the Spirit toward eschatology.—The question of certainty of possessing the Spirit. Works or faith? The circle for the second time.

Spirit and word. The circle for the third time. The relationship between the problem of faith and certainty. The sacrament. The problem of scripture; with Christ and the Spirit against scripture; the canon.

The *church* as the administrator of the word.—The problem of 'the theologian'.—(1) Sermon, the work of the Spirit for the congregation, apart from saving faith. Miracle. Fides heroica.[244] (2) Exegesis and dogmatics.

[237.] *NL* A 12, 4; handwritten. In *NL* 10f., the table of contents is incorrectly applied to the paper on the Holy Spirit by Frank. Cf. *DB-ER* 88, *DBW* 17:30–48, and below, 2/13a:404ff.

[239.] "Contrition as a work of the law."

[240.] "Spirit as gift."

[241.] "The hope of the new person."

[242.] "The imputation."

[243.] "The gift of perseverance."

[244.] "Heroic faith."

The formulae praescriptae Spiritus Sancti.[245]—The word constitutes the church in common possession.—Council and Spirit.—Gospel should be the succession.

3. The Trinity
Luther's interest in the subject

11. "Joy" in Early Christianity: Commemorative Paper for Adolf von Harnack[1]

[Overview of the plan of the work] [2]

I.	*Synoptics, Acts,* *Apocryphal Gospels*	*Mr. Goes, Göppingen, Würt-* *temberg, Blumenstr. 18 (2nd floor)* *Mr. Kern, Gaildorf, Württemberg*
411 II.	*John and the* *Apocalypse of Peter*	*Mr. Bonhoeffer* *Ms. Ludwig, Lichtenberg* *Realgymnasium*

[245.] "The formulas that have been prescribed by the Holy Spirit."

[1.] For Adolf von Harnack's 75th birthday on May 7, 1926, the participants of his seminar prepared a group paper investigating the concept of joy in the New Testament. This concept was especially loved by Harnack. Bonhoeffer, who organized and edited this undertaking (see *DB-ER*: 67–68), and Renate Ludwig, presented this paper with the following spoonerism. [A spoonerism is an accidental transposition of the initial or other sounds of two words. In this case, of course, the transposition is anything but accidental and the words '*heute freut*' in the first verse are transposed to '*Freude heut*' in the second. In the third verse '*Freude beut*' is transposed to '*Beute freut*' in the fourth.][MCN] The original poem reads: "*Drei Viertel eines Saeculums Dich heute freut. / Drum bringen wir Dir diese 'Freude' heut'. Das Seminar, das Dir die 'Freude' beut', / wünscht Glück und Freud', und daß die Beute freut!*" ("Three quarters of a century bring you joy today. / Now, therefore, we bring you 'joy' in this way. / The seminar, which today secured the 'pleasure' of this treasure, / wishes you happiness and joy, and that you will find pleasure in this treasure.") Only some of the contributions are preserved in Bonhoeffer's literary estate. In addition to the portions that are presented here, there is another investigation on "Joy in the Shepherd of Hermas, Barnabas, and the Didache," by Richard Ratter and Wilhelm Schäfer; see *NL* A 11, 6 (3). There is also a collection of citations of χαρά and related terms in the Pauline epistles from an unknown author; see *NL* A 11, 6 (4). The complete text could not be found either in the Harnack archives or anywhere else.

[2.] *NL* A 11, 6 (1); handwritten, except for two small additions not by Bonhoeffer. Documents in the archives of the Friedrich-Wilhelms University in Berlin (now Humboldt University) indicate that the following persons were involved: Helmut Goes, Dietrich Kern, Bertha Schulze, Anna Schümer, Elisabeth von Aschoff, Annemarie Nossen, Richard Ratter, Wilhelm Schäfer, Ewald Schmid, Dr. Gertrud Ferber, and Renate Ludwig; Frik and Tschuschner could not be identified. See the Index of Names for personal information about the contributors.

III. *Paul*	*Mr. Frik, Ulm a. D.,*
	Georgstr. 6
	Ms. Schulze, Nr. 31
	Ackerstr. 80 (3d floor)
IV. *Catholic Letters and*	*Ms. Schümer, Magdeburg,*
1 & 2 Clement	*Neustädterstraße 46*
	Ms. von Aschoff, Magdeburg,
	Halberstädterstraße 9 b.
V. *Ignatius, Polycarp*	*Mr. Tschuschner (?)*
Gnostics[3]	*Neukölln, Herzbergstr. 29*
	Ms. Nossen, Berlin
	Levetzowstraße 13
VI. *Hermas, Barnabas,*	*Mr. Ratter, Ulm a. D.,*
Didache	*Glöcknerstraße, shoe store*
	Mr. Schäfer, Steglitz,
	Maßmannstr. 12
VII. *Apologists*	*Mr. Schmid, Stuttgart*
	Gutenbergstr. 49 (2d floor)[4]
	Ms. Dr. Ferber, Wilmersdorf,
	Badnorickestr.[5] *35*

412

["Joy" in John][6]

Christian joy takes on a completely distinctive stature and meaning in the Johannine writings. The word χαρά is used most frequently and meaning-fully in those passages where John speaks most independently and pro-foundly. This occurs in the farewell speeches of chapters 14–17 (7 times) while it only occurs in the rest of the Gospel 5 times. Wherever John, in

---

[3.] Bonhoeffer added "Gnostics" by hand.

[4.] Bonhoeffer added the street address by hand.

[5.] Transcription uncertain.

[6.] *NL* A 11, 6 (2); handwritten plan by Renate Ludwig, written in cursive; the general editor was Bonhoeffer, whose edited version was printed. In order to document Bonhoeffer's editorial work, the passages in Renate Ludwig's text that Bonhoeffer deleted can be found in the editorial notes below. The Greek words, including those found in the passages edited by Bonhoeffer, come from Renate Ludwig. Preceding the text we find a collection of citations from John in Bonhoeffer's hand, which have been deleted. John: χαρά [joy] 3:29; 4:36; 9:56 [corrected to 8:56]; 11:15; 14:28; 15:11; 16:20, 21, 22, 25; 17:13; 21:20; ἀγαλλιᾶσθαι [be happy] 5:35; παρρησία [joyful assurance] 11:14; θαρσεῖν ["be of good courage"] 16:35; εἰρήνη [peace] 16:33. Under them one finds Bonhoeffer's comment, "Please place *all* of the citations of χαρά and χαῖρειν ["to be happy"], *with the text*, at the beginning; in addition place within the text the most important ones for παρρησία, εἰρήνη, δόξα ["glory"] etc., otherwise only chapter and verse numbers!"

413   truth, speaks of Christ's salvific meaning for us, of his and our relationship to
          God, there one must also speak of joy.[7]

          Two[8] *values stand in the center of the Johannine proclamation: "Life" and
          "Light."*[9] Ἐν αὐτῷ ζωὴ ἦν, καὶ ἡ ζωὴ ἦν τὸ φῶς τῶν ἀνθρώπων *(1:4)*[10]
          and[11] οὕτως γὰρ ἠγάπησεν ὁ θεὸς τὸν κόσμον, ὥστε τὸν υἱὸν τὸν μονο-
          γενῆ ἔδωκεν, ἵνα πᾶς ὁ πιστεύων εἰς αὐτὸν μὴ ἀπόληται ἀλλ᾽ ἔχῃ ζωὴν
          αἰώνιον[12] *(3:16). The*[13] *"eternal life" does not,*[14] *however, lie in the future
          (even if passages can be found to support this, 10:28; 11:25).*[15] *Instead* it is
          already present *in every moment of this earthly life.*[16] *It is indestructible and ever-
          lasting, untouched by* bodily *death*[17] *(11:25); it* fulfills and *surrounds time and
          eternity.*

          Faith in Jesus Christ brings ζωὴν αἰώνιον,[18] *faith, that is, in him who is the
          light of the world.*᾽Εγω ειμι το φῶς του κοσμου· ὁ ακολουθῶν μοι ου μη περι-
          πατήσῃ ἐν τῇ σκοτίᾳ, ἀλλ᾽ ἕξει τὸ φῶς τῆς ζωῆς[19] *(8:12 and similarly
          12:35-36). Light leads to life, as it can teach how one recognizes God and God's
          being.*[20]

          *Where "light" and "life" are, there "joy" rules as well. Where joy finds expression in
          the Gospel or the letters*[21] *of John, then it results from the knowledge of "light" and
          "life"* in and through Christ.[22]

          [7.] The first paragraph replaces the following passage, "*In John's religious life 'joy' is one
          of the primary factors. Sin, suffering—everything that separates humanity from God and disrupts the
          relationship to the Father—find no echo or only a very faint echo in his work. The deepest sources for
          this piety, which is the antithesis of Pauline piety, will be very difficult to discern, but perhaps a few
          points of departure might be found.*"

          [8.] Deleted: "*glorious.*"

          [9.] Deleted: "*At the beginning stands the elevated Word.*"

          [10.] "In him was life, and the life was the light of all people."

          [11.] Replaces: "*further, it means.*"

          [12.] "For God so loved the world that he gave his only Son, so that everyone who
          believes in him may not perish but may have eternal life" (John 3:16).

          [13.] Replaces: "*This.*"

          [14.] Deleted: "*anymore.*"

          [15.] Bonhoeffer adds a question mark to the Bible passages found in the parentheses
          and crosses out "*3:15.*"

          [16.] Replaces: "*can be fulfilled in any moment.*" At the end is written, "*It is mysterious full-
          ness.*"

          [17.] Deleted: "*in the usual sense.*"

          [18.] "Eternal life."

          [19.] "I am the light of the world. Whoever follows me will never walk in darkness but
          will have the light of life" (John 8:12).

          [20.] Deleted: "*to.*"

          [21.] Deleted: "in words."

          [22.] The phrase "in and through Christ" replaces "*In this way the highest shouts of joy
          resound where Christ is the subject.*"

In the light of John the Baptist, the people[23] wanted to rejoice for a 414
short time (5:35). Now they can rejoice for the first time in the light of
Christ![1] *Abraham already rejoiced in the day that he would come and, as he* was
allowed to see him from his heavenly home,[24] *he rejoiced in the fulfillment of
the promise (8:56). Joy ruled when he came. John the Baptist proclaimed it in a joyful
vision:* ὁ ἔχων τὴν νύμφην νυμφίος ἐστίν· ὁ δὲ φίλος τοῦ νυμφίου, ὁ
ἑστηκὼς καὶ ἀκούων αὐτοῦ, χαρᾷ χαίρει διὰ τὴν φωνὴν τοῦ νυμφίου. αὕτη
οὖν ἡ χαρὰ ἡ ἐμὴ πεπλήρωται[25] *(3:29).* But the light of the world comes
into the darkness, and joy arrives in suffering and grief. The joy in Christ's
coming is severely threatened by his death on the cross. It would have been
shattered if it had not been transcendent. In joy about Christ one does not
see a normal emotional response as much as one sees the certainty of an
inward possession that points beyond the world and its fears; cf. 16:33, see
previous page. True joy about Christ, therefore, can be found only where
peace in response to the suffering of the world can be found. Εἰρήνην ἀφίη-
μι ὑμῖν, εἰρήνην τὴν ἐμὴν δίδωμι ὑμῖν"...". μὴ ταρασσέσθω ὑμῶν ἡ καρδία
μηδὲ δειλιάτω *(14:27).*[26] This peace can be given to the soul only through
Christ; it is less "jubilation" than it is calm, certainty, and peace. It is not
something occasional or repeated, but something enduring, constant. The
disciples[27] *should be prepared for* Jesus' death.[28] Indeed they were supposed to
rejoice[29] *that he was going to his Father,* since indeed[30] the *Paraclete, the Com-* 415
forter, will come thereafter,[31] *in order to lead them into all truth.*[32] Εἰ ἠγαπᾶτε με,
ἐχάρητε ἂν ὅτι πορεύομαι πρὸς τὸν πατέρα[33] *(14:28).*

---

1. I very much doubt whether the word χαίρειν really had here the commonly
accepted sense of "to take pleasure," "to enjoy."

[23.] Deleted: "the disciples."

[24.] The phrase "was . . . home" replaces "saw."

[25.] "He who has the bride is the bridegroom. The friend of the bridegroom, who
stands and hears him, rejoices greatly at the bridegroom's voice. For this reason my joy has
been fulfilled" (3:29).

[26.] "Peace I leave with you; my peace I give to you. [. . .] Do not let your hearts be trou-
bled and do not be afraid." This citation is found in another place in Ludwig's text; cf. editorial note 32.

[27.] "The" replaces "*The light came into the darkness of the world but the darkness did not
understand it. In this way Jesus always had his death in his line of sight and also the . . .*"
(cf. John 1:5).

[28.] The words "Jesus' death" replace "him."

[29.] The phrase "Indeed . . . rejoice" replaces "*but they were not to be disturbed by his departure, instead they were to rejoice.*"

[30.] Difficult to decipher.

[31.] The phrase "since . . . come," replaces "*The Paraclete, the comforter will come after.*"

[32.] The quote from John 14:27 is found at this point in the preliminary text of Renate
Ludwig; cf. editorial note 26.

[33.] "If you loved me you would rejoice that I am going to the Father." The following
sentence is deleted: "*Here peace and joy are also found closely related.*"

It is not only the Paraclete who comes to the forsaken ones, instead yet another comfort is given to the believing community: they will[34] *see Jesus again.* For John the coming of the Paraclete, seeing Jesus, and the parousia are different expressions for the same thing, which will be experienced in the Easter-Pentecost joy. *From this point on, joy is a secure possession of the church-community;*[35] *this joy in the "parousia" will*[36] *be complete. All questions will then fall away (16:23).* This is the first time that the church-community can pray to the Father by calling on the exalted name of Jesus Christ.[37] Everything will be fulfilled for them, and their joy, their trust, their certainty in God will again[38] be complete (16:23ff.; 15:7, 16b; 1 John 5:15).[39] Once again we find an example of the breadth and depth of joy, χαρά,[40] in the Gospel of John. Joy is assurance in prayer and calmness in the face of the world's problems; both are given through spiritual unity with Christ and necessarily develop out of it. In this way the joy of Christ is brought to fulfillment in his disciples. Ἀμὴν ἀμὴν λέγω ὑμῖν ὅτι κλαύσετε καὶ θρηνήσετε ὑμεῖς, ὁ δὲ κόσμος χαρήσεται· ὑμεῖς λυπηθήσεσθε, ἀλλ᾽ ἡ λύπη ὑμῶν εἰς χαρὰν γενήσεται. ἡ γυνὴ ὅταν τίκτῃ λύπην ἔχει, ὅτι ἦλθεν ἡ ὥρα αὐτῆς· ὅταν δὲ γεννήσῃ τὸ παιδίον, οὐκέτι μνημονεύει τῆς θλίψεως διὰ τὴν χαπὰν ὅτι ἐγεννήθη ἄνθρωπος εἰς τὸν κόσμον. καὶ ὑμεῖς οὖν νῦν μὲν λύπην ἔχετε· πάλιν δὲ ὄψομαι ὑμᾶς, καὶ χαρήσεται ὑμῶν ἡ καρδία, καὶ τὴν χαρὰν ὑμῶν οὐδεὶς αἴρει ἀφ᾽ ὑμῶν. καὶ ἐν ἐκείνῃ τῇ ἡμέρᾳ ἐμὲ οὐκ ἐρωτήσετε οὐδέν *(16:20-23).*[41] Ταῦτα λελάλη-

416   κα ὑμῖν ἵνα ἐν ἐμοὶ εἰρήνην ἔχητε. ἐν τῷ κόσμῳ θλίψιν ἔχετε. ἀλλὰ θαρσεῖτε, ἐγὼ νενίκηκα τὸν κόσμον.[42] Καὶ ταῦτα λαλῶ ἐν τῷ κόσμῳ ἵνα

[34.] Replaces: "*instead.*"

[35.] Deleted: "*indeed.*"

[36.] Replaces: "*a.*"

[37.] The phrase "first . . . Christ" replaces "*above all they have the possibility to pray to the Father in the name of Jesus.*"

[38.] Difficult to decipher.

[39.] Difficult to decipher.

[40.] The words "Joy, χαρά" replace: "the word χαρά."

[41.] "Very truly, I tell you, you will weep and mourn, but the world will rejoice; you will have pain, but your pain will turn into joy. When a woman is in labor, she has pain, because her hour has come. But when her child is born, she no longer remembers the anguish because of the joy of having brought a human being into the world. So you have pain now; but I will see you again, and your hearts will rejoice, and no one will take your joy from you. On that day you will ask nothing of me." At the end is deleted: "Certainly this belongs to v. 33 [… illegible] as to the same chapter."

[42.] "I have said this to you, so that in me you may have peace. In the world you face persecution. But take courage; I have conquered the world!" (John 16:33). In the margin Bonhoeffer notes, "16:33; see the previous page." At the end of the Greek citation the following is deleted: "But the gospel goes beyond this promise of joy through the parousia, νῦν δὲ πρὸς σὲ ἔρχομαι (John 17:13a)." The words that were deleted connected directly to the text that followed.

ἔχωσιν τὴν χαρὰν <u>τὴν ἐμὴν</u> πεπληρωμένην <u>ἐν ἑαυτοῖς</u>[43] (17:13) and 15:11. Here the final *unio mystica with the Lord* is voiced.[44] *His followers overcome the world with him even when their bodies and souls suffer severe hardship.*

We bring these thoughts to full conclusion in conjunction with what is said in 17:22-23.[45] Ταῦτα λελάληκα ὑμῖν ἵνα ἡ χαρὰ ἡ ἐμὴ ἐν ὑμῖν ᾖ καὶ ἡ χαρὰ ὑμῶν πληρωθῇ[46] *(15:11)*. At the end of the speeches[47] the concept of δόξα once again stands in the forefront; unity with Christ in perfect joy, in life and in light, *is bound together with complete participation in* δόξα, *glory:* Κἀγὼ τὴν δόξαν ἣν δέδωκάς μοι δέδωκα αὐτοῖς, ἵνα ὦσιν ἓν καθὼς ἡμεῖς ἕν· ἕν· ἐγὼ ἐν αὐτοῖς καὶ σὺ ἐν ἐμοί, ἵνα ὦσιν τετελειωμένοι εἰς ἕν, ἵνα γινώσκῃ ὁ κόσμος ὅτι σύ με ἀπέστειλας καὶ ἠγάπησας αὐτοὺς καθὼς ἐμὲ ἠγάπησας *(17:22-23)*[48] *(see above). The only begotten Son possesses the* δόξα (1:14), *which the Father has given to him (8:54 and 13:31-32), or, as other passages attest,*[49] *which will be given to him at his death, at his exaltation (12:23 and 17:1-5). The raising up of Lazarus is meant to manifest the glorification of the Son (11:4); and Jesus therefore rejoices that he was not there at Lazarus's death. Seeing his* δόξα *(11:15) should lead the people to faith (11:15)* and thereby to participate in possessing δόξα themselves.[50] We thus recognize the Johannine concepts of faith, life, perfect joy in Christ, participation in δόξα as identical in content, only seen from different perspectives.

When, therefore, the faithful participate in δόξα,[51] *Jesus' joy is also fulfilled within them.*

417

[43.] "I speak these things in the world so that they may have *my* joy made complete *in themselves*" (John 17:13b; Bonhoeffer's emphasis).

[44.] The sentence "Here . . . Lord" replaces "What does this mean for the faithful? A final *unio mystica* [mystical union] with the Lord."

[45.] This sentence replaces: "*Now Jesus also calls his disciples his 'friends' (15:13ff.). The same joy in this union with Jesus is also expressed by the other phrase.*"

[46.] "I have said these things to you so that my joy may be in you, and that your joy may be complete."

[47.] Deleted: "in chaps. 14–17, in which the words of joy are the most numerous and meaningful."

[48.] "The glory that you have given me, I have given them, so that they may be one, as we are one, I in them and you in me, that they may become completely one, so that the world may know that you have sent me and have loved them even as you have loved me." The passage immediately preceding this ("is bound . . . (17:22-23)") is Bonhoeffer's abbreviated and rearranged version of the following Ludwig text, "*Beyond that, this also leads* [what follows is the Greek citation from John 17:22f. that Bonhoeffer left in the text]. *The unity in Christ is bound up with full participation in* δόξα, *glory. This was the highest hope of the early Christian congregation. It is a desideratum alongside of* φῶς [light], ζωή [life], *and* χαρά [joy] in John's gospel."

[49.] Deleted: "—*the statements are different here*—."

[50.] The phrase "should lead . . . themselves" replaces: "*should be sufficient for the people to believe* (11:15)."

[51.] The phrase "participate in δόξα" replaces "*to take this* δόξα *into themselves at the parousia.*"

418

In the First Letter of John[52] *joy is presented in a slightly different meaning.*[53] The position that χαρά occupied in the Gospel is taken by παρρησία.[54] Χαρά appears in the letters 2 times in a formula (1 John 1:4; 2 John 12), once (2 John 4), as does χαίρειν (2 John 4; 3 John 3), in no specific religious sense (that is, as in the gospel). Παρρησία 4 times (1 John 2:28; 3:21; 4:17; 5:14).

In the gospel this word is found nine times in essentially *ancient usage—speech characterized by sincerity. In the letters it would probably be translated as "joyous,* sincere *certainty." This term is very close to* χαρά, but is more active. If we assume the identity of the author of the gospel and the letters, the reason for this change in vocabulary is difficult to understand. There is certainly a connection between the practical character of the letters and the active-demonstrative meaning of παρρησία and between the religious educational character and the self-possessed contemplative disposition of the Johannine χαρά.[55] The term παρρησία points 2 times to the end times, to judgment and the parousia (2:28; 4:17). Joy and confidence should be in us at this time; faith, which exists in love, has no reason to fear the judgment. We believe that here we can already anticipate something of the confessional nature of early Christianity. At any rate we see that, for the characterization of this lifestyle, παρρησία was suited far better than was χαρά. Ἀμὴν ἀμὴν λέγω ὑμῖν, ἄν τι αἰτήσητε τὸν πατέρα δώσει ὑμῖν ἐν τῷ ὀνόματί μου. ἕως ἄρτι οὐκ ἠτήσατε οὐδὲν ἐν τῷ ὀνόματί μου· αἰτεῖτε καὶ λήμψεσθε, ἵνα ἡ χαρὰ ὑμῶν ᾖ πεπληρωμένη[56] (*John 16:23, 24*).[57]

[52.] Deleted: "2:28 καὶ νῦν, τεκνία, μένετε ἐν αὐτῷ, ἵνα ἐὰν φανερωθῇ σχῶμεν παρρησίαν καὶ μὴ αἰσχυνθῶμεν ἀπ' αὐτοῦ ἐν τῇ παρουσία αὐτοῦ [And now, little children, abide in him, so that when he is revealed we may have confidence and not be put to shame before him at his coming (1 John 2:28)] *and* 4:17 ἐν τούτῳ τετελείωται ἡ ἀγάπη μεθ' ἡμῶν, ἵνα παρρησίαν ἔχωμεν ἐν τῇ ἡμέρα τῆς κρίσεως [Love has been perfected among us in this: that we may have boldness on the day of judgment, because as he is, so are we in the world (1 John 4:17)]."

[53.] Deleted: "it is directed to the events at the end of history."

[54.] The sentence, "The position . . . παρρησία," replaces: "one could perhaps call it 'eschatological'. *Faith that remains in love has a sure hold on the inner similarity with God, the future judge, and does not need to fear a judgment.* Παρρησία, *i.e., joyful certainty, should therefore rule over him. In these passages in Greek it is not* χαρά; *that is present but* παρρησία."

[55.] The word "verte!" follows at this point. It refers to the reverse side, where the rest of Bonhoeffer's addition to this text can be found: "2 times the phrase . . . χαρά."

[56.] "Very truly, I tell you, if you ask anything of the Father in my name, he will give it to you. Until now you have not asked for anything in my name. Ask and you will receive, so that your joy may be complete." Regarding this citation Bonhoeffer noted in the margin: "See page 373f." Cf. above, 2/11:373f.

[57.] *"The same is also said in John 15:7, 16b; 1 John 5:13-14. This confidence in the hearing of prayer is a fortunate outpouring of eternal life. Believers possess this confidence 'in him', but only when they plead according to his will. Could they plead in any other way in accordance with the existing unio, but for what God wills?"*

In the letters, more than in the Gospel, the <u>communal nature of the religious possession</u> is stressed. The[58] *consciousness* of it *is a reason* for joy[59] *for the author of the Johannine epistles.* Καὶ ταῦτα γράφομεν ἡμεῖς ἵνα ἡ χαρὰ ἡμῶν ᾖ πεπληρωμένη.[60] *(1 John 1:3b* and *4)* . . . ἀλλὰ ἐλπίζω γενέσθαι πρὸς ὑμᾶς καὶ στόμα πρὸς στόμα λαλῆσαι, ἵνα ἡ χαρὰ ἡμῶν πεπληρωμένη ᾖ.[61] Joy, however, does not exist only when the presbyters rejoice in the path their spiritual children are following (3 John 4), but much more over newly won souls, that is, over the work of missions.[62] *This joy finds expression*[63] *in 4:36. The sower and the reaper may rejoice. The phrase "one sows and another reaps" does not usually have a joyful ring. Here it is different.* One Christian works for the other's gain; there is no ambition and no egotism, only common joy in the message that has been received. (I question whether καρπὸν φερεῖν, cf. 15:8, belongs here.) The odd fact that the term εὐαγγέλιον is completely missing from the gospel and letters of John and instead is replaced by φῶς and ζωή does not permit us to argue e silentio.[64]

419

Joy[65] *in the Gospel of John and the letters stands before us as a purely spiritual good that has* been given with the *person* of Christ—with his *coming*[66] *to earth as well as his glorification and "parousia." John does not speak of "joy" in the things of the world. We miss any ethical dimension in which joy could be seen as a start-*

420

[58.] The words "In the . . . stressed. The" replace: *"All the faithful, however, share communally in this possession of life,* δόξα, χαρά, *and this."*

[59.] Replaces *"to rejoice."*

[60.] "We are writing these things so that our joy may be complete" (1 John 1:4).

[61.] "I hope to come to you and talk with you face-to-face, so that our joy may be complete" (2 John 12).

[62.] The sentence "Joy . . . missions" replaces: *"And this also causes him joy when souls are won and have found the way to Christ and walk in truth."* Ἐχάρην λίαν ὅτι εὕρηκα ἐκ τῶν τέκνων σου περιπατοῦντας ἐν ἀληθείᾳ *(2 John 4)* ["I was overjoyed to find some of your children walking in the truth"] and μειζοτέραν τούτων οὐκ ἔχω χαράν, ἵνα ἀκούω τὰ ἐμὰ τέκνα ἐν τῇ ἀληθείᾳ περιπατοῦντα *(3 John 4)* ["I have no greater joy than this, to hear that my children are walking in the truth"]. Originally Bonhoeffer wanted to place the following sentence, now deleted, at this place in Ludwig's text: "This community [uncertain transcription; perhaps 'church-community'] of believers has, [uncertain] the greatest value [uncertain] and Christ rejoices in every newly won soul."

[63.] Replaces: *"This joy in the missionary movement stems from the gospel."*

[64.] The sentences "One Christian . . . e silentio" replace: *"In the harvest of the kingdom of God one person stands on the shoulders of another and the sower should rejoice just as the reaper does. The words in the gospel 15:8 and 15:16a belong perhaps in this context: the disciples should bring the fruit and sow the seeds of God in the hearts of other people.* [New paragraph] *The word* χαρά *is found also in 3 John v. 3 in a religiously neutral sense and* χαίρειν *= greeting in 2 John 10-11. The concept of* εὐαγγέλιον [gospel] *is missing in the Gospel of John. How can one explain this? Perhaps as follows? The message itself is already something that lies behind, something that happened, and was no longer so important. Now it is important that it is awakened to life in faithful hearts, and that is what the gospel will bring about."*

[65.] Replaces "χαρά."

[66.] The phrase "with the person . . . coming" replaces *"that is concentrated on the person of Jesus and his coming."*

ing point for moral behavior.[67] *This all fades into the background behind the other great experience, the unity between humanity, God, and Christ. The*[68] *"joy" that has its origins here is freed from the world and looks only toward its source: God and Christ.*

Χαρά appears in 3 John 3 without religious meaning, and χαίρειν is present in 2 John 10-11 where it means "to greet."[69]

Joy in the Revelation of John has a completely different character.[70] *It is not a religious possession, something that the faithful possess, but an emotional response. Although certain prerequisites are necessary before one can participate in it, it is accessible to everyone. One must understand that the words* χαίρωμεν καὶ ἀγαλλιῶμεν καὶ δώσομεν τὴν δόξαν αὐτῷ, ὅτι ἦλθεν ὁ γάμος τοῦ ἀρνίου καὶ ἡ γυνὴ αὐτοῦ ἡτοίμασεν ἑαυτήν . . . [71] *(19:7) contain within them the concept of apocalyptic*[72] *"joy." All the terrible things that the prophets had foretold and prophesied for the last days had come to pass. The only event that remains is the last judgment and final salvation.*[73] The seer sees this perfection and in the depiction of the end times develops an atmosphere that recalls some of the Psalms. The evil forces, those that oppose God, collapse; Babylon [Babel] falls; and the godly and those in heaven explode in jubilation (18:20). One seldom perceives anything like compassion or charity in this sharp dualism.[74] On the other hand, great jubilation[75] rings out when God, the Lord, and God's anointed establish dominion over the world and rule in all eternity (11:14ff.; 12:12). Here one cannot understand "joy" in the sense it has in the gospel. A

421

[67.] The phrase "We miss . . . dimension" replaces: *"We miss an ethical connection, which is suggested only once, in 1 John 3:21."*

[68.] Replaces: *"This."*

[69.] Cf. editorial note 65.

[70.] Replaces: *"is completely different."*

[71.] "Let us rejoice and exult and give him the glory, for the marriage of the Lamb has come, and his bride has made herself ready" (Rev. 19:7).

[72.] Deleted: *"or pertaining to the end time."*

[73.] The final passage of Ludwig's text, replaced by Bonhoeffer's editing, continues: *"It stands at the end of all things and looks backward from the state of perfection. Perhaps another passage belongs in this context, 20:6. There someone who takes part in the first resurrection is called* μακάριος ["blessed"]. . . . [New paragraph] *Those who have not loved their lives until they die are called happy (12:12* [the correct reference is Rev. 12:11]). *This passage points to another side of 'joy' in Revelation. An ethical moment comes to the fore and is emphasized in the same manner as is expressed in 18:20 over the fall of Babylon and in 11:15-19.* [New paragraph] *It is perhaps also necessary to note that* εὐαγγέλιον *is mentioned in 14:6. Here it is supplemented by the word 'eternal' and should therefore be seen as unchangeable and binding for all eternity. The last penitential sermon prior to the judgment is called 'gospel' and, like the message Jesus brought, includes a serious exhortation to repentance alongside of the 'good news'."* [Here, and in Bonhoeffer's replacement, 'Babylon,' a code name for Rome, is spelled by transcribing the Hebrew form of the name, 'Babel'.] [CG]

[74.] The word "seldom" replaces: *"not at all."*

[75.] Replaces: "great jubilation breaks out."

calmer word, such as "blessed" (14:13), might be more appropriate. All in all, "joy" is not an important term in Revelation. It is too closely connected with peace and is drowned out by the cries of battle, misery, and jubilation. All particulars can be omitted here.

The Apocalypse of Peter is likewise not productive here. The aesthetic moment distinctly outweighs the moral.[76] Neither the term χαρά nor related terms are present. We discover an almost childlike joy in the chiliastic passage in Papias (Irenaeus 5) when the harsh punishments that will take place during the 1000-year reign are described in minute detail. (In its everyday usage χαρά occurs in Papias, Eusebius, *H.E.* 3.39.)[77] The term itself does not occur.

"Joy" in Early Christianity

422

An Attempt at a Summary[78]

It is remarkable to see how much effort was put into the attempt to clarify how the Christian message evolved from its beginnings onward and how little one considered why this message was and remained a *joyful* message. If one asks about its development, one finds that what was perceived to be joyful and happy about the message most closely depended on the type of version that proclaimed this message.

From the colorful multiplicity of emotional impulses and thoughts that are connected with early Christian joy, we now will attempt to discover some guidelines for an understanding that is both historical and expresses its real meaning. On the one hand, one must take care that emotional complexes that have nothing to do with specifically Christian joy are differentiated fully from it. On the other hand, one has to pay attention to the extent in which Christian joy has infused "worldly" joy.

From the outset, early Christian joy is the joy of Christian believers in the exalted Lord. The joy of Easter stands at its beginning (see John 16:20-24), and with it we find the joy of Pentecost (see the separate paper on John).[79] However, because sending the Spirit has only interim character here, the concept is connected to the parousia. The source and focus of Christian joy

---

[76.] Deleted: "in Revelation."

[77.] *Papias,* bishop of Hierapolis around 150, composed a lost, five-volume collection of non-canonical sayings of Jesus from which the church fathers Irenaeus and Eusebius, among others, cite. A description of the 1000-year reign from Papias is preserved by Irenaeus, *Against Heresies* 5.33.3f., and Eusebius, *Ecclesiastical History* 3.39.21; both references are cited by Seeberg, *History of Doctrine* 1:70.

[78.] *NL* A 11, 6 (1); handwritten; first printed in *GS* 5:106–15. In the right margin at the top of the paper there is the instruction, "Please set the underlined text in boldface or underline it. Underline the title! 20 marks payment is included. (The citations for the paper on Paul follow.)"

[79.] See the paper of Renate Ludwig edited by Dietrich Bonhoeffer, above, 2/11:371ff.

therefore was found in the fulfillment of the salvific work of Jesus Christ (Easter), the actual founding of his church-community [Gemeinde] (Pentecost) or church [Kirche], and the hope of the parousia. Whether these three complexes are seen as being closely related or as being sharply distinct results in different variations in representing joy.

423   The first authentic report can be found in the letters of Paul; temporally later, though in content quite uninfluenced by him, the Gospel of John stands *beside* Paul. On the other hand, the whole development toward early Catholicism stands under Pauline influence.

It is very important for Paul's concept of joy that it be rooted in mission and not, as with John, in the religious life of the individual. Consequently, joy has a concrete and practical form. It emerges from the reality of Christ's resurrection and the hope of his (imminent) parousia. Yet joy is not primarily a human emotion, although it is naturally also that. Instead, it is an objective power that determines the Christian life, like righteousness and peace (see Rom. 14:17). It is similar to them, as these concepts are more than an individual's righteous and peaceful attitude, as necessary as this attitude is; instead, they are the foundation of the kingdom of God. They are values created by Christ, yet they have an independent ethos into which one must fully grow. They are not momentary surges of emotion but correspond in the nature of the case to the constancy of the new life. All of Paul's passages that speak generally of Christian joy and summon us to it are to be understood in this sense, especially those in which he refers to the joy of the Spirit (ἐν πνεύματι) (see separate paper on Paul).[80] Only thus can the striking concept of the joy of the angels and of God the Father be justified, which therefore cannot simply be understood as an anthropomorphism, as it might be in other cases.

The unheard-of energy and turbulent impatience that effervesces in joy, as Paul preaches it to the congregations, has its basis in the expectation of the parousia (Phil. 4:4, χαίρετε ἐν κυρίῳ πάντοτε . . . ὁ κύριος ἐγγύς,[81] even more strongly in the earlier letters like Thessalonians). The singularly

424   powerful tension between present possession and future fulfillment emerges from these expectations. This is where the work of mission, the building up and the growth of the congregations, plays the decisive role.

We can already see that John's point of departure lies completely elsewhere. The source of joy is obviously the exalted Lord. However, for John, the content of Easter, Pentecost, and the parousia coincides to such an extent that, in any case, no eschatological tension exists. Instead, the emphasis lies on the current possession of light and life. Thus from the outset

---

[80.] The only part of this paper that has been preserved is a collection of citations; cf. above, editorial note 1.

[81.] "Rejoice in the Lord always. . . . The Lord is near!" (Phil. 4:4-5).

Johannine joy reflects a quiet, reflective, and supra-worldly emphasis. The concept of mission also fades right into the background (see 4:35ff.), as does that of the church-community, and we get a picture of a highly personal joy resulting from participating in life and light. This results in John's unique association of the intimate connection of personal prayer with joy (see the separate paper on John).[82] In John, *eu*aggelion signifies complete joy in unity with Christ here and now as well as the overcoming of the world and the world's suffering; here as well, joy is not chiefly an emotional expression such as joyful agitation but rather is essentially identical with "certainty of faith." It is, as well, an inalienable, *religious*, and stable possession, which is always created or nurtured by reflecting upon the light that has come into the world. "We saw his majesty" (1:14; see Matt. 5:8; also 2 Esdras 7). For the Gospel of John the entire joy in Christ lies in this insight. In this contemplative method of observation there is no practical concretion. The Christian is not, as is the case in Paul, bound to the earth by the expectation of the parousia, but has in each moment eternal life and perfect joy.

Eternal life, the zoë aionios in John, corresponds to Paul's concept of the kingdom of God as present *and* future. Paul thinks collectively, always with the welfare of the church-community in mind. We also saw already that in Paul interest in the church-community and mission are closely connected to the temporal tension between present and parousia.[83] In the interim, Christian congregations were the God-ordained bearers of Christian proclamation and Christian joy. They were to rejoice in the things that had occurred in the past and those that would occur in the future. But they were also to be a joy to each other. This could only mean that one congregation [should] demonstrate to others that it is a member of the body of Christ. Here Paul introduces the term συγχαίρειν[84] (see the separate paper on Paul). Christians should rejoice in their neighbor's faith and way of life and be themselves a joy to the other. These thoughts necessarily arise from the life of the Christian congregation and also remind us of the letters of John (see special paper).[85] That they do not stray far from the concept of joy presented in the Gospel of John we see in 4:36ff., although in other instances only Christ can be seen as the object of joy. It hardly needs to be said that these are obvious in a perspective that sees joy as the foundation of the kingdom of God.

It is therefore important to be a joy to one another and to rejoice in the joy of others (2 Cor. 7:13), and thus to light a bonfire of joy. It is immediate-

425

[82.] See above, 2/11:371ff.

[83.] The words "that in . . . parousia" replace: "that in Paul interest in the church-community and mission especially resulted from the temporal tension between present and parousia."

[84.] "To rejoice with someone."

[85.] See above, 2/11:377ff.

ly clear that here we find how incredibly important the emotional aspect of joy is, and how much more important it is here than in the piety of John.

We must now address the practical considerations. How can one become an object of joy, and, as a Christian, what kinds of things can one rejoice over in one's neighbor? Paul is led to concretize joy and make it effective, not only because he emphasizes the Christian church-community and the life devoted to mission, but also because of the concept of sin, which was almost ignored in Johannine thought.

In Paul the notion of human sinfulness neither leads to giving up on joy, i.e., resignation, nor does joy's brightness drown out the message of sin. Instead, both stand next to or—better yet—over against each other. With this, however, joy obtains a practical ethical emphasis. It becomes the source of all virtues. (See the separate paper and 2 Cor. 1:24; especially 2 Cor. 8:2; compare Goethe's "Joy is the mother of all virtues"[86] with the fine distinction between "joy" and "joyous," which Paul presents as distinct in content, though not semantically.) Hence, Christian joy must be present in order for a work to be ethically good. Joy, justice, etc., are not sentiments that grow out of actions, but are values that make actions valuable. This new conceptual turn could never develop in John, because in him ethical dualism never exists.

In the following development joy continued to be connected with ethics, and it is precisely in this connection that what one called joy had its foundation. The relationship, however, has been turned on its head. Joy comes from the "good works" that one has done, and on the basis of these works one receives a foretaste of the coming glory. One already earns a bit of eternal joy in the present; joy is no longer the source of virtue and the foundation of the church-community. Consequently, it is no longer religiously based as the fruit of the Spirit but arises only in response to one's own ethical behavior as an expectant, reward-hungry hope. This is the type of joy that is primarily expressed in 1 Clement, and then in Hermas, Barnabas (see separate paper), and as it survived in the ancient Catholic church.[87]

Joy in the coming glory was strongly fed by Christian-apocalyptic literature, which was closely dependent upon Jewish apocalyptic literature. If one compares the description of the seven joys in 2 Esdras 7 with the Revelation to John, one will hardly be able to point to any specific differences. Exultation in heaven—which in this context equals joy—when one sees God and the fall and punishment of the evil one, etc., contains nothing specifically Christian. The crude chiliastic descriptions (Papias) of rewards for an ethical life pertain to this context. It is clear that these joys, which appeal to base

---

[86.] Goethe, *Götz von Berlichingen: A Play*, act 1.

[87.] See the outline of the plan of the whole work, above, 2/11:370f. and editorial note 1. The paper on 1 Clement has not been preserved.

human instincts, are not joys en pneumati.[88] To be sure, it did not enter the ancient Catholic church in this crass manner. The exact opposite occurred; severe moral discipline—in Paul it was based on the joy in the Spirit!—soon demanded much energy, and through initial organization the Spirit became dampened. Consequently one not only hears little about joy but one does not see much of it in life at all. In 1 Clement, the Pauline χαρά is "replaced" by a very pallid παρρησία.[89] The reversal in the understanding of joy and morality occurred automatically due to a deficient understanding of the Pauline concept of joy. (One cannot actually speak of a deficient understanding, at least not reproachfully. According to Paul one is either given the joy that emanated from the Spirit or one is not.[2] One cannot reconstruct it after the fact.) With this the door was opened for reward-hungry apocalyptic literature. Another characteristic of this reversal is the Christian attitude toward the suffering of the world. The suffering of the world could not affect John's inner bond with the Lord or the perfect joy of faith. He knew that fear belonged to the world, but that those who had been made perfect in joy had overcome the world with their Lord. It is nothing for them, not even an enemy. Paul also triumphs in faith over suffering despite adverse circumstances. Joy is haughty and victorious, "Death, where is your sting?"[90] (see the separate paper on Paul and John). Throughout history the church-community faced more and more misery; they were forced to confess and stand up for their faith, yes, even to be martyred for it. Victorious joy does not disappear; on the contrary, it becomes more distinct by the addition of something that is not found in Paul. Suffering itself was glorified. One rejoiced *because* of suffering, not *despite* suffering. Minucius Felix understood Christian martyrdom to be a glorious spectacle for God.[91] This developed from the idea of sacrifice, from imitation of Christ, etc., and certainly from a desire to reach an even more glorious hereafter through suffering as well. The first person in whom this mood of joyous suffering is clearly pronounced is Ignatius (Phil. 5,[92] cf. the separate papers).[93] However, Matt. 5:10-11 and the letters of James and Hebrews already point in this direction (see the separate papers on James and Hebrews).[94]

428

---

2. The objection that Paul often asked for joy is based on a deficient understanding of the relationship between the indicative and the imperative in Paul. The indicative is always the primary foundation.

[88.] "In Spirit." [The reference above to the seven joys in the Second Book of Esdras is to chapter 7, verses 90-99.] [CG]
[89.] In 1 Clement "joy is 'replaced' by a very pallid confidence."
[90.] 1 Cor. 15:55.
[91.] Cf. Minucius Felix, *Octavius*, 3.1.1.
[92.] Ignatius, "To the Philadelphians," 5.
[93.] No longer extant.
[94.] No longer extant.

Therefore, here we also see a broadening and softening of the Pauline concept of joy that is closely related to the reversal described above. This joy, however, could not be suppressed, either through organization or through moral discipline. It was powerful and pulsating, and because it was solely rooted in the individual it was an unabated power of early Christianity. Here one recognizes traces of Paul's spirit but, just as distinctly, elements of emerging Catholicism.

It was not the case that an impulse to renounce the world went hand in hand with this glorification of suffering. The exact opposite is true. One is able to observe that when Pauline thought infiltrated the Greco-Roman intellectual world, the Christian's indifference and enmity toward the world seems to have faded. What was retained and heightened was hatred against the "joy" of this world, especially in the Apologists with their distinct perception of the ideal of ἀπαθής.[95] However, joy in the cosmos and in creation already has a prominent place in 1 Clement and is prominent in the Apologists and here in Minucius Felix. A very unbiased attitude is assumed toward the "pure" joys of this world—nature, art, scholarship, play, etc. This would have been impossible for Paul with his concept of joy that was focused on parousia enthusiasm, and yet this joy has its foundation more in conventional philosophy than in religion. Therefore, it cannot be compared to the natural joy in Jesus' sayings, like that in Matt 6:29.

429

From our earliest sources onward this joy is presented as being powerfully active. It is joy in the life of the church-community led by Christ, in the *common* possession of faith, in familial love in social relationships, as well as in the life of faith of others and in the increase of members. This joy is central for Ignatius, Hermas, and others, and specifically in Paul's understanding of the word; but also here, out of the era of enthusiasm, organization had to form a structured cult. As we learn from 1 Clement, it was in Rome that this transition was naturally first noticeable. In Hermas, for example, joy and jubilation about the church as such, about the tower,[96] the pomp and majesty, prevail over the other about the common possession of faith and the other's life of faith.

We could be much more detailed here. Many more commonalties and differences could be discovered, but that is not our intention.

Before we close, we would like to point briefly to a type of Christian joy as yet unmentioned. It is joy according to the Gnostics. *Redemption* and *revelation* are objects of joy for these people. Consequently, they are values of the highest intellectual endeavor and result from the feeling of *moral* and *intellectual* inadequacy. We find the first already in Paul, even though it is not as one-

---

[95.] "Immunity to suffering."
[96.] In *The Shepherd*, Hermas uses 'tower' as a metaphor for the church, following its metaphorical use in the Song of Songs. [CG]

sided as it is in the Gnostic writings, and the way has been paved for the second by John (especially in passages like 16:23, and others). We see that both the concept of the church-community and inner personal *joy* in the *bond* with Christ are missing. Although the latter is missing to a lesser extent than the former, this gives their joy an aura that seems truly alien to reality.

To sum up, it can be said that the development of Catholicism favored one of the two main prototypes of Christian joy. The Pauline prototype, with its emphasis on the church-community, completely pushed aside the Johannine prototype. The process described above occurred as the era of the Spirit turned into the era of "morality" and organization. Christian joy could not find a foothold where the Spirit had departed. The early-Christian kingdom of God became the church. The Spirit was not in the church-community as such; instead it was in individual people. Christian joy was present only in individuals (martyrs!). This was the case because joy about the church could only in a very indirect way be called Christian. Johannine joy lived on in the individuals; up until the Middle Ages, it remained a corrective force for the distorted Pauline concept.

430

12. Paper on Early Lutheran Eschatology[1]

The Doctrine of Life after Death and
the Last Things in Early Protestant Dogmatics

Eschatology does not in fact belong to the controversial subjects of early Protestant dogmatics. There is essential agreement, and we seldom need to elaborate the disagreements.[2]

[1.] *NL* A 12, 3; handwritten. The title page reads, "Report on Early Protestant Eschatology. May 14, 1926." On the first page, upper left, is the name: "Dietrich Bonhoeffer." The paper was read in Seeberg's seminar (see the course list, Appendix 3 below, page 585) and was evaluated by him. Apart from the last two paragraphs and several critical comments, in this manuscript Bonhoeffer wove together two sources either verbatim or practically verbatim: Karl von Hase, *Hutterus redivivus* (12th edition, 1883) and Heinrich Schmid, *Die Dogmatik der evangelisch-lutherischen Kirche* (7th edition, 1893). [The English translation of the 5th edition, *The Doctrinal Theology of the Evangelical Lutheran Church*, differs considerably from the edition Bonhoeffer used; page numbers cited here are from the German 7th edition.] [PDM] Bonhoeffer owned editions of both compendiums and still had them in his personal library at Finkenwalde, according to Albrecht Schönherr. In order to demonstrate how they were used in this paper, the editorial notes will cite, after the page number, the numbers of the lines Bonhoeffer has incorporated; continuously quoted lines are joined by a hyphen, otherwise lines from which words are quoted are separated by commas—however, reference to specific words quoted from the two sources will not be given.

[2.] Bonhoeffer, like Hase (see V and often), understands "early Protestant Dogmatics" to be "early Lutheran Dogmatics" (VII) or "Lutheran Orthodoxy" (XI). As far as their "agreement" is concerned Bonhoeffer follows Schmid's judgment (VIf. and VIII). Bonhoeffer is not acquainted with the passages cited by von Hase and Schmid. Cf. editorial note 80.

The goal of human life is not yet reached with justification[3] but is completed only in the end time,[4] when the power of original sin is broken and the Holy Spirit takes possession of the whole person.[5] At that point the individual and the whole world will proceed toward the fulfillment of their existence, and the church triumphant will emerge from the church militant.[6]

431

Both sides of the consummation, the consummation of the μικροκοσ-μος,[7] i.e., the human being, and the consummation of the μακροκοσμος,[8] i.e., the world, are discussed in the *locus de novissimis*.[9] Consummation, or better the goal of an individual's life, which is the vita or damnatio acterna,[10] is associated very closely with the idea of predestination.[11] Consequently, Calixtus's analytical methodology discussed this article as the finis theologiae formalis[12] and placed it in the locus de Deo.[13] The four remaining articles, on mors, resurrectio mortuorum, extremum iudicium, and consummatio mundi, were discussed in the locus de novissimis.[14] Although there can be no doubt that placing the article on vita or damnatio aeterna in the locus [de] Deo can be objectively justified, it results in a rupture that is disadvantageous for the overall understanding of eschatology. This is the reason we follow the earlier discussion of eschatology, e.g., by Gerhard, and retain the order in which the articles are customarily presented: mors, resurrectio mortuorum, judicium extremum, consummatio mundi, vita or damnatio aeterna.[15]

For our early Protestant theologians death[16] was not actually a problem as we understand it.[17] Because of the rigid distinction between the substance of soul and body, belief in immortality is not threatened.[18] Soul and body separate themselves from each other,[19] as if they had never belonged

---

[3.] Schmid, *Dogmatik*, 461, 4.

[4.] Seeberg: "more likely the hereafter."

[5.] Hase, *Hutterus redivivus*, 278, 13, 15, 16.

[6.] Hase, *Hutterus*, 278, 20, 21, 16, 17; 264, 39–265, 1; Schmid, *Dogmatik*, 432, 31–33; 462, 22, 23, 25, 26.

[7.] "Microcosm."

[8.] "Macrocosm."

[9.] "Chapter on the last things." Hase, *Hutterus*, 278, 38–40, 11; Schmid, *Dogmatik*, 462, 37, 38; 463, 8–10.

[10.] "Eternal life or eternal damnation."

[11.] Seeberg: "Providence."

[12.] "Formal [i.e., inner] goal of theology [in itself]."

[13.] "Chapter, 'God'."

[14.] "Death, resurrection from the dead, final judgment, consummation of the world"; Schmid, *Dogmatik*, 462, 32–37, combined with Hase, *Hutterus*, 33, 17–20.

[15.] Like Schmid, *Dogmatik*, 462, 37.

[16.] See editorial note 2.

[17.] Cf. Hase, *Hutterus*, 279, 3–6.

[18.] Cf. ibid., 279, 6, 7.

[19.] Ibid., 279, 1, 2, 28, and Schmid, *Dogmatik*, 462, 17, 18; 463, 13, 14.

together, like two halves of a ball that had been pushed together or liquid being poured out of a container. Although their reciprocal effects on each other[20] were clear, no difficulty was perceived when their relationship with each other ceased. Gerhard proposed that the emotions and the passions of the soul no longer had any effect on the body following their separation from each other. Moreover, the body became dust and the soul no longer acted through the instrument of the body sed extra corpus subsistens immortalem agit vitam atque ab omni corporis commercio semota in certo ποῦ adversatur (Gerhard, 17:149).[21] The soul now lives on and is able to use its intellect and will far away from the body.[22] Certainty that this will occur is based on scriptural testimony,[23] as in Matt. 10:28, μὴ φοβεῖσθε ἀπὸ τῶν ἀποκτενόντων τὸ σῶμα, τὴν δὲ ψυχὴν μὴ δυναμένων ἀποκτεῖναι, etc.,[24] and is taken from the idea that God's breath created the soul.[25] This realization can be approached by reason,[26] as these proofs are very likely to contain a quandam veri similitudinis persuasionem (17:159).[27] The soul is cognitive substance. It is nonorganic, simple, invisible, immaterial, similar to God, and a self-moving essence. It also has an inborn ability to distinguish between good and evil, a "religious predisposition," ecstasin quandam, h.e. intentam partis rationalis ad res sublimes.[28] The sum total of these facts should have forced the philosophers e lumine naturae et historiae[29] to believe in the eternity of the soul, but certainty can only be attained through the Scriptures.[30]

Now whence does death, mors temporalis,[31] enter the world? Gerhard lists three ways: the devil's maliciousness, humanity's sin, and God's avenging wrath (17:30).[32] Through Christ, however, the fate of death has been trans-

432

[20.] Schmid, Dogmatik, 464, 39–43.

[21.] "But subsisting outside the body, it leads an immortal life and, removed from all communion with the body, it is preserved in a definite location" (Schmid, Dogmatik, 464, 47–165, 6). [The Gerhard work that Bonhoeffer cites from Schmid is Loci Theologici, the standard edition of which was 20 volumes plus index.] [CG]

[22.] Schmid, Dogmatik, 461, 23, 24.

[23.] Ibid., 461, 26–28; 465, 9, 10. Cf. Hase, Hutterus, 280, 5.

[24.] "Do not fear those who kill the body but cannot kill the soul" (Schmid, Dogmatik, 465, 11, 12).

[25.] Schmid, Dogmatik, 465, 17–25.

[26.] Ibid., 461, 25, 26.

[27.] "A certain persuasion of plausibility" (Hase, Hutterus, 280, 33–35; Schmid, Dogmatik, 466, 1–3). [Bonhoeffer cites Gerhard again.] [CG]

[28.] "A certain ecstasy in (its) rational part, i.e., directed toward sublime things" (Schmid, Dogmatik, 466, 5–11, 18, 19, 26–28.)

[29.] "From the light of nature and history."

[30.] Hase, Hutterus, 280, 6, 35–37.

[31.] "Death in time," death prior to the last judgment is meant (Hase, Hutterus, 279, 29, 30). Bonhoeffer did not take into consideration the distinctions in Schmid, Dogmatik, 463, 20ff.

[32.] Schmid, Dogmatik, 463, 40–43.

433 formed into something beneficial for all who believe in him. They merely proceed through death into life.[33] Where do the souls live after death but prior to the last judgment? In answer, Catholic scholasticism added the doctrine of purgatory into its geography of the hereafter. But these teachings were rejected by Protestants on solid theological grounds.[34] Humanity can be justified only through Christ, quidquid expiationibus vel purgatorii vel suffragiorum adscribitur, id omne Christi merito, quod solum nos a peccatis purgat, derogatur[35] (Hafenreffer, 667). The reason that these retorts could not stand up under critical reflection is clear. Why shouldn't Christ's purifying work also affect the hereafter?[36] It seems to me that here some wheat was pulled out along with the weeds. Views on the status intermedius,[37] such as the wandering of souls and the sleep of souls, etc., were rejected for similar reasons.[38] Consequently, one taught that there was an immediate transition from death to a life that was either eternally blessed or eternally damned.[39] The fate of every individual was decided in the iudicium particulare[40] during the final convulsions preceding death.[41] After death, some immediately enjoy eternal happiness while others suffer eternal damnation.[42] Beginning with Baumgarten and Mosheim, theology stipulated that this state was not final.[43] If it were, as Quenstedt[44] and others propose, then the meaning of the resurrection would be unclear.[45]

The Bible, however, teaches the resurrection[46] in the sense that the immortal soul will be reunited with a body at the end of time, and specifically, at the general resurrectio mortuorum.[47] Because it is biblically based, the necessity of this process is rarely pondered[48] but merely its form. The

434 most prevalent attitude, that only a corporeal being can live in community

---

[33.] Schmid, *Dogmatik*, 464, 2–5, is somewhat different.

[34.] Hase, *Hutterus*, 281, 9–282, 3, 24.

[35.] "Whatever is attributed to works of expiation, whether those in relation to purgatory or intercessions, takes away from Christ's merit, which alone cleanses us from sin" (Schmid, *Dogmatik*, 467, 39–43). [Bonhoeffer cites from Schmid the *Loci theologici* of Matthias Hafenreffer.] [PDM]

[36.] Cf. Hase, *Hutterus*, 282, 6, 7, 43–52.

[37.] The "intermediate state," between death and the last judgment.

[38.] Hase, *Hutterus*, 282, 8–10; Schmid, *Dogmatik*, 462, 4–6; 467, 1, 2, 7–14.

[39.] Hase, *Hutterus*, 282, 4, 5.

[40.] The phrase "particular judgment" refers to the judgment of the individual.

[41.] Hase, *Hutterus*, 282, 5, 6, 39, 40.

[42.] Seeberg: "!." Schmid, *Dogmatik*, 462, 1, 2; 466, 33–39.

[43.] See editorial note 36.

[44.] Hase, *Hutterus*, 282, 40–43, and Schmid, *Dogmatik*, 467, 2–7.

[45.] Cf. Hase, *Hutterus*, 282, 45, 46, and Schmid, *Dogmatik*, 468, 11–16; 470, 5–8.

[46.] Schmid, *Dogmatik*, 468, 5.

[47.] Ibid., 474, 2.

[48.] Cf. Schmid, *Dogmatik*, 468, 19–29, and Hase, *Hutterus*, 285, 3, 4.

with others and have an active intellectual life, is central to the discussion.[49] The new body must have completely different attributes from the old.[50] According to Quenstedt, certain traits will be shared by good and evil persons: the physical body will be restored and it will be imperishable, the differences between the sexes will remain, and, as far as age is concerned, it was agreed that the bodies of the faithful would be about the age of Christ, i.e., somewhere around thirty years old.[51] The bodies of the faithful will be glorificata, potentia, spiritualia, coelestia.[52] The bodies of the godless will also be eternal, but non impassibilia, aeternis cruciatibus obnoxia, nullo decore, nulla gloria, etc.[53] Understood in this way, the resurrection is particularly resurrectio carnis,[54] for death brings no changes to the soul. Only the flesh, which had turned to dust, will be reawakened.[55] However, at the time of the general resurrection[56] people will still be living[57] on earth. These people will not need to die first but will be transformed.[58] They will experience ad statum resurgentium transfiguratio.[59]

All of this will occur only following Christ's return.[60] No one, however, knows when the reditus Christi[61] will take place.[62] Christ has revealed the signs[63] and only from them can one conclude when the world will end.[64] Here as well, theologians hold fast to the biblical statements and work only in a quite formal way. Signa remota s. communia and signa propinqua s. propria are differentiated from each other.[65] The former repeat themselves and point more toward seriousness and holiness than to the exact time of Christ's reditus.[66] The latter immediately precede the last judgment.[67] To the former belong haeresium multiplicatio, securitatis et impietatis inunda-

435

[49.] Seeberg: "Where is this?" Bonhoeffer cites Hase, *Hutterus*, 285, 2, 3, 4, 5, 9–11, 45.

[50.] Cf. Schmid, *Dogmatik*, 468, 9–11.

[51.] Hase, *Hutterus*, 285, 19–23, and Schmid, *Dogmatik*, 469, 12–14.

[52.] "Glorified, powerful, spiritual, heavenly." Hase, *Hutterus*, 285, 28–33, and Schmid, *Dogmatik*, 469, 24–44.

[53.] "Not unable to suffer, subject to eternal tortures, without honor, without glory" (Schmid, *Dogmatik*, 469, 46–470, 2).

[54.] "Resurrection of the flesh" (Hase, *Hutterus*, 284, 39–43).

[55.] Cf. Hase, *Hutterus*, 284, 45, 46, and Schmid, *Dogmatik*, 468, 30–32.

[56.] Schmid, *Dogmatik*, 474, 42.

[57.] Schmid, *Dogmatik*, 470, 13, 14, and Hase, *Hutterus*, 284, 8, 9.

[58.] Hase, *Hutterus*, 284, 52.

[59.] "Transfiguration to the state of the resurrected" (Hase, *Hutterus*, 284, 9).

[60.] Ibid., 282, 14.

[61.] "The return of Christ" (Hase, *Hutterus*, 282, 12).

[62.] Schmid, *Dogmatik*, 471, 28–30.

[63.] Hase, *Hutterus*, 283, 1, 2.

[64.] Schmid, *Dogmatik*, 470, 12, 20, 21.

[65.] "Distant or general signs, and near or particular signs."

[66.] "Return." Schmid, *Dogmatik*, 471, 34–41.

[67.] Hase, *Hutterus*, 283, 35.

tio, universalis evangelii praedicatio.[68] The latter include the collapse of the fourth world kingdom, antichrists,[69] and powerful signs.[70] Some theologians also include in this list the final conversion of the Jews according to Rom. 11:25ff.[71] When referring to the antichrists, biblical accounts are used to differentiate between the antichristi parvi and the antichristus magnus.[72] Most of the time the idea of the conversio Judaeorum[73] is rejected as an unjustified transfer of a historically based concern into the discipline of theology.

We find, therefore, that the early Christian picture of the end of history has been adopted intact, even in details. In contrast to all evolutionary ideas, a sharp antithesis in the development of the world is emphasized, rendering impossible any weak eschatology or concept about the kingdom of God. Its purely transcendent character is maintained, but we miss any philosophical attempt to comprehend and to expound on the biblical statements. Religiously significant concepts are intermingled with pure biblical fantasies that have been accepted as dogmatic truths. Thus it becomes abundantly clear that no coherent dogmatic method is present.

The millenarians believed[74] that when Christ returns he would establish a glorious thousand-year kingdom and rule with his elect. This chiliasm,[75] however, is rejected on the grounds that the return of Christ, the universal resurrection, the last judgment, and the end of the world are so closely connected that there is no time at all in the middle of this process for the establishment of an earthly kingdom. One event follows the other with no time in between.[76] This objection, however, may have been apologetic in nature. The actual antipathy toward chiliasm[77] may have arisen from a justified awareness of the danger of losing one's self in the material world, as well as from an awareness of the revolutionary-sectarian and irreligious tendencies that often accompanied chiliasm.[78]

Christ will descend on the clouds in divine-human nature—a horror to the godless and a joy to the pious. Following the resurrection of the dead he

436

[68.] "The multiplication of heresies, the inundation of security and impiety, worldwide preaching of the gospel."

[69.] Schmid, *Dogmatik,* 471, 44, 45; 472, 22, 24–27.

[70.] Cf. Schmid, *Dogmatik,* 470, 20, 22, 23, and Hase, *Hutterus,* 283, 36.

[71.] Schmid, *Dogmatik,* 474, 2, 3, 8, 9.

[72.] Seeberg: "Is this one person?" Schmid, *Dogmatik,* 473, 15–18.

[73.] "The conversion of the Jews" (Schmid, *Dogmatik,* 474, 4, 5).

[74.] Millenarians are proponents of the belief in a kingdom lasting 1,000 years at the end of time (chiliasm).

[75.] Schmid, *Dogmatik,* 474, 31–39, and Hase, *Hutterus,* 284, 17.

[76.] Schmid, *Dogmatik,* 474, 41–47.

[77.] Seeberg: "The 1,000-year kingdom in the history of the church."

[78.] Cf. Schmid, *Dogmatik,* 475, 2–7, 11–13, 21–24, and Hase, *Hutterus,* 284, 29, 30.

will judge the virtuous and the evil at the extremum judicium.[79] Extremum iudicium universale est actio solemnis, qua Deus unitrinus per Christum in visibili forma summaque gloria apparentem, angelos malos omnesque homines ad normam Legis et Evangelii judicabit, piis aeterna gaudia, improbis aeternos cruciatus assignaturus (Gerhard).[80] The entire act of judgment certainly does not supplement the judicium particulare in agona mortis[81] and clothing with the body of either glory or shame. It is the solemn pronouncement and public declaration of the judgment that has already taken place.[82] The act of judgment takes places in several stages: (1) Solemnis praeparatio (a) Christi iudicis in throno collocatio (b) omnium hominum coram tribunali Christi congregatio (c) congregatorum separatio.[83] The iudicium then is divided into iudicium discussionis,[84] whereby all the sins of the godless will be enumerated, those of the faithful being barely mentioned in extenso, and into the iudicium retributionis,[85] that is, the pronouncement of guilt or innocence.[86] This concludes the court of justice proceedings. The site where the court will meet is not, as Catholic scholasticism asserts, the Valley of Jehoshaphat. Instead it will take place somewhere in space. No agreement can be found on the amount of time the last judgment will take.[87]

437

At judgment day the fate of the world is sealed. It will burn,[88] and a glorious world will arise.[89] The idea of a new world following the consummatio mundi, to be sure, seldom appears, and most theologians leave it at an abolitio substantiae[90] and do not teach, as Luther and Gerhard do, a qual-

---

[79.] Hase, *Hutterus*, 284, 47, 48; Schmid, *Dogmatik*, 476, 44, 45; 470, 27–29; and Hase, *Hutterus*, 285, 12, 13.

[80.] "The universal last judgment is a solemn act, in which the triune God, through Christ, who appears in visible form and in highest glory, will judge the evil angels and all people according to the norms of the law and the gospel, and the faithful will be assigned eternal happiness and the unfaithful will be assigned eternal damnation" (Hase, *Hutterus*, 286, 2–5). Hase reworks Hollatz's formulation (Schmid, *Dogmatik*, 476, 4–9), that Bonhoeffer traces back to Gerhard on account of Hase, *Hutterus*, 286, 21. He could not have read Gerhard's definition in "Tractatus de extremo iudicio," *Loci theologici*, 9:124a.

[81.] "The particular judgment during one's final death throes" (Hase, *Hutterus*, 286, 14; 285, 13, 14; 282, 4, 5, 39–42; cf. editorial notes 39–42).

[82.] Ibid., 285, 15–17.

[83.] "Solemn preparation (a) Christ seats himself as judge on the throne (b) all people congregate before the judgment seat of Christ (c) division of those who are assembled." Hase, *Hutterus*, 286, 21, 22, 26, 27.

[84.] "Judgment of discussion."

[85.] "Judgment of retribution."

[86.] Hase, *Hutterus*, 286, 27, 28, 33–36, 37, 38, and Schmid, *Dogmatik*, 477, 22–25.

[87.] Hase, *Hutterus*, 286, 40–44.

[88.] Schmid, *Dogmatik*, 478, 1; 477, 43, and Hase, *Hutterus*, 286, 16.

[89.] Cf. Hase, *Hutterus*, 286, 17.

[90.] "Annihilation of being."

itatum alteratio.[91] Luther's saying is well known: "Today heaven has on its work clothes; but then it will put on its Sunday best."[92] This view is very much like the other view about the new body. God does not allow anything in creation to pass away but purifies the bodily form into a higher way of being, the σῶμα πνευματικόν.[93] It is therefore astonishing to note the frequent absence of this type of parallel thought.[94] The analytical method ends its theological reflection with this article. In their conclusion, the earlier theologians add the teaching of the vita and damnatio aeterna at this point. We will follow them here.[95]

The fate of individuals is decided for eternity in the court of judgment.[96] The damned go to hell; where this is, is not revealed.[97] There they will suffer eternal tortures. We can only depict their horror with feeble images, because they greatly supersede our ability to imagine them.[98] The torture of deprivation (mala privativa) and the positive tortures that can be experienced are differentiated from one another. The descriptions follow directly from the biblical accounts.[99] Gradations of damnation, as, for example, Hutterus postulates, apparently contradict the absoluteness of the judgment, the infinity of our sin and guilt, as well as the degree of bliss that is posited by the confessional books.[100] We definitely see a vestige of Catholicism before us. The assumption that the period of punishment in hell could be temporally limited is persistently denied by theologians. CA 14:[101] damnant . . . qui sentiunt hominibus damnatis ac diabolis finem poenarum futurum esse.[102] This opinion either leads to Pelagianism, i.e., to the doctrine of conversion without the benefit of God's gracious judgment, or to the assumption that divine grace is also at work in hell.[103] Both positions must be rejected. So must the Origenistic ἀποκατάστασις πάντων.[104] The passages in the Holy Scriptures that appear to support this merely intend to speak of the

438

[91.] "Alteration of qualities."

[92.] Hase, *Hutterus*, 287, 1, 2, 13–16, 42–47, 27–29. Following Hase, Bonhoeffer misunderstood Gerhard; see Konrad Stock, *Annihilatio mundi*, 1ff.

[93.] "Spiritual body" (Hase, *Hutterus*, 287, 11–13, 16–19, 25, 26).

[94.] Like Hase, *Hutterus*, 287, 1, 2.

[95.] Cf. editorial notes 14 and 15.

[96.] Hase, *Hutterus*, 287, 31, 32, and Schmid, *Dogmatik* 478, 16, 17.

[97.] Schmid, *Dogmatik*, 479, 34, 35, and Hase, *Hutterus*, 288, 2, 4.

[98.] Hase, *Hutterus*, 288, 3, 32, 33.

[99.] Ibid., 288, 5–6, 39–45, and Schmid, *Dogmatik*, 480, 10–25.

[100.] Hase, *Hutterus*, 288, 9–11, 48, 49; 289, 19, 20, and Schmid, *Dogmatik*, 481, 15.

[101.] Hase, *Hutterus*, 288: "C.A. 14: (XVII)."

[102.] Augsburg Confession, Article 17: They "condemn [the Anabaptists] who think that there will be an end to the punishments of condemned human beings and devils"; *The Book of Concord*, 51; Hase, *Hutterus*, 288, 11–15; 289, 35, 36.

[103.] Hase, *Hutterus*, 288, 15, 19–20.

[104.] "Restoration of all [human beings to a state of grace]."

total victory of the kingdom of God.[105] As with the damned so there is a corresponding distinction between privativa and positiva bona for the blessed:[106] being far away from sin and evil, seeing God, visio et fruitio Dei,[107] joy and jubilation, and glorifying God in eternity.[108] Salvation takes place in heaven (Gerhard). In salvation, all the faithful are equal. Gradations exist only in their active effectiveness[109] in the kingdom of God, according to the good works done on earth (AC 135).[110] People will see their loved ones again in the same way that the apostles saw their Lord.[111] No compassion for the damned will disturb their blessedness because their wills shall have become one with the divine will.[112] Beati videbunt suos notos et cognatos inter damnatos, quotiescumque voluerint, sed absque ullo commiserationis afflatu.[113] Here the coelum gratiae or the ecclesia militans has become the coelum gloriae, that is, the ecclesia triumphans.[114]

439

This is where early Protestant theology ends. If we review what we have observed, we must note a few things especially critically. On the whole it appears that the biblical statements were simply accepted and developed further formally. Difficult problems in the scriptures, such as apokatastasis or chiliasm are ignored (i.e., damned) without sufficiently delving into their content. The doctrine of the immortality of the soul is very superficially combined with the doctrine of the resurrection. The relationship of predestination, iudicium particulare, and iudicium universale, is left undeveloped as far as its subject matter is concerned. The Johannine problem of eschatology is not even touched upon. The whole is actually without philosophical-metaphysical or historical-philosophical interest. Instead, a plethora of unimportant things is expressly discussed. Biblical fantasies and dogmatic statements are intertwined in a motley way. In short, as far as the development of eschatology is concerned, it has shown very little productive systematic strength. And yet this gap is compensated for by something else. First, everything that is important has been retained amidst the abundance of dogmatic rubbish:

[105.] Hase, *Hutterus*, 289, 11, 12, 14, 16–19.

[106.] "Good that exists because evil and wickedness are absent and good that exists because one enjoys the positive aspects of goodness."

[107.] "Seeing and enjoying God [by those who have been saved]."

[108.] Hase, *Hutterus*, 290, 16–20, and Schmid, *Dogmatik*, 481, 46; 482, 43, 44.

[109.] Replaces "activity."

[110.] Hase, *Hutterus*, 290, 5, 4, 6–8, 39, 40, and Schmid, *Dogmatik*, 481, 15, 17, 18.

[111.] Hase, *Hutterus*, 290, 9, 10.

[112.] Hase, *Hutterus*, 290, 12 and 291, 1.

[113.] "Those who are saved will see their acquaintances and their relatives among the damned, as often as they would like, but without any breath of compassion" (Hase, *Hutterus*, 291, 26–28).

[114.] "Here the heaven of grace or the church militant has become the heaven of glory, that is, the church triumphant." Cf. Hase, *Hutterus*, 287, 16, 17; 290, 21, 22; 264, 39–265, 1. Cf. above, editorial note 6.

the idea of the divided course of history[115] and the purely transcendent concept of the kingdom of God. These concepts and others like them are clear and unequivocally pronounced. Moreover, we may not overlook the fact that the acceptance of biblical eschatology involved considerable religious and moral power that enabled a seriousness to develop that has been unmatched by the following systematically independent generations. This seriousness is reflected in the absence of playful statements. Instead a valiant attempt was made earnestly to contemplate the ruggedness of the biblical images and ideas. The fact that a great deal of damage was done by the absence of a historical perspective as well as or—better yet—in connection with the excessive doctrines of inspiration cannot detract from the religious strength of such an attempt.

440

If we can learn little about methodology from the founders of early Protestantism, we can learn about the enormous seriousness and awe with which they approached every topic of theology.[116]

Summary[117]

Early Lutheran Eschatology
(mainly according to Joh. Gerhard)
Death, Resurrection
(Body-Soul Problem)
Return of Christ and its signs
Biblical findings *uncritically* handed down
Extremum judicium
Consummatio mundi
(Then the "New World")
Saved and Damned
Joys of the Good[118]
Rejection of Apokatastasis
Critique on the last two pages
1. Biblical tradition only formally handed down, not mastered.
2. Difficult complexes are ignored (for example, Johannine eschatology).
3. Generally, in this doctrine no systematic strength is demonstrated.
Positive: Great deal of emphasis placed upon the transcendent kingdom of God[119] in the biblical conception and the divided course of history.

[115.] See Bonhoeffer's seminar paper on "Luther's Feelings about His Work" (see above, 2/5:257ff.; cf. also 2/9:320).

[116.] Seeberg: "Quite good. Seeberg 5/14/26."

[117.] *NL* A 12, 6 (2); handwritten text on a scrap of paper. The summary of the above paper, written in great haste and very difficult to read, was clearly to be used as an aid in presenting the paper orally to the seminar.

[118.] See above, 2/11:371ff.

[119.] Difficult to decipher; the manuscript reads "Emphasis on t[ranscendent] k[ing-dom] of God."

13. Paper on John and Paul[1]

The Fifteenth Chapter of the Gospel of John and the Apostle Paul

The fifteenth chapter of the Gospel of John has the following structure: vv. 1-17, Christ and his disciples in their relationship to each other; vv. 18-24, their attitudes toward the world; vv. 24-27, testimony about Christ to the world. In greater detail: vv. 1-6, the allegory of the vine, vv. 7-17 further expand the ideas touched on in the allegory, especially "remaining in Christ";[2] the relationship of the Father to the Son as an image for the relationship of Jesus to the disciples and their relationship to him; "remaining in love" as meaning to keep the commandments of God and Jesus 9 and 10; (perfect joy of Jesus, 11); connected to the love commandment, the meaning of the death of Jesus as taking place for his friends v. 12 and 13. The disciples are the friends of Jesus, whom he himself has chosen 15-16. The κόσμος,[3] however, hates Jesus and the disciples 18-20; it does not know the Father 21; but only has itself to blame 22-24; when Jesus will no longer be there, then the Paraclete will witness to him 26-27. In order not to cause confusion by delving into the wealth of problems, we can follow the development of the chapter by focusing on its fairly clear and logical arrangement, beginning with v. 1.

¶When considering the allegory of the vine, we are entering a difficult area in the arena of comparative religions. Bultmann recently pointed to a striking parallel in Mandaean literature. It reads: "I am a vine, a vine of life, a tree on which there is no lie [. . .]. Everyone who repents, their branch will never be cut off [. . .]. But the evil ones, they who are liars . . . the evil ones sink of their own accord in the great Suf-sea."[4] The parallel is certainly striking but scarcely compelling, for the following reasons: (1) The specifically Johannine ἐν ἐμοί[5] is not present. (It could, of course, have been in the missing verses.) (2) Bultmann may be astounded by the detailed parallel

---

[1.] *NL* A 12, 1; handwritten; previously printed in *GS* 5:95–106. Paper for Adolf Deißmann's New Testament seminar on Paul and John in the summer semester 1926. The paper was neither corrected nor graded by the dozent. On the first page in the upper left Bonhoeffer has written "Deißmann" and on the right "Dietrich Bonhoeffer." Unless specified otherwise, the verses cited refer to John 15. For secondary literature Bonhoeffer relies on Rudolf Bultmann's article, "Die Bedeutung der neuerschlossenen mandäischen und manichäischen Quellen für das Verständinis des Johannesevangeliums." In addition, it is very likely that he used Walter Bauer, *Johannes*. [Paragraph signs from the German editor replace Bonhoeffer's dashes.] [CG]

[2.] Deleted: "especially regarding the problem of certainty about prayer."

[3.] "The world"

[4.] Bultmann, "Die Bedeutung der mandäischen und manichäischen Quellen," 117; Bultmann cites from the page proofs of the 1925 German translation of the *Ginza* by Mark Lidzbarski. Instead of "branch" the original has "soul." The Mandaeans were a gnostic baptizing sect who lived in southern Iraq and western Iran.

[5.] "In me."

of the "cutting off,"[6] which can be found in v. 2 of our chapter, yet the Mandaean vine is a vine in which there are no lies, while the Johannine vine is one on which unfruitful branches grow. Nonetheless, it is not impossible that the image of the vine is connected somehow to the Mandaean sources, but the connection can hardly be a literary one. Of course, closer points of connection might be the Old Testament prototypes such as Psalm 80 and Jeremiah 2, the wine of the Lord's Supper (ἀληθινή[7] in v. 1 should be understood in this way), or an incidental connection[8] by way of the Kidron Valley. Many elements could have come together. In short, we are not in a position to decide which of these is most likely.

¶But the theological perspective is much more important. The Johannine image of the vine has often been seen as a parallel to the Pauline image of the church as the body of Christ (1 Cor. 12:12; Rom. 12:5; Eph. 5). Is this justified? John uses this imagery to present the inner unity between Jesus and the disciples. We could say that the entire Johannine image crystallizes around the formula ἐν ἐμοί, "remain in me as I in you." Further in v. 1 ἡ ἄμπελος ἡ ἀληθινή[9] designates the entire organism, i.e., Christ *and* the individual members. When Paul speaks of the body of Christ, he primarily refers to familial love and its basis in the "*one* body." This is due to the fact that Paul thinks collectively and John individualistically. Here we have initially discovered a difference in emphasis. Now let us proceed to investigate the content.

¶Is the Pauline "being *one* body" identical with the Johannine "remaining in Christ, the vine"? Obviously the inclusive identification in v. 1, ἄμπελος = Christ, corresponds precisely to the interpretation of Christ in 1 Cor. 12:12: "For just as the body is one and has many members, and all the members of the body, though many, are *one* body, so it is with *Christ*."[10] Here we find agreement between the two. Christ is the whole body, in which the disciples are somehow present. In John, it is the vine's sap that feeds the tendrils. In Paul it is the Spirit that rules the body. How is the relationship of Christ to the disciples understood in both? Although Paul often speaks of the body of Christ, as far as I know he never uses the formula "we in Christ, Christ in us."[11] I believe we can use this formula to answer our question. The reason

443

[6.] Cf. Bultmann, "Die Bedeutung der mandäischen und manichäischen Quellen," 117, note 1.

[7.] "True."

[8.] Replaces: "a chance meeting."

[9.] "The true vine."

[10.] Cf. Bauer, *Johannes*, 143.

[11.] The formula that is presented by Bonhoeffer stands at the center of the interpretation of Paul by Adolf Deißmann. Cf. Deißmann, *Die neutestamentliche Formel 'in Christo Jesu' untersucht*, especially 91ff. and 130, and also Deißmann, *Paul. A Study in Social and Religious History*, 78f.

for this will be shown below. Therefore, in the words "Christ in us, we in Christ" we have come upon a formula that can be used to understand the thought processes that are common to Paul and John. We have to keep this in mind. In order to understand what this central formula meant for Paul we must proceed from the point at which his faith in Christ finds its center. This is his certainty of justification, his view of sin and grace, of law and gospel, of old and new Adam, of history and eschatology. The old person becomes justified and sanctified through faith and the Spirit. The new person's sin stands under grace and therefore the new person stands as a new creature in the world of God's grace, beyond history and *in Christ.* 'In Christ' means, "Our inclusion in the suspension [Aufhebung] of this person as revealed in Jesus as the Christ, in which the individual is founded as a *new* person" (Barth).[12] It is consequently primarily a statement of faith inspired by the Spirit and not some kind of mystical experience.[13] Corresponding to this, "Christ in us" for Paul is not an experience, even more because the word of God has become real in us *prior to* any experience. Forgiveness and healing are not accomplished by us, but through God-Christ. However, the entire community that is "in Christ" and in whom Christ is, is the body of Christ. Together they are *a unity that is beyond* all differences, namely, Christ. Regrettably, this is not the place to pursue this claim further. These Pauline ideas stand out most clearly in Rom. 8:1: "There is therefore now no condemnation for those who are in Christ Jesus. For the law of the Spirit of life has set you free from the law of sin and of death." Rom. 8:10: "But if Christ is in you, though the body is dead because of sin, the Spirit is life because of righteousness"; and finally Gal. 2:2:[14] "and it is no longer I who live," must also be added.

¶We now compare John with this. "We in Christ, Christ in us" is also central for his Christianity, but it finds its basis elsewhere. The doctrine of justification, and with it moral dualism, the problem of law and gospel, play no role for John. Christ, the revealer of his own divinity and his Father's, comes as light and love into the dark, hate-mongering κόσμος. He seeks to draw his disciples into his light and to live with them in intimate community. They are invited to enter into his love and his light and be in him so that he will be in them with his love, and give them "*his*" joy and *his* peace (14:27; 16:33). They should be in him like the branches of a vine, who can only live in him and wither without him. They should find their strength in him and his strength should be in them. Here we see a different image of "Christ in us" than in Paul. There is something of nature mysticism in the bond between Christ and the disciples. Yet we would incorrectly describe the Johannine form if we

444

445

[12.] See Barth, *Romans,* 272 [trans. altered], concerning Rom. 8:1-2.
[13.] Here and in the following, Bonhoeffer takes the opposite view to Deißmann's experiential theological interpretation of Paul; see Deißmann, *Paul,* especially 98ff.
[14.] The correct reference is Gal. 2:20.

wanted to call it simply mystical, because its interest in experiential piety is too weak. Bultmann believes that the unique characteristic of the Gospel can be found in the fact that it is based on a Mandaean myth. Consequently, the bond with Christ that is found in the Gospel of John is not mystical but mythical.[15] There is some support for this proposition. What is important for us is only to stress the essential difference between the foundation for the Johannine and Pauline concept of ἐν Χριστῷ[16] first as a statement about justification and second as a statement about the experienced inner bond with Christ's kingdom of light.[17] The presence of an almost identical formula, in spite of all their differences, is certainly striking. It is highly unlikely that this occurred accidentally.

¶However, since I do not know whether any similar formulas can be found in the mystery cults or whether this is a specifically Christian formula, I cannot say anything more precisely about their interdependence. In the first case, Paul as well as John would have found the formula (ἐν Χριστῷ or a similar one) in the Hellenistic cultic world. In the second case, however, one could hardly conceive of John being independent of Paul. John must have encountered this formula in the Pauline congregations and have transformed it to fit his needs.

Following this understanding of the basic ideas of vv. 1-17, we can proceed to the details. We can point to the interesting connections and differences in comparison with Paul. There are fruitful and worthless branches on the vine, just as there were good and worthless fish in the nets. The worthless branches are cut off, just as the man guilty of incest was driven out of the congregation (1 Cor. 5), though, of course, so that his spirit could be saved on the day of judgment (5b). The good branches will be purified by the γεωργός so that they bear more fruit.[18] In a repetition of 13:10 Jesus says that the disciples are already clean διὰ τὸν λόγον ὃν λελάληκα ὑμῖν.[19] Christ's word is spirit and life (cf. 6:63) and thus has purifying power. The purity of the disciples cannot be conceived as enduring but as something in principle,[20] that is, forgiveness of sins, effected by the word. One could cite here Rom. 10:10 and 17, which speak of faith that results from the preached word. A similar thought is expressed (1 Tim. 4:5) especially in Eph. 5:26, "in order to make her holy by cleansing her with the washing of water by the word" (cf. also 1 Pet. 1:23: "born anew . . . through the word").

446

[15.] Cf. Bultmann, "Die Bedeutung der mandäischen und manichäischen Quellen," 103ff. and 139ff.

[16.] "In Christ."

[17.] The words "as a statement . . . kingdom of light" are added by Bonhoeffer in the margin.

[18.] The phrase "by the γεωργός [gardener]," was added later by Bonhoeffer before "bear more fruit." He deleted: "This occurs by the γεωργός God the Father."

[19.] "By the word that I have spoken to you" (John 15:3).

[20.] Deleted: "or else the contradiction would be too great."

¶The word of God in John is conceived of as much more self-effecting than it is in Paul. In Paul only passages like Col. 3:16, "Let the word . . . ," lead to the concept of the special self-effectiveness of the word.[21] *In John* Jesus' words[22] must remain in the disciples. This is the same as when Christ is in them (v. 7). A branch can bring forth fruit only if it is on the vine (vv. 4 and 5) το καρπὸν φέρειν[23] and therefore not in the sense of success in missions, as is often the case in Paul (cf. Rom. 1:13; Phil. 1:22), but in the sense of healing. Cf. Gal. 5:22; Phil. 1:11, "filled with the fruits of righteousness," etc. But χωπίς ἐμοῦ οὐ δύνασθε ποιεῖν οὐδέν[24] is a sentence that we might find in Paul also. We can compare Eph. 2:12 χωρίς Χριστοῦ[25] and especially 2 Cor. 3:5, "Not that we are competent of ourselves to claim anything as coming from us; our competence is from God." In Paul this concept of the total impotence of human beings stems from the doctrine of justification. In John it results from his view that whoever does not belong to Christ belongs to the κόσμος and is therefore worthless. Humanity is certainly free to do evil. According to v. 2 they can be separated from Christ at any time.[26] In spite of 10:28, "No one will snatch them out of my hand," John knows nothing of a gratia inamissibilis.[27] Paul thinks somewhat differently in this case. Luther's *Lectures on Galatians* emphasize that, in spite of the Galatians' errors in matters of *faith*, according to Gal. 1:2 Paul still considers them to be part of the church. God's grace is thus not dependent on human decisions.[28] The fundamental difference is clear, in spite of agreement with the statement, "without Christ we can do nothing."

447

¶According to v. 6, unfruitful branches are burned. The sharp division in Paul (1 Cor. 3:15) between work and person can be compared to this. The work burns yet the person remains. If one remains bonded to Christ (μένειν ἐν,[29] one of John's favorite expressions), then what one prays for will also be fulfilled (v. 7). Paul never spoke in this way. People cannot pray by themselves; the Spirit intercedes for them (Rom. 8:26). Paul himself experienced

---

[21.] Replaces: "special meaning."

[22.] The words "*In John* . . . words" replace "In John the word is also the judge: 12:48. Jesus' words must. . . ."

[23.] "Bear fruit."

[24.] "Apart from me you can do nothing" (John 15:5).

[25.] "Without Christ."

[26.] The words "Humanity . . . at any time" replace "as we shall see. The individual who is incapable of doing good receives the strength to do it from Christ. It is clear that the subject here does not concern deterministic certainty. It can already be seen from vv. 2 and 6 that individuals are always free to do evil, i.e., individuals can always separate themselves from Christ."

[27.] "Grace that cannot be lost."

[28.] Cf. Luther, *Lectures on Galatians*, WA 2:456, especially lines 26–28, LW 27:169, especially the sentence beginning "The apostle calls them churches that were afflicted. . . ."

[29.] "Remain in."

failure in his prayers. In 2 Cor. 12:8 he recounts how he prayed in vain three times to be freed from sickness. A promise was considered to be this prayer's "success." This is an interesting difference from John's understanding. God is praised by bringing fruit (v. 8); cf. Phil. 1:11, "having produced the harvest of righteousness that comes through Jesus Christ for the glory and praise of God."

¶Following v. 9, we see the comparison between God's love for the Son and the Son's love for human beings. In the love that Christ has disciples must remain (μένειν!). One remains in Christ's love by keeping his commandments. His commandment, however, is that the disciples love one another, so the person who practices love is the one who remains in Jesus' love. Jesus tells his disciples all this in order that his joy might be in them, i.e., that the joy he has in God's love might be found in his disciples in the love of Jesus. In Jesus' farewell speeches, joy is seen as a religious value[30] (cf. 16:20; 17:13; and the Johannine letters). Joy also has other characteristics than it does in Paul. In John joy is individualistic while in Paul it is the foundation of the kingdom of God. Cf. Rom. 14:17, "For the kingdom of God is . . . righteousness, peace, joy." In Paul it is much more active than it is in John. Cf. Phil 4:4, "Rejoice . . . ," as well as 2 Cor. 8:2 for joy's bearing on missions and joy as the source of ethics. We do not have the time to delve into this any further here. I find it unnecessary to posit that the motif of joy was taken from the Mandaeans. It is characteristic of John, when discussing love, to see it in the relationship between the Father and the Son and the Son and the disciples. It is equally characteristic for Paul that joy is conceived of in this manner only in Phil. 2:5; yet even here the discussion centers on absolute obedience and not mystical unity. In particular, it seems to me that a completely nonmystical quality lies behind John's[31] emphasis on "keeping the commandments." As Jesus obeyed and remained in love, so must the disciples. "Everyone should have the same mind that was in Christ Jesus, who . . . became obedient to the point of death . . . *therefore* God highly exalted him." This means reward for being obedient to God's commandment and is our reward for being obedient to Jesus' commandments. But the commandment of Jesus is love. Cf. Gal. 5:14: "For the whole law is summed up in a single commandment, 'You shall love your neighbor as yourself,'" and Rom. 13:8, "for the one who loves the other has fulfilled the law"; v. 10, "therefore, love is the fulfilling of the law." It is characteristic of Paul that when he contemplates the love commandment he immediately reflects on the law that can be fulfilled only out of joy and love. In John, the love commandment (which, interestingly, is narrowed down to the love of friends) is seen in contrast to

---

[30.] Cf. Bonhoeffer's paper "'Joy' in Early Christianity," above, 2/11:370ff.
[31.] The correct word must be: "Paul."

the hated κόσμος. In Rom. 8:22[32] when Paul declares, "For I am convinced that neither death, nor life . . . will be able to separate us from the love of God through Christ Jesus our Lord," we find ourselves at a point that is beyond the contrasting views of Pauline-Johannine theology. Soon, however, we see the contrast come to the fore once more when John in v. 13 speaks of Christ's sacrificial death for his friends. The use of the preposition ὑπέρ[33] to refer to Christ's death certainly has its roots in early Christianity. The contrast between the motif of Jesus' dying for his friends and Rom. 5:10, "For if while we were enemies we were reconciled to God through the death of his son," is noteworthy; v. 8 reads, "while we still were sinners." What a remarkable abbreviation of the significance of the Savior of the world! In the Johannine statement there is certainly more to be seen than a dialectical reversal of the judgment of justification!

¶V. 15: Jesus calls his disciples friends and no longer servants, because he has told them everything. (According to 16:12, to be sure, he had not really told them everything, but this is an insignificant discrepancy.) Is this passage a conscious correction of the familiar Pauline use of the term of δοῦλος as found in Rom. 1:1; Gal. 2:22; and Rom. 6:6,[34] "Do you not know that if you present yourselves to anyone as obedient slaves, you are slaves of the one whom you obey?" Paul also rejects the use of the word in the servile sense, i.e., Rom. 8:15 and Gal. 4:7, "So you are no longer a slave but only a child." John seems only to have seen the servile nature of the term δοῦλος. In spite of this we find in 15:20 the disciples referred to as servants once again. The use of the term φίλος could have been derived from Abraham's designation as φίλος θεοῦ[35] (cf. James 2:25)[36] or even from Greek philosophy. This term did not prevail, because it was superseded by the much more personal ἀδελφοί.[37] The community of friends did not choose their own head, but it is chosen by Jesus. Ἐγὼ ἐξελεξάμην ὑμᾶς, καὶ ἔθηκα ὑμᾶς.[38] For ἔθηκα cf. 1 Cor. 12:28: οὓς μὲν[39] V. 18: νυνὶ δὲ θεὸς ἔθετο τὰ μέλη[40]—a remarkably similar use of language!

This community, however, is in the κόσμος, yet the κόσμος hates the disciples just as it hated the master, because all of them do not belong to the

---

[32.] The correct reference is Rom. 8:38.
[33.] "On behalf of."
[34.] The correct references are Gal.1:10 and Rom. 6:16.
[35.] "Friend of God." Cf. Bauer, *Johannes,* 145.
[36.] The correct reference is James 2:23.
[37.] "Brother."
[38.] "I chose you, and I appointed you" (John 15:16).
[39.] "Such as God has appointed in the church" (1 Cor. 12:28); see also Bauer, *Johannes,* 145.
[40.] "But as it is, God arranged the members" (1 Cor. 12:18).

450   κόσμος but, instead, ἐξελεξάμην [. . .] ἐκ τοῦ κόσμου.[41] What does John
mean by the term κόσμος? We find the word 70 times in his writings. It refers
to the entity that is radically opposed to the self-revealing God, and thus is
darkness, lack of understanding, and lovelessness. It is sin in its elemental
form, and is understood not as resulting from an act of will but as a force of
nature. It is seen in contrast with the ζωὴ αἰώνιος as the κόσμος οὗτος.[42]
Consequently it refers to death (John 12:35).[43] There is a prince of this
κόσμος, who stands against God and Christ. Apparently this ruler is conceived of as having existed since the beginning of time. This is the reason
one speaks of cosmological dualism in John. To a certain extent, two kingdoms have existed since the beginning of time. Even if members of the
divine kingdom were to be found in the satanic kingdom, they would still not
belong to this world; instead these members are elected from the satanic
kingdom for the divine kingdom. What is (v. 19) ἐξελεξάμην ἐκ τοῦ κόσμου,
and thus not of the κόσμος, is hated by the world; for its essence is the inability to love. The beginning of the chapter supports this proposition. A Mandaean text reads, "You have chosen us and have taken us out of the world of
hate."[44] This is a striking parallel to our text.

We turn our attention to Paul. He seems to be the first writer who took the
Greek concept of κόσμος, which referred to a world of order and harmony,
and reinterpreted it to refer to the Christian concept of a wicked world.
There is no cosmological dualism in Paul. Instead we find a pure anthropo-
logical, moral dualism. Thus the world is not *fundamentally* evil. For Paul, the
κόσμος is reconciled through Christ, an impossible concept for John (see
Rom. 11:15; 2 Cor. 5:19; and above). It is certainly the case that evil rules the
world. The wisdom of the world is nothing before God (1 Cor. 1:20). In Paul,
however, the view of the world still stands too strongly under the concept of
creation for him to reach the dualistic consequences of John. Paul can also
speak of being saved from the wicked world, ὅπως ἐξέληται ἡμᾶς ἐκ τοῦ
451   αἰῶνος τοῦ ἐνεστῶτος πονηροῦ[45] (Gal. 1:4), in the same way that he speaks
of the groaning of creation; these expressions are rare, but it is clear that they
are more in line with Johannine thought. We can compare to v. 19 also Eph.
1:4, "He chose us in Christ *before* the foundation of the world" and Gal. 1:15,
"God, who had set me apart before I was born." According to v. 21 the disciples will be persecuted because of Christ's name (cf. Mark 13:13; Matt. 5:11;

[41.] Add ὑμᾶς. "I have chosen [you] out of the world" (John 15:19).
[42.] "Eternal life," "this world."
[43.] The correct reference is John 12:31.
[44.] Cf. Bultmann, "Die Bedeutung der mandäischen und manichäischen Quellen,"
118; Bultmann cites Lidzbarski, *Mandäische Liturgien,* 75.
[45.] "To set us free from the present evil age" (Gal. 1:4).

10:22); cf. also Phil. 1:22,[46] "suffering for him as well," and Phil. 2:30, "because he came close to death for the work of Christ."

Μισεῖν[47] is very common in John but not in Paul. The world hates because it does not know God. If Jesus had not come with word and deed, then it would be guiltless. But now, it has seen and has still hated and thus the scriptures have been fulfilled.[48] According to Paul, even the Gentiles can know God (Rom. 1:20). The idea that it was only with Jesus' coming that guilt was brought into the world reminds us strongly of Paul's understanding of the coming of the law (Rom. 4:15) to places where the law has not been (5:13; 7:8).[49] In both cases, the divine word is the occasion for sin. This does not occur in opposition to the divine will but in order that the scriptures may be fulfilled (11:38).[50] Such an understanding at least softens the ensuing dualism.

¶All these words, however, stand in the shadow of Jesus' farewell. Thus the conversation seamlessly turns to the Paraclete, whom Jesus will send after returning to the Father. The Spirit of truth, who comes from God, will witness for Jesus and also for the disciples. The Spirit, who according to 14:7 will be sent by the Father, here is sent by the Son, who is "from the Father." The Spirit comes from God and is the Spirit of truth (18:37 provides an occasion to speak of ἀλήθεια).[51] By the way, we now find ourselves at the passage that occasioned the battle over the "filioque."[52]

V. 26 μαρτυρεῖν[53] is found 36 times in John. In Paul it appears only 6   452
times. According to Paul, the Spirit of the Son, which lives in people's hearts, has been sent by God the Father (Gal. 4:6). Paul's view of Spirit oscillates between a personal and an impersonal concept. In Rom. 8:26 it is definitely thought of as personal. In most of the other passages it is not. For John, the Spirit is always a person. This is already evident in the usage of the masculine παράκλητος[54] as opposed to the neuter πνεῦμα.[55]

With this our discussion is complete. To conclude, we can say that there are many points of contact between Johannine and Pauline thought, but few agreements in content. This conclusion does not at all exclude the possibili-

---

[46.] The correct reference is Phil. 1:29.

[47.] "Hate."

[48.] The preceding sentences are Bonhoeffer's paraphrase of John 15:18-25.

[49.] Here Bonhoeffer means Rom. 5:13 and 7:8.

[50.] This must mean John 13:18; but see also John 15:25.

[51.] "Truth."

[52.] Latin, "and the Son." This formula is a clause that the Western Church added to the Nicene-Constantinopolitan Creed so that it read, "the Holy Spirit proceeds from the Father and the Son." The Eastern Church objects strongly to this addition.

[53.] "Witness to."

[54.] "The Advocate."

[55.] "Spirit."

ty that John was influenced by Pauline thought, but it is precisely the manifold external agreement that allows one to see the inner divergence of both men so much more clearly.[56]

17:30   **13a. Paper on Spirit and Grace in Frank**[1]

Paper Given on November 19, 1926
"Frank's View of Spirit and Grace"
Presented according to the *System der christlichen Gewißheit*
and the *System der christlichen Wahrheit*.[2]

Frank's two main systematic works lead us back to the years 1880–1890. Since Schleiermacher, theology had partly been allowed to grow speculative and wild—this is especially evident in Hegel's student Biedermann—and partly was constrained by biblicism. At any rate it seemed to have distanced itself a long way from Lutheran-Reformed doctrine. Frank[3] opposed this development in the name of Lutheran theology. In principle he recognizes Schleiermacher's dogmatic starting point, but it appears to him to be presented too metaphysically and generally.[1] Frank limits the concept of the feeling of absolute dependence. For

17:31   The
theological
starting point

him the starting point for every specifically Christian theology is the consciousness of being reborn. This subjective anchoring must be confirmed by the objective[4] parallel of scholarly reflection. This is found in part one of his theo-

---

1. Frank, *System der Wahrheit* 1, §9, p. 108.

[56.] The manuscript contains, below the text, the following handwritten note by Bonhoeffer: "Please hand me the paper on Wednesday morning in the New Testament seminar between 1:15 and 1:45. If you cannot manage to do it at that time, please put it in the pigeonhole of the Johannine literature!"

[1.] *NL* A 12 , 4; handwritten, with corrections by Seeberg, in whose seminar it was presented. [Note that the page numbers to the German original in the margins refer to *DBW* 17, not *DBW* 9.] [CG]

[2.] On the lower righthand corner of the title page in handwriting is the name "Dietrich Bonhoeffer"; at the beginning of page 2 the title appears in a shortened form, "Spirit and Grace in Frank." Bonhoeffer cites Frank's *System der christlichen Gewißheit*, 2d edition, translated as *System of the Christian Certainty*, and his *System der christlichen Wahrheit*, 3d edition (not the 2d edition, as indicated in Bonhoeffer's heading by the superscript at the end of the title; cf. *DBW* 17:30).

[3.] Seeberg, marginal note: "Here one should have touched upon the relationship to Hofmann's outline! Cf. Schelling." Cf. Seeberg, *Aus Religion und Geschichte*, 1:385.

[4.] Frank, *Certainty*, 1:§17.

logical system—the system of certainty—without which part two which articulates positive theology[5]—the system of truth—hangs in the air. This in brief is Frank's starting point.

To anticipate the conclusion, Frank's doctrine of the Spirit is not exhausted by its combination with grace. This is why, in order to understand part of the problem, we must also start developing the doctrine of the Spirit at another point. Indeed, we will follow Frank's outline and begin with the problem of the Spirit within the system of certainty.

Frank observes the consciousness of the reborn Christian and, following the model of cause and effect promoted in the sphere of ethics, deduces the reality of the immanent, transcendent, and transeunt object of faith.[6] In this process of establishing certainty, the problem of the Spirit comes to the fore for the first time according to dogmatic

The testimony of the Holy Spirit

tradition. In contrast to Catholic doctrine, which sees the church as the final arbiter of certainty, orthodox Protestant theology develops doctrine from the testimonium Spiritus Sancti.[7] Agreeing with Michaelis[8] who, in spite of his firm stand on the importance of revelation, claims never to have felt the Holy Spirit and its testimony, Strauss[9] believed he found the Achilles' heel of Protestant theology in the doctrine of the Holy Spirit.[10] Frank also believes that this testimonium cannot be the last arbiter of certainty, as it is something that comes to the "I" from the outside. The certainty about whether or not this is really the Holy Spirit must be discovered from this "I." Frank does not ascribe to the old Protestant view that identifies the testimonium Spiritus Sancti with the act of assent. Instead, he

17:32

[5.] Cf. Seeberg, *Religion*, 1:390.

[6.] Cf. Frank, *Certainty*, part two, section 1 (pages 183ff.), section 2 (pages 295ff.) and section 3, dealing with the transeunt object of faith, is in volume 2 of the German edition and only volume 1 was translated. Briefly, "transeunt," the present participle of *transire*, 'to cross over', is the aspect of faith involving both the transcendent and the immanent dimensions.] [CG]

[7.] "The testimony of the Holy Spirit."

[8.] Cf. a work Bonhoeffer used frequently, Karl August von Hase, *Hutterus redivivus*, 90, footnote 3. There one finds a quote from Johann David Michaelis, "I must solemnly admit that, as firmly as I am convinced by the truth of revelation, never in my life have I understood this to be a witness of the Holy Spirit."

[9.] David Friedrich Strauss said, "What can convince us that this testimony in us is truly from the Holy Spirit and not from our own or even from an evil or lying spirit outside of us?"

[10.] Frank, *Certainty*, 1:§17.1.

separates the new "I" from the Spirit that is testifying in the person. The new situation in life in the individual who has been born again is created by the Spirit. The confidence that it must be the effect of the Holy Spirit, however, must arise from the new "I."[2] At this point the doctrine of the tes-timonium Spiritus Sancti is surmounted, but only in order to reactivate it at another point, that is, where in the system of certainty under the transcendent object of faith the doc-trine of the Trinity is developed out of the experience of the reborn. The reborn experience the work of the Spirit in their situation in three forms, yet essentially in unity. First, they experience the Spirit as the one who causes the consciousness of guilt, then as the one who establishes free-dom from guilt in principle, and finally as the one who cre-ates a new "I," who knows that it is actually transferred into this relationship of freedom from guilt. These are the three forms of the revelation of the Trinity in the reborn con-sciousness.[3] Here we are interested only in the way the Holy Spirit is experienced and how the "I" confirms this experience. "For though the efficiency and reality of those factors, (the Father and the Son) are then, it is true, recog-nised in their priority, yet they are recognized only under and in consequence of the operation of the [Holy Spirit], and the subject becomes actually sensible of that which in itself originates in the world beyond, the transcendent, per-ceives it in its acting and existing, in and with the influence of this factor operating within him [Diesseitigen], produc-ing the new *I*."[4] In other words, any act of salvation will be meaningful for us only through the work of the Holy Spir-it. Feelings of guilt and freedom from guilt can actually be understood and evaluated only from the new "I" created by the Holy Spirit. On the other hand, the new "I" will be cre-ated only in relationship to the recognition of the first two agents. The Holy Spirit comes to the human person in a relationship of immanence, which only indirectly appears in the first two agents, but which would not be possible without them. Here we already find the interwoven paths of the doctrine of the Trinity in the system of truth.[11] The

Margin notes:

Trinity from the experi-ence of the reborn

17:33

Spirit, Trinity, "I"

---

2. Cf. *System of Certainty*, §25.
3. *System of Certainty*, 1:335f. [§33.6 and §33.9, pp. 341-42.]
4. Ibid., §33.9, p. 342.

[11.] Deleted: "pointed to."

immanent Spirit and the new "I" now stand in a striking interrelationship. The latter recognizes the Spirit as its creator, and the Holy Spirit assures the subject of the reality of its state of grace. This event is designated as the testimonium Spiritus Sancti. The Spirit puts the "I" in relationship to God before whom it knows itself guilty and by whom freedom from guilt is effected. As such, the Spirit is the principle that unites both attitudes in relation to the subject and brings them into unity. For example, all that Luther affirms about the work of the Holy Spirit,[12] where he boldly uses God, Christ, and the Holy Spirit as synonyms, is omitted here. The agency of the Holy Spirit, according to Frank, is person-related and person-created, because the Spirit, of course, is person.[5] What the Holy Spirit actualizes in the individual is God's claim and the reconciliation through Christ. We see that the theory of reciprocal relationship between the Spirit and "I" appears artificial and requires a corrective.

17:34

Critique and positive statement

It is of utmost importance to the Protestant Christian to be able to say that the new "I" is somehow fundamentally—I would like to say, without being mystically or speculatively misunderstood, substantially—connected to the Holy Spirit in the sense of Gal. 2:20 and 4:6: "God has sent the Spirit of his Son into our hearts, *who* cries, 'Abba! dear Father!'" Frank himself emphasizes that it is important to note "how closely, in spite of every difference, the spiritual 'I' and the 'I' of the Holy Spirit come together in the believer."[6] This, however, is not a dogmatically formulated sentence. We also do not want to identify our "I" with the "I" of the Spirit. This identity exists as real only in Christ. However, we want to understand this "coming closer" more precisely. In actuality, the Holy Spirit itself must speak the word of consent to its own working in my soul. At the same time this is certainly the case for me as well. But finitum incapax infiniti.[13] Like can only comprehend like. God can be grasped only through God's Spirit. In the new subject, it must be God who is the subject of the knowledge of

---

5. *System of Certainty*, 1:342ff.
6. *System der Wahrheit* 2, §38.3 [257].

[12.] Cf. Bonhoeffer on Luther's views on the Holy Spirit, above, 2/10:325.
[13.] "The finite is not capable of the infinite."

17:35

The testimonium Spiritus Sancti

"System of Truth"

17:36

Doctrine of God

God's work.[14] But this process must not be thought of in a trans-subjective manner. Frank correctly puts great emphasis on this. If this were not the case, the Protestant concept of the Spirit would be lost in favor of a magical one. In the same way that the Holy Spirit in me knows and affirms me, I know in the Holy Spirit. This means that the Holy Spirit creates the organ of knowledge. In the same way, it is the Holy Spirit that says a self-affirming yes, as equally the "I" says yes to the Holy Spirit. Only in this sense has Frank not needed to set aside the testimonium Spiritus Sancti. The fact that Frank has uncovered truly new and decisive problems needs only to be mentioned. He also has responded earnestly to Strauss's objection, even though he does not fully refute it. His concept of the Spirit does not lead him "close enough" to the person.

Only after having solved the question of certainty does the actual positive work begin, "the presentation of the objective correlation of the truth of salvation" in the system of Christian truth. Without having solved the problem of certainty, however, the whole work threatens to be no more than talking into the wind.[7] In part two as well, Frank vehemently rejects everything metaphysical.[8] "Whatever is not suited to characterize God as the principle of everything whose principle God is does not belong to a dogmatic statement." Only on the basis of revelation can a dogmatically grounded perspective be attained. It seems more than reasonable to Frank that one can with certainty infer abstract statements about God's being from the knowledge of the content of revelation. These are the presuppositions which for the most part we agree with, and yet Ritschl's accusation that Frank is doing metaphysics proves not to be totally unsubstantiated.[15]

The positive presentation of the system of truth begins with the doctrine of God. God is the Absolute, which

---

7. *System der Wahrheit*, 1:114
8. Ibid.

[14.] Cf. Bonhoeffer's "Paper on the Historical and Pneumatological Interpretation of Scripture," above, 2/6:288f.
[15.] Cf. Frank, *Wahrheit*, 1, §9.4, page 114, cf. 225; see Ritschl, "Theology and Metaphysics," in *Three Essays*, 161–70; especially 164: "I can see in Frank's postulate [sc. the absoluteness of God], however, nothing but an unseemly mingling of metaphysics with revealed religion."

involves unity and completeness. As absolute being God is at the same time person, not in an incidental way but given with the concept of the absolute. God as person is Spirit and life.[16] According to Frank there is no Christian consciousness that does not have God's person as its object. Personality is given with absolute self-determination, not only as a human conception—in contrast to dogmatic thought, as Biedermann suggested—but also objectively, as witnessed in scripture. Moreover, human personality cannot be conceived as an ultimate unity without being grounded in God. Psalm 94, "He who planted the ear, does

God is Spirit

he not hear?"[17] As person, God is Spirit. Spirit does not suffice as the only definition. Yet in this context it is clear that Spirit[18] can be conceived only in the form of the concept of person, as a self-subsisting, self-empowering nature. With this the presuppositions for the doctrine of the Trinity are given. The absolute being of Christian consciousness is conceived as the trinitarian God, as we have seen, without any property that does not yet exist being added to its being. It would now be consistent to spell out an economic[19] doctrine of the Trinity. Frank does not do this, but instead teaches the immanent Trinity. His reasoning is that

17:37

Trinity is immanent, not economic

without the immanent Trinity, the economic Trinity is impossible.[20] In accord with the earlier principle, and in order to penetrate into the abstract nature of God on the basis of revelation, Frank teaches the immanent Trinity, common in Catholic theology but left behind by Luther, although it was taken up again[21] after his death by Protestant scholasticism.

Now the problem of the immanent Trinity has always been somehow to bring into an identity the three persons of God and the oneness [Einpersönlichkeit] of God. Also, here we can only speak more precisely of the functions of the Spirit only. The Spirit is person and bears hypostatic

---

[16.] Here Bonhoeffer summarizes Frank's sections on "The Nature of God," *Wahrheit,* 1, §§10–11, 116ff., and "The Personhood of God," *Wahrheit,* 1, §§12–13ff.

[17.] Frank, *Wahrheit,* 1, §12.2, 143; see Ps. 94:9.

[18.] Replaces: "God."

[19.] The doctrine of the economic Trinity sees the three persons of God in their various work as externally oriented, the immanent doctrine in their inner relationship to each other.

[20.] Frank, *Wahrheit,* 1, §14.4, 164–65.

[21.] Cf. Bonhoeffer's comments on Luther's feelings about his work, above, 2/5:368; but cf. Frank, *Wahrheit,* 1:165 and 1:201, and Seeberg, *Dogmengeschichte* 4.1, 233.

Scripture and
Trinity

17:38

Speculation

character. This comes to full expression in scripture for the first time following Jesus' transfiguration. Only after the Spirit received the consummation of Christ as the content of his work is the Spirit for scripture an independent "I," a hypostasis.[22] All earlier intimations concerning the Spirit do not yet reveal the Spirit as hypostasis. It is not that this is not yet present as such; that would reflect a wrong concept of time. It is only that the Spirit has not yet been revealed as hypostasis in salvation history. Jesus himself acts only in the power of the Spirit. The hypostatic division is not yet able to be perceived by our eyes. Passages like Rom. 8:16 and Gal. 4:6 exhibit the hypostatic independence of the Spirit over against God and also over against our "I." At the same time, however, John 15:26 and Gal. 4:6 prove the internal belonging-together of the Spirit with the hypostases, as the Spirit of the Father and the Son. The Spirit cannot be thought of without both; and this means the Spirit proceeds ex patre filioque;[23] nor can Father and Son be conceived of without the Spirit, because it is the Spirit who initially brings the Father and the Son to the human being. This is why scripture never speaks of the abstract, transcendent being of the Spirit but instead of the Spirit's relationship to us.[9]

But this is mainly a summary of the biblical material, and it presents an economic Trinity. "But why," Frank asks, "should we not allow the faithful to see what God's angels[24] wish to see: the depths of divine realities?"[10] If we hold fast to what we have attained from our experience of salvation and scripture, then the other cannot harm us. One must realize that it is only on this basis that Frank accepts speculation. As further basis for the immanent relationship of the Trinity, Frank uses the creaturely concept of personhood. The person is constituted by a threefold act of generation. First, it generates itself as such, but then it divides itself into generating and being generated and becomes aware of itself as generating. Third, however, it

---

9. Cf. *System der Wahrheit*, 1:193-204.
10. *Wahrheit*, 1, §15.12, p. 201.

[22.] Hypostasis is a form of being, a theological designation of the three persons in the Trinity.
[23.] "From the Father and the Son."
[24.] Cf. 1 Pet. 1:12. [CG]

recognizes itself [as] the unity of that which generates and
that which has been generated, and with this constitutes
itself as a whole.[25] At this point we will put aside the fact
that the problem of personhood has not been solved, when
I, recognizing *myself* as a unity, put myself in a position of
duality, in the relationship of object to subject that belongs
to the structure of our thought. Frank believes that it has
been solved and now imposes this process of creating personhood, "as the only permissible analogy"[11] to the inner-   17:39
trinitarian relationship. The Father is the Father only
because of the position of the Son. Unity in the Trinity is
created by the joining together of generating and being
generated, Father and Son, through the Holy Spirit.[12] Taking what has been said above about God as Holy Spirit one
step further, it appears significant that 2 Corinthians states,
ὁ κύριος τὸ; πνεῦμά ἐστιν.[26] The Spirit is present wherever there is life and motion. Here it is not used in the
sense of hypostasis, but neither does it exclude this possibility. In the equality of relationship the character of the
Spirit is proved "to bring into unity the original and the
copy," the Father and Son.[27] As *Holy* Spirit, God is self-
revealing in that the Spirit directs what has been created
toward God and brings what has been created into unity
with God.[28] This relationship of immanence first becomes
clear in the doctrine of creation. Therefore, the same Holy
Spirit who is a person of the Trinity is somehow immanent
in the world.[29] It is not gratia creata in contrast to gratia
increata.[30] Reformation and Catholic dogmatics differ
fundamentally on this point.

Critical   We now have some critical questions for Frank. (1) The
questions   analogy of the concept of person is self-evident, but where
is the really decisive thing, the hypostatic character of the
"I" of the begetter, the begotten, and the unity? If this is
what we want to express, then the example would not ring

---

11. *Wahrheit* 1:212, §15.13 [in the original, "as the only reliable, final analogy."]
12. [*Wahrheit* 1:] p. 206.

[25.] Frank, *Wahrheit*, 1, §15.12, 201.
[26.] "The Lord is the Spirit."
[27.] Frank, *Wahrheit*, 1, §15.13, 211. The citation is not verbatim.
[28.] Frank, *Wahrheit*, 1, §15.13, 212.
[29.] Frank, *Wahrheit*, 1, §26.14, 518.
[30.] "Created" and "uncreated grace."

17:40

true. (2) Does Frank truly restrain himself from all metaphysical speculation?[31] It is evident that this is what he wishes, but I don't think he achieves this. He thinks that the faithful are not forbidden to see what the angels desire "to see." However, doesn't he realize that we do not live by seeing, but by faith[32] and that we have to be satisfied with revelation? With this, however, the backbone of any immanent doctrine of the Trinity, including Frank's, is broken. Even he was unable to make three out of one by means of metaphysical speculation.

With the doctrine of the Trinity, however, (3) the problem of Spirit is now treated in a starkly metaphysical manner and is somewhat robbed of its Lutheran vitality. Certainly, the revelatory and moral character is not missing, but both stand in the background. Therefore what we have previously learned about the Spirit can be summarized briefly in the following manner.

Summary

(1) The Spirit is a hypostatic person. (2) The Spirit somehow comes into relationship with human beings and indeed more directly[33] than do the Father and the Son. (3) The Spirit has the tendency to bind together, to build unity. The Spirit closes the chasm that had developed, which we saw in the Trinity that was developed from the concept of rebirth, in which the Spirit sets consciousness of guilt and of freedom from guilt in one entity in that the Spirit creates the new "I." In the immanent Trinity, the Spirit creates the unity between the generating and the generated, and we have already noted the Spirit's unifying activity as creature and creator.

Now it is impossible that the "perfection of becoming," the creation, or "generation"[34] as Frank expresses it, occurs without the participation of the triune[35] principle of becoming, and so the Holy Spirit has its work as well.

17:41 The world as reflection of the Trinity

The world is a reflection of the Trinity in what is created, with respect not only to creation but also redemption. God places the image of God's majesty in the created order, but

---

[31.] Seeberg: "In the sense he wishes it to have, yes, as he really only means to describe religious experience in a dialectical manner."

[32.] Cf. 2 Cor. 5:7. [CG]

[33.] Seeberg underlines and puts "?" in the margin.

[34.] Frank, *Wahrheit*, 1, §20, 595ff.; §21, 324ff.

[35.] Replaces: "Trinity."

this corresponds to the function of the Son in the Trinity, as the generated image of the divine archetype. In this way, the Son participates in creation. We also hear of the participation of the Holy Spirit in Gen. 1:2, where the Spirit broods over creation.[36] The Spirit's nature is to realize and perfect the fate of the creature, which has its potential through the Son.[13]

The Holy
Spirit and
creation

"The Spirit, in whom from eternity the divine archetype, the Father, together with his essential image, the Son, hypostatically binds himself, also effects the unification of the created image of God, existing in the world as a result of its creation through the Son, with its archetype. Creatively, in shaping the divine idea of creator, and redemptively, in shaping and perfecting the salvation-mediating work of Christ, the Spirit establishes a real and complete community between God and God's creation."[37] It is through this work of the Son and the Holy Spirit in creation that the Pauline ἐξ αὐτοῦ καὶ δι'αὐτοῦ καὶ εἰς αὐτόν[38] has actual meaning. Again and again we see the same well-known concept of the Holy Spirit that originates from the doctrine of the Trinity. For that reason we do not need to go into more details here.

Degeneration,
conscience,
and the Holy
Spirit

At this point, humanity's degeneration as a result of the fall is addressed.[39] Nevertheless, at some point, one must demonstrate the redeemability of the human being. Sin must allow an open door for grace. According to Frank, this door is conscience[40] and natural religion.[41] If Frank were really as Lutheran as he would like to be, he would find the opportunity here to speak about the Holy Spirit instead of conscience. For Frank, conscience is "the result of two things, the immanence of the divine Spirit in humanity and the reciprocal effect of humanity on God's inner being and inner working."[14] Moreover, this imma-

17:42

---

13. *Wahrheit* 1, §21.5 [338ff.]
14. *Wahrheit* 1, §26.14, p. 518.

[36.] Frank, *Wahrheit*, 1, §21.5, 341.
[37.] Frank, *Wahrheit*, 1, §26.14, 518.
[38.] "From him and through him and to him" (Rom. 11:36). Compare Frank, *Wahrheit*, 1, §21.5, 344.
[39.] Frank, *Wahrheit*, 1, §26.14, 518.
[40.] Replaces: "sin."
[41.] Frank, *Wahrheit*, 1, §26.13, 511–12, and §26.15, 524ff.

nence is conceived of from the perspective of creation, whereby the Spirit works in all living creatures, even if primarily in human beings, "without prejudice to their degeneration."[15] For Luther every impulse of conscience is an intervention of the Holy Spirit in majestate sua, which, as such, is adversarius noster.[42] It is an intervention from transcendence, which now already stands in immediate relationship to the effect of faith. For Frank, it is only with the impulse of conscience that the possibility for grace is given; for Luther, conscience involves a positive step toward justification. The ethical character of the Spirit is thereby much more emphasized in Luther than in Frank. It goes without saying that here, in the movement of conscience, the Holy Spirit is much more likely to be perceived as *Holy* Spirit in Luther than at the same point in Frank. It might not be an accident that in the section on conscience, the Spirit as *Holy* Spirit is never mentioned. I need only to mention that, in other respects, Frank's doctrine of conscience corrects many old errors.

17:43

The doctrine of regeneration does not in itself provide us with any substantially new insights. The new humanity is, in principle, generated in Christ, and the actualizing belongs to the Holy Spirit, as did generation; "everywhere the Spirit is the mediator of the historically realized dimension of the divine salvific intention in shaping the divine economy of salvation."[16]

Only through the agency of the Holy Spirit does Christ come to us. In doing this, however, the Holy Spirit does not suppress Christ's efficacy. Instead, the Spirit speaks only of Christ and Christ thereby first comes to us—indeed, to speak properly—in us. In order, however, for Christ to come in us the Spirit uses the means of grace. But "no means of grace can be present and become active without being subject to the Holy Spirit. No effect of grace of any kind can occur without being mediated through the Holy Spirit."[17]

Spirit
and grace

Here is the place where Luther cannot but speak of the

---

15. Ibid.
16. §37, *System der Wahrheit* 2:[250].
17. §37.5, p. 251, *System der Wahrheit* 2

[42.] "The Holy Spirit in its majesty which, as such, is our adversary." Cf. above, 2/10:329f.
[43.] "Holy Spirit as gift and grace."

Spiritus Sanctus as donum and gratia.[43] Frank never took up this expression, and it is evident, but no accident, that one looks in vain in the index of Frank's work for "grace." I have also not read in Frank's work the juxtaposition of Spirit and grace, and the word "grace" rarely occurs. Now it is certain that Frank does not thereby abandon the subject; it shows only that he seeks the heart of the problem of Spirit elsewhere than does Luther, deferring the question.

17:44

Grace

Still, he essentially agrees with Luther in this matter. With this he remains true to the Lutheran position that as grace, the Spirit—the power that creates the new "I"—is truly the Holy Spirit as a trinitarian person and is gratia increata. Furthermore, grace, conceived as purely personal, is freely given to persons who do not have free will. It is actual power, not simply forensic judgment. Everything else that we say about the Spirit can be said—in this regard Frank is a genuine Lutheran—equally about grace.

The word and the incarnation of the Holy Spirit

The first means of grace through which the Holy Spirit "glorifies Christ to humanity"[18] (an expression Frank loves) is the word. This is primarily the human word, but it is capable of bearing the Holy Spirit and thereby "personally to mediate"[44] Christ and to create the new "I." In this human speaking of the Spirit's word, the Spirit's incarnation to a certain extent takes place, "to be sure, without hypostatic union," Frank adds.[45]

If, however, it is the word that personally mediates Christ to believers through the Holy Spirit, then we would have to say that an unmediated working of the Holy Spirit is impossible. Although it is certain that the Christian church-community is "a Spirit-filled community," and therefore begotten of the Spirit,[46] it can be such only as long as it draws its strength from the word. This means that the Spirit can never be possessed in the sense that one is "able to regulate it." The Spirit "blows where it will," but only in relation to the word, living and proclaimed in the present, the only means by which the Spirit is able to give individuals and the church-community the power to possess it. With the emphasis on the word, Frank erects a bar-

17:45

---

18. *Wahrheit* 2, §37.4 [and] 5[, 250] §38.3 [, p. 256f.]

[44.] Frank, *Wahrheit*, 2, §38, 252 ff.
[45.] Ibid., §38.3, 256f.
[46.] Frank, *Wahrheit*, 1, §37.4, 258.

rier against mysticism and fanaticism with Lutheran precision and clarity. But he is not speaking about mechanical verbal inspiration[47] of the word; instead the Spirit works ubi et quando visum est Deo (*A.C.* 5).[48]

Lex and evangelium

Following this Frank finally comes to the problem of lex and evangelium. Frank does not seem to be aware of Luther's notion that the first action of the Holy Spirit occurs in the law,[49] in the pure claim of the Spiritus Sanctus in sua maiestate. This is how the Spirit leads the person to the point of blasphemy, then grasps that person in flight and finally gives itself as donum. Luther's disputations[50] are full of such points. Frank states, "a sermon on the law that is preached purely for itself will never convey the Holy Spirit. For the same reason it will never be the source of healing repentance." What Frank says about the sacraments does not go beyond what is well known. After the person sees reality as the "object of becoming" in word and sacrament, the person as "the subject of becoming" should follow. This means it should be seen under the aspect of its

The call as freely given grace and action of the

17:46   Spirit

self-activation.[51] The beginning of spiritual life occurs through the call. The new "I" is contrasted with the old "I."[52] At first the call goes out to one who is disobedient. Deus nolentem trahit.[53] This means it is truly grace freely given. The perverse will is shattered in the act of faith, that means in "the turning of the new 'I' to salvation."[19] The new "I"[54] is created by the Holy Spirit *in the present*; thereby its faith is effected by the Spirit. This seems completely

Faith and Spirit

Lutheran. And yet faith according to Luther is more than a product of the Spirit. The Spirit is itself the subject of faith, in fact in the same way as we are. Both are just as nec-

---

19. *Wahrheit* 2 §41.3, p. 344.

[47.] Seeberg: "Here one must only think of the spoken word! Its inspiration!"

[48.] "Where and when it pleases God." [Augsburg Confession 5; see *The Book of Concord*, 41.][CG] See also Müller, *Die Symbolischen Bücher*, and Frank, *Wahrheit*, 2, §38.4, 259.

[49.] Seeberg: "?" See Seeberg, *Dogmengeschichte*, 4.1, 208 footnote 2 and 210ff.

[50.] Bonhoeffer studied Luther's teaching about the Holy Spirit as seen in the disputations; see the seminar paper above, 2/10:355ff.

[51.] Frank, *Wahrheit* 2, §40.1, 320–21.

[52.] Seeberg: "'The kernel of life' effect on the 'side of nature'." Frank, *Wahrheit* 2:281 and 337 and *Certainty*, pages 189, 193.

[53.] "God pulls the one who does not want to come."

[54.] Seeberg: "Here the important thing is the arbitrium liberatum [the freed will] in relationship to the old liberum arbitrium [the free will] (*Wahrheit*, 2:338)."

essary (see above).

For Frank, the center of the "I" becomes different through justification. The sinful "I" that is still present has moved to the periphery and only inhibits the good will.

Renewal, favor, and grace

This renewal is a "successive removal of the nature of Adam" and a "gradual restoration of the image of God"[20]— and all of this through the activity of the Holy Spirit. With this Melanchthon's favor dei[55] has been overcome in favor of the Lutheran gratia. God's Spirit or grace is real power. And yet Luther would not have spoken as Frank does here. Although renewal is for him a true activity of the Spirit and the grace of God, yet renewal always remains incomplete and is always hemmed in by sin and repentance. Luther's concept of "I" was different. It was conceived functionally. The evil will overpowered the good will again and again and made itself the center. It therefore does not remain on the periphery. The fact that the Holy Spirit remains in spite of sin, just as the individual continues to remain in a state of grace, is also an unsolved puzzle for Luther.

unio mystica

The crowning glory of the relationship of the Holy Spirit to the "I" is the unio mystica.[56] Here we are connected with the Father and the Son through the Holy Spirit. This immanence of God is not the same as God's creative force but is purely personal. It is "the correlation of the turning away from God by the created individual."[21] Here once again a genuinely Lutheran position is being proposed.

personal, ethical

The most intimate connection between Spirit and grace that takes place in the person is purely personal. This means that it is conceived as a corollary to the fall, in purely ethical terms, not as something natural, like the "little spark" of the mystics and the Anabaptists. Thus metaphysics is in fact routed at the apex of the content of Frank's presentation.

With increased renewal the unio mystica also grows and, although it is never completed in this life, it continually

17:47

---

20. *Wahrheit* 2, §42 [360]
21. *Wahrheit* 2, §42.7, p. 376f.

[55.] "God's favor."
[56.] "Mystical [i.e., inner] union" or "unifying."

advances. Once again it is the Holy Spirit that brings this connection to life and with this also restores the original unity of the trinitarian relationship in the world.

Here Frank's doctrine of the Holy Spirit and grace is essentially finished. We learn nothing new in his doctrine concerning the church, in which the problem of scripture[57] is also addressed. Precisely at the point where Schleiermacher pointed out new paths by skillfully identifying communal spirit and the Holy Spirit, Frank consciously holds back.[58] He does not agree with this identification. For him Spirit and grace remain individual principles. He does not find any relationship to the ideal of the collective.[59] This can rightly be surprising with a systematic theologian who can speak of Spirit as metaphysically as Frank did. For him, however, as soon as the Spirit took on the aspect of grace, it became a purely individual principle. Even Schleiermacher did not proceed in an exemplary way with his daring identification, but he certainly saw something that dogmatics should never be allowed to forget. If the relationship between the Holy Spirit and churchly community had been sufficiently considered early on, then the praxis could perhaps have been quite different. Similarly, Frank says nothing about the Holy Spirit when he speaks of the last things. Here Luther speaks very calmly about an end to the ministry of the Holy Spirit. Frank does not do this. For him, the activity of the Holy Spirit is essentially determined by an inner-trinitarian relationship.[60]

In conclusion, we can ascertain that one unified thought runs through the entire doctrine of the Holy Spirit in Frank's thought, even where Spirit becomes grace. The concept of Spirit, however, is not arrived at from the concept of grace but instead is developed from the doctrine of the Trinity. Frank tenaciously retains the orthodox Lutheran doctrine and often overcomes Melanchthon's concept of the Spirit. Yet he often remains only with what he knows to say about Spirit and grace, and that is ground-

Marginal notes:

Church and Holy Spirit

17:48

The last things

Conclusion

[57.] Frank, *Wahrheit*, 2, §45, 423ff.

[58.] Bonhoeffer refers to Frank, *Wahrheit*, 2, §43 and §44, 381ff.

[59.] Marked in the margin. Seeberg wrote beside it, "More clearly." Here we can recognize the beginnings of Bonhoeffer's dissertation. Cf. *SC* (*DBWE* 1):190.

[60.] Seeberg: "?"

ed in the origin of the concept of Spirit in the doctrine of the Trinity. Frank certainly knew that in the final instance Spirit can be completely understood only in connection with grace—pure Lutheran thought. However, he did not pursue his thoughts to the end, to the point where the origins of the system lie. Therefore, his presentation is weaker at this point.

So there remains at this point a great deal of critical and positive work to be done in later Lutheran dogmatics.[61]

[61.] Seeberg: "Very good. Seeberg 19/11 26." The number "19" is uncertain; it may be "13." [The date would thus be either November 19 or 13, 1926.] [PDM]

D. Papers in the Final Phase of His University Years, Doctoral Examination, and the First Theological Examination.[1] January 1927–January 1928

14. Seminar Paper on Job[2]

The Various Solutions to the Problem of Suffering in Job

As is so often the case, so too with this subject, questions of introduction are inextricably linked with the answer to problems of the content. But a formal introductory critique will not lead us to secure results before we delve into problems of content. Indeed it is virtually impossible to decide on a historical-critical question without already having come to some results regarding

---

[1.] The "first theological examination" is a church examination toward ordination, not a university examination for the doctorate. New paragraghs on pages 426 and 427 were created by the German editor.[CG]

[2.] *NL* A 12, 5; typewritten. Bonhoeffer wrote this seminar paper for Ernst Sellin, who evaluated it, in the winter semester of 1926–27 (see below, Appendix 3, page 586). On the first page in the upper left Bonhoeffer wrote by hand, "Dietrich Bonhoeffer." Of the commentaries and monographs we can conclude Bonhoeffer consulted, the two he used intensively were Karl Budde, *Das Buch Hiob*, and Bernhard Duhm, *Das Buch Hiob*. He also used Ernst Sellin, *Das Problem des Hiobbuches*; Carl Siegfried, *The Book of Job*; Rudolf Smend, *Lehrbuch der alttestamentlichen Religionsgeschichte*; Carl Steuernagel, "Das Buch Hiob," in vol. 2 of Emil Kautzsch, *Die Heilige Schrift des Alten Testaments*; and Harry Torczyner, *The Book of Job*. For literature used for the excursus see below, editorial note 40.

content. If this does not happen, the whole is suspended in thin air. This can be seen most clearly when we investigate the issues raised by the Elihu speeches and the speeches of God. Thus it becomes clear why the questions of form and content must be investigated by an integrated approach. We will now attempt as far as possible to determine from the content the introductory questions and thereby also the range of issues, although, as mentioned above, this method is not always successful. Proceeding from the established contents, we believe that we can arrive at a defensible view of the whole, without having to weigh the paper down with exhaustive exegesis of passages like 6:19 or 19:20.

The "Solutions" to the "Problem" of Suffering

Goethe once mentioned to Eckermann that it was an incorrigible German characteristic to view all artistic creation under the perspective of "idea." But this is a highly inartistic attitude that often does not get to the heart of the work of art.[3] If this had been recalled more often when addressing the problem of Job, a great deal of pedantic activity could have been avoided. Someone will say that wherever there is dialogue there must be an idea. Certainly there are topics around which there is debate, but, as we follow the dialogue, we will see that the form is inappropriate to the subject. How far one can speak of a "problem" in this case, or even of a "solution," remains to be seen.

454

It is well known that the *folktale*,[1] like the Faust saga, is an ancient narrative, to which the poet of Job 3–31 added his dramatic work. The content decisively shows this.[2] The folk-saga shows no awareness of the problem of suffering as a question of theodicy. Nothing in the whole tale is problematic. The fact that God tests the pious is as natural, although extraordinary, as is the expectation that the those who are tested will not protest but will humbly subject themselves to the trial. The fact that Job's suffering is presented as a

---

1. The designation "Volksbuch" is unfortunate, because the literary fixing is possibly of a later date and, in any case, the scope of the narrative is not that of a book.[4]

2. The external reasons: the use of the name Yahweh, the transcription of curse words, the difference between Job the shepherd leader (1:1, 4) and Job the city leader (29:7ff., 31:21, and often); the different type of suffering of the latter (16:10; 30:1; 19:3) needs only to be affirmed.

[3.] Cf. Goethe and Eckermann, *Conversations of Goethe with Johann Peter Eckermann*, conversation of May 6, 1827.

[4.] Contrary to Duhm, *Hiob*, VIIf., and Budde, *Hiob*, XIIIf.; on Bonhoeffer's critique see also Sellin, *Das Problem des Hiobbuches*, 22. [The English 'folktale' conveys the sense of an oral story that Bonhoeffer prefers better than the German *Volksbuch*; in the rest of the paper Bonhoeffer normally uses *Volkssage*, 'folk-saga', and sometimes *Volkserzählung*, 'folk-story'.]
[CG]

test is not recounted to explain Job's behavior (Job knows nothing of these motives) [5] but to let the reader know that God's action is not simply an arbitrary power play unconnected[6] to the afflicted person. God and the human person stand in a *personal* relationship, and this relationship must have ethical character. Whatever God has to say to the persons must be based on their ethical value. If human suffering is seen at all as the result of divine action, then one can conceive of only two possibilities: either God wants to test upright persons or God wants to punish the unrighteous. Expressed differently, God wants evidence of Job's piety, either (that is to say, if the passages about Satan are not original) because God himself doubts Job's piety or because God wants to present conclusive proof to those who do. Or again, God wants to requite evil. The Job of the folktale is supposed to be seen as righteous. If evil befalls him, then it necessarily follows that the divine motivation behind it must be to use this suffering as a test (of course, only under the presuppositions listed above). In this scheme there is nothing else to say. For Job the situation is as follows: he is certain of his righteousness and understands that his previous fortune was a divine gift (Yahweh has given it). There is no doubt that he attributes it to his righteous behavior. However, his good fortune is not bound so tightly to ethical behavior that its absence would point to unethical behavior. It is rather that its absence leads one to ask a question that leads one from the ethical arena into the dynamic.[3] Suffering is sent by Yahweh,[7] quite definitely to one individual, so it is not an act of caprice. Yet this is exactly why the only possible attitude in response is to retain one's ethical stance by refraining from all dynamic moments. In relationship to Yahweh one must accept fortune and disaster as they come, because Yahweh is just. The focal point of this book is found in the attitude that whenever a pious individual deals with God neither torment nor problems exist. What the attitude of the unrighteous individual may be when confronted by suffering is not even considered. The fact that Job is righteous is simply assumed by God, by Job, by the reader, and, apparently, by Job's wife. I doubt that the speeches made by Job's friends (assuming they belong to the folktale) originally questioned this. If one were to doubt Job's righteousness one would certainly have added a new complication to the simple, unified composition of the story of the pious Job. On the basis of everything that has been said above, one cannot even imagine this scenario, especially

455

---

3. I designate as dynamic a natural, strong protest without investigating the reason behind it.

[5.] Sellin: underlined with a wavy line.

[6.] The inadvertent *Ungezogenheit*, 'impertinence', in the original has been replaced by the German editor with *Unbezogenheit*, 'unconnected'.

[7.] Here and in what follows the typed word "Jawe" is corrected by hand to read "Jahwe." [The translation uses the customary English spelling, 'Yahweh'.] [PDM]

when one realizes that the friends' speeches could actually be omitted, and that if one were to delete the gloss in 42:10a one could see that 42:10 follows easily on 2:10.

Job remained righteous because he did not question but rather accepted what Yahweh sent him. Therefore, after rejecting Job's friends, Yahweh changed Job's fate. Job became twice as rich and just as happy as before. Thus, the 'problem' in the folktale [Volkssage] is resolved. There is certainly no need to offer any further explanation about the heavenly arrangement. There is also no need for a final act in heaven in which Satan has to admit that he lost the bet. To require this would be the construct of a rationalizing Christian theology of suffering. Job himself does not want to know any more about it. The reader knows it already. What more is there to say? 456

In summary: the folktale is a purely moral (not a theological) story about Job, who proved that he was pious by accepting tragedy and humbly assenting to it. Job is referred to as the epitome of a pious and patient man in Ezek. 14:14 and particularly in James 5:12.[8] The arrival of Job's friends is the introduction to the great series of *speeches in chapters 3–31*. They have come to comfort (2:11). Job recognizes this as well (16:2, v. 5; 21:2). Their first consoling witness is seven days of extended silence. This induces Job to regret his fate and to curse the day of his birth, as does Jeremiah in Jer. 20:24.[9] "The change in the tone from 2:10 . . . can be adequately explained by the amount of time that has passed (constant suffering reduces one's ability to withstand it) and by the actions of his friends, which served only to lower his morale" (Steuernagel, in Kautzsch, 2:330). Today we are no longer so hard-hearted that we cannot sympathize with a Job. It could happen in just this way, but it would undermine the intent of the folktale. The patient, stable, and therefore blessed Job does become impatient. He does not accept his fate at all and does not maintain his ethical stance. Instead, he begins his speeches by cursing his very existence. The narrator of the folktale would be much more than a little shocked at the metamorphosis that had been scripted for his pious Job. This shows with absolute clarity that something radically new begins in the content in chapter 3. This new stance must now be described quite distinctly from the foregoing.

Job curses, and the necessity of asking the first "why" is set in motion (3:11). Why did he have to be born and keep on living? Why do unhappy people live at all? Why must the one whose name is too terrible and holy to mention give light to those who are tortured (3:20)? The question thus is not, Why must *I* suffer? but rather, Why must I live if I have to suffer? The presupposition of everything—this must always be kept in mind—is that Job 457

[8.] The correct reference is James 5:11.
[9.] The correct reference is Jer. 20:14.

retains his righteousness, not in the sense of total sinlessness (13:25ff., 14:3ff., 7:21, 31:33ff.), but as a steady, upright attitude, which is just as unshakable as his awareness of being in a personal relationship with a personal God. He shares only one presupposition with his friends, and that is that the fate of the individual is necessarily related to his actions. "With this emphasis he certainly has taken a much more difficult stance than have his friends. They would only have to give up a friend. Job would have to give up God and therefore the whole world" (Budde, Comm[entary], XXIV). The first to answer is Eliphaz, "No human being is righteous before God" (4:17).[10] "Human beings are born to trouble" (5:7). Did Job question this? He never disputed the first, and the other must appear to him completely senseless. Eliphaz apparently begins from a completely different position than he. Finally, Eliphaz remembers Job's words about unbearable suffering and replies that suffering is happiness, "How happy is the one whom God reproves" (5:17), and with this he actually turns his back on Job. He calls for peace, for patience, for humility so that everything will end happily. The moral of the folktale is epitomized by him, Job's opponent, but apparently from an entirely different presupposition than that in the mind of Job. Disturbed, Job complains anew about the horror and the riddle of his suffering (6:2), then about the disloyalty of his friends. Finally he realizes Eliphaz's awful presupposition. He is supposed to be guilty of all of this. "Teach me, and I will be silent; make me understand how I have gone wrong" (6:24). But he knows that no one can do that. He immediately rejects this nonsensical idea of his own guilt, and once again he begins to complain. He concludes with his life and his fate. With this, however, new strength to struggle grows within him. He realizes that God, who had been his friend, has personally attacked him as if God were his enemy (7:13).[11] Would God ever be his friend again (7:8, 21)? Could God think that human beings are so important that it was worthwhile to torture them until they despair (7:17)? Could sin possibly be the reason for all of this? Why didn't God forgive them? At some point God's wrath will continue too long. Then if God wanted a truce, Job would be no more (7:21). All of this can be understood only on the basis of a very personal, ethical understanding of Job's relationship to God. The anthropomorphisms are preposterous. Bildad answers with the wisdom of the ancients that surely has an answer to every question. You are at fault; God is always in the right (chapter 8). With this latter statement he certainly has not told Job anything new (9:1). Job is more aware of this than is Bildad, i.e., if he believed that might is right (v. 3). "He is wise in heart, and mighty in strength—who has resisted him and succeeded?" (v. 4). God's might is great,

458

[10.] In Bonhoeffer's text this is a statement, not a question as in the Luther Bible and the NRSV. [CG]

[11.] The correct reference is Job 7:13-14.

so great that he can become capricious (12:14ff.) and cruel. "For he crushes me with a tempest and multiplies my wounds without cause" (9:17). "He mocks at the calamity of the innocent" (9:23). God wants him to be guilty, and God has the power. What can Job do against this? (9:29). The lonely call, "Let me know why you contend against me" (10:2), fades hopelessly away. God created him with the intention of ruining him, and so he is swiftly approaching death without turning back (10:20ff.). Like a bad refrain that either fits or does not fit after every verse, Zophar's buffeting speech clangs out that God is righteous and therefore Job is guilty, that God knows Job's sins, even though he does not know them himself (11:6ff.). But Job has quite rightly protected himself against such a concept of guilt.[12] This really was not an answer to Job, who in any case had not actually asked any questions; indeed, he frequently gets answers to questions that he does not ask. The dialogue form does not fit very well.

Job now risks it all and audaciously confronts Zophar with the statement that it is especially the pious who fall into ruin. The secure individuals, however, are those who stand fast (12:4).[4] God simply does what God wants to do. Who cannot see this? Yet especially because of this, "I desire to argue my case with God" (13:3). "He will surely rebuke you" (13:10). Yes, he will surely kill me, but come what may, I will prove my innocence to God. I know who I am, and I am standing my ground. Could a guilty person dare to speak in this way? Job has finally generated a standpoint from which everything can be discussed. His friends have driven him to it. He intends to call good what is good until the bitter end. Not even for God's sake will he call black white (13:7). What must occur is that God must personally acknowledge that such action is fraudulent (13:10). With this a completely new backdrop has been introduced into Job's concept of God. God is peevish, certainly, but nonetheless righteous. If God is showing one side to Job now, the time will come when Job once again will see God from the other. Both sides, however, stand in an indissoluble relationship to each other, and the subject of the poem's entire further development lies in the manner by which Job persistently forces his way through to the just God—but never[14] without forgetting the peevish God in his attempt. Job's attitude is thus two-pronged. A hopeful certainty echoes constantly in the foreground alongside of Job's

459

---

4. Considering vv. 4 and 6 to be inauthentic as Siegfried and Duhm do, is not supported by the arguments they present; certainly vv. 9 and 10 are inauthentic (the name Yahweh!).[13]

[12.] The words "that God . . . concept of guilt" are a handwritten addition by Bonhoeffer.

[13.] Cf. Siegfried, *The Book of Job,* 7 and 49, and Duhm, *Hiob,* 66ff.

[14.] The "never" contradicts the intention of Bonhoeffer's argument and should be ignored.

cacophony of hopeless lament. Along with or—better—within the dynamic attitude of the first chapter, an ethical attitude comes to the fore. Of course, this happens in a completely different way than it does in the folktale: not in humble acceptance but in the self-assured demand for a just judgment.

¶ *With this newly attained stance and hope, the question raised by the entire dialogue is transformed.* Had the Job of the first chapter remained calm at the terrible turn of events, as described in 42:10? Had everything that had occurred been nothing but *a* violent scream of one individual who had been mortally afflicted with a puzzling fate and was begging for either the coup de grâce or healing? If his own innocence had been a self-evident presupposition for him, which his friends tried to undermine, now everything was different. Job no longer wants any change of circumstance or, at any rate, this recedes into the background. Certainly he hopes, but he also knows how hopeless his situation is. With his imminent death everything will be over. He doesn't want to hear about resurrection (14:10ff.), but he will appeal to the righteous God. At least he wants to know that his innocence has been confirmed. His friends must recognize that he, a righteous person, fell into misfortune. But Job is able to think and hope like this only for fleeting milliseconds, and the return to revulsion follows even more frightfully (14:15-17 and 18-22). It is at this point that the first dialogue ends. Eliphaz repeats his refrain about human guilt without bringing any new perspectives to bear. Job wants to stop speaking. He finds himself in a depressed mood again (16:6-16), but he does not give in. "There is no violence in my hands, and my prayer is pure" (16:17); and now he strives forward. He will sue forever, but he knows that the witness to his innocence is already in heaven. At some point God will establish justice between humanity and God, who is humanity's friend (16:20ff.).[5] God is not only called a just God but—and that must mean the same—God is after all Job's friend. Here Job has uttered a statement that Job's friends must consider blasphemous. He, who is plagued by God, wants to consider himself God's friend. Preciely now, when Job seems most helpless, when God's wrath is most evident, when everything visible is rearing up against him (16:8), and when God's temper is raging, Job reaches toward the just and loving God. In all of this Job no longer hopes for an alteration of his fate. He knows that his death stands at the door, and he complains about this; but there is something much more important for him. This attitude reaches its apex in the chapter 19. Job knows that he is righteous, and that gives him

---

5. I am following Duhm's exegesis, who already in 20a conjectures, יִמְצָא לִי רֵעִי and understands God to be the friend in 21b.[15]

[15.] Duhm, *Hiob*, 89–90.

the audacious hope even in death[6] to see God,[7] and to hear God's justice 461 declaring judgment. With all the strength of his trust, he casts himself on the God who was his friend, and must become his friend again, and who truly still is. Statements like, "I will not let you go unless you bless me"[19] or Psalm 73:23ff. can be compared with this.

¶Zophar finds this steadily increasing certainty intolerable: "Even though they mount up high as the heavens, and their head reaches to the clouds, they will perish forever like their own dung" (20:6-7). From this point on, nothing new is said. Job becomes more and more certain of victory, but without changing the tenor of the complaints about his terrible fate. In chapter 21 he speaks openly about the unjust division of fortune and misfortune. In chapter 23 the old torment reawakens. Finally,[8] in chapter 29 Job sadly describes his former happiness and his devastating fate.[9] But in his powerful, purifying oath he reclaims and maintains his righteousness. He intends to sign his name under all his words and, like a prince, challenge God to a duel in proud consciousness of his friendship with God. With God and for God he 462 wants to go up against God. God's caprice should not cover up God's love and justice. "The speeches of Job are ended" (31:40).

We will now attempt to summarize what has been said. If the folktale tells us of Job's piety, the poet tells of Job's complaints. At first his only "problem" is to empty his own heavy heart and to drive himself to death. "And when man becomes silent in his suffering, a god enabled me to say what I suffer."[22] The tacit supposition upon which all is based is that Job is righteous

---

6. Not, as Duhm thought, after death,[16] which, in spite of his objections, seems to me to contradict everything earlier (cf. 14:10ff.). In fact, this does not have much to say about the actual problem. Torczyner places the words of 25/27[17] under 42:5.[18] This is fine, but only if you accept Torczyner's general presuppositions.

7. On the idea of seeing God see, e.g., Pss. 11:7; 17:5.

8. Chapter 28 is inauthentic. In Job's mouth it would be a striking anticipation of the speech of God. In addition, in the time period of our poet a hypostatization of wisdom would be unthinkable. The attempt of Budde to conceive this chapter as an increasing attack upon God fails with this alone. Torczyner places this chapter at the end of God's speech. The difficulty is not resolved even by this.[20]

9. In the psychological structure, the whole is not penetrable, and it says something in favor of Torczyner's argument for a later redaction of fragments.[21]

[16.] Ibid., 103.

[17.] This means Job 19:25-27.

[18.] Torczyner, *The Book of Job,* 130.

[19.] Gen. 32:26.

[20.] Cf. Budde, *Hiob,* 162ff., and "Die Capitel 27 und 28 des Buches Hiob," 193–274.

[21.] Cf. Torczyner, *Job,* 202–7.

[22.] The motto of the elegy from Goethe's *Torquato Tasso,* act 5, scene 5, 224. Cf. also above, 2/2:206, editorial note 86.

whether or not God is irascible or hostile toward him. The other presupposition is that one must stand in a personal ethical relationship to God, i.e., actually to live under God's enmity rather than God's indifference, even if this attitude is without foundation. Truly God intends individuals to have what God has given them. It is only when Job's friends try to rob him of the first presupposition that Job's specific question crystallizes out of the plethora of possible starting points. It is the question of Job's righteousness. Naturally, a poet would like to address many other related issues, but the tone is set by the proof of Job's righteousness, i.e., for the poet and the reader, *Job's truthfulness* about his actions despite everything that seemed to speak against it. Emphasized also is the triumph of the righteous individual, who does not forget that God is a just and loving friend even when God is irascible. Only when the central question of innocence is clarified can one approach the question of the rationale for innocent suffering. However, the "solution" presented by Job's friends was incorrect from the start. They understood the problem but approached it from false presuppositions.[23] The problem of suffering, in the sense of a metaphysical question, "Why do the pious suffer and the wicked prosper?" reappears again and again in the course of the dialogue, but it is not central. Instead it results from the debate. It could not even be addressed if one began from such different perspectives as do Job and his friends. One does not, however, come to terms with these perspectives until chapter 31. The differences have been sharpened to their utmost extent. For the poet and the reader, moreover, this problem had already been solved in the prologue. This is the main significance of it for this poetry and is proof that the poetry and the prose originally belonged together. But the main interest of the poet is the individual. According to the poet, the misfortune of a righteous person's suffering can be traced to God's irascibility. But a righteous individual does not allow for the concept of a just God and God's friendship to perish. Therefore one cannot, as Duhm cautiously does, identify as "the primary problem, whether the fate of this world and the course of the world can be made to agree with the traditional conceptions of God and God's rule of the world" (p. 42). This problem is solved the moment God speaks. To be sure, it lies alongside of the main problem, but it is not itself the issue at hand. We agree with Budde even less when he says that the righteous Job becomes a sinner when he defends his righteousness. The intent of the poem is to cleanse Job of his self-righteousness (XXXII). Duhm arrives at his conclusion on the basis of God's speeches, and Budde reaches his conclusion from the Elihu speeches. How could this be, however, when the original outline included neither one? We have tried to understand the dialogue purely on its own terms and to inquire: could the book of

463

[23.] The phrase, "but . . . false presuppositions," has been added by Bonhoeffer's hand.

Job once have ended with 31:40? Here the contradictions are sharpened. God has been challenged. God *must* appear. A simple transformation of external fate could no longer suffice. God does appear, and Job is not disappointed in his expectations. Apparently the friends see this too (I would like to interpret 19:27[10] "not as a stranger"). But God does this only after we "permit the childishness of a pompous rabbi to flow over us" (Duhm).[25] This is an exaggeration. Actually, after almost intolerably long speeches, with countless repetitions of what has already been said, Elihu advances a new thought: the pride of the righteous should be tempered by suffering (33:17; 36:9). This, however, is not connected to Job's outbursts, which had provoked his three friends, but instead to his earlier life of good fortune. And so Job should accept his suffering from God as having been sent to *purify* him. Elihu rises to the occasion and utters this exquisite sentence, God delivers the afflicted by their affliction (36:15). This is truly a fresh and perhaps redeeming thought, but first we could point out that it is not spoken clearly by Elihu, but remains hidden under the repetition of the friends' opinions. Second, this is not a solution to the question the poet raises in chapters 3-31 (see above); at best, it is a deepening and refining of the opinions of Job's three friends, as here also we find the assumption: misfortune, therefore guilty. Third, however, according to chapters 13,16; 19,31 the solution can no longer come from a human but only from God. These arguments from content, along with several linguistic points not adduced here, are evidence that the Elihu speeches did not belong to the original conception. Therefore 38:1 follows directly after 31:40. God appears in the whirlwind and might well now offer the solution, pronounce judgment on Job, confirm his righteousness, maybe even tell Job the reason for his suffering (although this is not necessary), and punish his friends. God also speaks just as Job said God would. God thunders and demands to know who takes it upon themselves to question the divine decree. God asks about the pillars of the earth and its founding, about the home of light and darkness, and Job cannot answer. God says that even where no people live, God causes it to rain and allows plants to grow (38:26).[11] God suggests mockingly to Job that he take the government of the world in his own hands (40:10), and asks whether God must become unjust because Job would like to be just (40:8-14). Job cannot stand up under this questioning or bring himself to answer. Instead he admits that

464

---

10. וְלֹא זָר (19:27) can also be translated: "not a foreigner."[24]

11. Cf. below, note 14.[26]

[24.] Bonhoeffer added note 10 by hand. For the translation of Job 19:27 Bonhoeffer follows Budde, *Hiob*, 107.

[25.] Duhm, *Hiob*, 152. On Bonhoeffer's immediately following reliance upon Duhm's judgment, see Sellin, *Hiobbuches*, 18.

[26.] Bonhoeffer added note 11 by hand.

465

he has spoken out of ignorance. Now that his eye has seen God, he recognizes this and repents with dust and ashes. It happened exactly as Job knew it would (chapter 9). God has shoved him to the side, "he crushed him in a tempest" (9:17). He knew of nothing to combat God's terrible command. Job admitted that he was defeated. The friends must have been right. He had overreached himself like the Titan Prometheus and now lay humbled in the dust. He repented, and the next thing that God says is addressed to his friends and contains the message: "Job was totally right; you were wrong." What is this? This is plainly a contradiction. Is it possible that the connection with chapter 9 does not make sense? The question whether God's speeches are genuine rests indeed on chapter 9. There, in his unbearable torment, Job gave up hope (cf. Jer. 12:1). Nothing would be of any help. If he were to cry out to God, who knows if he would get an answer? And if he received one, then it would not be an answer but a striking down by the dreadful power, and he would have to admit that he was guilty even though he was not. An encounter with God would not bring justice but violence. And this is what happened. Duhm thinks that one difference is very clear: Job's awareness that he had no answer to the speeches of God is humble, while in chapter 9 it is bitter.[27] We must admit that after chapter 9 one might have thought that God would ask other questions than were asked in chapter 38. Still the decisive point is the same in both. Duhm himself admits that if his objection is not valid, one would have to consider God's speeches inauthentic.[28] And so it is, because God does not answer Job. There is, however, the difference that in chapter 9 it is out of enmity and in chapter 38, indifference. But in both cases the power of nature is contrasted to Job's concept of justice. In the face of this, everything breaks apart, not because Job wants to humble himself but because he simply can do nothing else. Thus it necessarily follows (indirectly[29] with Duhm as well) that God's speeches are not original. To be

466

sure, it was the poet's goal to allow his Job to force his way through to an ethically just relationship to God, to allow him to put his rightful demands to God and to ensure that God become a witness to Job's innocence. Thus it was not the poet's intent to show that Job was basically wrong. He would have had to do this much more clearly instead of allowing him to be de facto right. In addition one cannot imagine an ancient poet capable of using the modern technique in plays and novels in which everyone is guilty. Budde claims that it is clear that the poet's intent was to allow Job to be presumptuous, even blasphemous, and therefore guilty. No reader from that time period could have overlooked this.[30] This is truly a more serious objection. That Budde

---

[27.] Cf. Duhm, *Hiob*, 182.

[28.] Ibid.

[29.] Added by Bonhoeffer's hand.

[30.] Cf. Budde, *Hiob*, chapters 39–49, especially 33f. and 40ff.

is correct in his second assertion is evident from God's speeches themselves. These assume a completely different interpretation of the entire poem. But we cannot agree with Budde's first assertion. It was exactly the unprecedented audacity of the poet of chapters 3-31 that sanctioned such invective as Job hurled at God on the basis of his own righteousness.

He wanted his Job to be so righteous that he had the right even to declare God unjust.[12] Prometheus was intended to receive moral consecration. To take offense at this was something that every conscience had to do, especially every Christian conscience. Job, however, had a good conscience, i.e., he didn't have one at all. That it is easy for us to apply a Christian judgment to the poet is self-evident, but it should nonetheless be avoided. The interpretation that God's speeches give to chapters 3-31 of constantly intensifying audacity, and with it of chapter 9 as profound insight, does not fit with the original plan. From this, however, it follows that God's speeches are the answer to something that was not even asked. This is the issue that Duhm sees as central to the text. It is the question of the relationship of human suffering and divine sovereignty of the world.[32] Hardly a word is spoken about Job's righteousness; only the outcome demonstrates his "unrighteousness" (but cf. 464ff. on 40:8-14).[33] God should not come as the Lord of nature, but only as the righteous friend of humankind. The encounter should not have been presented as a dynamic one but as ethical. If one were to say that this tension and solution are precisely the crowning glory of the whole, then one would have to handle the exegesis of chapter 9 differently and with it the whole personal-ethical development of the book. To be sure, God's speeches require total submission to the type of fate that Eliphaz and the folktale suggest, with the difference that the latter is ethically motivated. God's speeches, however, opine that God and divine power are far too great for a person to reproach God. Was not the world created for God and not for humanity? Is not God, then, the center of the world and not human

467

---

12. The self-justification of the Psalms, as in 7:1, 17:3ff., 26, etc., does not come into consideration here as a comparison. That the poet always had Satan before his eyes by the accusations of God—"according to the poet, the true God didn't abuse Job but rather the false God of doctrine"[31]—does not appear true to me. Would he not have clarified this intention, in that he, e.g., let the friends criticize Job, and that he spoke of God as if he were Satan? This is also the reason why I would not reject the originality of the pieces about Satan. In the Old Testament we certainly hear often enough of temptations by God (Gen. 15:6, 21:1, especially 2 Sam. 24:1, and 1 Chron. 21:1).

[31.] Sellin, *Hiobbuches*, 36; cf. also 23f., where Sellin objects to the originality of the pieces about Satan, and 25, where one find the biblical references given by Bonhoeffer (up to the reference from 1 Chron. 21:1).
[32.] Cf. Duhm, *Hiob*, IXf., 42 and 203.
[33.] The parenthetical comment is added by Bonhoeffer.

beings?[13] It is with such insight that God's speeches dismiss us. There actually is an answer to the problem of suffering, but from the perspective of the all-powerful, not the just God. This, however, could not have satisfied the poet of chapters 3-31.[14] Chapter 40:8-14 indirectly answers the actual question about whether Job is righteous. It is apparently the intention of the chapter that Job appear to be righteous. God's righteousness and Job's innocence do not exclude each other (Smend);[35] and the other thought, "What would happen then, if you, Job, would condemn every godless person?" seems to confirm this. Therefore, Job's innocence is not questioned here either. Thus we can perhaps assume that here is retained an undoubted snippet of the poet's original speeches of God, which were later completely reworked. But one cannot place too much emphasis on this. We must only adhere to the thought that the poet ended his drama of Job with a speech of God, onto which 42:7 could easily have been appended in the manner discussed above. Job's righteousness is thereby attested. He has proved himself and has triumphed. It is true that Job should actually have died at the moment he saw God (cf. 13:15ff.; 19:25ff.; etc.). (The fact that the Elihu speeches allow everything to end happily does not speak against their authenticity, contra Smend.)[36] There is little to be gleaned from God's speeches about this (contra Duhm).[37] According to the folktale something completely different is at work. Here, for better or for worse, the poet must have had to accommodate the tradition. It is evident that a contradiction lies before us.

We would like to respond to our topic with this summary. In the proper book of Job, chapters 3-31, there is neither a problem of suffering nor a solution to the problem of suffering in the sense of a theodicy. Still, so many problems are touched upon that it is difficult to formulate a unified method for framing pertinent questions. This results in completely different interpretations of chapters 3-31, depending on whether one interprets them from the perspective of chapters 32ff. or from chapters 38ff. It is thus relatively easy to force the interpretation. We have attempted to understand these chapters from their own perspective and came to the conclusion that their purpose was not to discover a theological truth but to tell the story of a suffering, righteous man. This is the reason why the dialogue form does not

---

13. Duhm sees the kernel of the speeches of God here (38:26ff.).[34]

14. The external reasons for the inauthenticity of the speeches of God: before 38:1 Job must have spoken, before 42:7 Yahweh. To the best of my knowledge, no one has remarked on the different conceptions of geophysics: 38:6 and 26:7b.

[34.] Duhm, *Hiob*, 180ff.
[35.] Cf. Smend, *Lehrbuch der alttestamentlichen Religionsgeschichte*, 476.
[36.] Smend, *Religionsgeschichte*, 475, footnote 1.
[37.] Cf. Duhm, *Hiob*, 180ff.

seem to fit the whole text. The problem of suffering and of theodicy, however, is addressed again and again by Job's three friends in the sense of a doctrine of retribution. This is how it was circulated among the people and advocated especially by Ezekiel. Elihu saw suffering in terms of purification and therefore presupposed that it was a *deserved* misfortune. The problem of undeserved misfortune, the real problem of Job, is solved in the prologue with the idea that suffering is a test, and in God's speeches with the idea of 469 the trifling significance of human suffering in the context of the immensity of the natural world. It is consciously left unsolved in chapter 28. Chapters 38ff. cannot be recognized as a solution, because they use a dynamic concept of God that prophetic Judaism had overcome. The concept in the prologue, the most profound in the whole book of Job, was superseded only by the more universal concept of Christianity, "all things work together for good for those who love God,"[38] and in the eschatological expectation.

The epilogue has buried within it an idea that leads to deeper contemplation. In it, through the testing of his suffering, Job has gained the strength to make a plea to God for his friends. Whether or not this idea was part of the original folk story is difficult to decide. We see it instinctively in connection with the suffering servant of God (Isaiah 53). We would, therefore, really like to give the poet credit for it. With this, the problem of the relationship between the poet and the author of the folk-story comes to the fore once again. How could the poet dare to bring his story about the lamenting Job into the context of the pious Job, who was a model of patience? Where is the tertium comparationis? Might there perhaps really be a break at this point and might the poem originally not have had the Job legend as its subject? Perhaps our whole thesis is false and Job really became guilty when he was tempted by his friends during their final visit to him? We are not forced to accept any of these hypotheses. The tertium comparationis lies in the personal ethical relationship to God, which Job never allows to be taken from him, and has its basis in his objective righteousness. If the poet had only addressed this, then the poet could easily have taken over the folk-story, which every reader would have recognized as such or perhaps already knew. (One only need think of the reworking of the tale of Faust.) Whether the whole book can be seen as the outgrowth of the work of *one poet* and that poet's attitude to suffering in the world remains to be tested. It is certainly possible to assume that an anxious conscience gradually informed the poet 470 of chapters 3–31 that titanism was blasphemous. But was it a higher moral solution to allow this strong individual simply to be cast to the ground by one even stronger? Should the poet then not have seen that he thereby had nullified his whole work to that point? Should he not rather have struck it out than versified like that? I believe that only someone who had already judged

---

[38.] Cf. Rom. 8:28.

Job's battle of faith as such and still had a secret joy in titanism could have produced the solution of God's speeches. Our poet could hardly have been transformed into such a person. It seems even more unfeasible that our poet could have finally become our Elihu since Elihu apparently begins with an assumption that does not reflect Job's attitude. Elihu's assumption is that the most secret fruit of injustice is self-righteousness. This is a deeper idea, but it does not belong here. Therefore, in both cases, we would have to assume that the poet completely changed his basic attitude. Would he really have allowed his old poem to prevail without being clearer about how it was finally to be interpreted? Should the original and later speeches of God be replaced by Elihu's speeches or be trumped by them? Could the speeches of Elihu hope for the approval of the reader when the speeches of God say something quite different? I believe that all these questions have to be answered in the negative and that the consequences are thereby clear.[39]

Excursus on R. Otto's presentation of the speeches of God in *The Idea of the Holy*, pages 77ff., and the assessment of the problem of suffering in Christendom according to Luther (cf. Holl, *What Did Luther Understand by Religion?*, 91ff.)[40]

In the speeches of God in Job, Otto is determined to find a "calming of the soul" and no overpowering by sheer superior force. How else can the passage about Job's repentance in dust and ashes be understood? "This is a witness to inner conviction."[41] Here we do not find a parallel to Rom. 9:20ff. but much more that the whole represents a powerful justification of God, not a denial of it. The "mystery," which here at the same time is fascinans and augustum, has as its content the "dysteleology" of world events.[42] Before this mysterious wonder, which contradicts all searching for meaning, Job becomes calm and his soul is stilled.

We cannot agree with Otto's presentation and evaluation of the problem of Job. An answer is not given to Job by chapters 3-31 with the speeches of God, and therefore he cannot find peace in these speeches.

It is noteworthy that Otto without further discussion correlates the feeling of the "quieted soul" with the ethical act of repentance (see above). That a soul tortured by terrible misfortune and focused on religious experience could find a certain peace in the feeling of the dysteleology of events cannot be doubted. Suddenly the soul would perceive universally that its objective dysteleology, which had been repressed, subjectively presents itself with an

471

[39.] The following excursus is handwritten.

[40.] Otto, *The Idea of the Holy*, 77ff.; Holl, *What Did Luther Understand by Religion?* 15ff.

[41.] Otto, *The Idea of the Holy*, 78.

[42.] "Fascinating," "sublime"; "dysteleology" (unsuitability, inappropriateness, inimical nature), a concept Otto used in *The Idea of the Holy*, 79.

undeniable universal feeling of liberation. It is precisely its existential unworthiness that is then transformed into the feeling of the worthiness of the unworthy. This is the paradox of the irrational. These are certain religious experiences that are all too common. Yet, Job is more than a "tortured soul." He is a person with an ethical mandate and an ethical-personal concept of God. He is the friend of God in spite of all friendship.[43] In spite of the long recognized dysteleology of world events, he holds fast to a personal relationship to God. The only important thing to him is the acknowledgment of this relationship. Can one then speak of a "justification of God" (see above) when nothing other than God's complete incomprehensibility is being taught to humankind? No, an ethical will can be broken only in confrontation with a positive personal will. Along with the poet of Job, we know of a "justification of God," if one is able to use this phrase, only in the sense of a personal relationship to humankind, i.e., in God's justification of the human person. That we are left with a final puzzle in the deus absconditus, namely, predestination (Rom. 9:20ff.),[44] is demonstrated by the relativity of the "justification" and also by the difference of an ethical and a naturalistic justification. Romans 9:20ff. far transcends the problematic of the speeches of God! Here, however, the ethical height had already been achieved. *Everything* else is a descent, even if it does have the privilege of being modern.

472

We cannot see that this presents a solution to the problem of Job in the speeches of God.

In the description of the lamenting Job has the poet of Job already arrived at a Christian solution of the problem? To a certain extent, this must be answered in the affirmative. (1) The poet traces suffering back to the personal God and not to a satanic force, a commandment that Luther repeatedly stressed. Luther calls it a sin against the First Commandment whenever people "ascribe to the devil or evil persons their misfortune and adversity . . ." (*WA* 1:252).[45] (2) The poet does not confuse profound peace with trust in God (*WA* 14:467);[46] here lies the 'religious' root of titanism. (3) The poet also sees that Job's faith is being tested and proved. (4) The poet still sees the loving God 'in' Job's misfortune. To be sure, there is a decisive difference here between the poet's perspective and the Christian perspective. Christianity finds God '*in*' the midst of misfortune. To a greater degree, Job finds God *despite* misfortune or *beyond* it. He could not yet conceive of God's wrath and God's love together. Certainly God is both friend and enemy at the same

---

[43.] Certainly a mistake. Bonhoeffer must have meant "enmity." [The two German words are somewhat similar, *Freundschaft* and *Feindschaft*.] [CG]

[44.] Here and further below Bonhoeffer means Rom. 9:20ff.

[45.] Luther, *WA* 1:252, 9, "Eine kurze Erklärung der zehn Gebote, 1518." Bonhoeffer cites from Holl, *Luther*, 91, footnote 1. [This note is not in the English translation.] [CG]

[46.] Cf. Luther, *WA* 14:467, 20ff., "Die Ascensionis domini. 5 Mai 1524." The reference is found in Holl, *What Did Luther Understand by Religion?*, 92, footnote 64.

time—"with God against God"—(Holl[47] and cf. above). The realization that God is angry *out* of love cannot yet be found in Job. In Job's concept of God, the chasm that Christianity closed is still open. The final reason, however, is found in the Christian deepening of the concept of righteousness, and so we find here an enormous chasm between Job and us. Here we also find the other root of Job's titanic protest, which we, along with Budde and others, are inclined to see as Job's worst guilt. But this should not[48] lead us to ignore the presupposition and the incredible achievement of the poet.[49]

473

15. Notes on Karl Barth's *Die christliche Dogmatik im Entwurf*[1]

Barth 335: Relationship of Scripture to the foundational history witnessed in it. The statement that the Bible is God's word harks back to the subject of this literature.

The church finds in Scripture the word *heard* by the authors.[2]

337: No intuition. *God* wrote the scriptures.[3]

474   338: The canon is to be believed as singled out by *God*.[4]

[47.] Holl, *Luther*, 91.

[48.] The German text has an inadvertent double negative in this sentence.[PDM]

[49.] Final grade: "Bibliography! Otherwise quite good. Sellin."

[1.] *NL* Appendix A 21, a), b), c); handwritten; date of composition uncertain. Three working notes were in Bonhoeffer's copy of Barth's *Die christliche Dogmatik im Entwurf*. Published in the late summer of 1927, it was probably read immediately by Bonhoeffer. Most of the notes refer to the third chapter: "Holy Scripture," §20: "God in the Witness of the Prophets and the Apostles" (*Christliche Dogmatik*, 334–62). Two notes pertain to the fourth chapter, "The Proclamation of the Church." The first refers to §23.3: "God in the Sermon: the Ministry of Dogmatics" (*Christliche Dogmatik*, 421); the second refers to §25.1: "Dogmatic Thinking: Formal and Material Principles (*Christliche Dogmatik*, 451). Cf. also the appropriation of *Christliche Dogmatik* in *SC* (*DBWE* 1):250–52.

[2.] "The acknowledgment of the Christian church that the Bible is God's word thus harks back to an acknowledgment in it regarding the *subject* of this literature. It finds in the Bible, not separated from it but also not confused with it, through the Bible both veiled and disclosed, both hidden and offered, a primary datum, the word that the authors of scripture not so much spoke and wrote as heard and perceived, the word of God in its initial form, *revelation*" (*Christliche Dogmatik*, 436).

[3.] Bonhoeffer's formulation is different from Barth's in that he argues for a non-dialectical identity of God's revelation and the Bible as a book. "If the church actually thinks that it has heard God in the witnesses of these people (i.e., the prophets and apostles), then it must in all seriousness think also the other, that God has spoken in them" (*Christliche Dogmatik*, 337). And this: "The reality of revelation is indirectly identical with the reality of the Bible. Indirect: we know that the Bible is one thing and revelation another. But identical: revelation does not occur in a vacuum, through historically determined facts and conjectures, only to fill and enliven the space behind the Bible. It occurs in their witness. It occurs in the Bible" (*Christliche Dogmatik*, 344).

[4.] "In choosing such and such writings out of the mass of those available as God's true word, one meant to do nothing more than to establish that they as such are already chosen,

421: Oral and written human communication is only an accident of the word of God.[5]

Does not make sense! The church exists only in this way.[6]

451: The formal and material principles of dogmatics are identical; the material principle is not one created from other sources, but rather also = scripture.[7]

i.e., therefore: the super formal principle. Calvinist?[8]

341: One may not, as Luther wants, adapt the Bible to a dogmatics; in the canon, John and James, *law and gospel,* are together; both are grace. For the word of God has no history. (Luther does not deny this; all of the word of God is spoken!)[9]

342:[10] "That it is law and indeed law of the church and not that it is somehow evident from experience is what confirmed the priority of the word of the prophets and apostles before other (Goethe's) words"—in part simply false![11]

Like[12] the incarnation of the Logos, the coming to speech of the word is eternal, 343.[13]

344: The reality of revelation is indirectly identical with the reality of the Bible, Christianity is a religion of the book.[14]

But the gospel is the humanity of Christ, which is certainly no book.[15]   475

---

that such and such writings have already shown themselves to be God's word" (*Christliche Dogmatik*, 338).

[5.] Bonhoeffer here refers to Barth's statement about the significance of the Bible for dogmatics: "Just as Holy Scripture is *Holy* Scripture only in the divine *act* of lordship, which is at the same time absolute authority and absolute freedom, so the proclamation of the church is also not in itself God's word but rather only in the *act* of divine speech occurring today" (*Christliche Dogmatik*, 542). [The word '*act*' is italicized by the German editor.] [PDM]

[6.] Concerning this critique of Bonhoeffer, cf. *AB* (*DBWE* 2):83ff. and 98–99.

[7.] Uncertain; perhaps "scriptures."

[8.] "That the formal and material principles are therefore one and the same" (*Christliche Dogmatik*, 451).

[9.] A summary recap of Barth's argument on page 340f. The sentence in parenthesis is to be interpreted as a defense of Luther against Barth.

[10.] Beginning of the second page; with the exception of the word in parenthesis, a verbatim citation (*Christliche Dogmatik*, 342).

[11.] Concerning this critique cf. Bonhoeffer's paper on the interpretation of Scripture, above 2/6:285ff., especially 289ff.

[12.] Replaces: "with the."

[13.] Barth contrasts the eternal incarnate Logos with the earthly human word in the Bible. Bonhoeffer's formulation is a criticism of this passage. (See *Christliche Dogmatik*, 343.) [For Barth they are to be distinguished, but not separated. See his explication of the threefold form of the word of God, *Church Dogmatics* 1/1:88ff.] [PDM]

[14.] "If one for this reason wants to call Christianity a 'religion of the book', one can always do that" (*Christliche Dogmatik*, 344).

[15.] The following, "Determine . . . is lost," is in Roman script and probably not from Bonhoeffer; after this it is once again in Bonhoeffer's handwriting.

Determine (with Luther) the relationship of the *humanity* of Christ and the Bible

Word about Christ = sermon   (*Christ's spiritual body*)

Bible *human* witness. *Indirect* communication; otherwise the character of the scriptures as calling for decision is lost. It will not *be* God's word, but rather be *heard*[16] (good! but!)

The scandal [addition above "scandal": "lies not here"] is overcome[17] in *faith*: therefore no theory of inspiration, *which Calvin also did not have*, 345–6 exactly as unfortunate as God in history.[18]

356:[19] The crux, that only with the bondage of our reason can one grasp God,[20] does not mean yet that one sets in the place of the paradox of Christ the paradox of "Scripture."[21] [22]

358: Doctrine of inspiration, theology of experience—wrong way[23]

testimonium Spiritus Sancti $\underset{\textstyle\diagup}{\overset{\textstyle\diagdown}{}}$ Spirit in the Bible
Spirit in us[24] not abstract
appropriated for itself[25]

Openness (inspiration) is not revelation![26]

[16.] Summary of Barth, *Christliche Dogmatik*, 345.

[17.] Uncertain, perhaps "overcame."

[18.] "It is not about being blind to the possibility of scandal, not about the impossibile attempt to demonstrate the word of God directly from the Bible, but rather about seeing the scandal, about it being in faith—but really only to be overcome in faith" (*Christliche Dogmatik*, 345). After the colon is a summary recap of *Christliche Dogmatik*, 345.

[19.] Beginning of page 3.

[20.] Replaces: "the Scripture."

[21.] Replaces: "church."

[22.] Justification of Luther against Barth's statement: "Luther's foundation, that the scripture is God's word insofar as it impels one to Christ—if it be not a hidden form of rationalism or in any case not understood and reworked in the sense of some proof from experience—does not in itself involve the circumventing of the crux. All real knowledge of God can begin only with God himself in the obedience of Christ and therefore with the imprisonment of our reason, including our religious reason" (*Christliche Dogmatik*, 356).

[23.] Summary recap.

[24.] *Christliche Dogmatik*, 358.

[25.] Ibid., 359.

[26.] Verbatim citation from *Christliche Dogmatik*, 359. The word "(inspiration)" is added by Bonhoeffer. [Barth's play on the words *Offenbartheit* and *Offenbarung* cannot be reproduced in English.] [PDM]

16. Graduation Theses[1]

476

Theological Theses

Which with approval
of
The Dean of the Honorable Theological Faculty
of the
Friedrich-Wilhelm University
of Berlin
Will Be Publicly Defended
Toward the Attainment of the Licentiate of Theology
On December 17, 1927, at 12 o'clock Noon
In the Old Lecture Hall
Dietrich Bonhoeffer

Opponents:[2]
Robert Stupperich, cand. theol.
Walter Dress, Lic. Theol.
Pastor Helmuth Roessler

Berlin
Emil Ebering Publisher. Mittelstrasse 29

Dean theological[3] *faculty. Effort. Advice and action most friendly*
It is my sincere wish at this moment.
Seeberg.[4] *Many memories of the semester. Theological scholarship. Dogma, life. Discipline of thought piece from the heart.*
Harnack.[5] *Promise.*

477

What I have learned and understood in your seminar is too closely bound to my entire person for me ever to forget it.
1.   The speeches of God in Job 38–41 do not belong to the original plan of the book of Job.[6]

[1.] *NL* A 17, 2; previously published in *GS* 3:47 and *NRS* 32–33, cf. *DB-ER* 96. Bonhoeffer's personal copy has handwritten notes that are printed here in italics.

[2.] Cf. Bonhoeffer's letters from 1925 onwards to Walter Dress in this volume, above 1/89a and following. Concerning Helmuth Roessler and Robert Stupperich, see the Index of Names.

[3.] In the manuscript this is the beginning of the next page.

[4.] Cf. *DB-ER* 69–72.

[5.] Cf. *DB-ER* 66ff., and often.

[6.] Cf. Bonhoeffer's paper on the problem of suffering in Job in this volume, above, 2/14:420ff., especially 429ff.

2. The identification of "being in Christ" and "being in the church-community" are in Paul in unresolved contradiction with his concept of Christ in heaven.[7]

    1 Cor. 12:12; 6:15; 1:13. Put on Jesus R 13:14; G 3:27.[8]
    The new human being
    Col 3:10; Eph 4:24, Col 3:10f. Heaven Eph 4:8; 1 Thess 4:16; 1 Cor 15:23;
    2 Thess 1:7; Phil. 3:20.

3. Every Protestant Christian is a theologian.[9]

    The 'Word.'[10]

4. The introduction of the concept of potentiality in the *Christian* concept of God means a limitation of divine omnipotence.[11]

    1. Something outside of God 2. Speculation 3. Sentimentality. Self-empowerment. World empowerment.
    The primal cause for the actualization of a potential either alone in God (potential superfluous); or in humanity (God's omnipotence abolished).

5. There is no sociological concept of the church that is not theologically based.[12]

6. The church is to be understood as Christ "existing as church-community" and as a collective person.[13]

    'One' Gal 3:28; Eph 2:5.

7. In its sociological structure the church embraces in itself all possible types of social association and transcends them in the 'community of spirit'; this rests on the fundamental social law of vicarious representation.[14]

8. Logically considered, faith is based not on psychological experiences but on itself.[15]

    Sola fide! The whole act. Intellect and will.
    Haec vita non habet experientiam sui, sed fidem; nemo enim [. . .] experitur se esse justificatum, sed credit et sperat II.[16]

478

[7.] Cf. *SC* (*DBWE* 1):140 and *AB* (*DBWE* 2):112, footnote 39.

[8.] The intended references are Rom. 13:14 and Gal. 3:27.

[9.] Cf. *SC* (*DBWE* 1):190 and Karl Barth, dictated sentences (*NL* A 10, 11 (1)), §13.

[10.] Cf. Bonhoeffer's paper on the historical and pneumatological interpretation of scripture, above, 2/6:285ff., and especially 292f.

[11.] This thesis goes back to the reading of Scheiermacher, *The Christian Faith*, 212ff., §54, 2; cf. the note concerning Schleiermacher in *NL* A 10, 10 (8). Further *GS* 3:78ff. and *NRS* 64ff.

[12.] *SC* (*DBWE* 1):31–33.

[13.] *SC* (*DBWE* 1):120f., 140f., 189ff., and 213–15; see also *AB* (*DBWE* 2):110–11.

[14.] *SC* (*DBWE* 1):141ff. and 252ff.

[15.] Cf. the note on Luther's lectures on Romans, above, 2/7:300, and also 2/5:271 and 2/10:338ff.

[16.] The complete Latin citation in Ficker's edition of Luther's *Römerbriefvorlesung* 1:54 reads, "*Si autem mortui sumus* spirituali (morte) per baptismum, ad finem peccati *cum Christo; credimus* Quia hec Vita non habet experientiam sui, Sed fidem. Nemo enim scit se vivere aut experitur se esse Justificatum, sed credit et sperat *quia simul etiam vivemus* in spiritu et

> *Faith doesn't require experience, knowledge, security; instead it calls for*
> *free surrender and joyful daring that trusts God's unfelt, untested, and*
> *uncomprehended kindness. XV.*[17]
> *Non cognoscendus deus secundum fülen, sed secundum fidem.*[18]
> *The new human being, Hegel. Paradox.*

9. The dialectic of the so-called dialectical theology bears logical, not real character and is in danger of neglecting the historicity of Jesus.[19]
10. Protestant proclamation and Protestant teaching must be doctrinally oriented.
11. There is no Christian teaching of history.[20]

> *There is Christian philosophy of history and there are historical times of edifi-*
> *cation. The teaching of history has as a goal the most objective possible pres-*   479
> *entation of historical entities and relationships, including the most adequate*
> *judgment of the same. We do not see the <u>heart</u>, but rather the <u>person</u>. Not world*
> *judge. For this reason all historical things are essentially withdrawn from*
> *<u>Christian</u> judgment.*

17. Doctrinal Examination on the Certainty of Salvation[1]

To What Extent Is the Question of Certainty of Personal Salvation
the Decisive Difference between Catholicism and Protestantism?

We seek to demonstrate that the decisive difference between Catholic and Protestant doctrine and piety lies in the problem concerning the certainty of salvation. This question is to be formulated so that the nature of both confessional stances is clarified on this point. From a purely theological and

---

novitate incipiente usque in eternum *cum illo*." See WA 56:58, 14–18. *LW* 25:52: "But if we died in spiritual (death) through baptism, thereby sin has an end with Christ. We believe that this life does not have experiential knowledge of itself, but only faith. For no one knows that he has life or experiences that he is justified, but he believes and hopes that we shall also live with him in the spirit and in a newness which is beginning and will continue into eternity with him." Cf. *SC* (*DBWE* 1):173–74, footnote 35 and Holl, *Luther*, 139, footnote 1; in addition Seeberg, *Textbook of the History of Doctrine*, 4/1:232–33. [Regarding the Roman numerals II and XV after the quotations from Luther connected to thesis 8, it is not yet known to what they refer.] [CG]

[17.] *WA* 10/3:239, 19–21, "Predigt am Jakobstage. July 25, 1522"; cf. *DB-ER* 70 and Seeberg, *Textbook*, 4/1:255–56, footnote 4.

[18.] "God cannot be known through feeling but rather [only] through faith" (*WA* 15:536, 34, "Predigt über Joh. 10:12ff., 1524").

[19.] Cf. concerning this: *AB* (*DBWE* 2):85–86 and the summary of the second article of faith, below, page 3/8:546ff.

[20.] Cf. *SC* (*DBWE* 1):150ff. and often.

[1.] *NL* D 11, 25; handwritten. This the first of three proctored examinations that Bonhoeffer wrote during January 14–16, 1928. In the upper margin is the note of the person who evaluated the paper: "Quite good. [Ernst] Vits 1/16/28."

dogmatic stance one could just as easily put the concepts of penance, the church, the law, or the word at the center of the discussion in order to understand the Protestant theological conceptualization and the Catholic one. There are two reasons, however, why the question of salvation constitutes the seminal point for both confessional positions. First, seen historically, it was the impetus for his new understanding of the gospel.[2] As such, here we have uncovered not only *a* theological focal point but religiously precisely *the* absolute focal point. When confronting the question of personal "salvation"—how this concept should be understood will be discussed later—Protestant Christians wake up and nourish their lives on the answer they have been given.

480   In his work *Luther,* Holl has made us aware that Luther believed that there was a double certainty, the certainty of justification and the certainty of salvation.[3] Protestant Christians must gain the former but not the latter, i.e., everyone must come to the realization that they have a gracious God but not to the realization that they are predestined to eternal salvation. Luther takes a double-sided attitude toward salvation. On the one hand, all who believe that they are predestined are certainly predestined. On the other, it is also possible for mature Christians to accept the idea that they are eternally condemned and subject also here to the will of God. Yet, by following this train of thought, Luther unintentionally arrives at the belief that whoever subjugates themselves to the will of God—regardless of how faithful or unfaithful they are—still remains in community with God. This means that they still believe in a gracious God—even if they are in hell, which is now no longer hell but heaven. In this way Luther constantly returns to the idea of the gracious God. One could paraphrase Luther's certainty of his salvation with the words (in spite of Holl) "*having found a gracious God.*"[4] How did Luther come to this realization?

Luther had become conscious of the overpowering fact of sin and guilt, a guilt for which there is no healing in this world. Personal "righteousness" dissolves into nothing when confronted by this guilt. The only thing that can be of any help is a gracious word from God which attests that God wants to have community with the sinner. There is only one possible attitude of the person to such a word of God. It is to accept it in the manner that it had been given, to place one's entire trust in it, i.e., to believe that God is gracious to me and to be assured of my salvation.

The concepts of sin, of repentance, and God all arose for Luther out of the question of a gracious God. God desires the sinner, God enters into per-

---

[2.] Vits: "whose!" [Bonhoeffer means Luther].[CG]

[3.] Holl, *Luther,* 111–54. ["Die Rechfertigungslehre in Luthers Vorlesung über den Römerbrief mit besonderer Rücksicht auf die Frage der Heilsgewissheit."][CG]

[4.] Vits: "Correct." Here one can assume Seeberg's influence. See Seeberg, *Textbook,* 4/1:231f.

sonal community with the sinner, and the sinner should accept this. This is what Luther discovered and what his heart had cried out for when he was in the monastery. Here, in the certainty of a merciful God, he had thrown off 481 the chains with which Catholicism had bound him. These chains, however, comprised an un-Protestant [unevangelisch] concept of sin, of repentance and skewed ideas about the righteousness of a human being and the person's relationship to God.

Since the Middle Ages it has been official Catholic doctrine that ordinary Christians could never achieve certainty about their relationship to God and their salvation. Only certain people in specific situations are given the gift of certainty on the basis of a revelatio specialis.

The most profound reason for this lies in the Catholic concept of God[5] and, more precisely, in the definition of the relationship between God and human beings. One could follow this theologically back to the doctrine of creation. For the sake of brevity, we will set our starting point somewhat later. In spite of sins, the individual is capable of works that have a certain influence over God. How human works and divine action meet in these works—Thomas and Duns have different opinions on this—is immaterial for our purpose. It is sufficient that the person is thought of as standing in a certain judicial relationship of give and take with God. Certainly, in order to arrive at works that have a certain influence on God in any direction, one has to use the sacraments of the church. This means that the church becomes a middle ground between God and humanity, which magically pours its powers of grace into people by means of the sacraments. Now, the fact arises[6] that people pile up 'good works' on top of good works in order to incline God to be gracious; conversely, God records sin after sin. The only thing left to be done is to tally up the total, which people can never do because they cannot see the entire picture of their lives. In short, they are condemned never to be certain of salvation. They know that God has forgiven this sin or that sin, but they never know what God's attitude toward them is on the whole. In other words, people are condemned to look at their own works and, being serious persons, must acknowledge that they will be continually judged by them and 482 will always stand under God's wrath. Consequently, the question concerning the certainty of salvation, as soon as it is asked by the inquiring Catholic, is thrown back upon the question, "How do I create the greatest grace, i.e., good works?" This means, however, that it becomes a question concerning the *church*, which is the mistress of grace. The church alone dares to comfort torn and tortured humanity. Whoever gives themselves up to her completely will be led to salvation. *Therefore, the place that God occupies for Protestants is*

[5.] Cf. on the following, the paper on the Catholic church, below 3/14:525ff., especially 526ff.

[6.] The phrase "Now, the fact arises" replaces "Now the situation emerges."

occupied for Catholics by the church. This fact explains the power that the Catholic church has over the members of its congregations. It recruits its power from the crushed consciences of the insecure and ignorant. The church, which dares to take responsibility completely away from the people, continually points them to their works. Whether this is good or bad it makes them uncertain, precisely because of the promises it has made.

The church, which in Luther is nothing other than a finger pointing to God, or to the cross and resurrection of Christ, has become in Catholicism a finger pointing to humankind.

Thus we recognize that with the idea of the certainty of salvation all the reservations that we carry in our hearts against our sister church emerge. And theologically, at its basis, the question about the certainty of salvation is the question of one's concept of God. If people need to speak to God about their affairs, well and good. Then they forfeit the right to be certain about God because of this apparent prerogative. But if God's grace alone has the final word, then people must only listen and accept. From this position as a servant they will receive the magnificent reward of being certain of God and of the grace of God, from which even the commandments of a church cannot separate them.

In the question of the certainty of salvation, the differences between Catholicism and Protestantism always remain alive.

17a. New Testament Examination on Baptism[1]

New Testament Statements concerning Christian Baptism
Collected and Explained

The early Christian church-community traced baptism back to institution by Jesus and indeed[2] by the risen Lord, and we have no cause to criticize this. If one says that such a command contradicts the possibility of a revelation of the risen one, that would not be easy to prove. To be sure, whether the transmitted formula of the command to baptize is "authentic" is a completely different question, which will be answered in the negative. Our Lord before he was raised,[3] however, cannot have given the command because baptism

---

[1.] *NL* D 11 (26), a personal file of the consistory; handwritten. This is the second examination, January 14–17, 1928. On the upper-left margin is written, "Dietrich Bonhoeffer." Next to the title is a note by Albert Coulon, who evaluated the paper, stating, "quite good C[oulon] Jan. 16," 1928; not previously published. On Coulon, see below in the Index of Names.

[2.] Above the next word "by" is the addition "as," probably inserted by Coulon.

[3.] Coulon puts a question mark and writes "Matt. [uncertain transcription] 28!"

occurs εἰς τὸ ὄνομα . . . τοῦ υἱοῦ[1] (Matt. 28:19; Acts 19:2ff. and often.) and 17:66
therefore assumes his death and exaltation. Matt. 28:19f. contains the command to extend baptism over the whole world. This means that baptism was seen as an important aspect of Christian mission. The inauthentic ending to the book of Mark (Aristion?)[4] therefore declares that baptism is necessary for salvation (Mark 16:16). Faith is the requirement for baptism (Mark 16:16; Acts 8:37 only in h).[5] This is demonstrated by the gift that baptism brings with it and also by the fact that the church-community was still in its first generation. With this infant baptism is excluded (1 Cor. 7:14 can much more easily be used against infant baptism than for it). In the earliest church-community baptism is so self-evident and widespread[6] that here again there is every reason to assume institution by Jesus Christ.[7]

If John the Baptist said that he baptizes with water but that Jesus would baptize with the Holy Spirit (Mark 3:8),[8] it seems that in the earliest congregations baptism by water and baptism by the Spirit were sometimes[9] seen as separate (in Acts 8:16 the Spirit is not given until the laying on of hands [Acts 6:6, 13:3][10] Acts 19:2ff.).

The *theological* connection of baptism and the gift of the Spirit was first made by Paul (but cf. Acts 2:38). Forgiveness of sins and the gift of the Holy Spirit were the two gifts that the community received through Christ. Both, however, are given to the Christian in baptism. The passages that speak of this the most clearly are 1 Cor. 6:11 ἀλλὰ ἀπελούσασθε, ἀλλὰ ἡγιάσθητε ἀλλὰ ἐδικαιώθητε and Titus 3:5 and 7, the latter of which was used by Luther, in a fortunate stroke, for his Small Catechism. Col. 2:12 and 13 also give expression to the twofold gift as new life and forgiveness of sins. The Holy Spirit is our pledge; with which we are 'sealed' (σφραγίς is an Hellenistic-cultic expression for baptism; cf., for example, Eph. 4:30; 2 Cor. 1:22). Christ's gift, however, is bound up together with his death and so Paul, in a mean- 17:67
ingful way, placed our baptism in relationship to Christ's death on the cross

---

1. This means, "By calling on the name of"; cf. Heitmüller, *Im Namen Jesu.* Here, perhaps, we can see that the Johannine assertion that Jesus did not baptize is based on the intention to anchor baptism in [the] death and resurrection of the Lord (John 3:22 and 4:2).

[4.] Mark 16:9-20. According to an Armenian manuscript from the year 989, the "inauthentic ending of Mark" was written by the "Presbyter Aristion," who is mentioned by Papias as well. Cf. Lohmeyer, *Markus-Evangelium*, 361.

[5.] Acts 8:37 is seen by exegetes as an interpolation into the Western textual tradition. Cf. Jacob Jervell, *Die Apostelgeschichte*, 273, footnote 860.

[6.] Difficult to decipher.

[7.] Bonhoeffer uses the name "Jesus Christ" to designate the risen Lord.

[8.] See Matt. 3:11; Mark 1:8.

[9.] Replaces: "often."

[10.] Bonhoeffer's square brackets.

(Rom. 6:3ff., Col. 2:12). We are baptized into Christ's death, we die with him, and that means that we die to our sins.[2] Yet, just as Christ was resurrected,[11] a new person will be resurrected in us (cf. Luther). We die to our old self and put on the new person (Col. 3:9; Rom. 13:14 and often). With this we have been led back to the formula *forgiveness of sins and the gift of the Holy Spirit as the effects of baptism* because Christ died for our sins and was resurrected for our new life.

Baptism is not only fundamental for [the] individuals and their standing as Christians, but for the church-community as well. In 1 Cor. 12:13 we are all baptized into a body. Baptism is the unifying bond that binds us together (cf. Eph. 4:5). Those who have been baptized in Christ are no longer Jew or Greek but are one in Christ (Gal. 3:27). They have been fused together into a collective person.[12] They have put on Christ (Rom. 13:14; Col. 3:9 the new person = Christ?). Therefore, baptism is as basic for the individual as for the church. For the individual it gives the Holy Spirit[3] and the forgiveness of sins, and for the church it creates the moment of unity.

John sees baptism together with the Last Supper as based on the death of Christ (cf. John 19: [34] 35). He designates baptism, Spirit, and the Last Supper as fundamental elements of Christianity ([1] John 5:6, the "Johannine Comma").[13] I believe that baptism is also referred to in John 3:5 and seen there as necessary to enter the kingdom.

A peculiar debasement of baptism, which at the same time is evidence of the enormously high value that was placed on baptism, can be seen in 1 Cor. 15:29, where the living allow themselves to be baptized for the dead, a practice that Paul does not reject.

Finally, we would also like to ask whether[14] baptism is a "sacrament" in the New Testament. Baptism is a divine gift of grace mediated through a symbol, water,[15] and commanded by our risen Lord and, as such, can be designated a sacrament.

We know little about the outward performance of baptism. The practice of baptism in a river would generally be followed, which implies immersion (cf., for example, Acts 8:36).[16]

17:68

---

2. Jesus already calls his death a baptism; see Mark 9:35.

3. 1 Corinthians 12:3, with its demand of faith, stands prior to baptism in an odd, but necessary contradiction.

[11.] Replaces: "was awakened."
[12.] Cf. *SC* (*DBWE* 1):192ff. and above, 2/16:440.
[13.] The Johannine Comma refers to a late, Western interpolation into the text of 1 John 5:7f. that has been omitted from modern English translations since the Revised Version; see the apparatus of the NRSV. [CG]
[14.] Replaces: "whether already."
[15.] Deleted: "and as such."
[16.] The correct reference is Acts 8:38.

In the above I have to a great extent been influenced by Reinhold Seeberg's presentation[17] of baptism in the New Testament.

17b. Old Testament Examination on Amos 9[1]

Amos 9:11-15
Translation, Form Analysis, Interpretation

[1] On that day I will raise up the booths of David[2] that have fallen, and repair its breaches and raise up its ruins and rebuild it as in eternal[3] (that means old) days; for they[4] might possess the remnant of Edom and all the nations who are called by my name—saying of Yahweh who will accomplish this. See, the days are surely coming, says Yahweh, when the one who plows will overtake the one who reaps, and the treader of the grapes the one who draws (this means sows) the seeds (sc. in the furrows); (Luther: then the one who plows will *overtake* the one who reaps . . .) the mountains shall drip sweet wine, and all the hills shall be moved[5] (that means be populated). I will restore the fortunes of my people Israel (The word שׁוּב should be understood as referring to their fate in general as well as to their return from exile), and they shall build rebuild the ruined cities and inhabit them; and they shall plant vineyards and drink their wine, and they shall make gardens and eat their fruit. And what has been planted (their plantings) is on their land and they will never again be driven off their land that I have given them says Yahweh, your God.

17:69

[2][6] אָקִים	from	קוּם	1 p. imp. hiph.
יִירְשׁוּ	from	ירשׁ	3 p. pl. imp. qal
נִקְרָא			3 sing. niph.
בָּאִים	from	בא	part. act.

[17.] Coulon underlines "Seeberg's presentation" and writes "Alfred Seeberg!!" This can only refer to Alfred Seeberg, *Die Taufe im Neuen Testament.*

[1.] *NL* D 11 (27), a personal file of the consistory; handwritten. This is the third examination, dated January 14–17, 1928. In the upper-left margin is written, "Dietrich Bonhoeffer." Above it is the remark of Ernst Sellin, who evaluated it, "Good. S." See also the certificate of his First Theological Examinations, above, 1/114:183f. Sellin was very generous in evaluating the paper and did not mark the smaller mistakes.

[2.] Sellin wrote "sing[ular]!" and underlined "the booths of David." Cf. Luther's translation, "David's booth that has fallen." [The NRSV version is used here except where Bonhoeffer's translation of the Hebrew differs from it.] [PDM]

[3.] Difficult to decipher.

[4.] Sellin underlined "for they" and wrote beside לְתִצָּן.

[5.] Sellin: "Better: dissolve." In the text he changes Bonhoeffer's translation to read "will move."

[6.] The analysis, in the form of grammatical notes, here follows the translation.

x)	נָגַשׁ	touch, approach, hit	niph. 3 pers. sing. perf.
	תִּתְמוֹגַגְנָה from מגג move		hithpolel, to move oneself, = to become populated
	שַׁבְתִּי		1[7] perf. qal
	נְשַׁמּוֹת from שׁמם		part. niph.
	נְטַעְתִּים from נטע		part. niph.
x)[8]	הֵטִיפוּ from טף		hiph. 3 plur. qal[9]
	יִנָּתְשׁוּ		impf. niph. 3 plur.

[3][10] The text at hand is declared by most exegetes to be inauthentic, as it stands in sharp contrast to the prophet's proclamations of doom. The same man who composed Amos 9:11-15 could not have written Amos 3:1ff. nor have flung those terrible threatening words at Amaziah in chapter 7 nor be identified with the one who had the four terrifying visions of Israel's destruction, the one who was called away from his herds to preach Yahweh's sermons of doom. In addition, 9:11-15 and especially v. 14f. refers directly to the exile. Amos, however, preached around 750. Do these reasons hold up?

1. Other prophets have pointed to a majestic future in spite of the harshest words of doom. This is well known and does not need to be discussed further.

2. Could not precisely this promise about the house of David be identical with the prophecy of doom over Israel?[11] Amos expressly aimed his threats at Israel (Bethel). Therefore, vv. 11-13 in any case should be considered authentic.

Due to naming of Israel, etc., vv. 14f. present a difficult problem. Was this added later? The odd "vineyard prophecy" could support this.[12] This question remains open.

[7.] Add "pers." at this place in the text.

[8.] Bonhoeffer's indication that these two lines, which were written in the lower margin, should be placed above, where the first x) is.

[9.] Perhaps crossed out.

[10.] The interpretation of the text, the third section named in the title, begins here.

[11.] Sellin: "Arguments for and against are missing." Sellin thought that this passage was authentic. In it he saw a continuation of Amos 7:10-17. Cf. Sellin, *Introduction to the Old Testament*, pages 169–70. Bonhoeffer used this work to prepare for the examination. See Bonhoeffer's postcards of August 3, 1926, and January 28, 1927, above, 1/97f:164 and 1/99b:167.

[12.] Deleted: "at any rate."

PART 3
Sermons, Catechetical Lessons, and Addresses

A. Congregational Sermons and Children's Sermons before Taking Part in Seminars in Practical Theology. October 1925–May 1926

---

1. Sermon on Luke 17:7-10[1]   485

Sermon for Sunday, October 18, 1925
Delivered in the Church of Stahndorf. Luke 17:7-10.

Christianity entails decision, repentance, renunciation, yes, even enmity toward the old humanity that is past. To forget this would be to forget the strength with which the Reign of God confronts human frailty and false meekness.[2] Christ completely tears down the old humanity until only vestiges remain. He attacks and severs the most fundamental life force with the sword he promised to bring with him. His blow hurts the most when his

---

[1.] *NL* A 13/1. The text has been handed down in two manuscripts. Manuscript 1 is in Bonhoeffer's handwriting with comments made by an unknown evaluator and supplements made to the text based on these comments. Manuscript 2 is in the handwriting of Bonhoeffer's mother. It indicates awareness of the comments in manuscript 1 but does not refer to them. It incorporates Bonhoeffer's changes in the text and has been reworked by him in a few places. As such, it is the final form of the sermon. Changes in the text, except those that are purely stylistic, are mentioned in the editorial footnotes, as are the comments. Manuscript 1, entitled "Sermon for Sunday, October 18, 1925, as Pastor Koller's substitute; Stahnsdorf Church. Luke 17:7-10," was published in Bonhoeffer, *Predigten, Auslegungen, Meditationen*, 1:96-101.
[2.] The phrase "confronts human . . . meekness" is not in manuscript 1.

sword strikes idealized morality's seemingly highly honorable sentiments. But we ask, "What about this old humanity we are talking about?" Is it the person in their natural physicality over against the spiritual person? Is it the sinner over against the justified person? Is it the immoral person over against the moral person, the lawbreaker over against the law-abiding person? Is it the tax collector over against the Pharisee?[3] Above all, is it the person who has done nothing over against the person who has done everything? We would like to answer these questions superficially and comfortably with a yes. If we do this, however, then Christ has come into the world in vain. He would have died on the cross in vain, and he would have been resurrected in vain. It is before this deep divide that we stand with our question.

The hastily self-assured community of Pharisees, which stands before God all too comfortably, answered this question with a distinct yes. It did so in the past and continues to do so today. Those who answer with yes suppose that if they ordered their lives according to the rules of moral spirituality, as opposed to natural sensuality, then they could comfortably keep track of every day and period of their lives. If they should happen to make one mistake—well, this one mistake is erased by the great number of superb deeds that they can recount. Thus at the end of our lives, we stand before God with a reconciled account and demand that it be approved without question. Two thousand years ago people spoke like this, and today[4] some still do (even if somewhat more cunningly conceded). It was to shake people out of this Pharisaic self-satisfaction that Christ came, and it is against the background of this incredible arrogance[5] that our passage must be understood. These intelligent people made a big mistake in their calculations;[6] they forgot that God remains God, and humans remain human.[7] It is God who can demand things from humans, not humans from God. It is not that humans take, but that God gives.

The question concerning the old humanity is answered in another way. It is not a question of the natural-physical person over against the spiritual-moral person. No, the whole person, body *and* spirit, is the person of the past, and the word of the Lord is directed toward the whole person. Truly we can give to charity over and over again, go to church every Sunday, and read the[8] Bible at home every day; but as terrific and wonderful as this may be, the moment that we believe we have a claim on God, we are trying to grab God's omnipotence and holiness with unholy hands, and with this we slander

---

[3.] The question "Is it the . . . Pharisee?" is not in manuscript 1.
[4.] Manuscript 1 reads, "and today one does not speak differently."
[5.] This is also in an address on prayer by Bonhoeffer. See *NL* A 15/9.
[6.] The phrase "in their calculations," is missing in manuscript 1.
[7.] Cf. Barth, *Romans*, 153.
[8.] Manuscript 1 reads "their."

God. Before God we are all sinners and remain so.[9] "When you have done all that you were ordered to do, say, 'We are worthless slaves; we have done only what we ought to have done!'"[10] Jesus says, "When you have done all that you were ordered to do." Our question is, "What indeed have we[11] been ordered to do, and what can we do?" We have been commanded to follow the law, which addresses us with uncompromising harshness, and to follow the moral requirements that govern our entire lives. Jesus believes[12] that it is entirely possible to fulfill these expectations. Even if it requires energy, work, renunciation, sacrifice, and devotion, they must be fulfilled. When we have accomplished this difficult task, we are to say, "We are worthless slaves; we have only done what we ought to have done."

What a terrible about-face! With great pains we scaled a high mountain. Now a chasm has opened up under our feet, and we are asked to leap into it with open eyes. Soaring and climbing, we almost conquered heaven. The tower of Babel almost touched the clouds;[13] then with a sudden blow we lie in the abyss in gloom and darkness, in filth and sin.[14] The righteous person, who has done everything, is an unworthy servant! Those who thought they were so near are miserably far[15] from God. We are standing at the limits of humanity, a limit that the human being cannot transgress.[16] On the oppo-   488
site side of this boundary God reigns on God's throne at an infinite distance away and directs God's people, God's servants, on this side of the boundary.

If human beings are servants, then God is all-powerful, almighty, and the sublime Lord.[17] As such, God should be acknowledged and believed in, not understood and proved. This also means that humans do not have their own will[18] or[19] their own life and that everything that they own belongs to God—their property, their life, their will, their reputation, and their honor. As such they are indebted to God for their life, their labor and work, and their renunciation. They can do nothing that is not for the Lord. Their rep-

---

[9.] See Rom. 3:23.

[10.] Luke 17:10.

[11.] Manuscript 1 has the German word for "they" instead of "we."

[12.] In manuscript 1 it reads, "seems to think."

[13.] Cf. Barth, "The Righteousness of God," in *The Word of God and the Word of Man*, 14; cf. also *DB-ER*, 90 and 450.

[14.] The words "filth and sin" are underlined, but not by Bonhoeffer.

[15.] The evaluator: "does not apply to δοῦλος [servant or slave]."

[16.] "The human being" is not in manuscript 1. [The word *Grenze*, translated here as "limit" (or when the imagery is spatial, "boundary," as in the next sentence) will prove to be a central term in Bonhoeffer's later writings, such as *Sanctorum Communio* and *Creation and Fall*, n.b. the section entitled "The Center of the Earth."] [WF]

[17.] The phrase, "all powerful . . . sublime," is handwritten and put in parentheses by someone other than Bonhoeffer; evaluator: "these attributes are not present in κύριος [Lord]."

[18.] Cf. Luther, *Lectures on Romans*, 66-67; cf. Holl, *Luther*, 119.

[19.] In manuscript 1 one finds "instead."

utation and honor do not belong to them. They belong to the Lord. Yet Jesus says, "When you have done all that you were ordered to do, say, 'We are worthless slaves!'"[20] With this, one takes yet another large step forward into the abyss. We are not merely servants; no, we are worthless servants. Our Pharisaic nature in all its excellence rebels at this notion.

This requirement exceeds the amount of humiliation we can be expected to swallow. Yet it is precisely this last step that we must take with an open mind. Is it not true? Do we not remain sinners? Even with "life at its best"[21] we remain inadequate, and in the end we do not want what God wants but what we want. We want our salvation more than God's honor. We therefore love ourselves more than we love God, even though we should love God more than anything else. With our moral lifestyle we want to have a claim on God, to speak first and not wait until God speaks. We want to strike a bargain with God for our salvation; we want to forestall God's sentence. We want to intrude into God's judgments, although we know that "a servant should not know his master's secrets."[22] We do not begin by taking a submissive stance

489 in the fight between grace [Gnade] and a fall from grace [Ungnade]. Instead we pretend to be combatants, although this is something we can never be. We find it impossible to accept, yet we must acknowledge that, if it is God's will that we be among the unjustified and condemned,[23] we must accept our condemnation as completely legitimate.[24] We should joyfully acknowledge it, just as Luther always advocated.[25] We want peace and self-satisfaction, and not the saving divine unrest that is effected by the Lord.

Consequently we are completely selfish and are truly unworthy servants. This is the reason that the first thing we must say to God before all else is, "Lord, we are unworthy servants!" Without this insight into this most serious situation in which we humans find ourselves in relationship to God, there can be no conversation with God. If we clearly understand ourselves, we will guard against making demands on God. A powerful change takes place in our lives with these words. We recognize that the very best that we are able to do appears servile, sinful, and worthless before God. We confess that we are worthless and that, in our relationship with God, God alone is the one who demands, speaks, and gives, while we are the ones who perform, listen, and

---

[20.] Evaluator: "See the original text."

[21.] See the hymn by Martin Luther, "Out of the Depths I Cry to You," verse 2, *Lutheran Book of Worship*, 295).

[22.] Martin Luther, *Sendschreiben an die Christen zu Antwerpen (WA* 18:549, 35). Cf. Holl, *Luther*, 52, footnote 3.

[23.] Underlined, but not by Bonhoeffer.

[24.] In manuscript 1, the German word for "happily" is used instead of the word for "accept."

[25.] Cf. Holl, *Luther*, 111ff.

receive. We therefore must acknowledge that "all our good works are done in vain, even in the best life."[26] A tempting question intrudes: "If everything ultimately remains sinful, should we perhaps give up all striving and efforts for the kingdom of God?" "Let God be proved true," the apostle answers, when he asks himself this question.[27] No, being a Christian means to struggle for the honor of God, to work, and yet to understand clearly that it is only God who can complete the work. To explain this away would be blasphemy, because this is the way God intended it to be. We should work and struggle in gratitude[28] for God's honor, not for our own perfection and blessedness.

But does all our Christian[29] preaching end with the recognition of our worthlessness and sinfulness? Yes, it is so ended, but we should never forget the other.[30] A great promise lies in the words "unworthy servants," because this humiliation cannot be the work of humanity. If it were, then humanity would have a claim on God for[31] its own work. No! Here God steps in and helps. Once again we find ourselves at a dangerous point. Woe unto us if we substitute a vain, artificial, self-deprecating stance and servanthood for repentance and contrition.[32] We cannot by our own power cancel our efforts so completely and fully as we would have to if they were to stand in God's presence. Only God's mercy can help us. This holy self-recognition is a gift of the Holy Spirit. If any of us were its source, it would lead us to despair. But since this self-recognition comes from God, it leads to prayer in the presence of a merciful God. This is not the prayer of the Pharisee but the

490

[26.] Cf. above, editorial note 22.

[27.] Rom. 3:4.

[28.] The phrase "We should work and struggle . . . blessedness" is added by Bonhoeffer in the margin of manuscript 1.

[29.] The German words for "all" and "Christian" are added by Bonhoeffer to manuscript 1 as a correction.

[30.] The words "but we . . . the other" are added by Bonhoeffer in the margin of manuscript 1 in response to this comment by the evaluator: "The basis is missing. The strongest and surest [uncertain reading] motivation is thankfulness, not a striving for perfection. The strongest sense of thankfulness is present when knowledge of forgiveness is present. The relativity of all accomplishments and all *satisfaction* about one's accomplishments, as well as over the *favor* of the world."

[31.] Instead of "for" in manuscript 1, we find "still through."

[32.] The words "Once again we find ourselves . . . contrition" are added by Bonhoeffer in the margin of manuscript 1. They replace the following: "The greatest danger exists when we are tempted to submit to artificial self-deprecation and the love of servility, and thereby attempt to be pleasing to God. God helps us avoid this danger at that point." Both additions were in response to the comments by the evaluator: "Whatever else, no artificial, vain self-deprecation! No servility on the way to true self-understanding, i.e., understanding God in one's human servanthood. (I am what I am due to the grace of God—and God's grace has not been in vain—a *you*, a pious and faithful servant, in contrast to *I*, an unworthy servant.)"

prayer of the tax-collector who prayed in the Temple, "God be merciful to me, a sinner."[33]

Our reflections have come full circle. God does not desire Pharisees who see themselves as righteous and moral,[34] but repentant sinners who have acquired holy self-recognition and do not demand but instead pray. God is pleased by the prayer of servants and sinners, full of regret and repentance stimulated by God, asking for forgiveness for their sins. To such a sinner God says, "Yes, you pious and faithful servant."[35] God defends humanity. God comes to humanity so that humanity can come to God in prayer. "Neither with sorrow, grief, nor self-inflicted pain, but only with prayer can anything be asked of God."[36]

2. Address on the Decalogue[1]

All of you can answer my first question. What is better: school or vacation? Are there a few upstanding students who would really say that school is better? Oh no, I don't think so. All in all, vacations are much nicer than school. You all basically think so too. Let's see now, why are vacations so much nicer than school? Because you can do what you want to do? And what do we call it when we can do what we want to do and nobody is there to stop us? In these cases we say that we are free. And why isn't it as nice at school? Because too often when we are there, we have to do what we don't want to do. In these cases we say that we are not free but are forced to do things and to submit to definite regulations. Which is nicer: freedom or force? Well, I hardly need to ask any further because it is so clear. Freedom to do what you want to do in the time you want to do it is the best thing in the world. It is a bad sign if someone loves force more than freedom. That kind of person has the soul of a slave,[2] and we don't want that. There are, however, subjects in school that you like—natural science, gymnastics, history,[3] maybe even reli-

---

[33.] Luke 18:13.

[34.] Instead of "as righteous and moral," one finds in manuscript 1 "as the righteous and moral."

[35.] Bonhoeffer adds the sentence from "To . . . servant." to the margins of manuscript 1. Cf. Matt. 25:21.

[36.] Paul Gerhardt, "Befiel du deine Wege" ("Commend your way"), verse 2 (*Evangelisches Kirchengesangbuch*, 294).

[1.] *NL* A 15/1; handwritten children's meditation without a title (presumably on the Ten Commandments), February or March 1926. On the date of it, see below, pages 580. The talk was given in the Grunewald church, Bonhoeffer's home parish; see *DB-ER*, 91–2.

[2.] Cf. Nietzsche, *Beyond Good and Evil*, 204–37, and *On the Genealogy of Morals*, 36–43. Cf. Bonhoeffer's catechetical talk on "honor," below, pages 3/15:529–40.

[3.] In place of "mathematics."

gion. What is it like when you are in those classes? Aren't you also forced to   492
learn how certain animals live, or what kinds of battles people fought 2000
years ago? Yes, of course. But you see, you don't even notice it, and you
shouldn't. You only notice force when you are forced to do something you
don't want to do. You see, a horse that is trotting or walking like it is supposed to doesn't even notice the reins. But if it wants to run away suddenly,
then it notices that it is held tight. It is the same way with people. If people
do what they are forced to do willingly and well, then they don't feel the
reins. We call that doing our duty. They notice the reins only when they fight
against them, when they get angry at their math homework or their dates in
history.

Now what would reasonable people do when they know that they are
forced to do too many things? This certainly applies to all of you, just as it
does to everyone else.[4] They would try not to get angry and upset about it
and instead to do it as willingly as possible. In such a case they would be
doing it freely, as if they were on vacation, because they are always free. Think
about this. They are always on vacation! Vacation even during school time.
That would be a strange thing, don't you think? Strange, but wonderful.[5]
Now we all have our different duties. You have your homework, I study at the
university, the pastor has to preach, the workman has to make shoes or do
carpentry. Behind all of these different duties, however, we all have the same
duty. The cobbler and the professor, you, your teacher, and I. To whom do
you think we have this duty? You could say, "the nation." But if I were to tell
you that in one respect all people everywhere have the same duty, then you
would be able to tell me what it is. It is their duty to God, who is the Father
of us all. Yes, we say, "God is our Father, and we should be God's children."
This means that the whole world is a big house in which there are many,
many little rooms where people live. But all the people in the house have *one*   493
father. All have their own work to do in their room and have to keep them
neat, but all have one common duty, which is to be obedient to their
Father.[6]

Now tell me, why do we compare this to our house? All in all, do we or
don't we like to do what our parents want us to do? Do we think that we live
in a jail at home where we are forced to do everything? Don't we rather think
that it is our own decision to obey our parents? Is this duty forced or free?
Surely, for the most of us, it is a duty that we do freely. When we come home
from school, we don't say, "Now we are going to be forced to do something
again." Instead, it is as if we are free. We don't feel the reins that guide us. We
like being at home. Most of what we have to do—sometimes this isn't the

---

[4.] Difficult to decipher; perhaps "us."
[5.] The sentences "In such a case . . . wonderful" replace "That reflects daily life."
[6.] No new paragraph in the manuscript.

case—but most of what we have to do we do willingly. Yes, that's how it is when we are at home. We are free, just as if we were on vacation. We are happy to do everything that there is to do. If things are sometimes difficult and hard, and if sometimes there are tears, then our mothers stroke our heads gently and we know that we are at home with father and mother. Where you are at home, then you are loved; and where you are loved, there is no force. You see, if you are interested in a subject at school, then you love it and you don't feel that you are forced to do it. You feel only the freedom. If I really love my father, then I don't say, "Oh no, I have to visit my sick father." Instead I want to do it freely, even if I have to travel a long distance. And you don't say, "Oh, it's too bad that I have to make my mother a birthday present." No, you do this by yourself. You get to work with great love, freely. Think about it, vacation in the middle of work!

Now, let's say that all of us are really together in the house of our loving Father in heaven. Our parents and grandparents and all of us are children in the house. Think about it—only *children*, not servants; we don't need to be forced to do things. Instead, we belong to the house in which there are no servants. We do everything out of love, freely, out of love for our Father and our many, many brothers and sisters. There is a lot to do, to help with, to make use of, and we always do it freely. We always have vacation in the middle of work. Oh, it must be wonderful in that house where no angry words are ever spoken, in which no one is forced to do anything, because all do their work out of love for the Father and the others. Yes, we would love to be at home in a house where things are like that; and we may be at home there—think about it carefully. Yes, we yearn to be there and away from any place where ugly, scolding, harsh words are spoken. Oh, if we really sought that and took no pleasure in crude things, then it would be much better here.

But now horrible things began to happen in this beautiful house. The Lord God had just barely shown the first people their rooms, had let them enjoy themselves, had given them everything that they wanted, and then one day they all ran out of the house and wanted to try to live on their own. But, oh, how terribly they had fooled themselves! They came to desert places where they had to work very hard to get bread[7] to eat.[8] When they had children, it didn't take long before one killed the other out of jealousy and hate.[9] The more people there were in the world, the worse it became. None wanted to live in God's house, where everyone loved each other. They would rather be where people killed each other. Then came the flood,[10] which

494

[7.] Difficult to decipher; perhaps "their bread."
[8.] Gen. 3:19.
[9.] Gen. 4:8.
[10.] Genesis 6 and following.

washed away everyone except the one person who still lived in God's house, Noah. But his children turned to evil[11] again, and soon there was no one left who knew what it was like in God's house. There were many peoples [Völker], and all of them came from God's house, but they had run away. No one knew very much about the rules that were established there. Then the Lord God took pity on all these poor runaway children and decided to tell them once again how to act in God's house. And that is what happened. From the small number of Jewish people one man, called by God, appeared. With God's help, he led the people out of Egypt, where they had been held captive. In the middle of the desert, on Mount Sinai, God called to him (Exod. 20:32-33) and, as you all know, gave him the Ten Commandments that we still know today.[12]

Now, at first everything seemed to go well. Many faithful people tried to follow everything exactly; 1000 other commandments were added and they followed each one of them. But do you know what happened? Everyone felt forced to follow them. Everyone was terribly anxious, just as people always are when they are forced to do something. No one loved their Father in heaven anymore. But God never forgets those who come from his house. He still loves them. So he sent more and more men to show them that the only truly important thing is to love God, and that in God's house no one is a servant and all are children who are happy and full of love in everything they do. But the disobedient people did not listen. Then God sent God's own son. He showed the people, especially the poorest and most evil people, that God had not forgotten them. Out of love he was so obedient to his Father in heaven that he allowed himself to be nailed to a cross before the eyes of the whole world.[13] And when he was asked what the greatest commandment in his Father's house was, he answered, "you shall *love* the Lord your God. . . ."[14] He showed us that only when we first truly love the Father are we happy to do the Father's will, even if it is sometimes very difficult. How often does your mother ask you to do something that you really don't want to do? I know a boy who had to help his mother earn money one summer instead of going on vacation. He did it so willingly and was so happy while he was helping her that he had the nicest vacation amidst the hardest work. Now if we love our mother that much, shouldn't we love even more the one who gave us everything—our mother and our house, our work and our holidays? Yes, even if our good Father in heaven often requires very difficult things

495

496

[11.] Gen. 9:20-29.

[12.] No new paragraph in the manuscript.

[13.] Cf. below, Bonhoeffer's children's meditation on the first Commandment (3/3: 461–464), and on Matt. 21:28-31 (3/4: 465–70). The following sentence "He truly loved humanity" is crossed out.

[14.] Luke 10:27.

from us, we should do what we are asked to do with a joyful heart. God is love, and those who abide in love. . . .[15] The next few Sundays we will talk about the difficult things we are supposed to do[16] in God's house. Let's be joyful, and then God the Father will be happy too. Our Lord Jesus also knew that there are such difficulties, challenges we must face that test the power of love to see if it is real, alarming situations.[17] Pass through the narrow gate. The gate is narrow, and the path is hard that leads to life.[18] Yes, climbing a steep path is always more difficult than walking on a level path. The steeper it is, the harder it is, but the higher one climbs.

There is only one more thing left. Alone we can do nothing. All of us know this. Those who do try end up on a lonely mountaintop, far off the path that leads to God's house. Those who want to hike safely need someone to stand by their side, to hold their hands when they come to an obstacle, and to guide them past the wrong path, which might seem tempting and easier, onto the correct path, even though it might be more difficult. We should ask again and again for God to give us Jesus as our guide. We ought never to be alone on our hikes through the mountains. Jesus will be with us. Show me your way, O Lord, so that I may walk in your truth.[19] Jesus will go ahead of us all through life.[20] We won't become faint or get tired when he leads us; "those who wait for the Lord shall renew their strength."[21]

There was once a king who had a magnificent park and a beautiful palace in the park. Children were allowed to play in this park all day long. One day a child got the idea that he would like to see what it was like outside the park; but they knew that his father had forbidden it. One of them told the others, and soon they were all outside of the magnificent park and were far away. Suddenly they were afraid and wanted to go back, but they couldn't find the way and began to fight among themselves. They all tried to go their own way and fought with the others, but none of them found their way back. A few of the brothers and sisters liked being away from their father's house, and they didn't want to go home. The others, however, searched for the way back and couldn't find it.[22]

Because he was a wise king, their father knew what had happened, but he still loved his children even though they had disobeyed him. And so finally he sent a man out to bring them home. The first thing this man had to do

497

[15.] 1 John 4:16.

[16.] Difficult to decipher; perhaps "that exist."

[17.] Difficult to decipher.

[18.] Matt. 7:13-14.

[19.] Ps. 86:11.

[20.] See the hymn by Zinzendorf, ("Jesus, Still Lead On," *Lutheran Book of Worship*, 341).

[21.] Isa. 40:31.

[22.] No new paragraph in the manuscript.

was to tell them about their father, what it was like at home, that their father still loved them, and that they should still love him. Then he would show them the way to their father, and they would once again live in his house just like before. When their father's messenger told them this, many did not believe him, but some of them did. The messenger took these children by the hand and showed them the correct path, which they were not able to find alone. He led them past the gorges, past the obstacles; and it was odd, they always saw the lights of the father's house shining in the distance. Every one of their steps was brightened by it. When they were very near, their old father rushed towards them with outstretched arms. Crying in sorrow and in joy, they all went into the radiant house.[23]

You see, whoever loves God, the good Father, and asks for the guidance of the Lord Jesus Christ will find the way, even in the dark when everything is difficult and much is required. These persons will find that they are drawn ever more securely to God, and the Father's house shines ever more brightly. There at home, everything is love. There is no force, no difficult commandments. There, one freely does everything without being asked. There, one is a child of the house. But we are not there yet. We still have to pray and plead that our Father will allow us to find the right way and will send us the true guide. "Teach me your way, O Lord, so that I may walk in your truth."[24]

3. Address on the First Commandment[1]   498

Do you know what an orphanage is? Many children who don't have parents anymore live together in a big house. They are called orphans. Have you ever seen such a house? Every day I see a house in which many, many children live, children who have lost their father, or rather don't know their father anymore. You see, I don't mean a real orphanage, because these children's father is still living, but the children don't know him and don't want to know him. But it is just as sad in this house as if it were a real orphanage. Think about what it would be like at your house if your father and mother were suddenly gone; this is exactly what it is like in this house that I am telling you about. And all of you know which house I am talking about. It is the big

---

[23.] No new paragraph in the manuscript.
[24.] Ps. 86:11.

[1.] *NLA* 15/4: handwritten; children's meditation without a title (probably on the first commandment), March 1926; on the dating of the text, see below, Appendix 1, pages 579–80. In the margins of the first page, we find Bonhoeffer's handwritten note: "214, 1.2.7.8; 266." This indicates two hymns by Martin Luther, both found in the *Evangelisches Gesangbuch:* no. 214, "Ein feste Burg ist unser Gott" ("A Mighty Fortress Is Our God"), and no. 266, "Gott sei gelobet und gebenedeiet" ("To God Be the Honor and Glory"). Cf. Holl, *Luther*, 60ff.

house that we talked about last time,[2] not the one that God built, but the one that the people built themselves. Haven't you noticed it yourselves? The whole world acts as if it has lost its father. Its face is always so serious, so weighed down, so important looking, and so full of sorrow. There is not the slightest trace of happiness and laughter, nor is it filled with true light heartedness and love.

But we don't want to belong to the kind of people who look as if they don't have a father anymore and as if they are orphaned. Instead, anyone should be able just to glance at us and see what a good father we have. Someone who has a bad father might look sad and worried. But those who have a father like we all have will have a merry twinkle in their eyes. We also spoke about the things we are supposed to do in our heavenly Father's house that are not very easy. We thought about the Ten Commandments and some other things. But God begins by reassuring us of God's faithfulness before insisting that we take these 10 commandments to heart. Tell me where the commandments actually begin? Surely there where it says, "You should have no other gods. . . ." What precedes this isn't a commandment, nor an order. Instead it is a—how can we put it—it is the word in which God gives himself to each and every one of us. "I am the Lord your God." Think carefully about each word! God speaks to us, to me, to you. It is truly God, the Almighty, the one who smashes nations into pieces like pottery,[3] who is speaking to you. Think about it and be alarmed, alarmed in your innermost being, because it really is God who is speaking to you. Be frightened and tremble at the thought that it is God, the Almighty, who speaks to you, the runaway. Humble yourself before God, who is the king of kings, whose throne is the heavens and whose footstool is the earth.[4] Tremble and cheer, rejoice and thank God, that God has come to you. Lift yourself up, for God is speaking to you! Think about it carefully. The one who is the Lord of Lords is your God, you disobedient child of humanity—your God, who hears everything for which you plead. God is your helper, your master, your comforter, and your savior. Can you imagine it? Oh no, we can't even begin to imagine it. If we try, suddenly everything gets so cold again that we brood and don't understand it at all. Believe it, take it to heart. Do you want to reject what God has given you? Is it too grand for you? Would you rather the king gave you a cup of water instead of a kingdom? "I am the Lord, your God." God gives us the greatest thing that there is. God gives us himself.

You know, we talk so much about God—every Sunday, a few times every day—but do we really think about the fact that someone like God really exists? We may think about it. But do we realize what this means for us? Oh,

---

[2.] Cf. above, 3/2: 457ff.
[3.] Cf. Jer. 18:1-11; Rom. 9:21-29 and the "Sermon on Psalm 127:1," 3/5: 470–75.
[4.] Cf. Isa. 66:1.

how proud some of us would be if we could just speak a few words to an important person like Hindenburg[5] and he would speak a few words to us. We would remember every word. Yes. And yet we aren't impressed by the fact that we can talk a few times each day with the King of Kings. We just take that for granted. Oh, if we would just wake up and hear that it is really God who speaks to us, and with whom we can speak so easily. At times, realizing our thoughtlessness would truly frighten us to death. The Lord is *your* God. You can be certain of this above all else. Another way to say the same thing is that the Lord is *your* Father. Oh, if we really took these words seriously, what happy children we would be! Before God commands, God gives; and if God gives, then God gives everything. God never gives anything less than himself. And what do we say to such a royal gift? Just think about it. The only thing that is required of us is that we accept it. But that is *required* of us. Woe unto us if we don't. "I am the *Lord, your* God." Yes, don't we feel it in our own bodies? Who gave us life? Who gave us our parents? Who saves us from grave illnesses and great danger? Who comforts us when we are unhappy and in need? Who saves us when our conscience troubles us? "I am the Lord, your God." "Bless the Lord, O my soul." When in his monastery cell Luther[6] began to despair under the weight of the commandments and began to suffer when his conscience repeatedly condemned him, when he grew faint-hearted and terrified at the thought of a gracious God, he ran to the Bible and opened it up to the page where words clearly stated, "I am the Lord your God." And then he knew that God had spoken. What can anyone add to that? And he found certainty in his distress. And the serious care-worn face of Doctor Martin Luther was transformed into the joyful laughter of a child in the house of the heavenly Father. We should do the same thing when sorrow begins to crease our foreheads or when our conscience constantly bothers us and won't leave us in peace. At those times we will want to flee to the words, to which many before us have fled for shelter: "I am the Lord your God." God knows what troubles us. God will comfort our sadness and will give our tortured conscience certainty. In this way, we will become little children and not orphans in God's house.

500

If we realize that God is talking to us, then there is no other voice we would rather listen to than our heavenly Father's voice. When we know that we are only at home with God, why would we want to go abroad? God is our God, our only God, from whom nothing can separate us. That is why God says in the First Commandment, "You shall have no other gods before me." As humans we have only one home. God alone is God, and if anyone wants to serve another god they take away the honor that they owe the one true God. Think about the many pagans who still know so little about God that

501

[5.] Paul von Beneckendorff Hindenburg, Reich President 1925–34.
[6.] See above, "Seminar Paper on the Holy Spirit according to Luther," pages 325–70.

[they] think animals, trees, yes, you know, wooden dolls and pieces of metal are gods, and they pray to them. They live in terrible fear of their gods; quite often they even hate them and pray to them only out of fear. You see, these human children have lost their true Father. They also belong to the house that we spoke about in the beginning, where it is so sad and gloomy. Now, you might say that we aren't pagans but Christians, so the First Commandment isn't aimed at us. But think about it. Do we really think only about serving God, who speaks to us in the commandments? Do you know what it means to serve a false god? It means to serve something that is not God but opposed to God. As the apostle Paul says, a person's false god can be the stomach.[7] These are the people whose only concern in life is what they will eat and drink.[8] Our false god could be laziness in everything. It could be riches, or all kinds of unrighteous tendencies. Anything that we listen to more than we listen to God's voice is a false god. Jesus said once, "You cannot serve two masters, God and mammon."[9] Do you know that the people who serve a false god don't look so different from those who are the true children in God's house? They go to church and do all sorts of good things. But in one part of their lives, they serve not God but a false god. This means that they run away from God and act as if nothing is wrong. "You should love the Lord your God with all your heart, and with all your soul, and with all your mind."[10] You should love God more than anything else.[11]

502

So you see, where you love, there you are at home. Whoever loves God the Father will listen to God first, belong to God, and be a true child in God's house. But whoever loves a false god, money, or pleasure more than God has run away from God's house and is imprisoned in the great, sad, gloomy house of the world. The only thing that God says is, "Here, human child, you have my word, my promise, and my commandment. Do with it what *you* will. At the end of your days, we will see each other again." What will happen to the person who has loved only this world and has acquired only worldly treasure? The Lord Jesus spoke harsh words about those people. But what will God say to those people who have loved God's house, God's promises, and God's commandments? Oh, we can't even begin to imagine how wonderful it will be at the place where we are eternally at home. We want to sit quietly and rejoice over it. God has given us the divine self. Won't God give us everything? God has spoken, "I am the Lord *your* God." Who can separate us from the love of God?[12]

[7.] Phil. 3:19.

[8.] Cf. Matt. 6:25.

[9.] Matt. 6:24 (NRSV, alt.).

[10.] Matt. 22:37.

[11.] Luther, "Ten Commandments" from the "Small Catechism," in *The Book of Concord*, 351.

[12.] Rom. 8:35.

4. Address on Matthew 21:28-31[1]

Matthew 21:28-31: The Different Sons

[1.] The Fortress

Easter is almost here and that means promotion from one grade to the next. At home you hear more often than usual, "Well, how was it at school? How did your paper go? How did you do on your math test? How are you doing with your French verbs? Have you been called on often? What did your teacher have to say about it? And so on. And some of you don't feel very good about it all. Some of you have a guilty conscience, because you know that you have been lazy to the bone and are now going to receive the punishment you deserve.[2]

503

There was once a boy, a young fellow who was the youngest of many brothers. He had been sick for a long time and therefore was far behind in his schoolwork. Now, one morning he had to take the final French exam, and he didn't do at all well with it. His mother had to go out, his father wouldn't be home until late, and all his brothers were gone except for the oldest. "You'll help the little one, won't you, Fritz?" his mother said to the oldest son. "Oh, mother." "What is it?" "Don't you remember that the boy from next door was going to come over to play soldiers[3] today? We're going to build a fortress and now. . . ." "You'll just have to play tomorrow." "I've looked forward to it so much, and tomorrow I'll have a lot of homework to do myself." "But, son, what will happen to the little one?" "But Mother, it isn't my fault that he got sick and now will fail. No, Mother, I won't do it. Not today. No, I don't want to." Their mother has gone out the door, when the doorbell rings. Fritz opens. It is the neighbor boy. "My, my, you look awful, as pale as the moon. You look as if you've been crying," he calls out when he sees Fritz. "Oh don't be silly," Fritz says huffily. "Come on in, let's play. But let's be a little quiet, because the little one is sitting in the next room doing his French homework." In the next room they hear the little boy saying his French verbs out loud. The game of soldiers begins, but Fritz's heart isn't in the game. The fire is getting closer and closer to his fortress, and now his enemy is right at his outer wall, and Fritz has to pay close attention or it will all be over.[4]

Then in the next room he hears a book fall to the ground and bitter crying. He can't stand it anymore. He runs to the door and flings it open. The little boy is sitting at his reading desk, his eyes and face filled with tears, and

---

[1.] *NL* A 15/2; handwritten. Children's meditation given in March 1926; on the date see below, page 580.

[2.] No new paragraph in the manuscript.

[3.] Cf. below, "Exegesis and Catechetical Lesson on Luke 9:57-62" (3/6:476–88); see above, 1/8:26 and 1/12:30.

[4.] No new paragraph in the manuscript.

504 his book and notebook lying on the ground. "I can't do it. I can't remember anything." Hopelessly sobbing, he looks up at his big brother. He can't stand by any longer. Quickly he picks up the book and the notebook, seats himself next to his little brother on the bench and pats him on the head. "Come on now, we'll try it together." The little one can hardly believe it, but they begin, and just as he has understood the first page, Fritz looks up and sees his friend, who is standing confused at the door. "Why are you still waiting? We're not going to play anymore today." "But what about the fortress that I was just about to conquer?" "Oh yes; the fortress, well you know I believe that the fortress that I made has already been conquered by someone else. And its walls were so thick, yes so thick that I had imprisoned myself in it. But suddenly someone tore the wall down. It happened just a little while ago, when you wanted to conquer my fortress and the little one was crying so much. It was then that someone tore my wall down and I was free." "Fritz, what are you talking about? Your fortress is still standing. No one has torn your wall down. I don't understand at all." "No, no person has. It was definitely not a person that tore them down, but believe me, the walls of my fortress are destroyed. Good-bye till tomorrow."[5]

The neighbor boy slowly drags himself out the door. He finally understood a little of what Fritz had said. Page by page the work progresses. The eyes of the little boy light up, as he sees that things are moving along. And now, as the clock chimes 7, they both slam the terrible book and notebook shut. That very instant their mother comes in the door and sees both of them standing up from their work. The whole time she was gone she had been so upset about her oldest son. Now she gives them both a hug, and even her oldest, who had spoken to her so horribly, is once again her good boy. And, just in case you were wondering, the next day the little boy got the best grade on his French test in the class, and he was promoted to the next grade.

505 ## 2. The Devil's Paint Jar

When the world was created with all its flowers, animals, butterflies, mushrooms, and people, and when every flower and animal had been painted by the angels with lovely colors and had been placed on the earth, the devil longed to steal some of the leftover paint in the angels' big paint jars. One night, when the angels were sleeping, the devil crept up and stole some of the most beautiful colors and some of the most wonderful floral scents and fled down to earth with them. Then the devil walked through the woods and met many of the flowers and the mushrooms. The devil came to a place where a mushroom stood, which had been painted completely gray. It was

---

[5.] No new paragraph in the manuscript.

unassuming and looked a little dirty, but it was a good mushroom variety and not poisonous. This mushroom stood there next to the chanterelles and the edible boletus and the saffron milk caps, and was sad that it was the ugliest of them all. Now no one would like it or look at it and admire it. The devil came up to it and said, "What would you give me if I painted you in the most glorious colors that I have found in heaven? I would adorn you so beautifully that everyone will think that God loves you more than all the rest. Everyone will admire you and think that you can do no wrong, that you are the most beautiful of all the mushrooms, and that you glorify God's magnificence and goodness with your coat and your stature." The little mushroom became very happy and said, "You may have everything that is now good about me."[6]

So the devil took the paint jar and began to paint the mushroom's cap with the most beautiful red. His stem was painted a gorgeous white, the kind of white that exists only in heaven, and his cap was decorated with little white dots. A terrible poison flowed into the body of the mushroom with the paint that the devil used so that every good thing drained out. Yet the mushroom grew prouder and prouder, and when the first people saw him they thought that God's favorite stood in front of them. "Only God could have decorated a creature like that. Look at the way his coat glorifies God." No one saw the terrible poison that was in its body, that it was now dangerous and evil, and that its coat was the work of the devil.[7]

506

Satan, however, walked on and painted mushrooms and snakes, bestowing the most beautiful scents to flowers, and pouring a terrible poison into everything he touched. And Satan walked on and came to the people, but this time Satan didn't have his paint jar, and[8] here as well Satan asked, "Do you want to look like God's favorites? Would you be willing to give me everything that is good about you in exchange? Do you want to have faces like God's saints and give me your hearts in exchange? Do you want everyone to be jealous of your beautiful faces and be admired and adored because of them? I will give you all of this." And there were many who came to terms with the devil and gave him their hearts. This is how hypocrites and deceitful people came into the world, full of pomp and poison. The devil walked on. Even today the devil stands at our door and flatters us, "Give me your heart, and I will make it look like you gave it to God. I will adorn you with holy jewels, as if God had adorned you. My poison is sweet and God's goodness is often harsh. Come with me!" Children, if you hear this voice, then stand fast. Hold on to God with all your might. God, we prefer your harshness to the devil's sweetness. Lead us not into temptation. Let us be humble and unassuming,

---

[6.] No new paragraph in the manuscript.
[7.] No new paragraph in the manuscript.
[8.] Difficult to decipher.

but true. Let us trust in you and not in our holiness. Dress us in sorrow and misery, but let us see your everlasting glory, truth, and purity.

3. [The Different Sons]

Think about these two preceding stories, while I now tell you a story that our Lord Jesus told. The owner of a vineyard had two sons, who were perhaps 15 and 17 years old. One of the boys gave his father a lot of trouble and caused him a lot of worry. He was often insolent, defiant, obstinate, and rude. He often rudely confronted his father. Today we would say that he had a "rough exterior." The other boy was always friendly to his aging father. He was never angry or wretchedly[9] rebellious. His father must have loved him dearly.[10]

One day their father became ill and there was a lot of work to do in the vineyard. The father called to his older son in a friendly manner, "Dear child, today you have to work in the vineyard." "Father, it is hot today. Hardly anyone is working." "My child, it is absolutely necessary. The grape vines are falling down." "Father, I worked yesterday. Today I want to go swimming with my friends." "My child, please, go." "No, Father, it's too much. I won't do it. Today I just don't want to." He glances back one last time at his pleading father and dashes angrily out the door. His father remains behind, saddened. Just then the younger son comes in with a friendly smile. "How are you doing, Father?" "Not very well, my son. I have something to ask you, something that your brother has refused to do. Go to the vineyard and see that everything is taken care of. The grapevines are falling down. I can't go again today, I'm too weak." "Certainly, dear Father," his son tells him, "I'll go this very instant and take care of everything. Don't worry." And he bends over and gives his father a good-bye kiss on the forehead.[11]

In the meantime, the older brother is on the way to the swimming pool. But one thing keeps coming to mind: the face of his pleading father and his request. He knows that he has now sent his younger brother and that his younger brother had agreed to go. Anger is still raging within him. To go to the vineyard in such heat—no, that's too much. But he doesn't want to go swimming anymore either. He now hated the idea. But he is dissatisfied with himself. Surely he did the right thing to refuse to go. In his mind he sees his father's pleading face. He doesn't know what to do with himself. He is angry both at his father and at himself. He stops on the road. The hot sun shines down upon him. But, the look on his pleading father's face! He doesn't know how or why, but he finds himself on the path to the vineyard, going faster and faster until finally he arrives. The pickax from yesterday is still lying there.

507

508

[9.] Difficult to decipher.
[10.] No new paragraph in the manuscript.
[11.] No new paragraph in the manuscript.

He grabs it quickly and with every strike the difficult work progresses. But now he looks around. Is he alone? Where is his brother? He should have arrived a long time ago. He doesn't have time to think. The work is getting done and as the sun sets he is finished. He lays his pickax down, looks around, wipes the sweat from his forehead, and thinks. Once again he sees his father's pleading face. He rushes out of the garden gate. He must go to his father to ask for forgiveness.[12]

When he reaches home, his younger brother drives up in a car filled with friends and with the happiest face in the world. What happened? As he kissed his father good-bye he knew that that was all he had to do. He didn't really intend to go to the vineyard. After he left the house, he also remembered the face of his pleading father, and as he recalled it he laughed out loud, because the poor betrayed man really thought that he was his loving son. The more he thought about his imploring father, the louder his laughter grew and the uglier his eyes grew. Then he reached his friends. When he told them the story of what happened, a disgusting, loud, jarring laughter rang out from every mouth. They all continued gambling, eating, and drinking; and again and again someone called out, "Well now, how do you like the work in the vineyard? How many kisses did your old betrayed father give you to thank you?" The day passed in this way until they drove home, hooting with glee.[13]

The story ends here. Jesus asks—he actually doesn't even need to ask—"Which of the two did the will of the father?" Even the Pharisees understood. Jesus says, "Truly, the sinners and the tax collectors who repent will enter the kingdom of heaven before the hypocrites, who say yes and do nothing."[14] He could also have uttered another saying at that time, "Not everyone who says to me, 'Lord' . . . will enter the kingdom of heaven."[15]

Now do you understand the story about the fortress and the devil's paint jar? If we are ever in danger of saying, "Yes, dear Father," while in our hearts we are saying "No" and intend to do "nothing," then we should think about the devil's paint jar and the younger brother. Are we as beautiful but as poisonous as the toadstool or a beautiful stone that hides a disgusting crawling worm. It is certainly not nice to say no when someone asks for help. But it is more honest and therefore better. We should not pretend to be better than we are. All those who have the devil's poison in them will find it difficult to get rid of. They look like God's loving children but are really nothing else but the home of the devil.

Think about what we promise to do in church every Sunday when we say, "Your will be done." If we don't pretend to be better than we are, then we are

509

[12.] No new paragraph in the manuscript.
[13.] No new paragraph in the manuscript.
[14.] Cf. Matt. 21:31b.[MJ]
[15.] Matt. 7:21.

saying a great deal. Perhaps it would be better if some of us would say, "No, no." Then maybe one day the hour would come when the walls of our fortress fall and we could say with a joyful and serious heart, "Yes, dear Father."

Children, because hypocrisy is such a terribly comfortable thing we have to be so careful. Just think about school and how many hypocrites there are. How often have each of us said to our mothers, "Yes," and then done the opposite? Hypocrisy makes itself at home in our souls in the same way that ugly weeds take root quickly in fertile soil and then choke out the good plants. Hypocrisy poisons to its core everything good that grows; and you know how difficult it is to get rid of deeply rooted weeds. You rarely have enough strength on your own, and others have to help. Only by working and suffering together for a long time can one master this challenge. Let us guard against letting the seeds of this weed fall on our souls. If we do, then the story of the devil's paint jar will also apply to us.

There was once a man who for years said no to everything that he heard from the Lord Jesus. Then the day came when his fortress fell, and he was able to say a much stronger yes. The name of this man was Paul. There has only been one person on this earth who has always said yes and then followed through, doing yes, for whom word and deed were one thing, who not only talked about God's word but was and lived God's word. God gave him a name above all other names. You all know him.

510

5. Sermon on Psalm 127:1[1]

Psalm 127:1. "Unless the LORD builds the house, those who build it labor in vain. Unless the LORD guards the city, the guard keeps watch in vain."

Today we live in a time when more than ever we speak—and have to speak—of reconstruction and rebuilding again and over again. We talk about how our economy has to be strengthened and which trade agreements negotiated today or tomorrow will help us reach this goal most swiftly. We think about the best way to regulate workers' wages and how we can ensure that workers and employers are interested in achieving the same goal. How can we begin, we ask ourselves, to work toward becoming a wealthy, carefree, happy, respected nation once again? Today we are probably working harder

---

[1.] *NL* A 132; handwritten; a sermon preached before a congregation. The following note was added to it, "This sermon can be preached to a congregation. Berlin, May 20, 1926. Prof. Dr. Mahling." A note written by an ordained theologian was required if someone who had not yet passed his or her theological examinations wanted to preach to a congregation. Because this sermon was not prepared for Prof. Mahling's seminar, there are no corrections. On the first page in the left upper corner is the note, "Dietrich Bonhoeffer, Grunewald."

than ever before to reach this goal. All of us truly want to do our best to add a brick to this building.

God knows there are also others. Let us pray that God grants them insight! But here we are only talking about those who take the word "reconstruction" seriously, who are putting their lives and their strength on the line. And there truly are many, many of them. Woe unto us if we do not belong to them!

Another question presents itself, a burning social question closely related   511
to this economic question. How much has already been said and done in this arena! And we thank the men and women who have invested so much time and have done such productive work here. Every one of us wants to join those men and women who work with great earnestness for brotherly and sisterly love. Woe be unto our Christianity if we did not. We want our nation to become prosperous, healthy, and strong. To achieve this goal scientists sit at their desks, in their institutions, and before their instruments day and night. The academic sciences and the technological sciences are all focused on building a sound structure for the coming years. Read any paper. You can see it spelled out or read it between the lines; one word cries out piercingly from the page: "reconstruction, reconstruction."

Insofar as we count ourselves among truly earnest people, we don't merely or solely want to become a prosperous, admired nation but one that is healthy both in body and soul. We want to make it possible for the youth who live in big cities to hike, do gymnastics, and play; and we rejoice that they go outdoors and experience nature instead of finding pleasure in dingy and questionable areas of the cities. At the same time we talk about moral renewal,[2] without which nothing can be accomplished, and we know that such a construct will never be completed unless we begin with ourselves.[3] Many men and women see their vocation as training youth to be morally fit. They devote all their strength to this task and never complain, because they are proud of their vocation. We are happy to have men and women like this! Don't we all want to join this group of men and women, as far as we are able, even if it is only for a little while? Woe be unto us if we do not! If we did not, and restricted our Christian activities to Sunday from 9 to 10, it would be useless to call ourselves Christians!

And certainly not least: people from every part of our nation, from churches and schools, blame the misery of our age on the failure of religious education. They accuse the schools and the churches of being careless and   512
lenient in performing their duty. God knows that this is true. People are beginning to teach children about our holy, almighty God and God's com-

---

[2.] Cf. Holl, "Der Neubau der Sittlichkeit," in *Luther*, 155–287.

[3.] The words "and we know . . . ourselves" are added by Bonhoeffer in the margin. The word "and" was subsequently crossed out.

mandments with renewed energy.[4] The schools are at work. The church is at work, renewing and enlivening its worship services and strengthening pastoral care. Happy are we that we have men and women who have found their vocation in doing this! And woe unto us if we don't incorporate our vocation into theirs.

Many laborers are joining to complete the task and are moved by a good and strong sense of purpose. Everyone is working toward rebuilding the collapsed structure, contributing a brick, and thereby creating a memorial for history; laborers, farmers, professors, teachers, industrial leaders, and pastors—all are at work on the same building. Every building, however, needs to be able to withstand assaults. Just as a terrible storm, an earthquake, or a military offensive can destroy a building or a whole city, powers are always at work trying to destroy what others have built with great care. These powers threaten to destroy in one night what has taken decades to build. These are the powers of destruction that develop within any effort and constantly threaten it, which are, to a certain extent, part of every building. Thus, reconstruction and destruction—that is the enduring struggle, the great exigency, in which human intentions are found.[5]

Now let us listen once again to the words of the psalm, "Unless the Lord builds the house. . . ." Whoever understands these words correctly sees that judgment is incurred in all times of rebuilding as well as all times of secure possession. Wherever anything is built by human hands instead of by the Lord it is built in vain. We want to focus on these two things: "Unless *the Lord* builds," and "those who build it labor *in vain*." What can it mean that God builds? Has there ever been a building, a house, or a city on this earth that has fallen from heaven and has not been built by human hands? Could it be that our passage is encouraging us to wait until such a miracle occurs? If all our building is in vain, truly in vain and worthless, why should we even begin to rebuild what has fallen down instead of waiting until God rebuilds it? Why are we still working on the church in order to put it back where it belongs? Why are we working for the moral and religious education of children if all *our* work is in vain?[6]

A lot of people who take the words "in vain" seriously will ask this question. Yet other comforting voices can also be heard. Certainly our actions are in vain if we do only what we want. In these cases we can expect nothing. But if we try seriously to do what God wants and not what we want, then it is the same thing as if God is doing the building. How else can the Lord build except through us? Therefore our building is in vain only when we don't

---

[4.] This is similar to Bonhoeffer's "Address on the First Commandment," see above, 3/3:461–64.

[5.] No new paragraph in the manuscript.

[6.] No new paragraph in the manuscript.

513

build with our whole heart in accordance with God's will! It is true that the people who tell us these things are right about one thing: Woe unto us if we do not commit ourselves to our work with our whole heart and mind! Yet do we really want to join them in saying that if we put forth our best effort in building it is the same thing as when the Lord builds? Isn't there something substantially different about the Lord's building and building that is done with a pious and good will? None of us doubts that many try to improve themselves and work on the whole project with true goodwill. But do we want to say that God is at work here when only people are working? Do we really want to claim that our goodwill renders God's deed unnecessary? Are we so blind that we don't see that *all* our deeds *always* and necessarily carry with them a sign of impermanence and thus sinfulness? Do we no longer see that we are in the world and remain in the world *with all* our thoughts, even the most pious ones, and that we can't do God's will unless God wills it or say yes to God's will unless God has already said yes to us?[7]

Yes, it is so. We don't see that we are in danger of building the tower of   514
Babel anew,[8] saying that we intend to reach heaven on our own. We claim that we don't need God's action but instead intend to replace it with our own. By merely speaking of religious and moral renewal we truly believe that we have done not only enough but everything we can do. We don't even think that someone other than us has to say, "It is very good." We want only to say, "We all would rather be a contented, wealthy nation and a fortunate, good person than be subject to a merciful God." Oh, none of us will admit this or believe it about ourselves. But let's look at ourselves seriously for a minute. Who would not recoil from the person they really are? It is dubious praise for a person not to have anything to recoil from. Family, folk, nation, church, club, and—last but not least—the growth of our own "personality" are the idols around which we dance! Who still thinks about the one who gives everything meaning, who judges and forgives everything? Who still thinks about the fact that our God is a God who smashes nations like pottery, and that it is up to God whether our effort is in vain. Who still thinks about the fact that it does not depend on a person's desire or effort but instead on God's mercy whether that person receives the light of eternity and the light of divine grace in the midst of sinfulness.

Why have we forgotten all this? Because our merciful God lets it rain on the just and the unjust,[9] because even a building that God has not built can last for a time, and because God might allow a building that God has built to last only for a short time. We understand this "in vain" to refer to the world. God is speaking about eternity. Truly, those who sang the psalms knew as well

---

[7.] No new paragraph in the manuscript.
[8.] Cf. Genesis 11. See above, 3/1:453, editorial note 13.
[9.] Matt. 5:45.

as we do that godless people also built houses and towns that had permanence in this world and were not built for this world in vain—and that the
cities that housed God's chosen ones were often destroyed. Yet the psalmist
said, "Unless God builds the house, those who build it labor *in vain.* . . ." Not
in vain for this world. The tower of Babel was higher than all other towers.
Not in vain for the economic and "moral" health of a nation. Not in vain for
the furious competition of the world marketplace. In vain for eternity—in
vain! Because the light of God's magnificence does not shine upon it, in
vain! Because God's mercy is distant, in vain! Because God's love has not covered its damage! The psalmist goes on to say, "Unless the Lord guards the
city. . . ." In vain, perhaps not for the world, in vain, not in the eyes of humanity, but in vain for eternity, in vain in God's eyes, in vain! Because its establishment stands under God's judgment, in vain! Its establishment in earthly
time is its death in eternity.

At this point temptation raises its head, seemingly of its own accord. "Well
then," we might say, "let us lay our hands in our lap, pray, and wait for God
to intervene." Let us not delude ourselves. God will not drop a city from the
heavens, and God's holy commandments insist on being fulfilled. We must
work with our dirty hands. We must labor, even if it is only God who labors for
eternity. We must work on ourselves, our families, our people, and our
church, and still realize that everything is in vain if it is only *we* who build.
This means that we must work with our eyes turned toward heaven, with the
prayer that God will overlook the sinfulness of our accomplishment. Do we
now understand what the psalm means when it says that the Lord has to
build and not we? We remember the words that the wise Gamaliel said about
the first Christians, "If this plan or this undertaking is of human origin, it will
fail; but if it is of God, you will not be able to overthrow them."[10]

The Lord, however, always builds for eternity, even when the Lord does
not build for earthly time. God builds by giving us grace, when God affirms
us and our actions, our work on ourselves, our striving to improve our economy, health, morality, and religion. God does this by letting mercy shine
upon the sins of the big cities and by letting forgiveness shine on the competition of the powerful in this world. The Lord guards us, when out of the
flow of time he saves those things that are pleasing to him for eternity. It is
only when God sees our selves and our deeds that we don't build in vain. It
is only there where God lets the light of eternity fall upon us and our accomplishments that the watchman does not watch in vain. God builds when God
creates a new humanity from an old humanity, which becomes a humanity fit
for God's eternal kingdom. It is where God says yes to us in the midst of sin
that we are already justified, yet remain completely sinful. Because God does
not see the temporal but instead the perfected, the light of perfection falls

---

[10.] Acts 5:38-39.

upon our sinful actions. God's edifice for eternity is forgiveness and over-powering divine love. As long as we remain on earth both we and our work will remain full of sin. It is transitory like everything else. But God has seen it. God has built it. God has forgiven.

As long as *we* act we will not build God's kingdom but, to the extent that God sees us and our work and has had mercy on our godlessness, God will build God's house, God's eternal kingdom, where God's spirit is everything. God the Father will reveal God's lordship to us, who through Jesus Christ, God's Son, have access to God and have received forgiveness for all our sins. And the Holy Spirit will be in us. And God will be everything. Your kingdom come! Marantha, yes come, Lord Jesus.[11]

[11.] Cf. 1 Cor. 16:22 and Rev. 22:20.

B. Texts from the Homiletics and Catechetical Seminar. Summer Semester 1926

6. Exegesis and Catechetical Lesson on Luke 9:57-62[1]

Catechetical Lesson on Luke 9:57-62 for Boys Ages 12–14,
The 4th and 5th Grades of Gymnasium[2]

Exegesis

The Synoptic parallel for Luke 9:57-60 is Matt. 8:19-22. The material seems to have been taken from Q, which is the common source of Luke and Matthew. Luke 9:60-62 probably comes from the Lukan special source. The two or three stories were placed together, not because they follow one another chronologically, but because their subject matter is similar. In contrast to Matthew, the story in Luke is reported in a context meaningful to both what precedes and what follows. The imperfections of Jesus' disciples are eminently clear from Luke 9:40-56. In 9:57-62, however, we hear the thoughts of the true followers—although without any real reference to what has gone before. Luke 10:1ff. follows the sending out of the disciples in a definite context. And the entire content of 9:57-62 is substantially illuminated by its inclusion into the narrative of Jesus' journey to Jerusalem.

[1.] *NL* A 14/1; handwritten; catechetical lesson for Prof. Mahling's seminar, summer semester of 1926. Cf. below, Appendix 3, page 585. In addition to the title, the first page contains the words "23 June 1926—Dietrich Bonhoeffer." See also *D* (*DBWE* 4):59–69, 115–16. The instructor made many detailed comments, indicated below as Mahling followed immediately by a colon.

[2.] The nine high school grades of a Gymnasium in Bonhoeffer's time were named Sexta, Quinta, Quarta, Untertertia, Tertia (or Obertertia), Untersekunda, Obersekunda, Unterprima, and Oberprima.[WF]

Verse 57, ἐν τῇ ὁδῷ seems to belong to εἶπέν τις through an otherwise incomprehensible pleonasm. According to Matthew, the person referred to is a scribe. This is a thoroughly characteristic description of someone who thinks of Jesus as the διδάσκαλος (cf. Matt. 8:19) but not as the wandering holy one, the "Lord" (8:21). His temperament can be described as excitable, open, warm, fairly impressionable, and, using Wundt's terminology,[3] sanguine. Understanding and will are ruled by feeling; reflection is often completely nonexistent. One is able to discern these characteristics from his own words as well as from Jesus' answer. This answer emphasizes the absence of any true reflection by the young scribe prior to making his proposal, without denying his genuine (yet very youthful) enthusiasm. This enthusiasm is placed exactly where it is needed. If we can assume an original historical relationship of Luke 9:46-56 and 57-58, Jesus' statement about the "Son of Man [who] has nowhere to lay his head" was no doubt inspired by the event in Samaria. If this is not the case, then we have before us a Lukan scribal artifice. Whether the designation "Son of Man" at this point emerged out of an original "I," analogous to the passages foretelling Jesus' passion and other passages, should be seriously considered. In this instance the title sounds unnecessarily solemn. Interpreting it as ironic can hardly be justified, since such an ironic response would presuppose a correspondingly appropriate address by the disciples. The meaning of the whole is to characterize the restless, even dangerous life Jesus and every one of his disciples[4] led—a life that Luke knew well, since even following Jesus outwardly is no easy task.

518

In v. 59 Jesus invites the second person to join him. According to Clement, *Strom.* 3.25, this person is the "evangelist" (not the apostle!) Philip,[5] a claim that cannot be further pursued. This second person has a completely different temperament than the first: slow, brooding, resigned; the technical term for it would be melancholy.[6] His nature demands a completely different treatment by Jesus. He needs a push, a sharp, specific allusion to his duty. He must be awakened from his dreams, and at this point only a harsh word will do. The interpretations of v. 60 diverge greatly. Greßman[7] attempts to explain the statement about the dead burying the dead as being derived from a fairy tale in which the dead actually do bury the dead. With such questions it is methodologically extremely difficult to prove dependence, and I believe that in order to get to the truth we have to look for an explanation

519

[3.] Wundt, *Grundzüge der physiologischen Psychologie*, 612.

[4.] Mahling: "correct."

[5.] Clement of Alexandria, *Stromateis* 3.25.3 in "On Marriage," Library of Christian Classics, 2:51. Bonhoeffer may have found this citation in Zahn, *Das Evangelium des Lucas*, 406, note 53.

[6.] Also one of Wundt's distinctive temperaments; cf. Wundt, *Grundzüge*, 612.

[7.] Greßmann, "Die Bibel im Spiegel Ägyptens," in *Protestantenblatt* 49:281.

different from Greßman's. The objection to the phrase is always the inexplicable harshness and severity with which Jesus uncovers a conflict between filial piety and discipleship, and how he "solves" the conflict by ruthlessly favoring discipleship. One scarcely believes Jesus capable of such a statement and we think that this statement does not need any such explanation. The dead are really dead, the father is already buried, and the statement is really another way of saying, "Let the dead remain dead."[8] With this the whole conflict really would be solved. After long reflection, however, I cannot agree with this interpretation. I believe the θάψαι in vv. 59 and 60 simply cannot be ignored. If v. 60 were also considered rhetorical, then v. 59 would be a charming, spontaneous statement.[9] The father therefore cannot already be buried. Who are the "dead"' who should bury the dead remains to be explained. If we compare this sentence with Luke 15:24, and then John 5:24, Eph. 2:1, 5; 5:14; 1 Tim. 5:6, and the Pauline thought about death or being dead in sin, it seems to me that the appropriate interpretation would correspond with the Pauline understanding of spiritual death. Those who do not want to follow Jesus but are caught up in the ceremonial aspects[10] of the law, are, for Jesus, dead. Jesus seems to be talking about specific people, perhaps the relatives of "Philip,"[11] who could have performed the burial. With this, the harshness of the statement has been somewhat mitigated. Yet how can we expect Jesus to speak these words with the harshness that doubtless still remains in them? First, we must realize that this phase is not isolated in the Gospel tradition. Matt. 10:34ff. and Luke 14:24ff. far surpass this phrase in Luke 9.[12] But, Jesus knew that sometimes people who were melancholy could not be helped unless they were forced to make a radical break with the past,[13] even if it meant neglecting a pious duty. Individuals should be able to "lord it over" even their most pious duties[14] and should not be tyrannized by them. If Jesus saw a person's soul threatened and put in danger by a law,[15] he then used radical methods and broke through barriers. Following

520

[8.] Mahling: "Rest, while the wish of the one addressed perhaps amounted to: Let me first finish my year of mourning."

[9.] Mahling: "Except when burial is thought of as a daily process of renewal: we would then perhaps say: Weep! Lament!"

[10.] Mahling: "Is this in the text? Is burial—understood literally—really only a legal ceremony for the Son?"

[11.] Mahling: "But how does Jesus come to characterize them as totally dead? And how is the Son [uncertain reading] thought of as totally living? And would not this distinction have led to hatred of the family member and to the pride of arrogance about it?"

[12.] Mahling: "Here nothing new has been said that can or may be understood as a neglect of duty or a neglect of love."

[13.] *LPP*, 275–76; *D* (*DBWE* 4):50–52, 92ff., and 210–11.

[14.] Mahling: "Better here—expressions (such as weeping, lamenting)."

[15.] Mahling: "See the remark at the previous spot [difficult to decipher]."

him was primary; love of people came *after* love of God.[16] When God orders the neglect of human love, called for in the fourth commandment, then God must be obeyed. Everything else will be taken care of by the one who issued the commandment. Shrinking back at the last minute therefore calls forth the severe tone of Jesus' commands. In addition to this is the fact that Jesus needed workers for the harvest (Luke 10). Once again Luke's artful hand can be seen at work. It is evident that he was no less shocked by this harshness than were the hearers of it. It is in this light that I believe vv. 59 and 60 must be interpreted. For διάγγελλε v. 60 cf. Acts 21:26.

Verses 61ff.: cf. the Mishnah: "R. Jacob said: If a man was walking by the way and studying and he ceased his study and said, 'How fine is this tree! . . .' the Scripture reckons it to him as though he was guilty against his own soul."[17] The third man is phlegmatic.[18] He is delighted about his heroic decision but does not go straight to work. Instead once more (and who knows how many times?) he wants to reminisce about the past and, like Elisha (1 Kings 19:20), celebrate his departure (cf. Acts 2:35 for τοῖς εἰς τὸν οἶκόν μου = the ones who came to his house to see him one last time). This person needed the warning that Jesus' disciples should not delight in the past but must do battle in the present with their sights focused on the future. This person's weakness is the inability to take the initiative[19] in any direction at all. What is curious here is the amalgamation of word and interpretation in v. 62. Εἰς τὰ ὀπίσω is taken by several commentators to refer to the winter rest, now over. I find that far-fetched. Images taken from the realm of farming that are used to speak about building the kingdom of God can be found, for example, in Luke 10:2; John 4:35; 2 Tim. 2:6; Luke 8:5.[20]

521

[16.] Mahling: "Cf. also on this Matt.15:1-9, where Jesus certainly very strongly upholds the duty to parents." On Bonhoeffer's development of the problem of one's duty to one's parents, cf. *E* 114, 210, 266, 280f, 363f, 367f. [In Bonhoeffer's late ethical thought, this problem is treated as he develops his doctrine of mandates. He remains essentially Augustinian in his treatment of worldly duty. For Bonhoeffer the love of God precedes all otherworldly loves. This is how he develops his thesis that the world of earthly things is not immune to the command of God. He goes much further than Augustine, however, by critiquing "two kingdoms thinking" and arguing that love for the world does not contradict love for God when one loves the world as God loves it. Cf. *E* 196ff., especially 204–5. In *Discipleship* this problem is conspicuously absent. Yet in *D* (*DBWE* 4):297 he writes, "The world must be contradicted within the world. That is why Christ became a human being. . . ."] [PDM]

[17.] Mishnah, *'Aboth* 3.8.

[18.] The third type of Wundt's doctrine of temperaments; Wundt, *Grundzüge*, 612.

[19.] Mahling adds: "lacking initiative."

[20.] Mahling: "To speak of the 'building' of God's kingdom is easily inappropriate [difficult to decipher]." In the following, the answers Bonhoeffer anticipates are set in italics.

Catechesis

Catechist   *Children*
    1. Who can name any of the great famous, important, brave armies from the past? *1. The armies of Alexander, Napoleon, the armies of the world war.*
    2. Do you know approximately how big the army in the world war was? *2. Seven million Germans were out in the field and there were even more enemy soldiers.*
    Just think what a huge army that was. We can't even imagine that many people. But you will be amazed when I tell you that there is an army that is greater than all the armies of this war put together. At first this army was very small. There was a captain and about 12 soldiers and, just think, these soldiers weren't knights but fishermen and poor people who were down on their luck.[21] This army slowly grew, but when it was just a little bit larger the captain was taken prisoner and accused of being a rabble-rouser and a disturber of the peace. He was treated cruelly and finally was sentenced to death with two[22] criminals.[23] His soldiers, however, ran away, and his most faithful soldier denied him in front of everyone.[24] Now everything seemed to be at an end.
    3. You already know who the executed man was. Who was he? *3. Jesus.*
    Yes. It was God's Son, and you also know what happened next. After Jesus' death on the cross, it became very clear to his soldiers that their Lord was not dead but alive, though no longer among them. Then they began to tell everyone about what had happened, and the army grew. It grew and grew, and the message went out to the whole world. This army still exists today, and there are always new people who join up, sometimes even whole nations.
    4. Who were the first soldiers? *4. The disciples.*
    5. Who were the other fighters in the army? *5. All the people from the disciples until today.*
    6. Who belong to the soldiers today? *6. All of us.*
    The early Christians often talked about the *militia Christi* and every Christian called themselves a *miles Christi.*[25] You can translate that, can't you? A soldier has to have an enemy. Do you[26] know who the enemy of the *miles Christi* is? It is sin. We will say more about this enemy in a little while.
    7. Now tell me: How can one fight in an army whose commander died long ago? *7.*—Sub-question 7a. Who was the commander? *7a. Jesus Christ.* 7b.

[21.] Mahling: "Should we say this? More likely the people not esteemed by humanity."
[22.] Mahling adds: "real."
[23.] Cf. Luke 23:32.
[24.] See Matt. 26:69-75.
[25.] "Army of Christ" and "soldier of Christ;" cf. Harnack, *Militia Christi.*
[26.] Difficult to decipher; Mahling replaces "you know" with "who knows."

What happened to our Lord Jesus after his death? *7b. He was raised from the dead.* 7c Is he then really still dead?[27] *7c. No, he is alive.* 7(d) Then I will ask question 7 again. *7(d) The commander isn't dead at all. He just doesn't live among us anymore.*

8. Yes, if the commander is still living, then we certainly can fight in his 523 army. Now, from playing soldiers, you all know what is needed most in an army so that everything is done correctly and there is no disorder in the ranks.[28] *8. Obedience to the commander's orders.*

9. In which large army must we then also find such commands and obedience to them?[29] *9. In Jesus' army.*

10. But how do we learn about these commands? *10. From other soldiers.* 10a. And how do they know about them?[30] *10a. From the Bible.*

11. The New Testament tells us what Jesus required of the people who wanted to be his soldiers. And if Jesus still lives today, then we have to listen closely to what he is saying to us. When you are playing soldiers what do you think when there are always children on the other side who don't obey the rules, who do stupid things or even bad things? Or what would one have said about Napoleon's Legion of Honor if there were soldiers in it who were cowardly and evil? Or what would you say if your class had to present something to the whole school and one of you did his part poorly?[31] *11. One would say that they had disgraced the entire class or the entire Legion of Honor.*

12. And would others think highly of that class?[32] *12. No.*

13. It is exactly the same in Christ's army. If those who don't want to be in it because they are lazy see that the soldiers in this army do bad things, what will they think? *13. That the army isn't worth much, that those soldiers disgrace the whole army.*

14. Now think about what it would be like if someone had to say about us that we were disgracing the army of Jesus Christ and most of all the com- 524 mander himself. How disgraceful would that be for us? That's why we want to pay close attention to the commands we hear from the mouth of our captain. Do you think that these commands are very strict or very gentle?[33] *14. Strict—gentle.*

[27.] Mahling replaces the question and answer with: "For what was he resurrected? For life. What must we therefore say of him? He lives."

[28.] Mahling adds: "what is needed most?"

[29.] Mahling brackets: "to them."

[30.] Mahling "This saying falls outside the context of this image. And from which command or law book have they taken it?"

[31.] Mahling: "Do not all at once raise a lot of questions but let each individual question stand alone."

[32.] Replaced by Mahling with: "How would the others judge the class?"

[33.] Mahling: "A command is always strict. . . . Here we may therefore presuppose from Jesus' commands: that they were conceived as serious and strict."

15. Both groups are correct. Jesus can be wonderfully gentle. You have all heard such words out of his mouth. Who can remember one? *15. Come to me. . . .*[34]

16. But he can also be terribly harsh, so harsh that we wince when we hear him call. And today we want to talk about the things that this harsh Lord Jesus demands of us. Turn to Luke 9:57-62.—Read—The student reads the passage out loud again.

16. What is the subject of all three stories? *16. Following Jesus.*

17. What phrase could we use for this if we put it in the perspective of our previous discussion? *17. What it takes to be in the Lord Jesus' army.*

18. Now, are these three men very similar to each other or very different[35] from each other? *18. Very different from each other.*

19. Let us look at the first story. A young scribe (this is who he is according to Matthew) had heard about Jesus and believed that he had never heard smarter, wiser, or more beautiful words than those of Jesus of Nazareth. Then he heard that Jesus was on a journey and was passing through his little town. He hurries out and sees Jesus and his small band in the distance, coming toward him. Full of joy he runs to him and, before Jesus has even reached him, calls out, "Dear Master, I want to follow you wherever you may go." Jesus sees great joy and enthusiasm in his eyes and looks at him for a long time. And what does he say then? *19. The foxes have holes. . . .*

20. What did Jesus mean by this? *20. He means that animals are often better off than he is.*

525

21. Did this answer encourage the young scribe to join Christ's army? *21. No.*

22. Why not?[36] *22. Because no one wants to follow someone who has such an uncertain life.*

23. Why did Jesus tell him this at all? *23. Because he did not know it.*

24. Why did he not know it? *24*—24a. What do we call a person who treats someone the way the scribe acted toward Jesus?[37] *24a. Impetuous, hasty, rash.* 24(b). Now do you know why he didn't know all this? *24(b). Because he hadn't thought about the whole situation very seriously.*

[34.] Matt. 11:28. Concerning this Mahling notes: "The saying listed here is not a military command; therefore it cannot be included as an expression of a command."

[35.] Replaced by Mahling with: "We become acquainted with three people; when we reflect on all that is said here, what must we say then about their relationship?"

[36.] Mahling: "Here one can use a yes-no question; the subsequent basis is necessary and correct."

[37.] Mahling replaces "who treats . . . toward Jesus" with "who makes a decision quickly without recognizing the significance of the decision?"

25. Yes, he didn't use his mind to think about the situation. What did he use? *25. Feeling.*[38]

26. You see, Jesus says about feeling that it is not thoroughgoing enough. One also has to have considered it carefully. What happens with people who don't think carefully about something that they decide to do based on emotion? *26. They don't finish it. They become disappointed.*

27. We have to consider carefully every little thing that we do. How much more important is it to consider carefully an important decision, like the one the scribe was making! If someone is not able to consider carefully something on their own, then Jesus plainly tells them the truth about what it means to follow him. He doesn't want any of his followers to be disappointed. Is it easy for them? *27. No.*[39]

28. No, it is often harder for them than it is for animals. Animals have a place where they can find shelter, but Jesus' followers often can't find shelter. They haven't slept on featherbeds at night nor eaten at a table at noon. Instead they live an uncertain life, in danger and need, in hunger and want. Now perhaps you think that this was a long time ago, that today you and I sleep in a warm featherbed at night and at noon we eat at a fine table so that what was said above shouldn't be taken so seriously. But, boys, there you are terribly mistaken. Do you know where people who confessed Christ were executed not at all long ago? *28. The pastors in the Baltic states.*[40]

29. As you see, up until the present day there have been people who have laid down their lives to be soldiers of Christ. Many others have given all they had[41] and "have nowhere to lay their head." But tell me, is this type of distress related only to external things? Or can you already think what it would be like for the followers of Christ to experience this type of inward misery? What is it that makes a Christian[42] feel all sorts of inward anxiety and misery? What is it[43] that always accuses us? *29. Our conscience.*

30. Yes, the conscience gives Christians their greatest sense of misery. Conscience tells Christians that there is a lot that they should be doing and are not. The misery is that their conscience is always accusing them so that they would rather suffer great external pain than the great misery that arises from the battle of the heart. If you wanted to do something really bad in school

---

[38.] Mahling replaces question and answer 25 with: "By what alone did he allow himself to be led? By his feeling."

[39.] Mahling replaces "Is it easy for them?" with: "Then what must they expect? Difficult thorny situations and tasks."

[40.] During the Latvian revolution of 1905–7 five pastors were executed. During the communist revolution in the Baltics in 1918–19 thirty-two Baltic pastors were executed. See Otto Schabert, *Baltisches Märtyrerbuch.*

[41.] Difficult to decipher.

[42.] Replaces "human being."

[43.] Mahling replaces "What is it" with "And" and remarks in the margin, "Usually two questions are raised."

with all your friends but you know that someone else is watching you who
doesn't want you to do it, then something burns deep down inside your heart
so that you almost burst with fire, ardent desire, and conscience. See, boys,
you all already know the uneasiness of being a Christian soldier. Do we still
think that today the life of a Christian is quiet and comfortable? We have
learned two things from our short story. What was the first thing?[44] *30. Whoever follows Jesus has to know beforehand what will be required of them.*

31. And the second thing? *31. To follow Jesus is sometimes outwardly difficult
but always inwardly difficult.*

32. We now come to the second story. None of us has really understood
it—or have we?! Who is offering discipleship in this case? *32. Jesus.*

527   33. What do you imagine the man was like to whom Jesus is speaking? Is
he tumultuous and cheerful like the first? *33. No, he is sad.*

34. Why is he so sad? *34. His father died.*

35. What was going to happen next? *35. The funeral.*

36. Funerals like that lasted 8 days.[45] Now, there he sat on the road, this
young farmer, sad, drawn into himself as if he were no longer a part of this
world. He hears nothing, sees nothing, and was himself hardly a living person anymore. Then Jesus comes along with his small army. The young farmer
had often heard about Jesus, had come to love him, and had hoped very
much to see him. Now he sits there and doesn't know anything about what is
happening around him. Suddenly a voice frightens him and calls[46] out to
him. Now what words are spoken?[47] *36. Follow me.*

37. He is startled, recognizes Jesus, and understands his command.
Thoughts race through his head—the master—his dead father—following
Jesus—the funeral—his relatives, his mother—how, if Jesus had come a few
days earlier, he would have followed him eagerly, but now, when he is so sad.
. . . And what does he answer? *37. Let me first. . . .*

38. He said this with pleading eyes. He asked only for a short time, for a
delay of one or two days. But then he has to hear the words out of Jesus'
mouth that pierce his heart, "Let the dead. . . ." What can be meant by the
"dead" who are suppose to bury? "Dead" cannot bury. Therefore these
"dead" must be living people. Turn to Luke 15:24; Eph. 2:1 and 5. What
therefore does it mean to be dead?[48] *38. To live in sin.*

39. Why is this called "being dead"? Is one dead to this world?[49] *39. No,
to God's world.*

[44.] Mahling: "Good!"

[45.] Mahling: "There is a difference between burial and celebration. Burial must be
done on the same day. Cf. Jesus; Ananias and Sapphira in Acts 5:1-12."

[46.] Mahling inserts: "something."

[47.] Mahling adds, "did Jesus say to him."

[48.] Mahling: "Cf. concerning this statement the remarks in the exegesis."

[49.] Mahling replaces "Is one dead to this world?" with "For which world is one dead?"

40. Who then always lives a sinful life? *40. Whoever does not want to follow*   528
Jesus.

41. Who then are these dead whom Jesus is talking about? *41. Those who do not follow him should bury the farmer's father.*

42. Was it very friendly of our Lord Jesus to tell the son that he should let other people bury his father? *42. No.*

43. Did the son say anything unkind when he asked to be allowed to bury his father and said that he would then come soon?[50] *43. No.*

44. We would all do exactly the same thing, wouldn't we? Why then does Jesus use such terribly sharp words? Could he possibly believe that a son is not responsible for burying his father? He couldn't possibly have meant that. Why then does he use such harsh words? *44.—44a. What kind of person was this young farmer? 44a. He was a slow, sad person.* 44b. We call this type of person melancholic. How must one have to talk to that type of person so that they awaken from their dreams? *44b. Harshly and strictly.*[51] [44c.] Now do we know why Jesus spoke that way to the young farmer and why he forbade him to prepare a long funeral? *44(c). Because he wouldn't have awakened from his dreams otherwise.*

45. Do you know people like this? Maybe one of your classmates is always sad, hangs his head, and wants to be left alone? Then you know that often nothing else helps others than a well-meaning but sharp word. This will shock that person inwardly and she will be able to start a new life. You see, boys, Jesus first had to call the person who wore his heart on his sleeve back to responsibility and peace. Jesus had to warn him about the dangers of following him. Jesus knew that excitement easily wears thin in such people, just as a flame will be blown out by a soft wind. He knew, however, that once the second person had decided to undertake any new project he would hang on tenaciously to his new work with all his strength. A decision had to be made. First, however, a thick wall had to be torn down, and this could not be done   529
without force. Just think, "What does Jesus require?" *45. The disciple should come with him and let others bury his father.*

46. What therefore is more important—to follow Jesus or to bury one's father?[52] *46. To follow Jesus.*

47. Wasn't a funeral important in Israel? Which commandment do you think of in this context? *47. The fourth commandment.*

48. Honoring your parents also included burying them properly when they die. If you know the many regulations that the Jews had for funerals, then you know how serious and holy this occasion was for the Jews. In

---

[50.] Mahling: "Due to their difficulty, the decisive questions must remain open with respect to divine judgment."

[51.] Mahling: "This is incorrect!"

[52.] Mahling: "This either-or cannot be retained in this generalization."

which book was all of this written down. *48. In the Law, and this was holy for the Jew.*

49. If a funeral and everything surrounding it is so important, how important must following Jesus be! One must leave everything for Jesus' sake. What does he want when he calls us?[53] *49. That we be obedient.*

50. Did Jesus call the farmer away from his duty without giving him another one?[54] *50. He said, "Proclaim God's kingdom."*

51. Now, tell me, is there anything that is more urgent than proclaiming the kingdom of God, which means that God wants to be our ever-loving Father? No, there is nothing more urgent or more important. Jesus called us; let us follow him. When Jesus calls we need to stop doing everything else, listen, and go to work immediately, even if we think we have very important things to do at home, at work, or at play. Often one not only has to stop doing bad things—that goes without saying—but also stop doing some things that aren't actually bad at all because we are called to do something infinitely better. The main point is that we should not make any excuses and say, "Oh, only one moment more, one hour, one day!" Jesus never calls us at an incorrect time. When he calls, there is always a reason. Remember this, boys! Did Jesus think it was bad that the farmer wanted to bury his father?[55] No, but what did the farmer do that Jesus thought was bad? *51. He didn't follow immediately. Instead he made excuses[56] and put conditions on following the Lord Jesus.*

52. Yes, because he said, "Only one more day." That was what was dangerous. Can Jesus still call us? And how and where can he do that?[57] *52. He does it through our conscience; he does it wherever he wants to, at home or at school.*

53. He can do that everywhere. He can do it where we see ugly, disgraceful things on the street or in our schoolmates and revel in them. He calls to us and makes us uncomfortable. "Go away, go away," our conscience tells us. Then we want to ignore it or drown it out with, "Be still, you in there," or "Oh, just a second; I'm coming right away." And then the knocking at our heart's door often becomes weaker and weaker until it finally stops altogether. At that point, God[58] would have left. Who knows, it might be for a long time, because God did not want to "bother" us any more. Boys! It might be

530

[53.] Mahling rearranges this: "from us when he calls us?"

[54.] Mahling replaces question 50 with: "What has Jesus encouraged the man to do in contrast to what he should stop doing?"

[55.] Mahling: "One must be very careful with rhetorical questions when doing catechesis."

[56.] Mahling: "His protest is not previously characterized as such."

[57.] Mahling rearranges the last sentence: "How and where, then, can Jesus still call?"

[58.] Mahling: "Earlier Jesus was consistently the subject of the lesson. One would have to introduce this topic with the questions, "Who comes to us in Jesus, and to whom does Jesus want to lead us?"

forever! We didn't want to let God in. We locked the door against God. Do we hear God calling only when we want to do something bad?[59] *53. God also calls when we have the opportunity to do something good, like helping an elderly woman on the street, or our little brother.*

54. Boys, no one can tell me, "I don't have a conscience like that." "God has never called me." Just listen closely, deep down inside yourselves. When bad things begin to happen, you will surely hear someone knocking. Oh boys, then, we don't want to say, "Only one more minute" again. Instead we want to show that we are courageous and strong and want to join our Lord Jesus' army as one of his brave soldiers. Being a brave soldier in this army is more than being a brave soldier in Napoleon's army. And if one of you feels like hanging his head because his mother is sick or even because he has failed a class, then he should go back to work. Jesus does not like to see people hang their heads. He wants brave soldiers. We want to be wherever there is work to do, and not where no battle is taking place. You now know better who our enemy is. Everyone must fight this fight alone. Some think, "I won't go to a lot of trouble for nothing when no one is looking." This is a bad thing to say. Is it really true that no one is watching our battles?[60] *54. God watches over us even when everything is quiet.*

531

55. Well, then, not when we are back in the communication zone but when we are on the front lines. Nothing risked, nothing gained. Put everything or nothing on the line. Put on the armor of light, fight against the works of darkness![61] Wage God's holy war!

56. Now the third story. Who has decided to begin following Jesus here? *56. The disciple.*

57. What else does he still want to do? *57. He wants to have a last meal with his relatives.*

58. Is that still necessary[62] after he has offered Jesus his services? *58. No.*

59. You see, he wanted to be admired by his friends because of his courageous decision, and he couldn't disengage himself from this outward need. He is still attached to his old way of life. When he tells Jesus this, Jesus points his finger at a man who is plowing a field and says, "What would happen if he should turn around while he is plowing and look at what he had already plowed"? "He would plow uneven furrows," was the answer. Here Jesus says, "Anyone who puts the hand to the plow, to plow in the field of God's king-

---

[59.] Mahling replaces the last question with: "But on what occasions does Jesus call us to discipleship through our conscience?"

[60.] Mahling replaces this sentence with: "Who, then, observes us in all circumstances?"

[61.] Cf. Rom. 13:12, Eph. 5:11.

[62.] Mahling replaces "Is that still necessary" with "What necessity is exhibited here?"

dom, and looks back is not fit for the kingdom of God." Who was this phrase referring to?

532   *59. The disciple.*

60. What does Jesus mean when he says this? *60. When one enters into his service, one is not allowed to look back at what lies behind or what one has done before.*

61. That's true. Jesus' disciple was not allowed to look back at what he left behind, and certainly not when he asked to be allowed to serve Jesus. Oh, how lovely it was in all the comfort, in all the dirt and slime, where one was so cozy, and how icy and hard it often is in Jesus' army. Whoever thinks like this and looks back does not fight and will soon be wounded by the evil enemy. Do you understand this?[63]

Well, then, we have learned three things that are vital for Christ's army. We want to summarize the watchwords of this army in three short phrases. From the first story: First think, then act! From the second story: All or nothing. From the third story: Forward to the enemy! Fie on anyone who stays behind! All of this is just as relevant today as it was then. Come, boys, let's be brave soldiers! Who would want to stay behind?[64]

533   **7. Exegesis and Sermon on James 1:21-25**[1]

Be Doers of the Word!
Sermon on James 1:21-25

Exegesis

The exegetical understanding of our passage can be arrived at only after observing the literary character of the entire letter. Some have thought that they could demonstrate that the letter of James is basically not a Christian letter, but one whose origins are purely Jewish.[2] By deleting as Christian inter-

---

[63.] No new paragraph in the manuscript.

[64.] Mahling's final comment: "The technique of questioning in the catechesis still contains some shortcomings. The content of the second case suffers in the explanation and from the difficulty of understanding the text. The third case, in relation to the other two, falls somewhat suspiciously short; the second, in contrast, could have been a bit shorter. In its entire structure, in its entire tendency, in the manner of its presentation, in the liveliness with which the children were seized, in the rich connection to real practical life, the catechesis is to be described as really good."

[1.] *NL* A 13/3; handwritten; the sermon was previously published in Bonhoeffer, *Predigten, Auslegungen, Meditationen,* 1:109-17. This paper originated as a sermon for the homiletics seminar of Prof. Mahling, who is the evaluator, during the summer semester of 1926; see below, Appendix 3, page 584. In addition to the title, the title page includes this handwritten note from Bonhoeffer: "For 7/17/26. Dietrich Bonhoeffer." For the exegesis Bonhoeffer used: Dibelius, *James: A Commentary on the Epistle of James,* von Soden, *Hebräerbrief,* and Hollmann, "Der Jakobusbrief."

[2.] See Friedrich Spitta, *Der Brief des Jakobus;* cf. Dibelius, *James,* 5, notes.

polations the two critical passages (1:1 and 2:1) where Jesus Christ is mentioned (deleting the second passage does seem justified),[3] they thought they had solved the puzzle. The violence done to the text by this type of argument is generally recognized today and has finally been shown to be untenable by the work of von Soden and Dibelius.[4] But this has by no means solved the problem. In order to solve the problem, one first needs to recognize the close relationship of our letter to 1 Clement and the letter to the Hebrews.[5] The analysis of 1 Clement shows that, with the exception of very few passages, this letter could also have been written by a Hellenistic Jew.[6] On the other hand, there is nothing at all in the letter that only a Jew could have written. (This is quite evident in 1 Clement but is precisely what is in question for James.) With this one can conclude that the writer of James was in all probability a Jewish Christian.[7] Could it be possible that our Lord's brother James was the author of the letter? This possibility must be excluded.[8] (1) The letter assumes conditions that James, who died shortly after 60, could not possibly have known. (2) The writer was acquainted with the letter to the Romans. But this is not a compelling argument. (3) The brother of our Lord would not have placed the figure of Jesus Christ in the background and placed the Old Testament in the foreground (the citations, by the way, are from the LXX). The period in which this letter was written would have to be about the time when 1 Clement and the Shepherd of Hermas[9] were written. Thus the writer was a Jewish Christian who opposed Pauline theology and perhaps admired James. The letter is probably not written to Jewish Christians. One could not presume to find among them the contemptuous attitude toward the law and works-righteousness that is presupposed in this

534

[3.] Replaced by Mahling with: "possible."

[4.] Mahling: "Correct." Cf. Dibelius, *James*, 5, and von Soden, *Hebräerbrief*, 171.

[5.] Mahling: "But not closer than to the Synoptics; Matt. 5, oath; Matt. 7, action." In disagreement with this comment is von Soden, *Hebräerbrief*, 141.

[6.] Cf. above, "Seminar Paper on First Clement," 2/4: 216.

[7.] Mahling: "The entire letter corresponds in content well with that of James, the righteous one, as he was called, the brother of the Lord." Both von Soden and Dibelius disagreed with this. Neither believed that a Jewish Christian could be the author of the letter. See von Soden, *Hebräerbrief*, 176 and 178; Dibelius, *James*, 2–4.

[8.] Mahling: "This cannot be said with certainty. The circumstances of the church-community that had been dispersed by the first persecution in Palestine correspond very well. The interpretation of Abraham's faith and works is not a polemic against the letter to the Romans but rather an argument from a totally different standpoint on the question of how believers can prove that they believe. How can painters prove that they paint or musicians that they compose? It can only be done through the work they present. Is not here the relationship to the Sermon on the Mount obvious: 'By their fruit you shall know them!' We learn directly from James that he uses the Old Testament as the basis of his life. I would therefore like to propose that the letter should be dated very early, perhaps A.D. 45." Bonhoeffer's position is supported by von Soden, *Hebräerbrief*, 178ff.

[9.] A penitential writing from the first half of the second century in the form of an apocalypse.

letter.[10] The characteristics of the letter, comprehensible from its Jewish-Christian drafting and rather late genesis, are its moralism, didactic flavor, and complete absence of early Christian enthusiasm.[11] These had their origins in its Jewish-Christian composition and the relatively late date of composition. We must keep this in mind whenever we do an exegesis of the individual passages.

535

Verse 21. ἀποθέσθαι[12] is used often in early Christian literature, perhaps a cultic expression for absolving someone of sin (see Rom. 13:12; Eph. 4:22; Col. 3:8; etc.). περισσείαν[13] is most likely meant to be taken as an adjective. Ἐν πραΰτητι is most often related to δέξασθε.[14] Dibelius rejects this and sees it as superfluous and self-evident, and suggests that it stands on its own in opposition to ὀργή[15] in vv. 19 and 20. I believe that one can maintain the contextual contrast without losing the grammatical relationship.[16] "Welcome with meekness" means that one should submit to it and be subject to it, not contradict it. The term ἔμφυτος λόγος[17] is problematic. What is meant by it? One often thinks in terms of the Stoic concept of λόγος σπερματικός,[18] which later plays a part in Christian philosophy and dogmatics. This hypothesis should not be rejected out of hand, but it seems unnecessary when seen in correlation with a passage like Jer. 31:33 (see Heb. 8:10; 10:10). This expression may already have attained formal character at the time the letter of James was written; cf. Ep. Barn. 9:9, οἶδεν ὁ τὴν ἔμφυτον δωρεὰν τῆς διδαχῆς αὐτοῦ θέμενος ἐν ἡμῖν,[19] and Ep. Barn. 1:2; Ps. Ign., Eph. 17:2. But I don't agree that the content thereby becomes shallow (Dibelius).[20] In Rom. 1:19f. and 2:14f., the thoughts are still very alive. Given the context of a letter written to a community beset by trials, I believe that the meaning of λόγος ἔμφυτος must be found primarily in the baptismal ritual. This community was also one in which every believer had heard the word

536

preached since childhood. It is in conjunction with these two facts that the

---

[10.] Mahling: "The author wishes to show that a new morality for life does not replace strict self-discipline. Is this not a message for a congregation that has just found faith that comes from the Law?"

[11.] Mahling: "This coheres with the person of the author; it can appear in every time."

[12.] "Lay [something] aside."

[13.] "Surplus, abundance."

[14.] "With meekness," "receive, welcome."

[15.] "Wrath, anger."

[16.] Mahling: "Correct." Against this opinion, see Dibelius, *James*, 78-79.

[17.] "The implanted word."

[18.] "The seminal word," or "the word that is present as seed." Meant is the Stoic doctrine of universal reason that permeates and rules the world.

[19.] "He who put in us the implanted gift of his teaching knows this well"; cf. Dibelius, *James*, 79.

[20.] Ibid.

decidedly practical meaning of λόγος ἔμφυτος may lie, whereby the possibility that Jer. 31:33 and the concept of λόγος σπερματικός could have been in the back of the author's mind is not excluded. Gratia praeveniens is here dogmatically taught.[1] [22] At first glance the challenge to accept this implanted word seems contradictory. Calvin declares, "Accept it so that it can grow in you."[23] But that is not what is stated here; the word is actually already planted. I believe that this apparent contradiction can be solved by realizing that God's gift wants to be accepted. The word ἔμφυτος means only that God has already paved the way for communication to take place. A person has only to say yes, and the covenant will be established. The fact that even this yes has value only because it has been elicited by God lies outside the conceptual realm of this passage. It is clearly stated here that at the same time it must nevertheless remain truly *our* yes. It is not "without internal coherence"(Hollmann).[24] Instead, the statement about doing the word follows the statement about hearing the word in a natural, objective sequence. Could there possibly be Christian concepts that are more tightly woven together than faith and obedience?[25] The subject of our text is none other than this relationship. Following the statement that the word has the power to save souls (cf. Rom. 1:16, 1 Cor. 1:18; etc.), the text does not name the conditions for attaining blessedness; in fact, the only condition actually is accepting the word. Instead, the self-evident result of having accepted the word is described.[26] The use of the imperative mood in the following verse seems to contradict the above statement, but actually it does not. The relationship between the indicative and imperative in Christian ethics can in principle not be abolished but simply points to an observation from two different perspectives. From God's perspective every ethical coming-into-being is an organic occurrence (tree, fruit, the field!). From a human perspective it is

537

---

1. Verse 18 is also to be read in this sense; cf. "Today I have begotten you," at the baptism![21]

[21.] Cf. Ps. 2:7, cited in the context of the baptism of Jesus in several manuscripts of Luke 3:22.

[22.] Mahling: "ἔμφυτος λόγος refers to the preceding image ἀπεκύησεν λόγῳ ἀληθείας = he brought us forth (in the world of God's life) by the word of truth [James 1:18]. Thereby the word is inseparably bound with you; ἔμφυτος from the first beginning, present, inborn. Receive without contradiction the word inseparably bound to your life.—All life, even when it is received as a gift of God, presupposes that it needs the care of human hands to survive. Without this care it will die.—So there is here no talk of baptism or of infant baptism. There is also no talk of the λόγος σπερματικός, of gratia praeveniens ("prevenient [to faith] grace") but only of the natural connection of the λόγος with ἀπεκύησεν, i.e., of the word with the placement within the life of God."

[23.] Cited according to Dibelius, *James*, 79.

[24.] Hollmann, *Der Jakobusbrief*, 7, who says, "an interconnectedness is lacking."

[25.] Mahling: "Good."

[26.] Mahling: "Good."

something that occurs in starts and fits, and that means in the dialectical imperative mood. The passages Matt. 7:26, Rom. 2:13, Ezek. 33:32; and others demonstrate that the problem[2] of hearing and action is not unique to this "epistle of straw."[28] Verse 22. ποιητὴς λόγου[29] must have been understood by the Greeks as denoting the speaker. Semitic usage clearly lies in the background of this genitive compound (cf. 1 Macc. 2:67).[30] The image of the mirror in vv. 23 and 24 has received the most varied interpretations, ranging from allegorical interpretations to strongly parabolic interpretations in Jülicher's sense.[31] Dibelius advocates the latter. Those who don't act according to the word retain as much of the word as those who see their image in a mirror—they forget it.[32] It is certainly right to highlight the intended fleetingness in our image. But I would like to follow von Soden's interpretation,[33] in which also another thought is found, namely, that believers see themselves mirrored in the law in their total, natural imperfection just as people commonly notice their flaws in a mirror. But those who only hear the word are just like the second person who, when he had scarcely turned away from the mirror, forgot everything he could correct about his appearance.[34] The law is thus the mirror, which also fits very well with v. 25.[35] Further interpretations don't seem to me to be permissible. All in all, the difference between the two interpretations is not considerable as far as the content is concerned[36] but has more to do with a sense for the language. The image of a mirror appears often in ancient literature (cf. also 1 Cor. 13).

538

---

2. There can scarcely be a sharper contrast than between the Schleiermacherian definition of religious terms (knowing and doing as mutually exclusive)[27] and the conception of the letter of James.

[27.] Schleiermacher, *The Christian Faith*, §3, 5–12.

[28.] Luther, "Preface to the New Testament," in *Martin Luther's Basic Theological Writings*, 117 (*WA* DB 6:10, 33–34).

[29.] "Doers of the word."

[30.] Dibelius, *James*, 77.

[31.] Jülicher, *Die Gleichnisreden Jesu*, volumes 1 and 2.

[32.] Dibelius, *James*, 80–81.

[33.] Von Soden, *Hebräerbrief*, 183–84.

[34.] Mahling: "Forgetting is not the main thing but instead the thought that repeated glances into the mirror are useless if the task of cleansing does not take place every time between the glances. One looks in the mirror only in order to see whether one still has a blemish. The blemish does not go away even when I look many times into the mirror. Such behavior is meaningless: one goes away, forgets one's image and that one has a blemish, and afterwards all remains as it was."

[35.] Mahling: "The word—not only the law but the word—through its proclamation makes possible and effects transformation to new life."

[36.] Mahling: "That is certainly the case."

For the Jewish Christian, the thought of doing the word of God is automatically linked to the law. In the writings of the Jewish-Christian James, however, the law does not appear as a burdensome force but as a law of freedom. Some have thought they had to see here pure Hellenistic influences or the influence of Stoic philosophy, for it called to mind the "freedom of the wise at the Stoa" expounded by Epictetus[37] and its "relationship" with Christianity in general. But I am not certain that this path is necessary in this case. There are similar thoughts in Mishnah *'Aboth* and already in Jeremiah 31 that could have stimulated a gentile Christian to develop such a concept. *'Aboth* 6:2, "You will find no free person except the one who is occupied in the study of the Torah." If we would think that the expressions in James sharply contradict the apostle Paul,[38] then we should remind ourselves of phrases like "the law of faith" in Rom. 3:27; Gal. 6:2; and Rom. 8:2. It is clear that we cannot exclude the possibility that a Jewish Christian, writing in Rome, would be subject to Stoic influences.[39] In conjunction with ἔσται, which must almost be understood in the present tense, μακάριος is not some eschatological state but the possession of certainty that one is obedient to God.[40] Verses 21-25 lay the general groundwork for the individual warnings that are elucidated in vv. 26ff.

539

Sermon

The sermon is intended to be preached at a worship service for young people 16–20 years old who are educated or are somehow spiritually advanced (members of the youth movement, etc.).

We do not live in a classical era of world history, but it is much less a time that someone [in a][41] later century will be able simply to ignore as ordinary. A time in which death has been so close at hand and so frightful and which has known war, distress, hunger, and scarcity has too many horrors to have a classical mien, not to mention a complacent countenance. Distress has all too distinctly etched furrows on her countenance. And where do you most unmistakably see the face that a particular era displays? You see it in the young people! Youths who have seen death, hunger, and a lost war look dif-

---

[37.] Cf. Dibelius, *James*, 81, note 2.

[38.] Mahling: "That is certainly not the case."

[39.] Mahling: "The expression νόμος ἐλευθερίας [law of freedom] does not lead to this conclusion. Instead it points to the fact that the law becomes my freedom. No longer does it mean: I must become pure, and I should become pure. The law would free me from stain when I put forth the effort to wash away [uncertain reading] the stain."

[40.] "Will be . . . blessed." Mahling: "To be praised as fortunate, as in Matt. 5:1-10."

[41.] Added by Mahling.

ferent from youths who have spent those years in a bucolic landscape or *playing* war. Why shouldn't we just say it? We all know it. May God preserve us that we take pride in it. Truly, we would be more childish than any young people have ever been.

Yes, the young people of today display different characteristics. But are these solely the marks of distress? God help us, no! But they still are the marks of unrelenting severity; not the severity of resignation but a severity that searches and knows that it must continue to search lest everything else be lost. I know that none of us wants to be dependent on our parents; we want to be able to support ourselves. We don't want to breathe only the air of our parents' home. We want to find a place where the wind blows more freely. We want, we seek, we hope, we desire, we fight—always we, we! Always full of longing to do great things! In the midst of this activity and urgency the question about God raises itself with terrible seriousness. It is the question about the reality of the divine. In the midst of this so-called antiauthoritarian era we ask again about an authority, about who is worthy of being called an authority. In the midst of an era of amorality and immodesty we hear words of judgment and forgiveness shouted aloud. We ask, we try, we philosophize, we attempt to find a way to sneak into another world, we don't sleep, we are completely awake and, in truth, not sober. Among the cacophony of voices we hear one voice that we want to listen to today. This voice does not cry in the marketplace; it is not sensational, but it is awake and it is sober. "Therefore rid yourselves of all sordidness . . . and welcome with meekness the implanted word that has the power to save your souls."

"One path among many" is what we might want to say. "And in addition, it is a highly old-fashioned one and not terribly clear." Yes, it is one path and still the only one. It is not one of the human paths that truly are no paths at all. It is the path of God to humanity. Listen carefully! The word that must be grasped is clearly *God's* word. It is true. But how can we human beings understand God's exalted word? If it is *God's* word, then it is too exalted and powerful for humans! Yes, certainly, it is God's word. Long ago God had already planted it in us.[42] Perhaps we just haven't noticed it yet. God has planted his word in the midst of our sordid existence. It lives there in silence and for many it is completely hidden. God is already with us; indeed, God is truly already *in* us. Believe it! Accept it! God has taken up residence in our evil hearts. It is there that God has deposited God's word, the word that can save your souls. God made this promise at your baptism,[43] and God is faithful. Perhaps we have felt this already when being accused or at the assurance of pardon and have therefore not paid attention to it. We have arrogantly and conceitedly driven it from us. We have uttered impressive words, mumbled

540

541

[42.] Mahling: "Exegesis, page 491" [see above, editorial note 22].
[43.] Mahling: "Cf. exegesis, page 491" [see above, editorial note 22].

something about philosophy and Nietzsche and about being bigger than our sins,[44] and have carried our wise heads exceedingly high. Oh! You know that if it weren't so sad it would be funny. I can't help but think that our heavenly Father also knows how to laugh at human arrogance. Oh, how terrible if God didn't!

Accept with humility the word that has been implanted in you. Simply believe that God's word is already there. It directs you and forgives you. Be humble by making yourselves subservient to it. Take it seriously when your conscience calls out to you, "You have sinned." Believe that it is true that God wants to live with you and always has wanted this. Take it seriously, because it is God's word. Here we are talking about God's faithfulness, and in this case one either says yes or no—"I believe" or "I don't believe." Here one accepts it with humility, trusting in God's word and way, or one rejects it with arrogance, trusting in one's own way. Saying a simple yes and listening obediently is to believe, hear, and accept the word as James intended.

But what does it mean that God speaks and that *we hear*? If God, who is absolute holiness and absolute duty, speaks, then God's word always commands the fulfilling of this absolute duty. This is the command of holiness, "You shall be holy, for I am holy."[45] And it is with this command that God confronts our conscience. God agitates us violently. God makes us tremble in the presence of divine holiness.[46] What should happen then when we speak about hearing this word? Yes, certainly, we hear it, we believe it completely, we know with whom we are dealing, and yet is this enough? Even the demons believe and tremble.[47] If God requires something of me, should I really only say, "I have heard it," and have that be the end of it? No, that will not do at all if I know that *God* has said it. In this case there is only one answer. Obedience! *Bow down* beneath God's almighty hand.[48] Belief that hears but does not obey can certainly not be called belief![49]

542

Yes, actual obedience—we can't let anyone diminish this. Obedience is a word that we don't like to hear very much today and whose meaning we don't want to understand. It is a word that, since the time of Nietzsche, we have contemptuously driven out from ethics and especially from religion.

[44.] Cf. Nietzsche's criticism of the consciousness of sin, e.g., *On the Genealogy of Morals*, 31–32.

[45.] Lev. 11:44-45; cf. 19:2; 20:7; and 26.

[46.] Mahling: "Should not a relationship with the Word become flesh, Jesus Christ, a reference to him, be cited here? In him the holy, beloved, pure, righteous, and good Word of God appeared in bodily form; in him God lures and calls us to new life. So wouldn't the connection with ἀπεκύησεν ("he gave us birth") be made and thereby awaken the joy of being obedient to this word?"

[47.] James 2:19.

[48.] 1 Peter 5:6. Cf. Bonhoeffer's children's meditation on Matt. 21:28-31, above, pages 465–70.

[49.] Cf. *D* (*DBWE* 4), especially pages 63–64.

Ethics is an individual's free self-determination. How can obedience possibly have anything to do with this? Religion is somehow an emotional fusion with the divine or maybe the theoretical recognition of the divine. But what is the meaning of obedience, if I myself become God? This is what many in our circle think. Slaves obey. People who think for themselves are free. But I want to tell you something different. Religion is submission to a clearly acknowledged authority. It is absolute submission. Ethics is the attempt to obey this authority. Our actions in this world demonstrate[50] how we honor this authority. Reflect on this for a minute. Wherever there is obedience, there is authority. It is simply unthinkable that serious persons would refuse to acknowledge some form of authority, even if it be simply the authority of their intellect that rejects all authorities.

Now, however, all imaginable authorities are merely faint reproductions and shadows of the one authority who really earns that name and without whom there would be no earthly authority at all. When we do not recognize all earthly authorities as being dependent on that one authority, we make them our idols, be they state, church, reason, or genius. Is it discernible for us anywhere else than where it reveals itself to us in its absolute otherworldliness? God is revealed in God's holy word. Jesus Christ is the path from God to humanity.[51] All human road signs are subject to rigorous questioning when seen in the light of this path, regardless of the words they carry: to God, to the mysteries, to the world of the spirits, to the soul, or to a super-human race [Übermenschen]. "Welcome with meekness the implanted word that has the power to save your souls. But be doers of the word, and not merely hearers who deceive themselves." Therefore God's authority commands obedience. God's word comes to us with this command. Now we have seen that. Should we be ashamed of this?

Does it not depend upon the one to whom we are obedient? Is there not a certain pride in being obedient to a powerful person? But it comes to the same thing whether it is comfortable[52] or not, since we are not on this earth to have fun. Assume, just for a moment, that it is true and real that there is a God, a holy claim, and a holy path from God to humanity,[53] and that this is Jesus Christ. Then try once again to open your mouths and speak about the superhuman and about being "greater than one's sin," or to preach a shallow Epicurianism. I tell you, the words will stick in your throat at the mere

543

[50.] Mahling: "Is this expression, which is repeated later, understandable? Meant is certainly: proof, application?" Here Bonhoeffer takes up Barth, *Romans*, 431-32.

[51.] Mahling: "Cf. the remark on page 495 [see above, editorial note 46]. Also here this thought should have been more thoroughly discussed."

[52.] Mahling asks, "Comfortable?"

[53.] On the term "claim" cf. Barth, *Romans*, 64, 74ff., 93, etc. On the expression "a holy path from God to humanity" cf. Barth, "The Problem of Ethics Today," in *The Word of God and the Word of Man*, 179–80.

thought. Onward to duty and to obedience! We all know people who don't think this way. They come to church often to "hear," as they say, God's word. As someone told me recently, they also allow themselves to be criticized a little by the sermon. They take pleasure in the "wonderful" paradoxes of the Gospels. They take a certain pride in having at least been honest with themselves once again and having discovered certain evil things about themselves. With the thought "Know thyself"[54] they think they have done enough. Then they go home, having had enough for a while. They are no different from those who look at themselves in the mirror for a moment and see that a lot of things are not the way they should be. But they have barely turned away when they forget the image, and everything remains a mess.[55] Their glance in the mirror is as fleeting as their desire to take anything seriously. These people are deceiving themselves. They convince themselves that they have already done enough. Because they believe[56] this, we see that they have not really heard what is being said to them. How can anyone who has truly listened to God believe that it is enough merely to hear? God's word forces us to act obediently. It is a living and a powerfully creative force that one [cannot][57] take up as if it didn't exist at all. It was when God's word became flesh that "we saw his glory."[58] Truly, we saw and we heard. But when God's word became[59] flesh, it was then that God's holy claim became flesh and we were required to obey!

544

Be *doers* of the word! Whoever does not[60] is like the man who built his house on the sand and it was soon torn down by the wind. Be *doers* of the word! One really doesn't even have to say this, because it is so obvious for the person who has really heard *God* and who knows that a good tree bears good fruit.[61] Be doers of the *word*! These are therefore not laws and moral rules that have been self-discovered, even if they appear so important to you. Be doers of the word! Be obedient to God and to no one else. But when you are bound to God in obedience, then you have become truly free. You are free from everything from which you should be free; free from people and powers, because you are bound to God. To be free from God, however, means to be god-less! Think about it! If we are God's through obedience, then we

---

[54.] The γνῶθι σεαυτόν of the Delphic oracle.
[55.] Mahling: "Then he has nothing with which to dispose of the known blemish."
[56.] Replaced by Mahling here and on two lines further below by: "think."
[57.] Added by Mahling: "think to."
[58.] Cf. John 1:14.
[59.] Addition of Mahling.
[60.] Mahling: "Does, or is a doer."
[61.] Cf. Matt. 7:17, 26-27.

have a law of freedom,[62] a law that makes us free from everything that controls us. It is a law that we fulfill out of free obedience. But once again: How do we come to this obedience? Is it born in us? Oh no, that is certainly not the case. At first, when God calls us, we want to flee and to hide like Adam. We become afraid and frightened at the thought that we will have to deal with God. It is horrible to fall into the hands of the living God.[63] No, this obedience certainly does not come from us. But when we hear the word of God correctly we become obedient. The word about the claim and about the gift of God, about holy love, is the word that coaxes our will. God *has* loved—should we therefore hate? God is already there—should we turn God away? The word has been planted—should we not accept it and become doers of the word?

We have been confronted by words and thoughts that are very uncomfortable for all of us: authority, obedience, and law. And can it be that here we want to speak about freedom? Yes. Freedom is always there where our will says yes to God—but indeed to God and not to an idol.[64] Through this people become bound, because they bind themselves to something earthly. But if they truly bind themselves to God, then they are truly free from earthly concerns, through obedience—free! If they are steadfast in their obedience, then they will be blessed[65] in their actions. God will be with them, and they will have the certainty of their being bound to God in all that they do. But our letter does not say [anything][66] to suggest that everything Christians do is pure and admirable. A word of warning needs to be issued! We are not allowed to dream about being holy.[67] Our deeds remain sinful, they remain demonstration[68] and an allusion. Our work is daily repentance, precisely because we are obedient to God. Repentance is the first and the last thing that anyone who has become a doer of the word must do. Repent, *because* the kingdom of heaven is near![69] Those who have been called by God, who are constrained to obedience to God, are those who know what daily repentance means. Take my obedient deeds as my offering[70] and nothing else. "We are worthless slaves; we have done only what we ought to have done!"[71] But because the deeds are obedient deeds, God does not speak judgment but grace.

[62.] Mahling: "So it becomes for us the law to freedom, i.e., to a free action of our will obedient to our God."

[63.] Heb. 10:31.

[64.] Mahling: "Good."

[65.] Mahling replaces "blessed" with "praised as happy."

[66.] Mahling's addition in the margin.

[67.] Mahling: "Instead of dream, better another word."

[68.] Mahling: "Cf. concerning the demonstration page 496" [above, editorial note 50].

[69.] Matt. 4:17.

Now we know that the phrase "be doers" does not mean "Gather laurels   546
on which you can rest before God." It means, rather, demonstrate that your
belief in God is really a belief in *God*, that this belief is submission to the
authority, that it shows that you are obedient. "Work, but not for your own,
but for God's glory." "Work out your own salvation with fear and trembling."[72] God's claim and love has preceded you. Accept God's word, hear
it and do it!

Do we really still want to ask what there is to do? Must we really still talk
about putting aside uncleanness and wickedness? About the love that is self-
less? Should we dictate to the tree what kind of fruit it should bear, or to the
wheat kernel what kind of wheat sheaf it should grow, or to the lily what kind
of bloom it should bear? Do what comes to hand. Adam, where are you?
Adam, don't hide.[73] The Lord also sees behind the bulwarks. Come out,
humanity, from the foxhole. Come out to where the breeze is blowing free,
where the bullets whistle by. There, brother, you are vulnerable, exposed.
This means for you: "Decide, act! Believe and obey!"[74]

8. Catechetical Outline concerning the Second Article of Faith[1]

Summary of the Second Article

1. In discussing the Second Article one must recall that the congregation
confesses in it that Jesus Christ, their Lord, is the basis of their faith.   547

The relative clauses with "who" are nothing other than translations of the
original participial appositions, which answer the question, "Who then is this
Jesus whom you recognize as your Lord?" Answer, "He is Jesus, whom the
apostles and the Gospels declare was conceived by the Holy Spirit"—etc., up
to the words, "to judge the living and the dead" (cf. 1 Cor. 15, κατὰ τὰς
γραφάς).[2] Therefore, because we are given only a summary synopsis of the
Gospel accounts and the course of Jesus' life from the beginning until the
end, the work of Jesus during his earthly life is not mentioned at all. This reference is sorely missed and can be understood only as indicated.

[70.] Cf. Barth, *Romans*, 430–33.

[71.] Luke 17:10. See above, "Sermon on Luke 17:7-10," 3/1:451–56.

[72.] Phil. 2:12.

[73.] Cf. Eccl. 9:10 and Gen. 3:9.

[74.] Final remarks by Mahling: "The sermon is directed toward youth. In view of its
content and form, its style of dashing manliness and heartfelt goodness, pure truthfulness
and conscientious seriousness, it is to be described as a very good interpretation and application of the text at hand."

[1.] *NL* A 14/2; typed. Address given on July 21, 1926, in Prof. Mahling's class. On its
date see *NL* A 1/12.

[2.] "According to the scriptures." Bonhoeffer added this Greek note in the margin.

2. It is also true for the Second Article that faith must be understood as personal submission to Jesus Christ as the Lord of the faithful and of the community. The notion that it has to proceed in this way, "I believe in Jesus Christ our Lord," "I believe in the conception by the Holy Spirit," "I believe in the birth from the Virgin Mary," is an error. This would immediately equate faith, the personal submission of one's life, with belief, holding something to be true. Faith in the Protestant sense cannot mean the deeming of something to be true.[3]

3. Concerning the assertions "God's only begotten son" or "true God begotten of the Father from eternity," we must protect ourselves from every kind of mythological conception. As our Lord Jesus Christ revealed to us, God is Spirit. It follows that these expressions should be understood only from this perspective. God's Spirit dwells in Christ or, as Paul said in 2 Cor. 5:19, God is "in Christ." Jesus' living bond with the Spirit of God was such that a change never took place. Jesus manifested God in his earthly life in such a unique way that anyone who saw purity and goodness, holiness and faithfulness in Jesus immediately saw the purity, holiness, and faithfulness of God himself. "Whoever sees me, sees the Father."[4] Jesus thereby is distinguished as the highest of all humankind. He is the mediator between God and humanity. We therefore regard him with the deepest reverence and confess that he is our Lord.

4. In his exposition of the Second Article,[5] Luther summarized his experience of the blessings and gifts of his Lord Jesus Christ. He knew that through Jesus, his life and suffering, his death and resurrection, he was redeemed from the power of sin, which had erected a wall between himself and God and made him one of the condemned. Luther knew that he was most inwardly united with his Lord Jesus and through him was won for a life of thankfulness and service. Luther praises this, his personal possession of salvation, with words that he again places in the mouth of the father of the household, as he did also with the First Article.

5. The treatment of the Second Article and its exposition for children requires that we also here attempt to translate what Luther the mature Christian articulates about truth from his experience of sin and grace into the experiential possibility of children. Just as with the First Article, Luther's melody of faith is to be transposed into the musical key of children.

6. It would most closely approximate the understanding of children if one summarized the Second Article and its explanation in this simple and

548

[3.] Cf. *SC* (*DBWE* 1):200, 275–76 for more on Bonhoeffer's understanding of the Apostles' Creed.

[4.] John 14:9.

[5.] Cf. Luther's exposition of the Second Article in his "Small Catechism," in *The Book of Concord*, 355.

short manner: "I believe in Jesus Christ, my Lord—meaning that I give my heart to my Lord Jesus. I am certain that he who called the children to himself and blessed them will also bless me and will help me to become a pure and thankful child of God."

7. A somewhat expanded summary, especially for more mature children, could be formulated in this manner:

549

a. I give my heart to Jesus Christ as the mediator and Lord of my life.

b. While he lived on earth he wanted to win humankind over with his word and his life so that people might belong to God with their whole will and life and thus become God's obedient and trusting children.

c. And he died in order to demonstrate to us through his death in battle with sin the extent of his love for us and the disgrace of the evil that brought him to the cross. John 10.[6]

d. As the one who died on the cross and became alive again, he calls me to himself. He does so in order to free and redeem me from everything that is not in accord with the will of God and therefore will not allow me to become a true person as God desires, thus robbing me of peace, happiness, and strength.

e. God is love. God is joy. God is holy seriousness. If I walk hand in hand with my Lord Jesus on my life's path, then I will be guided by him so that I will be allowed to delight in being a child of God forever. For this I should be thankful to the Lord Jesus from my whole heart!

[6.] "John 10" is a handwritten addition on Bonhoeffer's carbon copy. The reference is to vv. 11 and 15.

C. Addresses for Children's Worship Services. November 1926–April 1927

550

9. Address on Luke 12:35ff.[1]

All Saints Sunday, Luke 12:35ff.

Recently, when we were taking an evening walk, we spoke about the end of the world and what would happen then. We'll use this as our starting point today.[2] You know that Jesus often spoke about the things that would happen at the end of the world. Why do you think he did that? What do you think will

---

[1.] *NL* A 15/5; handwritten; children's meditation on November 22, 1926. The manuscript consists of two folio sheets, each with four pages of text, and a half folio sheet with two pages of text. The progression of the text cannot be easily determined because of the uncommonly large number of deletions, additions, and rearrangements of the text made by Bonhoeffer. Page numbers are missing. The second folio sheet is marked with a "2." It is very difficult to relate the half sheet of folio to the rest of the text. The solution is suggested by Bonhoeffer's note on page 1 of folio 2: "p. I 2." This indicates that a text should be inserted here, beginning on the bottom of page 2 of folio 1 and covering the whole of page 3 of folio 1; in its place should be inserted the text that begins on page 1 of the half folio and concludes on page 4 of folio 1. Following Bonhoeffer's notation, the larger portion of text found on page 2 of the half folio was inserted into page 1 of folio 2. Accordingly, the pages of the manuscript appear here in this order: folio 1: pages 1 and 2 are pages I and II. The half folio: page 1 is page III. Folio 1: page 4 is page IV. On the half sheet of folio page 2 is page V. Folio 1, page 3, is page VI. Folio 2, pages 1–4 are pages VII–X. In the micofiches of these manuscripts there is a transcription that organizes the pages differently.

[2.] The first two sentences replace the following original passage, which is crossed out: "Today we will talk about something none of us likes to talk about. It is something that some big boys and some grown-ups as well feel awkward about, because it is something that one cannot really prove rationally. In this way it goes far beyond what we commonly think, and in such cases it is good that we listen closely to what the Bible has to say to us. We really want to see if there isn't something there that speaks directly to us."

happen after the world ends? God's kingdom will be established all by itself. That is why the Lord Jesus spoke so often about it. And so he often painted in his mind a picture of how it would look during the world's final days. He always saw new pictures in his mind's eye and discovered new ways of telling others about it in parables. The early Christians wrote some of them down and preserved them for us. Once he told the disciples this story. In the middle of deep dark night he sees a large house, but the house is brightly lit. One could see many servants on the inside peering out of the windows. They stand there in the middle of that dark night and each one holds a lamp that shines brightly onto the long, dark street. What are they doing? No one says a word. Then one of them almost falls asleep, but his fellow servant calls softly to him, and they peer out alertly into the darkness again. Who could they be waiting for? Why don't they go to their rooms to get some sleep? Who will come that late at night? They hear the night watch called out. Then it is almost morning. The servants still remain at the windows. They have to encourage each other to stay awake, because their tired eyes are beginning to fall shut. They are waiting for their lord, who is coming home from a wedding. By now they have waited many days and nights, and he still hasn't come. Yet the faithful servants don't get tired of waiting. They want to welcome him when he comes home to them. They don't want to be sluggish when he knocks at the gate, but rather to open the door for him swiftly and go toward him with their lamps, even if it be midnight.[3]

Jesus pauses slightly. Silent and amazed, the disciples listen to Jesus' words. Then he continues, "Blessed are those slaves whom the master finds alert when he comes; truly I tell you, he will fasten his belt and have them sit down to eat and he will come and serve them." Speechless, the disciples look their Lord in the eyes; they have not understood what he means. Then he makes it clear to them: "You also must be ready, because the Son of God and his kingdom will come at an hour when you are not expecting it. Let your loins be girded and your lights shine like those of the servants." Then it becomes clear to the disciples what the Lord Jesus wants of them. Has it become clear to us what, if anything, the story means to us? You can't know how much!

So[4] it's true, isn't it, that we are the servants in the parable, and the lord whom they await so faithfully[5] is the Lord Jesus and his kingdom. But what does that have to do with us? His kingdom, as we know, will not come until the world ends, when the earth and the stars collide or some other sort of terrible catastrophe occurs. Astronomers have calculated that this won't happen for another thousand or million years; what does it matter to us what might

551

552

[3.] No new paragraph in the manuscript.
[4.] Page III begins here (see above, editorial note 1).
[5.] Difficult to decipher; perhaps "gladly."

be important in a million years, when the end of time comes? It is quite natural to ask this now, and you are quite right. The time period at the end of the world really has nothing at all to do with us. Others can rack their brains about it. It is better that we ignore it. But what now? Does the story really have nothing to say to us? What would you say if I told you that every moment could be the end of the world, the "last days"? What could I mean? It's true, isn't it, that there is only one end, just as there is only one beginning to our human lives and to everything? But shouldn't we think about this more carefully? Instead of end, let us use a very similar word, "fulfillment." So instead of talking about the end of the story or the end of our lives, let's talk about fulfillment. Perhaps now its meaning can become clear to us. When is a person's life fulfilled? Surely when such persons have become the kind of persons they are put on the earth to be.[6] But when does this happen in a person's life? To know this, we must listen carefully to our Lord Jesus and to his word. When we do God's will as God's true children, when God has personally moved into our hearts and helps us sweep them out, "there a heav'n on earth must be,"[7] and we are fulfilled. This is what Jesus taught.[8]

553   And now let us turn again to the story of the servants and the lord, the story of the people and of the kingdom that the Lord Jesus wants to usher in. Here, you see, we come in the story to what is especially relevant to us. We readily believe that we will not experience the end of the world; none of us will. The world will last many thousands of years until God decides to make everything new. Yet we don't need to wait that long. Christ's kingdom and Jesus Christ's lordship[9] are much closer to us than we think. Christ's kingdom should already be a part of us; we should already be children in his kingdom. Our Lord Jesus calls to us every day, if we just listen. He knocks at our

---

[6.] The phrase "put on the earth to be" replaces "what they were meant to be."

[7.] From a hymn by Benjamin Schmolck, "Open Now Thy Gates of Beauty," *Lutheran Book of Worship*, 250.

[8.] The insertion from page 3 ends here. It replaces the following passage from the beginning of page 4 on folio 1: "First, Jesus wants to tell us, 'At some point everything that exists will pass away, and then God will establish God's kingdom in which we should all live from then on.' But he adds, 'Let. . . .' That doesn't mean, for example, that we shouldn't sleep anymore until all of this occurs or that from now on we can't think of anything other than the end; we would then be completely useless dreamers. No, it doesn't mean anything other than that in everything you do you should think that at this very moment God's kingdom perhaps will come, and that you are now at this very moment supposed to stand before God's judgment throne. 'Whether or not he is ready he must stand in front of his judge' (Friedrich Schiller, *William Tell*, Act IV, Scene 3). This is what you yourselves sang recently when a beloved friend died." It can no longer be established which of the "many choral pieces" of this song the children sang (Heinrich Riemann, "Schiller in die Musik," in *Bühne und Welt* 7, 656).

[9.] In the manuscript, "H" perhaps refers to the German word "Herrlichkeit," which means "majesty."

door, just as the lord in the story knocked at the servants' door. He asks, "Are you ready for me to enter? Have you swept your chamber clean for the important guest who wants to come?" "Listen," says the Lord, "I am standing at the door, knocking."[10] In this way, the Lord Jesus and the Holy Spirit come to us. It is just as it is when we pray, "Where we find thee and adore thee. . . ."[11] It is a bad servant who is asleep when the Lord knocks and does not open swiftly the door for the Lord. Happy is the servant whom the Lord finds awake. We already spoke about this "being awake" on Repentance Day, when we said that we have to listen deep within ourselves to discover whether we hear a voice that has something to say to us. You see, in the beginning the voice is very quiet. We must be wide awake and attentive in order to hear it. The harder we try, the more distinctly and easily we understand it. This is how we prepare ourselves so that we can truly welcome the Lord Jesus. See how closely together the thoughts of Repentance Day and All Saints' Sunday lie. And we sense a hint of the coming already on the First Sunday of Advent.[12]

554

Now you'll say to me, "We'll never be able to be the children of God that God wants us to be while we are here on earth, no matter what we do." Therefore, "heaven cannot truly be in us." Here you are very right. We are never so perfect that we can say while we are here, "Now I am perfect." Jesus showed us that again and again; we note it very clearly. This is the reason that we are often so sad, for we are not quite able to achieve it. We don't always pay attention to the knocking of the Lord Jesus. Yet we know that God nonetheless wants to be with us here on this earth. The kingdom of heaven is very near. At one point, though, it will happen. At that moment it will be the last time the Lord Jesus knocks at our door; and this time it will be so loud that no one can sleep through it. This is the moment when we die.[13] If we think about it, we will suddenly recognize that the story about the servants has much more to say to us. It says to us, "You should be awake, not only when the Lord Jesus calls to you for the first time, but each time, until our Lord Jesus knocks at your door for the last time and says, 'Now it is time to go. Are you ready?'" At that point, many people become aware for the first time in their lives that they had never thought about what would happen. Whether they are prepared to go or not, they must now stand before their judge, as stated in the song you've recently sung.[14] You see, they did not

---

[10.] This sentence is a direct quote of Rev. 3:20.

[11.] Cf. above, editorial note 7 ("Open Now Thy Gates of Beauty," verse 2).

[12.] At this point in the manuscript there is a mark that indicates that page 5 should be inserted.

[13.] The insertion (page 5) indicated on the half folio ends here. The sentence that stands directly before the mark, indicating that something is to be inserted here, should apparently be crossed out. The sentence is as follows: "It is true, is it not, that this is the moment when we have to die."

[14.] See above, editorial note 8.

want to hear the Lord Jesus and the Holy Spirit, even though both had often knocked at their door. They had closed their eyes and ears, and slept. They are now on their final journey and know they have no treasure stored in heaven. They had their treasure and their hearts in this world only.[15]

Recently we took a walk and talked about serious things. One[16] of you said something that I remember quite well. He said, "If I knew that I would die in 3 days, I would take my money out of the bank, buy a huge piece of Swiss cheese and eat incessantly. Now we laugh about this, and the one who said it meant it only as a joke; but, you know, one really shouldn't make a bad joke about dying, even if it isn't meant maliciously, because there are quite a few people who really would do something very similar to what that boy said. They think about nothing else but the movies, eating, and drinking. The people of Jerusalem told the prophet, "Let us eat and drink, for tomorrow we die."[17] Why, indeed, can so many treat this issue so lightly, in a way that we ought not at all? You know the answer! Surely it is because so many people believe that with death everything is finished and at an end. The older ones among you have often discussed and argued with someone who believes this as well. You have noticed how difficult it is to change a person's opinion. We have so little to say about death because none of us is acquainted with it or has experienced it. I readily admit that you will never be able to prove what we are discussing today. Thanks be to God that it can't be proved, but you can believe it. You see, if we know that God has entered into a relationship with us, then how can we imagine that the good Lord is capable of rejecting us completely? We should, after all, rely on God's faithfulness. Otherwise, everything certainly is at an end.[18]

Now, if we make up our minds to believe courageously in our Lord Jesus' words (one cannot believe without courage), then we have to go all the way. The time will come for all of us when Jesus will knock at our door for the last time and will call us to go. Who knows when it will be! Maybe when we're 80

[15.] The mark "p. I 2.," mentioned above in editorial note 1, follows this paragraph. This is why the text from folio 1 should be inserted here.

[16.] Replaces: "In order to understand this completely, we will begin at a completely different point. During the same trip, when we talked about the reality of the Holy Spirit, we spoke of something else as well. We spoke about the end of the world and about the people who do not do anything other than go to the movies and to dance halls. At that time you spoke of the Indians and of reincarnation. And so."

[17.] Isa. 22:13.

[18.] The words, "You see . . . everything certainly is at an end" replace "But you can believe it. It is no great thing to pursue something that has been proved. What would happen to all of those who do not understand that kind of proof? You have to have courage to believe. Being completely free to rely on it solely because the Lord Jesus said it. That is what it means to believe. It is just as difficult and just as easy for everyone." The following text is located at the bottom of page 1 of folio 2.

years old,[19] maybe this very week. A dear friend was torn from our midst only a very short time ago. Who knows why? Who could have imagined it, when the week before he sat with us in the children's worship service. Children, it is truly frightening how often death comes so suddenly. "Quickly death approaches,"[20] you sang. Those who talk about nature's law or some other sophistry talk foolishly. No, it is horrible, terrible. Whoever doesn't feel this certainly doesn't have a Christian heart. Now think how terrible it is for those who don't want to hear the Lord Jesus knock and don't realize that they have to stand before their judge when this life is over.[21]

Oh no, death is not the end for humanity. It is a horror for some and a delight for others.[22] Jesus tells us that death is God's arrival, a call and a knock at our door. Now we stand closer to the kingdom[23] of glory than ever before; it stands before the door. Yes, the kingdom of God is very close to us. Oh, the righteous persons of the Bible were able to tell us splendid things about the kingdom of God toward which we should all strive.[24] They described the Holy City of everlasting light, with its golden streets and gates of pearls,[25] the majesty of God the Father, and the joy of God's immense kingdom. All these pictures are really only very faint images of reality, the reality that will become ours one day. But, Jesus says, only the true servants who wait for the coming of their Lord, will sit with the Lord at the table. Only those who don't let their lights go out will see the eternal light. Those who do not light their lamp won't be able to see the Lord coming. They will go to sleep in the dark. 557

This serious warning from Jesus about letting the light burn means two things. First, be on the lookout for the Lord. Show the Lord that you are waiting. For us this means, "Listen for the Lord's knock." It also means, "By candlelight look to see if you are well girded and ready to receive him." For us it means that we should make sure we have swept our house clean so that the Lord can enter and make sure we are ready to go when the Lord knocks at our door for the last time.[26] We can never start too soon to prepare our-

---

[19.] Difficult to decipher; perhaps "90."

[20.] Schiller, *William Tell*, Act IV, Scene 3 (see above, editorial note 8).

[21.] The words "who don't want to hear" replace "that one doesn't have to fear death, that one can look forward to it gladly." With the following paragraph, the last portion of the address begins (pages VIII–X). This portion is free of any transpositions.

[22.] The words, "Oh no . . . others" replaces "Jesus told us more about this, and said that you should prepare yourself for it. He told us that everything is not at an end when we die; instead, everything really begins anew. At that time, it will be revealed whether a person has lived for eternity or not."

[23.] In the manuscript "R" is used for the German word, *Reich*, "kingdom."

[24.] Crossed out is, "People have imagined beautiful scenes."

[25.] Rev. 21:18-21.

selves. At any moment the last time for us might come, and then it may be too late. Let your lights shine. God has lit the light in you, don't let it be extinguished! See that no evil one blows it out, because then it will be dark and cold in and around you.[27]

Once it was completely dark in the world, and everything slept in darkness. People didn't know up from down, and bad things were done in the darkness of night. It was then that God sent the light from heaven into the world. In the middle of the night a man stood with a glowing torch and shined a light into the darkness. Around him stood men and women. They stood there, seized torches, lit them from his flame, and carried them into the dark night. And more and more men and women came to the strange and extraordinary man[28] with enormous torches and lit them from his flame and ran out into the world. Oh, how careful they were that this wonderful flame wasn't extinguished. But a lot of them turned around. They didn't pay attention to their flames and stumbled so that their flame was extinguished. Oh, how difficult it was to find the way back to the man with the torch! The light spreads farther and farther, because each person lights his torch on someone else's, and so on and so on until the world becomes lighter and lighter and warmer and warmer. When the man with the torch returned to his home away from the world, his light shined in many hearths in the world. To be sure, there were many who had become used to the night, and the light burned their eyes so much that they fled from it. But once people had it, they took care of it just as if it were the most precious holy relic so that they might never lose it again. In this way the light of the fire burns on and on. We are the ones who guard it.[29] Let your lights shine! Blessed are the servants whom the Lord finds watching.[30]

So as we pay attention to the little flame, the Lord Jesus Christ glorifies us even now; but we are glorified for eternity first in God's kingdom, when we leave the world of darkness to enter the kingdom of everlasting light, when we bring our light back to his home. Suddenly we don't have any fear of death at all, if only our little light shines so that we may gain entrance into the kingdom of eternal light. We are also not quite so sad when someone dies who has guarded his flame well. God alone sees whether it really shined or if it just seemed to us to do so. We, the children, can't see this. Let us remem-

558

[26.] Crossed out are the words: "The people about whom we just spoke do all of this. There is nothing to laugh about here. Instead, it is terribly sad. What will become of those who sleep until their last hour? Wake up. . . ."

[27.] No new paragraph in the manuscript.

[28.] The phrase "strange and extraordinary man" replaces "wonderful man."

[29.] The words "on and on . . . who guard it" replace "a time will come when it will burn to high heaven, and then there will be no more darkness. God has made everything new. God's kingdom has come."

[30.] No new paragraph in the manuscript.

ber that God intends for all people to be helped. Let us remember this All Saints' Sunday those people who have entered into the eternal kingdom as faithful guardians of their lights; and let us in complete stillness be of good cheer for all people as well as for ourselves. No picture is adequate to depict for us the extent of joy that will be there, when we see God and our Lord Jesus face to face and rejoice in their service. Until that time Jesus calls to us, "Do not be afraid, little flock, for it is your Father's good pleasure to give you the kingdom."[31]

559

10. Children's Address on Psalm 24:7[1]

1. A long time ago on a very ordinary day during vacation far away from here in the south of Germany, I took my morning walk to one of the most beautiful old castles that I have ever seen. Almost every morning at the very old castle with its magnificent massive portal, I sat on the low wall and looked for a long time down upon the countryside and the river. On that day early morning hikers[2] came out of the gate of the castle to meet me as usual. With a greeting, they passed me walking through the courtyard of the castle toward the street.[3] How often in the many weeks that I lived there had I seen that. But today something felt a bit strange to me. I remained standing and watched the two people until they were out of sight. They were naturally not a little puzzled. "No doubt he has never seen two people before," one said, and they went on, laughing. I continued to lean against the wall and looked up at the high castle gate.[4] How many people have already entered and exited here? I thought. How long have they done this? And how different they have looked: knights and nobles, lords of the castle and servants, children and old people, beggars and musicians, bishops and warriors, wanderers and hoboes. How many happy and how many sad messages have been carried through this tall portal? How many devious and bad plans, and how many good and pious thoughts has one brought in here? Against how many enemies has one slammed the door shut, and how many friends have been

560

[31.] Luke 12:32.

[1.] *NL* A 15,6; handwritten; untitled children's address for the First Sunday in Advent, presumably on Ps. 24:7; delivered November 29, 1926 (see below, Appendix 1, pages 579–80).

[2.] Difficult to decipher.

[3.] The text up to this point is a new version of the beginning of the address; it replaces: "It was on a completely ordinary day, when I returned home from work; and just as I wanted to enter the house, two strange men came out of the door of the house toward me, and then went past me through the garden onto the street."

[4.] The words "I continued to lean . . . castle gate" replace "I still sat at the entrance to the house, and then I made a decision. I went quickly into the house and to my room. I sat there a long time and thought about this in silence."

heartily welcomed? Now it was a magnificent summer morning. The gates were opened wide, and the warm rays of the bright sun reached far into the enormous entrance hall. But at night one had to close the door tight so that the cold night breeze and perhaps all sorts of rabble couldn't force their way into the castle. This was what the resourceful head of the house had ordered, and the faithful servants followed his orders every day. What danger threatened the whole castle if just once the gate were left open without being guarded? Too much depended on the vigilance of the gatekeepers. The entire responsibility was theirs; the whole castle depended on them. How often might it be possible for a bad guard to let evil people in, and how often might it be possible for him to sleep through the master's return from the hunt or from a military expedition?[5]

After I pondered this for a long time I suddenly thought of another castle—I didn't quite know why. It was much smaller than the immense one before me. But infinitely more people trafficked in and out of the small castle than the big one. There was a continuous movement in and out the whole day long. An incredible variety of things entered it, from the most beautiful to the ugliest, from the best to the most repulsive. And there was also a gatekeeper in this castle, who opened and shut the lock. How very securely this castle could be barricaded, much more tightly than the other one. At this castle one could pound and pound on the gate with the steel knocker, yet no one inside would hear it, or at any rate no one would open up. Here it was important to be wary of evil intruders who would in an instant completely destroy the little fortress if they could ever get in. They would ruin every beautiful thing and would seize the place. Yet the door often stands wide open in order to let the sun and the warmth in, but the gatekeeper has to be there. Now it often happened that the gatekeeper was inattentive, even when the sky was dark and a driving rain splashed into the house, upsetting everything that stood in its way. Then he couldn't wake up fast enough from his dreams to close the door tightly. Or he slept in when the sun rose in the morning, or when the master of the castle returned. Then the master had to stand before the gate and wait; no one let him into his own house. He had even built it himself and furnished it and given it into the charge of the gatekeeper when he had to go away, and now the gatekeeper wouldn't let him in.

He must stand there and wait a long time. Day after day he returns and wants to gain entrance to his property, but no one hears him, no one opens the gate. Who knows how long the owner will have patience and will come and knock? Maybe today is the last time before he stays away completely and leaves the little castle alone behind him. You know what the castle is—the heart of a person. The gatekeeper didn't notice any of this; and we, as you know, are the gatekeepers. What will it be like if the Lord leaves us, the ones

561

[5.] No new paragraph in the manuscript.

who are denying the Lord his own property, alone for eternity? We did not want a master, and now we have gotten our way for eternity! We are alone without a master and without a God, because we did not want to hear when there was still time, and the master knocked at our door.[6] Lord, let us not miss your holy hour, when you call out and seek to enter your property. Let us be upright gatekeepers and watchful servants of your house. Open the doors wide.[7]

2. Christmas is not a celebration for the individual but for everyone together. Why is that? God comes into God's kingdom, and God's kingdom is the whole world. Every person belongs to God, because God has created everyone. We are all God's possession, which God now comes to claim. Who wants to refuse to give the Master his own property? Who wants to steal God's property? Who wants to seize what does not belong to him? Let us rejoice that God is coming to occupy God's kingdom and that we have been God's possession from the beginning of the world. God wants everyone—not only us but also others—everyone. God will bring God's kingdom to bear on the crimes of the large cities. The magnificence of God's kingdom triumphs over the power struggles of the kingdoms of the world. Everyone should become a citizen of God's kingdom. The one who began the endeavor will bring it to fulfillment.[8]

562

3. Recently I heard someone in a streetcar complain loudly and say, "Then I was sent to these rich people to deliver something, and they let me wait a whole hour before they came down. Who still has time today to wait around?" He was completely right, because it could happen that with these delays he could not complete a job and therefore no one would give him work any longer. He and his family would be unemployed, even though it was not his fault. Now tell me, is there anything worse than to have to wait for a friend, or wait when we are on an errand, or when someone is sick in bed and really wants to get well, or to wait at any time? No, all of us really dislike waiting. Think for a moment about another person, a mother, whose son has done something terrible to her, and now she waits for him to come and say, "Forgive me, mother." She waits for him to open the door of his heart to her and cleanse everything from his heart that is untrue to her; she wants only to let love live in it. Just think how she has to wait, often days and weeks. But the son closes himself completely off, and perhaps the mother has to wait her

---

[6.] Rev. 3:20.

[7.] Ps. 24:7.

[8.] On the back of this page there is a passage that is upside-down that perhaps was intended for the second part of the address. It reads: "Do you know the most powerful man on the earth who rules over untold millions of souls? He does not have a large kingdom like the other rulers, and yet he is the most powerful king of the world. He is the pope in Rome. Do you also know what he calls himself? He would be the Vicar of Christ on earth. So actually he only administers a kingdom that belongs to someone else.

563 whole life. Perhaps you already know about something similar. Or remember how the father had to wait for the prodigal son.[9]

Now think how, day after day, someone who would like to come in waits patiently outside our hearts, knocking tirelessly. We hear the knocking but ignore it, due to the cries and noise of the voices that can't wait and seek to drown everything else out. Tell me, do the loudest criers always bring the best with them? So the patient stranger has to stand aside and wait, and he can wait. If he couldn't have done so from eternity, then he would have to learn how to do it from us. God is the great unknown Father standing before our hearts, the one whom we ignore so easily, although God stands near to our door and knocks. Won't we finally listen and open up? Do we want to let so many less important things in but let the Master wait like a servant? Certainly God has enduring patience for those who don't know about him and his will. Yet for us who know that he waits but then don't even open the door, the time could come when we no longer find God standing at the door. "How we will seek him with tears."[10] Be serious about this. Don't you also think: "Yes, yes, certainly he is right about all of this." Open the door wide!

4. Now if we have really resolved to open the doors of our hearts to the Master, how do we do it? We must truly try to open the door when we are alone by ourselves. It doesn't happen just by talking about it. Certainly the door is often rusted shut and difficult to open, but we have to try. First, we have to silence all the voices in us that wish to speak about school, our friends, about the games, and the boy we just fought. It must become very still within us, and when it has become very still we can call out to the one who hopes to come to us. You can be certain that that person will come, even if, for some reason, you can't tell if he is with you, and you have suddenly become a completely different person. When we then return to work we 564 can't allow ourselves again to become so busy that we can't hear God's voice. If it should get to that point again then we should very quietly come before God in prayer. It just cannot happen without prayer. God once again will let his voice speak within us and will be with us. In this way we celebrate Advent, the arrival of the Master, every day.

5. I want to tell you an ancient legend. It was winter far up in the north on a dark night just before Christmas. A snowstorm blew and howled around the sturdy walls of a brightly lit house. Far and wide one saw nothing but fields of snow. But within the house lived cold, hard people—a man and his wife. With doleful faces they were eating their evening meal when someone hammered on the door ever louder and ever harder. The man didn't want to go to the door. He waited until it seemed as if the door would burst open. The storm howled even more terribly outside. Then he hurriedly jumped up and,

---

[9.] No new paragraph in the manuscript.
[10.] See Heb. 12:17.

with a curse, opened the door to let in the mischief-maker. He had just touched the door handle when the door flew open and icy air and snow rushed in, but no one was outside. It was the storm. Enraged, he closed and slammed the door shut as firmly as he could. "So did you throw the person out?" the woman asked when he returned. Without answering, the man sat down at the table. It didn't take long before there was a knock again at the door. Neither of them paid attention. The knock was not as loud as before, but it came again and again. "Oh don't bother; it's the storm again," said those who were inside the house. Then they heard an exhausted, strained voice calling out, but they didn't want to listen. They didn't want to be bothered. The voice called out ever more urgently. "Listen how the storm howls," the woman said. And she knew that it was not the storm. Once again there was a frantic knock and a final call, which sounded like a distinct cry. Then once again it was still inside. The only thing to be heard was the usual rushing of the wind and the crackling of the wood stove on which the food cooked. They thought silently to themselves, "Praise God that we are rid of that person. Insolent beggars." But in front of the door, soon to be covered with snow, lay an old man without a coat or a jacket, and next to him a little boy tightly wrapped in the clothes of the old man. Both were frozen to death. That same night the man who had lived in the house died, and his soul flew away to heaven's gate. Next to his soul two other souls flew along on the same 565 day, and they whispered softly to each other. The soul of the wretched man suddenly became frightened and miserable. In this way they flew on. The two flew always a little ahead, and then they finally arrived at heaven's gate. There they knocked at the door, and immediately a friendly man opened the door, letting the two souls into a most beautiful garden. The angel of the Lord had known both of the souls for a long time and had seen how, just before he died, the old man had taken his jacket from his body in order to protect the child. The door had hardly closed again when the miserable soul, full of fear, knocked at the door. When no one came to open up, he knocked louder and louder; but the door remained closed. Then a terrible storm arose before the door, and the soul froze terribly. Full of distress, he cried out for help. Then he heard a voice (Matt. 25)[11] and knew at once that it was the voice of the Lord Jesus Christ. "I was hungry and you gave me no food, I was thirsty and you gave me nothing to drink, I was . . . naked and you did not give me clothing." Then the miserable soul cried out, "Lord, when did we see you hungry, or as a stranger among us?" The Lord answered, "What you did to one of the least of these you also did to me. When you did not open the door to the poor man who knocked at your door, you shoved the Lord Jesus out of your house." Now do you know what it means when the Lord says, "Behold I stand at the door. . . ."? Don't open your heart and house only for the Lord

---

[11.] Matt. 25:42-43, 45.

Jesus, but do the very same thing also for your poor starving brother. With every poor brother who comes into your house the Lord Jesus enters in. Our collection for Bethel[12] is at hand. Think about this. Even though poor and sick brothers don't always knock on our door, they do rap at our heart and ask to be let in. The Lord comes with them. Open the gates wide!

11. Address on Jeremiah 27–28[1]

566

Jeremiah 27–28

Jeremiah had warned them. He realized that a terrible fate was concealed in the clouds that gathered in the sky. Yet they had listened to him less than to any other prophet. He was the fool, the object of derision, but also the terror of the city. They ridiculed and abused him out of a deep fear of the one who stood behind him. They knew that this was decisive. They could either believe him and repent *or*—or indeed seek to get rid of him by any means possible. Insolent and cold mockery seemed to be the best way to disguise the terrible dread they felt. Jeremiah had long ago recognized the ultimate failure of his words, but God still spoke to him and as long as that happened he had to continue to speak. "The Lord has spoken; who can but prophesy?"[2] Jeremiah was the unhappiest person in the whole city, because he knew both God *and* the people. Some knew only the people, but most did not even know them. Jeremiah first came to know the people when he spoke God's word to them, and he came to realize that his own people, rather God's people, couldn't behave any differently from the way they were behaving. "Can Ethiopians change their skin or leopards their spots? Then also you can do good who are accustomed to do evil."[3] When Jeremiah realized this he cursed the day of his birth.[4] Just think what it would be like to know that the people you love will have to die soon; this would not be easy. But to know that God has rejected them and that they were to blame for evil having become an integral part of their nature—oh, no one can stand this kind of pain! Let us thank God for not initiating us into these, his final resolutions. Let us pray daily that we don't belong to those for whom evil has become an integral part of their being. Jeremiah's close relationship with God made him

567   curse his life. Children, being with God does not make one happy. We learn this from Jeremiah.

[12.] Bethel, near Bielefeld, is a well-known Protestant institution for epileptics and chronically mentally handicapped persons.[HP]

[1.] *NL* A 15/10; handwritten; children's meditation thought to be from the beginning of 1927.
[2.] Amos 3:8; cf. Jer. 25:3.
[3.] Jer. 13:23.
[4.] Jer. 20:14.

War came to Jerusalem. The king had died in battle.[5] In Jerusalem there was dismay. Yet after a short time everyone was once again on their high horse. They believed this defeat was punishment for their past sins. Those who saw more clearly made fun of this proud excuse, "The parents have eaten sour grapes, and the children's teeth are set on edge!"[6] Oh! if only these people, who at any other time were so self-absorbed, had thought more about themselves this once! Jeremiah was not susceptible to such talk. Once again his time had come. He appeared in the marketplace amidst a large crowd and predicted the complete destruction of the temple if the people did not repent. God did not live in a temple built by human hands.[7] God lived with those who listened to him. Their hearts were God's temple. Because he knew this, Jeremiah could boldly speak of God personally destroying the temple. The priests take him prisoner, accuse him of blasphemy against the temple and God. They want to execute him; but his time has not yet arrived. He is allowed to go free in response to the ominous voices of the people.[8] No one wants to take responsibility for innocent blood. The words of Jeremiah were too clear and plain, and resembled too closely the words that they felt in their innermost hearts for them to consider him crazy or a dreamer. So they freed him with feelings of dread.[9]

Years pass. Jeremiah doesn't change, but neither does Jerusalem. The harvest, which Amos had already seen as a basket of summer fruits,[10] this harvest descends upon Jerusalem. Jerusalem revolts against its ruler, Nebuchadnezzar of Babylon, and is conquered after a short siege. The temple and the king's palace are plundered. The king and his court are taken to Babylon as prisoners. Nebuchadnezzar places on the throne a new vassal king named Zedekiah.[11] Jeremiah is proved correct. Yet no person who has ever lived would rather have his prophecy proved wrong than Jeremiah. Jerusalem was deeply shocked. But it was still standing, and it didn't take long to regain its arrogance. Priests and soldiers made plans for war and liberation. With few exceptions the people cheered them on. The king wavered between his oath of allegiance to Babylon and the advice of his general. [He] is too afraid of Jeremiah to ask his advice. One day envoys from Jerusalem's neighboring counties arrive at the king's palace. At first secretly, Zedekiah receives them. They propose a unified defection from Babylon and suggest the formation of an alliance. Zedekiah asks them to wait, and summons his

568

[5.] It is possible that Bonhoeffer is thinking of 2 Chron. 25:22-27.

[6.] Jer. 31:29.

[7.] Acts 7:48.

[8.] Cf. Jer. 26:1ff.

[9.] No new paragraph in the manuscript.

[10.] Amos 8:1f.

[11.] Cf. 2 Kings 24:10-12.

advisers.[12] With one voice they advise revolution, war. The news is spread among the people by the servants of the palace, and everyone runs to the king's palace. Here and there the shouts are heard, "Rise up and free Jerusalem," "War against Babylon," "God is with us," "It is a holy war." The tumult before the palace and the temple grows louder and louder. Zedekiah deliberates in his chamber and can't decide. The high priest and Hananiah, the prophet of the city, are summoned. Once in a great while a voice is heard shouting, "Where is Jeremiah? He should speak!" Then it fades away amidst the uproar.

At the same hour Jeremiah sat alone in his room and brooded. He did not hear the uproar. But he did hear something completely different. He conversed with God and heard how he was given a peculiar mission: "Make a yoke for yourself and hang it on your neck. Go to the king Zedekiah and to the messengers, and tell them what I will say to you." It didn't take long for Jeremiah to understand what this action symbolized, and he went out and began to make for himself a yoke. Do you know that a yoke is something placed on the necks of strong oxen so that they can be led and controlled? Perhaps you also know the story about the yoke[13] that the entire Roman army once had to bear when they had been conquered. Walking in a yoke was the greatest humiliation one could heap on a people or a person. And now this is the commission that Jeremiah gets from God. In a short time he made the wooden yoke, immediately threw it upon his shoulders, and went to the city.[14]

From afar he hears the noise of the people and guides his heavy footsteps toward the king's palace. He thinks of nothing other than his mission. Behind him women berate him and children throw stones at him. Vulgar curses ring out of the mouths of the men. As he abruptly turns a street corner, the people standing around see him so near that they flee with a cry of fear. Skittishly they press themselves against the walls. When he has barely passed, stones fly at him. He doesn't feel anything. Now he is very near the square. [He] hears the people becoming louder and more frenzied. He barely rounds the corner of a street and walks into the square when he sees the high priest[15] Hananiah standing above him in the king's palace. The people are cheering him. They call for war, for freedom from the yoke of Babylon. Without many people noticing him, Jeremiah makes his way through the crowd. With heavy strides under his burden, he climbs the broad palace steps. A deadly quiet falls upon the crowd. Full of horror they look at this ter-

569

[12.] Cf. Jer. 27:3.

[13.] Replaces "the Caudine." This refers to the defeat of Rome at the Caudine Forks in 321 B.C.E. by the Samnites in what is known as the Second Samnitic War.

[14.] Jer. 27:1-22. No new paragraph in the manuscript.

[15.] According to Jeremiah 28, Hananiah was a prophet, a contemporary of Jeremiah.[MJ]

rifying person, who never joins in when the people cheer, who proclaims judgment when Jerusalem celebrates, who laments when Jerusalem laughs, who now carries a yoke when Jerusalem breathes freedom. There he, the terrible torturer of the people, stands next to the high priest, the one who blesses. Vulgar words are hurled at him. Fists are raised and stones fly.[16]

Then he raises his voice. All about are silent as he calls out, 'The Lord of hosts, who made everything that is made, people and cities, kings and servants, countries and kingdoms, who has power over everything that was made, speaks through me. God will subject all of God's kingdoms to the power of the king of Babylon. He should be our king and we should be his people, until it pleases the Lord of hosts[17] to take away his kingdom from him and to make him a servant of another. Therefore it is God's will that Jerusalem bend its neck under the yoke of the king, just as God commanded me to appear before you bearing a yoke. Become humble, bow down, because not only the king of Babylon is your lord but rather God who elected him to be king over us. Woe to the people that does not bow its neck when Yahweh commands it! It will not be an enemy of Babylon but of Yahweh. By war, famine, and pestilence this people will be wiped from the face of the earth, which belongs to God.'[18]

He spoke loudly to the crowd. It answered him in a wild confusion of opinions for and against him. "Away with the coward, he has been bribed by the king of Babylon." And others again, "No, listen to him, God's word speaks through him." Then Hananiah respectfully strides over to Jeremiah, and the people wait to see what will happen. Jeremiah stretches himself to his full height. Powerfully he stands there under his yoke, raises his right hand, and calls out, "Don't be led into temptation by your prophets, who vie for your approval, by your priests, your teachers of wisdom, like this Hananiah who flatters you with predictions of good days and victory and freedom from Babylon, and lies. Only the people who obey God's call and bow before Babylon will stay on their land to plant and build."[19] At this point his speech is interrupted. Zedekiah has walked out of the palace gates, accompanied by his whole court and the envoys. He is astounded, and shudders when he sees the man under the yoke, whom he fears more than the enemy. On the steps of his palace he speaks to the people and the high priest. When Jeremiah sees the king he slowly and powerfully strides over to him. With a trembling voice he cries out, half pleading, half furious with a holy fury, for the third time, Bow your necks under the yoke of the king of Babylon, serve him and his people. In this way you will live. Don't believe the liars and flatterers,

570

[16.] No new paragraph in the manuscript.
[17.] Difficult to decipher; perhaps "lords."
[18.] Jer. 27:4ff; paraphrase by Bonhoeffer.
[19.] Jer. 27:9-11. [NRSV differs significantly.] [WF]

571   because Yahweh declares, 'I have not sent them. You will die together with your prophets.' You will have God as an enemy if you do not bow down to Babylon.

Fully shocked, the king withdraws and looks away from Jeremiah to the people, and then again to the high priest Hananiah, as if he were looking for help. Then Hananiah steps up next to the king and the envoys and declares, "Thus says Yahweh, 'I have broken the yoke of Babylon. Before two years have past, I will bring all of the prisoners and the king home from Babylon, because I will soon break the yoke of Babylon!'" He shouted this loudly, and the people responded to him and to the king with a resounding cry of rejoicing. "Freedom from Babylon." "Off to holy war." Jeremiah stretched his arms up to the sky and said, "Amen; thus may the Lord do. May the Lord validate your words, Hananiah." And from the people the call cried out, "Amen, may the Lord do this." Jeremiah spoke again, "But hear this message, 'Throughout the ages prophets have predicted disaster, war, and pestilence. God always sent them to warn that hard times were coming. Remember Isaiah and Amos. A prophet who predicts peace and good times can be proved true only after his words have been fulfilled.'" Full of fury, Hananiah strode over to Jeremiah, ripped the yoke from his neck, shattered it to pieces on the stone steps and cried out, "Yahweh will break the yoke Babylon holds over Jerusalem in the same way as I have broken this yoke. May the freedom of redemption be Jerusalem's."[20] And again the echo of the people rang out.[21]

Jeremiah remained silent while this happened to him; then he slowly walked down the steps, across the marketplace, and through the crowd. Everyone retreated from him, fearing his silence almost more than his words. They anticipated something terrible. Jeremiah passed through the empty streets of Jerusalem. No one could have wished more than he that Hananiah would be proved correct! But he knew that it was not Hananiah but he himself who spoke God's word. When home, he spoke to God in prayer, and he received a new task. Again he went out. It was evening. This

572   time he bought a yoke made of iron and with this much heavier burden went to the marketplace. The crowd was still in a frenzy. They celebrated the establishment of an alliance[22] with the neighboring states. Terror strikes the crowd when they see Jeremiah approaching. They run to Hananiah. It is directly to him that Jeremiah guides his steps. They meet again, the proud victor and the one who can never be vanquished. Jeremiah speaks, "Thus says God, 'I have hung an iron yoke on the necks of the people so that they will serve the king of Babylon. God is with Babylon and punishes you. Do not

----

[20.] Jer. 28:1-17; Bonhoeffer's paraphrase.
[21.] No new paragraph in the manuscript.
[22.] Difficult to decipher.

oppose what can and will destroy you.' Hananiah, God has not sent you. You have led the people astray so that they have revolted against God's will. Therefore thus says God, 'I will uproot you from the earth. You will die this very year.'"[23]

After these foreboding words Jeremiah strides through the crowd. In three months Hananiah was dead. For months Jeremiah was never seen without the iron yoke on his back. He carried the yoke that God had placed upon him, and although it was truly an iron yoke, it never weighed him down to the ground. If the people had helped him carry it, it would have been lighter. He carried the heaviest burden that any person has ever carried. There was only one other time that a person carried a wooden burden a thousand times heavier than Jeremiah's iron yoke. He carried his burden not just for his people but for the whole world. His burden was a wooden cross. It's true, isn't it children; we all know who he was!

12. Address on John 19[1]

573

Good Friday: John 19 and Parallels

When God's Son said to God the Father, "I am drawn to the people," God-Father said to the Son, "It will have to be a path of degradation and humiliation that God's Son will walk among the people." And the Son answered, "I want to travel along that path." Then God-Father speaks, "My wrath is great because of the evil of humanity. I have to deliver a severe punishment." And the Son speaks, "Lay all of your wrath and your punishment on me. I will stand before you in the place of the people that you created and will obediently carry the burden of your wrath for the sin of the world." The Father speaks, "Son, my wrath is great." And the Son answers, "Father, your love is greater. I want to be the herald of your love while carrying the burden of your wrath and all humiliation. I myself want to be your love, which also goes where sin and malice and misery are, the love that will love the criminal, that tastes what it is to be abandoned by God, and proclaims that your love is brought even to those who lost faith in it. Wherever I will be on the earth, there will your love be." Then God-Father kisses the Son with a holy kiss. In a narrow stall in Bethlehem a boy was born to poor, pious parents.

Three things marked the way of Jesus Christ among us. His boundless love, the humiliation he experienced day after day, and the wrath of God that

---

[23.] Jer. 28:12-17. [14–16] No new paragraph in the manuscript.

[1.] *NL* A 15/8; handwritten children's meditation delivered on April 15, 1927.

brought his work to ruin in the eyes of the world. We have often spoken about these things. Today we remember them as we talk about that hour of Jesus' life when all three, united together, found their highest purpose.

Jesus was taken from Caiaphas and brought to Pilate, the Roman governor. When he is interrogated by Pilate, he states that he is a king whose kingdom is not of this world. He is a king of truth.[2] How could this dreamer, standing so quietly and meekly before the court, harm him, Pilate, or even the Roman emperor? Pilate somehow feels touched by the clarity and confidence with which this king of truth looks him in the eye. A word is spoken to the effect that it is not Pilate but God alone who has power over the life and death of Jesus. This pierces Pilate's heart, and he wants to free him. But the people, who have been stirred up by the high priest, rebel: "If you free that one, then you are not Caesar's friend." "We only have one emperor, the emperor of Rome."[3] Pilate could not stand his ground against this. Asserting his own innocence, he hands the accused over to the enraged masses and frees the political criminal Barabbas. While shouting, "Crucify him. Let his blood be on us and our children,"[4] the crowd takes pleasure in Jesus' scourging. Ill-mannered soldiers grab Jesus, and with an echo of laughter they bring adornments of kingship to the failed king of the Jews. The crown, a wreath of sharp thorns, is pressed upon his forehead. The first drops of blood fall on the earth, upon which he, the love of God, walked. The earth drinks the blood of its creator's beloved Son, who loved it as no one had loved it before. Then the king's cloak, a purple mantle as red as blood, is thrown over him. The only thing missing is a mighty king's scepter. They press a fragile cane into his right hand and bend their knees before the likeness of their own madness. Finally they grab the cane, hit his head with it, and spit in his face.[5] Ecce homo, a picture of gruesome reverence, a picture of infinite loving mercy.

We now see in the distance a troop of people coming. Above them tower three crosses. The time has come to get ready. They strip Jesus of the purple mantle and silently await those who approach. We can clearly recognize two criminals carrying two huge crosses on their shoulders. Behind them a third cross is carried by a soldier. They descend the stairs of the judgment hall into the square where the arrivals wait. Silence reigns. Then a convulsion ripples through the crowd. The soldier has placed the cross on Jesus' neck. The procession sets itself in motion. At this moment, the screaming, hooting, and ridicule begins anew. They pass through the gates of Jerusalem. Children play on the path. When they see the procession, they run away

---

[2.] John 18:33-37.
[3.] John 19:12, 15.
[4.] Matt. 27:25.
[5.] John 19:2, 5.

frightened. Soon they recognize the person under the cross as the one who had spoken to them so often and so kindly, and their hearts skip a beat. Sobbing and frightened, they want to run to the Lord Jesus. A cruel fist yanks them out of the way. They catch only the quick glance that the Lord Jesus offers them, full of love. Their game is over. Deep sadness fills their hearts. As they return they hear only the noise in the distance. The sun flees. People want to get to work even more quickly. Without a sound, Jesus crumbles to the ground beneath his burden. A commotion arises among the masses. Loud crying is heard in the procession. It is Mary, the mother of the Lord, who leans on a young man, John, the beloved disciple of the Lord. She stumbles slowly in the procession. Her heart has been torn in two. Women and mothers who know her cannot stand the sight. Crying with an inner, regretful sorrow, they abandon the procession and turn away. The head of the procession arrives at the summit. From there they can see out over the endless crowd that seems to reach to the gates of Jerusalem. Soon Jesus has also reached his destination. An old man passes by on his way to the city. Recognizing Jesus, he trembles and calls out, "God is with you." Softly he whispers the words of the prophet, "He was wounded for our transgressions, crushed for our iniquities; upon him was the punishment that made us whole."[6] Jesus' eyes light up. The man was one of those whom Jesus had healed and who had followed Jesus devotedly from that time. A blow from the soldier threw him aside.[7]

They arrive, and the cross lies on the ground. Jesus is stripped and is laid on the cross. Nail after nail fixes his body to the wood. The soldiers grab the cross and raise it up. The body of Jesus is now suspended high above everyone. A shudder runs through the crowd. "He was numbered with the transgressors," one hears a voice saying.[8] "The deed has been done." The crowd stands staring at the 3 crosses. The ridicule begins again, "If you are God's Son, come down from the cross."[9] Then, clearly audible, these words come from Jesus' mouth, "Father forgive them. . . ."[10] They pierce the hearts of the crowd. Now they watch his mother, Mary, walking slowly with John beneath the cross. With composed eyes, with indescribable pain and love, she looks up at Jesus. Then Jesus' voice is heard, and it becomes quiet all around him. "Woman, here is your son." And to his disciple, "Here is your mother."[11] In the meantime the guards gamble beneath the cross for the Lord's clothing. Then one hears both of the criminals speak. The one, who

576

[6.] Isa. 53:5.
[7.] No new paragraph in the manuscript.
[8.] Isa. 53:12.
[9.] Cf. Matt. 27:43.
[10.] Luke 23:34.
[11.] John 19:25-30.

dared to ridicule the Lord, is being admonished by the other. "Do you not fear God, since you are under the same sentence of condemnation? And we indeed have been condemned justly, for we are getting what we deserve for our deeds, but this man has done nothing wrong." And to Jesus he calls out, "Jesus, remember me when you come into your kingdom!" And Jesus says, "Truly I tell you, today you will be with me in paradise."[12] Minutes pass like hours. The crowd slowly disperses. Some go on ridiculing, some meditating, others bickering. Could someone who could speak such words while on the cross be a blasphemer against God? The sun bakes his naked body. Then Jesus says, "I am thirsty," and someone offers him vinegar.[13] Now the end is at hand. His blood rages in his fevered body.[14]

Death has already touched his heart. Then a cry of fear forces its way through the air, "My God. . . . ?"[15] Some look with pity upon the miserable one. Finally he also knows what others have known for a long time; his life was a pleasant dream. Yes, truly terrible was the wrath of God upon Jesus for the sins of the world. Jesus not only was to experience death but also the horror of having been abandoned by God. Yet at that exact moment he remained the obedient Son of God. He was to feel the fear of those who are far from God so that they may realize that God's love itself[16] is more powerful and real. This didn't last long, and the final hour had come. Jesus and all near him became silent. "Father, into your hands I commend my spirit," he prays loudly.[17] "It is finished," and with that he bows his head and dies.[18] When, around evening, servants came to break the legs of the crucified ones in order to hasten their death, they see with astonishment that Jesus is already dead. They don't break his legs, but by thrusting a lance into his side they convince themselves that he is really dead. More terribly than ever, darkness descends upon Jerusalem. The workers in the vineyard have killed the Son. What should the owner of the vineyard do?[19] Jesus had prayed, "Father forgive them."[20] Jesus, the Lord, not only died for his friends but for his enemies as well. Everything had happened as it had to happen. In humiliation, disgrace, and shame the love of God appeared on the earth. On the cross God's wrath lashed out at God's own Son for the evil of the world—or the evil of the world lashed the Son to the cross. Today, on Good Friday, we should not too soon recall how these events took on new

577

[12.] Luke 23:39-43.
[13.] John 19:28-9.
[14.] No new paragraph in the manuscript.
[15.] "My God, my God why have you forsaken me?" (Matt. 27:46).
[16.] "God's love itself" replaces "God personally."
[17.] Luke 23:46.
[18.] John 19:30.
[19.] Matt. 21:39-40.
[20.] Luke 23:34.

meaning on Easter Sunday. We should recall that with the death of Jesus the disciples saw all their hopes dashed. Separated from each other, in hopeless sorrow, they dwelt upon what had happened. Only when we take the death of Jesus as seriously as they did can we correctly understand what the proclamation of the resurrection might bring with it.

D. Paper for a Youth Group, Catechetical Lessons for Youth, and an Examination Sermon. April–October 1927

13. Invitation to the "Thursday Circle"[1]

Invitation to an evening of reading and talks
Every Thursday 5:25–7:00 p.m.
Beginning on 4/29/27

Program:
1. The Christians and their God
   a. What Christians think about God and what they want from God
      α. Did God create the world? Does Providence exist?
      β. What is the purpose of prayer?
      γ. Who is Jesus Christ?
      δ. What is the purpose of a church (confirmation)?
      ε. What is the soul, and is there life after death?
   b. What God wants from Christians
      α. Beatitudes[2] Matt. 5:1ff. Are we able to love our enemies?[3] Matt. 5:38ff. Are we then allowed to engage in war?[4]

[1.] *NL* A 15/11 (1); handwritten.
[2.] Cf. *D* (*DBWE* 4):100–10.
[3.] Cf. *D* (*DBWE* 4):137–45.
[4.] Cf. the lecture in the Ciernohorské Kúpele in *NRS*, 163.

β. Is there such a thing as a necessary lie?[5]

γ. What is Christianity's stand on
   (1) Political parties?
   (2) The poor and the rich?
   (3) The Jews?
   (4) Sports and hiking?

2. The gods of the ancient Germans
3. The gods of Negro tribes
4. The gods of the classical world[6]   579
5. The mystery cults
6. The Muslims and their God[7]
7. The Indians[8]
8. Famous poets and their God (Goethe, Schiller)
9. Famous painters and their God (Grünewald, Dürer, Rembrandt)
10. Religious songs of 1000 years (folk songs and hymns)
11. The Catholic church
12. Luther

Every evening begins with a report by a participant followed by discussion and a summary. Please bring the New Testament with you! We will also read excerpts from various authors.

14. Paper on "The Catholic Church" for the Thursday Circle[1]

Like the holy Church itself, the *sacraments* dispensed by her priests carry with them an objective, sacred character. They are divine gifts of grace, completely separate from anything humanity may add to them, and are beneficial to humanity *regardless of the frame of mind in which they are received* (ex opere operato).[2] Baptism, penance, and Holy Communion stand at the center. Confirmation, marriage, ordination of priests, and the last rights ensure that a Catholic's whole life is sacramentally accompanied. In all of this, God is   580

[5.] Cf. Bonhoeffer's essay "What Is Meant by 'Telling the Truth'?" in *Ethics*, 363–72.

[6.] Cf. Bonhoeffer's work on the philosophy of Euripides, *NL* A 5/2, and his study of Walter F. Otto's *Die Götter Griechenlands*, in *LPP*, 331–33.

[7.] Cf. above, the letter from Tripoli on April 9, 1924 (1/66:118).

[8.] Cf. the letter to Helmuth Rößler of October 18, 1931, in *DB-ER*, 166.

[1.] *NL* A 15/11 (2); handwritten; written somewhere between the beginning and middle of July 1927. The first page is no longer extant. Prior to our text, the following sentence has been crossed out: "The priests and faithful are not only to bring about a mystical effect with the sacraments [illegible]. . . ."

[2.] "It works out of the work done" [the idea that the sacrament is objectively effective in itself as an instrument of God when the conditions of its institution are validly fulfilled].

thought of as the one who reveals before all eyes God's power in this world. God is the one who becomes flesh every day in the visible church.

How does the *individual* in this church gain salvation, and how can the individual be certain of salvation? Human salvation is an act of God performed out of sheer compassion. It is through grace that God creates a supernatural person out of a natural person. For this to occur, however, the persons must have prepared themselves beforehand. If they have obtained grace, then by their *good works*, i.e., by following the commandments of the church, they *earn* the increase of grace, eternal life, and the increase of glory. Of course, all this can only occur through the assistance of grace. The individual can also do more than God actually requires by following the so-called evangelical counsels: poverty, chastity, and obedience (the monastic vows). By following these, a monk becomes the perfect Christian. And so a higher and a lower morality are taught. This parallels the distinction between venial and mortal sins. If Christians fall into sin only the priest can restore them. This is accomplished through the sacrament of penance, which is composed of these parts: (1) contrition (which is sufficient even if it is imperfect and consists only of fear of punishment), (2) confession of mortal sins (auricular confession; venial sins are to be confessed only[3] upon advice), and (3) the performance[4] of the required penance. Through receiving the sacrament, the merit that would have become totally invalid[5] through sin, is restored. However, because Christians always sin repeatedly, they can never be sure of their salvation or the state of grace in which they find themselves. They can never be sure of their standing with God and how their sins balance their merits. The only thing that could give them assurance is special revelation.[6]

With this we arrive at their most seminal notion: God's relationship with humanity is thought of in legal terms. Individuals have certain justifiable claims on God, and God must answer these claims on the basis of the individual's merits. One can easily satisfy God with little, but the reward grows with the size of the accomplishment.[7] The believer, however, can never be thought of in isolation. The believer exists at the center of the community of saints, which lives in faith, love, and intercession for one another. The believer receives from its perfected members the help and the gift of their merits.[8] From this perspective, formed by worshipping the saints, the notion of

581

[3.] Difficult to decipher.

[4.] Difficult to decipher.

[5.] Difficult to decipher; perhaps "would have become."

[6.] Cf. above, 2/17:441–44.

[7.] Deleted: "It no longer helps us to speak of God's grace [. . . illegible] would that God's grace be so great."

[8.] Deleted: "The doctrine of the communion of saints as the nature of the church is the polar opposite to the doctrine of the church as heavenly institution."

an overflowing treasury of merit becomes understandable. This teaching inherently has an extraordinarily great power to build community.

Our main objection is aimed at the Catholic view of God:[9]

1. God is revealed as redeemer *once and for all* in Christ. For us, that means in scripture, not in visible glory, but in the form of a servant, in poverty and humility.

2. In this way God alone is the Lord, so that the individual cannot demand anything of God. God always places the highest demand on individuals, that of constant love of God and love of neighbor. *Every* person is broken by this divine will. No one can flee from God to a lower but adequate morality. Everything that does not arise from faith is sin (Rom. 14:23), and no one can have faith without God's help. Everyone stands alone before God; no church and no saint can remove any of the burden. God comes to an individual's aid through the realization of his or her complete helplessness. God sends individuals a healing, *perfect*, honest penance, forgives them their sins, and in their hearts gives them *infinite trust*, i.e., Christian *faith* in the grace of God. Because God *justifies* humanity in this way, God also wishes to sanctify it. Throughout the ages,[10] God views people from the perspective of eternity, perfected as saints. In this way the sinful are holy in God's eyes. But humanity never has a right to demand anything from God, because we remain sinners as long as we live. With *every* sin we cut the cord that connected us to God. It is precisely such sinners as these that God seeks.[11]   582

But we have God in us, because God has placed faith in our hearts. Luther says, "However much you believe, that is how much you have."[12] Thus all are fully assured of their state of grace. Any doubt is a mistrust of God's grace, and therefore the severest sin.[13] The word of God stands at the center of the Protestant life of faith. There is no authority on earth other than the word of Christ[14] that we read or hear. And it stands without mediation as its own witness.[15] Our church is a church of the *word*. It rests alone on the authority of the word. All who believe and are obedient, who congregate around the word, are true priests and are the true church, regardless of which visible church they belong to. Sacraments are the visible signs through

---

[9.] The sentence "Our main objection . . . view of God" replaces "Compare placing at the center: the Protestant church has an image of God different from that of the Catholic, and from this stems all the differences." Compare this with Bonhoeffer's sermon on the church in Bonhoeffer, *Predigten, Auslegungen, Meditationen*, 1:165–73.

[10.] Difficult to decipher; perhaps, "during all time."

[11.] The sentence "Again and again God must come to humankind in order to forgive" is deleted.

[12.] Martin Luther, "Sermon on the Sacrament of Penance, 1519," *LW* 35:12.

[13.] Cf. above, 2/10, 325.

[14.] The phrase "There is . . . other than" replaces "God comes to humankind not directly, rather through."

[15.] This sentence replaces "this does not need any human witnesses."

which divine grace is distributed. Like the word, however, they only work toward salvation in faith. Only two sacraments have their origins in Christ: baptism and the Lord's Supper.[16] Every external action of the church is the work of humanity. God is not revealed in external institutions, as the Catholic church supposes, but solely in Spirit, in an unpretentious form. The Protestant pastor is a member of the congregation. The pastor serves as preacher and distributor of sacraments, and nothing more. Like everyone else the pastor is allowed to marry. Being unmarried is not a merit. There is absolutely no Christian occupation that is better than any other. One can serve God everywhere. For this reason, one should not flee from the world and its troubles, as do the monks. No one can do more than is required. Luke 17:10.[17] With this we come to our point number 2.

583   Our position

It is hard to overestimate the importance of the Catholic church's value for European culture and for the whole world. It Christianized and civilized barbaric peoples and for a long time was the only guardian of science and art. Here the church's cloisters were preeminent. The Catholic church developed a spiritual power unequaled anywhere, and today we still admire the way it combined the principle of catholicism with the principle of one sanctifying church, as well as tolerance with intolerance. It is a world in itself. Infinite diversity flows together, and this colorful picture gives it its irresistible charm (Complexio oppositorum).[18] A country has seldom produced so many different kinds of people as has the Catholic church. With admirable power, it has understood how to maintain unity in diversity, to gain the love and respect of the masses, and to foster a strong sense of community (see above). But it is exactly because of this greatness that we have serious reservations. Has this world really remained the church of Christ? Has it not perhaps become an obstruction blocking the path to God instead of a road sign[19] on the path to God? Has it not blocked the only path to salvation? Yet no one can ever obstruct the way to God. The church still has the Bible, and as long as she has it we can still believe in the holy Christian church. *God's* word will never be denied (Isa. 55:11), whether it be preached by us or by our sister church. We adhere to the same confession of faith, we pray the same Lord's Prayer, and we share some of the same ancient rites. This binds us together, and as far as we are concerned we would like to live in peace with

[16.] Deleted: "Only the otherworldly is holy [difficult to decipher] but is invisible."
[17.] See above, 3/1, 453. In addition cf. Harnack's "Was wir von der römischen Kirche lernen," in *Reden*, 247–64.
[18.] "That which embraces the opposite."
[19.] On the church as a road sign, see above, page 2/9:315.

our disparate sister. We do not, however, want to deny anything that we have recognized as God's word. The designation Catholic or Protestant is unimportant. The important thing is God's word. Conversely, we will never violate anyone else's faith. God does not desire reluctant service, and God has given   584 everyone a conscience. We can and should desire that our sister church search its soul and concentrate on nothing but the word (1 Cor. 2:2).[20] Until that time, we must have patience. We will have to endure it when, in false darkness, the "only holy church" pronounces upon our church the "anathema" (condemnation). She doesn't know any better, and she doesn't hate the heretic, only the heresy.[21] As long as we let the word be our only armor we can look confidently into the future.

[Literature]

Heim, *The Nature of Protestantism*
Heiler, "Das Wesen des Katholizismus"[22]
Holl, *Luther*
Fendt, "Warum evangelisch?"[23]
Adam, *The Spirit of Catholicism*
Fendt, "Die religiösen Kräfte des katholischen Dogmas"[24]
von Zezschwitz, "Warum katholisch?"[25]

15. Meditation and Catechetical Lesson on "Honor"[1]   585

Meditation

Honor, Christianity, young people who are 16 or 17 years old—how can these be brought together? The Nietzsche complex about the slave morality of Christianity[2] comes into play here as also the other side, the tired wisdom of philosophical rationalism that asks, "What is honor? What is insult? No one can insult me. I bear my honor in me. Any insult is a reflection of the

---

[20.] The correct reference is 1 Cor. 2:12-13. Deleted: "In the Third Article we confess our faith in the holy Christian church. We can only pray that she develop and grow."
[21.] Deleted: "But neither can we become proud; if God does not say yes to it, all our action remains human work. Nor should we forget that whoever praises, praises the Lord." 1 Cor. 1:31.
[22.] Heiler, The nature of catholicism.
[23.] "Why protestant?" refers to Fendt, *Erfahrung: Ein Büchlein vom wohlgemuten Luthertum.*
[24.] Fendt, The religious power of catholic dogma.
[25.] "Why catholic?"

[1.] *NL* A 14/4; untitled handwritten catechetical lesson presented to Prof. Mahling's seminar in the summer semester of 1927; comments by Mahling. The answers expected from the youth are set in italics.
[2.] Cf. above, 3/2:456, editorial note 2.

person who insulted me."[3] Both groups of ideas must be analyzed here as we approach the New Testament. The Bible speaks of God's honor and humanity's dishonor.[4] Humanity in itself has no honor but only when God grants it, i.e., it has honor as the creation of God. But, as God's creation, the individual human exists in the context of social life. From this observation follows first the honor of the social community[5] and second the will of God that humans live in community, i.e., that God intended the human being to have outward honor. Outward honor, however, relies[6] on inner honorableness.[7] Christians' inner honor rests on their relationship with God, God's grace and justification.[8] Thus we arrive at the central problem of the Christian life of faith. No external assault can destroy this relationship with God.

586   But it should not be treated with indifference or ignored. Much rather, every malicious assault is an injury not only to our honor but also to God's honor, from which we receive "our" honor. It is therefore the duty of Christians to repulse any malicious assault. It might seem that Matt. 5:39 contradicts this statement. The meaning of the Christian love commandment, however, is to overcome evil, and boundless outward patience is only one—and not the only—means to the goal. We are therefore obliged to defend our honor whenever it is threatened by malicious intention, just as we are obliged to defend the honor of our neighbor, our communities, and our position. Only when personal reconciliation has failed will we go public. We reject duels as a means of restoring wounded honor as we do war insofar as it serves only this purpose. Courts of honor in school and the workplace are indispensable. Whatever means we choose to overcome evil and defend God's will, the first and the last means within the Christian community must be prayer for the offender (Matt. 5:44). Only the person who has inwardly forgiven may punish and prosecute. Only then can it be recognized that all our deeds are done to the glory of God (1 Cor. 10:31).

I believe that it is more important to introduce young people to a full understanding of Christian honor than to proceed casuistically.[9]

[3.] On Thales see below, editorial notes 10 and 11.

[4.] Mahling: "But certainly only concerning God. Are not honor and dishonor here juxtaposed equally? Jesus says also, 'You dishonor me' (John 8:49). Does he not expect that the Son be honored as you honor the Father (5:23)? So the Bible also acknowledges human honor. Cf. especially John, chapters 5 and 8. Does not the fourth Commandment say: 'Honor your father and your mother'?"

[5.] Mahling: "Does this statement really follow from the previous sentence?"

[6.] Mahling changes this to "should rely."

[7.] On the distinction between inner and outer honor, see Wundt, "Die Ehre als Quelle des sittlichen Lebens," 34.

[8.] Mahling: "I.e., his behavior developing from the reception of grace and justification, or the inner relationship of the justified in their conscience before God."

[9.] Mahling: "Correct."

Catechetical Lesson

In every religion class we should be able to imagine that we are standing at the brink of a wide sea where we hear the waves of eternity roar against the shores of our time. Often it happens that our ears remain deaf. We know that the sea is before us and that we are standing at the shore, but we don't hear it. How often does it happen that we talk about God and Christ in religion class, but when it is over we may as well have talked about history and natural science!

We don't even notice that we should be able to see eternity from the shores of our time, that God was speaking and we only heard human voices. 587 May God grant that during this hour our hearts are able to understand this lesson about God's honor and humanity's dishonor, about God's honor and the honor that is God's gift to humanity. May God grant that the cup of eternity quench our thirst!

When I was your age, our first-year class [Prima] was badly insulted by a teacher. At that time we asked ourselves the same question that I am asking you to consider today: the perplexing and weighty question of the nature of human honor, its preservation and its violation. I remember a class session in which we were divided into two camps. I'm telling you this only because I believe that the discord we experienced then is significant for the positions we take today in response to this problem. Our differing opinions were based on what we understood by violation of someone's honor.

What would one group have said? *Violation of our honor is any deliberate insult.*

What would the others have said? *No one can violate our honor.*

What did the first group understand by honor? *Something outward.*

What did the others understand by honor? *Something internal.*

What might be another name for the "internal" honor? *Inner integrity.*

What would it mean for it to be lost? *Dishonor.*

How could the second group be justified in saying that no one could injure their honor? *Their inner integrity cannot be taken away by outward violation.*

How do such people react to outward insults? *They are indifferent.*

This attitude is as old as Greek philosophy. Thales[10] was walking with a student on the street. Another student met them and proudly walked by without greeting the master. In answer to the question his student posed as 588 to what he intended to do now to rectify this insult, Thales answered that he wasn't in the habit of hitting a donkey in retaliation if it happened to bump

---

[10.] Thales of Miletus (ca. 624–546 B.C.E.)was a Greek philosopher, mathematician, astronomer, and politician.

into him.[11] You understand the analogy. How would we describe Thales' behavior? *Reasonable.*

Certainly. But what foreign word [could] we use to make of Thales' attitude a fundamental principle? *Rationalistic.*

What sort of position does the offended individual take over against the person who insulted him? *A position that is indifferent, superior, disdainful, and removed.*[12]

What kind of societal relationship between people is made impossible by this type of attitude?[13] *A relationship in community.*

How is such a relationship made impossible? *Through the fact that one person sets himself or herself above all the rest so that communication is made impossible from the outset.*[14]

How do individuals who think like Thales see their position in the world? *They look upon it with complete indifference.*[15]

What term do we use for people for whom the only important thing is their own honor, who don't want to communicate with other people, who are content to be by themselves, and who are indifferent or annoyed by the social environment in which they live? *We call them individualists.*

We have now learned about the rationalistic, individualistic concept of honor, which is present in many levels of society today. It is at this point that difficult problems arise for the Christian view of honor. But first we would like to discuss the limits of the concept of inner honor. A brief example will help us do this. In class a boy slanders one of his classmates. He knows that the classmate tries to ingratiate himself with the teacher for selfish reasons but that behind the teacher's back this classmate says lots of horrible things about the teacher. In addition, the boy supposedly claims to know that the teacher does not earn his money by tutoring but gets it by illicit means. The question now is, what is actually involved in this type of slander? What does the slanderer hope to achieve? *He wants his classmate to be seen as a bad person by his other classmates. He wants his classmate to lose the respect of his other classmates and to lose his honor.*

How does the slanderer achieve his goal of having his classmate lose his honor? *He does it by stripping his classmate of his honorableness.*

589

[11.] Mahling: "Cf. the other story of Thales."

[12.] Mahling: "Couldn't it also be imagined that he doesn't consider the matter worth the trouble; yes, even that he is free from the thought of revenge!" Cf. below, editorial note 40.

[13.] Mahling: "And if Thales had returned like for like, would a community have been made possible through this?"

[14.] Mahling: "This result does not follow from the example of Thales."

[15.] Mahling: "Must not this mean: as fully secure in themselves, and therefore not to be unnerved by failing to be greeted properly or by an insult."

What is understood by honor in this context? *Outer, civic honor. The respect that one person enjoys from other people.*

What are the consequences of losing this civic honor? *The consequences are social disgrace.*

Who are the recipients of this civic honor? *Everyone who has a sense of personal honorableness.*

What term should we therefore use to describe an insult to someone's honor? *An intentional denial of someone's civic honor, i.e., maliciously, consciously contesting someone's personal honorableness is injuring someone's honor.*

It is still conceivable that we could ignore everything in our environment so that we could accept this civic disgrace, this doubting of our personal honorableness. But the possibility exists that an offense is not directed at my personal honor. Against what could this offense be directed for me to feel personally wounded? *Against a community of which I am a part or against a member of it.*

Which social group would come into question in this case? *Family, friends, nation, schoolmates, workplace colleagues.*

Give me an example from your school years of such an injury to a group's honor. *One class accuses another of having played unfairly during a sports event. Or a member of another class makes serious slanderous accusations against someone in my class, etc.*

How would you judge the behavior of a class if it remained silent in the face of such accusations? *As cowardly and without honor.*   590

What does one expect a class do if it has been insulted like this? *That it publicly defend its internal and external honor, or that of one of its members.*

How would the class do this? *By declaring a class feud, by appeal to the school's court of honor.*

Which occupations especially cultivate this concept of honor? *The military, students.*

How would one here consider avenging an insult? *With a duel.*

What happens in a duel? *The insulted person challenges the person who has insulted him to back his words with his life. By dueling, honor is considered to have been restored.*

What would have happened to an officer of our former army if he didn't rise to the challenge of a duel? *He would have had to resign his commission.*

Why would he have had to resign his commission? *Because he not only lost his own public honor but also left a black mark on his whole social group.*

The individual stands for the social group in matters of honor, as does the social group for the individual. Once again the question is raised whether it matters what other people think about me and my group. The important thing is that my group is faultless. Let the others gossip all they want, whether the assaulted group be my family, friends, classmates, or nation. They all bear their value within. Should a social group that holds its honor within itself allow itself to be drawn into innumerable feuds and legal battles with people who don't deserve it? Odi profanum vulgus et arceo.[16] Once again we are confronted with ancient Thales' wisdom: "Who would shove a donkey that had bumped into him?" This view diametrically opposes the view that people are without honor, cowardly, and have a slave mentality if they do not defend themselves against any and all insults with whatever methods are available. How can we decide? Should we assume this aristocratic, noble withdrawal from the world or this pugnacious attitude that is completely caught up in the world? This was the situation in our first-year class [Prima], and most of the class would have decided for the former position.

We have now uncovered enough problems and, laden with them, knock on the door of the New Testament with the hope of being set free from them. Will we receive an answer? Will the door be opened to us?[17] These questions are not under our control. We pray to God that we will be allowed to hear God's word and that God gives us divine truth as the guide for our understanding.

Whose honor does the Bible discuss most? *God's honor.*

Whose honor does the Bible mention only rarely?[18] *A person's honor.*

Which Bible passages can you list for me that address the latter? *Ps. 8:6; Gen. 1:26; 1 Cor. 1:31, 2 Cor. 12:9.*

In which context is a person's honor the subject of the text? *In the context of the will of God.*

How then is it impossible to conceive of human honor? *As absolutely separate from God.*

From whom then does a person receive honor?[19] *A person receives it from God.*

In what relationship to God does a person possess honor? *As God's creation.*

Which people "possess" this kind of honor? *All people.*

In what type of relationship to each other has God created people? *In a relationship of community.*[20]

[16.] "I shun and keep removed the uninitiate crowd." Horace, *The Complete Odes and Epodes,* 129. Cf. above, 2/2:198–214.

[17.] Cf. Matt. 7:7.

[18.] Mahling: "Cf. above, especially the fourth commandment." See above, editorial note 4.

[19.] Mahling replaces this question with, "Through what, when, and by which manner has God given humanity honor? For which fact does humanity give thanks for the honor that God has given to them?"

[20.] Mahling replaces this question and answer with: "And in which relationship should human beings stand in relation to each other? *They should form a community.*" On this and the following questions cf. *SC* (*DBWE* 1):39–57.

And so, what has God created in addition to individuals?[21] *Human* 592
communities.[22]

Now if all individuals have honor as God's creatures, what else receives honor as a result of having been created by God? *Human communities.*[23]

If God has created people to live in communities, where does God wish their honor to be preserved? *In social life.*[24]

What did we call the honor that is associated with life in society? *Public honor.*

To whose honor does the will of God extend?[25] *To the public honor of individuals as well as of societies.*

God intended for us to live among nations, families, and friendships. This is why God also intends that communities have honor and that we have honor within these communities. God intends that our class have honor and that we have honor, because both are God's honor.[26]

What does this mean for the way we behave toward other people? *It means that we must give them the honor due to them.*

What do we call this type of behavior? *Respectful, honorable, reverential.*

What do we respect in others? *God's creative activity and God's intention that we live in communities.*

How do we express our respect for others? *In preserving the civic forms of* 593
behavior.

What type of people are to be treated with special respect? *Those who are especially active in community life, and those who have great accomplishments.*

Give me some examples. *President of Germany, national ministers, etc., scholars.*

The New Testament refers to giving respect to governmental authorities and kings (Rom. 13:1; 1 Pet. 2:17; 1 Tim. 6:1). What method does our country have for honoring particular people? *Titles, medals.*

[21.] Cf. *CF* (*DBWE* 3):91ff.

[22.] Mahling replaces the question and answer with: "To what has God called humanity? *To society.* And in what way can this society express itself? *In different ways.*" Mahling adds in explanation: "It would at best follow in the singular, but cannot be found in or result from this [uncertain reading] that God created societies." Mahling then adds the following question: "What different societies can humanity put together?"

[23.] Mahling corrects with: "human society."

[24.] Mahling corrects with: "In the life of the community. What do we call this, using a non-German word?"

[25.] Mahling: "That can here be demonstrated for the family from the fourth commandment. From there other circles of society can be drawn in."

[26.] Deleted: "What is the moral presupposition of outward honor? *The inner honorableness of honored persons.* What does it mean? *Honorableness, i.e., a certain moral value that expresses itself in truthfulness, courage of conviction, moral life.*"

We also have the possibility of treating particular people with extraordinary respect. But where are the limits that a Christian has to place on any bestowal of honor? *Wherever it might lead others to lose humility before God.*

Let us guard ourselves from making the persons we honor slaves to vanity, since we would then lose respect for them.

What is the requirement for public honor?[27] *The inner honorableness of the honored person.*

What does this mean? *Honorableness, i.e., a certain moral dignity that expresses itself in truthfulness, the courage of their convictions, and in a moral way of life.*

Where do Christians see their inner honor most profoundly? *In their relationship to God.*

Can people see themselves as having an unbroken relationship to God? *No.*

Why not? *Because they know that they are guilty before God.*

How can people reestablish their original relationship with God? *Through the forgiveness of sins, through the grace of God, through "justification."*

But what[28] is reborn after a relationship with God has been reestablished? *A person's inner honor.*

594   Through what does a person acquire[29] inner honor? *Through God's gift of justification.*

An individual's honor rests entirely with God. Individuals receive honor only from God; they have no honor in themselves and seek no honor[30] for themselves. Christ's power and honor live wherever individuals boast of their weakness before God. Therefore, "Let the one who boasts, boast in the Lord."[31] What is the measure of humanity's honorable deeds? *God's honor manifest in humanity.*

Our honor in its entirety should, as Paul said, consist in being God's temple.[32] God's honor should be our honor. We honor God when we hold on to our honor in thoughts, word, and deed, in body and soul.

Who alone can injure this inner honor? *Only we.*

Who alone can restore this inner honor? *God.*

[27.] Replaced by Mahling with: "What should be the unspoken presupposition of all public honor?"

[28.] Replaced by Mahling with: "What possibility . . . ?"

[29.] Mahling adds "the possibility of."

[30.] Mahling: "From this point on it must be shown how this possibility becomes a reality through the progressive self-expression of humans in their conscience before God, and how this is the concept of inner honor."

[31.] Mahling: "No more desire for merit before God, but everything is owed solely to God's grace—does the concept of 'honor,' really fit here?" Bonhoeffer cites 1 Cor. 1:31.

[32.] Cf. 1 Cor. 3:16.

What then can we say about[33] insults? *They affect only outer, not inner honor.*[34]

May we therefore treat such injury with indifference, as if it did not affect us? *No.*

Why not? *Because, as we already saw, outer honor also rests on God's will.*

What effect does this have on the way an insulted person should act? *An individual must repudiate the insult.*

What can an individual or a community be accused of if they let an insult rest upon them? *Cowardice, dishonor, infidelity, tolerance of sin and thereby of sin itself.*

The repudiation of a malicious[35] insult is therefore a Christian duty. You 595 may want to raise several objections that are taken from the New Testament, which seem directly to contradict our thoughts. Which objections, for example, can be derived from the Sermon on the Mount? *Matt. 5:39ff. seems to indicate that we are to abstain from resisting evil wherever the commandment to love your neighbor is followed.*[36]

It is similar in 1 Cor. 6:7. To defend yourself when you are unjustly treated evidently contradicts the Christian love commandment. Which Christian virtue should much rather be expressed when one is insulted and offended? *Patience and the power of forgiveness.*

You know that the passage from the Sermon on the Mount cited above was the occasion to accuse Christianity of having a slave morality, of knowing nothing about human honor and pride. And some of you may agree with this. It is true; we cannot accept being publicly abused and insulted and remain silent, as if the person insulting us were justified in doing so. Who could stand by while the honor of their mother or sister is assailed, while a friend is slandered, or while our nation is reviled and our church ridiculed?—Is it really only a vestige of our unrefined nature that comes to the fore here or is it perhaps something different, something more? What is it that enrages us the most as Christians when, for example, someone in the class says bad things about us? *That in the end the slanderer is thought to be right and is victorious.*

[33.] Mahling adds: "baseless."

[34.] Mahling: "*Substantiation*, of course, concerns also inner honor; we would prefer then to say accusations instead of insults."

[35.] Mahling: "This expression is first introduced here now, and it modifies the discussion somewhat."

[36.] Mahling: "Cf. on this the fact that Matt. 5:38-42 stands under the point of view of *retaliation*, and in all four cases it should become clear that another's incorrect behavior may not be made the measure of my behavior, since I also might walk [uncertain reading] in sin."

Certainly. Then what does the New Testament mean when it says that one should not resist evil?[37]———

I will help you. What is the goal of Jesus' love commandment? *The establishment of God's kingdom on earth.*

Hence, what must be done away with? *The evil will.*

Love's goal is to overcome evil. What then is the goal of infinite patience and nonresistance? *The defeat of evil.*

Where then does the Sermon on the Mount have its limitations?[38] *Wherever, by following it, evil is not defeated but furthered.*

In Rom. 12:21 Paul says, "Overcome evil with good." There are many ways to overcome evil. One is boundless patience. Give me an example where this has its limitations. *Self-defense.*

In this case, evil must be actively deterred through any means possible. What follows from all this regarding the upholding of my offended honor or the honor of my family, etc.? *It is God's commandment.*

Whose honor is being upheld? *God's honor.*

Whenever we promote the victory of the good we uphold God's honor and will. Every step that we take in upholding our honor must be done ad maiorem gloriam Dei.[39] But where must we see an insult as an offense to our honor? *There where the danger exists that evil will overcome good, where an evil will is systematically at work.*

Certainly a child's misbehavior, unfriendly service in a store, or the insolence of a crude person are not things that should offend our honor. What kind of attitude should we have in response to them? *The attitude of Thales, i.e., indifference toward trifles.*[40]

How do we respond to his conclusion, however, that there is no such thing as an insult? *We find this conclusion to be false.*

Evil intentions and slander can really rob us of "our" honor if we do not contest them vehemently, promptly, and energetically. What means are available to us in public life to protect our injured honor? *A lawsuit.*

As Christians, when should we avail ourselves of this option? *When all attempts at personal reconciliation have failed.*

Certainly. The first thing we must do is to attempt a personal understanding that would correct those who have insulted us, bearing up with them

596

597

[37.] Replaced by Mahling with: "One should not oppose evil with evil." Bonhoeffer had in mind Matt. 5:39; Mahling had in mind texts such as Rom. 12:17, 1 Thess. 5:15, and 1 Pet. 3:9.

[38.] Cf. *D* (*DBWE* 4):133–37, and *LLP* 6–7.

[39.] "To the greater glory of God."

[40.] Mahling: "Cf. above [see above, editorial notes 11–14]. There the assessment of Thales was apparently not quite right. For here the same thing [uncertain reading] is brought forward as a model, an ideal."

patiently, and forgiving them. If that fails, then we have to resort to other means. What should these means be weighed by? *Christian love.*

What, for example, are the usual methods of upholding one's honor in military and student life? *The duel.*

How should we regard this from a Christian standpoint? *As inadequate.*

Why? *Because it*[41] *does not assist good in overcoming evil.*

Since today no one in the military can any longer be forced to fight a duel, it is the duty of the Christian community to eliminate the need for duels.

What means are available to offended nations in order to reestablish their honor? *War.*

Without being able to elaborate this here, it seems to me that war is also an improper means to overcome evil with good and as such it is to be rejected. Wars must arise, not be made. Wherein ultimately lies the definition both of what is considered an offense to honor and what it takes to reestablish honor? *In the conscience of the individual or that of the community.*

The Christian community has means at its disposal with which to overcome evil with good, ranging from patient suffering to ardent persecution. One means seems to me to have been used too infrequently, namely, the use of courts of honor. Certain fights between school classes and certain duels could have been prevented if these had been used. It is true that all these methods have all too often been used as a cover for despicable vindictiveness. Since the Sermon on the Mount was preached, the Christian community has had a weapon against evil that is stronger than all others, because it brings God into the battle. What means am I speaking of? *Prayer for the one who has insulted you.*

This prayer is the basis for all proceedings against the offender.

How must Christians respond to the act of someone who has insulted them, prior to any action against this person? *They must have forgiven the act.*

598

What is the only attitude one can and must have before one, if the case arises, disgraces the offender himself?[42] *An attitude of love and forgiveness.*

It is the chief duty of Christians to forgive where they would otherwise punish. We cannot attempt to uphold our own honor without first having begged God to forgive the one who has insulted us. Pray for those who persecute you![43] According to Christian understanding, what then is the social relationship between the offended and the offender? *A relationship in community.*

[41.] Mahling: "Apart from all other considerations. . . ."

[42.] Mahling underlines "disgraces . . . himself" and replaces it with the following comment "This expression can lead to misunderstanding. Become yourself responsible or transfer it to the court for responsibility."

[43.] Matt. 5:44.

How can this be proved? *It is proved by fighting evil with the harshest means available, the community's will to overcome evil with good and to be united with the offender in God's community.*

Woe to those who try to defend their honor with vindictiveness instead of with humility before God, with anger that does not include forgiving, patient love—because it is from God alone that we receive our honor. Out of fear of working for their own interest instead of for God's, some people will silently endure evil. Only those who have completely overcome their insult and who can forgive the offender can publicly transform the evil of the injustice suffered. We have our honor, and our honor is both a gift of and a duty to God. We should uphold the honor of others in the same way as we uphold our own. We uphold this honor as God's honor, because only God is honorable. Everyone else is dishonorable. "Let the one who boasts, boast in the Lord."[44] This is the sum total of our honor. Our actions, however, should be guided by the following passages, "Overcome evil with good,"[45] "Love your enemies and pray for those who persecute you,"[46] and "Whatever you do, do everything for the glory of God."[47]

599   ## 16. Meditation and Sermon on Luke 9:51-56 for the Theological Examination[1]

Sermon on Luke 9:51-56

Meditation

The fact that, with the exception of D and some fragments, our manuscripts end our story with v. 55, ἐπετίμησεν αὐτοῖς, shows that the essential thought

---

[44.] 1 Cor. 1:31.

[45.] Rom. 12:21.

[46.] Matt. 5:44.

[47.] 1 Cor. 10:31. Final comment of Mahling: "Three points in the catechesis remain to be examined: (1) Thales. (2) Justification. (3) Interpretation of Matt. 5:38-42. Other details are noted. On the whole the catechesis in layout and execution as well as form and content is quite good."

[1.] *NL* A 13/4; typed. The sermon below was previously published in Bonhoeffer, *Predigten, Auslegungen, Meditationen,* 1:118–29. Written in October and November 1927 (cf. above, page 180). The handwritten title page contains the following text, "Sermon on Luke 9:51-56/Dietrich Bonhoeffer." The numerous grammatical corrections made by Superintendent Bronisch, the evaluator, are not noted individually here. The sermon was given on January 8, 1928, in the Hochmeister Church in Halensee. Superintendent Diestel assessed its presentation. The assessments of Bronisch and Diestel are found above, 1/114:183–187. On the literature used by Bonhoeffer see above, Bonhoeffer's letter of November 8, 1927, 1/110:180; see also the letter from his father of March 13, 1928 (*DB-ER*, 90–91).

of the narrative must have already been expressed by this point and that the sentences that follow in D serve only to interpret what has gone before. (Whether v. 56b ἐπορεύθησαν εἰς ἑτέραν κώμην belongs to our pericope, or should be considered part of the following, one is uncertain. D does not even have v. 56a.)[2] So it is. The general statements in D acquire their distinctive interpretation only when seen in relationship with what precedes[3] them. They in turn highlight the particularity of the story and make it generally valid. For the reader the center of the story is Jesus' threatening posture in response to a vehement declaration by the Zebedee brothers. What is the reason for this division between Jesus and his disciples? The disciples wanted to call down fire from heaven upon a Samaritan village[4] that refused to receive Jesus, in order to destroy the village.[5] They were enraged because of their zealous love for Jesus. In them we see zealots. Jesus, however, cuts them off abruptly and warns them. The reason for this is not found simply in the gist of Jesus' words. Jesus' words received their definitive character from what is reported in v. 53, where it is said that the Samaritans[6] rebuff Jesus because he is traveling to Jerusalem, i.e., because he is a Jew. It is when we realize this that the meaning of the whole story first becomes clear. The Samaritans are not acting out of malice, enmity, or hate against Jesus personally. They may not even know that Jesus is on a pilgrimage or even who he is. They reject Jesus because of the Jews, among whom he found himself. This means that they rejected him out of ignorance, without knowing him. For this the disciples want to destroy the village. But the reason Jesus warns them now becomes very clear. Jesus is saying, "Haven't you heard that they are not rejecting me, but the pilgrims journeying to Jerusalem? They don't know me at all. They don't know anything about me, and you want to judge and condemn them?" The words "You do not know what spirit you are of" must be interpreted in light of what precedes, as must the following phrase, "for the Son of Man has not come to destroy the lives of human beings but to save them." The spirit of which Jesus speaks is the spirit of patient love that certainly does not condemn where there is ignorance of the facts.

It is apparently at this point that the practical utilization of the text sets in. The text recounts Jesus' arrival and reception, and the disciples' anger, its[7] condemnation and suppression. Before us we see the big city[8] we live in. It

600

[2.] Here Bronisch wrote, "This is an extraordinarily fruitful sentence." In more recent Bible translations, vv. 55b and 56a are printed only in the notes.

[3.] Bronisch: "Preceding."

[4.] In the manuscript is written, "a Samaritan there." Bronisch comments in the margin: "Expression."

[5.] Replaced by Bronisch with "it." In the margin is: "style [uncertain reading]."

[6.] A line was drawn through these words by Bronisch.

[7.] Bronisch adds: "his."

[8.] Bronisch: "Only the big city."

601

is easy for us to compare it with that Samaritan village. People see the church members, and they reject Jesus[9]—a typical deed for the Samaritans. At the same time, the analogy between our own attitude and the attitude of the Zebedee brothers becomes evident to those of us who are secure in the church, as does the realization that Jesus uses threatening words to respond to such sentiments. It is also apparent that zealots themselves,[10] like the Zebedees, no longer share Jesus' spirit. We now have to examine ourselves and ask whether perhaps our own church-community, and not just the outside world, is like the Samaritan town that refuses to receive Jesus. What does it mean to accept Jesus? It means to recognize him as Lord without reservation, to yield one's entire self to him. Do we do this? Do we even want to do this? All of us forget what the picture of Jesus Christ looks like, even if we have seen it at some point. An endless number of things rush in upon us, and they blind our vision to the surpassing authority of Jesus and to the absolute urgency of his call. We are blind and deaf in response to his word. In this way we recognize that we are in the same situation as the Samaritans in that all of us also live solely through the love of Jesus Christ. And[11] here we find that the words of Jesus in v. 56a apply also to us. It is in him that we find our way and find a foothold when we are in distress. With this our unbridled anger is shattered. Our desire to destroy life is overcome by Jesus Christ's desire to preserve life[12] with patient, alluring love. With this comes the task of thinking and acting according to the spirit of these words and to represent Jesus by remaining patient in alluring love, even when we face rejection.

The difficulty in evaluating the text methodologically lies in the fact that we cannot simply place ourselves at the side of the disciples and experience Jesus' judgment from their vantage point. We also are made aware of the penitential power of the text, because we know that we are not substantially better than the Samaritans. We therefore see ourselves as belonging both on the side of the disciples and on the side of the Samaritans. We still have something of the spirit of both in us. Because of the recognition of the need for repentance, the disciples' wrath, which leads them to repudiate the Samaritans, condemns them, since in their anger they have separated themselves from the Spirit. In this way they became like the Samaritans—broken, vanquished, and purified[13] by receiving Jesus' words of grace and being turned to good. It is in this double-sidedness that the text can be fully understood, and so it would not be right to avoid it in favor of a simple one-sidedness.

602

[9.] Bronisch adds: "Barth."

[10.] Bronisch places "themselves" next to "Jesus," so that the text reads, "Jesus' spirit itself."

[11.] Deleted by Bronisch.

[12.] Marked through by Bronisch, who comments in the margin: "Style."

[13.] The passage from "Because" to "purified" is marked by Bronisch: "Style."

Further, regarding the structure of the material, the attempt to avoid the double thrust by combining the second and third part of the sermon (by thoroughly discussing first the model of the Samaritans and then the disciples, and finally Jesus' words) does not work.[14]

Finally, we should mention that our text supports Ritschl's conclusions about the relationship of guilt, forgiveness, and ignorance.[15] In spite of its one-sidedness it must be presented when talking about this text.

*A Sermon about the Coming of Jesus and His Rejection,
about the Disciples' Wrath and Its Defeat by the Savior*[16]

Outline

I.   The story will be made understandable in its psychological and historical context.
II. How the characters in the story and their behavior can be seen as being typical.
   1.   The Samaritans are the ones who do not see and thus reject; they see Jesus only as a Jew, the unremarkable wrapper covering his essence.
   2.   The two disciples as wrongheaded zealots for Jesus' honor.
   3.   Jesus as he judges the disciples: not blind enthusiasm but obedience to the word and the spirit of Jesus. The disciples are destroyers of Jesus' work. Jesus' promise: Jesus' spirit preserves understanding[17] and alluring love.   603
III. The story of Jesus' arrival in the Samaritan town—a mirror of our time.
   1.   The world of the big city as the Samaritan town.
   2.   We in the church are inclined, apparently rightly, to agree with the disciples' way of thinking.
   3.   But after careful reflection we see that by doing this we are sentencing ourselves. Even we in the church belong to the Samaritan town.
      a.   Have we really accepted Jesus?
      b.   Do we really want to accept Jesus?
      c.   Are we not also ignorant, blind, and deaf like the Samaritans?
   4.   To preserve the word of Jesus Christ concerning his will and human life, his patient, alluring, understanding love is, for us,
      a.   A gift.

[14.] On the entire paragraph, Bronisch comments: "Style."

[15.] Ritschl, *The Christian Doctrine of Justification and Reconciliation*, 253ff.

[16.] Handwritten postscript by Bonhoeffer that gives the theme of the sermon. Bronisch comments on this: "No unified theme."

[17.] Bronisch: "Unclear! Style!"

(aa) We are assured of the love of Jesus Christ as the power
from which alone all of us live,

(bb) and so the wrath of the disciples is broken by their
recognition of the superior power of Jesus Christ's
love.

b.   An assignment.

(aa) The love by which we live should lead to compassion
for everyone.

(bb) The prerequisite for this is that we tirelessly help people see Jesus Christ and do not judge them.

Sermon on Luke 9:51-56

Our story draws us into the time of Jesus' life when[18] he is preparing to die
and is traveling down the road to Jerusalem for the final time. "He set his
face to go to Jerusalem." He knows the fate that awaits him at the end of the
road. He knows that now everything is compelling him to make a decision.
His disciples, who are with him, know this as well.[19]

604

Yet they have not yet understood that Jesus' path is the path of divine love,
not the path of ultimate judgment. It is evening. Once again they have come
one day closer to the final battle. The thoughts of the wanderers circle fever-
ishly around the coming events. Exhausted from the trip, the little band[20]
looks for a night's lodging. Jesus sends messengers to the nearest place. It
belongs to the Samaritans.[21] Hundreds of years of hatred lay between them
and the Jews. All communication between them had been broken off. For a
long time the path taken by pious pilgrims from Galilee to Jerusalem followed the eastern bank of the Jordan and bypassed Samaria in a roundabout
way. Jesus, on the way to the cross, the path of compassionate love, travels
along the road through Samaria, directly toward Jerusalem. We can only
infer, for the text does not tell us, why Jesus took this path. But he might have
talked often with his disciples about what would soon happen. He might
have tried to make them understand that this path was a path of God's love
among the people, that the Jews needed this love as much as the Samaritans
did, and that he wanted to demonstrate this love to the Samaritans as much
as he did to the Jews. In order to witness to this conviction he may have
taken this path through Samaria. This step would have obliged the disciples
to exercise a great deal of self-control. Piercing, heartfelt aversion might

[18.] Replaced by Bronisch with: "for."

[19.] Bronisch adds "?"

[20.] Bonhoeffer's spelling "Scharr" ("band") for "Schar" is corrected by Bronisch here
and in the following in the German edition.

[21.] Bronisch corrects Bonhoeffer's spelling of the German word for Samaritans:
"Samariter! Always Samariter instead of Samaritaner."

have accompanied the small band when they arrived on Samaritan soil as the sun went down. But the disciples had conquered their inner selves. They wanted to demonstrate that they shared Jesus' spirit, and so they went with him. They wanted to prove, especially to the Samaritans, that they paid no attention to these outer battles. They wanted to travel with their Savior through Samaria. Yes, they really had conquered their inner selves. They came as human beings to human beings. This was the Master's spirit.

Night had fallen and they needed lodging. Jesus had sent several of his disciples ahead to inquire where a tired group of Jews on a pilgrimage to Jerusalem might find shelter. It was the ancient right of foreigners to ask for shelter, even in enemy territory. Jesus and his disciples waited in front of the place for news from the messengers. They return. Their motions, their stride, their face, and their eyes spew agitation and rage. "They won't accept the master. They have refused to give him shelter." Great agitation seizes the band. Angry words reach Jesus' ear. But he remains undisturbed and silent. Their rage increases. "Why have they turned him away? What did they say?" "A pilgrim on the way to Jerusalem can't find shelter in Samaria." The brothers James and John push themselves through the band toward Jesus. Their eyes are ablaze with zealous love for their Lord and with zealous wrath against anyone who would turn him away. "Lord, do you want us to command fire to come down from heaven and consume them?" Jesus now turns around toward the voices that had spoken to him behind his back. And he warns the speakers with righteous solemnity, "You do not know what spirit you are of, for the Son of Man has not come to destroy the lives of human beings but to save them." Then they went on to another village.

It was only a minor incident, played out in only a few brief minutes—but what a forceful sermon for our time about the disciples' wrath and the Savior's mind, about the coming of Jesus Christ and his reception.[22] It deals with the Samaritans, the angry disciples, Jesus' harsh words about the latter, and his comforting words for the former.[23] How does this affect us?

Let us thoroughly examine the text until the walls of the centuries that divide us from it disappear and we comprehend the timeless kernel of the story.[24] In order to do this, we first must ask what kind of people these Samaritans actually were. According to everything thus far, we must take them for very rough and hard people. We can easily understand and sympathize with the disciples' anger. Shouldn't heavenly fire consume anyone who shuts the door in Jesus' face? Yet we must pay careful attention to the text. We

605

606

[22.] Bronisch: "Theme."

[23.] Bronisch underlines the words "comforting words for the former." In the margin this phrase is marked by several question marks.

[24.] Cf. Barth, *Romans*, 4–5; and Harnack, *What Is Christianity?*, 10–15. See above, 3/15; see also *DB-ER*, 90–91.

learn from[25] our text not only that the Samaritans do not receive Jesus but also why—in this case because "he set his face to go to Jerusalem." What does this mean? Their rejection apparently was not aimed particularly at Jesus but at all Jewish pilgrims and therefore Jesus as well. We don't hear that the Samaritans knew about Jesus, let alone his true importance, or that they were personally hostile to him. Jesus is rebuffed, turned away. Why? Because he was a Jew and a member of his people. The Samaritans as a people had hostile attitudes toward the Jews as a people. They see only outward appearance, the unremarkable wrapper in which our eternal God hides from the eyes of those who see and yet don't believe. In Jesus they see a Jew—they, the "church people"—and they draw their conclusion about the Master from this. That means that basically they don't see Jesus at all but reject him, perhaps even reject him for that very reason. This is the kind of people the Samaritans were.

And now to the disciples. Full of great hopes and pious thoughts they followed their Lord on the path through Samaria, and now they receive this stern rejection. Oh, it didn't center on them. But their Lord, their Master—it was he who was rejected. The Samaritans showed him the door, and that deeply affected the disciples' fiery hearts. All right, if you don't want to, then go to hell! Whoever refuses to accept Jesus should be wiped off the face of the earth. That person has incurred eternal divine wrath.

Now Jesus speaks. It immediately becomes clear to us that he breaks out in wrath not at the Samaritans, but at his disciples.[26] Those who had just heard why the Samaritans refused to accept Jesus were blind and hard-hearted enough to pass eternal judgment on a situation that was still unclear, and where the people were blind. Didn't they see that in one stroke they would have called down fire on not only the Samaritan village but also on Jesus' entire work, indeed on the whole world? Did they really misunderstand Jesus' final journey to Jerusalem so completely that they failed to realize that it was a journey of patience and love? Must Jesus leave this world so misunderstood by his inner circle? Would this be his legacy? Oh, but the disciples were burning with love and zeal for their Lord. They wanted to protect their Lord's honor at all costs. This was certainly not concealed from Jesus; but here he knew no tenderness. To love Jesus means to obey him, to walk in his spirit, and not to forget that one should be a child of that spirit. "For the love of God is this, that we obey his commandments" (1 John 5:3). No overdone enthusiasm! No excess emotion! Instead pay attention to the word. Be obedient! Truly honoring Jesus is not attending to and cherishing[27] his physical life but obeying his commandment. Giving Jesus the honor he deserves

607

[25.] Bronisch here replaces the German word "von" with "aus."
[26.] Bronisch: "!"
[27.] Bronisch: "Unclear."

means winning lives, not destroying them. Now we understand his harsh words, "But he turned and rebuked them, and said, You do not know what spirit you are of." Of course, it becomes clear to us which spirit Jesus is referring to only when he contrasts the summary of his entire work among humans with the angry outburst of the disciples: "The Son of Man has not come to destroy the lives of human beings but to save them."[28] Jesus speaks to the disciples of the spirit that preserves life,[29] a spirit of redemption and patience that never tires, an understanding, alluring spirit. Woe unto them who act contrary to this spirit! May patience be given to those who are the focus of Jesus' work.

Now all the facets of the picture are clear and transparent. Even the wall of the centuries that has separated us from this story has fallen. We face Jesus eye to eye. We see the Samaritans, hear the disciples. Now doesn't this picture   608 frighten us? Won't we wake up? Do our ears remain deaf? Don't we recognize our own time in this picture? Can't we all easily find a place in this picture where[30] we could stand?

Today also is such a day when Jesus wants to come, just as he did then. Aren't there also today, as then, Samaritans and zealous disciples? Could they at that time have been the last of their ilk and their spirit? Is not Jesus' arrival today very, very similar to the arrival of Jesus then? Sunday after Sunday during winter we ring the bells of the Christmas message.[31] They sing quietly and tenderly about the stable in Bethlehem; powerfully and intensely they ring out in our big cities the word about love's arrival. Who among us hasn't been extraordinarily affected when they passed by the Kaiser Wilhelm Memorial Church in the evening as the bells were ringing, while[32] the noise of the cars and streetcars, the fantastic neon signs, and the push of the crowds on their way to countless places of amusement wouldn't let them think clearly?[33] How incredibly lost the peal of the bells sounds in this environment! How strange and alone the house with the high tower looks![34] Fear and bitter pain often assail us at such a sight. Is there something like a Christmas message in the tumult of the big city? A message about the coming of the Lord Jesus?

Maybe we are filled with zeal to stand up and shout with all the power we possess, to scream into the frantic frenzy, "People, can't you hear anything?" But who would hear it? And if some did hear it they would pass by laughing

---

[28.] Bronisch: "Literally: 'save'." The German translation in the Luther Bible used by Bonhoeffer reads "preserve."

[29.] Bronisch: "Style."

[30.] Bronisch changes to: "in den" ["in which"].

[31.] Bronisch: "Only?"

[32.] Bronisch here changes the placement of a German word.

[33.] Bronisch: "Style."

[34.] Bronisch: "Exaggerated."

609 and say, "One more curiosity in the big city." Blinded, they pass by the message[35] of the coming of the eternal God to human beings through Jesus Christ. "It is one of many," they say. Perhaps they glance at the people who are going to church, the church folk, and, thinking they know what is going on, pass by.[36] The message of Jesus Christ's coming has forced its way into the Samaritan village.

We would rise up in anger and pain. We would intervene for our rejected, despised Lord, and perhaps would call down a terrible curse on our big city, perhaps even call down heavenly fire to destroy this Babylon. None of us is a stranger to this wild, passionate, roiling pain and this boundless indignation. If they don't want to listen, well and good; let the judgment of[37] Sodom and Gomorrah fall on them. Oh, now we begin to understand the disciples well! Perhaps we have even been active, have worked with people, have told them about Jesus, have gone about our work with the highest hope of showing them who Jesus is and how he is and what he brings and will bring—with the result being a firm No and a haughty smile.[38] We think about the quiet, pious work of missions, not only far away in distant lands but also here in the cities. Consider the pastoral duties of ministers in urban churches. They joyfully accept all kinds of scorn, if only the Holy One, their Lord, is untouched—and their reward is cold rejection. Oh, it is not we who are important. They can laugh and ridicule us as much as they want. But how painful it is when we see how they put our Lord on the same level as us, how they ridicule him with us, and drag him through the mud. How much time have we waited in vain on people who even now only have rejecting and scornful words for the mission of Jesus Christ! "Won't this ever end?" we ask bitterly. We don't need any more illustrations. All of us know about this. It is the disciples' anger that flares up in us, an anger that seems so righteous and so holy. We want to condemn and to judge. We want to turn away with the wish that heavenly wrath descend and destroy. Indeed, do we really want

610 this? Do we want to pass judgment upon those who haven't even seen yet? Do we want to pass judgment upon those who are inattentive,[39] foolish, and superficial? It might become clear to us that with such desires and actions we prove that we have not accepted Jesus, have not felt his spirit, and have forgotten whose spirit we are descended from. We have pushed our Lord away from us with our excessive[40] love for him and have fallen from the community of his spirit.

[35.] Bronisch: "Metabasis εἰς ἄλλο γένος" ["transfer to a different genus"].

[36.] Bronisch: "!"

[37.] Bronisch: "?"

[38.] Added by hand are the words "of the others."

[39.] Bronisch marks the phrase "judgment . . . inattentive" and remarks concerning it "The presupposition may perhaps not be true."

[40.] Bronisch: "?"

Serious reflection leads us to ask, Can we really be so completely without understanding for the Samaritans that we[41] judge them so severely? Are the Samaritans really beyond the church walls? One glance at ourselves and at our church-community teaches us that things are very different from what we would perhaps want them to be. It teaches us that perhaps the game would be lost for us[42] and the mission of Jesus Christ finished if the likes of John and James would perform the duties of their office.[43] We not only discover these kinds of 'Samaritan villages' out in the world. No, we discover them right here in our midst. It is a horrible thing to think and to say, The whole story that we heard not only took place 2000 years ago far away in the east, but also it takes place today in the hubbub of world metropolises. It is taking place over and over again in our own circles.[44] In our midst, the story comes alive for the millionth time in the history of the world. What does that mean? What is going on?

Jesus Christ is looking for lodging. He is looking for entrance into our spirits and our hearts. Do we really understand what this means? Jesus Christ is a controlling, willful guest.[45] He wants our hearts completely.[46] He will not tolerate competition, even if the competition only wants to dispute Jesus' right to the least bit of his possession.[47] Jesus Christ is a discomforting, imperious guest. He will rule whoever invites him in, and whoever invites Jesus in must serve him. Let us understand fully to whom we give shelter when we invite Jesus in. Do we want to take the risk of having this unusual[48] guest? Oh yes! All of us "want" to—at least this is what we say and think. It is in this that we are different from the Samaritans. But before we speak these words too quickly, what does "want" mean? Half and half is unacceptable here. Only yes or no will do. The issue here is either to desire God completely or not at all, because whoever wants God halfway does not desire *God.* To desire God completely, however, means already to have God. Can we dare say that we desire Jesus to be our guest completely and with our whole soul?

611

If it turns out to be the case that many of us don't want to take this risk, then there may be another way for us to be justified. We could say, "We know about Jesus Christ and have been baptized and confirmed. We have heard enough about him in every sermon on Sunday. We are certainly not blind like the Samaritans." Don't be angry if I ask one more time: Do you really

---

[41.] Bronisch: "!"
[42.] Bronisch: "Expression."
[43.] Bronisch: "Skewed expression."
[44.] Bronisch: "In our Christian circles."
[45.] Bronisch: "Clumsy."
[46.] Bronisch: "For himself."[MCN]
[47.] Bronisch: "!"
[48.] Bronisch: "!"

know Jesus *Christ?* Do we really hear Jesus Christ knock at our door every Sunday? We might be able sincerely to answer this question with yes for certain moments and hours of our lives, but we would certainly be hesitant to answer the question with yes for the entirety our lives. I believe that we could say the following: For every one of us, Jesus Christ disappears not merely once but day after day. Either we don't even see or hear him anymore, or we still see him but our eyes have lost their ability to see that everything depends on our either accepting or rejecting him. We ignore the absolute urgency of his call. And thereby we are blind, like the Samaritans in our story, even if it is true that we still hear his call. Let us now remember the anger of the disciples, our own bitterness and indignation, and our anger that wished to destroy those who rejected us. This anger appeared to be so righteous, so understandable, and so holy—and now look at ourselves! How fitting it is that we are terrified at this thought! In truth we don't have the slightest reason to proclaim judgment and death where ignorance and blindness rule. We[49] who think we know and yet don't act, and they[50] who barely know and don't act either.

612

If all this is clear to us and has touched our hearts, then I implore in the name of our Lord Jesus Christ: let us[51] not be alarmed by people like John and James. Instead let us examine the words of Jesus, with which he warns these men, and the final comforting words of our story: "The Son of Man has not come to destroy the lives of human beings but to save them." Comfort comes only from the one who makes it so difficult for us to offer him hospitality. He doesn't want to destroy but to preserve. He wants to capture us with everlasting love. He wants to give us sight. He desires our life, i.e., wants us to live in community with God and with him. And when we can't find our way to him, he will find the way to us. He will live in us. He will make our heart his temple. He himself will do what we are too weak to do. He has promised. He will do it.

If we have understood this and have taken it to heart, then we no longer feel the disciples' anger. It has been completely overcome and broken because we recognize our own inadequacy and our need for the love and the patience of Jesus Christ as much as anyone else. Jesus' love is our only foothold. Anger dissolves in response to its overpowering force. Love is the spirit Jesus speaks of, and it is solely from this love that we live, and it is this love which should now live in us. When we begin to doubt our own power, it is then that we place our whole trust in the eternal power and love of God and our Lord Jesus Christ.

613

With this a tremendous task has been given to us and, of course, the strength to fulfill it. It is to guide our thoughts and actions according to the

---

[49.] Underlined by Bronisch.
[50.] Marked by Bronisch, who comments in the margin: "Style [difficult to decipher]."
[51.] Bronisch inserts "Also."

words of Jesus, "The Son of Man did not come to destroy the lives of human beings but to save them." This is true for our attitude toward those "out there" as well as to those "in here." Let us think about the fact that we are children of the spirit of love.[52] The act of Christian love is to save souls with alluring love and above all to manifest Jesus, the bearer of eternal divine love, so that we don't remain ignorant and blind like those Samaritans but begin to see. The act of Christian love is to manifest Jesus not as a religious genius, an ethical thinker, or a philosopher, but as the Lord of death and of life; as the Word of God made flesh, for whom command and promise are the same. This is the act of Christian love that we owe everyone. Let us not forget that!

Let us look at life today within our church and in the world. Truly, it seems from a human perspective that God would have reason enough to condemn the world. But we have just heard that God wants to save. Should we then destroy? God would be patient. Should we become impatient? God would give life. Should we kill? No! With the eyes of the alluring love of Jesus Christ let us look at our time, the suffering out there in the world and the suffering here in the church, the suffering of blindness and deafness, both here and there. We all have a bit of the Samaritans' spirit and the disciples' anger in us. We all live from the love of Jesus Christ and the love of his Father. May God grant that we put the disciples' anger and the Samaritans' spirit behind us, and carry only the Savior's spirit within us! Then we can accept Jesus, and our anger will be overcome by Jesus' spirit, and through this love we can become Christ to our brothers and sisters.[53]

May the Lord open our eyes so that we may see. May the Lord open our ears so that we may hear. May the Lord open our hearts so that the Lord may find a dwelling place there. Christ speaks, "Listen! I am standing at the door, knocking." We want to call out, "Amen. Come, Lord Jesus![54]

[52.] Bronisch: "Expression."
[53.] *SC* (*DBWE* 1):183–84.
[54.] Rev. 3:20 and 22:20.

17:53   **16a. Catechetical Exam on Matthew 8:5-13**[1]

Catechetical Lesson[2]
on Matt. 8:5-13
for a class of 14–15-year-old boys
in secondary school

[5:When he entered Capernaum, a centurion came to him, appealing to him 6: and saying, "Lord, my servant is lying at home paralyzed, in terrible distress." 7: And he said to him, "I will come and cure him." 8: The centurion answered, "Lord, I am not worthy to have you come under my roof; but only speak the word, and my servant will be healed. 9: For I also am a man under authority, with soldiers under me; and I say to one, 'Go,' and he goes, and to another, 'Come,' and he comes, and to my slave, 'Do this,' and the slave does it." 10: When Jesus heard him, he was amazed and said to those who followed him, "Truly I tell you, in no one in Israel have I found such faith. 11: I tell you, many will come from east and west and will eat with Abraham and Isaac and Jacob in the kingdom of heaven, 12: while the heirs of the kingdom will be thrown into the outer darkness, where there will be weeping and gnashing of teeth." 13: And to the centurion Jesus said, "Go; let it be done according to your faith." And the servant was healed in that hour.]

Reading of the text by a catechist.[3]
First we want to go through our text purely superficially to see whether something in the wording cannot be understood.—What kind of illness does the servant have? He has palsy.—How does the palsy manifest itself? The servant cannot walk, is lame, must lie in bed, and is in a great deal of pain.—What does "from the morning and from the evening"[4] in v. 11 mean? It means from the east and from the west.—What does the narrator mean in v. 12 by heirs of the kingdom? He means the Jews.[5]
Second reading of the text, this time by one of the children.[6]
Where does our story take place? In Capernaum.—Where is Capernaum?
17:54   On the Sea of Gennesaret in Galilee. To which people do most of the inhabitants of Capernaum belong? The Jewish people.—During the time in which

---

[1.] *NL* S 11(20/21), a personal file in the Consistory; a typed paper with handwritten corrections in the margin made by Pastor Gustav Posth, who evaluated it (see above, 1/114, editorial note 7, 184). The date is corrected to November 10, 1927. Bonhoeffer's own copy is cataloged *NL* A 14/5. Unpublished.
[2.] Posth: "Literature?"
[3.] Posth: "Preparation."
[4.] The German Bible translates it this way. The English translation, "as the east is from the west" suggests the solution to Bonhoeffer's difficulty.
[5.] Posth: "They won't answer that quickly."
[6.] Posth: "For what reason?"

Jesus lived, who had political power over the Jews? The Romans. Which people did the Romans use to exercise their power? Their administrative officials and their military.[7] Who would the centurion have served? The Romans.— What social status did a Roman centurion have?[8] He had the most important position in the city. What kind of relationship[9] did the Jews have to the Romans? They were enemies.—This was certainly the case in general. There were certainly people among the Jews—the Sadducees—who wanted to have friendly relations with Rome, but these were considered by the devout Jews, especially by the Pharisees, practically to be traitors. Apparently there were also pagan people of importance who sought to ingratiate themselves with the Jews by building synagogues or schools. Luke tells us that the centurion of Capernaum did this as well. At any rate this was most likely a later embellishment.[1] [10] In our story there is no mention of this. Therefore one can accurately say that all pious and strict Jews saw the Romans as enemies. What was the deepest reason for this attitude? The Romans were pagans, and the pagans had enslaved God's people.—Thus it happened again and again that the Jews tried to throw off the tyranny of the Romans.—What, in general, did the Romans think about the Jews? They thought that they were a peculiar and despicable people, and they hated them. And so it happened that the pious and strict Jew and the self-satisfied and proud Roman walked past each other with glances on both sides full of disdain and smoldering hatred. A sharp divide had been created between them. Any Roman who had anything to do with the Jews made himself ridiculous. Any Jew who had anything to do with the pagans would have been forgetting their unique position in the world. Iron was pitted against iron. The Romans had set foot on explosive ground. Hail to the man who freed Israel from the pagans, who would surrender Rome into Israel's hands so that Israel could enjoy putting its heel on the pagan's head. This was the situation when Jesus descended the mountain where he had been teaching and came to Capernaum. When does our story take place? At the moment when Jesus entered the city. Did Jesus come

17:55

---

1. The assertion that the text in Luke 7:1-7 is less authentic is demonstrated already by the fact that the Jews came to Jesus by order of the centurion, but apparently against the centurion's will (v. 7). In line with the position of the centurion vis-à-vis the Jews in Luke, the statement in Matt. 8:11f. must be missing, and thereby the point of the story is lost. In addition, the direct confrontation of Jesus and the centurion is better suited to a catechetical lesson than is the account in Luke.[11]

[7.] Posth: "Doesn't an 'older' schoolboy answer?"
[8.] In the original: "head centurion."
[9.] Posth: "Expression."
[10.] On Bonhoeffer's text-critical reflections, cf. Heinrich Julius Holtzmann, *Die Synoptiker. Die Apostelgeschichte*, 128f., which, however, Bonhoeffer does not always follow.
[11.] Posth: "Why this critique in front of [illegible] children? Neither is of any interest to the students."

alone?[12] No, v. 10 mentions some followers.—What kind of people could they have been? Jews from the surroundings or from Capernaum itself who had heard him preach on the mountain and now continued to follow him.

The Jews had heard Jesus speak of many things, but it was one theme that they wanted to hear again and again. It was the central message of Jesus' teaching. Which thought had Jesus put at the center of his entire proclamation? The thought of the kingdom of God and the sovereignty of God.[13]—It was the message about the imminence of the kingdom of God that captivated the Jews so extraordinarily. Now the time had surely arrived, if this man were correct, when the eternal kingdom of Israel would be established and the Romans finally subdued. The Jews could not grasp this thought in any other way, and they still did not understand it differently eight[14] days before Jesus' death. The crowd of Jews entered the city filled with such hopes. It was an impressive troop that now entered through the city gate. Only a few steps into the city the crowd is suddenly held up. The city's centurion, the man who was known, feared, and respected by everyone approached the crowd and rushed over to Jesus. What expression would one have seen reflected in his face? Worry and need. One would certainly have seen the centurion approach Jesus with a sorrowful, fear-ridden, and care-worn face. Now what? Could one believe one's ears? The centurion speaks to Jesus, he asks, he begs, saying,[15] "Sir, my servant is lying at home paralyzed, in terrible distress." Astonishment and complaints rumble through the crowd. How can a Roman centurion approach a Jewish rabbi with his problems? What is this? Why should our rabbi be concerned about a pagan soldier? Then they heard Jesus answer—words that no one expected, so puzzling, even terrible to the Jewish hearers[16]—"I will come and heal him." What do you think is remarkable when you combine the words of the centurion and Jesus' answer? (If no one answers, ask the following questions, "What kind of sentence do the words of the centurion compose?" An affirmation.[17] After hearing Jesus' answer what kind of sentence would one have expected the centurion to have said? A sentence expressing hope. Now repeat the above

---

[12.] Posth: "This is not the way to ask a question!"

[13.] This sentence, in which Bonhoeffer uses Albrecht Ritschl's differentiation of God's sovereignty from the kingdom of God, is crossed out by Pastor Posth. Cf. Ritschl, *Die christliche Lehre von der Rechtfertigung und Versöhnung*, 2:29–30, "that through Christ God's sovereignty has found a community that allows itself to be ruled by God." On the differentiation of "the kingdom of God" and "God's sovereignty" in Ritschl compare, among others, Walther's *Typen des Reich-Gottes-Verständnisses*, 135–55, especially chapter 7, "Das Reich Gottes als die im Sittlichen zu realisierende Herrschaft Gottes."

[14.] Luke 19:38 is apparently meant.

[15.] Posth: "Question!"

[16.] Posth marked in the margin the sentences "Then they . . . Jewish hearers" and commented "This will still be developed."

[17.] Posth: "How tedious!"

17:56

question.) Jesus offers to come although the centurion did not specifically ask him to do so. We would ask, "Why does Jesus do this?" In order to understand this, we must first ask whether there was a particular reason why the centurion did not ask Jesus directly. Try to remember a time when you had a particular wish that you wanted your parents to fulfill. Perhaps it was a trip or a visit to the theater or something else. You probably would do the same thing with your parents when you tell them how nice it would be to go there. Why do you think that you do this or something like this? Because you don't want to pester them and want to put the whole affair into their hands.[18] Now, why do you think the centurion did not specifically ask Jesus but instead only told him briefly of his distress? He did not want to be obtrusive but wanted to put the whole matter into Jesus' hands.—What attitude does the centurion show that he has toward Jesus when he does this?—Trust that Jesus will do what is best in this situation. You see, we stand here before a very interesting point in our story from which we can learn a great deal for our own religious life. Which part of our religious life could be affected by the way the centurion behaved in his misery?[19] Our prayer life.—What can we learn about this passage for our prayer life? We see that a type of prayer exists that does not badger and attack but only tells God of our distress and leaves everything else to God.[20]—Yes certainly,[21] and we learn even more. In the end, all of our praying, as turbulent as it may become, can never be anything more than an indication of our distress and a humble appeal to God. God knows my distress, and only does what is good and right. The decision is God's. May God's will be done. So now we understand Jesus' answer.— Why does Jesus immediately declare himself ready to come and to heal? Because, in the centurion's words, he sees a humble trust in his power as the savior.[22] What, in particular, would have allowed Jesus to recognize this in the centurion? In the fact that he came at all, in his manner of speaking, and in his eyes.[23] All of this certainly appeared to Jesus to be something unusual. But something else happened as well that we haven't spoken of yet, and this is a very nice feature of our story.—For whom does the centurion actually come to Jesus? For his servant.—He does not come for himself but instead for his sick servant. What danger does he expose himself to when he comes with this kind of request to a Jewish rabbi? Rejection, mockery, and derision by the Jews and especially by his Roman soldiers.[24] You see, to go

17:57

17:58

[18.] Posth: "Children?"

[19.] Posth: "It really is asked in a much too difficult a manner!"

[20.] Posth: "Is a child supposed to answer this?"

[21.] Posth: "Unnecessary."

[22.] This sentence is handwritten, probably by Bonhoeffer, and put in single quotation marks. Pastor Posth has underlined it with wavy lines.

[23.] Posth: "Thus three answers at once."

and ask for someone else's sake, to ask with the danger of being rejected and being made ridiculous, is perhaps not such a small thing. It is a deed for which we perhaps have much more respect than if the centurion had won an entire battle. Think sometimes about the fact that one can go to people and also to Jesus to plead for another person![25] Even when it is often difficult for us! This may also have persuaded Jesus to offer the centurion his help.

In which case might all this not have been anything unusual in the eyes of the Jews?[26] If a Jew had been standing in front of Jesus.—But how did the Jews take[27] Jesus' dealings with a pagan? They found it repulsive.—Certainly, think of yourself as one of these Jews who even yet had imagined what it would be like when the pagans would crawl to crosses,[28] when the Romans would be their subjects.—Imagine these Jews, and there, in front of their eyes, the one whom they expect to fulfill all their hopes offers to go to a pagan's house and help him. This was a blow to the head that ripped all their illusions to shreds. What does the kingdom of God have to do with a pagan? What kind of a claim could they have on God? Now the story develops bit by bit. The centurion does not accept Jesus' offer to come.—What were his reasons? He says that he is unworthy for Jesus to come to his house.—What would the Jews have felt when they heard these words from the centurion? The feeling of satisfied pride.[29]

Certainly, the centurion humbles himself in everyone's eyes, in the eyes of his subjects, and he even makes himself into a ridiculous figure[30] in the eyes of his soldiers. A Roman man is not worthy to have a Jewish rabbi visit him? Such a man is a disgrace to Rome. All ears and eyes were anxiously focused on the centurion as he continued, "But only speak the word, and my servant will be healed. For I also am a man under authority, with soldiers under me; and I say to one, 'Go,' and he goes, and to another, 'Come,' and he comes, and to my slave, 'Do this,' and the slave does it."[31]

In order fully to understand these words, we have to think back to a time when we still loved to play soldiers or war.[32] What is the first prerequisite when you play war?[33] That there are two armies.—What does such an army

17:59

[24.] Posth: "The answers are too scholarly."

[25.] Posth: "It is awkward that the explanations and the application are always mixed together."

[26.] Posth: "Too difficult."

[27.] So, instead of, "feel about."

[28.] Posth: "Expression."

[29.] Posth: "Children!?"

[30.] Posth: "?"

[31.] The passage "Only speak the word . . . does it" is marked. Beside it Pastor Posth has written "Ask questions."

[32.] Cf. below, page 570.

consist of? Of a commander and subordinates.—What is the necessary relationship between the commander and those who are being led, if one group
hopes to be victorious?[34] The subordinates must obey their commander.—
Obedience is the fundamental rule that must be observed in any army,
whether it is a game or it is serious.—What is the only thing that matters in
any army? The leader's command.—And what is the characteristic of a commander? That he can command and that he is obeyed.

You see, the commander's *word* is the only thing that is valuable in a skillful army. If the commander says something, then one can be sure that it will
happen. One doesn't have to check.[35] One can absolutely rely on it happening and each commander must be able to rely on it happening. Isn't it
true that it's the same with you. The ability to command makes a leader, and
the word of a leader is the only thing that makes an army an army. Now,
there are small and great commanders and armies. Alexander and Caesar,
Frederick the Great and Napoleon were commanders of such immense and
powerful armies.—Which commander of a small troop does our story tell us
about? About the centurion of Capernaum.—How does one know that he
was a leader? Because he could give commands and be obeyed.—In his
army, then, what was the only thing that counted? His word and his command.—What does the centurion say about this himself? Answer with v. 9.   17:60

Yes, this is the way it was, because the centurion only needed to say a word
and it happened. No one would have doubted him or have thought that it
could have been different. It was completely obvious that this is the way it was
in the Roman army. Anyone who would have tried to test if this was really the
case would have been stupid and a coward at the same time. You understand
this, don't you? Now, in our story, the centurion himself is telling us about
another commander.—Which commander is he talking about? About
Jesus.—You see, the Roman centurion could not think of the wonderful Jewish rabbi in any other terms than as a powerful army leader who could give
commands to the whole world and has power over all the spirits in the world.
He therefore also had power over the evil spirits who, according to the worldview of that time, plagued people with sickness. How would the centurion
have thought about the success of Jesus' command?—He would have
thought that everything would happen as Jesus had commanded it.—At this
point, what is the characteristic of an army leader? His command.—What is
the only thing of meaning to his army? His word.[36]

Therefore the centurion believes that if every minor leader of a minor
troop has only to say the word and his word is immediately followed, and that

---

[33.] Posth: "This also is asked in a much too mature manner."
[34.] Posth: "So doctrinaire! The same thing could be asked in a much simpler form."
[35.] Posth: "Why so terribly tedious?"
[36.] Cf. above, 2/6:285–300.

the leader can depend on this happening without personally helping, then how much more effective would be the word of someone whose power extends to the whole world! A word—and the most wondrous thing becomes reality, a command—and someone who is terminally ill becomes healthy. Just think what a unique and wonderful view of the world this centurion must have had! He believed that the Jewish rabbi Jesus was the person who had authority over the whole world, whose word was sufficient to make a blind person see and a lame person walk. If his word alone is enough to heal a sick person, then what is not needed? Jesus' personal presence.[37] Yes, and due to the immense trust that the centurion had, Jesus spoke the fearful words to the shocked and indignant[38] Jews, "in no one in Israel have I found such faith." And what is new and unheard-of in the words of the pagan centurion? I will tell you already that it is the centurion of Capernaum who has opened the door of our faith for all of us by his example.[39]—On what does he place his entire certainty? On a word from Jesus.—Now, what is this strange thing, "the word" that, as you know, the Reformers spoke with such emphasis. "God's word forever shall abide," "Lord, keep us steadfast in your word."[40] We hope to understand this. What is usually expressed in a word, for example, of your parents? Your parents' thought or will.—Whose word is the only word that the Reformers talk about? The word of God, Jesus Christ.—What, therefore, is expressed in the word of God? The thought and the will of God.—Is the will of a person present in a word? Who then is present to us in the spiritual sense? The person.[41]—Who, then, is always present in Jesus' words? Jesus himself.—Of course, Jesus is not present bodily but spiritually, where his word is and where his will is heard. It is similar to our mothers being present in their words. You know that one feels this presence even when you do not see your mother. The matter becomes even more important for us, doesn't it, when we realize that in the words we are dealing with the thoughts and the will, yes, even with the person of our Lord Jesus and our God. Now we should probably try to discover where we can find such a "word." Where have all Christians throughout the centuries found such a word? In the Bible.—It is certainly true that a great deal is in the Bible, a great deal about God's thought and God's will, but one thought and will is of primary importance and is always referred to.—What kind of thought and

17:61

[37.] Posth: "Children?"

[38.] Posth: "Fantasy."

[39.] Posth: "Always too stilted for the children."

[40.] Citations from hymns of Martin Luther. See *Lutheran Book of Worship*, hymn 228, "A Mighty Fortress Is Our God," verse 4, and hymn 230, "Lord Keep Us Steadfast in Your Word," verse 1).

[41.] The passage "Your parents' thought or . . . The person" is underlined with wavy lines. Next to it is written, "Always so formal."

will of God is this? (If no answer is given, ask the following questions: "What do we call the part of the Bible that talks about Jesus?" The Gospels. And what does Gospel mean? Good news.—What is the good news about? That God wants to be our most loving father and that God wants to establish God's kingdom among us.—The previous question will be asked once more and the answer given immediately above will follow.) Now, a message can be valid for the present and the future.—What is it valid for in Christianity? For the present and the future.—What do we call a message concerning the future? A pledge and a promise. 17:62

Jesus gives us a promise in his word, which is that God will establish God's kingdom and rule through him. He also says, however, that God has already begun to do this. Of course, it will be completed only in eternity. God wants to be our loving father now, but we will see God only in eternity. Jesus calls to us, addresses us, speaks his word: "I want you, God wants to be your father." You see, you cannot confirm the truth of this promise in any way and you cannot prove it either. Several things even speak against it.—What attitude can we have toward such a word, a pledge, a message?

We can say, "Yes," and rely on it or say, "No," and reject it.[42] What do you call this type of "saying yes" and "trusting in it"? Faith.—What, therefore, is the only way that we can accept Jesus' word? By believing.—Word and faith belong together. But it is a necessary part of faith that you rely on the word even when much speaks against doing so. When the centurion spoke to Jesus and trusted completely in his word, there seemed to be a number of things that spoke against it, as some may have thought: "This centurion is a fool to rely on *one* word of Jesus." Now tell me, what does Jesus say to the centurion at the end of our story? He says, "Go, let it be done according to your faith."—What caused Jesus to say these words? The centurion's faith in his power.—And what happened to the centurion's servant? He became well in that same hour. You see, we have reached a point here where we have to stop thinking. Nothing helps here other than reverential silence and the acceptance of what is being told, or a frank "No." There is nothing in between. Naturalistic explanations do not help at all because the evangelist's story tells us of a deed which points to Jesus' power as the savior. Jesus' word becomes deed. "For he spoke, and it came to be; he commanded, and it stood firm."[43] Here our power has completely failed, and it does not make any sense to talk about it anymore. Whoever has ears can hear in this the source of eternity opening up and roaring powerfully. That person sees in 17:63

[42.] Posth marks the section "Jesus gives . . . reject it" and writes next to it "How much more vividly this could have been developed!"

[43.] Ps. 33:9. Pastor Posth writes in the margin, "Jesus?"

this a sign that God will fulfill the divine promise in time.[44] Whoever is deaf is not helped a great deal by thinking. May God give all of us ears to hear.

Today it is the case that we have nothing, nothing at all from Jesus except his word, his command, and his promise. Nowhere else can we understand Jesus, and that means understanding our God's will, than in his word, "I want you." Do we wish to hear it? Do we want to trust in such a word alone? Do we wish to risk building our whole lives on this word? There is one thing that is necessary in order to do this: valiant courage. This is the choice: either we risk placing our lives on Jesus' word or we are without hope[45]—for we have no other support than the word. No one proves to us that we are really God's children and that God's kingdom truly comes. The word says it, no one else. Or we stay with what we can see and feel and in our lives we rely on ourselves, our minds, and our energy. We have the choice. May God grant us the courage to risk resting our lives in God's word just as the centurion obeyed Jesus' word alone. Come, let us try it. Whoever has courage, come and serve the army of Christ, and by doing so serve the word. Lord, sustain us in your word! It's true, isn't it, that we now understand that the centurion of Capernaum has many very important things to tell us.

17:64   How is the centurion's relationship to Jesus different from the relationship of Jesus' Jewish followers to him? The Jews wanted to see in Jesus the bodily king of a worldly kingdom of God. The centurion saw in Jesus a powerful sovereign lord who ruled his spiritual kingdom through his word.[46]

Recognizing this, the words that Jesus now speaks to the Jews in vv. 10 and 11 become clear.—Who are the people who will come together from all the world to the eternal kingdom? The pagans.—And who are those who will be subject to harsh judgment? The Jews.—Why does Jesus emphatically give the pagans preference over the Jews? Because the pagans understood Jesus better than the Jews.—In what respect did the pagans understand Jesus better? They knew that Jesus' kingdom was a kingdom of his word and our faith, which goes to all the world[47] not a kingdom in which Jesus would physically lead Israel to dominion over the world.—When must the Jews' hope have collapsed? When they saw Jesus dying on the cross.—The pagan's hope could not fall to pieces at this point. No, it is especially at this point that it became powerful, as you all know. Now you also understand what I said to you earlier. In what respect is it that the centurion of Capernaum opened the door of faith to us for the first time? In that he trusted completely in Jesus' word and thus overcame all temporality.[48]

[44.] Posth: "All of this for 14-year-old children?"

[45.] Posth marks the section "Nowhere else . . . on Jesus' word" and comments "Ask questions!"

[46.] Posth: "Does the catechist believe that he will get this kind of an answer?"

[47.] Posth marks the section "Because the pagans . . . all the world."

[48.] Posth: "Children?"

On what did the Jews base their claim to participate in the kingdom of God?[49] On their Jewish heritage.—They were descended from Abraham and had received Moses' law. They believed that this gave them priority over everyone else.—On what did this claim collapse?[50] On Jesus' word and on the way in which Jesus proclaimed and understood the kingdom of God.

There are no claims on God, either by Jews or by pagans. There is, however, obedient listening to the word, which is the power of the kingdom. It 17:65 expands our perspective of our story to take in the whole world. It is the word that holds the eternal kingdom together and rules it. To set our whole lives upon the word, to listen to God's thoughts and to do them—that is the faith that was not found in Israel. This is the faith for which the centurion of Capernaum remains a shining example. This faith is the victory that has conquered the world. Pay attention, remain in faith, be valiant and be strong![51]

[49.] Posth: "You could have asked this question much more elegantly!"

[50.] Marked out.

[51.] Posth's final remarks: "In spite of all of the erudition, it will only have meager application to the hearts of children!" The complete evaluation of the catechesis can be found above in 1/114:183–87.

HANS PFEIFER

EDITOR'S AFTERWORD
TO THE GERMAN EDITION

In *Fiction from Tegel Prison* Dietrich Bonhoeffer himself had put into words his legacy from childhood. In that work a member of the proletariat describes the privileges of a son from a well-off family. "People like you have a foundation; you have ground under your feet; you have a place in the world. There are things you take for granted, that you stand up for, and for which you are willing to put your head on the line, because you know that your roots go so deep that they will sprout new growth again."[1] In the home of Bonhoeffer's parents the 'deep-lying roots' of the traditions of two families were intertwined, participating fully in the formative cultural richness offered by the previous centuries. Members of this family saw themselves as "guardians of a great historical inheritance and intellectual heritage,"[2] which included the liberal thinking formative of the revolutionary movement for human rights. Several members of both families had taken part in this movement and had to accept the consequences for having done so.[3] Bonhoeffer was indebted to his parents' home for a "certainty of judgment and manner that cannot be acquired in one generation."[4] The sixteen-year-old gave evidence of this decisiveness in his response to the murder of Rathenau, which he condemned with disgust.[5] A fellow schoolmate remembered this event because, he said, "I was surprised at that time that someone could know so exactly where he stood."[6]

[1.] *FP* (*DBWE* 7):68.
[2.] *LPP* 294 [trans. altered].
[3.] *DB-ER* 11–12.
[4.] *DB-ER* 13.
[5.] See above, 1/27:49.
[6.] *DB-ER* 33.

His father was largely responsible for the fact that this heritage did not simply harden into mere convention. The neighborhood children—and certainly often his own—felt "totally unraveled" by the elder Bonhoeffer's judgment, even if at the same time they also felt "understood in a kindly way."[7] Naturally the young Bonhoeffer did not refer directly to this "self-evident fact" in his letters, but when the student in the sixth form refuses to use "terribly longwinded phrases" in a German essay,[8] one sees the enduring influence of his father's example. This influence not only gave Bonhoeffer a decided advantage over his schoolmates and his fellow students but also served him well in his studies when it came time to analyze theological ideas with independence and impartiality (see below).

Parents and children in the Bonhoeffer household were unified by the expectation that the family was and would remain the deciding factor in the way the children were raised. Bonhoeffer continued to profess this view even when in prison.[9] The responsibility for the daily management of the maturing children lay in the hands of their mother. In Breslau she taught the younger children herself, and in the first years they lived in Berlin she allowed them to be taught at home by Ms. Käthe Horn.[10] In later years, when the children were on trips, she awaited their reports. The Bonhoeffer brothers and sisters were always sure daily to send her a short note or at least to telephone. It is in this context that the letters of this volume can best be understood. They contain reports about many ordinary events. For example, Bonhoeffer, among other things, writes about collecting mushrooms, about a forest fire, about the crash of an airplane, about a visit to a Roman Catholic church, as well as church, his impressions of nature during an excursion on the Brocken.[11]

We will discuss the journey to Italy below. But he also mentioned the most important political events, as well as the concrete problems that arose due to the war or the period of inflation, and the difficulties that their grandmother had with her underhanded landlord.[12] It goes without saying that this served primarily to give the expected information about the children's well-being. At the same time, however, it served to form the background from which their mother could shoulder her responsibility for her children. She expended an unusual amount of effort to fulfill this task. When Dietrich

---

[7.] "The House on Wangenheimstraße" by Emmi Bonhoeffer, née Delbrück, *FP* 135 [trans. altered].

[8.] See above, 1/18:000; cf. *LPP* 275 and the letter from Robert Held, to whom Dietrich Bonhoeffer openly conveyed this attitude (1/89:38).

[9.] *LPP* 295f.

[10.] Cf. above, 1/1:20, editorial note 8.

[11.] Cf. above, 1/16:35f.

[12.] Cf. above, 1/42:65f.

concerned himself with Troeltsch and Barth, she read articles by them[13] in order to give him good advice during his university years. When the question arose about the subject of his doctorate, she wrote to him, "I keep wondering whether you shouldn't write a history of doctrine thesis under Holl."[14]

It would never have occurred to Bonhoeffer to find this patronizing, since his parents only gave advice; it was their son who had to make the final decision, and it could be a different one from what they had advised. So he could write with confidence, "I'll stay with him in any case. I proposed a subject to him that is half-historical and half-systematic. He readily agreed with it."[15]

II

Bonhoeffer grew up in an academic section of Grunewald, that is, his parents' home was not located in anonymous, inconsequential surroundings. Perhaps nothing more characterized the atmosphere of the neighborhood than the fact that four of his siblings found spouses from among their friends in this area of the city.[16] Along with all the differences[17] there was in this neighborhood a common intellectual, political, and ethical attitude that went far beyond mere physical proximity. Eberhard Bethge described this by using the example of a soirée at the Delbrück's home.[18] The letters allow one to recognize just how important were the friendships with the neighborhood children, the school friends, and the fellow students in confirmation class. Even what one often hears about joint excursions, especially about hiking during vacations,[19] is a description of the establishment of a mutual trust and common attitude that certainly can be considered among the most important prerequisites for a conspiracy against the Nazi regime. Moreover, it is significant for this milieu that a considerable number of these friends had to emigrate after 1933, because they were subject to the race laws, while, on the other hand, not a few of them took active part in the resistance and were persecuted because of it.[20] In an aside, let it be noted that Bonhoeffer's fellow fraternity brother Theodor Pfizer during his semester in Berlin

617

[13.] See above, 1/92:147f.

[14.] Ibid.

[15.] See above, 1/93:148.

[16.] Karl-Friedrich Bonhoeffer married Margarete von Dohnanyi, Klaus married Emmi Delbrück, Christine married Hans von Dohnanyi, and Sabine married Gerhard Leibholz.

[17.] On this see Emmi Bonhoeffer, "The House on Wangenheimstraße," in *FP* 133f.

[18.] *DB-ER* 29.

[19.] Compare especially the extensive tour of the Bodensee (see above, 1/29:51f., and others).

[20.] Among others mentioned in *DBWE* 9, Gerhard Leibholz with his family, their neighbor Maria Weigert, their friends Bärbel Hildebrandt and Anneliese Schnurmann, Felix and Mary Gilbert and their cousin Lotte Leubuscher, all had to emigrate. In addition

found the Bonhoeffer house a "refuge"—a word that took on deeper meaning with the emergence of the Nazi regime. There was substance in these homes that was not easy to destroy. The childhood years shared with siblings and friends effected a strength of character that led to Bonhoeffer being sought out as a friend, becoming the center of a circle of university friends, and being a mentor and adviser for his students. These experiences, however, also taught him how to value community.

618

Politically, the Bonhoeffer family was fairly down to earth. It is remarkable how little resentment is found in Bonhoeffer's school essay "Germany's Situation before the World War."[21] It is true that at first the names of the new political leaders of the republic led to spontaneous protest by Bonhoeffer. "It surely is absurd that Scheidemann is Minister-President and Ebert should be the Provisional President."[22] Soon, however, one can sense a level of acceptance. The radical right-wing murders are condemned[23] in exactly the same way as is the [communist] Spartacus rebellion.[24] His judgment during the difficult crisis in November 1923 is noteworthy: "Everyone is just waiting for the moment when Ludendorff will pull off the matter with more effective support, i.e., the support of the Imperial Army. This is the complete opposite opinion of all the people up at the [Hedgehog] house, who want to murder Ludendorff. Today it seems that everyone is stirred up in one direction or other."[25] In this intellectual climate of liberality, moderation, and openness to the world, there was no room for fanaticism or resentment, nor for any type of prejudice that stems from unwillingness to take responsibility for the less fortunate. His friend and later brother-in-law Leibholz had Jewish forebears. This is not mentioned, because it was considered unimportant in their relationship. When a cousin refused to go on a hiking trip with their Jewish friend Anneliese Schnurmann, his sister Susanna asked, a bit derisively, "Could his parents be against it because they are anti-Semitic?"[26] The conscious anti-Semitism of these years found no resonance in this climate. Bonhoeffer also approached Roman Catholicism in a remarkably unprejudiced

to immediate members of the family—Hans von Dohnanyi, Klaus Bonhoeffer, and Rüdiger Schleicher—the conspiracy against Hitler was to draw in the future husband of his classmate Marion Winter, Peter Count Yorck von Wartenburg, Bonhoeffer's confirmation classmate Hans Bernd von Haeften, his brother Werner, and, of course, Dietrich Bonhoeffer himself. These seven were actively involved in the conspiracy and all were executed. The number of persons involved in the resistance was, of course, greater and cannot be completely listed here.

[21.] See above, 2/1:191–97.

[22.] See above, 1/10:28.

[23.] See above, 1/27:49f.

[24.] See above, 1/9:27, including editorial note 2.

[25.] See above, letter 1/50:75.

[26.] See above, 1/101:171. The following report from Werner Milch about confirmation classes he shared with Bonhoeffer reveals something of the latter's position on anti-

manner, which was just as unusual in Berlin during that era. Without the
ecumenical openness with which he began his trip to Italy, he would never   619
have had the formative experience he did in the ecclesiastical city of Rome
(see below).

Although we see in those accounts the image of an especially privileged
youth full of intellectual ideas, this should not mislead us, for during the war
and during the period of high inflation everyone's financial situation was
highly precarious. A festive meal was rare during the war.[27] And not only
was it difficult to allow one's son to study for two semesters away from one's
hometown, but also during the era of high inflation, purchasing books—or
even shoelaces and cheese—could be a noteworthy event.[28] Only if one for
a moment ignores his grandmother's difficulties and anxieties in her old
age about being able to pay the rent[29]—and who therefore was invited by
Bonhoeffer's parents to move from Tübingen to Berlin—can one say that
these periods of material scarcity had no lasting impact on these children.

Problems arose for Bonhoeffer in other relationships. It was never easy for
him to establish himself with respect to his older brothers. This is expressed
in a singular note, "Even as a boy he had enjoyed imagining himself on his
deathbed, surrounded by everyone who loved him, and to whom he now had
to say his final words."[30] He had the feeling that he had to fight for recognition and for room for his own development.[31] His father's unimpeach-
able judgment, and the not very gentle critique of his brothers, had an
impact on his behavior. He was always deliberately self-controlled in his letters. If he was not quite sure of an impression or an experience, then he was
more comfortable keeping it to himself. This becomes especially evident
when one compares his diary with his letters from Italy. The diary is full of
spontaneous ideas and thoughts, for example, about fantasy and reality,[32]   620
about art,[33] and about Catholicism and Protestantism[34] that do not occur
in his letters. This becomes most clear in his reticence to express feelings that
were out of the ordinary, for example, during the time the brothers Klaus
and Dietrich spent in Africa. This adventure left its mark on Dietrich. It had
been a shock and an experience completely foreign to him, which he did not
know how to process. On the return trip to Sicily he wrote, "For the first time,

---

Semitism, "When Pastor Priebe asked a question about original sin, Bonhoeffer answered
without hesitating: 'anti-Semitism'!" (Milch, "Werner Milch über Manfred Resa," 31).

  [27.] See above, 1/1:19.
  [28.] See above, 1/35:58f. and 1/44:68.
  [29.] See above, 1/42:65f.
  [30.] *GS* 6: 232, *DBW* 11:373.
  [31.] Cf. *LPP* 386–87.
  [32.] See above, 1/57:95.
  [33.] See above, 1/57:103.
  [34.] See above, 1/57:88f., 90f., and 106.

one was able to breathe freely again. It was as if fetters had been removed from our limbs,"[35] and, "Soon, however, real reinforcement through extensive study will be necessary in order to avert the catastrophe [in one's own consciousness], because what one had seen was enormous."[36] Nothing of this can be seen in the letters except for a small hint to his twin sister, Sabine.[37] He felt much freer to express himself to his grandmother in Tübingen, who consequently becomes one of the most important correspondents of his youth. At her funeral he would say about her, "She had time, patience, and counsel, always and for everything. And although she entered wholly into the lives of each, still her judgment and counsel always came out of a broad perspective on whatever was at hand, out of an incomparable knowledge about all human affairs, and out of a great love."[38] It would be ridiculous to argue that there was conflict between Bonhoeffer and his parents' home. In prison he testifies to the contrary, "Most people have forgotten nowadays what a home can mean, though some of us have come to realize it as never before. It is a kingdom of its own in the midst of the world, a stronghold amid life's storms and stresses, a refuge, even a sanctuary."[39] He nonetheless needed to find elbowroom for the search for his own path— room also beyond his family circle.

621

Bonhoeffer was able to absorb new ideas almost without limit, and he had a great need to do so. Walking tours and trips were important to him, as they certainly were for the youth movement.[40] His reports about his experiences on his trips are among the most lively and vivid descriptions in his letters. These trips enabled him to encounter the unknown outside of the family circle, which is certainly not an unusual way to discover the extraordinary. For this reason the trip to Italy is among the most important experiences of these years. The announcement itself was filled with excitement: "the most fabulous thing that could happen to me."[41] "But reality is, quite certainly, more beautiful than fantasy,"[42] he wrote in his first reports. He experienced his return as a decisive break, "and then took the fateful steps over the Italian border [Grenze]."[43] He was practically entranced by the land, the art, and the church. It is therefore, not accidental that his statement, "I think I'm

---

[35.] See above, 1/57:98.

[36.] See above, 1/57:101.

[37.] *NL*, Appendix A 1–6, 5 (6).

[38.] *TF* 270.

[39.] *LPP* 44.

[40.] Bonhoeffer loved and took part in the practices of the youth movement, but already by 1925 "he didn't like it anymore" (letter of August 10, 1985, from Robert Held to Hans Pfeifer).

[41.] See above, 1/54:78.

[42.] See above, 1/57:83.

[43.] See above, 1/80:129.

beginning to understand the concept of 'church',"[44] was written in Italy, rather than after having visited a congregation in Berlin. It is not by chance that Carl Friedrich von Weizsäcker labeled Bonhoeffer's life as a "a journey to reality."[45]

III

Bonhoeffer's announcement that he wanted to study theology came as a surprise to his schoolmates and his teachers.[46] For a long time he was undecided as to whether it would be a better idea to study music.[47] We have no   622
direct witnesses about the reasons for his final decision. Space limitations, moreover, prevent us from documenting the schoolboy's first attempts at theological discourse, intriguing as this would be. In an essay on Julian the Apostate he seems to be thinking of his own situation when he describes two vocations that were difficult to reconcile but at the same time important to him: the ideal of a congenial military leader and that of a religious reformer.[48] At the same time, the early death of the Roman Emperor Julian gave him the opportunity to come to terms with the death of his brother Walter. In his paper on Euripides' philosophy, written as part of his final exams for graduation from high school, he argued—under the influence of his philosophy professor, a Nietzsche scholar—that ethics as grounded in the philosophy of religion was the answer to radical skepticism.[49] In his earliest semesters it seemed that he concentrated primarily on problems of philosophy of religion, as letters from his friend Wilhelm Dreier demonstrate.[50]

[44.] See above, 1/57:89.

[45.] Von Weizsäcker, "Thoughts of a Non-Theologian on Dietrich Bonhoeffer's Theological Development."

[46.] See GS 6:229, DBW 11:369ff. Bonhoeffer's godfather Hans von Hase wrote about this in a family circular-letter ("Family Circular-Letter" no. 16) dated March 20, 1923: "It will also interest you that Dietrich Bonhoeffer received his school graduation certificate and definitely wants to study theology. He would like to become an academic and brings good qualifications to this task. So once again the old tradition breaks through. In addition to the image of his grandfather and great-grandfather, he has probably been influenced by Harnack, who knows him from the neighborhood and advises him." In July 1986 Hans Christoph von Hase writes about this: "I still remember his visit to us in the parsonage in Waldau as he [Bonhoeffer] displayed great interest when he was shown my father's library. In it could be found many examples of books personally owned by my great-grandfather Karl August (von) Hase. My father gave him a whole series of books to be used as his personal library at the university. At that time the old tomes did not interest me in the least."

[47.] See above, 1/36:60.

[48.] NL A 5, 1 (3).

[49.] NL A 5, 1 (4); Bonhoeffer's philosophy teacher Martin Havenstein published a book Nietzsche als Erzieher.

[50.] See above, 1/81:131f. and 1/83:133f.

The only theologian from Tübingen who continued to be important to him was Adolf Schlatter. He later distanced himself from Karl Heim, whom he initially found very interesting.[51] The philosophical seminars of Groos, which he attended both semesters, were important for him.

623   Otherwise the letters from Tübingen demonstrate that he spent as much time at the house of the Hedgehog fraternity as he did in the lecture rooms. In becoming a Hedgehog he was simply following his father's example: "I took the customary step for every dutiful son and became a Hedgehog."[52] Bonhoeffer took a fencing course ("never a problem for Dietrich")[53] as well as dance lessons given at the Hedgehog. Robert Held tells us, "I still remember very clearly the grace and the musicality with which Dietrich Bonhoeffer always danced, especially the folk dances and the elegant country dances."[54] At the house he played the piano and sang songs to the lute from the Zupfgeigenhansl. He found the specific demands of fraternity life, that is, the visits to the "Venerables," a bit tedious and annoying, but he did not question them.[55] The Hedgehog fraternity, to which he felt associated, was what was called a "black" fraternity, meaning that it was a reformed fraternity that did not wear colors and "was, at that time, in good form and attractive."[56] The fact that "the Hedgehog fraternity and really all of the other fraternities are going in full strength"[57] was an important argument for Bonhoeffer's participation in the brief military training course. The true importance of the Hedgehog can be seen in a coterie of close friends, who made him the center of a circle with whom he could discuss things and go hiking.[58]

As a schoolboy Bonhoeffer did not want to attend a party of his friends because Lent had begun (*DB-ER* 37). Early on—for example, with the professors in Tübingen—he was interested in the question of the Christian life, that is, of discipleship (also see above, 3/6). During his Italian trip this issue

624   surfaced in a particular way. The dogmatic and apologetic discussions he had with the Catholic theologian Platte-Platenius did not make any impression on Bonhoeffer. "Catholic dogma veils every ideal thing in Catholicism, without knowing that this is what it is doing. There is a huge difference between

---

[51.] Cf. *GS* 3:138ff., *DBW* 12 (2.5): 213–31.

[52.] See above, 1/36:60.

[53.] Letter dated August 10, 1985, from Robert Held to Hans Pfeifer.

[54.] Ibid. A warning issued by Held to the editor of the German edition of this volume also belongs here. "Don't present my young Dietrich as someone who is too serious and ponderous! He had a radiant light and a joy with life that dominated his personality, at least in his younger years" (letter of September 9, 1985).

[55.] Concurring report from Theodor Pfizer and Robert Held.

[56.] Letter of Robert Held dated August 10, 1985, to Hans Pfeifer.

[57.] See above, 1/45:69.

[58.] The letters of Robert Held, Walter Dreier, and Theodor Pfizer support this.

confession and dogmatic teachings about confession—unfortunately also between 'church' and the 'church' in dogmatics."[59] In contrast, when he followed a worship service with the Missal in his hands, he could say, "For the most part the texts are wonderfully poetic and lucid. Every text flows from the main theme of the Mass: the sacrificial death and its continuous reenactment in the sacrificial Mass of communion."[60] "It was almost indescribable" and "worship in the true sense. The whole thing gave one an unparalleled impression of profound, guileless piety."[61] But he rejected Catholic theology's symbolic interpretation of the Mass.[62] In these worship services he suspected—probably for the first time—the identity of a reality that exists in faith, and one that exists concretely.[63] Even though this experience was not based on theological reflection, it nevertheless made such a great impression on him that it became the focal point of his orientation from then on.

In Berlin, Bonhoeffer studied the works of Max Weber and Ernst Troeltsch on the sociology of religion, and he often discussed them with his friend Robert Held.[64] On the doctrine of the church, he was first influenced by the academic theology he encountered in Berlin. Clearer than is evident from his letters, Bonhoeffer was also interested in the social question as addressed, for example, by Siegmund-Schultze's study group on social issues on the east side of Berlin.[65] In addition, his literary estate contains summaries prepared for him by Bertha Schulze, the senior student in Harnack's seminar, on the issues of the relationship between the Protestant and Roman Catholic churches as well as the workers' movement.[66] In his first two semesters at Berlin, Bonhoeffer's interest revolved around the theme "The Church and the Social Question." It appears that temporarily he was here seeking the possibility of a legitimation of Christianity. It is certain that his interest was many-sided. He read Schleiermacher and Husserl,[67] but the subject of church took on a special importance. In his first seminar paper, he specified that one of the two important Christian themes of 1 Clement is "the ἐκκλησία τοῦ θεοῦ. Everyone is united in a fellowship. The work within this and beyond this (1:2) is Christianity."[68]

625

[59.] See above, 1/57:93.
[60.] See above, 1/61:111.
[61.] See above, 1/57:88f.
[62.] Ibid.
[63.] See the quote from Joachim von Soosten, below, page 573, editorial note 84.
[64.] Letter from Robert Held of August 10, 1985, to Hans Pfeifer.
[65.] Ibid.
[66.] *NL* A 10,11 (1)–(4).
[67.] See above, 1/82:133.
[68.] See above, 2/4:241.

IV

The summer semester of 1925 began a first decisive stage in Bonhoeffer's orientation for his future studies. He wrote two long seminar papers, got to know the Swabian theologian Widmann, and at the beginning of vacation came to an agreement with Reinhold Seeberg about his doctoral dissertation. Widmann met him in Karl Holl's seminar. The first recognizable and profound theological stimulus that affected Bonhoeffer came from these two: Holl introduced him to an approach to Luther's theology and Widmann to dialectical theology. His mother was acutely aware of this situation. She expressed surprise at the fact that Dietrich did not want to do his doctoral work under Holl and, at the same time, asked him to send her Barth's collection of articles, *The Word of God and the Word of Man,* so that she could read it.[69] Bonhoeffer wrote his paper "Luther's Feelings about His Work"[70] under Holl, in which he summarized and expanded on Holl's article "Luther's Judgment of Himself."[71] In this paper Holl developed the idea of the "consciousness of being an instrument" for Luther's perception of himself. He wrote, "Every Christian who had found unity with God through justification could and must feel it, too."[72] Bonhoeffer refers to this when he writes, "God works in and through us, i.e., the work that 'we' do is God's work"[73] and, "In spite of the most emphatic pessimism about the world, his characteristic inner religious certainty remains intact—a fact we can't forget."[74] This is also the case in light of massive self-criticism. "Luther believed he was the worst of all sinners and felt truly unworthy of the great proclamation. Nevertheless, no one would ever be worthy of the task of proclaiming God's word. It is too great even for the angels. If one were to follow this premise, then Christ could never be proclaimed on this earth."[75] With this, theology at once gained an existential meaning for him, even though in his own introspection he was unsure of his motives for studying theology. The thoughts "Who then speaks . . . my faith? My vanity? . . . God . . . I want to study theology" are written in a self-critical report.[76]

A further aspect of Luther's theology is important to him; he later referred to it several times and called it a sign of good theology when this thought was held fast:[77] "The entire history of the world is to be seen under the aspect of this battle between gospel and devil. This was especially true in

---

[69.] See above, 1/92:148.

[70.] See above, 2/5:257ff.

[71.] Cf. Holl, *Luther,* 381–419; translated as "Martin Luther on Luther."

[72.] Holl, "Martin Luther on Luther," 31.

[73.] See above, 2/5:260.

[74.] See above, 2/5:280.

[75.] See above, 2/5:261.

[76.] *GS* 6:232; *DBW* 11 (2/21):372; *DB-ER* 41.

[77.] See above, pages 263 and 320.

this final crisis that had emerged as the gospel was proclaimed anew, i.e., in Luther's work."[78] With this emphasis on Luther's apocalyptic understanding of history, Bonhoeffer separates himself from all optimistic theology of progress, which was represented in Berlin in different ways. At this point the problem of the legitimacy of theological statements came to the fore for the young Bonhoeffer. It seems obvious to suspect here the influence of Widmann and of dialectical theology.

627

The second paper of this semester treats the relationship of the word of God and historical-critical research.[79] Here Bonhoeffer directly espouses the interests of dialectical theology. He writes, "Christian religion stands or falls with the belief in a historical and perceptibly real divine revelation, a revelation that those who have eyes to see can see and those who have ears to hear can hear."[80] "The first statement of spiritual interpretation is that the Bible is not only a word about God but God's word itself."[81] If, in accepting Luther's "knowledge of being an instrument" he was interested in authentically legitimizing the existence of theologians, here he strives to establish the same type of legitimization for theology as such. Seeberg was not especially happy with this paper, as can be seen in his notes in the margin. He gave it a poor grade.[82] A certain distance from Karl Barth's theology is nonetheless evident. Bonhoeffer tried to avoid a paradoxical situation to which the dialectical theology of the twenties could lead. If Barth wanted to hold fast to the sovereignty of the word of God in every case over against all historical reality as well as over against the written word in the Bible, he had to address the question of how to avoid the danger of completely removing revelation from historical reality, because in this case revelation could only be demonstrated dialectically. Did not the danger exist, as Bonhoeffer formulated in his outline of the paper on Luther, that the existence of a theologian would be divided into an earthly being and a "heavenly double"?[83] "From its very beginning, Bonhoeffer's theology is informed by the conviction that the truth which is believed must have a concrete locus within the reality of the world."[84] That the theologians in Berlin wanted to hold fast to the concrete demonstration of divine truth in history impressed him; that in doing so they lost credibility because of their historical-theological or ethical optimism led Bonhoeffer to agree with Barth's critique.

628

[78.] See above, 2/5:263, and cf. 2/9:320.

[79.] See above, 2/6:285ff.

[80.] See above, 2/6:285.

[81.] See above, 2/6:287.

[82.] Cf. above, 2/6:286, editorial notes 12 and 14; 2/6:287, editorial note 19; and 2/6:299, editorial note 101.

[83.] See above, 2/10:343.

[84.] Joachim von Soosten in the "Editor's Afterword" to *SC* (*DBWE*):291–92.

In the summer of 1925, Bonhoeffer found himself in a mediating theological position between Barth and the Berlin theologians. His unwillingness simply to attach himself to Barth is demonstrated in the fact that, despite the advice of his cousin Christoph von Hase, he did not want to go to Göttingen to study under Barth. His mother was not the only one who was surprised that he chose Seeberg as his doctoral adviser. He had the possibility of choosing among different professors. On the basis of his paper on Clement, Harnack wanted to have him as a doctoral student. And, as Bonhoeffer's speech at Harnack's funeral demonstrates, his respect for the great multidimensional historian remained unbroken.[85] However, he considered Harnack's foundation of theology in the "holy spirit of Christianity"[86] too optimistic and incompatible with Luther's theology of history.

It is even harder to understand why he chose not to do his doctoral work under Holl. An observation might be helpful at this point. Since the winter semester of 1925/26, the third article of faith had become the central theme of his seminar papers, and one would not be wrong in placing his dissertation in this context. Several reasons can be found for his interest in the Holy Spirit, in the church, and in eschatology. The concrete presence of God in history can be not only christologically based, i.e., through the doctrine of revelation and from the holy word. To a greater degree it takes on other forms in history, "God the Father, in God's majesty, sends the Son and the Holy Spirit as gifts (in the larger meaning of the word!) . . ."[87] The Holy Spirit works not only in each individual Christian but in the church. This is "God's mask [larva]."[88] This means that one must have faith in the church: "Therefore the credo ecclesiam."[89] Holl could also speak in this way. But when we read in Holl, "In the same way as it [the church] is created from above through Christ and his word, it is reborn from below through the inner feeling of the communion of the faithful,[90] he is leading up to a "reconstruction of morality."[91] Bonhoeffer, however, in complete agreement with Barth, could not accept this moral optimism.[92] The church needed a more fundamental theological basis.

He found the best point of departure for a work on the church in Seeberg's dogmatics, even though he did not agree with him that the church

629

[85.] *NRS* 29–31.
[86.] *NRS* 31. This is Bonhoeffer's formulation.
[87.] See above, 2/10:368.
[88.] See above, 2/5:261, footnote 17 and editorial note 19.
[89.] See above, 2/10:365, and cf. 2/9:315f.
[90.] Holl, *Luther*, 322.
[91.] Holl, *Luther*, 155–287, especially 250f.
[92.] See above, 3/5:470.

would, in the course of history, develop into the kingdom of God.[93] Nonetheless, in Seeberg's anthropology the notion can be found that being human is grounded not only in "historicity" but also in "sociality." Bonhoeffer believed that he found in this sociality the true place of revelation and the human community based on it. "The more one considers the significance of the sociological category for theology, the more clearly has emerged the social intention of all basic Christian concepts."[94] With this he was able finally to bridge the gap between the theology of revelation and tangible concrete reality. For him the doctrine of the Holy Spirit and the social nature of human beings, founded in creation, were mediating concepts. And this is precisely the area that he addressed in his dissertation.

It is not our intention here to speak of the remarkable feat that Bonhoeffer accomplished in *Sanctorum Communio.*[95] It is sufficient to point to the fact that he was aware of the limits of the work from its inception. He found it necessary to assert that God is fully present in the "sanctorum communio." If God in the divine revelation of Jesus Christ is and allows himself to be identified with a concrete historical person, then the same must be true for the presence of the Holy Spirit in the church. For the sake of the unity of the triune God, one cannot weaken at this point. "The introduction of the concept of potentiality in the *Christian* concept of God means a limitation of divine omnipotence."[96] With this thought, taken from Schleiermacher's *The Christian Faith*,[97] he positions himself in confrontation with Barth as well as Seeberg. He therefore substantiates his doctrine of the church in a very independent manner. To a certain extent he comes at the same time into conflict with eschatology. He was aware of this, and this is why he writes in his Graduation Theses, "The identification of 'being in Christ' and 'being in the church-community' are in Paul in unresolved contradiction with his concept of Christ in heaven."[98] It may be that this is the reason why he occupied himself so intensively during the year 1926 with eschatology. Under Luther's influence he did not want to lessen the importance of eschatology in any way whatsoever. But if God is present in full actuality in the church,[99] then it is truly difficult to retain the distinctive theological sense of the doctrine of the future of God. Bonhoeffer did not solve this problem during his university years. With his dissertation he stands before us, not as a systematic theologian who has a full-blown dogmatics, but as a theologian who has created a start-

630

[93.] Cf. Seeberg, *Christliche Dogmatik*, 2:348: "The church is therefore the kingdom of God on earth built upon the foundation of the new covenant."

[94.] *SC* (*DBWE* 1):21.

[95.] On this see Joachim von Soosten, "Editor's Afterword," in *SC* (*DBWE* 1):290ff.

[96.] See above, 2/16:440.

[97.] See above, 2/16:440, editorial note 11.

[98.] See above, 2/16:440.

[99.] *SC* (*DBWE* 1):157ff.

ing point for his own theological path and a concrete engagement with ecclesial reality.

631   V

This presentation is incomplete without referring to the Part 3 of Bonhoeffer's writings in this volume. The church consistory expected that the students who took its exams could prove that they had taken part in the life of the church.[100] For Bonhoeffer this was anything other than a bothersome expectation. He enthusiastically devoted himself fully to the children's worship services in his congregation. This is shown by the very elementary introduction that he chose for the first of his addresses, recollecting his own childhood. This is evident from the role that the "house" plays, which then becomes synonymous with "castle" and further evident in the examples of playing soldiers, his relationship to his younger sisters (wherein his youngest sister, Mrs. Susanne Dreß, recognized herself), and of course also in examples from his school days. The questions that can be reconstructed from Widmann's answers are noteworthy. Can one discuss anything with children? (See on this Widmann's fine reference to Dostoyevsky.)[101]Must one be a good pedagogue in order to hold children's worship services? Should children's worship services lead to religious conversations with the children? How does one tell the biblical story to children? How should the children's sermon end, full of feeling and emotion? Should one worry about being "successful" with children? How does one react if children from another group want to switch over into one's own group? Widmann's answers in each case are noteworthy as well.[102] Bonhoeffer called upon his sister Susanne to help him in his work, for which, to their mother's surprise,[103] she was ready to return early from her vacation. Together they took the children on outings.[104] When after confirmation the group became too old for the children's worship service, Bonhoeffer founded the "Thursday Circle" for them, even while he was in the middle of preparing for his doctoral and ecclesial exams.[105] In his meditations he did not shy away from speaking to the children directly and forcefully: "Now if we love our mother that much, shouldn't we love even more the One who gave us everything—our mother and our house, our work, and our holidays?"[106] Or, "At that moment it will be the last time the Lord Jesus knocks at our door; and this time it will be so loud that no

632

[100.] Cf. above, 1/109:179.
[101.] See above, 1/96:155.
[102.] Ibid.
[103.] See above, 1/99:165.
[104.] *DB-ER* 91–92.
[105.] *DB-ER* 94–95 and above, 3/13:524.
[106.] See above, 3/2:459.

one can sleep through it. This is the moment when we die."[107] Or, "No picture is adequate to depict for us the extent of joy that will be there, when we see God and our Lord Jesus face-to-face and rejoice in their service.[108]

In this practical work, Bonhoeffer found his own style of interacting with the children, which they appreciated. Meanwhile his professors sometimes rather severely criticized his composition of the catechetical lessons for their seminars. The discrepancy between the corrections of his written catechetical exam papers and the actual handling of his class is noteworthy. Whereas the evaluator of the paper wrote, "The application would not touch the children's hearts . . . [because it is] often so patently doctrinal that the children would be bored,"[109] after seeing the catechetical lesson taught, Superintendent Diestel writes, "Bonhoeffer teaches with a great deal of liveliness. He captivates the children."[110]

At the same time, the catechetical and homiletic pieces in Part 3 are an important mirror of Bonhoeffer's own theological development. The first addresses from the year 1926 are defined very clearly by Luther's theology, which he learned from Holl. Here we encounter the concept of duty transformed into joy, "fear in the face of the majesty of God."[111] In the sermons preached at the same time, Barth's influence can be seen more clearly. Here he can also be critical of Holl, when he rejects "reconstruction of morality" as a theological error.[112] Luther also is well represented in the later children's-worship sermons, and it is worthy of note that it is Luther's "consciousness of being an instrument" that comes to the fore.[113] On the other hand, during the year 1926 Bonhoeffer's interest in the problem of eschatology, with which he struggles in his academic papers, is more evident than earlier was the case (see above). In the children's church address preached on All Saints' Day, present and future eschatology are found juxtaposed but disconnected.[114] He did not find this subject easy to address, as the substantial revisions of this address demonstrate. But the academic problematic finally—here this is especially evident—fades into the background, losing its importance in relation to the message proclaimed. In the papers on practical theology the future themes of Bonhoeffer's theology begin to emerge. It

633

[107.] See above, 3/9:505.

[108.] See above, 3/9:509.

[109.] See above, 1/114:186.

[110.] Ibid.

[111.] Holl, *Luther,* iv.

[112.] See above, 3/5:470f.

[113.] See above, 3/11:514ff. and 3/12:519f.

[114.] Compare 3/9:503f., above, with 3/9:505f.; one must to some extent agree with Bethge's correction of Martin Honecker's criticism that Bonhoeffer's lacked an adequate understanding of eschatology (cf. *DB-ER* 87).

is especially significant to see in this light his seminar's catechetical lesson on discipleship.[115]

Under the impression of the later direct encounter with Karl Barth and the subsequent Church Struggle, Bonhoeffer's own judgment of his university years in Berlin was a critical one.[116] Only in prison did he begin to correct aspects of this view. "Continuity with one's own past is a great gift, too."[117] When one reads Bonhoeffer's early texts, one must respect his later critical distance as well as his awareness of continuity. Only from the interrelation of the two can one find the key to an understanding that is fair to these texts. It appears to this editor that continuity and change not only are a meaningful criterion in viewing the relationship between the early and the late Bonhoeffer, but also are important time and again in every phase of his life, thereby presenting a significant key to understanding his entire work.

634

[115.] See above, 3/6:476ff.
[116.] Cf. *NRS* 20f. and *DB-ER* 157–59.
[117.] *LPP* 276.

APPENDICES

636

APPENDIX 1.
DATING THE MANUSCRIPTS

THE BASIS FOR DATING THE *larger works* in this volume (reports, seminar papers, sermons, and catechetical lessons) rests mainly on Bonhoeffer's own statements, his study books, and university syllabi. In this way all such texts can be dated with great certainty. Dating the *notes*, however, must remain in the area of probability when a terminus ad quem cannot be determined from a remark made by Bonhoeffer himself (see above, 2/7, "Note on Luther's Lectures on the Letter to the Romans," and 2/16, "Graduation Theses" no. 8).

Bonhoeffer seldom dated his *letters* completely and rarely noted the place from which they were sent. Eberhard Bethge therefore dated the letters according to the postmark—not found on the microfiches—on the envelope. These dates have been used. It hardly needs to be mentioned that differences could exist between the day and place the letter was written and the day and place that it was mailed. These vagaries cannot be overcome. This is also true for his postcards, which usually have the postmark only as an indication of the date. At times references to dateable events can be adduced (see above, 1/27:49, the letter of June 25, 1922).

The addresses at children's worship services present a special problem. Here a distinctive chronology had to be established, which should be explained briefly. Bonhoeffer's request to be admitted to the first examinations is accompanied by a certificate from Pastor Meumann, which certifies that Bonhoeffer "spent two years as an assistant in children's worship services" (see above, 1/109:179). This statement can be made more precise. In a letter of March 13, 1926, Widmann answers Bonhoeffer's questions about the children's worship services and gives the general impression that this was from the early phase of this activity. When the earlier letter of February 25, 1926 was written, these questions were obviously not in the air. As Bonhoeffer was busy with three long papers in the winter semester 1925/26, of which two were unfinished until the end of the semester, it is also unlikely that he took on new responsibilities in the congregation before the end of that semester. The early sermons are therefore to be placed in March 1926 at the earliest. This means that the sermon for All Saints' Sunday (see above, 3/9) and the one for Advent (see above, 3/10) were given not in 1925 but in 1926. This is supported by the fact that the sermon on All Saints' Sunday presupposes trips with the children, which Bonhoeffer did not begin until somewhat later. On the other hand, Bonhoeffer probably began working on the children's sermons during the vacation between winter semester 1925/26 and summer semester 1926 in order to be able to demonstrate that he had had practical experience prior to the beginning of his first homiletics seminar.

Four children's addresses make a good impression (above, 3/2–4 and *NL* A 15, 9). They are carefully written, refer to his own childhood memories, work with stories based on examples, and also reflect the influence of Holl's interpretation of Luther, which in 1925 became very important to Bonhoeffer. The first sermon refers to the others, which speak of God's demands on us, and the fourth (*NL* A 15, 9) reflects back on this series. Sermons 3/3 and 3/4 (above) are easily placed in the same category as these sermons. Of these, 3/4 seems to be the later. It was given shortly before the Easter holidays.

The sermons for All Saints' Sunday and Advent (above, 3/9 and 3/10, as well as *NL* A 15, 7) allow one to see a situation of changed theological interest. They deal with the theme of eschatology, to which Bonhoeffer turned several times during 1926. The fall of 1927 would be too late for these addresses, because at that time he was busy preparing for his examinations and in the congregation had given himself primarily to the Thursday Circle (see above, 3/13).

The Good Friday sermon, and the one related to it on Jeremiah 27–28, presuppose that he knows the children well. They could therefore hardly have been held in the spring of 1926. They are composed in such a way that they could have been understood only by children who were a bit older, perhaps ready to be confirmed. This would have been the case for the majority of the children from Bonhoeffer's group in the spring of 1927, as he created the Thursday Circle for them after Easter (and their confirmation). Lent 1927 is a good fit for dating these two sermons.

Based on Bonhoeffer's own statements and the syllabus for Professor Mahling's homiletics seminars, Bonhoeffer's catechetical lessons are to be dated to the summer semester of 1926 (see *NL* A 15, 12). The undated catechetical lesson on "honor" (above, 3/15) can therefore have been held only during the second homiletics seminar that Bonhoeffer attended, i.e., in summer semester 1927.

637

Appendix 2.
Chronology of *The Young Bonhoeffer: 1918–1927*

February 4, 1906
Dietrich and Sabine are born in Breslau

August 22, 1909
Susanne is born in Breslau

Easter 1912
Move to Berlin due to their father's appointment as the director of the University Psychiatric Clinic

Easter 1913
Begins school in the Friedrich Werder Gymnasium
Parents purchase a vacation home in Friedrichsbrunn

March 1916
Family moves to Berlin-Grunewald, Wangenheimstr. 14

1918
Karl-Friedrich and Walter serve in the military

April 28, 1918
Walter dies in the field hospital Marcel Cave in France

June 1918
Summer vacation in Boltenhagen on the Baltic Sea

September 1918
Fall vacation in Waldau with the family von Hase

Easter 1919
Changes schools and enters the Grunewald Gymnasium

July 1920
Vacation in Friedrichsbrunn

March 1921
Confirmation

June 1922
Hiking tour of the Lüneburg Heath with Max Delbrück

July 1922
Trip to Lake Constance with his siblings and friends

March 1923
Qualifying exams

Summer semester 1923
First semester, in Tübingen
(under Groos, Hauer, Müller,
Schlatter et al.)
Entered the "Hedgehog" fraternity
(friends: Dreier, Held, Pfizer,
Weynand)

August 1923
Vacation in Friedrichsbrunn

Winter semester 1923/24
Second semester, in Tübingen
(under Groos, Heim, Heitmüller,
Rudolph et al.)

November 1923
Military volunteer for a time
as a rifleman in Ulm

April 1924
Sojourn in Rome and Sicily

May 1924
Visit to North Africa

May/June 1924
Second stay in Rome

June/July 1924
Third semester, in Berlin (under
Greßmann, Harnack, Holl, Lietz-
mann, Maier et al.)

September/October 1924
Hiking tour with Held in Schleswig-
Holstein

639 **Winter semester 1924/25**
Fourth semester, in Berlin (under
Bertram, Deißmann, Köhler, Sellin,
Titius et al.)

April 1925
Hiking tour with siblings von Hase
in the Riesengebirge (now the
Krkonose mountains in the Czech
Republic)

Summer semester 1925
Fifth semester, in Berlin (under
Harnack, Holl, Seeberg, Sellin,
Stutz et al.)
Friendship with Widmann;
concerns himself with Karl Barth's
theology

August 1925
Vacation in Lesum (north of
Bremen) with the Dreiers

September 1925
Discussion with Seeberg about his
doctoral dissertation

Winter semester 1925/26
Sixth semester, in Berlin (under
Deißmann, Holl, Mahling, Seeberg,
Stolze et al.)

October 1925
First sermon, in Stahnsdorf

February and onward 1926
Assisted at the children's worship
services in the Grunewald church

Summer semester 1926
Seventh semester, in Berlin (under
Biehle, Deißmann, Galling,
Mahling, Seeberg et al.)

August 1926
Trip with Karl-Friedrich and Held to
the Gardasee (Italy)

Winter semester 1926/27
Eighth semester, in Berlin (under
Michaelis, Seeberg, Sellin,
Spranger)

March 1927
Vacation in Friedrichsbrunn

April 1927
Began the Thursday Circle for the youth in the congregation

Summer semester 1927
Ninth semester, in Berlin (under Lietzmann, Mahling, Seeberg et al.)

July 1927
Submits his doctoral dissertation and registers for examination

October/November 1927
Works on his sermon and catechetical lessons for examination

December 1927
Doctoral examinations and defense of his doctoral thesis

January 1928
First theological exam, acceptance as a candidate for ordination by the consistory

APPENDIX 3.
LECTURES AND SEMINARS
IN WHICH BONHOEFFER
PARTICIPATED

An Overview[1]

Tübingen

Summer semester 1923
Prof. Dr. Groos, Logic
University Instructor Dr. Hauer, History of Religions I, the
    Oriental Religions
Prof. Dr. von Müller, Church History II
Prof. Dr. Schlatter, Explanation of the Gospel of John
Prof. Dr. Volz, Explanation of Selected Psalms
Prof. Dr. Hasse, Forms in Beethoven's Symphonies

Winter semester 1923/24
Prof. Dr. Heim, Dogmatics II
Prof. Dr. Heitmüller, Explanation of the Epistle to the Romans
Prof. Dr. von Müller, Church History III
Prof. Dr. Rudolph, Old Testament Theology
Prof. Dr. Groos, History of Modern Philosophy
Prof. Dr. Groos, Seminar in Philosophy
Prof. Dr. Wilbrandt, Political Science

[1.] According to his departure certificate from Tübingen dated March 13, 1924, and according to the Berlin enrollment book where Bonhoeffer was matriculated on June 16, 1924. He finished on August 13, 1927.

Berlin

Summer semester 1924
Prof. von Harnack, History of Dogma (enrolled 6/21)
Prof. Holl, Church History II (enrolled 6/25)
Prof. Greßmann, Explanation of Genesis (audit)
Prof. Lietzmann, Introduction to the New Testament (enrolled 6/25)
Prof. Heinrich Maier, Epistemology (enrolled 6/21)
Prof. Holl, The Confessions (enrolled 6/26)

Winter semester 1924/25
Prof. Sellin, Introduction to the Old Testament (enrolled 11/12)
Prof. Titius, Dogmatics I (enrolled 11/11)
Prof. Deißmann, The Synoptics (enrolled 11/11)
Prof. Köhler, Introduction to Gestalt Theory (enrolled 11/11)   641
Prof. Wertheimer, Psychology (enrolled 12/1)
University Instructor Rieffert, History of Ideas of Logic (enrolled 11/13)
Prof. H. Maier, Seminar, Freedom and Necessity (enrolled 12/1, not
    completed)
Licentiate Bertram, Proseminar, Resurrection of Jesus (enrolled 11/20,
    completed 2/26)

Summer semester 1925
Prof. Holl, Church History I (enrolled 5/15)
Prof. Seeberg, Ethics (enrolled 5/15)
Prof. Sellin, History of the Israelite-Judaic People (enrolled 5/15)
Prof. Stutz, Church Law (audit)
Prof. Holl, Seminar in Church History (enrolled 5/20, completed 7/29)
Prof. Seeberg, Seminar in Systematics (enrolled 5/29, completed 7/31)
Prof. von Harnack, History of the Development of the New Testament and
    the Apocryphal Gospels (enrolled 5/27, not completed)

Winter semester 1925/26
Prof. Holl, History of Protestant Theology (enrolled 11/17)
Prof. Mahling, Practical Theology I (enrolled 11/9)
Prof. Deißmann, Theology of the New Testament (audit)
Prof. Holl, Seminar in Church History (enrolled 11/12, not completed,
crossed out 5/23/26)
Prof. Seeberg, Seminar in Systematics (enrolled 11/20, completed 3/15)
Licentiate Stolzenburg, Introductory Seminar in Systematics (enrolled
    11/10, completed 3/11)

Summer semester 1926
Prof. Mahling, Practical Theology II (enrolled 5/17)
Prof. Seeberg, Theology of the New Testament (enrolled 5/21)
Licentiate Dr. Galling, Isaiah (enrolled 6/15)
Prof. Biehle, Liturgy (enrolled by Mahling 5/17, as well as certified completed 7/27)
Prof. Mahling, Seminar in Homiletics (enrolled 5/17, completed 7/28)
Prof. Mahling, Seminar in Catechetics (enrolled by Biehle 5/18, as well as certified completed 2/24/27)
Prof. Seeberg, Seminar in Systematics (enrolled, completed)
Prof. Deißmann, Seminar in New Testament (enrolled 6/16, completed 7/28)

Winter semester 1926/27
Prof. Spranger, Philosophy of Culture (enrolled 12/17)
Licentiate Michaelis, Letter to the Corinthians (audit)
642　　Prof. Sellin, Old Testament Seminar on Job (enrolled 12/10, completed 3/1)
Prof. Seeberg, Seminar in Systematics I (enrolled 1/25, completed 3/15)
Prof. Biehle, Lectures in Liturgy and Church Music (enrolled 12/8, completed 2/24)

Summer semester 1927
Prof. Lietzmann, Church History IV (audit)
Prof. Seeberg, Seminar in Systematics (audit)
Prof. Mahling, Seminar in Catechetics (enrolled 6/15, completed 7/27)

Note in the Berlin Matriculation Book, "The bearer has not taken academic courses in physical education."

In addition this special attestation,
Prof. Biehle-Bautzen.
Theology Student Dietrich Bonhoeffer took part for two semesters in the lectures in Music of Liturgy I and II.
Signed, Prof. Biehle.

APPENDIX 4.
UNPUBLISHED MATERIAL
FROM THIS PERIOD

1. Letters, Diary, Documents
(not including letters from others)

Addressee or content	Date	NL reference
Parents	2/16/1918	A 3, 1 (1)
"A Dream" (Play)	3/5/1918	Appendix A 16
Parents	6/29/1918	A 3, 1 (2)
Parents	7/3/1918	A 3, 1 (3)
Julie Bonhoeffer	7/3/1918	A 3, 2 (3)
Parents	8/11/1918	A 3, 1 (4)
Julie Bonhoeffer	August 1918	A 3, 2 (4)
Parents	9/28/1918	A 3, 1 (5)
Vaccination Certificate	10/15/1918	A 6 (5)
Parents	5/28/1919	A 3, 1 (8)
Julie Bonhoeffer	7/11/1919	A 3, 2 (9)
Siblings	7/20/1919	A 3, 3 (4)
Parents	7/29/1919	A 3, 1 (9)
Julie Bonhoeffer	5/3/1920	A 4, 2 (1)
Parents	7/22/1920	A 4, 1 (1)
Julie Bonhoeffer	8/19/1920	A 4, 2 (2)
Parents	11/1/1918	A 4, 1 (4)
Parents	End of December 1920	A 4, 1 (5)

List of Confirmands	Beginning of 1921	A 4, 3 (7)
Blessing from Wohlgemuth	3/1/1921	A 4, 3 (6)
Postcard with handwritten grave inscriptions	5/17/1921	A 4, 3 (5)
Parents	July 1921	A 4, 1 (6)
Parents	7/8/1921	A 4, 3 (1)
Parents	7/12/1921	A 4, 1 (8)
Parents	Mid-July 1921	A 4, 1 (9)
Parents	7/18/1921	A 4, 1 (7)
Karl-Friedrich Bonhoeffer	7/24/1921	A 4, 1 (10)
School certificate	9/28/1921	A 6 (6)
Hans von Dohnanyi	7/22/1922	A 4, 3 (4)
Parents	8/29/1922	A 4, 1 (14)

644

Hans von Dohnanyi	12/31/1923	A 7, 2 (8)
Book of courses attended in Tübingen	Summer semesters 1923 and 1924	D 11 (12) and (13)
Registrar's final record, Tübingen	3/13/1924	D 11 (12)
Julie Bonhoeffer	4/11/1924	A 7, 2 (1)
Parents	4/29/1924	A 7, 1 (25)
Sabine Bonhoeffer	April 1924	Appendix A 5 (6)
Ursula Schleicher	5/26/1924	A 7, 2 (5)
Robert Held	6/2/1924	(Held)
Sabine Bonhoeffer	6/25/1924	Appendix A 5 (10)
Sabine Bonhoeffer	June 1924	Appendix A 5 (11)
Sabine Bonhoeffer	10/4/1924	Appendix A 5 (12)

Play (von Dohnanyi Wedding)	Beginning of 1925	A 9, 3
Parents	3/13/1925	A 9, 1 (1)
Parents	4/3/1925	A 9, 1 (2)
Parents	April 1925	A 9, 1 (3)
Parents	4/7/1925	A 9, 1 (4)
Parents	4/9/1925	A 9, 1 (5)
Ursula Schleicher	5/21/1925	A 9, 1 (10)
Sabine Bonhoeffer	8/14/1925	A 9, 1 (11)
Dreier guest book	8/23–9/1/1925	(Dreier)
Poem (Leibholz marriage)	4/5/1926	A 9, 4
Dreier guest book	7/23–27/1926	A 9, 1 (13)
Parents	8/16/1926	A 9, 1 (8)
Certificate of participation in liturgy	12/30/1926	D 11 (9)
Faculty of Theology	July 1927	(Archives of Humboldt-University)
Book of courses attended in Berlin	Summer semesters 1925–1927	D 11 (11)
Acceptance of his dissertation	8/1/1927	D 11 (33)
Dreier guest book	8/2–6/1927	(Dreier)
Registrar's final record, Berlin	8/13/1927	D 11 (10)
Examination exercises	9/27/1927	D 11 (14)
Diestel (of the Consistory)	12/15/1927	D 11 (18a)
Certificate of oral doctoral examinations	December 1927	D 11 (32)
Invitation to oral examination	January 1928	D 11 (23)

2. Writings, Seminar Presentations, Notes

Subject	*Date*	*NL Reference*
Caesar	December 1920	A 5, 1 (2)
Julian the Apostate	2/4/1921	A 5, 1 (3)
Euripides' Philosophy	August 1922	A 5, 2 (1)
Introduction to the Old Testament (lecture notes)	Winter 1922?	A 5, 2 (2)
Groos, Logic (lecture notes)	Summer semester 1923	A 10, 3
Questions of Logic	Summer semester 1923?	A 10, 1 (3)
Müller, Church History II (lecture notes)	Summer semester 1923	A 10, 1 (4)
Schlatter, Gospel of John (lecture notes)	Summer semester 1923	A 10, 1 (6)
Volz, The Psalms (lecture notes)	Summer semester 1923	A 10, 2
Psalms 34 and 40	Summer semester 1923?	A 10, 1 (2)
Heitmüller, Romans (lecture notes)	Winter semester 1923/24	A 10, 4
Rudolph, Old Testament Theology (lecture notes)	Winter semester 1923/24	A 10, 5
Groos, History of Philosophy (lecture notes)	Winter semester 1923/24	A 10, 6
Lietzmann (?), Introduction to the New Testament (lecture notes)	Winter semester 1923/24	A 10, 1 (5)
Harnack, History of Dogma (lecture notes)	Summer semester 1924	A 10, 7
Lietzmann, Introduction to the New Testament (lecture notes)	Summer semester 1924	A 10, 8
Rough note on the Apostolic Fathers	Undated	Appendix A 19
Barth, Dictated notes (lecture notes)	Winter semester 1924/25	A 10, 11 (1)

Sellin, History of Israel (lecture notes)	Summer semester 1925	A 10, 9 (1)
Holl, Church History I (lecture notes)	Summer semester 1925	A 10, 9 (2)
Seeberg, Ethics (lecture notes)	Summer semester 1925	A 10, 9 (3)
Schulze, Workers' Movement	Summer semester 1925?	A 10, 11 (2)
Schulze, The Labor Unions	No date	A 10, 11 (3)
Schulze, For Rome— Against Rome	No date	A 10, 11 (4)
Note on evil	August 1925	A 9, 2 (2)
Study papers and Notes	No date	A 10, 10 (1–12)
Church and Eschatology, *Copy B*	January 1926	A 12, 2 (b)
Theses on the Form of the Church	May 1926	A 15, 12
Seeberg, New Testament Theology (lecture notes)	May 1926	A 15, 12
Excerpts from Paul on "Joy"	May 1926	A 11, 6 (4)
Joy in Hermas etc.	May 1926	A 11, 6 (3)
Excerpt from Schleiermacher on faith	1926?	A 10, 10 (8)
Excerpt from Natorp, *Sozialpadagogik*	1926	Appendix A 18
Rough note on Schmid, *Doctrinal Theology*	1927?	Appendix A 22

646

3. Sermons for Seminars and Early Congregational Sermons, Catechetical Lessons for Seminars, and Addresses at Children's Worship Services

Bible Text or Theme	Date	NL Reference
Sermon on Luke 17, handwritten by Bonhoeffer	10/18/1925	A 13, 1 (a)
Meditation on prayer	April/May 1926	A 15, 9
List of catechetical themes from Mahling	Beginning of May 1926	A 15, 12
Meditation on Luke 9: 57ff.	June/July 1926	A 15, 3
Meditation for the Fourth Sunday in Advent	December 1926	A 15, 7
Catechesis on Luke 19: 1–9	Summer semester 1927	A 14, 3

APPENDIX 5.
TEXTS PUBLISHED IN BOTH
GESAMMELTE SCHRIFTEN
AND *DBWE* 9

BIBLIOGRAPHY

---

1. Literature Used by Bonhoeffer

Adam, Karl. *Das Wesen des Katholizismus.* 3d ed. Düsseldorf, 1926. English translation: *The Spirit of Catholicism.* Translated by Dom Justin McCann. Introduced by Robert A. Krieg. New York: Crossroad, 1997. *NL* 6 B 1

Alexis, Willibald. *Der Wärwolf* (The werewolf). Berlin: O. Janke, 1879.

Althaus, Paul. *Das Erlebnis der Kirche* (The experience of the church). 2d ed. Leipzig, 1924.

———. *Die letzten Dinge: Entwurf einer christlichen Eschatologie.* (The last things: outline of a Christian eschatology). 3d ed. Gütersloh: Bertelsmann, 1926. *NL* 3 B 3.

Baedeker, Karl. *Italien. II: Mittel-Italien und Rom: Ein Handbuch für Reisende* (Italy II: Central Italy and Rome: A handbook for travelers). Leipzig: Baedeker, 1903.

Barth, Karl. *Die christliche Dogmatik im Entwurf* (Christian dogmatics in outline). Vol. 1: *Die Lehre vom Worte Gottes: Prolegomena zur christlichen Dogmatik* (The doctrine of the Word of God: Prolegomena to Christian dogmatics). Munich, 1927. Also published in *Gesamtausgabe* (Collected works), edited by Gerhard Sauter. Zurich, 1982. *NL* 3 B 9.

———. "Menschenwort und Gotteswort in der christlichen Predigt" (The human word and the Word of God in Christian proclamation). *Zwischen den Zeiten* 3/2 (1925): 119–40.

———. *Der Römerbrief.* 2d ed. of the new, revised edition of 1922. Munich, 1923. English translation: *The Epistle to the Romans.* Translated from the 6th German edition by Edwyn C. Hoskyns. London: Oxford University Press, 1933, 1960.

———. "Das Schriftprinzip der reformierten Kirche" (The scriptural principle in the Reformed church). *Zwischen den Zeiten* 3/3 (1925): 215–45.

———. *Das Wort Gottes und die Theologie.* Munich: Chr. Kaiser, 1924. English translation: *The Word of God and the Word of Man.* Translated by Douglas Horton. London: Hodder and Stoughton, 1928. *NL* 3 B 11.

Bartmann, Bernhard. *Lehrbuch der Dogmatik* (Textbook of dogmatics). 6th ed. 2 vols. Freiburg, 1923, 1929. *NL* 6 B 3.

Bauer, Walter. *Die Evangelien. II. Johannes* (The gospels. II. John). Tübingen: Mohr, 1912.

Beck, Johann Tobias. *Einleitung in das System der christlichen Lehre oder Propädeutischen Entwicklung der christlichen Lehrwissenschaft* (Introduction to the system of Christian doctrine or propaedeutical development of the discipline of Christian education). Stuttgart, 1870.

Bellarmin, Robert. *Prima controversia generalis de verbo Dei quatuor libris explicata* (First general controversies on the word of God, book four explicated). In Vol. 1 of *Opera omnia* (Complete works). Edited by J. Fèvre. Paris, 1870.

Bengel, Johann Albrecht. *Gnomon Novi Testamenti.* German translation by C. F. Werner. Basel, 1876. English translation: *New Testament Word Studies.* 2 vols. Translated by Charleton T. Lewis and Marvin R. Vincent. Reprint of 1864 edition. Grand Rapids: Kregel, 1971.

Bernheim, Ernst. *Lehrbuch der historischen Methode und der Geschichtsphilosophie mit Nachweis der wichtigsten Quellen und Hilfsmittel zum Studium der Geschichte.* (Textbook of historical method and the philosophy of history with an indication of the most important sources and aids for the study of history). 6th ed. Leipzig: Duncker & Humblot, 1908.

Bode, Wilhelm: *Der weimarische Musenhof* (The Muses' Court at Weimar). 2d ed. Berlin: E. S. Mittler & Sohn, 1925.

Bousset, Wilhelm. *Die Religion des Judentums* (The religion of Judaism). Berlin, 1903.

———. *Kyrios Christos. Geschichte des Christusglaubens von den Anfängen des Christentums bis Irenäus.* Forschungen zur Religion und Literatur des Alten und Neuen Testaments, Neue Folge 4/2. Revised edition. Göttingen, 1913. English translation: *Kyrios Christos: A History of the Belief in Christ from the Beginnings of Christianity to Irenaeus.* Translated by John Steely. Nashville: Abingdon, 1970.

Brevarium Romanum ex decreto SS. concilii Tridentini restitutum. (The Roman breviary restored in accordance with the decree of the most holy council of Trent.). Ratisbonae: Augustae Taurinorum, 1898.

Bucer, Martin. *Ordnung der christlichen Kirchenzucht. Für die Kirchen in Fürstenthum Hessen.* (Order of Christian church discipline: For the church in the principality of Hessen.) Marburg, 1539.

———. *Ordnung der Kirchenübung. Für die Christen zu Cassel.* (Order of church practice: For the Christians of Kassel.) Marburg, 1539.

Budde, Karl. *Das Buch Hiob* (The book of Job). 2d ed. Göttingen, 1913.

———. "Die Capitel 27 und 28 des Buches Hiob" (The 27th and 28th chapters of the book of Job). *Forschungen zur Religion und Literatur des Alten und Neuen Testaments,* Neue Folge 4 (1882): 193–274.

Bultmann, Rudolf. "Die Bedeutung der neuerschlossenen mandäischen und manichäischen Quellen für das Verstandinis des Johannesevangeliums" (The significance of the newly discovered Mandaean and Manichaean sources for understanding the Gospel of John). *Zeitschrift für die neutestamentliche Wissenschaft* 24 (1925): 100–146.

———. *Jesus.* Berlin: Deutsche Bibliothek, 1926. English translation: *Jesus and the Word.* Translated by Louise Pettibone Smith and Erminie Huntress Lantero. New York: Charles Scribner's Sons, 1962, 1989.

Burckhardt, Jacob. *Der Cicerone: Eine Anleitung zum Genuss der Kunstwerke Italiens.* 8th ed. 2 Parts. Leipzig & Berlin, 1900–. English translation: *The Cicerone: An Art Guide to Painting in Italy.* London: T. Werner Laurie, 1908.

Caspari, Walter. *Die evangelische Konfirmation, vornehmlich in der lutherischen Kirche.* (Protestant confirmation, primarily in the Lutheran church.) Erlangen, 1890.

Cohn, Leopold and Paul Wendland, eds. *Philonis Alexandrini opera quae supersunt.* (The extant works of Philo of Alexandria.) 6 vols. Berlin: George Reimeus, 1896–1915. Reprint: Berlin: Walter DeGruyter, 1962.

Cremer, Hermann. *Biblisch-theologisches Wörterbuch der neutestamentlichen Grazität.* 4th ed. Edited by J. Kögel. Gotha, 1915. English translation: *Biblico-theological Lexicon of New Testament Greek.* 3d ed. Translated by William Urwick. Translated from second German edition. Edinburgh: T. & T. Clark, 1883; New York: Charles Scribner's Sons, 1895.

Cyril of Jerusalem. *Catecheses.* In J.-P. Migne, *Patrologiae cursus completes, series graeca, accurante,* volume 33. Paris, 1857. English translation: *Cyril of Jerusalem and Nemesius of Emesa.* The Library of Christian Classics, volume 4. Philadelphia: Westminster Press, 1955.

Dahn, Felix. *Ein Kampf um Rom* (A battle for Rome). Leipzig: Breitkopf & Härtel, 1920.

Deißmann, Gustav Adolf. *Die neutestamentliche Formel 'in Christo Jesu' untersucht* (An investigation of the New Testament formula "in Christ Jesus"). Marburg, 1892.

———. *Paulus; eine kultur- und religionsgeschichtliche Skizze.* 2d ed. Tübingen: Mohr, 1925. English translation: *Paul: A Study in Social and Religious History.* 2d ed., revised and enlarged. Translated by William E. Wilson. Gloucester, Mass.: Peter Smith, 1972.

Dibelius, Martin. *Der Brief des Jakobus.* Kritisch-exegetischer Kommentar über das Neue Testament 15. Göttingen, 1921. Reprint: Göttingen, 1956. English translation: *James: A Commentary on the Epistle of James.* Revised by Heinrich Greeven. Translated by Michael A. Williams. Edited by Helmut Koester. Philadelphia: Fortress Press, 1976.

———. *Die Formgeschichte des Evangeliums.* Tübingen, 1919. English translation: *From Tradition to Gospel.* Translated from the revised 2d edition by Bertram Lee Woolf. Cambridge: Cambridge University Press, 1971.

Diestel, Ludwig. *Geschichte des Alten Testamentes in der christlichen Kirche* (History of the Old Testament in the Christian church). Jena, 1869.

Dieterich, Albrecht. *Eine Mithraslithurgie.* 2d ed. Leipzig: Teubner, 1910. English translation: *A Mithraic Ritual.* Translated by George R. S. Mead. London & Benares: Theosophical Publishing Society, 1907.

Dilthey, Wilhelm. "Die Entstehung der Hermeneutik." In *Philosophische Abhandlungen. Christoph Sigwart zu seinem siebzigsten Geburtstag, gewidmet von B. Erdmann et al.*, 185–201. Tübingen, Freiburg, Leipzig, 1900. Reprinted in *Gesammelte Schriften* 5:317–31. Leipzig, Berlin, 1924. English translation: "The Rise of Hermeneutics." In *Selected Writings 1833–1911*, 246–63. New York: Cambridge University Press, 1976.

—————. "Weltanschauung und Analyse des Menschen seit Renaissance und Reformation (Worldview and human analysis since the Renaissance and Reformation). In *Gesammelte Schriften* 2. Stuttgart: B. G. Tuebner, and Göttingen: Vandenhoek & Ruprecht, 1964.

Dorner, Isaak August. *Entwicklungsgeschichte der Lehre von der Person Christi von den ältesten Zeiten bis auf die neueste.* Part I: *Die Lehre von der Person Christi in den ersten vier Jahrhunderten.* Berlin, 1851. English translation: *History of the Development of the Doctrine of the Person of Christ.* Vol. 1, part 1, translated by W. L. Alexander and D. W. Simon. Edinburgh, 1861.

—————. *Grundriß der Dogmengeschichte* (Outline of the history of dogma). Berlin: G. Reimer, 1899.

Dreß, Walter. *Die Mystik des Marsilio Ficino.* (The mysticism of Marsilio Ficinio) Vol. 14 of *Arbeiten zur Kirchengeschichte.* Edited by E. Hirsch and H. Lietzmann. Berlin and Leipzig, 1929.

Drews, Paul, ed. *Disputationen Dr. M. Luthers in den Jahren 1535–1545 an der Universität Wittenberg gehalten* (The disputations of Dr. M. Luther held in the years 1535–1545 at the University of Wittenberg). Göttingen, 1895. See Luther.

Duhm, Bernhard. *Das Buch Hiob* (The book of Job). Freiburg, Leipzig, Tübingen, 1897.

Egelhaaf, Gottlob. *Geschichte der neuesten Zeit vom Frankfurter Frieden bis zur Gegenwart* (History of the modern era from the Peace of Frankfurt until the present). Stuttgart, 1917.

Enders, Ernst Ludwig, ed. *Dr. Martin Luthers Briefwechsel* (Dr. Martin Luther's letters). 18 vols. Vols. 1–11, ed. Ernst Enders; vols. 12–16, ed. G. Kawerau; vol. 17, ed. P. Fleming, vol. 18, ed. O. Albrecht. Frankfurt and Leipzig, 1884–1923..

Erasmus, Desiderius. *Paraphrasis in Evangelium Matthaei.* (A paraphrase of the Gospel of Matthew.) Basel, 1521.

Evangelisches Gesangbuch, nach Zustimmung der Provinzial-Synode vom Jahre 1884 zur Einführung in der Provinz Brandenburg mit Genehmigung des evangelischen Oberkirchenrats (Protestant hymnal; according to the agreement of the provincial Synod of the Year 1884 for introduction into the Province of Brandenburg with permission of the provincial council). Edited by the Royal Consistory. Berlin, 1894.

Evangelisches Kirchen-Gesangbuch. Kassel: Bärenreiter Verlag, 1950.

Fendt, Leonhard. *Die religiösen Kräfte des katholischen Dogmas* (The religious powers of Catholic dogma). Munich, 1921. *NL.*

———. *Erfahrung. Ein Büchlein vom wohlgemuten Luthertum (Warum evangelisch?)* (Experience: A small book of good-humored Lutheranism. Why be Protestant?). Berlin, 1923.

Fontane, Theodor. *Der Stechlin.* Berlin, 1909. English translation: *The Stechlin.* Translated, with an introduction and notes, by William L. Zwiebel. Columbia, S.C.: Camden House, 1995.

Frank, Franz Hermann Reinhold. *System der christlichen Gewißheit.* Two volumes. 2d ed. Vol. 1, Erlangen, 1884; vol. 2, Erlangen, 1881. English translation: *System of the Christian Certainty.* Translated by M. J. Evans. Edinburgh: T. & T. Clark, 1886.

———. *System der christlichen Wahrheit* (System of Christian truth) 3d ed. Two volumes in one. Erlangen, 1894.

Gebhardt, Otto von, and Adolf von Harnack, eds. "Clementis Romani ad Corinthios quae dicuntur epistulae. Textum ad fidem codicum et Alexandrini et Constantinopolitani nuper inventi" (Letters of Clement of Rome to the Corinthians. Faithful codices from Alexandria and Constantinople). *Patrum Apostolicorum Opera* (Works of the Apostolic Fathers) 1/1. Leipzig, 1876.

Gerhard, Johann. *Loci Theologici* (Systematic theology). 20 volumes. Edited by J. F. Cotta, Tübingen, 1762–89. New edition edited by E. Preuss. 9 volumes. Berlin: Schlawitz, 1863 (1610–21).

———. "Tractatus de extremo iudicio." (Treatise on the last judgment.) *Loci theologici.* New edition, vol. 9, §126. Leipzig: Hinrichs, 1875.

Girgensohn, Karl. "Die Inspiration der Heiligen Schrift" (The inspiration of the Holy Scriptures). *Pastoral Blätter für Homiletik, Katechetik und Seelsorge* 1/67 (1924–25): 121–30, 161–76, 225–56. *Die Inspiration der Heiligen Schrift.* Dresden: Ungelenk, 1925.

Greßmann, Hugo. "Die Bibel im Spiegel Ägyptens. IV. Tobit" (The Bible in the mirror of Eygpt. 4 Tobit). *Protestantenblatt Berlin* 49 (1916): 278–82.

Gundert, E. "Der erste Brief des Clemens Romanus an die Corinther" (The first letter of Clement of Rome to the Corinthians). *Zeitschrift für die lutherische Theologie und Kirche* 14 (1853): 638–58.

Hafenreffer, Matthias. *Loci theologici* (Systematic theology). Wittenberg, 1612.

Harnack, Adolf von. "Der erste Klemensbrief. Eine Studie zur Bestimmung des Charakters des ältesten Heidenchristentums" (1 Clement: A study on determining the character of earliest gentile Christianity). *Sitzungsberichte der preußischen Akademie der Wissenschaften* (1909): 38–63. *NL.*

————. *Lehrbuch der Dogmengeschichte.* 4th ed., rev. and enlarged. Tübingen, 1909, 1910; Darmstadt, 1983. English translation: *History of Dogma,* 5 vols. Translated by E. B. Speiers and Neil Buchanan from the 3d German ed. New York: Russell & Russell, 1958. *NL.*

————. *Militia Christi. Die christliche Religion und der Soldatenstand in den ersten drei Jahrhunderten.* Tübingen, 1905. English translation: *Militia Christi: The Christian Religion and the Military in the First Three Centuries.* Translated and introduced by David M. Gracie. Philadelphia: Fortress Press, 1981.

————. *Die Mission und Ausbreitung des Christentums.* 2d ed. Leipzig, 1924. English translation: *The Mission and Expansion of Christianity in the First Three Centuries.* Translated and edited by James Moffat. 2d ed., revised and enlarged. New York: Harper, 1962. *NL.*

————. "Was wir von der römischen Kirche lernen und nicht lernen sollten" (What we should and should not learn from the Roman church). In Harnack, *Reden und Aufsätze* (Speeches and essays) 2:247–64. Giessen, 1906.

————. *Das Wesen des Christentums. Sechzehn Vorlesungen vor Studierenden aller Facultäten im Wintersemester 1899/1900 an der Universität Berlin.* Leipzig, 1920. English translation: *What Is Christianity?* Translated by Thomas Bailey Saunders. 2d ed. revised. New York, London, 1901. *NL.*

Hase, Karl August von. *Gnosis oder protestantisch-evangelische Glaubenslehre für die Gebildeten in der Gemeinde* (Gnosis or Protestant doctrine for the educated members in the parish). 2 vols. Leipzig, 1869—.

————. *Handbuch der protestantischen Polemik gegen die Römisch-Katholische Kirche* (Handbook of Protestant polemic against the Roman Catholic Church). Leipzig, 1865.

————. *Hutterus redivivus oder Dogmatik der evangelisch-lutherischen Kirche* ([Leonhart] Hutter revived, or the dogmatics of the evangelical Lutheran church). 12th ed. Leipzig, 1883. *NL* 3 B 33.

————. *Kirchengeschichte. Lehrbuch zunächst für akademische Vorlesungen.* Leipzig, 1877. English translation: *A History of the Christian Church.* Translated from the 7th edition by Charles E. Blumenthal and Conway P. Wing. New York, London, 1855.

Hauck, Albert. *Kirchengeschichte Deutschlands* (Church history of Germany). 5 vols. Leipzig : J. C. Hinrich'sche Buchhandlung, 1911–. *NL* 2 B 8.

Hegel, Georg Wilhelm Friedrich. *Erste Druckschriften.* (First pamphlets.) Vol. 1 of *Sämtliche Werke.* Edited by Georg Lasson. Leipzig: Felix Meiner, 1928.

————. *Phänomenologie des Geistes.* Vol. 2 of *Sämtliche Werke.* Edited by Georg Lasson. Leipzig: Felix Meiner, n.d. English translation [but not of the Lasson edition]: *Phenomenology of Spirit.* Translated by A. V. Miller. Oxford: Oxford University Press, 1977.

————. *Vorlesung über Philosophie der Religion.* Pt. 1, *Der Begriff der Religion* [*NL* 7 A 26]; Pt. 2, *Die Bestimmte Religion*; Pt. 3, *Die absolute Religion.* Edited by Georg Lasson. Vols. 12–14 of *Sämtliche Werke.* Leipzig: Felix Meiner, 1925,

1927, 1929. English translation: *Lectures on the Philosophy of Religion.* 3 volumes. Edited by Peter C. Hodgson. Translated by R. F. Brown, P. C. Hodgson, and J. M. Stewart, with the assistance of J. P. Fitzer and H. S. Harris. Berkeley: University of California Press, 1984–87. [Note: This is not a translation of the Lasson edition of Hegel's *Vorlesungen über die Philosophie der Religion.* Only vol. 14 of Lasson's edition of Hegel's *Sämtliche Werke* (*Philosophie der Religion,* Pt. 3: *Die absolute Religion*) has ever been translated into English. It appeared as *The Christian Religion.* Edited and translated by Peter C. Hodgson. Missoula, Mont.: Scholars Press, 1979.]

Heiler, Friedrich. *Der Katholizismus: Seine Idee und seine Erscheinung* (Catholicism: Its essence and appearance). Completely new edition of six lectures previously published as *Das Wesen des Katholizismus* (The nature of Catholicism). Munich: E. Reinhardt, 1920.

Heim, Karl. *Leitfaden der Dogmatik. Zum Gebrauch bei akademischen Vorlesungen* (Guide to dogmatics: for use in academic lectures). 2 parts. Halle, 1912; 3d ed., 1923–25.

———. *Das Wesen des evangelischen Christentums.* Leipzig, 1926. English translation: *The Nature of Protestantism.* Translated by John Schmidt. Philadelphia: Fortress Press, 1963.

Heitmüller, Wilhelm. *In Namen Jesu: Ein sprach- und religionsgeschichtliche Untersuchung zum Neuen Testament, speziell zur altchristlichen Taufe.* (In Jesus' name: a linguistic and religion-historial examination of the New Testament, particularly of ancient Christian baptism.) Göttingen, 1903.

Hesse, Herman. *Knulp: Drei Geschichten aus dem Lebens Knulps* (Knulp: Three stories from the life of Knulp). Berlin: Fischer, 1931.

Heußi, Karl. *Kompendium der Kirchengeschichte* (Compendium of church history). 2d ed. Tübingen: Mohr Siebeck, 1919.

Hirsch, Emanuel. *Die idealistische Philosophie und das Christentum* (Idealist philosophy and Christianity). Gütersloh: Bertelsmann, 1926.

———. *Die Reich-Gottes-Begriffe des neueren europäischen Denkens: Ein Versuch zur Geschichte der Staats- und Gesellschaftsphilosophie* (The idea of the kingdom of God in recent European thought: Toward a history of the philosophy of state and society). Göttingen, 1921.

Holl, Karl. "Der Neubau der Sittlichkeit." ("The new construction of morality.") In Holl, *Gesammelte Aufsätze zur Kirchengeschichte* 1:155ff.

———. *Gesammelte Aufsätze zur Kirchengeschichte* (Collected essays on church history). Vol. 1: *Luther.* Tübingen: J. C. B. Mohr, 1923.

———. "Luthers Urteile über sich selbst." In *Gesammelte Aufsätze zur Kirchengeschichte* (Collected essays on church history). Vol. 1: *Luther,* 381–419. Tübingen: J. C. B. Mohr, 1923. English translation: "Martin Luther on Luther." Translated by H. C. Erik Midelfort. In *Interpreters of Luther. Essays in Honor of Wilhelm Pauck,* 9–31. Edited by Jaroslav Pelikan. Philadelphia: Fortress Press, 1968.

————. "Was verstand Luther unter Religion?" In Holl, *Gesammelte Aufsätze zur Kirchengeschichte* 1:1–110. English translation: *What Did Luther Understand by Religion?* Edited by James Luther Adams and Walter F. Bense. Translated by Fred W. Meuser and Walter R. Wietzke. Philadelphia: Fortress Press, 1977.

Hollatz, David. *Examen theologicum acroamaticum universam theologiam thetico-polemicam complectens* (1707) (A consideration of theological issues, including polemical theology). Leipzig, 1763; reprint: Darmstadt, 1971.

Hollenberg, Wilhelm, and Karl Ferdinand Reinhardt Budde. *Hebräisches Schulbuch.* (Hebrew Schoolbook). Berlin, 1919. *NL* 8 B 3.

Hollmann, Georg. "Der Jakobusbrief" (The letter of James). *Schriften des Neuen Testaments* 2/3: 2–24. Göttingen, 1907.

Holtzmann, Heinrich J. *Die Synoptiker. Die Apostelgeschichte* (The Synoptics. The Acts of the Apostles). Hand-Commentar zum Neuen Testament 1. 2d ed., improved and enlarged. Freiburg, 1892. *NL* 1 B 2.

Husserl, Edmund. *Ideen zu einer reinen Phänomenologie und phänomenologischen Philosophie: Allgemeine Einführung in die reine Phänomenologie.* Halle, 1922. *NL.* English translation: *Ideas: General Introduction to Pure Phenomenology.* Translated by W. R. Boyce Gibson. New York: Collier Books, 1962. *NL.*

Ihmels, Ludwig. *Centralfragen der Dogmatik* (Central questions of dogmatics). Leipzig, 1918.

Jülicher, Adolf. *Die Gleichnisreden Jesu* (The parables of Jesus). 2 vols. Freiburg, 1899.

Kaftan, Julius Wilhelm. *Dogmatik* (Dogmatics). Vol. 1. Tübingen, 1901. *NL.*

————. "Zur Dogmatik 3/5: Schrift und Bekenntnis" (Concerning dogmatics 3/5: Scripture and Confession). *Zeitschrift für Theologie und Kirche* 13 (1903): 519–59.

Kautsch, Emil, ed. *Die Apokryphen und Pseudepigraphen* (The Apocrypha and Pseudepigrapha). 2 vols. Tübingen, 1900. *NL.*

Klostermann, Erich. *Das Matthäusevangelium* (The Gospel of Matthew). Handbuch zum Neuen Testaments 4. Tübingen, 1927.

Klostermann, Erich, and Hugo Greßmann. "Das Lukasevangelium" (The Gospel of Luke). In *Die Evangelien* (The Gospels), 359–612. Handbuch zum Neuen Testaments 2/1. Tübingen, 1919.

Knackfuß, Hermann, and Max Gg. Zimmermann, eds. *Allgemeine Kunstgeschichte.* (A popular history of art). 3 vols. Bielefeld & Leipzig: Velhagen & Klasing, 1897–1903.

Knopf, Rudolf. "Der Erste Clemensbrief" (1 Clement). In Handbuch zum Neuen Testament, supplemental vol.: *Die Apostolischen Väter* (The Apostolic Fathers) 1: *Die Lehre der Zwölf Apostel. Die zwei Clemensbriefe* (The teaching of the Twelve Apostles: The two letters of Clement), 41–150. Tübingen, 1920.

Kropatschek, Friedrich. *Das Schriftprinzip der lutherischen Kirche* (The scripture principle of the Lutheran church). Vol. 1. Leipzig, 1904.

Lemme, Ludwig. "Das Judenchristenthum der Urkirche und der Brief des Clemens Romanus" (Jewish Christianity of the early church and the letter of Clement of Rome). *Neue Jahrbücher für deutsche Theologie* 1 (1892): 325–480.

Lightfoot, Joseph Barber. "Clement of Rome." In *The Apostolic Fathers* 1/1 and 2. London, New York, 1890.

Lipsius, Richard Adelbert. *De Clementis Romani epistula ad Corinthios priore disquisitio* (On the letter of Clement of Rome to the Corinthians). Leipzig, 1855.

Luther, Martin. *Disputationen Dr. Martin Luthers in den Jahren 1535–1545 an der Universität Wittenberg gehalten* (The disputations of Dr. Martin Luther held in the years 1535–1545 at the University of Wittenberg). Edited by Paul Drews. Göttingen, 1895. English translation: Some disputations translated in *LW* 34.

———. *Dr. Martin Luthers Briefwechsel* (Dr. Martin Luther's correspondence). 19 vols. Edited by E. L. Enders et al. Frankfurt am Main: Evangelische Vereins, 1883–. See above, Enders.

———. *Dr. Martin Luther, Siebenzig Predigten auf all Sonn- und Festtage des Kirchenjahres* (Dr. Martin Luther, seventy sermons on every Sunday and festival of the church year). Edited by H. Planck. Stuttgart, 1888.

———. "The Large Catechism." *The Book of Concord*, 377–480.

———. *Sämtliche Werke* (Erlanger Ausgabe) (Collected works, Erlangen edition). Vols. 10 and 63. Frankfurt, Erlangen, 1868/1854.

———. "Sendbrief von Dolmetschen." *WA* 30/2:632–48. "On Translating. An Open Letter." *LW* 35:175–202.

———. *Vorlesung über den Römerbrief 1515/1516*. Vol. 1 of *Anfänge der reformatorischen Bibelauslegung*. Edited by Johannes Ficker. Part 1: Die Glosse; Part 2: Die Scholien. Leipzig: Dieterich'sche Verlagsbuchhandlungen, 1908; 3d ed. 1925. The definitive version of Ficker's edition was published as *WA* 56 in 1938. English translation: *Lectures on Romans*, *LW* 25. Edited by Hilton C. Oswald. "Glosses": chaps. 1–2, translated by Walter G. Tillmanns; chaps. 3–16 translated by Jacob A. O. Preus. "Scholia": chaps. 1–2 translated by Walter G. Tillmanns; chaps. 3–15 translated by Jacob A. O. Preus. St. Louis: Concordia Publishing House, 1972.

———. *Werke. Kritische Gesamtausgabe* (Weimarer Ausgabe = *WA*), 58 vols. Weimar, 1883ff. English translation: *Luther's Works*. Vols. 1–30 edited by Jaroslav Pelikan. St. Louis: Concordia, 1958–67. Vols. 31–55 edited by Helmut Lehmann. Philadelphia: Muhlenberg Press and Fortress Press, 1957–67.

———. "Wider Hans Worst. 1541." *WA* 51:461–572. English translation: "Against Hanswurst." Translated by Eric W. Gritsch. *LW* 41:179–256.

Müller, D. Karl. *Kirchengeschichte* (Church history). Two vols. Freiburg: J. C. B. Mohr, 1892–1919.

Müller, Johannes Tobias. *Die symbolischen Bücher der evangelisch-lutherischen Kirche, deutsch und lateinische* (The confessional books of the evangelical-Lutheran church, German and Latin). Third edition. Gütersloh, 1869.

Nägelsbach, Karl Friedrich. *Die nachhomerische Theologie des griechischen Volksglaubens bis auf Alexander* (Greek folk theology after Homer up to Alexander). Nuremberg, 1857.

Novum Testamentum Graece et Germanice (Greek and German New Testament). Edited by D. Eberhard Nestle and Erwin Nestle. 13th ed. Stuttgart, 1929. *NL.*

Otto, Rudolf. *Das Heilige. Über das Irrationale in der Idee des Göttlichen und sein Verhältnis zum Rationalen.* Gotha, 1921. English translation: *The Idea of the Holy: An Inquiry into the Non-rational Factor in the Idea of the Divine and Its Relation to the Rational.* Translated by John W. Harvey. New York, London: Oxford University Press, 1923, 1980.

Overbeck, Franz. *Über die Christlichkeit unserer heutigen Theologie* (On the Christianness of our contemporary theology). Leipzig, 1903. Reprint: Darmstadt, 1974.

Pfleiderer, Otto. *Der Paulinismus.* Leipzig, 1890. English translation: *Lectures on the Influence of the Apostle Paul on the Development of Christianity.* Translated by J. Frederick Smith. London, 1885.

Philo of Alexandria. *Philonis Judaei opera omnia* (Philo of Alexandria, collected works). 8 volumes. Edited by M. Carol Ernest Richter. Leipzig: Schwickerti, 1828–30. *Graece et latine* (Greek and Latin). Latin translation by Thomas Mangey. Edited by August F. Pfeiffer. Erlangen: Heyderiana, 1820.

Planck, Heinrich, ed. *Dr. Martin Luther, Siebenzig Predigten auf all Sonn- und Festtage des Kirchenjahres* (Dr. Martin Luther, seventy sermons on every Sunday and festival of the church year). Stuttgart, 1888. See Luther.

Plutarch, *Moralia.* Translated by Frank Cole Babbit et al. The Loeb Classical Library. Cambridge: Harvard University Press, 1960.

Przywara, Erich. "Metaphysik und Religion" (Metaphysics and religion). *Stimme der Zeit* 104 (1923): 132–40. *NL.*

Raabe, Wilhelm. *Die schwarze Galeere* (The black galley). Wiesbaden, 1917.

Raesfeld, Ferdinand von. *Im Wasgewald. Jäger- und Kriegsroman aus dem Grenzland* (In the Wasge woods: A novel of hunting and war from the frontier). Neudamm: J. Neumann, 1919.

Reitzenstein, Richard. *Die hellenistischen Mysterienreligionen, ihre Grundlagen und Wirkungen.* Leipzig, Berlin, 1918. English translation: *Hellenistic Mystery-Religions: Their Basic Ideas and Significance.* Translated by John E. Steely. Pittsburgh, 1978.

Ritschl, Albrecht. *Die christliche Lehre von der Rechtfertigung und Versöhnung.* Vols. 1 and 2. 2d edition, revised. Bonn, 1882. Vol. 3, 2d edition, revised. Bonn, 1882f–. *NL* 3 B 58. English translation: Vol. 1: *A Critical History of the Christian Doctrine of Justification and Reconciliation.* Translated by John S. Black.

Edinburgh: Edmonston and Douglas, 1872. Vol. 3: *The Christian Doctrine of Justification and Reconciliation: The Positive Development of the Doctrine.* Edited by H. R. Mackintosh and A. B. Macaulay. Edinburgh: T. & T. Clark; New York: Charles Scribner's Sons, 1900. Reprint: Clifton, N.J., 1966. *NL.*

————. *Die Entstehung der altkatholischen Kirche. Eine kirchen- und dogmengeschichtliche Monographie* (The origin of the early Catholic church: A monograph on the history of the church and dogma). Bonn, 1857.

Rothe, Richard. *Theologische Ethik* (Theological ethics). 5 vols. 2d, fully revised edition. Wittenberg, 1867–71. *NL.*

Schanz, Martin. *Geschichte der römischen Literatur* (History of Roman literature). Handbuch der klassischen Altertumswissenschaft (Handbook of the study of classical antiquity, 8). 2 pts. Munich, 1909, 1911.

Schlatter, Adolf. *Das christliche Dogma* (Christian dogma). 2d ed.. Stuttgart, 1923 *NL.*

————. "Wie sprach Josephus von Gott?" (How did Josephus speak of God?). *Beiträge zur Förderung christlicher Theologie* 14/1 (1910): 3–82.

Schleiermacher, Friedrich Daniel Ernst. *Der christliche Glaube—nach den Grundsätzen der evangelischen Kirche im Zusammenhange dargestellt.* 2d ed. 2 vols. Berlin, n.d. *NL.* English translation: *The Christian Faith.* Edited by H. R. MacKintosh and J. S. Stewart. 2d ed. Edinburgh: T. & T. Clark; Philadelphia: Fortress Press, 1976.

————. *Monologen/Weihnachtsfeier.* Berlin, n.d. *NL.* English translations: *Soliloquies.* Translated by Horace Leland Friess. Chicago: Open Court, 1957; *Christmas Eve: Dialogue on Incarnation.* Translated by Terrence N. Tice. Richmond: John Knox Press, 1967.

————. *Reden über die Religion.* Critical edition edited by G. C. B. Pünjer. Braunschweig, 1879. English translation: *On Religion: Speeches to Its Cultured Despisers.* Translated and with an introduction by Richard Crouter. Cambridge and New York: Cambridge University Press, 1988.

Schmid, Heinrich. *Die Dogmatik der evangelisch-lutherischen Kirche dargestellt und aus den Quellen belegt.* 7th ed. Gütersloh, 1893. New edition edited by H. G. Pöhlmann, Gütersloh, 1979. English translation: *The Doctrinal Theology of the Evangelical Lutheran Church.* Translated from the 5th edition by Charles A. Hay and Henry E. Jacob. 3d edition, revised, 1899. Reprint: Minneapolis: Augsburg, 1972. [The English translation differs markedly from the volume Bonhoeffer owned.] *NL.*

Seeberg, Alfred. *Die Taufe im Neuen Testament* (Baptism in the New Testament). 2d ed. Berlin, 1913.

Seeberg, Erich. *Geschichte der Kirche im 19. Jahrhundert* (History of the church in the nineteenth century). Leipzig, 1903.

Seeberg, Reinhold. *Aus Religion und Geschichte. Gesammelte Aufsätze und Vorträge* (From religion and history: Collected essays and lectures). 2 vols. Leipzig: Deichert, 1906–09.

———. *Christliche Dogmatik* (Christian dogmatics). Vol. 1; *Religionsphiloso-phischapologetische und erkenntnistheoretische Grundlegung* (Foundations in the philosophy of religion, apologetics, and epistemology). Erlangen and Leipzig, 1924. Vol. 2: *Die spezielle christliche Dogmatik* (The specifically Christian dogmatics). Erlangen and Leipzig, 1925.

———. *Die Kirche Deutschlands im neunzehnten Jahrhundert: eine Einführung in die religiösen, theologischen und kirchlichen Fragen der Gegenwart* (The church of Germany in the nineteenth century: An introduction to contemporary religious, theological, and ecclesial questions). 3d ed. Leipzig: Deichert, 1910.

———. *Lehrbuch der Dogmengeschichte*, 4/1: *Die Lehre Luthers*. Leipzig, 1917; 4/2: *Die Fortbildung der reformatorischen Lehre und die gegenreformatorische Lehre*. Erlangen/Leipzig, 1920. *NL* 2 C 4.44. English translation: *Textbook of the History of Doctrine*, 2 vols. in 1. Translated by Charles E. Hay. Grand Rapids: Baker Book House, 1956. The English translation follows a 1904 revision by the author; its organization and pagination do not correspond to those of the 1917 edition used by Bonhoeffer.

———. *Offenbarung und Inspiration*. In *Biblische Zeit und Streitfragen zur Auf-klärung der Gebildeten* 4/7, 8. Berlin, 1908. English translation: *Revelation and Inspiration*. London & New York: Harper & Brothers, 1909.

Sellin, Ernst. *Einleitung in das Alte Testament*. Leipzig, 1914. English transla-tion: *Introduction to the Old Testament*. Nashville: Abingdon Press, 1968.

———. *Das Problem des Hiobbuches* (The problem of the book of Job). Leipzig, 1919.

Siegfried, Carl. *The Book of Job: Critical Edition of the Hebrew Text*. Sacred Books of the Old and New Testament 17. Leipzig and Baltimore, 1893.

———. *Philo von Alexandrien als Ausleger des Alten Testamentes an sich selbst und nach seinem geschichtlichen Einfluß betrachtet* (Philo of Alexandria as inter-preter of the Old Testament and his historical influence). Jena, 1875. *NL*.

Sigwart, Christoph. *Logik*. 2 vols. Tübingen, 1873/1878. English translation: *Logic*. Translated by Helen Dendy. 2d ed., revised and enlarged. 2 vols. London: Sonnenschein; New York: Macmillan, 1895. Reprint. New York and London: Garland, 1980.

Smend, Rudolf. *Lehrbuch der alttestamentlichen Religionsgeschichte* (Textbook of Old Testament history of religion). In *Sammlung theologischer Lehrbücher: Alttestamentliche Theologie* (Collection of theological textbooks: Old Testa-ment theology), 2d edition, revised. Freiberg, Leipzig, Tübingen, 1899.

Soden, Hans von. *Hebräerbrief, Briefe des Petrus, Jacobus, Judas* (Letter to the Hebrews, letters of Peter, James, and Jude). Hand-Commentar zum Neuen Testament 3/2, 3d edition, improved and expanded. Frieburg, Leipzig, Tübingen, 1899.

Spitta, Friedrich. *Der Brief des Jakobus*. Göttingen: Vandenhoeck & Ruprecht, 1896.

Steuernagel, Carl. "Das Buch Hiob" (The book of Job). In E. Kautsch, editor, *Die Heilige Schrift des Alten Testaments* (The Holy Scripture of the Old Testament) 2:323–89. 4th edition, revised. Tübingen, 1923.

Teneromo, J. *Die Gespräche mit Tolstoi* (Conversations with Tolstoy). Berlin: Erich Reuss, 1911.

Thurneysen, Eduard. "Schrift und Offenbarung" (Scripture and revelation). *Zwischen den Zeiten* 3 (1924): 3–30. Reprinted in *Anfänge der dialectischen Theologie* (Beginnings of dialectical theology) 2:247–76. Munich: Chr. Kaiser Verlag, 1977.

Torczyner, Harry (Naphtali Herz Tur-Sinai). *Das Buch Hiob. Eine kritische Analyse des überlieferten Hiobtextes.* Vienna and Berlin, 1920. English translation: *The Book of Job: A New Commentary by N. H. Tur-Sinai.* Jerusalem: Kiryath Sepher, 1957.

Troeltsch, Ernst. *Der Historismus und seine Überwindung* (Historicism and its overcoming). Aalen, 1966.

———. *Die Soziallehren der christlichen Kirchen und Gruppen.* Vol. 1, first half of *Gesammelte Schriften.* Tübingen, 1919. Reprint: Aalen, 1977. English translation: *The Social Teaching of the Christian Churches.* 2 vols. Translated by Olive Wyon, with a foreword by James Luther Adams. Reprint, Louisville: Westminster/John Knox, 1992.

———. *Vernunft und Offenbarung bei Johann Gerhard und Melanchthon. Untersuchung zur Geschichte der altprotestantischen Theologie* (Reason and revelation according to J. Gerhard and Melanchthon: An investigation of the history of early Protestant theology). Göttingen, 1891.

———. "Zur Frage des religiösen Apriori" (On the question of the religious a priori). In *Gesammelte Schriften* (Collected works). 2:754–68. Tübingen, 1913. *NL* .

Tur-Sinai, Naphtali Herz. See Torczyner, Harry.

Vischer, Eberhard. *Die Offenbarung des Johannes—eine jüdische Apokalypse in christlicher Bearbeitung, mit einem Nachwort von Adolf Harnack* (The Revelation of John: A Jewish apocalyse in Christian form, with an afterword by Adolf Harnack). Texte und Untersuchungen zur Geschichte der altchristlichen Literatur 2/3. Leipzig, 1886.

Weber, Hans Emil. *Der Einfluß der protestantischen Schulphilosophie auf die orthodox-lutherische Dogmatik* (The influence of Protestant academic philosophy on orthodox Lutheran dogmatics). Leipzig, 1908.

Weber, Max. *Gesammelte Aufsätze zur Religionssoziologie.* 3 vols. Tübingen, 1920f. Vol. 1: *Die protestantische Ethik und der Geist des Kapitalismus. Die protestantischen Sekten und der Geist des Kapitalismus. Die Wirtschaftsethik der Weltreligion.* Vol. 2: *Hinduismus und Buddhismus.* Vol. 3: *Das antike Judentum.* Tübingen, 1920f. English translation: Vol. 1: (a) *The Protestant Ethic and the Spirit of Capitalism.* Translated by Talcott Parsons. New York: Charles Scribner's Sons, 1976 (1958). (b) *From Max Weber: Essays in Sociology.* Translated, edited, and introduced by Hans H. Gerth and C. Wright Mills. New York: Oxford University Press, 1958 (1946). (c) *The Religion of China: Confucianism and Taoism.* Translated and edited by Hans H. Gerth. New edition, with an introduction by C. K. Yang. New York: Macmillan, 1964 (1951). Vol. 2: *The Religion of India: The Sociology of Hinduism and Buddhism.* Translated and edited by Hans H. Gerth and Don Martindale. Glencoe, Illinois: Free Press, 1958. Vol. 3: *Ancient Judaism.* Translated and edited by Hans H. Gerth and Don Martindale. New York: Free Press, 1967 (1952); and *Ancient Judaism.* Translated and edited, with an introduction, by Hans H. Gerth and C. Wright Mills. New York: Oxford University Press, 1946, 1958. *NL.*

Weiß, Johannes. "Das Lukas-Evangelium" (The Gospel of Luke). In *Schriften des Neuen Testaments* 1/1: 378-484. Göttingen, 1906.

————. *Die Predigt Jesu vom Reiche Gottes.* 2d, revised edition. Göttingen, 1900. New edition edited by Ferdinand Hahn, Göttingen, 1964. English translation: *Jesus' Proclamation of the Kingdom of God.* Translated, edited, and with an introduction by Richard H. Hiers and David L Holland. Philadelphia: Fortress Press, 1971.

Wendland, Paul. *Die hellenistich-römische Kultur in ihren Beziehungen zu Judentum und Christentum* (Hellenistic-Roman culture in their relationship to Judaism and Christianity). Handbuch zum Neuen Testament 1/2. Tübingen, 1907.

Worringer, Wilhelm. *Abstraktion und Einfühlung.* Munich: R. Piper & Co., 1919. English translation: *Abstraction and Empathy: A Contribution to the Psychology of Style.* Translated by Michael Bullock. New York: International Universities Press, 1967.

Wrede, William. *Untersuchungen zum Ersten Klemensbriefe* (Investigations of 1 Clement). Göttingen: Dieterich, 1891.

Wundt, Max. "Die Ehre als Quelle des sittlichen Lebens in Volk und Staat" (Honor as source of moral life in people and state). In *Fr. Mann's Pedagogical Magazine,* no. 1172, Langensalza, 1927.

Wundt, Wilhelm. *Grundzüge der physiologischen Psychologie.* Leipzig, 1911. English translation: *Principles of Physiological Psychology.* Translated by E. B. Titchener from the 5th edition, 1902. London, 1904.

Zahn, Theodor. *Das Evangelium des Lucas* (The Gospel of Luke). Kommentar zum Neuen Testament 3. Leipzig, 1913.

Zauleck, P. *Deutsches Kindergesangbuch* (German children's hymnal). Edited by J. Zauleck. Gütersloh, 1924.

Zezschwitz, Gertrud von. *Warum Katholisch? Begründung meines Übertritts* (Why Catholic? The reasons for my conversion). Freiburg, 1922.

Zündel, Friedrich. *Jesus in Bildern aus seinem Leben* (Jesus in pictures from his life). Munich, 1923. *NL* 1 D 37.

2. Literature Mentioned by Bonhoeffer's Correspondents

Barth, Karl. *Die Auferstehung der Toten: Eine akademische Vorlesung über 1. Kor 15.* Munich: Chr. Kaiser Verlag, 1924. English translation: *The Resurrection of the Dead.* Translated by H. J. Stenning. London: Hodder and Stoughton, and New York: Fleming H. Revell Co., 1933. Reprint: New York: Arno Press, 1977.

————. "Wünschbarkeit und Möglichkeit eines allgemeinen reformierten Glaubensbekenntnisses." In *Die Theologie und die Kirche.* Munich, 1928. English translation: "The Desirability and Possibility of a Universal Reformed Creed." In *Theology and Church: Shorter Writings, 1920–1928,* 112–35. Translated by Louise Pettibone Smith; introduction by Thomas F. Torrance. New York: Harper & Row, 1962.

Bismarck, Otto von. *Gedanken und Erinnerungen.* Stuttgart, 1920. English translation: *The Memoirs, Being the Reflections and Reminiscences of Otto, Prince von Bismarck.* Written and dictated by himself after his retirement from office. Translated from the German under the supervision of A. J. Butler. New York: H. Fertig, 1966.

Dostoyevsky, Fyodor. *Die Brüder Karamosoff. Roman in vier Teilen mit einem Epilog.* Sämtliche Werke 9 and 10. Edited by A. Moeller van den Bruck. Munich, 1920. English translation: *The Brothers Karamozov.* Translated by Constance Garrett and revised by R. E. Matlaw. New York, 1976.

————. *Der Idiot. Sämtliche Werke* 2 and 4. Edited by A. Moeller van den Bruck. Munich, 1910. English translation: *The Idiot.* Translated by Constance Garrett. New York, 1958.

Gogarten, Friedrich. "Nachwort" (Afterword), in Martin Luther, *Vom Unfreien Willen* (On the bondage of the will), 344–71. Munich, 1924. Reprinted in *Anfängen der dialectischen Theologie* (Beginnings of dialectical theology), 191–218, under the title "Protestantimus und Wirklichkeit." Edited by Jürgen Moltmann. 3d ed. Munich: Chr. Kaiser, 1977.

Kierkegaard, Søren. *Angriff. Die agitatorischen Schriften und Aufsätze.* Translated and edited by A. Dorner and Chr. Schrempf. Stuttgart, 1896. English translation: *Attack upon "Christendom" 1854–1855.* Translated and introduced by Walter Lowrie. Princeton: Princeton University Press, 1944. A greatly expanded English translation: *The Moment and Late Writings.* Edited and translated with introduction and notes by Howard V. Hong and Edna H. Hong. Princeton: Princeton University Press, 1999.

————. *Der Augenblick. Gesammelte Werke* 12. Edited by Chr. Schrempf. Jena, 1909. An abridgement of *Angriff.* English translation: See above.

Kutter, Hermann. *Das Bilderbuch Gottes für Groß und Klein. Römerbrief—Erstes bis Viertes Kapitel* (The picturebook of God for old and young: Letter to the Romans, chapters 1–4). Basel, 1925.

Oppenheimer, Franz. *Die Siedlungsgenossenschaft* (The fellowship of settlers). 3d ed. Jena: G. Fisher, 1922.

Sellin, Ernst. *Einleitung in das Alte Testament* (Introduction to the Old Testament). 3d ed. Leipzig, 1920.

Spengler, Oswald. *Der Untergang des Abendlandes. Umrisse einer Morphologie der Weltgeschichte.* 2: *Welthistorische Perspektiven.* Munich, 1922. *NL* 7 A 83. English translation: *The Decline of the West,* three vols. in one. Translated by Charles Francis Atkinson. New York: A. A. Knopf, 1946, and London: Allen and Unwin, 1954. *NL.*

Tillich, Paul. "Kirche und Kultur. Vortrag vor dem Tübinger Jugendring im Juli 1924." In *Sammlung gemeinverständliche Vorträge und Schriften* 111. Tübingen, 1924. English translation: "Church and Culture," in *The Interpretation of History,* 219–41. Translated by N. Rasetzski and E. Talmey. New York: Charles Scribner's Sons, 1936. Also in Main Works/ Hauptwerke 2, *Writings in the Philosophy of Culture/Kulturphilosophische Schriften.* Edited by Michael Palmer. Berlin and New York: DeGruyter, 1990, 101–14.

Troeltsch, Ernst. *Der Historismus und seine Überwindung. Fünf Vorträge, eingeleitet von F. von Hügel* (Historicism and its overcoming: Five lectures introduced by F. von Hügel). Berlin, 1924. Reprint: Aalen, 1979.

Weber, Max. *Gesammelte Aufsätze zur Sozial- und Wirtschaftsgeschichte* (Collected essays on social history and economic history). Tübingen, Mohr, 1924.

3. Literature Consulted by the Editors

Alterverein der Tübinger Verbindung Igel e. V. Membership list as of March 1, 1955.

Anschütz, Gerhard. "Die Bayrischen Kirchenverträge von 1925" (The Bavarian ecclesial agreements of 1925). In *Das Bayrische Konkordat und die Schule* (The Bavaria concordat and the schools), 313–26. Edited by the Central Academic-Political Office of the Association of Bavarian Teachers. Nuremberg, 1925.

Aquinas,Thomas. *Opera Omnia* (Complete works). Vol. 1. Edited by R. Busa. Stuttgart, 1982. [Contains Aquinas's commentary on Peter Lombard's *Four Books of Sentences, Scriptum in IV Libros Sentiarum,* written in 1254–56, as well as the *Summa Theologica.*]

Aristotle. *The Complete Works of Aristotle.* The Revised Oxford Translation. Edited by Jonathan Barnes. Two volumes. Princeton: Princeton University Press, 1984.

The Babylonian Talmud. 34 volumes. General Editor, Isidore Epstein. *Shabbat.* 2 volumes. Translated by H. Freedman. London: Socino Press, 1935–52.

Barth, Karl. *Church Dogmatics* 1/1: The Doctrine of the Word of God. Edited by G. W. Bromiley and T. F. Torrance. Second edition. Edinburgh. T. & T. Clarke, 1975.

Die Bekenntnisschriften der evangelisch-lutherischen Kirche. Edited in 1930, the Anniversary year of the Augsburg Confession. Göttingen, 1930, 1952. *NL* 2

C 3. Twelfth edition. Edited by Hans Lietzmann, Heinrich Bornkamm, Hans Volz, and Ernst Wolf. Göttingen: Vandenhoeck & Ruprecht, 1998. English translation: *The Book of Concord: The Confessions of the Evangelical Lutheran Church.* Edited by Robert Kolb and Timothy J. Wengert; translated by Charles Arand, Eric Gritsch, Robert Kolb, William Russell, James Schaaf, Jane Strohl, and Timothy J. Wengert. Minneapolis: Fortress Press, 2000.

Bernard of Clairvaux. *De diligendo Deo.* In Migne, *Patrologia Latina.* Volume 185. Paris, 1844–64. English translation: *On Loving God.* Translated and with an analytical commentary by Emero Stiegman. Kalamazoo, Mich.: Cistercian Publications, 1995.

Bethge, Eberhard. *Dietrich Bonhoeffer. Theologe—Christ—Zeitgenosse: Eine Biographie.* Munich: Chr. Kaiser Verlag, 1968; 8th ed. 1994. English translation: *Dietrich Bonhoeffer: A Biography.* Edited and revised by Victoria Barnett. Minneapolis: Fortress Press, 2000.

Bethge, Eberhard, and Renate Bethge, eds. *Letzte Briefe im Widerstand: Aus dem Kreis der Familie Bonhoeffer.* Munich: Chr. Kaiser Verlag, 1984. English translation: *Last Letters of Resistance: Farewells from the Bonhoeffer Familiy.* Translated by Dennis Slabaugh. Philadelphia: Fortress Press, 1986.

Binding, Karl, and Alfred Hoche. *Die Freigabe der Vernichtung lebensunwerten Lebens* (Freedom to destroy unworthy life). Leipzig, 1920.

Bodenstein, Walter. *Die Theologie Karl Holls im Spiegel des antiken und reformierten Christentums* (Karl Holl's theology in light of ancient and Reformation Christianity). In *Arbeiten zur Kirchengesichte 40.* Berlin, 1968.

Bonaventura, *Opera Omnia* (Complete works). Vol. 2. Florence, 1885. Partial English translation in *Works of Saint Bonaventure.* Edited by P. Boehner and M. F. Laughlin. Saint Bonaventure, New York, 1955f.

Bonhoeffer, Dietrich. *The Cost of Discipleship.* Translated by Reginald H. Fuller, revised by Irmgard Booth. New York: Macmillan, 1963.

Dietrich Bonhoeffer Werke. 17 vols. Edited by E. Bethge et al. Gütersloh: Chr. Kaiser Verlag, 1986–99. English translation: *Dietrich Bonhoeffer Works.* 17 vols. Edited by Wayne Whitson Floyd Jr. et al. Minneapolis: Fortress Press, 1995–.

Vol. 1: *Sanctorum Communio: Eine dogmatische Untersuchung zur Soziologie der Kirche.* Edited by J. von Soosten. Munich: Chr. Kaiser Verlag, 1986. English translation: *Sanctorum Communio: A Theological Study of the Sociology of the Church.* Edited by Clifford Green. Translated by Reinhard Krauss and Nancy Lukens. Minneapolis: Fortress Press, 1998.

Vol. 2: *Akt und Sein: Transzendentalphilosophie und Ontologie in der systematischen Theologie.* Edited by Hans-Richard Reuter. Munich: Chr. Kaiser Verlag, 1988. English translation: *Act and Being: Transcendental Philosophy and Ontology in Systematic Theology.* Edited by Wayne Whitson Floyd, Jr. Translated by H. Martin Rumscheidt. Minneapolis: Fortress Press, 1996.

Vol. 3. *Schöpfung und Fall.* Edited by Martin Rüter and Ilse Tödt. Munich: Chr. Kaiser Verlag, 1989. English translation: *Creation and Fall: A Theological*

Exposition of Genesis 1–3. Edited by John W. De Gruchy. Translated by Douglas Stephen Bax. Minneapolis: Fortress Press, 1996.

Vol. 4: *Nachfolge.* Edited by Martin Kuske and Ilse Tödt. Gütersloh: Chr. Kaiser Verlag, 1989; 2d edition 1994. English translation: *Discipleship.* Edited by Geffrey B. Kelly and John D. Godsey. Translated by Barbara Green and Reinhard Krauss. Minneapolis: Fortress Press, 2001.

Vol. 5: *Gemeinsames Leben. Das Gebetbuch der Bibel.* Edited by G. L. Müller and A. Schönherr. Munich: Chr. Kaiser, 1987. English translation: *Life Together.* Edited by Geffrey B. Kelly. Translated by Daniel W. Bloesch. *The Prayerbook of the Bible.* Edited by Geffrey B. Kelly. Translated by James Burtness. Minneapolis: Fortress Press, 1996.

Vol. 6: *Ethik.* Edited by Ise Tödt, Heinz Eduard Tödt, Ernst Feil, and Clifford Green. Gütersloh: Chr. Kaiser Verlag, 1992.

Vol. 7: *Fragmente aus Tegel.* Edited by Renate Bethge and Ilse Tödt. Gütersloh: Chr. Kaiser Verlag, 1994. English translation: *Fiction from Tegel Prison.* Edited by Clifford J. Green. Translated by Nancy Lukens. Minneapolis: Fortress Press, 2000.

Vol. 8: *Widerstand und Ergebung.* Edited by Christian Gremmels, Eberhard Bethge, and Renate Bethge, assisted by Ilse Tödt. Gütersloh: Chr. Kaiser Verlag, 1998.

Vol. 9: *Jugend und Studium, 1918–1917.* Edited by Hans Pfeifer, with Clifford Green and Carl Jürgen Kaltenborn. Munich: Chr. Kaiser Verlag, 1986.

Vol. 10: *Barcelona, Berlin, Amerika: 1928–1931* (Barcelona, Berlin, America, 1928–1931). Edited by Reinhart Staats and Hans Christoph von Hase, assisted by Holger Roggelin and Matthias Wünsche. Munich: Chr. Kaiser Verlag, 1991.

Vol. 11: *Ökumene, Universität, Pfarramt: 1931–1932* (Ecumenical, academic, and pastoral work, 1931–1932). Edited by Eberhard Amelung and Christoph Strohm. Gütersloh: Chr. Kaiser Verlag, 1994.

Vol. 12: *Berlin: 1932–1933.* Includes "Christologie," 279–348, and "Die Kirche vor der Judenfrage," 349–58. Edited by Carsten Nicolaisen and Ernst-Albert Scharffenorth. Gütersloh: Chr. Kaiser Verlag, 1997.

Vol. 13: *London: 1933–1935.* Edited by Hans Goedeking, Martin Heimbucher, and Hans-Walter Schleicher. Gütersloh: Chr. Kaiser Verlag, 1994.

Vol. 14: *Illegale Theologenausbildung: Finkenwalde 1935–1937* (Theological education at Finkenwalde, 1935–1937). Edited by Otto Dudzus and Jürgen Henkys, assisted by Sabine Bobert-Stützel, Dirk Schulz, and Ilse Tödt. Gütersloh: Chr. Kaiser Verlag, 1996.

Vol. 15: *Illegale Theologenausbildung: Sammelvikariate 1937–1940* (Theological education underground, 1937–1940). Edited by Dirk Schulz. Gütersloh: Chr. Kaiser Verlag, 1998.

Vol. 16: *Konspiration und Haft. 1940–1945* (Conspiracy and imprisonment, 1940–1945). Edited by Jørgen Glenthøj, Ulrich Kabitz, and Wolf Krötke, Gütersloh: Chr. Kaiser Verlag, 1996.

Vol. 17: *Register und Ergänzungen* (Indices and supplements). Edited by Herbert Anzinger and Hans Pfeifer, assisted by Waltraud Anzinger and Ilse Tödt. Gütersloh: Chr. Kaiser Verlag, 1999.

———. *Ethics.* Translated by Neville Horton Smith. New York: Macmillan, 1965; Simon and Schuster, 1995.

———. *Gesammelte Schriften* (Collected works). 6 vols. Edited by Eberhard Bethge. Munich: Chr. Kaiser Verlag, 1958–74.

———. *No Rusty Swords: Letters, Lectures, and Notes, 1928–1936.* Translated by Edwin H. Robertson and John Bowden. London: Collins; New York: Harper & Row, 1965.

———. *Predigten, Auslegungen, Meditationen* (Sermons, interpretations, meditations). 2 vols. Vol. 1: 1925–1935; vol. 2: 1935–1945. Edited by Otto Dudzus. Munich: Chr. Kaiser Verlag, 1984, 1985.

———. *A Testament to Freedom: The Essential Writings of Dietrich Bonhoeffer.* Edited by Geffrey B. Kelly and F. Burton Nelson. San Francisco: Harper Collins, 1990. Revised and expanded edition, 1995.

Bonhoeffer, Karl. "Lebenserinnerungen" (Life memories). In *Karl Bonhoeffer zum hundertsten Geburtstag* (Karl Bonhoeffer for his one hundredth birthday), 8–107. Edited by J. Zutt, H. Scheller, and E. Straus. Berlin, Heidelberg, New York, 1969.

Bonhoeffer, Lothar. *Erinnerungen. Ein Beitrag zur Familiengeschichte* (Memories: A contribution to a family history). Munich, 1974.

Bonhöffer, Eugen. "500 Jahre Boenhoff–Bonhoeffer" (500 years Boenhoff–Bonhoeffer). Manuscript, 1934.

Bosanquet, Mary. *The Life and Death of Dietrich Bonhoeffer.* London: Hodder & Stoughton, 1968.

Bracher, Karl Dietrich. *Die Auflösung der Weimarer Republik* (The dissolution of the Weimar Republic). Villingen, 1964.

———. *The German Dictatorship.* Translated by Jean Steinberg with an introduction by Peter Gay. New York: Penguin Books, 1970.

Calvin, Jean. *Institutes of the Christian Religion.* Vols. 20–21 of *The Library of Christian Classics.* Edited by John T. McNeill. Translated by Ford Lewis Battles. Philadelphia: Westminster Press, 1960.

Catullus, Gaius Valerius. *Liebesgedichte und sonstige Dichtungen* (Love poems and other poetry.) Latin and German. Translated into German by Otto Weinreich. Reinbek: Rowohlt, 1960.

———. *The Poems of Catullus.* Translated with an introduction by Peter Whigman. London: Penguin Books, 1966.

Cicero, Marcus Tullius. *De natura deorum; Academica* (The nature of the gods). Latin and English. Loeb Classical Library. Vol. 19. Translated by H. Rackham. Cambridge: Harvard University Press, 2000.

———. "Pro Flacco." "In Defense of Lucius Flaccus." Translated by Louis E. Lord. *The Speeches.* Latin and English. Loeb Classical Library. Vol. 10. Cambridge: Harvard University Press, 1977.

———. "Pro Milone." "On Behalf of Titus Annius Milo." Translated by N. H. Watts. *The Speeches.* Latin and English. Loeb Classical Library. Vol. 14. Cambridge: Harvard University Press, 1992.

Clement of Rome. "The Letter of the Church of Rome to the Church of Corinth, commonly called Clement's First Letter." Translated by Cyril C. Richardson. In *Early Christian Fathers,* 33–73. Translated and edited by Cyril C. Richardson et al. The Library of Christian Classics. Vol. 1. Philadelphia: Westminster Press, 1953.

Corpus Reformatorum (Works of Melanchthon and Calvin). 87 vols. in 53. Edited by Karl Gottlieb Bretschneider. Bad Feilnbach: Schmidt Periodicals, 1990.

Deissmann, Adolf. *Paul: A Study in Social and Religious History.* Translated by W. Wilson. 2d ed. New York, 1926.

Delbrück, Hans, and James Wycliffe Headlam-Morley, *Deutsch-Englische Schulddiskussion* (German-English discussion of guilt). Berlin, 1921.

Deutsches Kirchliches Adreßbuch (German church directory). Edited by the Protestant Press Association for Germany, Berlin, 1927.

Dickens, Charles. *The Personal History of David Copperfield.* London & Toronto: J. M. Dent; New York: E. P. Dutton, 1919.

Dreß, Walter. *Evangelisches Erbe und Weltoffenheit* (Protestant heritage and openness to the world). Edited by von W. Sommer. Berlin: CZV-Verlag, 1980.

Dudzus, Otto, ed. *Bonhoeffer Brevier.* Munich: Chr. Kaiser Verlag, 1971. English translation: *Bonhoeffer for a New Generation.* London: SCM Press, 1986.

Eckermann, Johann Peter. *Gespräche mit Goethe.* Edited by Rudolf Otto. Berlin and Weimar, 1982. English translation: *Conversations of Goethe with Johann Peter Eckermann.* See Goethe.

Epictetus. *The Discourses.* Two volumes. English and Latin. Translated by C. H. Oldfather. Loeb Classical Library. Cambridge: Harvard University Press, 2000.

Eschenburg, Theodor. *Matthias Erzberger.* Munich, 1973.

Eusebius, Bishop of Caesarea. *The Ecclesiastical History.* Loeb Classical Library, 2 vols., Greek and English. Edited and translated by Kirsopp Lake et al. Cambridge: Harvard University Press, 1994.

Feder, Alfred Leonhard. *Lehrbuch der geschichtlichen Methode* (Textbook of historical method). 3d ed. Regensburg: Kosel & Pustet, 1924.

————. *Lehrbuch der historischen Methodik* (Textbook of historical methodology). 2d ed. Regensburg: Kosel & Pustet, 1921.

Fichte, Johann Gottlieb. *Versuch einer Kritik aller Offenbarung* (1792). *Sämmtliche Werke.* Edited by I. H. Fichte. Berlin, 1854–, 11–174. English translation: *Attempt at a Critique of All Revelation.* Translated with an introduction by Garrett Green. Cambridge and New York: Cambridge University Press, 1978.

50 Jahre Walther Rathenau-Schule (vormals Grunewald-Gymnasium) 1903–1953 (Fifty years of the Walther Rathenau School [previously the Grunewald Gymnasium] 1903–1953). Edited by W. Padberg. Berlin, 1953.

Gandhi, Mahatma K. *Die Botschaft des Mahatma Gandi* (The message of Mahatma Gandhi). Edited by Z. Husain and A. Ehrentreich. Berlin-Schlachtensee: Volkserzieher-Verlag, 1924.

Goethe, Johann Wolfgang von. *The Autobiography of Johann Wolfgang von Goethe.* Translated by John Oxenford. Chicago: University of Chicago Press, 1974. Translated from *Aus meinem Leben: Dichtung und Wahrheit.*

————. *Conversations of Goethe with Johann Peter Eckermann.* Translated by John Oxenford. Edited by J. K. Moorhead. Introduced by Havelock Ellis. New York: Da Capo Press, 1998.

————. *Faust.* Translated with introduction and notes by Peter Salm. New York, 1985.

————. *Götz von Berlichingen mit der eisernen Hand: ein Schauspiel.* Commentary by Wilhelm Grosse. Frankfurt am Main: Suhrkamp, 2001. English translation: *Götz von Berlichingen. A Play.* Translated by Charles E. Passage. Prospect Heights, Ill.: Waveland, 1991.

————. *Plays: Egmont, Iphigenia, Torquato.* Edited by Frank Glessner Ryder. New York: Continuum, 1993.

————. "Torquato Tasso." Translated by Anna Swanwick. In *The Works of F. W. von Goethe.* Volume 11. Edited by Nathan Dole. London and Boston: F. A. Niccolls, 1902.

————. "Trilogie der Leidenschaft." *Werke.* Hamburger Ausgabe, vol. 1. Edited by Erich Trunz. Twelfth edition. Munich, 1981ff.

————. *Werke.* Hamburger Ausgabe. 14 vols. Edited by Erich Trunz. Munich: Beck, 1981ff. English translations: "Tarquato Tasso" and "Götz von Berlichingen" in *The Works of Goethe* 11:91–356. Edited by Nathan Dole; translated by Sir Walter Scott, Sir Theodore Martin, John Oxenford, Thomas Carlyle, and others. "Tarquato Tasso" is translated by Anna Swanwick and "Götz von Berlichingen" by Sir Walter Scott. London, 1902.

————. *Wilhelm Meisters Lehrjahre.* Edited by Ehrhard Bahr. Stuttgart: Reclam, 1982, 1990. English translation: *Wilhelm Meister's Apprenticeship.* Edited and translated by Eric A. Blackall in cooperation with Victor Lange. Princeton: Princeton University Press, 1995.

Gramm, Erich. "Die soziale Arbeitsgemeinschaft Berlin-Ost" (The social workers' association East Berlin). In *Lebendige Ökumene. Festschrift für Friedrich Siegmund-Schultze*, 84–118. Witten, 1965.

Green, Clifford. *Bonhoeffer: A Theology of Sociality*. Grand Rapids: Eerdmans, 1999. Revised edition of *Bonhoeffer: The Sociality of Christ and Humanity: Dietrich Bonhoeffer's Early Theology 1927–1933*. American Academy of Religion Studies in Religion 6. Missoula, Mont.: Scholars Press, 1975.

——————. "Bonhoeffer in the Context of Erikson's Luther Study." In Roger A. Johnson, ed., *Psychohistory and Religion: The Case of 'Young Man Luther'*. Philadelphia: Fortress Press, 1977.

——————, ed. "Dietrich Bonhoeffer: Seminararbeit 'Luthers Anschauungen vom Heiligen Geist nach den Disputationen von 1535–1545' aus dem Jahr 1926." In Christian Gremmels, *Bonhoeffer und Luther*, 185–232.

Green, Clifford, and Wayne Whitson Floyd Jr. *Bonhoeffer Bibliography*: see Floyd.

Gremmels, Christian, ed. *Bonhoeffer und Luther. Zur Sozialgestalt des Luthertums in der Moderne* (Bonhoeffer and Luther: On the social form of Lutheranism in modernity). Internationales Bonhoeffer Forum 6. Munich: Chr. Kaiser Verlag, 1983.

Gremmels, Christian, and Hans Pfeifer. *Theologie und Biographie. Zum Beispiel Dietrich Bonhoeffer* (Theology and biography: The example of Dietrich Bonhoeffer). Munich: Chr. Kaiser Verlag, 1983.

Groos, Karl. *Der Aufbau der Systeme. Eine formale Einführung in die Philosophie* (The development of the system: A formal introduction to philosophy). Leipzig, 1924.

——————. *Naturgesetze und historische Gesetze* (Natural law and the laws of history). Tübingen, 1926.

Hase, Gottfried von. *Familientafel. Die Nachkommen von Karl August von Hase and Pauline Amalie von Hase* (Family tree: The descendants of Karl August von Hase and Pauline Amalie von Hase). Stuttgart, 1984.

Hauptmann, Gerhart. *Die versunkene Glocke. Eine deutsches Märchen-drama* (The lost bell: A German fairy-tale drama). Berlin: Fischer, 1922.

Havenstein, Martin. *Nietzsche als Erzieher* (Nietzsche as educator). Berlin: Mittler, 1922.

Hermas. *The Shepherd*. In *Fathers of the Second Century. Ante-Nicene Fathers*, vol. 2. Edited by Alexander Roberts and James Donaldson. Grand Rapids: Eerdmans, 1975.

Holl, Karl. "Luther und der Heilige Geist." Notes gathered by Emanuel Hirsch. In Walter Bodenstein, *Die Theologie Karl Holls*. See above.

——————. "Die Rechtfertigungslehre in Luthers Vorlesung über den Römerbrief mit besonderer Rücksicht auf die Frage der Heilsgewissheit" (The doctrine of justification in Luther's lectures on Romans with special attention to the question of the certainty of salvation). *Gesammelte Aufsätze zur Kirchengeschichte* (Collected essays on church history). Vol. 1: *Luther*, 111–54. Tübingen: J. C. B. Mohr, 1923.

————. *The Holy Bible: New Revised Standard Version.* Division of Christian Education of the National Council of the Churches of Christ in the United States of America. New York: Collins, 1989.

Honecker, Martin. *Kirche als Gestalt und Ereignis. Die sichtbare Gestalt der Kirche als dogmatisches Problem* (Church as form and event: The visible form of the church as dogmatic problem). Munich: Chr. Kaiser Verlag, 1963.

Horace (Quintus Horatus Flaccus). *The Art of Poetry.* Translated by Burton Raffel and James Hynd. Albany: State University of New York Press, 1974.

————. *The Complete Odes and Epodes, with the Centennial Hymn.* Translated with notes by W. G. Shepherd. London: Penguin Books, 1983.

————. *Horace: The Odes and Epodes.* Latin and English. Translated by C. E. Bennett. Loeb Classical Library. Cambridge: Harvard University Press, 1978.

————. *Satires. Epistles, and Ars Poetica.* Translated by H. Rushton Fairclough. Latin and English. Loeb Classical Library. Cambridge: Harvard University Press, 1978.

————. *Sermones. The Satires of Horace.* Edited, with notes, by Arthur Palmer. 4th edition reprint. London: Macmillan; New York: St. Martin's Press, 1964.

Ignatius, Saint, Bishop of Antioch. "To the Philadelphians." Translated by Cyril C. Richardson. In *Early Christian Fathers,* 107–111. Edited by Cyril C. Richardson et al. Philadelphia: Westminster Press, 1953.

Inter-Lutheran Commission on Worship. *Lutheran Book of Worship.* Minneapolis: Augsburg; Philadelphia: Board of Publication, Lutheran Church in America, 1978.

Irenaeus, Bishop of Lyons. *Adversus haereses.* In *Sources chrétiennes,* vols. 210–11. Edited and translated by A. Rousseau and L. Doutreleau. Paris, 1974. English translation: *Irenaeus Against Heresies.* Vol. 1 of the *Ante-Nicene Fathers.* Edited by Alexander Roberts and James Donaldson. Grand Rapids: Eerdmans, 1956.

Jervell, Jacob. *Die Apostelgeschichte, übersetzt und erklärt* (The Acts of the Apostles, translated and explained). 17th ed. Göttingen: Vandenhoek & Ruprecht, 1998.

Josephus, Flavius. *Against Apion.* Greek and English. Translated by Henry St. John Thackeray. Loeb Classical Library. Volume 1. Cambridge: Harvard University Press, 1993.

————. *Jewish Antiquities.* Nine volumes. Translated by Henry St. John Thackeray et al. Latin and English. Loeb Classical Library, volumes 5–9. Cambridge: Harvard University Press, 1998.

————. *The Jewish War.* Greek and English. Translated by Henry St. John Thackeray. Loeb Classical Library, volumes 5–13. Cambridge: Harvard University Press, 1997.

Kaltenborn, Carl-Jürgen. *Adolf von Harnack als Lehrer Dietrich Bonhoeffers* (Adolf von Harnack as a teacher of Dietrich Bonhoeffer). Berlin: Evangelische Verlagsanstalt, 1973.

Kant, Immanuel. *Critique of Pure Reason.* Translated by Norman Kemp Smith. New York: St. Martin's Press, 1933.

———. *Die Religion innerhalb der Grenzen der blossen Vernunft.* Leipzig, 1919. English translation: *Religion within the Limits of Reason Alone.* Translated by Theodore M. Green and Hoyt H. Hudson. New York: Harper, 1960.

Kierkegaard, Søren. *Philosophische Brocken. Gesammelte Werke* 10. Edited by Emanuel Hirsch and Hayo Gerdes. Düsseldorf: Diederichs Verlag, 1952. English translation from the Danish original: *Philosophical Fragments.* Edited and translated with introduction and notes by Howard V. Hong and Edna H. Hong. Princeton: Princeton University Press, 1985.

Korn, Elisabeth, ed. *Die Jugendbewegung* (The youth movement). Düsseldorf, 1963.

Köstlin, Julius. *Luthers Leben.* Leipzig: Fues, 1891. English translation: *Life of Luther.* London: Longmans, Green, 1905.

Krummacher, Friedrich Adolf, and Albert Wucher. *Die Weimarer Republik: Ihre Geschichte in Texten, Bildern und Dokumenten* (The Weimar Republic: Its history in texts, pictures, and documents). Munich, 1965.

Kupisch, Karl. *Studenten entdecken die Bibel* (Students discover the Bible). Hamburg, 1964.

Leibholz-Bonhoeffer, Sabine. *Vergangen, Erlebt, Überwunden.* Gütersloh: Gütersloher Verlaghaus, 1968. English translation: *The Bonhoeffers: Portrait of a Family.* London: Sidgwick and Jackson, 1971.

Lessing, Gottfried Ephraim. "Über den Beweis des Geistes." In *Sämtliche Schriften* 3:1–8. Leipzig, 1897. English translation: "On the Proof of the Spirit and Power." In *Theological Writings: Selections in Translation,* 51–56. Introduced by Henry Chadwick. Stanford: Stanford University Press, 1957.

Lidzbarski, Mark. *Ginza, der Schatz, oder das grosse Buch der Mandäer* (Ginza, the treasure, or the great book of the Mandaeans). Göttingen: Vandenhoek & Ruprecht, 1925.

———. *Mandäische Liturgien.* (Mandaean liturgies). Hildesheim and New York: George Olms Verlag, 1971.

Lohmeyer, Ernst. *Das Evangelium des Markus.* (The Gospel of Mark). 14th ed. Göttingen: Vandenhoeck & Ruprecht, 1957.

Lombard, Peter. *Magistri Petri Lombardi Parisiensis episcopi Sententiae in IV libris distinctae.* 3d ed. 2 vols. Edited by I. Brady. Grottaferrata: Editiones Collegii S. Bonaventurae ad Claras Aquas, 1971–81. English translation: *The Books of Opinions of Peter Lombard.* 4 vols. Translated by Robert E. O'Brien. Photocopy, Graduate Theological Union Library, 1970, 1992.

Lütgert, Wilhelm. "Wichern und Mahling. Rede zum Gedächtnis an D. Friedrich Mahling am 29. Juni 1933" (Wichern and Mahling: Address in memory of D. Friedrich Mahling on June 29, 1933). *Zeitschrift für systematische Theologie* (1934): 171–87.

Luther, Martin. "Die Ascensionis domini. 5 Mai 1524" (On the ascension of the Lord). *In Predigten über das erste Buch Mose* (Sermons on the first book of Moses). *WA* 14:466–471.

———. "Assertio omnium articulorum. 1520" (Defense of all the articles). *WA* 7:91–151.

———. "Dictata super Psalterium." 1513–16. *WA* 4:1–462. English translation: *First Lectures on the Psalms. LW* 11:3–553.

———. "Disputation concerning Justification." Translated by Lewis W. Spitz. *LW* 34:145–96.

———. "Eine kurze Erklärung der Zehn Gebote" (A brief explanation of the Ten Commandments). *WA* 1:247–56.

———. *In epistolam Pauli ad Galatas M. Lutheri commentarius.* 1519. *WA* 2:436–618. English translation: *Lectures on Galatians. LW* 27:153–410.

———. "Exempel, einen rechten, christlichen Bischof zu weihen" (Example, to ordain a proper Christian bishop). *WA* 53:219–60.

———. *Galaterkommentar WA* 2:495.1; *LW* 27:227 (Commentary on Galatians);

———. *The Letters of Martin Luther.* Selected and translated by Margaret A. Currie. London: Macmillan, 1908.

———. "Luther's Letter to His Wife. Eisleben. February 6, 1546." *Luther's Works* 50:300.

———. *Martin Luther's Basic Theological Writings.* Edited by Timothy Lull. Minneapolis: Fortress Press, 1989.

———. "Predigt am Jakobstage. July 15, 1522." (Sermon on St. James' day). *WA* 10/3:235–41.

———. "Predigt [über Johannes 10:12ff.] am Sonntage Misericordias Domini 1524." (Sermon [John 10:12ff] on Misericordia Sunday 1524). *WA* 15:533–37.

———. "Preface to the Epistles of St. James and St. Jude." *LW* 35:395–98.

———. "Preface to the New Testament." *LW* 35:355–62. Translated by Charles M. Jacobs and E. Theodore Bachmann.

———. *Reformation Writings of Martin Luther.* Translated with notes by Bertram Lee Woolf. 2 vols. New York: Philosophical Library, 1953.

———. "Sermon on the Sacrament of Penance, 1519" *LW* 35:12.

———. "Sermon von Sankt Jakob. 25.7.1522." *WA* 10/3:133–35.

———. "A Sincere Admonition by Martin Luther to All Christians to Guard against Insurrection and Rebellion." *LW* 45:51–74.

———. "Supputatio annorum mundi. 1541–1545." (A reckoning of the years of the world). *WA* 53:1–184.

———. "Theses concerning Faith and Law." *LW* 34:109.

———. "Verhandlungen mit D. Martin Luther auf dem Reichstage zu Worms." *WA* 7:814–87. "Luther at the Diet of Worms." Translated by Roger A. Hornsby. *LW* 32:101–31.

———— . "Vermahnung zum Gebiet wider die Türken" *WA* 51:585–625. "An Appeal for Prayer against the Turks." *LW* 43:213–41.

————. *The Works of Martin Luther.* The Philadelphia Edition. Translated by C. M. Jacobs. Philadelphia: Muhlenberg Press, 1932.

Marcus Aurelius. *Marcus Aurelius: Communings with Himself* [Meditations]. Translated by Charles R. Haines. Greek and English. Loeb Classical Library. Cambridge: Harvard University Press, 1994.

Melanchthon, Philipp. "De lege naturae." (Of natural law). *Loci praecipui Theologici* (1551). In *Corpus Reformatorum* 21:711–16.

Melito, Saint, Bishop of Sardis. *On Pascha and Fragments.* Translated and edited by Stuart George Hall. Oxford: Clarendon Press, 1979.

Milch, Werner. "Werner Milch über Manfred Resa" (Werner Milch on Manfred Resa). *Die Alte Schule* (The old school) 91 (1979): 29–32.

Minucius Felix, Marcus. *The Octavius of Marcus Minucius Felix.* Ancient Christian Writers, vol. 39. Translated and annotated by Graeme W. Clarke. New York: Newman Press, 1974.

Mishnah, 'Aboth 3.8. Translated by H. Danby. Oxford: Oxford University Press, 1933.

Nachlaß Dietrich Bonhoeffer: Ein Verzeichnis. Archiv–Sammlung–Bibliothek (Dietrich Bonhoeffer's literary estate: A bibliographical catalog—Archive, collection, library). Edited by Dietrich Meyer and Eberhard Bethge. Munich: Chr. Kaiser Verlag, 1987.

Nachlaß Dreß (The literary estate of the Dreß family). Property of Andreas and Ruprecht Dreß, Bielefeld, Germany, and San Diego, California.

Nietzsche, Friedrich. *Werke. Kritische Gesamtausgabe* 6/6.2. Edited by G. Colli and M. Montinari. Berlin, 1968. English translations: (1) *Beyond Good and Evil.* Translated by Walter Kaufmann. New York: Random House, 1966. (2) *On the Genealogy of Morals* and *Ecce Homo.* Translated by Walter Kaufmann and R. J. Hollingdale. New York: Random House, 1967.

Otto, Walter F. *Die Götter Griechenlands.* Bonn, 1929. English translation: *The Homeric Gods: The Spiritual Significance of Greek Religion.* Translated by Moses Hadas. New York, 1954.

Pascal, Blaise. *Pensées.* Introduced and translated by Martin Turnell. New York: Harper & Row, 1962.

————. *Pensées and Other Writings.* Translated by Honor Levi. Introduction and notes by Anthony Levi. New York: Oxford University Press, 1995.

Perrone, Giovanni. *Praelectiones theologicae.* (Preliminary theological readings). 9 vols. in four. Edition 31. Taurini: Hyacinthi-Marietti, 1865.

Pfeifer, Hans. "Die Gestalten der Rechtfertigung" (The forms of justification). *Kirche und Dogma* (1972): 177–201.

————. "Das Kirchenverständnis Dietrich Bonhoeffers. Ein Beitrag zur theologischen Prinzipienlehre" (Dietrich Bonhoeffer's understanding of the church: A contribution to basic theological doctrine). Diss., Heidelberg, 1963.

Pfizer, Theodor. *Im Schatten der Zeit 1904–1949* (In the shadow of time 1904–1949). Stuttgart, 1979.

Philo of Alexandria. *Philo von Alexandria. Die Werke in deutscher Übersetzung.* 2d ed. 6 vols. Edited by Leopold Cohn and Paul Wendland. Berlin: de Gruyter, 1962. English translation: *Works.* Greek and English in 10 vols. and 2 supplementary vols. Translated by Francis Colson, George Whitaker, and Ralph Marcus. Loeb Classical Library. Cambridge, Mass.: Harvard University Press, 1971.

Plato. *Werke.* 8 vols. Translated by F. Schleiermacher et al. Edited by G. Eigler. Darmstadt, 1970ff. English translation: *Complete Works.* Edited by John M. Cooper and D. S. Hutchinson. Indianapolis: Hackett Publishing Co., 1997.

Plutarch. "Quomodo adolescens poetas audire debet." "How the Young Man Should Study Poetry." *Moralia in fifteen volumes.* Vol. 1. Latin and English. Translated by Frank C. Babbitt. Loeb Classical Library. Cambridge: Harvard University Press, 1992.

Ranke, Leopold von. *Über die Epochen der neueren Geschichte.* Darmstadt, 1982. English translation: "On Progress in History." In *The Theory and Practice of History.* Edited by Georg G. Iggers and Konrad von Moltke. New York: Irvington, 1993.

Reventlow, Ernst Graf zu. *Politische Vorgeschichte des Grossen Krieges* (Political prehistory of the Great War). Berlin, 1919.

Riemann, Heinrich. "Schiller in der Musik" (Schiller in music). In *Bühne und Welt* (Theater and world) 7 (1905): 651–56.

Schabert, Otto. *Baltisches Märtyrerbuch* (Baltic book of martyrs). Berlin, 1926.

Schiller, Friedrich. *Sämtliche Werke.* Munich: C. Hanser, 1958–. English translation: *Complete Works.* Translated by S. T. Coleridge and Baron Lytton. 2 vols. Philadelphia, 1870.

———. *William Tell.* Translated and edited by William F. Mainland. Chicago: University of Chicago Press, 1972.

Scholder, Klaus. *Die Kirchen und das Dritte Reich.* Vol. 1: *Vorgeschichte und Zeit der Illusionen, 1918–1934.* Frankfurt, 1977. English translation: *The Churches and the Third Reich.* Vol. 1 of 2 vols. Translated by John Bowden. Philadelphia: Fortress Press, 1988.

Die Schuld am Kriege. Dokumente, geschichtliche Überlegungen, zusammengestellt vom Verein Auslandskunde e.V. (Guilt over the war: Documents, historical reflections, collected by the Association for Foreign Information). Mitteilungen des Vereins Auslandskunde (Communications of the Association for Foreign Information). Publication nos. 13/14. Berlin, 1919.

Schwarz, Albert. "Die Weimarer Republik" (The Weimar Republic). In *Handbuch der Deutschen Geschichte* 4/1. Edited by O. Brand, A. O. Meyer, and L. Just. Constance, 1958.

Seneca, Lucius Annaeus. *Ad Lucilium epistulae morales.* 3 vols. Latin and English, Loeb Classical Library. Translated by Richard M. Gummere. Cambridge: Harvard University Press, 1989.

———. "De beneficiis." *Moral Essays.* Vol. 3. Loeb Classical Library, Latin and English. Translated by John W. Basore. Cambridge: Harvard University Press, 1989.

———. *Philosophische Schriften* 3. Edited and translated by M. Rosenbach, Darmstadt, 1974. English translation: *Moral Essays.* 7 vols. Translated by John Barore. Cambridge: Harvard University Press, 1928–35.

75 Jahre Walther Rathenau-Schule (vormals Grunewald-Gymnasium) 1903–1978 (Seventy-five years of the Walther Rathenau School [previously the Grunewald Gymnasium] 1903–1978). Berlin, 1978.

Sifra: An Analytical Translation. 3 vols. Translated by Jacob Neusner. Brown Judaic Studies 138–140. Atlanta, GA: Scholars Press, 1988.

Sombart, Nikolaus. *Jugend in Berlin* (Youth in Berlin). Munich, 1984.

Staats, Reinhart. "Adolf von Harnack im Leben Dietrich Bonhoeffers" (Adolf von Harnack in the life of Dietrich Bonhoeffer). *Theologische Zeitschrift* 77 (1981): 94–122.

Staats, Reinhart, and Matthias Wünsche. "Dietrich Bonhoeffer's Abschied von der Berliner 'Wintertheologie'. Neue Funde aus seiner Spainienkorrespondenz 1928" (Dietrich Bonhoeffer's farewell to Berlin's 'Winter theology': New discoveries from his Spanish correspondence, 1928)," *Zeitschrift für Neuere Theologiegeschichte / Journal for the History of Modern Theology* (1994): 179–200.

Stählin, Otto, ed. *Clemens Alexanrinus.* 4 vols. Vol. 1. *Protrepticus und Paedagogus.*—Vol. 2. *Stromata, Buch I–VI.*—Vol. 3. *Stromata, Buch VII-VIII. Excerpta ex Theodoto. Eclogae prophetica. Quis dives salvetur. Fragmente.*—Vol. 4. *Register.* Volumes 12, 15, 17, and 39 of *Die griechischen christlichen Schriftsteller der ersten drei Jahrhunderte* (The Greek Christian authors of the first three centuries). Edited by the Prussian Academy of Science. Leipzig: J. C. Hinrichs, 1897–.

Stock, Konrad. *Annihilatio mundi. Johann Gerhards Eschatologie der Welt* (*Annihilatio mundi*: Johann Gerhard's eschatology of the world). Forschungen zur Geschichte und Lehre des Protestantismus 10/42. Munich, 1971.

Suetonius, Gaius Tranquillus. *The Lives of the Caesars.* 2 vols. Loeb Classical Library, Latin and English. Translated by J. C. Rolfe. Introduction by K. R. Bradley. Revised edition. Cambridge: Harvard University Press, 1998.

Tacitus, Cornelius. *The Annals.* Translated by John Jackson. Latin and English. Loeb Classical Library, vols. 4–5. Cambridge: Harvard University Press, 1986.

Tatian. *Oratio ad Graecos and Fragments.* Edited and translated by Molly Whittaker. New York: Clarendon Press, 1982.

Tertullian. "De Carne Christi." In vol. 2, *Opera Omnia* (Complete works). *Patrologiae cursus completus,* Latin Series. Edited by J.-P. Migne. Paris, 1841. English translation: "On the Flesh of Christ," *Ante-Nicene Fathers,* 3:521–43. Reprint, Hendrickson Publishers: Peabody, Mass., 1994.

Tödt, Hans Eduard, et al., eds. *Wie eine Flaschenpost. Ökumenische Briefe und Beiträge für Eberhard Bethge* (Like a bottle cast into the sea: Ecumenical letters and contributions for Eberhard Bethge). Munich, 1979.

Troeltsch, Ernst. *Psychologie und Erkenntnistheorie in der Religionswissenschaft. Eine Untersuchung über die Bedeutung der Kantischen Religionslehre für die Heutige Religionswissenschaft* (Psychology and epistemology in the study of religion: A study of the significance of the Kantian doctrine of religion for the study of religion today). 2d ed. Tübingen: Mohr, 1922.

Walther, Christian. *Typen des Reich-Gottes-Verständnisses; Studien zur Eschatologie und Ethik im 19. Jahrhundert* (Types of understanding of the kingdom of God; studies on eschatology and ethics in the 19th century). Forschungen zur Geschichte und Lehre des Protestantismus, Reihe 10. Munich: Chr. Kaiser Verlag, 1961.

Weizsäcker, Carl Friedrich von. "Gedanken eines Nichttheologen zur theologischen Entwicklung Dietrich Bonhoeffers." In *Der Garten des Menschlichen: Beiträge zur geschichtlichen Anthropologie,* 454–78. Munich and Vienna: C. Hanser, 1977. Previously published in *Genf '76: Ein Bonhoeffer Symposion,* 29–50. Internationales Bonhoeffer Forum 1. Edited by Hans Pfeifer. Munich: Chr. Kaiser Verlag, 1976. English translation: "Thoughts of a Non-Theologian on Dietrich Bonhoeffer's Theological Development." In Weizsäcker, *The Ambivalence of Progress: Essays on Historical Anthropology.* New York: Paragon House, 1988. Previously translated in *The Ecumenical Review* 28/2 (April 1976): 156–73.

Widmann, M. "Zum Gedenken an Paul Schempp" (In memory of Paul Schempp). *Evangelische Theologie* 42 (1982): 366–81.

Wright, Jonathan Richard Cassé. *"Above Parties": The Political Attitudes of the German Protestant Church Leadership, 1918–1933.* London, New York: Oxford University Press, 1974.

Xenophon. *Memorabilia* and *Oeconomicus.* Greek and English. Translated by Edgar C. Marchant. Loeb Classical Library. Cambridge: Harvard University Press, 1992.

Yorck von Wartenburg, Marion. *Die Stärke der Stille. Erzählung eines Lebens aus dem deutschen Widerstand.* Cologne, 1984. English translation: *The Power of Solitude: My Life in the German Resistance.* Edited and translated by Julie M. Winter. Lincoln: University of Nebraska Press, 2000.

Zabarella, Giacomo. *De Methodis Libri Quatuor* (Four books on methods). Introduction by Cesare Vasoli. Bologna: Clueb, 1985.

Zahn-Harnack, Agnes. *Adolf von Harnack.* 2d ed. Berlin, 1951.

Zimmermann, Wolf-Dieter. *Begegnungen mit Dietrich Bonhoeffer.* Munich: Chr. Kaiser Verlag, 1964. English translation: *I Knew Dietrich Bonhoeffer: Reminiscences by His Friends.* Edited by Wolf-Dieter Zimmermann and Ronald Gregor Smith. Translated by Käthe Gregor Smith. London: Collins; New York: Harper, 1966.

Zwingli, Huldreich. *Werke.* (Works) 8 vols. Edited by Melchior Schuler and Johannes Schulthess. Zurich: Friedrich Schulthess, 1842, 1828.

INDEX

OF SCRIPTURAL REFERENCES

INDEX

OF NAMES

This index lists persons mentioned in this volume, including authors of literature cited in notes. It provides brief profiles of the people listed, and differs from the German edition by also including information about all persons mentioned in the text and notes, not just the Bonhoeffer family. It does not include personal names mentioned in book titles, or the names of people that only appear in the bibliography.

Barth, Karl (1886–1968): Swiss Reformed theologian; early leading voice of dialectical theology; leader in the Confessing Church; important influence on Dietrich Bonhoeffer and the pastors of his circle—148, 151, 153–54, 156, 158–60, 291, 299, 342, 436–38, 565, 573–75, 578

Bauer, Walter (1877–1960): professor of New Testament theology, mainly at Göttingen; initiator of *A Greek English Lexicon of the New Testament and Other Early Christian Literature*—395, 396, 401

Baumgarten, Siegmund Jacob (1706–57): follower of Christian Wolff; applied Wolff's demonstrative method to dogmatics—388

Bazzi, Giovanni (1477–1549): Italian Renaissance painter of the Siena school; influenced by Leonardo da Vinci and Raphael: see Sodoma—108

Beck, Johann Tobias (1804–78): pastor and professor of systematic theology, Tübingen—292

Beethoven, Ludwig van (1770–1827): German composer—32, 93

Bellarmine, Robert (1542–1621): Jesuit theologian; Cardinal; Archbishop of Capua—298

Bellini, Giovanni (1430–1516): Venetian Renaissance painter; teacher of Titian; worked with his father and brother in Padua—106

Benedict of Nursia (d. ca. 547 C.E.): Italian monk; founder of the monastery of Monte Cassino and the Benedictine monastic order—112

Bengel, Johann Albrecht (1687–1752): Württemberg theologian; "Father of Swabian Pietism"; associated astrology with redemption history; known for his commentaries and text-critical works on the New Testament—299

Bernard of Clairvaux (ca. 1090–1153): influential Christian mystic and preacher; founder of the Cistercian Order—292

Bernheim, Ernst (1850–1942): historian and professor, Greifswald—286, 299

Bernini, Giovanni Lorenzo (Gianlorenzo) (1598–1680):Italian sculptor and architect; dominant figure of the Italian baroque—85

Bertram, Georg (b. 1896): lecturer in New Testament, Berlin—175, 585

Bethge, Eberhard (1909–2000): pastor, educator, theologian, and friend and biographer of Dietrich Bonhoeffer; 1935–37 at the Finkenwalde Preachers' Seminary of the Confessing Church led by Bonhoeffer; 1937–40, inspector of studies at one of the two Pomeranian collective pastoral training programs led by Bonhoeffer preparing ministers for the Confessing Church; 1940–44, missions inspector, Gossner Mission in Berlin; 1943 married Renate Schleicher, Bonhoeffer's niece; 1943 military service; October 1944 arrested in Italy and imprisoned in Berlin following the attempted assassination of Hitler; April 25, 1945 freed from Lehrter Strasse Prison; after WWII, assistant to Bishop Otto Dibelius; 1946–53, student pastor, Berlin; 1953–61, overseas pastor, London; 1961–75, director of the Pastoral College of the Rhineland Church at Rengsdorf; editor of Bonhoeffer's works and author of the biography; after 1976, emeritus—active in lecturing, conferences, publications; particularly devoted to

Euripides (ca. 485/480–406 B.C.E.): Greek tragic poet—52, 525, 569, 590

Eusebius: The name of the verger at St. Peter's when Bonhoeffer visited there—90

Eusebius of Caesarea (Eusebius Pamphili) (ca. 263–339 C.E.): Bishop of Caesarea, Palestine; Christian apologist and church historian—379

Eve: biblical figure—266

Ezekiel: biblical figure—433

Fabriano, Gentile da (1370–1427): Italian painter of the so-called weak style at the end of the Gothic period—100

Fahland, Paul (b. 1878): pastor in Berlin-Lichtenberg, witness at Bonhoeffer's first theological exam; assessor of Bonhoeffer's catechetical work for his second theological exam—184

Fauser: unidentified discussion partner of Robert Held and Dietrich Bonhoeffer—144

Feder, Alfred Leonhard (1872–1927): German religious historian; wrote works on Justin Martyr, Jerome, Hilary of Poitiers, Ignatius Loyola, and historical methodology—299

Fendt, Leonhard (1881–1957): 1915, professor of Catholic theology, Dillingen; 1917, Halle; 1918, converted to Protestantism; 1927, pastor, Berlin; 1931, postdoctoral lecturing qualification, then private lecturer; 1934–45, professor of practical theology, Berlin; university preacher, Berlin-Wilmersdorf; 1945, instructor, the mission school in Liebenzell—529

Ferber, Gertrud (b. 1889): 1910–13, teacher in Danzig; from October 1913, Berlin, where she taught the history of religion, French, and German; 1924 doctorate, Hamburg, in the field of education; participated in Harnack's seminar—370, 371

Fichte, Johann Gottlieb (1762–1814): philosopher of German idealism—301

Fick, Rudolf (1866–1936): professor of anatomy; 1892–1905, Leipzig; 1909, Innsbruck; 1917–34, Berlin—46

Ficker, Johannes (1861–1944): church historian, Luther scholar; 1900, professor, Strasbourg; 1919, Halle—300, 440

Fischer, Alfred (1874–1940): 1930, consistory councilor and member of the Evangelical Central Council—184

Floyd, Wayne Whitson (b. 1950): theologian, educator, author, and editor; 1985, Ph.D., systematic theology, Emory University; 1986–90 assistant professor of theology, University of the South; from 1993, visiting professor of theology and director of the Bonhoeffer Center, Lutheran Theological Seminary at Philadelphia; from 1993, general editor, *Dietrich Bonhoeffer Works,* English edition; 1995–2001, canon theologian, Cathedral Church of St. Stephen, Harrisburg, Pennsylvania; from 1996, also dean's fellow, Dickinson College; from 2002, director, Anglican Center for Theology and Spirituality, Diocese of Southern Virginia, Norfolk—16

Julius III (John Maria del Monte) (1487–1555): pope—79
Just, Mr.: the German consul, Casablanca, Morocco, during the crisis of 1905/6—192

Kaftan, Julius Wilhelm (1848–1926): Protestant theologian, philosopher of history; 1874, professor of systematic theology, Basel; 1881, Leipzig; 1883, Berlin; 1921, vice president of the Old Prussian Church; cofounder of the Evangelical-Social Congress—285, 288, 289, 296, 299
Kahr, Gustav Ritter von: monarchist; 1923, named General Staff Commissioner—66
Kalckreuth, Pauline Countess von (Aunt Lina?) (1856–1928): married Leopold; daughter of Count Stanislaus von Kalckreuth and Anna Eleonore, née Cauer; sister of Clara von Hase and Countess Helene Yorck von Wartenburg; great aunt of Dietrich Bonhoeffer—5, 41
Kaltenborn, Carl-Jürgen (b. 1936): student, theology, the Baptist Seminary of Hamburg and the Humboldt-University of [East] Berlin; 1969, Th.D. on Harnack as teacher of Bonhoeffer; involved in the ecumenical activities of the Christian Peace Conference (Prague); 1983, professor of Ecumenics; 1993, left the University—15, 175
Kant, Immanuel (1724–1804): German philosopher; professor of logic and metaphysics; described his philosophy as transcendental or critical idealism—66, 93, 100, 300, 301, 318
Kappus, Carl: Bonhoeffer's Hebrew teacher—54
Kautsch, Emil (1841–1910): professor of Old Testament, Basel, Tübingen, and Halle—256
Kayser, Wolfgang (1904–44): law student; Bonhoeffer's fraternity brother in Tübingen—130, 132
Kern, Dietrich (b. 1905 Tübingen): student, Tübingen and October 1925–March 1926, Berlin; member of Harnack's seminar—370
Kiderlen[-Wächter], Alfred von (1852–1912): German diplomat and politician; before WWI, German Undersecretary of Foreign Affairs; attempted to enlarge Germany's influence and economic presence in Africa—193
Kierkegaard, Søren Aaby (1813–55): Danish theologian, author, and philosopher; critic of the Danish Lutheran church; influenced the development of existentialism and modern philosophy—151, 159
Kircher, Athanasius (1602–80): Jesuit mathematician and music scholar—104
Klinger, Max (1857–1920): German neo-classical painter, etcher, and sculptor—37
Klostermann, Erich (1870–1963): Protestant New Testament and patristic scholar—180
Knackfuß, Hermann (1848–1915) German art historian; professor, the Academy of Art in Düsseldorf—76
Knopf, Rudolf (1874–1920): professor of New Testament and historian of early Christian thought—216, 223, 227, 236, 237, 239, 251, 256

Octavian (Gaius Julius Caesar Octavianus Augustus) (63 B.C.E.–14 C.E.), first Roman emperor; adopted son and heir of Julius Caesar; became known as Caesar Augustus—198

Oppenheimer, Franz (1864–1943): German economist and sociologist—143

Osborn, Robert: American theologian, Duke University—15

Otto, Rudolf (1869–1937): Protestant theologian and philosopher of religion; professor, Göttingen, Breslau, and, from 1917, Marburg—329, 434

Otto, Walter (1874–1958): classical philologist; 1897, doctorate, Bonn; until 1911, editor and author for the Onomasticum Latinum; 1905, postdoctoral lecturing qualification; 1911, professor in Vienna; 1913, Basel; 1914, Frankfurt am Main; 1934, forced to move to Königsberg; 1944, forced to flee from there; 1945, professor, Munich, then Göttingen; 1946, Tübingen; his *Die Götter Griechenlands* (1929) impressed Bonhoeffer while in prison—525

Overbeck, Franz Camille (1837–1905): German Protestant theologian, professor, Jena and then Basel; friend of Nietzsche; held that the gospel was wholly eschatological; influenced the young Barth—162, 287

Pacelli, Eugenio: see Pius XII

Pamphili, Cardinal: see Pompilij, Basilio

Papias (2nd century C.E.): Christian bishop of Hierapolis in Phrygia; recorded early traditions about the origin of the gospels—379, 382, 445

Pascal, Blaise (1623–62): French scientist and religious philosopher; became Jansenist—151,153, 155, 292, 313

Paschal I (d. 824): 817–824, pope—105

Paul: biblical figure—10, 104, 159, 223, 225, 228, 229–30, 233, 238, 240–41, 243, 245, 247–48, 250–51, 253, 255–56, 261, 270, 273, 275, 293, 297, 313, 316, 323, 327, 337, 341–42, 346, 371, 379, 380–84, 395–404, 440, 445–46, 464, 470, 493, 500, 536, 538, 575, 591

Pernice, Klara: see Hase, Klara von

Perrone, Giovanni (1794–1876): Italian Jesuit theologian; active in the formulation of the dogma of the Immaculate Conception—287–88, 291

Perugino II (Pietro Vannucci) (1446–1523): Italian painter; the leading Umbrian master of early Renaissance; teacher of Raphael; among the painters who worked on the Sistine Chapel frescoes —102, 103, 106

Peruzzi, Baldassare (1481–1536): Italian architect and painter of the High Renaissance—90

Peter: biblical figure—84, 102, 103, 225, 335, 346, 370, 379

Pfeifer, Hans Martin (b. 1930): theologian, teacher, pastor, and editor; studied theology, Heidelberg, Basel, Göttingen, and Princeton; 1964, doctorate in theology, Heidelberg, with a dissertation on Bonhoeffer's doctrine of the church; until 1995, variously employed as student chaplain, school department head, instructor in religion, and pastor; 1975–78, secretary of the International Bonhoeffer Society, West German Section; from 1986,

Rembrandt (Rembrandt Harmensz van Rijn) (1606–69): painter, draftsman, etcher; greatest artist of the Dutch school—525

Reni, Guido (1575–1642): Italian painter of the early baroque period—87, 100, 101

Resa, Fritz: member of the commission that examined Bonhoeffer for his Abitur at the Gymnasium in Berlin-Grunewald—54

Reventlow, Count Ernst of (1869–1943): journalist and pan-Germanist; during World War I, on the staff of the influential newspaper *Deutsche Tageszeitung;* until 1936, member of the national parliament and of the NSDAP; leading member of the German Faith Movement—195

Richter, Julius (1862–1940): 1913, professor of mission history, Berlin; 1928, member of the German Evangelical Mission Board and of the World Alliance for Promoting International Friendship through the Churches; from 1928, professor of mission studies, Berlin; September 1933, participated with Bonhoeffer in the conference of the WAPIFC in Sofia and 1934 on Fanø—177

Richter, M. Carol Ernest: author of an 1828 edition of the works of Philo—216

Riemann, Heinrich S.: author of article on the use of Schiller's poetry and plays in musical compositions—504

Ritschl, Albrecht (1822–89): German Protestant church historian, systematic theologian, and New Testament scholar; 1852, professor, Bonn; 1864, Göttingen; founder of the Ritschlian school, which emphasized social ethics and an appreciation of the inner life of Christ—162, 248, 312, 313, 408, 543, 554

Roger II of Sicily (1095–1154): grand count of Sicily; of Norman ancestry; 1130, King; waged war against the Byzantine emperor Manuel Comnenus—96

Rohloff, Miss: viola player; 1924, violin teacher of Sabine Bonhoeffer—130

Rohrer, Kurt (1904–92): 1933–69, pastor; acquaintance of Dietrich Bonhoeffer—140

Rondinello, Niccolo (1500–61): Italian religious painter—101

Rößler, Helmuth (1903–82): German Protestant theologian; one of Bonhoeffer's fellow students in Berlin; from 1929, pastor, Beveringen/Ost-Prignitz; 1933–39, Heerlen in southern Holland; 1939–41, director of the preachers' seminary in Düsseldorf; 1942–45, consistory councilor there; 1944, member of the Provisional Church Administration of the Rhineland Church; 1948–68, High Church councilor in the Rhineland—152, 169, 439, 525

Rothe, Richard (1799–1867): Protestant theologian; 1837–49 and 1854–67, professor of theology, Heidelberg; 1849–54, Bonn; ethicist and dogmatician who developed a speculative systematic theology; advocated the sublimation of the church in a cultural state—321

the impact of Christian faith on the Gospel tradition; applied Hegelian dialectic to the interpretation of the Gospels—405, 408

Stresemann, Gustav (1878–1929): German statesman; 1918, founded the German People's Party; 1923, chancellor of Germany; 1923–29, minister of foreign affairs; 1926, shared Nobel peace prize with Aristide Briand—66, 74

Stumm, Karl Ferdinand (1836–1901): from 1888, Baron von Stumm-Halberg; entrepreneur and politician; founder of important companies in the steel industry—143

Stupperich, Robert (b. 1904 Moscow): student of theology with Bonhoeffer, Tübingen; 1932, Lic. theol., Berlin; 1942, lecturer in eastern European history, Berlin; 1946–72, professor of church history, Münster; editor of the critical edition of Melanchthon's works—439

Suetonius (Gaius Suetonius Tranquillas) (ca. 69–ca. 140 C.E.): Roman biographer and historian—219

Sulayman II (1642–91): Ottoman emperor; son of Ibrahim I; fought the Austrians over Bulgaria, Serbia, and Transylvania—274

Sydow, Reinhold von (1851–1943): German lawyer and politician—196

Tacitus, Publius Cornelius (ca. 55–ca. 117 C.E.): Roman orator, politician, and historian—219

Tatian (b. ca. 120 C.E.): Christian writer and apologist; studied under Justin; later adopted the heretical doctrines of the Encratites—224, 226

Teneromo, J.: journalist; well acquainted with Leo Tolstoy—34

Tertullian (Quintus Septimius Florens Tertullianus) (ca. 160–230 C.E.): African theologian from Carthage; a father of the Latin church—145, 287–288, 301, 303

Thales of Miletus (ca. 624–546 B.C.E.): earliest known Greek philosopher; mathematician, astronomer, and politician—530, 531–32, 534, 538, 540

Thomas Aquinas (ca. 1225–74): Italian philosopher and Dominican theologian; from 1252, taught in Paris and elsewhere; from 1262, head of the new course of general studies in Naples; 1322, canonized; 1567, declared a Doctor of the Catholic Church; his use of Aristotelean categories had a formative influence on Roman Catholic theology—306, 308, 443

Thurneysen, Eduard (1888–1974): Swiss pastor and practical theologian; close friend and associate of Karl Barth; contributed to the beginnings of dialectical theology—285–93, 295, 297, 299

Tillich, Paul (1886–1965): systematic theologian; taught in Germany and, after emigrating prior to World War II, in the United States—131

Titian (Tiziano Vecelli) (1477–1576): Italian painter; chief master of the Venetian school—86, 87, 101, 103

Tödt, Ilse (b. 1930): studied anthropology and indigenous religion at the Technical University, Hannover, at the Universities of Göttingen, Hamburg, and Frankfurt, and at Ohio State University; 1957, Ph.D., Göttingen; 1957, married Heinz Eduard Tödt; since 1961 at the Protestant Research Institute (FEST) in Heidelberg, concentrating on editing and translating, particularly many volumes of the *Dietrich Bonhoeffer Werke;* since 1992, member of the *DBW* editorial board; 1995, honorary doctorate in theology, University of Basel—175

Tolstoy, Count Leo Nikolayevich (1828–1910): Russian novelist, philosopher, moralist, and Christian mystic—34, 35, 318

Torczyner, Harry (Naphthali Herz Tur-Sinai) (1886 Galicia [modern Ukraine]–1973): Israeli scholar of Semitics; biblical scholar, and translator—420

Troeltsch, Ernst (1865–1923): Protestant theologian and philosopher of religion; scholar of the history of Christian social thought—106, 133, 148, 176, 300–309, 317, 565, 571

Tschuschner: unidentified member of Harnack's seminar—370–71

Tur-Sinai, N. H.: see Torczyner, Harry

Velasquez, Diego Rodriguez de Silva y (1599–1660): Spanish painter; representative of naturalism—101

Vilmar, Wilhelm (1870–1942): Dr.Phil.; from 1916, director of the University Preparatory Academy; later Bonhoeffer's German teacher; a frequent guest of the historian Hans Delbrück, whose family were friends of the Bonhoeffer family and lived in the same neighborhood—29, 54

Vischer, Eberhard (1865–1946): father of Wilhelm Vischer; New Testament scholar, Basel—225

Vits, Ernst: Dr.Theol.; General Superintendent of Neumark and Niederlausitz; representative of the consistory at Bonhoeffer's first theological examinations; November 15, 1931, ordained Bonhoeffer; 1934, retired—184, 441, 442

Volkmann (Volkmann-Leander), Richard von (1830–89): Dr. med. and surgeon general of the Prussian army; son of Alfred Volkmann and Adele, née Härtel; German author and surgeon; first cousin of Karl Alfred von Hase—3, 20

Volkmann, Antonie (Toni or Tony): Italian adopted daughter of Dr. Richard Volkmann—20, 52, 63

Walker, N. (or W.): Baltic person mentioned in a letter in connection with Karl-Friedrich Bonhoeffer—67, 80

Walther, Christian: German theologian, writing in mid-twentieth century—554

Weber, Hans Emil (1882–1950): 1912, professor of systematic theology, Bonn; 1935, Münster; 1946, Bonn—303

Weber, Max (1864–1920): German social economist, economic historian, and sociologist; contributed to the sociology of knowledge and to the

Xenophon (ca. 430–ca. 355 B.C.E.): Greek historian, author, soldier, disciple of Socrates—247

Yorck von Wartenburg, Helene Countess, née Kalckreuth (1852–1925): daughter of Stanislaus Count von Kalckreuth and Anna Eleonore, née Cauer; sister of Bonhoeffer's grandmother, Clara von Hase and Pauline, Countess von Kalckreuth; Bonhoeffer's great-aunt; married Hans Count Yorck von Wartenburg, a godfather of Bonhoeffer—67

Yorck von Wartenburg, Marion Gräfin, née Winter: classmate of Bonhoeffer; married Peter Count Yorck von Wartenburg, who participated in the conspiracy against the Nazis and was murdered by the regime—47, 53, 54, 93, 566

Yorck von Wartenburg, Peter Count, Dr. jur. (1904–44): 1936, adviser to the Reich Commissar for Price Controls; 1939, drafted as a reserve officer; 1942, with the economic staff (east) of the high military command; from 1940, in close contact with Helmuth von Moltke; alongside Moltke a leading member of the Kreisau circle; after July 20, 1944, arrested; September 8, 1944, executed—566

Zabarella, Giacomo (Jacopo) (1532–89): late Aristotelian; author of the influential *De methodis libri quatuor*—304

Zahn, Theodor von (1838–1933): German Lutheran New Testament and patristics scholar; professor at various universities, ultimately Erlangen—180

Zahn-Harnack, Agnes (1884–1950): daughter of Adolf von Harnack—148, 216

Zebedee brothers: biblical figures—541–42

Zedekiah: biblical figure—515–16, 517

Zezschwitz, Gertrud von: member of a well-known aristocratic family with a history of military leadership—529

Zimmermann, Max Georg: art historian—76

Zimmermann, Wolf-Dieter (b. 1911 Berlin): 1932–33, pastor; among Bonhoeffer's circle of students in Berlin; winter semester 1932–33, attended the lecture-course on contemporary systematic theology and the course on "theological psychology"; summer semester 1933, attended the Christology lectures; summer 1936, participated in the third Finkenwalde course; 1936, special commissions for the Old Prussian Council of Brethren; 1938, pastor under General Superintendent Otto Dibelius; from 1939, "illegal" pastoral service in Werder/Havel; 1946, in Berlin-Tegel; 1950, personal adviser for Bishop Dibelius; 1954, radio work for the Evangelical Church of Berlin-Brandenburg; cofounder of the Unterwegs-circle and editor of the periodical *Unterwegs;* 1954, radio represen-

INDEX

OF SUBJECTS

GREEK TERMS

ἀγάπη, 228, 246, 256
ἀδελφοί, 401
ἀδελφότης, 241
ἀλήθεια, 248
ἁματιῶν, 255
ἀπαθής, 384
ἀποθέσθαι, 490
ἀποκατάστασις πάντων, 322, 392
βασιλεία, 252
δεσπότης, 229
δικαιοσύνη, 228, 231, 283, 247, 254
δόξα, 371, 375
δοῦλος, 228f., 401
γνῶθι σαυτόν, 497
εἰρήνη, 371
ἐκλεκτοιν, 242
ἐκκλησια, 241, 253
ἔμφυτος, 490ff.
ἐν χριστῷ, 251
εὐαγγέλιον, 377f.
εὐεργεσίας, 236
εὐσέβεια, 247, 253
θαρσεῖν, 371
θεάνθρωπος, 305
κανών, 232
κόσμος, 395ff., 402
κύριος, 221, 453
λειτουργία, 229
λόγος, 235
λόγος σπερματικός, 490f.
λύτρωσις, 250
μακάριος, 493
μετάβασις εἰς ἄλλο γένος, 305, 308
μετάνοια, 248f., 255f.

παιδεία θεου`, 230f.,246
πανάγιος, 227
παντοκράτωρ, 226, 228, 243, 323
παρακλητος, 403
παρρησία, 249, 371
πατήρ, 225
περισσείαν, 490
πίστις, 247, 256
πνεῦμα, 235, 403
σοθία, 231, 235
συγχαίρειν, 381
συνείδησις, 238
σφραγίς, 445
σῶμα πνευματικόν, 392
σῶμα τοῦ ἀνθρώπου, 159
σῶμα τοῦ χριστοῦ, 159
σωφροσύνη, 256
ταπεινοφροσύνη, 245, 253
ὑπακοην, 229-31, 246
φόβος θεοῦ, 230f., 246
χαρά, 371ff.
χάρις, 244
χάρισμα, 244

absolute, 134
absolution, 89
acroamatic, 303
Adam, old and new, 397
Africa. *See* Morocco; Congo; Tripoli
alcohol use, 130–31
Alexandria, 219
Algeciras Act, 192
All Saints Sunday, 505
Allah, 118
allegory, 221

Editors and Translators

Wayne Whitson Floyd Jr. (Ph.D., Emory University) is General Editor of the *Dietrich Bonhoeffer Works*, English edition, and Director of the Anglican Center for Theology and Spirituality of the Episcopal Diocese of Southern Virginia. Previously he has been visiting professor and director of the Dietrich Bonhoeffer Center at the Lutheran Theological Seminary at Philadelphia; a Dean's Fellow on the faculty of the Religion Department of Dickinson College; the Canon Theologian for the Episcopal Cathedral of St. Stephen in Harrisburg, PA; and a faculty member of St. Luke's School of Theology (Sewanee) of The University of the South. He is the author of *The Wisdom and Witness of Dietrich Bonhoeffer* (Fortress Press, 2000) and *Theology and the Dialectics of Otherness: On Reading Bonhoeffer and Adorno* (University Press of America, 1988); he co-authored with Clifford Green the *Bonhoeffer Bibliography: Primary Sources and Secondary Literature in English* (American Theological Library Association, 1992); and he co-edited with Charles Marsh *Theology and the Practice of Responsibility: Essays on Dietrich Bonhoeffer* (Trinity Press International, 1995). Dr. Floyd's articles on Bonhoeffer have appeared in *Union Seminary Quarterly Review, The Lutheran, Modern Theology, Religious Studies Review, Dialog, Modern Theology,* and *Christian Century,* as well as numerous anthologies.

Clifford J. Green (Ph.D., Union Theological Seminary, New York) is Executive Director of the *Dietrich Bonhoeffer Works*, English edition, and Professor Emeritus of Theology, Hartford Seminary. A native of Australia, his early education was at Sydney University, Melbourne College of Divinity, The University of London (Richmond College), and the World Council of Churches'

Graduate School of Ecumenical Studies (University of Geneva). His main teaching appointments were at Wellesley College, Goucher College, and Hartford Seminary. He was the founding president of the International Bonhoeffer Society, English Language Section from 1972-1992. He is the author of *Bonhoeffer: A Theology of Sociality* (Eerdmans, revised edition, 1999); co-editor of *Ethik* and *Jugend und Studium* in the German *Dietrich Bonhoeffer Werke;* editor of *Sanctorum Communio, Fiction from Tegel Prison,* and *Ethics* in the *Dietrich Bonhoeffer Works,* English edition; and author of numerous articles and bibliographical works on Bonhoeffer. His other publications include *Karl Barth: Theologian of Freedom* (Collins, 1989; Fortress Press, 1991); *Churches, Cities, and Human Community* (Eerdmans, 1996); and chapters on Tillich, Marx, Cone, and Gutierrez in *Critical Issues in Modern Religion* (Prentice-Hall, 1973, 1990).

MARSHALL D. JOHNSON (Th.D., Union Theological Seminary, New York), now retired as director of Fortress Press, is a free-lance editor and author in Minneapolis. A graduate of Augsburg College and Seminary, Minneapolis, he studied also at the University of Minnesota, the Pacific School of Religion, and Yeshiva University. He was pastor of Bronx Lutheran Church, New York; held teaching positions at the Lutheran Theological Seminary at Philadelpha and Wartburg College, Iowa; and was Fulbright Professor at the University of Bergen, Norway. He is the author of *The Purpose of the Biblical Genealogies* (Cambridge University Press, second edition, 1989), *Making Sense of the Bible: Literary Type as an Approach to Undrstanding* (Eerdmans, 2002), curricular materials, and numerous scholarly articles, and has translated "The Life of Adam and Eve" and "Apocalypse of Moses" for *The Old Testament Pseudepigrapha* (Doubleday, 1985).

PAUL DUANE MATHENY (Dr. Theol., Heidelberg University) is a professor of systematic theology at Union Theological Seminary in the Philippines. He has worked as a pastor, ecumenist, professor, missionary, theologian and editor. He studied theology at Princeton Theological Seminary, the divinity schools of Chicago and Yale University and at Heidelberg University, where his doctoral work was with Prof. Dr. Dietrich Ritschl. He is a member of the Pastor-Theologian program of the Center of Theological Inquiry, Princeton, and a member of the Advisory Committee to the Editorial Board of the *Dietrich Bonhoeffer Works,* English Edition.

MARY C. NEBELSICK (Dr. Theol. [candidate], University of Heidelberg), is a member of the faculty of Union Theological Seminary in the Philippines. Previously she served as a lecturer in German; as a research assistant at the University of Heidelberg; as professor's assistant at Louisville Presbyterian Theological Seminary; and as Director of Christian Education at St. Timothy's Episcopal Church, Wilson, North Carolina. She received her M.Div. from Princeton Theological Seminary following a B.A. from Wellesley College. She is the editor of *The Renaissance, the Reformation and the Rise of Science* by Harold P. Nebelsick (T&T Clark, 1992). Her dissertation at Heidelberg, "Yahweh's Honeymoon: Love Poems in Their International Literary Context," is being supervised by Prof. Dr. Manfred Weippert. She is a member of the Advisory Committee to the Editorial Board of the *Dietrich Bonhoeffer Works*, English edition.

DOUGLAS W. STOTT (Ph.D., Northwestern University), is a freelance editor and translator in Atlanta. A graduate of Davidson College, Northwestern University, and Emory's Candler School of Theology (M.T.S.), he studied also in Germany at the Philipps University in Marburg and at the University of Stuttgart. He held a teaching position at Davidson College in North Carolina, including serving as director of the year-abroad program and self-instructional language program. He is the translator of several volumes of the *Theological Dictionary of the Old Testament* and the *Exegetical Dictionary of the New Testament*; commentaries on Leviticus and Amos for the *Old Testament Library*; *DBWE* 10, *Barcelona, Berlin, New York: 1928-1931* (forthcoming); F.W.J. Schelling's *Philosophy of Art*; and numerous other theological works and scholarly articles by Claus Westermann, Jürgen Moltmann, Otto Kaiser, Dorothée Sölle, Wolfhart Pannenberg, Walther Zimmerli, and others.